THE SCHEME PROGRAMMING LANGUAGE

ANSI Scheme

Second Edition

R. Kent Dybvig
Indiana University

For book and bookstore information

http://www.prenhall.com

Prentice Hall PTR
Upper Saddle River, New Jersey 07458

Editorial/production supervision: *Joanne Anzalone*
Manufacturing manager: *Alexis R. Heydt*
Acquisitions editor: *Gregory Doench*
Editorial assistant: *Leabe Berman*
Cover design: *Bruce Kenselaar*
Cover illustration: *Jean-Pierre Hébert*
Cover design director: *Jerry Votta*

ISBN 0-13-454646-6

Prentice-Hall International (UK) Limited, *London*
Prentice-Hall of Australia Pty. Limited, *Sydney*
Prentice-Hall Canada Inc., *Toronto*
Prentice-Hall Hispanoamericana, S.A., *Mexico*
Prentice-Hall of India Private Limited, *New Delhi*
Prentice-Hall of Japan, Inc., *Tokyo*
Simon & Schuster Asia Pte. Ltd., *Singapore*
Editora Prentice-Hall do Brasil, Ltda., *Rio de Janeiro*

to Bob and Iva

Contents

Preface

Scheme was introduced in 1975 by Gerald J. Sussman and Guy L. Steele Jr. [23, 24], as the first dialect of Lisp to fully support lexical scoping, first-class procedures, and continuations. In its earliest form it was a very small language intended primarily for research and teaching, supporting only a handful of predefined syntactic forms and procedures. Scheme is now a complete general-purpose programming language, though it still derives its power from a small set of key concepts. Although early implementations of the language were interpreter-based and slow, some modern Scheme implementations boast sophisticated compilers that generate code on par with code generated by the best optimizing compilers for lower-level languages such as C and Fortran.

This book is intended to provide an introduction to the Scheme language but not an introduction to programming in general. The reader is expected to have had some experience programming and to be familiar with terms commonly associated with computers and programming languages. The author recommends that readers unfamiliar with Scheme or Lisp also read *The Little Schemer* [10] to become familiar with the concepts of list processing and recursion. Readers new to programming should begin with an introductory text on programming, such as *Structure and Interpretation of Computer Programs* [1], *Scheme and the Art of Programming* [21], or *The Schematics of Computation* [17].

This book is not a formal language definition or standard document and is not intended for use as such by implementors of Scheme. The "IEEE Standard for the Scheme Programming Language" [15], describing the ANSI/IEEE Standard for Scheme, is such a document. A separate series of documents, the "Revised Reports on the Algorithmic Language Scheme," contain extensions to the standard dialect that are not formally standardized but which most implementations support. Some of these extensions may be formally standardized at some future date. The current report in this series is the "Revised^4 Report on the Algorithmic Language Scheme" [4], although as this book goes to press, there is already agreement on features to be included in the Revised^5 Report.

In spite of the foregoing statement that this book should not be taken as a language definition, it does describe all of the language features documented in the ANSI/IEEE Standard, the Revised^4 Report, and the forthcoming Revised^5 Report (as proposed). Features that are in the Revised[4] or Revised[5] Report but not in the ANSI/IEEE standard are identified as such when they are described.

The first edition of this book described a number of extensions supported by the *Chez Scheme* implementation of Scheme. They have been removed from this edition. The primary rationale for including *Chez Scheme*-specific features in the first edition was that the standard language was really too small to be viable and including the extensions was necessary to show the full flavor of the language. The standard language has expanded considerably since then and now stands on its own. Features specific to *Chez Scheme* are described in *The Chez Scheme System Manual* [7].

A large number of small- to medium-sized examples are spread throughout the text, and one entire chapter is dedicated to the presentation of a set of longer examples. Many of the examples show how a predefined Scheme syntactic form or procedure might be implemented. Nearly all Scheme systems are interactive, and all of the examples can be entered directly from the keyboard into an interactive Scheme session.

This book is organized into nine chapters. Chapter 1 describes the properties and features of Scheme that make it a useful and enjoyable language to use. Chapter 1 also describes Scheme's notational conventions and the typographical conventions employed in this book.

Chapter 2 is an introduction to Scheme programming for the novice Scheme programmer that leads the reader through a series of examples, beginning with the simplest Scheme expressions and working toward progressively more difficult ones. Each section of Chapter 2 introduces a small set of related features, and at the end of each section is a set of exercises for further practice. The reader will learn the most from Chapter 2 by sitting at the keyboard and typing in the examples and trying the exercises.

Chapter 3 continues the introduction but covers more advanced features and concepts. Even readers with prior Scheme experience may wish to work through the examples and exercises found there.

Chapters 4 through 8 make up the reference portion of the text. They present each of Scheme's primitive procedures and syntactic forms in turn, grouping them into short sections of related procedures and forms. Chapter 4 describes operations for creating and changing variable bindings; Chapter 5, program control operations; Chapter 6, operations on the various object types (including lists, numbers, and strings); Chapter 7, input and output operations; and Chapter 8, syntactic extension.

Chapter 9 contains a collection of complete example programs or packages, each with a short overview, some examples of its use, the implementation with brief explanation, and a set of exercises for further work. Each of these programs demonstrates a particular set of features, and together they provide a picture of the author's style of programming in Scheme.

Following Chapter 9 are a bibliography, a detailed description of the formal syntax of Scheme programs and data, a concise summary of Scheme syntactic forms and procedures, and the index. The summary of forms and procedures is a useful first stop for programmers unsure of the structure of a syntactic form or the arguments expected by a primitive procedure. The page numbers appearing in the summary of forms and procedures and the italicized page numbers appearing in the index indicate the locations in the text where forms and procedures are defined.

Because the reference portion describes a number of aspects of the language not covered by the introductory chapters along with a number of interesting short examples, most readers will find it profitable to read through most of the material to become familiar with each feature and how it relates to other features. Chapter 6 is lengthy, however, and may be skimmed and later referenced as needed.

About the illustrations: The cover illustration and the illustrations at the front of each chapter are monohedral tilings created with the help of a Scheme program by artist Jean-Pierre Hébert. In a monohedral tiling, all tiles are congruent: they have the same size and shape but may be flipped. The base tile is called the prototile of the tiling. Many familiar and trivial monohedral tilings are known. No known algorithm exists, however, to decide whether a tile is the prototile of a monohedral tiling. Some of the most interesting tilings are spiral shaped, and the spirals may have from one to many arms. They come from a number of known prototiles, the first one having been discovered by Voderberg in 1936. Illustrations of the curious Voderberg tile (on the cover and at the front of Chapter 3) show how two tiles can surround one or even two similar ones and how they can be assembled to generate straight lines, arcs or circles, random paths, or regular paths.

In the process of creating the illustrations, a Scheme program was used to define tiles and placement rules for these tiles, resulting in diverse monohedral spiral and non-spiral tilings of the plane. Monohedral tilings were output directly as plane geometries in Postscript to produce the illustrations appearing at the front of Chapters 1, 4, and 7. For the remaining illustrations, the tilings were warped in various ways and augmented with the help of Geomview (Geometry Center, Minneapolis), which allows for spatial manipulations, insertions, and adjustments in color, perspective, light, and material.

Acknowledgements: I would like to thank the many individuals who contributed in one way or another to the preparation of the first edition of this book, including Bruce Smith, Eugene Kohlbecker, Matthias Felleisen, Dan Friedman, Bruce Duba, Phil Dybvig, Guy Steele, Bob Hieb, Chris Haynes, Dave Plaisted, John Curry, Frank Silbermann, Pavel Curtis, John Wait, Rob Vollum, Arol Ambler, Gyula Magó, Don Stanat, George Cohn, Mr. Jerry Neff, and my parents, Roger S. Dybvig and Elizabeth H. Dybvig. I would like to thank as well those who contributed to the preparation of the second edition, including Bob Hieb, Carl Bruggeman, Dan Friedman, Sam Daniel, Oscar Waddell, Mike Ashley, John LaLonde, John Zuckerman, and John Simmons. Many others have offered minor corrections and suggestions since the first edition was published, for which I am also grateful. Fred

pretty much slept through the writing of this edition, but I still appreciate his
presence. Finally, I wish to thank my wife, Susan Dybvig, who suggested that I
write this book in the first place and who lent her expertise and assistance to the
production and publication of both editions.

R. Kent Dybvig
Bloomington, Indiana

CHAPTER 1

Introduction

Concentric rings from a crescent shaped prototile.

Scheme is a general-purpose computer programming language. It is a high-level language, supporting operations on structured data such as strings, lists, and vectors, as well as operations on more traditional data such as numbers and characters. While Scheme is often identified with symbolic applications, its rich set of data types and flexible control structures make it a truly versatile language. Scheme has been employed to write text editors, optimizing compilers, operating systems, graphics packages, expert systems, numerical applications, financial analysis packages, and virtually every other type of application imaginable. Scheme is a fairly simple language to learn, since it is based on a handful of syntactic forms and semantic concepts and since the interactive nature of most implementations encourages experimentation. Scheme is a challenging language to understand fully, however; developing the ability to use its full potential requires careful study and practice.

Scheme programs are highly portable across implementations of the same Scheme system on different machines, because machine dependencies are almost completely hidden from the programmer. Also, because of two related Scheme standardization efforts, it is possible to use a standard dialect of Scheme to write programs that are portable across different Scheme implementations. The standard dialect is defined by an ANSI/IEEE Standard described in the "IEEE Standard for the Scheme Programming Language" [15]. The ANSI/IEEE standard grew out of an ongoing effort by a group of Scheme designers, who have published a series of less formal reports, the "Revised Reports" on Scheme. The most recent revised report, the "Revised^4 Report" [4], describes a dialect very close to the standard dialect, differing primarily in the addition of a few primitives. A "Revised^5 Report" is expected to appear soon, highlighted by the addition of a high-level syntactic extension system, an `eval` procedure, and multiple return values.

Although some early Scheme systems were inefficient and slow, many newer compiler-based implementations are fast, with programs running on par with equivalent programs written in lower-level languages. The relative inefficiency that sometimes remains results from run-time checks that help the programmer detect and correct various common programming errors. These checks may be disabled in most implementations.

Scheme handles data values quite differently from most languages. Data values, or *objects*, are dynamically allocated in a heap where they are retained until no longer needed, then automatically deallocated. Objects are *first-class* data values; because they are heap-allocated and retained indefinitely, they may be passed freely as arguments to procedures, returned as values from procedures, and combined to form new objects. This is in contrast with most other languages where composite data values such as arrays are either statically allocated and never deallocated, allocated on entry to a block of code and unconditionally deallocated on exit from the block, or explicitly allocated *and* deallocated by the programmer.

Scheme supports many types of objects, including numbers, characters, strings, symbols, and lists or vectors of objects. A full set of numeric data types, including complex, real, and arbitrary-precision rational numbers, allows Scheme to support many numerical applications typically coded in lower-level languages.

3

At the heart of the Scheme language is a small core of syntactic forms from which all other forms are built. These core forms, a set of extended syntactic forms derived from them, and a library of primitive procedures make up the full Scheme language. An interpreter or compiler for Scheme can be quite small, and potentially fast and highly reliable. The extended syntactic forms and many primitive procedures can be defined in Scheme itself, simplifying the implementation and increasing reliability.

Scheme programs share a common printed representation with Scheme data structures. As a result, any Scheme program has a natural and obvious internal representation as a Scheme object. For example, variables and syntactic keywords correspond to symbols, while structured syntactic forms correspond to lists. This representation is the basis for the syntactic extension facilities provided by most Scheme systems for the definition of new syntactic forms in terms of existing syntactic forms and procedures. It also facilitates the implementation of interpreters, compilers, and other program transformation tools for Scheme directly in Scheme, as well as program transformation tools for other languages in Scheme.

Scheme variables and keywords are *lexically scoped*, and Scheme programs are *block-structured*. Identifiers may be bound at top level (as are the names of primitive Scheme procedures and syntactic forms) or locally, within a given block of code. A local binding is visible only lexically, i.e., within the program text that makes up the particular block of code. An occurrence of an identifier of the same name outside this block refers to a different binding; if no binding for the identifier exists outside of the block, then the reference is invalid. Blocks may be nested, and a binding in one block may *shadow* a binding for an identifier of the same name in a surrounding block. The *scope* of a binding is the block in which the bound identifier is visible minus any portions of the block in which the identifier is shadowed. Block structure and lexical scoping help create programs that are modular, easy to read, easy to maintain, and reliable. Efficient code for lexical scoping is possible because a compiler can determine before program evaluation the scope of all bindings and the binding to which each identifier reference resolves. This does not mean, of course, that a compiler can determine the values of all variables, since the actual values are not computed in most cases until the program executes.

In most languages, a procedure definition is simply the association of a name with a block of code. Certain variables local to the block are the parameters of the procedure. In some languages, a procedure definition may appear within another block or procedure so long as the procedure is invoked only during execution of the enclosing block. In others, procedures can be defined only at top level. In Scheme, a procedure definition may appear within another block or procedure, and the procedure may be invoked at any time thereafter, even if the enclosing block has completed its execution. To support lexical scoping, a procedure carries the lexical context (environment) along with its code.

Furthermore, Scheme procedures are not always named. Instead, procedures are first-class data objects like strings or numbers, and variables are bound to procedures in the same way they are bound to other objects.

As with procedures in most other languages, Scheme procedures may be recursive. That is, any procedure may invoke itself directly or indirectly. Many algorithms are most elegantly or efficiently specified recursively. A special case of recursion, called tail recursion, is used to express iteration, or looping. A *tail call* occurs when one procedure directly returns the result of invoking another procedure; *tail recursion* occurs when a procedure recursively tail calls itself, directly or indirectly. Scheme implementations are required to implement tail calls as jumps (gotos), so the storage overhead normally associated with recursion is avoided. As a result, Scheme programmers need master only simple procedure calls and recursion and need not be burdened with the usual assortment of looping constructs.

Scheme supports the definition of arbitrary control structures with *continuations*. A continuation is a procedure that embodies the remainder of a program at a given point in the program. When a continuation is invoked, the program immediately continues from that point. A continuation may be obtained at any time during the execution of a program. As with other procedures, a continuation is a first-class object and may be invoked at any time after its creation. Continuations allow the implementation of complex control mechanisms including explicit backtracking, multithreading, and coroutines.

Many Scheme implementations support the `syntax-rules` syntactic extension (macro) system adopted for inclusion in the Revised[5] Report on Scheme. This system allows programmers to define extended syntactic forms in terms of existing syntactic forms using a convenient high-level pattern language. Of those implementations that do not support `syntax-rules`, virtually all provide some other mechanism for defining extended syntactic forms. Syntactic extensions are useful for defining new language constructs, for emulating language constructs found in other languages, for achieving the effects of in-line code expansion, and even for emulating entire languages in Scheme. Most large Scheme programs are built from a mix of syntactic extensions and procedure definitions.

Scheme evolved from the Lisp language and is considered to be a dialect of Lisp. Scheme inherited from Lisp the treatment of values as first-class objects, several important data types, including symbols and lists, and the representation of programs as objects, among other things. Lexical scoping and block structure are features taken from Algol 60 [18]. Scheme was the first Lisp dialect to adopt lexical scoping and block structure, the notion of first-class procedures, treatment of tail calls as jumps, and continuations.

Common Lisp [22] and Scheme are both contemporary Lisp languages, and the development of each has been influenced by the other. Like Scheme but unlike earlier Lisp languages, Common Lisp adopted lexical scoping and first-class procedures. Common Lisp's evaluation rules for procedures are different from the evaluation rules for other objects, however, and it maintains a separate namespace for procedure variables, thereby discouraging the use of procedures as first-class objects. Also, Common Lisp does not support continuations or require proper treatment of tail calls, but it does support several less general control structures not found in Scheme. While the two languages are similar, Common Lisp includes more specialized operators, while Scheme includes more general-purpose building blocks out of which such operators (and others) may be built.

The remainder of this chapter describes Scheme's syntax and naming conventions and the typographical conventions used throughout this book.

1.1. Scheme Syntax

Scheme programs are made up of keywords, variables, structured forms, constant data (numbers, characters, strings, quoted vectors, quoted lists, quoted symbols, etc.), whitespace, and comments.

Keywords, variables, and symbols are collectively called identifiers. Identifiers may be formed from the following set of characters:

- the lowercase letters a through z,
- the uppercase letters A through Z,
- the digits 0 through 9, and
- the characters ? ! . + - * / < = > : $ % ^ & _ ~.

Identifiers normally cannot start with any character that may start a number, i.e., a digit, plus sign (+), minus sign (-), or decimal point (.). Exceptions are +, -, and ..., which are valid identifiers. For example, hi, Hello, n, x, x3, and ?$&*!!! are all identifiers. Identifiers must be delimited by whitespace, parentheses, a string (double) quote ("), or the comment character (;). All implementations must recognize as identifiers any sequences of characters that adhere to these rules. Other sequences of characters, such as -1234a, that do not represent numbers or other syntactic entities may be recognized as identifiers in some implementations, although it is best to avoid such identifiers in code that may need to run in more than one Scheme system.

There is no inherent limit on the length of a Scheme identifier; programmers may use as many characters as necessary. Long identifiers are no substitute for comments, however, and frequent use of long identifiers can make a program difficult to format and consequently difficult to read.

Identifiers may be written in any mix of uppercase and lowercase letters. The case is not important, in that two identifiers differing only in case are identical. For example, abcde, Abcde, AbCdE, and ABCDE all refer to the same identifier. Scheme systems typically print an identifier in either all uppercase or all lowercase letters regardless of the way it is entered.

Structured forms and list constants are enclosed within parentheses, e.g., (a b c) or (* (- x 2) y). The empty list is written (). Some implementations permit the use of brackets ([ ]) in place of parentheses, and brackets are sometimes used to set off particular subexpressions for readability.

The boolean values representing *true* and *false* are written as #t and #f. Scheme conditional expressions actually treat #f as false and all other objects as true.

The ANSI/IEEE standard requires that () and #f be distinct objects, but the Revised[4] Report allows them to be the same. If they are the same, () counts, naturally, as false; otherwise, it counts as true. Scheme implementations in which () and #f are the same object always choose one way or the other to write the object when it is printed, which can lead to some confusion. This book always uses () for the empty list and #f for false.

Vectors are written similarly to lists, except that they are preceded by #(and terminated by), e.g., #(this is a vector of symbols). Strings are enclosed in double quotation marks, e.g., "I am a string". Characters are preceded by #\, e.g., #\a. Case is important within character and string constants, unlike within identifiers. Numbers may be written as integers, e.g., -123, as ratios, e.g., 1/2, in floating-point or scientific notation, e.g., 1.3 or 1e23, or as complex numbers in rectangular or polar notation, e.g., 1.3-2.7i or -1.2@73. Details of the syntax for each type of constant data are given in the individual sections of Chapter 6 and in the formal syntax of Scheme given in the back of the book.

Scheme expressions may span several lines, and no explicit terminator is required. Since the number of whitespace characters (spaces and newlines) between expressions is not significant, Scheme programs are normally indented to show the structure of the code in a way that is pleasing to the author of the program. Comments may appear on any line of a Scheme program, between a semicolon (;) and the end of the line. Comments explaining a particular Scheme expression are normally placed at the same indentation level as the expression, on the line before the expression. Comments explaining a procedure or group of procedures are normally placed before the procedures, without indentation. Multiple comment characters are often used to set off the latter kind of comment, e.g., ;;; The following procedures ....

1.2. Scheme Naming Conventions

Scheme's naming conventions are designed to provide a high degree of regularity. The following is a list of these naming conventions:

- Predicate names end in a question mark (?). Predicates are procedures that return with a true or false answer, such as eq?, zero?, and string=?. The common numeric comparators =, <, >, <=, and >= are exceptions to this rule.

- Type predicates, such as pair?, are created from the name of the type, in this case pair, and the question mark.

- The names of most character, string, and vector procedures start with the prefix char-, string-, and vector-, e.g., string-append. (The names of some list procedures start with list-, but most do not.)

- The names of procedures that convert an object of one type into an object of another type are written as *type₁*->*type₂*, e.g., vector->list.

- The names of procedures and syntactic forms that cause side effects end with an exclamation point (!). These include set! and vector-set!. Procedures that perform input or output technically cause side effects, but their names are exceptions to this rule.

1.3. Typographical and Notational Conventions

Often, the value of a procedure or syntactic form is said to be *unspecified*. This means that an implementation is free to return any Scheme object as the value of the procedure or syntactic form. Do not count on this value being the same across implementations, the same across versions of the same implementation, or even the same across two uses of the procedure or syntactic form. Some Scheme systems routinely use a special object to represent unspecified values. Printing of this object is often suppressed by interactive Scheme systems, so that the values of expressions returning unspecified values are not printed.

Scheme expressions usually evaluate to a single value, although the multiple values mechanism described in Section 5.8 allows an expression to evaluate to zero or more than one value. To simplify the presentation, this book usually refers to the result of an expression as a single value even if the expression may in fact evaluate to zero or more than one value.

This book sometimes says "it is an error" or "an error will be signaled" when describing a circumstance in violation of the rules of Scheme. Something that is an error is not valid in Scheme, and the behavior of a Scheme implementation in such a case is not specified. A signaled error results in the invocation of an implementation-dependent error handler, which typically results in an error message being printed and a reset of the interactive programming system or entry into a debugging subsystem.

The typographic conventions used in this book are straightforward. All Scheme objects are printed in a `typewriter` typeface, just as they are to be typed at the keyboard. This includes syntactic keywords, variables, constant objects, Scheme expressions, and example programs. An *italic* typeface is used to set off syntax variables in the descriptions of syntactic forms and arguments in the descriptions of procedures. Italics are also used to set off technical terms the first time they appear. In general, names written in typewriter font are never capitalized (even at the beginning of a sentence). The same is true for syntax variables written in italics.

In the description of a syntactic form or procedure, a pattern shows the syntactic form or the application of the procedure. The syntax keyword or procedure name is given in typewriter font, as are parentheses. The remaining pieces of the syntax or arguments are shown in italics, using a name that implies the type of expression or argument expected by the syntactic form or procedure. Ellipses are used to specify zero or more occurrences of a subexpression or argument. For example, (`or` *exp* `...`) describes the `or` syntactic form, which has zero or more subexpressions, and (`member` *obj* *list*) describes the `member` procedure, which expects two arguments, an object and a list.

CHAPTER 2

Getting Started

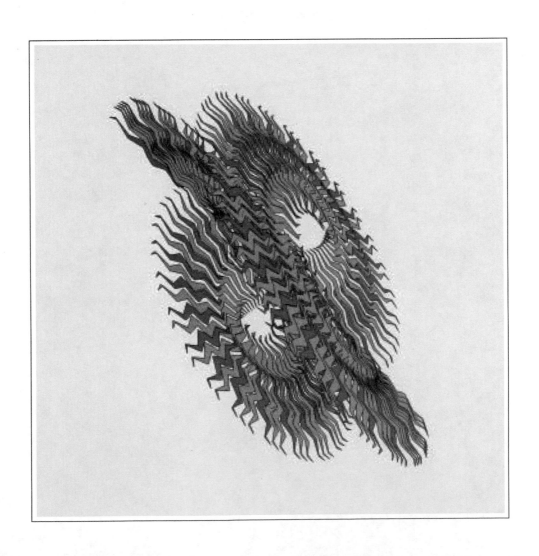

Two warped, two-armed spirals.

This chapter is an introduction to Scheme for programmers who are new to the language. You will get more from this chapter if you are sitting in front of an interactive Scheme system, trying out the examples as you go.

After reading this chapter and working the exercises, you should be able to start using Scheme. You will have learned the syntax of Scheme programs and how they are executed, along with how to use simple data structures and control mechanisms.

2.1. Interacting with Scheme

Most Scheme systems provide an interactive programming environment that simplifies learning and experimentation. The simplest interaction with Scheme follows a "read-evaluate-print" cycle. A program (often called a *read-evaluate-print loop*, or REPL) reads each expression you type at the keyboard, evaluates it, and prints its value.

With an interactive Scheme system, you can type an expression at the keyboard and see its value immediately. You can define a procedure and apply it to arguments to see how it works. You can even type in an entire program consisting of a set of procedure definitions and test it without leaving the system. When your program starts getting longer, it will be more convenient to type it into a file (using a text editor), load the file (using `load`), and test it interactively. Preparing your program in a file has several advantages: you have a chance to compose your program more carefully, you can correct errors without retyping the program, and you can retain a copy for later use. Scheme treats expressions loaded from a file the same as expressions typed from the keyboard.

While Scheme provides various input and output procedures, the REPL takes care of reading expressions and printing their values. Furthermore, if you need to save the results for later use, you can make a transcript (using `transcript-on` and `transcript-off`; see Section 7.4) of an interactive session. This frees you to concentrate on writing your program without worrying about how its results will be displayed or saved.

The examples of this chapter follow a regular format. An expression you might type from your keyboard is given first, possibly spanning several lines. The system's response is given after the ⇒, to be read as "evaluates to." The ⇒ is omitted when the value of the expression is unspecified or not of interest.

The example programs are formatted in a style that "looks nice" and conveys the structure of the program. The code is easy to read because the relationship between each expression and its subexpressions is clearly shown. Scheme ignores indentations and line breaks, however, so there is no need to follow a particular style. The important thing is to establish one style and keep to it. Scheme sees each program as if it were on a single line, with its subexpressions ordered from left to right.

If you have access to an interactive Scheme system, it might be a good idea to start it up now and type in the examples as you read. One of the simplest Scheme expressions is a string constant. Try typing `"Hi Mom!"` (including the double quotes)

in response to the prompt. The system should respond with "Hi Mom!"; the value
of any constant is the constant itself.

"Hi Mom!"   ⇒   "Hi Mom!"

Here is a set of expressions, each with Scheme's response. They are explained
in later sections of this chapter, but for now use them to practice interacting with
Scheme.

```
"hello"  ⇒  "hello"
42  ⇒  42
22/7  ⇒  22/7
3.141592653  ⇒  3.141592653
+  ⇒  #<procedure>
(+ 76 31)  ⇒  107
'(a b c d)  ⇒  (a b c d)
```

Be careful not to miss any single quotes ('), double quotes, or parentheses. If
you left off a single quote in the last expression, you probably received an error
message. Just try again. If you left off a closing parenthesis or double quote, the
system may still be waiting for it.

Here are a few more expressions to try. You can try to figure out on your own
what they mean or wait to find out later in the chapter.

```
(car '(a b c))  ⇒  a
(cdr '(a b c))  ⇒  (b c)
(cons 'a '(b c))  ⇒  (a b c)
(cons (car '(a b c))
      (cdr '(d e f)))  ⇒  (a e f)
```

As you can see, Scheme expressions may span more than one line. The Scheme
system knows when it has an entire expression by matching double quotes and
parentheses.

Next, let's try defining a procedure.

```
(define square
  (lambda (n)
    (* n n)))
```

The procedure **square** computes the square n^2 of any number n. We say more
about the expressions that make up this definition later in this chapter. For now it
suffices to say that **define** establishes variable bindings, **lambda** creates procedures,
and * names the multiplication procedure. Note the form of these expressions. All
structured forms are enclosed in parentheses and written in *prefix notation*, i.e.,
the operator precedes the arguments. As you can see, this is true even for simple
arithmetic operations such as *.

Try using **square**.

```
(square 5)  ⇒  25
(square -200)  ⇒  40000
(square 0.5)  ⇒  0.25
(square -1/2)  ⇒  1/4
```

Scheme systems that do not support exact ratios internally may print 0.25 for (square -1/2).

Even though the next definition is short, you might enter it into a file. Let's assume you call the file "reciprocal.ss."

```
(define reciprocal
  (lambda (n)
    (if (= n 0)
        "oops!"
        (/ 1 n))))
```

This procedure, `reciprocal`, computes the quantity $1/n$ for any number $n \neq 0$. For $n = 0$, `reciprocal` returns the string `"oops!"`. Return to Scheme and try loading your file with the procedure `load`.

```
(load "reciprocal.ss")
```

Finally, try using the procedure we have just defined.

```
(reciprocal 10)   ⇒   1/10
(reciprocal 1/10)   ⇒   10
(reciprocal 0)   ⇒   "oops!"
(reciprocal (reciprocal 1/10))   ⇒   1/10
```

In the next section we will discuss Scheme expressions in more detail. Throughout this chapter, keep in mind that your Scheme system is one of the most useful tools for learning Scheme. Whenever you try one of the examples in the text, follow it up with your own examples. In an interactive Scheme system, the cost of trying something out is relatively small—usually just the time to type it in.

2.2. Simple Expressions

The simplest Scheme expressions are constant data objects, such as strings, numbers, symbols, and lists. Scheme supports other object types, but these four are enough for many programs. We saw some examples of strings and numbers in the preceding section.

Let's discuss numbers in a little more detail. Numbers are constants. If you enter a number, Scheme echoes it back to you. The following examples show that Scheme supports several types of numbers.

```
123456789987654321   ⇒   123456789987654321
3/4   ⇒   3/4
2.718281828   ⇒   2.718281828
2.2+1.1i   ⇒   2.2+1.1i
```

Scheme numbers include exact and inexact integer, rational, real, and complex numbers. Exact integers and rational numbers have arbitrary precision, i.e., they can be of arbitrary size. Inexact numbers are usually represented internally using IEEE standard floating-point representations. Scheme implementations, however, need not support all types of numbers and have great freedom where internal representations are concerned. Experiment to determine what kind of numbers the Scheme system you are using supports.

Scheme provides the names +, -, *, and / for the corresponding arithmetic procedures. Each procedure accepts two numeric arguments. The expressions below are called *procedure applications*, because they specify the application of a procedure to a set of arguments.

```
(+ 1/2 1/2)  ⇒  1
(- 1.5 1/2)  ⇒  1.0

(* 3 1/2)  ⇒  3/2
(/ 1.5 3/4)  ⇒  2.0
```

Scheme employs prefix notation even for common arithmetic operations. Any procedure application, whether the procedure takes zero, one, two, or more arguments, is written as (*procedure arg ...*). This regularity simplifies the syntax of expressions; one notation is employed regardless of the operation, and there are no complicated rules regarding the precedence or associativity of operators.

Procedure applications may be nested, in which case the innermost values are computed first. We can thus nest applications of the arithmetic procedures given above to evaluate more complicated formulas.

```
(+ (+ 2 2) (+ 2 2))  ⇒  8
(- 2 (* 4 1/3))  ⇒  2/3
(* 2 (* 2 (* 2 (* 2 2))))  ⇒  32
(/ (* 6/7 7/2) (- 4.5 1.5))  ⇒  1.0
```

These examples demonstrate everything you need to use Scheme as a four-function desk calculator. While we will not discuss them in this chapter, Scheme supports many other arithmetic procedures. Now might be a good time to turn to Section 6.3 and experiment with some of them.

Simple numeric objects are sufficient for many tasks, but sometimes aggregate data structures containing two or more values are needed. In many languages, the basic aggregate data structure is the array. In Scheme, it is the *list*. Lists are written as sequences of objects surrounded by parentheses. For instance, (1 2 3 4 5) is a list of numbers, and ("this" "is" "a" "list") is a list of strings. Lists need not contain only one type of object, so (4.2 "hi") is a valid list containing a number and a string. Lists may be nested (may contain other lists), so ((1 2) (3 4)) is a valid list with two elements, each of which is a list of two elements.

You may notice that lists look just like procedure applications and wonder how Scheme tells them apart. That is, how does Scheme distinguish between a list of objects, (*obj₁ obj₂ ...*), and a procedure application, (*procedure arg ...*)?

In some cases, the distinction may seem obvious. The list of numbers (1 2 3 4 5) could hardly be confused with a procedure application, since 1 is a number, not a procedure. So, the answer might be that Scheme looks at the first element of the list or procedure application and makes its decision based on whether that first element is a procedure or not. This answer is not good enough, since we may even want to treat a valid procedure application such as (+ 3 4) as a list. The answer is that we must tell Scheme explicitly to treat a list as data rather than as a procedure application. We do this with `quote`.

```
(quote (1 2 3 4 5))  ⇒  (1 2 3 4 5)
(quote ("this" "is" "a" "list"))  ⇒  ("this" "is" "a" "list")
(quote (+ 3 4))  ⇒  (+ 3 4)
```

The `quote` forces the list to be treated as data. Try entering the above expressions without the quote; you will likely receive an error message for the first two and an incorrect answer (7) for the third.

Because `quote` is required fairly frequently in Scheme code, Scheme recognizes a single quotation mark (') preceding an expression as an abbreviation for `quote`.

```
'(1 2 3 4)  ⇒  (1 2 3 4)
'((1 2) (3 4))  ⇒  ((1 2) (3 4))
'(/ (* 2 -1) 3)  ⇒  (/ (* 2 -1) 3)
```

Both forms are referred to as `quote` expressions. We often say an object is *quoted* when it is enclosed in a `quote` expression.

A `quote` expression is *not* a procedure application, since it inhibits the evaluation of its "argument" expression. It is an entirely different syntactic form. Scheme supports several other syntactic forms in addition to procedure applications and `quote` expressions. Each syntactic form is evaluated differently. Fortunately, the number of different syntactic forms is small. We will see more of them later in this chapter.

Not all `quote` expressions involve lists. Try the following expression with and without the `quote`.

```
(quote hello)  ⇒  hello
```

The symbol `hello` must be quoted in order to prevent Scheme from treating `hello` as a *variable*. Symbols and variables in Scheme are similar to symbols and variables in mathematical expressions and equations. When we evaluate the mathematical expression $1 - x$ for some value of x, we think of x as a variable. On the other hand, when we consider the algebraic equation $x^2 - 1 = (x - 1)(x + 1)$, we think of x as a symbol (in fact, we think of the whole equation symbolically). Just as quoting a list tells Scheme to treat a parenthesized form as a list rather than as a procedure application, quoting an identifier tells Scheme to treat the identifier as a symbol rather than as a variable. While symbols are commonly used to represent variables in symbolic representations of equations or programs, symbols may also be used, for example, as words in the representation of natural language sentences.

You might wonder why applications and variables share notations with lists and symbols. The shared notation allows Scheme programs to be represented as Scheme data, simplifying the writing of interpreters, compilers, editors, and other tools in Scheme. This is demonstrated by the Scheme interpreter given in Section 9.7, which is itself written in Scheme. Many people believe this to be one of the most important features of Scheme.

Numbers and strings may be quoted, too:

```
'2  ⇒  2
'2/3  ⇒  2/3
(quote "Hi Mom!")  ⇒  "Hi Mom!"
```

Numbers and strings are treated as constants in any case, however, so quoting them is unnecessary.

Now let's discuss some Scheme procedures for manipulating lists. There are two basic procedures for taking lists apart: `car` and `cdr` (pronounced *could-er*). `car` returns the first element of a list, and `cdr` returns the remainder of the list. (The names "car" and "cdr" are derived from operations supported by the first computer on which a Lisp language was implemented, the IBM 704.) Each requires a nonempty list as its argument.

```
(car '(a b c))  ⇒  a
(cdr '(a b c))  ⇒  (b c)
(cdr '(a))  ⇒  ()

(car (cdr '(a b c)))  ⇒  b
(cdr (cdr '(a b c)))  ⇒  (c)

(car '((a b) (c d)))  ⇒  (a b)
(cdr '((a b) (c d)))  ⇒  ((c d))
```

The first element of a list is often called the "car" of the list, and the rest of the list is often called the "cdr" of the list. The cdr of a list with one element is (), the *empty list*.

The procedure `cons` constructs lists. It takes two arguments. The second argument is usually a list, and in that case `cons` returns a list.

```
(cons 'a '())  ⇒  (a)
(cons 'a '(b c))  ⇒  (a b c)
(cons 'a (cons 'b (cons 'c '())))  ⇒  (a b c)
(cons '(a b) '(c d))  ⇒  ((a b) c d)

(car (cons 'a '(b c)))  ⇒  a
(cdr (cons 'a '(b c)))  ⇒  (b c)
(cons (car '(a b c))
      (cdr '(d e f)))  ⇒  (a e f)
(cons (car '(a b c))
      (cdr '(a b c)))  ⇒  (a b c)
```

Just as "car" and "cdr" are often used as nouns, "cons" is often used as a verb. Creating a new list by adding an element to the beginning of a list is referred to as *consing* the element onto the list.

Notice the word "usually" in the third sentence of the preceding paragraph. The procedure `cons` actually builds *pairs*, and there is no reason that the cdr of a pair must be a list. A list is a sequence of pairs; each pair's cdr is the next pair in the sequence. The cdr of the last pair in a *proper list* is the empty list. Otherwise, the sequence of pairs forms an *improper list*. More formally, the empty list is a proper list, and any pair whose cdr is a proper list is a proper list.

An improper list is printed in *dotted-pair notation*, with a period, or *dot*, preceding the final element of the list.

```
(cons 'a 'b)  ⇒  (a . b)
(cdr '(a . b))  ⇒  b
(cons 'a '(b . c))  ⇒  (a b . c)
```

Because of its printed notation, a pair whose cdr is not a list is often called a *dotted pair*. Even pairs whose cdrs are lists can be written in dotted-pair notation, however, although the printer always chooses to write proper lists without dots.

```
'(a . (b . (c . ()))) ⇒  (a b c)
```

The procedure `list` is similar to `cons`, except that it takes an arbitrary number of arguments and always builds a proper list.

```
(list 'a 'b 'c)  ⇒  (a b c)
(list 'a)  ⇒  (a)
(list)  ⇒  ()
```

Section 6.2 provides more information on lists and the Scheme procedures for manipulating them. This might be a good time to turn to that section and familiarize yourself with the other procedures given there.

Exercise 2.2.1. Convert the following arithmetic expressions into Scheme expressions and evaluate them.

 a. $1.2 \times (2 - 1/3) + -8.7$
 b. $(2/3 + 4/9)/(5/11 - 4/3)$
 c. $1 + 1/(2 + 1/(1 + 1/2))$
 d. $1 \times -2 \times 3 \times -4 \times 5 \times -6 \times 7$

Exercise 2.2.2. Experiment with the procedures +, -, *, and / to determine Scheme's rules for the type of value returned by each when given different types of numeric arguments.

Exercise 2.2.3. Determine the values of the following expressions.

 a. `(cons 'car 'cdr)`
 b. `(list 'this '(is silly))`
 c. `(cons 'is '(this silly?))`
 d. `(quote (+ 2 3))`
 e. `(cons '+ '(2 3))`
 f. `(car '(+ 2 3))`
 g. `(cdr '(+ 2 3))`
 h. `cons`
 i. `(quote cons)`
 j. `(quote (quote cons))`
 k. `(car (quote (quote cons)))`
 l. `(+ 2 3)`
 m. `(+ '2 '3)`

    n. `(+ (car '(2 3)) (car (cdr '(2 3))))`
    o. `((car (list + - * /)) 2 3)`

Exercise 2.2.4. `(car (car '((a b) (c d))))` yields a. Determine which compositions of `car` and `cdr` applied to `((a b) (c d))` yield b, c, and d.

Exercise 2.2.5. The behavior of `(car (car (car '((a b) (c d)))))` is undefined because `(car '((a b) (c d)))` is `(a b)`, `(car '(a b))` is a, and `(car 'a)` is undefined. Determine all legal compositions of `car` and `cdr` applied to `((a b) (c d))`.

Exercise 2.2.6. Try to explain how Scheme expressions are evaluated. Does your explanation cover the last example in Exercise 2.2.3?

2.3. Evaluating Scheme Expressions

Let's turn to a discussion of how Scheme evaluates the expressions you type. We have already established the rules for constant objects such as strings and numbers; the object itself is the value. You have probably also worked out in your mind a rule for evaluating procedure applications of the form (*procedure* arg_1 ... arg_n). Here, *procedure* is an expression representing a Scheme procedure, and arg_1 ... arg_n are expressions representing its arguments. One possibility is the following.

- Find the value of *procedure*.
- Find the value of arg_1.

    $\vdots$

- Find the value of arg_n.
- Apply the value of *procedure* to the values of arg_1 ... arg_n.

For example, consider the simple procedure application `(+ 3 4)`. The value of `+` is the addition procedure, the value of 3 is the number 3, and the value of 4 is the number 4. Applying the addition procedure to 3 and 4 yields 7, so our value is the object 7.

    By applying this process at each level, we can find the value of the nested expression `(* (+ 3 4) 2)`. The value of `*` is the multiplication procedure, the value of `(+ 3 4)` we can determine to be the number 7, and the value of 2 is the number 2. Multiplying 7 by 2 we get 14, so our answer is 14.

    This rule works for procedure applications but not for `quote` expressions because the subexpressions of a procedure application are evaluated, whereas the subexpression of a `quote` expression is not. The evaluation of a `quote` expression is more similar to the evaluation of constant objects. The value of a `quote` expression of the form (`quote` *object*) is simply *object*.

    Constant objects, procedure applications, and `quote` expressions are only three of the many syntactic forms provided by Scheme. Fortunately, only a few of the other syntactic forms need to be understood directly by a Scheme programmer; these are referred to as *core* syntactic forms. The remaining syntactic forms are *syntactic extensions* defined, ultimately, in terms of the core syntactic forms. We will discuss the remaining core syntactic forms and a few syntactic extensions in the remaining sections of this chapter. Section 3.1 summarizes the core syntactic forms and introduces the syntactic extension mechanism.

Before we go on to more syntactic forms and procedures, two points related to the evaluation of procedure applications are worthy of note. First, the process given above is overspecified, in that it requires the subexpressions to be evaluated from left to right. That is, *procedure* is evaluated before arg_1, arg_1 is evaluated before arg_2, and so on. This need not be the case. A Scheme evaluator is free to evaluate the expressions in any order—left to right, right to left, or any other sequential order. In fact, the subexpressions may be evaluated in different orders for different applications even in the same implementation.

The second point is that *procedure* is evaluated in the same manner as arg_1 ... arg_n. While *procedure* is often a variable that names a particular procedure, this need not be the case. Exercise 2.2.3 had you determine the value of ((car (list + - * /)) 2 3). Here, *procedure* is (car (list + - * /)). The value of (car (list + - * /)) is the addition procedure, just as if *procedure* were simply the variable +.

Exercise 2.3.1. Write down the steps necessary to evaluate each of the following expressions.

 a. ((car (cdr (list + - * /))) 17 5)
 b. (cons (quote -) (cdr (quote (+ b c))))
 c. (cdr (cdr '(a b c)))
 d. (cons 'd (cdr (cdr '(a b c d e f))))
 e. (cons (+ '2 1/2) (list (- '3 1/3) (+ '4 1/4)))

2.4. Variables and Let Expressions

Suppose *expr* is a Scheme expression that contains a variable *var*. Suppose, additionally, that we would like *var* to have the value *val* when we evaluate *expr*. For example, we might like x to have the value 2 when we evaluate (+ x 3). Or, we might want y to have the value 3 when we evaluate (+ 2 y). The following examples demonstrate how to do this using Scheme's let syntactic form.

```
(let ((x 2))
  (+ x 3))  ⇒  5
(let ((y 3))
  (+ 2 y))  ⇒  5
(let ((x 2) (y 3))
  (+ x y))  ⇒  5
```

The `let` syntactic form includes a list of variable-value pairs, along with a sequence of expressions referred to as the *body* of the `let`. The general form of a `let` expression is

```
(let ((var val) ...) exp₁ exp₂ ...)
```

We say the variables are *bound* to the values by the `let`. We refer to variables bound by `let` as `let`-*bound* variables.

A `let` expression is often used to simplify an expression that would contain two identical subexpressions. Doing so also ensures that the value of the common subexpression is computed only once.

```
(+ (* 4 4) (* 4 4))  ⇒  32

(let ((a (* 4 4)))
  (+ a a))  ⇒  32

(let ((list1 '(a b c)) (list2 '(d e f)))
  (cons (cons (car list1)
              (car list2))
        (cons (car (cdr list1))
              (car (cdr list2)))))  ⇒  ((a . d) b . e)
```

Since expressions in the first position of a procedure application are evaluated no differently from other expressions, a `let`-bound variable may be used there as well.

```
(let ((f +))
  (f 2 3))  ⇒  5

(let ((f +) (x 2))
  (f x 3))  ⇒  5

(let ((f +) (x 2) (y 3))
  (f x y))  ⇒  5
```

The variables bound by `let` are visible only within the body of the `let`.

```
(let ((+ *))
  (+ 2 3))  ⇒  6

(+ 2 3)  ⇒  5
```

This is fortunate, because we would not want the preceding to change the value of + to the multiplication procedure everywhere.

It is possible to nest `let` expressions.

```
(let ((a 4) (b -3))
  (let ((a-squared (* a a))
        (b-squared (* b b)))
    (+ a-squared b-squared)))  ⇒  25
```

When nested `let` expressions bind the same variable, only the binding created by the inner `let` is visible within its body.

```
(let ((x 1))
  (let ((x (+ x 1)))
    (+ x x)))  ⇒  4
```

The outer `let` expression binds `x` to 1 within its body, which is the second `let` expression. The inner `let` expression binds `x` to `(+ x 1)` within its body, which is the expression `(+ x x)`. What is the value of `(+ x 1)`? Since `(+ x 1)` appears within the body of the outer `let` but not within the body of the inner `let`, the value of `x` must be 1 and hence the value of `(+ x 1)` is 2. What about `(+ x x)`? It appears within the body of both `let` expressions. Only the inner binding for `x` is visible, so `x` is 2 and `(+ x x)` is 4.

The inner binding for `x` is said to *shadow* the outer binding. A `let`-bound variable is visible everywhere within the body of its `let` expression except where it is shadowed. The region where a variable binding is visible is called its *scope*. The scope of the first `x` in the example above is the body of the outer `let` expression minus the body of the inner `let` expression, where it is shadowed by the second `x`. This form of scoping is referred to as *lexical scoping*, since the scope of each binding can be determined by a straightforward textual analysis of the program.

Shadowing may be avoided by choosing different names for variables. The expression above could be rewritten so that the variable bound by the inner `let` is `new-x`.

```
(let ((x 1))
  (let ((new-x (+ x 1)))
    (+ new-x new-x)))  ⇒  4
```

Although it is sometimes best to avoid confusion by choosing different names, shadowing can help prevent the accidental use of an "old" value. For example, with the original version of the preceding example, it would be impossible for us to mistakenly refer to the outer `x` within the body of the inner `let`.

Exercise 2.4.1. Rewrite the following expressions, using `let` to remove common subexpressions and to improve the structure of the code. Do not perform any algebraic simplifications.

    a. `(+ (- (* 3 a) b) (+ (* 3 a) b))`

    b. `(cons (car (list a b c)) (cdr (list a b c)))`

Exercise 2.4.2. Determine the value of the following expression. Explain how you derived this value.

```
(let ((x 9))
  (* x
    (let ((x (/ x 3)))
      (+ x x))))
```

Exercise 2.4.3. Rewrite the following expressions to give unique names to each different `let`-bound variable so that none of the variables is shadowed. Verify that the value of your expression is the same as that of the original expression.

```
a. (let ((x 'a) (y 'b))
     (list (let ((x 'c)) (cons x y))
           (let ((y 'd)) (cons x y))))
b. (let ((x '((a b) c)))
     (cons (let ((x (cdr x)))
             (car x))
           (let ((x (car x)))
             (cons (let ((x (cdr x)))
                     (car x))
                   (cons (let ((x (car x)))
                           x)
                         (cdr x))))))
```

2.5. Lambda Expressions

In the expression `(let ((x (* 3 4))) (+ x x))`, the variable `x` is bound to the value of `(* 3 4)`. What if we would like the value of `(+ x x)` where `x` is bound to the value of `(/ 99 11)`? Where `x` is bound to the value of `(- 2 7)`? In each case we need a different `let` expression. When the body of the `let` is complicated, however, having to repeat it can be inconvenient.

Instead, we can use the syntactic form `lambda` to create a new procedure that has `x` as a parameter and has the same body as the `let` expression.

```
(lambda (x) (+ x x))   ⇒   #<procedure>
```

The general form of a `lambda` expression is

```
(lambda (var ...) exp₁ exp₂ ...)
```

The variables *var* ... are the *formal parameters* of the procedure, and the sequence of expressions exp_1 exp_2 ... is its body. (Actually, the true general form is somewhat more general than this, as you will see later.)

A procedure is just as much an object as a number, string, symbol, or pair. It does not have any meaningful printed representation as far as Scheme is concerned, however, so this book uses the notation `#<procedure>` to show that the value of an expression is a procedure.

The most common operation to perform on a procedure is to apply it to one or more values.

```
((lambda (x) (+ x x)) (* 3 4))   ⇒   24
```

This is no different from any other procedure application. The procedure is the value of `(lambda (x) (+ x x))`, and the only argument is the value of `(* 3 4)`, or 12. The argument values, or *actual parameters*, are bound to the formal parameters within the body of the `lambda` expression in the same way as `let`-bound variables are bound to their values. In this case, `x` is bound to 12, and the value of `(+ x x)` is 24. Thus, the result of applying the procedure to the value 12 is 24.

Because procedures are objects, we can establish a procedure as the value of a variable and use the procedure more than once.

```
(let ((double (lambda (x) (+ x x))))
  (list (double (* 3 4))
        (double (/ 99 11))
        (double (- 2 7))))  ⇒  (24 18 -10)
```

Here, we establish a binding for `double` to a procedure, then use this procedure to double three different values.

The procedure expects its actual parameter to be a number, since it passes the actual parameter on to `+`. In general, the actual parameter may be any sort of object. Consider, for example, a similar procedure that uses `cons` instead of `+`.

```
(let ((double-cons (lambda (x) (cons x x))))
  (double-cons 'a))  ⇒  (a . a)
```

Noting the similarity between `double` and `double-cons`, you should not be surprised to learn that they may be collapsed into a single procedure by adding an additional argument.

```
(let ((double-any (lambda (f x) (f x x))))
  (list (double-any + 13)
        (double-any cons 'a)))  ⇒  (26 (a . a))
```

This demonstrates that procedures may accept more than one argument and that arguments passed to a procedure may themselves be procedures.

As with `let` expressions, `lambda` expressions become somewhat more interesting when they are nested within other `lambda` or `let` expressions.

```
(let ((x 'a))
  (let ((f (lambda (y) (list x y))))
    (f 'b)))  ⇒  (a b)
```

The occurrence of `x` within the `lambda` expression refers to the `x` outside the `lambda` that is bound by the outer `let` expression. The variable `x` is said to *occur free* in the `lambda` expression or to be a *free variable* of the `lambda` expression. The variable `y` does not occur free in the `lambda` expression since it is bound by the `lambda` expression. A variable that occurs free in a `lambda` expression should be bound by an enclosing `lambda` or `let` expression, unless the variable is (like the names of primitive procedures) bound at top level, as we discuss in the following section.

What happens when the procedure is applied somewhere outside the scope of the bindings for variables that occur free within the procedure, as in the following expression?

```
(let ((f (let ((x 'a))
           (lambda (y) (cons x y)))))
  (f 'b))  ⇒  (a . b)
```

The answer is that the same bindings that were in effect when the procedure was created are in effect again when the procedure is applied. This is true even if another binding for x is visible where the procedure is applied.

```
(let ((f (let ((x 'a))
           (lambda (y) (cons x y)))))
  (let ((x 'i-am-not-a))
    (f 'b)))   ⇒   (a . b)
```

In both cases, the value of x within the procedure named f is a.

Incidentally, a let expression is nothing more than the direct application of a lambda expression to a set of argument expressions. For example, the two expressions below are equivalent:

```
(let ((x 'a))
  (cons x x))
```

```
((lambda (x) (cons x x))
 'a)
```

In fact, a let expression is a syntactic extension defined in terms of lambda and procedure application, which are both core syntactic forms. In general, any expression of the form

```
(let ((var val) ...) exp₁ exp₂ ...)
```

is equivalent to the following.

```
((lambda (var ...) exp₁ exp₂ ...)
 val ...)
```

See Section 3.1 for more about core forms and syntactic extensions.

As was mentioned above, the general form for lambda is a bit more complicated than the form we saw earlier, in that the formal parameter specification, $(var \ldots)$, need not be a proper list, or indeed even a list at all. The formal parameter specification can be in any of the following three forms:

- a proper list of variables, $(var_1 \ldots var_n)$, such as we have already seen,
- a single variable, var_r, or
- an improper list of variables, $(var_1 \ldots var_n \cdot var_r)$.

In the first case, exactly n actual parameters must be supplied, and each variable is bound to the corresponding actual parameter. In the second, any number of actual parameters is valid; all of the actual parameters are put into a single list and the single variable is bound to this list. The third case is a hybrid of the first two cases. At least n actual parameters must be supplied. The variables $var_1 \ldots var_n$ are bound to the corresponding actual parameters, and the variable var_r is bound to a list containing the remaining actual parameters. In the second and third cases, var_r is sometimes referred to as a "rest" parameter because it holds the rest of the actual parameters beyond those that are individually named.

Let's consider a few examples to help clarify the more general syntax of `lambda` expressions.

```
(let ((f (lambda x x)))
  (f 1 2 3 4))  ⇒  (1 2 3 4)

(let ((f (lambda x x)))
  (f))  ⇒  ()

(let ((g (lambda (x . y) (list x y))))
  (g 1 2 3 4))  ⇒  (1 (2 3 4))

(let ((h (lambda (x y . z) (list x y z))))
  (h 'a 'b 'c 'd))  ⇒  (a b (c d))
```

In the first two examples, the procedure named `f` accepts any number of arguments. These arguments are automatically formed into a list to which the variable `x` is bound; the value of `f` is this list. In the first example, the arguments are 1, 2, 3, and 4, so the answer is (1 2 3 4). In the second, there are no arguments, so the answer is the empty list (). The value of the procedure named `g` in the third example is a list whose first element is the first argument and whose second element is a list containing the remaining arguments. The procedure named `h` is similar but separates out the second argument. While `f` accepts any number of arguments, `g` must receive at least one and `h` must receive at least two.

Exercise 2.5.1. Determine the values of the expressions below.

```
a. (let ((f (lambda (x) x)))
     (f 'a))
b. (let ((f (lambda x x)))
     (f 'a))
c. (let ((f (lambda (x . y) x)))
     (f 'a))
d. (let ((f (lambda (x . y) y)))
     (f 'a))
```

Exercise 2.5.2. How might the primitive procedure `list` be defined?

Exercise 2.5.3. List the variables that occur free in each of the `lambda` expressions below. Do not omit variables that name primitive procedures such as + or `cons`.

```
a. (lambda (f x) (f x))
b. (lambda (x) (+ x x))
c. (lambda (x y) (f x y))
d. (lambda (x)
     (cons x (f x y)))
e. (lambda (x)
     (let ((y (cons x y)))
       (list x y z)))
```

2.6. Top-Level Definitions

The variables bound by `let` and `lambda` expressions are not visible outside the bodies of these expressions. Suppose you have created an object, perhaps a procedure, that must be accessible anywhere, like + or `cons`. What you need is a *top-level definition*, which may be established with `define`. Top-level definitions are visible in every expression you enter, except where shadowed by another binding.

Let's establish a top-level definition for the `double-any` procedure of the last section.

```
(define double-any
  (lambda (f x)
    (f x x)))
```

The variable `double-any` now has the same status as `cons` or the name of any other primitive procedure. We can now use `double-any` as if it were a primitive procedure.

```
(double-any + 10)   ⇒   20
(double-any cons 'a)   ⇒   (a . a)
```

A top-level definition may be established for any object, not just for procedures.

```
(define sandwich "peanut-butter-and-jelly")
```

```
sandwich   ⇒   "peanut-butter-and-jelly"
```

Most often, though, top-level definitions are used for procedures.

As suggested above, top-level definitions may be shadowed by `let` or `lambda` bindings.

```
(define xyz '(x y z))
(let ((xyz '(z y x)))
  xyz)   ⇒   (z y x)
```

Variables with top-level definitions act almost as if they were bound by a `let` expression enclosing all of the expressions you type.

Given only the simple tools you have read about up to this point, it is already possible to define some of the primitive procedures provided by Scheme and described later in this book. If you completed the exercises from the last section, you should already know how to define `list`.

```
(define list (lambda x x))
```

Also, Scheme provides the abbreviations `cadr` and `cddr` for the compositions of `car` with `cdr` and `cdr` with `cdr`. That is, (`cadr` *list*) is equivalent to (`car` (`cdr` *list*)), and similarly, (`cddr` *list*) is equivalent to (`cdr` (`cdr` *list*)). They are easily defined as follows:

```
(define cadr
  (lambda (x)
    (car (cdr x))))
```

```
(define cddr
  (lambda (x)
    (cdr (cdr x))))

(cadr '(a b c))  ⇒  b
(cddr '(a b c))  ⇒  (c)
```

Any definition (**define** *var exp*) where *exp* is a **lambda** expression can be written in a shorter form that suppresses the **lambda**. The exact syntax depends upon the format of the **lambda** expression's formal parameter specifier, i.e., whether it is a proper list of variables, a single variable, or an improper list of variables. A definition of the form

```
(define var₀
  (lambda (var₁ ... varₙ)
    e₁ e₂ ...))
```

may be abbreviated

```
(define (var₀ var₁ ... varₙ)
  e₁ e₂ ...)
```

while

```
(define var₀
  (lambda varᵣ
    e₁ e₂ ...))
```

may be abbreviated

```
(define (var₀ . varᵣ)
  e₁ e₂ ...)
```

and

```
(define var₀
  (lambda (var₁ ... varₙ . varᵣ)
    e₁ e₂ ...))
```

may be abbreviated

```
(define (var₀ var₁ ... varₙ . varᵣ)
  e₁ e₂ ...)
```

For example, the definitions for **cadr** and **list** may be written as follows.

```
(define (cadr x)
  (car (cdr x)))

(define (list . x) x)
```

This book does not often employ this alternative syntax. Although it is shorter, it tends to mask the reality that procedures are not intimately tied to variables, or names, as they are in many other languages. This syntax is often referred to, somewhat pejoratively, as the "defun" syntax for **define**, after the **defun** form provided by Lisp languages in which procedures are more closely tied to their names.

Top-level definitions make it easier for us to experiment with a procedure interactively because we need not retype the procedure each time it is used. Let's try
defining a somewhat more complicated variation of `double-any`, one that turns an
"ordinary" two-argument procedure into a "doubling" one-argument procedure.

```
(define doubler
  (lambda (f)
    (lambda (x) (f x x))))
```

`doubler` accepts one argument, `f`, which must be a procedure that accepts two
arguments. The procedure returned by `doubler` accepts one argument, which it
uses for both arguments in an application of `f`. We can define, with `doubler`, the
simple `double` and `double-cons` procedures of the last section:

```
(define double (doubler +))
(double 13/2)  ⇒  13
```

```
(define double-cons (doubler cons))
(double-cons 'a)  ⇒  (a . a)
```

We can also define `double-any` with `doubler`:

```
(define double-any
  (lambda (f x)
    ((doubler f) x)))
```

Within `double` and `double-cons`, `f` has the appropriate value, i.e., `+` or `cons`, even
though the procedures are clearly applied outside the scope of `f`.

What happens if you attempt to use a variable that is not bound by a `let` or
`lambda` expression and that does not have a top-level definition? Try using the
variable `i-am-not-defined` to see what happens.

```
(i-am-not-defined 3)
```

Most Scheme systems print an error message to inform you that the variable is
unbound or undefined.

The system will not complain about the appearance of an undefined variable
within a `lambda` expression, until and unless the resulting procedure is applied.
The following should *not* cause an error, even though we have not yet established
a top-level definition for `proc2`.

```
(define proc1
  (lambda (x y)
    (proc2 y x)))
```

If you try to apply `proc1` before defining `proc2`, you should get an error message.
Let's give `proc2` a top-level definition and try `proc1`.

```
(define proc2 cons)
(proc1 'a 'b)  ⇒  (b . a)
```

When you define `proc1`, the system accepts your promise to define `proc2`, and does not complain unless you use `proc1` before defining `proc2`. This allows you to define procedures in any order you please. This is especially useful when you are trying to organize a file full of procedure definitions in a way that makes your program more readable. It is necessary when two procedures defined at top level depend upon each other; we will see some examples of this later.

Exercise 2.6.1. What would happen if you were to type

```
(double-any double-any double-any)
```

given the definition of `double-any` from the beginning of this section?

Exercise 2.6.2. A more elegant (though possibly less efficient) way to define `cadr` and `cddr` than given in this section is to define a procedure that composes two procedures to create a third. Write the procedure `compose`, such that (`compose` *proc₁* *proc₂*) is the composition of *proc₁* and *proc₂* (assuming both take one argument). Use `compose` to define `cadr` and `cddr`.

Exercise 2.6.3. Scheme also provides `caar`, `cdar`, `caaar`, `caadr`, and so on, with any combination of up to four `a`'s (representing `car`) and `d`'s (representing `cdr`) between the `c` and the `r` (see Section 6.2). Define each of these with the `compose` procedure of the preceding exercise.

2.7. Conditional Expressions

So far we have considered expressions that perform a given task unconditionally. Suppose that we wish to write the procedure `abs`. If its argument x is negative, `abs` returns $-x$; otherwise, it returns x. The most straightforward way to write `abs` is to first determine whether the argument is negative or not, using the `if` syntactic form.

```
(define abs
  (lambda (n)
    (if (< n 0)
        (- 0 n)
        n)))
```

```
(abs 77)   ⇒   77
(abs -77)  ⇒   77
```

An `if` expression has the general form (`if` *test consequent alternative*). *consequent* is the expression to evaluate if *test* is true; *alternative* is the expression to evaluate if *test* is false. In the expression above, *test* is (`< n 0`), *consequent* is (`- 0 n`), and *alternative* is `n`.

   The procedure `abs` could be written in a variety of other ways. Any of the following are valid definitions for `abs`.

```
(define abs
  (lambda (n)
    (if (>= n 0)
        n
        (- 0 n)))))
(define abs
  (lambda (n)
    (if (not (< n 0))
        n
        (- 0 n)))))
(define abs
  (lambda (n)
    (if (or (> n 0) (= n 0))
        n
        (- 0 n)))))
(define abs
  (lambda (n)
    (if (= n 0)
        0
        (if (< n 0)
            (- 0 n)
            n)))))
(define abs
  (lambda (n)
    ((if (>= n 0) + -)
     0
     n)))
```

The first of these definitions asks if n is greater than or equal to zero, inverting the test. The second asks if n is not less than zero, using the procedure not with <. The third asks if n is greater than zero or n is equal to zero, using the syntactic form or. The fourth treats zero separately, though there is no benefit in doing so. The fifth is somewhat tricky; n is either added to or subtracted from zero, depending upon whether n is greater than or equal to zero.

Why is if a syntactic form and not a procedure? In order to answer this, let's revisit the definition of reciprocal from the first section of this chapter.

```
(define reciprocal
  (lambda (n)
    (if (= n 0)
        "oops!"
        (/ 1 n))))
```

When the second argument to the division procedure is zero, the behavior is unspecified, and many implementations signal an error. Our definition of reciprocal avoids this problem by testing for zero before dividing. But were if a procedure, its arguments (including (/ 1 n)) would be evaluated before it had a chance to choose between the consequent and alternative. Like quote, which does not evaluate its only subexpression, if does not evaluate all of its subexpressions and so cannot be a procedure.

The syntactic form or operates in a manner similar to if. The general form of an or expression is (or *exp* ...). If there are no subexpressions, i.e., the expression is simply (or), the value is false. Otherwise, each *exp* is evaluated in turn until either (a) one of the expressions evaluates to true or (b) no more expressions are left. In case (a), the value is true; in case (b), the value is false.

To be more precise, in case (a), the value of the or expression is the value of the last subexpression evaluated. This clarification is necessary because there are many possible true values. Usually, the value of a test expression is one of the two objects #t, for true, or #f, for false.

```
(< -1 0)  ⇒  #t
(> -1 0)  ⇒  #f
```

Every Scheme object, however, is considered to be either true or false by the conditional expressions if and or and by the procedure not. Only #f is considered false; all other objects are considered true. (Although forbidden by the ANSI/IEEE standard, the Revised[4] Report permits () to be the same object as #f, and in those implementations in which this is the case, () is of course considered false as well.)

```
(not #t)  ⇒  #f
(not #f)  ⇒  #t

(not 1)  ⇒  #f
(not '(a b c))  ⇒  #f

(or)  ⇒  #f
(or #f)  ⇒  #f
(or #f #t)  ⇒  #t
(or #f 'a #f)  ⇒  a
```

The and syntactic form is similar in form to or, but an and expression is true if all its subexpressions are true, and false otherwise. In the case where there are no subexpressions, i.e., the expression is simply (and), the value is true. Otherwise, the subexpressions are evaluated in turn until either there are no more subexpressions or the value of a subexpression is false. The value of the and expression is the value of the last subexpression evaluated.

Using and, we can define a slightly different version of reciprocal.

```
(define reciprocal
  (lambda (n)
    (and (not (= n 0))
         (/ 1 n))))

(reciprocal 3)  ⇒  1/3
(reciprocal 0.5)  ⇒  2.0
(reciprocal 0)  ⇒  #f
```

In this version, the value is #f if n is zero, 1/n otherwise.

The procedures =, <, >, <=, and >= are called *predicates*. A predicate is a procedure that answers a specific question about its arguments and returns one of the two values #t or #f. The names of most predicates end with a question mark (?); the common numeric procedures listed above are exceptions to this rule. Not all predicates require numeric arguments, of course. The predicate null? returns true if its argument is the empty list (), false otherwise.

```
(null? '())   ⇒   #t
(null? 'abc)   ⇒   #f
(null? '(x y z))   ⇒   #f
(null? (cdddr '(x y z)))   ⇒   #t
```

It is an error to pass the procedure cdr anything other than a pair, and most implementations signal an error when this happens. Some Lisp languages, including Common Lisp, define (cdr '()) to be (). The following procedure, lisp-cdr, is defined using null? to return () if its argument is ().

```
(define lisp-cdr
  (lambda (x)
    (if (null? x)
        '()
        (cdr x))))
```

```
(lisp-cdr '(a b c))   ⇒   (b c)
(lisp-cdr '(c))   ⇒   ()
(lisp-cdr '())   ⇒   ()
```

Another useful predicate is eqv?, which requires two arguments. If the two arguments are equivalent, eqv? returns true. Otherwise, eqv? returns false.

```
(eqv? 'a 'a)   ⇒   #t
(eqv? 'a 'b)   ⇒   #f
(eqv? #f #f)   ⇒   #t
(eqv? #t #t)   ⇒   #t
(eqv? #f #t)   ⇒   #f
(eqv? 3 3)   ⇒   #t
(eqv? 3 2)   ⇒   #f
(let ((x "Hi Mom!"))
  (eqv? x x))   ⇒   #t
(let ((x (cons 'a 'b)))
  (eqv? x x))   ⇒   #t
(eqv? (cons 'a 'b) (cons 'a 'b))   ⇒   #f
```

As you can see, eqv? returns true if the arguments are the same symbol, boolean, number, pair, or string. Two pairs are not the same by eqv? if they are created by different calls to cons, even if they have the same contents. Detailed equivalence rules for eqv? are given in Section 6.1.

Scheme also provides a set of *type predicates* that return true or false depending on the type of the object, e.g., pair?, symbol?, number?, and string?. The predicate pair?, for example, returns true only if its argument is a pair.

```
(pair? '(a . c))  ⇒  #t
(pair? '(a b c))  ⇒  #t
(pair? '())  ⇒  #f
(pair? 'abc)  ⇒  #f
(pair? "Hi Mom!")  ⇒  #f
(pair? 1234567890)  ⇒  #f
```

Type predicates are useful for deciding if the argument passed to a procedure is of the appropriate type. For example, the following version of reciprocal checks first to see that its argument is a number before testing against zero or performing the division.

```
(define reciprocal
  (lambda (n)
    (if (and (number? n) (not (= n 0)))
        (/ 1 n)
        "oops!")))
```

```
(reciprocal 2/3)  ⇒  3/2
(reciprocal 'a)  ⇒  "oops!"
```

By the way, the code that uses reciprocal must check to see that the returned value is a number and not a string. It is usually better to report the error, using whatever error-reporting facilities your Scheme implementation provides. For example, *Chez Scheme* provides the procedure error for reporting errors; we might use error in the definition of reciprocal as follows.

```
(define reciprocal
  (lambda (n)
    (if (and (number? n) (not (= n 0)))
        (/ 1 n)
        (error 'reciprocal "improper argument ~s" n))))
```

```
(reciprocal .25)  ⇒  4.0
(reciprocal 0.0)  ⇒  error
(reciprocal 'a)  ⇒  error
```

The first argument to error is a symbol identifying where the message originates, the second is a string describing the error, and the third and subsequent arguments are objects to be inserted into the error message. The message string must contain one ~s for each object; the position of each ~s within the string determines the placement of the corresponding object in the resulting error message.

Let's consider one more conditional expression, cond, that is often useful in place of if. cond is similar to if except that it allows multiple test and alternative expressions. A cond expression usually takes the following form.

```
(cond (test exp) ... (else exp))
```

Recall the definition of abs that employed two if expressions:

```
(define abs
  (lambda (n)
    (if (= n 0)
        0
        (if (< n 0)
            (- 0 n)
            n))))
```

The two `if` expressions may be replaced by a single `cond` expression as follows.

```
(define abs
  (lambda (n)
    (cond
      ((= n 0) 0)
      ((< n 0) (- 0 n))
      (else n))))
```

Sometimes it is clearer to leave out the `else` clause. This should be done only when there is no possibility that all the tests will fail, as in the new definition of `abs` below.

```
(define abs
  (lambda (n)
    (cond
      ((= n 0) 0)
      ((< n 0) (- 0 n))
      ((> n 0) n))))
```

These definitions for `abs` do not depend on the order in which the tests were performed, since only one of the tests can be true for any value of n. The following procedure computes the tax on a given amount of income in a progressive tax system with breakpoints at 10,000, 20,000, and 30,000 dollars.

```
(define income-tax
  (lambda (income)
    (cond
      ((<= income 10000)
       (* income .05))
      ((<= income 20000)
       (+ (* (- income 10000) .08)
          500.00))
      ((<= income 30000)
       (+ (* (- income 20000) .13)
          1300.00))
      (else
       (+ (* (- income 30000) .21)
          2600.00)))))
```

```
(income-tax 5000)   ⇒   250.0
(income-tax 15000)  ⇒   900.0
(income-tax 25000)  ⇒   1950.0
(income-tax 50000)  ⇒   6800.0
```

In this example, the order in which the tests are performed, left to right (top to bottom), is significant.

Exercise 2.7.1. Define the predicate `atom?`, which returns true if its argument is not a pair and false otherwise.

Exercise 2.7.2. The procedure `length` returns the length of its argument, which must be a list. For example, `(length '(a b c))` is 3. Using `length`, define the procedure `shorter`, which returns the shorter of two list arguments.

```
(shorter (a b) (c d e))   ⇒   (a b)
```

2.8. Simple Recursion

We have seen how we can control whether or not expressions are evaluated with `if`, `and`, `or`, and `cond`. We can also perform an expression more than once by creating a procedure containing the expression and invoking the procedure more than once. What if we need to perform some expression repeatedly, say for all the elements of a list or all the numbers from zero to 10? We can do so via recursion. Recursion is a simple concept: the application of a procedure from within that procedure. It can be tricky to master recursion at first, but once mastered it provides expressive power far beyond ordinary looping constructs.

A *recursive procedure* is a procedure that applies itself. Perhaps the simplest recursive procedure is the following, which we will call **goodbye**.

```
(define goodbye
  (lambda ()
    (goodbye)))
```

```
(goodbye)   ⇒
```

This procedure takes no arguments and simply applies itself immediately. There is no value after the ⇒ because **goodbye** never returns.

Obviously, to make practical use out of a recursive procedure, we must have some way to terminate the recursion. Most recursive procedures should have at least two basic elements, a *base case* and a *recursion step*. The base case terminates the recursion, giving the value of the procedure for some base argument. The recursion step gives the value in terms of the value of the procedure applied to a different argument. In order for the recursion to terminate, the different argument must be closer to the base argument in some way.

Let's consider the problem of finding the length of a list recursively. We need a base case and a recursion step. The logical base argument for recursion on lists is nearly always the empty list. The length of the empty list is zero, so the base case should give the value zero for the empty list. In order to become closer to the empty list, the natural recursion step involves the cdr of the argument. A nonempty list is one element longer than its cdr, so the recursion step gives the value as one more than the length of the cdr of the list.

```
(define length
  (lambda (ls)
    (if (null? ls)
        0
        (+ (length (cdr ls)) 1)))))
```

```
(length '())     ⇒  0
(length '(a))    ⇒  1
(length '(a b))  ⇒  2
```

The if expression asks if the list is empty. If so, the value is zero. This is the base case. If not, the value is one more than the length of the cdr of the list. This is the recursion step.

Most Scheme implementations allow you to trace the execution of a procedure to see how it operates. In *Chez Scheme*, for example, one way to trace a procedure is to type (trace *name*), where *name* is the name of a procedure you have defined at top level. If you trace length as defined above and pass it the argument '(a b c d), you should see something like this:

```
|(length (a b c d))
| (length (b c d))
| |(length (c d))
| | (length (d))
| | |(length ())
| | |0
| | 1
| |2
| 3
|4
```

The indentation shows the nesting level of the recursion; the vertical lines associate applications visually with their values. Notice that on each application of length the list gets smaller until it finally reaches (). The value at () is 0, and each outer level adds 1 to arrive at the final value.

Let's write a procedure, list-copy, that returns a copy of its argument, which must be a list. That is, list-copy returns a new list consisting of the elements (but not the pairs) of the old list. Making a copy may be useful if either the original list or the copy may be altered via set-car! or set-cdr!, which we discuss later.

```
(list-copy '())       ⇒  ()
(list-copy '(a b c))  ⇒  (a b c)
```

See if you can define list-copy before studying the definition below.

```
(define list-copy
  (lambda (ls)
    (if (null? ls)
        '()
        (cons (car ls)
              (list-copy (cdr ls)))))))
```

The definition of `list-copy` is similar to the definition of `length`. The test in the base case is the same, `(null? ls)`. The value in the base case is `()`, however, not 0, because we are building up a list, not a number. The recursive call is the same, but instead of adding one, `list-copy` conses the car of the list onto the value of the recursive call.

There is no reason why there cannot be more than one base case. The procedure `memv` takes two arguments, an object and a list. It returns the first sublist, or *tail*, of the list whose car is equal to the object, or `#f` if the object is not found in the list. The value of `memv` may be used as a list or as a truth value in a conditional expression.

```
(define memv
  (lambda (x ls)
    (cond
      ((null? ls) #f)
      ((eqv? (car ls) x) ls)
      (else (memv x (cdr ls)))))))
```

```
(memv 'a '(a b b d))  ⇒  (a b b d)
(memv 'b '(a b b d))  ⇒  (b b d)
(memv 'c '(a b b d))  ⇒  #f
(memv 'd '(a b b d))  ⇒  (d)
(if (memv 'b '(a b b d))
    "yes"
    "no")  ⇒  "yes"
```

Here there are two conditions to check, hence the use of `cond`. The first cond clause checks for the base value of `()`; no object is a member of `()`, so the answer is `#f`. The second clause asks if the car of the list is the object, in which case the list is returned, being the first tail whose car contains the object. The recursion step just continues down the list.

There may also be more than one recursion case. Like `memv`, the procedure `remv` defined below takes two arguments, an object and a list. It returns a new list with all occurrences of the object removed from the list.

```
(define remv
  (lambda (x ls)
    (cond
      ((null? ls) '())
      ((eqv? (car ls) x) (remv x (cdr ls)))
      (else (cons (car ls) (remv x (cdr ls))))))))
```

```
(remv 'a '(a b b d))  ⇒  (b b d)
(remv 'b '(a b b d))  ⇒  (a d)
(remv 'c '(a b b d))  ⇒  (a b b d)
(remv 'd '(a b b d))  ⇒  (a b b)
```

This definition is similar to the definition for `memv` above, except `remv` does not quit once it finds the element in the car of the list. Rather, it continues, simply ignoring the element. If the element is not found in the car of the list, `remv` does the same thing as `list-copy` above: it conses the car of the list onto the recursive value.

Up to now, the recursion has been only on the cdr of a list. It is sometimes useful, however, for a procedure to be recursive on the car as well as the cdr of the list. The procedure `tree-copy` defined below treats the structure of pairs as a tree rather than as a list, with the left subtree being the car of the pair and the right subtree being the cdr of the pair. It performs a similar operation to `list-copy`, building new pairs while leaving the elements (leaves) alone.

```
(define tree-copy
  (lambda (tr)
    (if (not (pair? tr))
        tr
        (cons (tree-copy (car tr))
              (tree-copy (cdr tr))))))
```

```
(tree-copy '((a . b) . c))   ⇒   ((a . b) . c)
```

The natural base argument for a tree structure is anything that is not a pair, since the recursion traverses pairs rather than lists. The recursive step in this case is *doubly recursive*, finding the value recursively for the car as well as the cdr of the argument.

At this point, readers who are familiar with other languages that provide special iteration constructs, e.g., *while* or *for* loops, may wonder whether Scheme supports similar constructs. The answer is that such constructs are unnecessary; iteration in Scheme is expressed more clearly and succinctly via recursion. Recursion is more general and eliminates the need for the variable assignments required by many other languages' iteration constructs, resulting in code that is more reliable and easier to follow. Some recursion is essentially iteration and executes as such; Section 3.2 has more to say about this. Often, there is no need to make a distinction, however. Concentrate instead on writing clear, concise, and correct programs.

Before we leave the topic of recursion, let's consider a special form of repetition called *mapping*. Consider the following procedure, `abs-all`, that takes a list of numbers as input and returns a list of their absolute values.

```
(define abs-all
  (lambda (ls)
    (if (null? ls)
        '()
        (cons (abs (car ls))
              (abs-all (cdr ls))))))
```

```
(abs-all '(1 -2 3 -4 5 -6))   ⇒   (1 2 3 4 5 6)
```

This procedure forms a new list from the input list by applying the procedure `abs` to each element. We say that `abs-all` *maps* `abs` over the input list to produce the output list. Mapping a procedure over a list is a fairly common thing to do, so Scheme provides the procedure `map`, which maps its first argument, a procedure, over its second, a list. We can use `map` to define `abs-all`:

```
(define abs-all
  (lambda (ls)
    (map abs ls)))
```

We really do not need `abs-all`, however, since the corresponding direct application of `map` is just as short and perhaps clearer.

```
(map abs '(1 -2 3 -4 5 -6))  ⇒  (1 2 3 4 5 6)
```

Of course, we can use `lambda` to create the procedure argument to `map`, e.g., to square the elements of a list of numbers:

```
(map (lambda (x) (* x x))
     '(1 -3 -5 7))  ⇒  (1 9 25 49)
```

We can map a multiple-argument procedure over multiple lists, as in the following example:

```
(map cons '(a b c) '(1 2 3))  ⇒  ((a . 1) (b . 2) (c . 3))
```

The lists must be of the same length, and the procedure must accept as many arguments as there are lists. Each element of the output list is the result of applying the procedure to corresponding members of the input list.

Looking at the first definition of `abs-all` above, you should be able to derive, before studying it, the following definition of `map1`, a restricted version of `map` that maps a one-argument procedure over a single list.

```
(define map1
  (lambda (p ls)
    (if (null? ls)
        '()
        (cons (p (car ls))
              (map1 p (cdr ls))))))
```

```
(map1 abs '(1 -2 3 -4 5 -6))  ⇒  (1 2 3 4 5 6)
```

All we have done is to replace the call to `abs` in `abs-all` with a call to the new parameter `p`. A definition of the more general `map` is given in Section 5.5.

Exercise 2.8.1. Describe what would happen if you switched the order of the arguments to `cons` in the definition of `tree-copy`.

Exercise 2.8.2. Consult Section 6.2 for the description of `append` and define a two-argument version of it. What would happen if you switched the order of the arguments in the call to `append` within your definition of `append`?

Exercise 2.8.3. Define the procedure `make-list`, which takes a nonnegative integer n and an object and returns a new list, n long, each element of which is the object.

```
(make-list 7 '())  ⇒  (() () () () () () ())
```

[*Hint*: The base test should be (= n 0), and the recursion step should involve (- n 1). Whereas () is the natural base case for recursion on lists, 0 is the natural base case for recursion on nonnegative integers. Similarly, subtracting 1 is the natural way to bring a nonnegative integer closer to 0.]

Exercise 2.8.4. Consult Section 6.2 for the descriptions of `list-ref` and `list-tail`. Define both.

Exercise 2.8.5. Exercise 2.7.2 had you define the procedure `shorter`, which returns the shorter of its two list arguments, in terms of `length`. Write `shorter` without using `length`.

Exercise 2.8.6. All of the recursive procedures shown so far have been directly recursive. That is, each procedure directly applies itself to a new argument. It is also possible to write two procedures that use each other, resulting in indirect recursion. Define the procedures `odd?` and `even?`, each in terms of the other. [*Hint*: What should each return when its argument is 0?]

Exercise 2.8.7. Use `map` to define a procedure, `transpose`, that takes a list of pairs and returns a pair of lists as follows:

```
(transpose '((a . 1) (b . 2) (c . 3)))  ⇒  ((a b c) 1 2 3)
```

(Remember, ((a b c) 1 2 3) is the same as ((a b c) . (1 2 3)).)

2.9. Assignment

Although many programs can be written without them, assignments to top-level variables or `let`-bound and `lambda`-bound variables are sometimes useful. Assignments do not create new bindings, as with `let` or `lambda`, but rather change the values of existing bindings. Assignments are performed with `set!`.

```
(define abcde '(a b c d e))
abcde  ⇒  (a b c d e)
(set! abcde (cdr abcde))
abcde  ⇒  (b c d e)
(let ((abcde '(a b c d e)))
  (set! abcde (reverse abcde))
  abcde)  ⇒  (e d c b a)
```

Many languages require the use of assignments to initialize local variables, separate from the declaration or binding of the variables. In Scheme, all local variables are given a value immediately upon binding. Besides making the separate assignment to initialize local variables unnecessary, it ensures that the programmer cannot forget to initialize them, a common source of errors in most languages.

In fact, most of the assignments that are either necessary or convenient in other languages are both unnecessary and inconvenient in Scheme, since there is typically a clearer way to express the same algorithm without assignments. One common practice in some languages is to sequence expression evaluation with a series of assignments, as in the following procedure that finds the roots of a quadratic equation.

```
(define quadratic-formula
  (lambda (a b c)
    (let ((root1 0) (root2 0) (minusb 0) (radical 0) (divisor 0))
      (set! minusb (- 0 b))
      (set! radical (sqrt (- (* b b) (* 4 (* a c)))))
      (set! divisor (* 2 a))
      (set! root1 (/ (+ minusb radical) divisor))
      (set! root2 (/ (- minusb radical) divisor))
      (cons root1 root2))))
```

The roots are computed according to the well-known quadratic formula,

$$\frac{-b \pm \sqrt{b^2 - 4ac}}{2a}$$

which yields the solutions to the equation $0 = ax^2 + bx + c$. The let expression in this definition is employed solely to establish the variable bindings, corresponding to the declarations required in other languages. The first three assignment expressions compute subpieces of the formula, namely $-b$, $\sqrt{b^2 - 4ac}$, and $2a$. The last two assignment expressions compute the two roots in terms of the subpieces. A pair of the two roots is the value of quadratic-formula. For example, the two roots of $2x^2 - 4x - 6$ are $x = 3$ and $x = -1$.

```
(quadratic-formula 2 -4 -6)   ⇒   (3 . -1)
```

The definition above works, but it can be written more clearly without the assignments.

```
(define quadratic-formula
  (lambda (a b c)
    (let ((minusb (- 0 b))
          (radical (sqrt (- (* b b) (* 4 (* a c)))))
          (divisor (* 2 a)))
      (let ((root1 (/ (+ minusb radical) divisor))
            (root2 (/ (- minusb radical) divisor)))
        (cons root1 root2)))))
```

In this version, the `set!` expressions are gone, and we are left with essentially the same algorithm. By employing two `let` expressions, however, the definition makes clear the dependency of `root1` and `root2` on the values of `minusb`, `radical`, and `divisor`. Equally important, the `let` expressions make clear the *lack* of dependencies among `minusb`, `radical`, and `divisor` and between `root1` and `root2`.

Assignments do have some uses in Scheme, otherwise the language would not support them. Consider the following version of `cons` that counts the number of times it is called, storing the count in a variable named `cons-count`. It uses `set!` to increment the count; there is no way to achieve the same behavior without assignments.

```
(define cons-count 0)

(set! cons
  (let ((old-cons cons))
    (lambda (x y)
      (set! cons-count (+ cons-count 1))
      (old-cons x y))))

(cons 'a '(b c))  ⇒  (a b c)
cons-count  ⇒  1
(cons 'a (cons 'b (cons 'c '())))  ⇒  (a b c)
cons-count  ⇒  4
```

`set!` is used both to establish the new top-level value for `cons` and to update the variable `cons-count` each time `cons` is invoked.

Assignments are commonly used to implement procedures that must maintain some internal state. For example, suppose we would like to define a procedure that returns 0 the first time it is called, 1 the second time, 2 the third time, and so on indefinitely. We could write something similar to the definition of `cons-count` above:

```
(define next 0)

(define count
  (lambda ()
    (let ((v next))
      (set! next (+ next 1))
      v)))

(count)  ⇒  0
(count)  ⇒  1
```

This solution is somewhat undesirable in that the variable `next` is visible at top level even though it need not be. Since it is visible at top level, any code in the system can change its value, perhaps inadvertently affecting the behavior of `count` in a subtle way. We can solve this problem by `let`-binding `next` outside of the lambda expression:

```
(define count
  (let ((next 0))
    (lambda ()
      (let ((v next))
        (set! next (+ next 1))
        v))))
```

The latter solution also generalizes easily to provide multiple counters, each with its own local counter. The procedure `make-counter`, defined below, returns a new counting procedure each time it is called.

```
(define make-counter
  (lambda ()
    (let ((next 0))
      (lambda ()
        (let ((v next))
          (set! next (+ next 1))
          v)))))
```

Since `next` is bound inside of `make-counter` but outside of the procedure returned by `make-counter`, each procedure it returns maintains its own unique counter.

```
(define count1 (make-counter))
(define count2 (make-counter))
```

```
(count1)   ⇒   0
(count2)   ⇒   0
(count1)   ⇒   1
(count1)   ⇒   2
(count2)   ⇒   1
```

Local state is sometimes useful to allow a computation to be evaluated *lazily*, i.e., only once and only on demand. The procedure `lazy` below accepts a *thunk*, or zero-argument procedure, as an argument. Thunks are often used to "freeze" computations that must be delayed for some reason, which is exactly what we need to do in this situation. When passed a thunk t, `lazy` returns a thunk that, when invoked, returns the value of invoking t. Once computed, the value is saved in a local variable so that the computation need not be performed again. A boolean flag is used to record whether t has been invoked and its value saved.

```
(define lazy
  (lambda (t)
    (let ((val #f) (flag #f))
      (lambda ()
        (if (not flag)
            (begin (set! val (t))
                   (set! flag #t)))
        val))))
```

The syntactic form `begin`, used here for the first time, evaluates its subexpressions in sequence from left to right and returns the value of the last subexpression, like the body of a `let` or `lambda` expression. We also see that the *alternative* subexpression of an `if` expression can be omitted. This should be done only when the value of the `if` is discarded, as it is in this case.

Lazy evaluation is especially useful for values that require considerable time to compute. By delaying the evaluation, we may avoid computing the value altogether, and by saving the value, we avoid computing it more than once.

The operation of `lazy` can best be illustrated by printing a message from within a thunk passed to `lazy`.

```
(define p
  (lazy (lambda ()
          (display "Ouch!")
          (newline)
          "got me")))
```

The first time `p` is invoked, the message `Ouch!` is printed and the string `"got me"` is returned. Thereafter, `"got me"` is returned but the message is not printed. The procedures `display` and `newline` are the first examples of explicit input/output we have seen; `display` prints the string without quotation marks, and `newline` prints a newline character.

As a more complex example using `set!`, let's consider the implementation of stack objects whose internal workings are not visible on the outside. A stack object accepts one of four *messages*: `empty?`, which returns `#t` if the stack is empty; `push!`, which adds an object to the top of the stack; `top`, which returns the object on the top of the stack; and `pop!`, which removes the object on top of the stack. The procedure `make-stack` given below creates a new stack each time it is called in a manner similar to `make-counter`.

```
(define make-stack
  (lambda ()
    (let ((ls '()))
      (lambda (msg . args)
        (cond
          ((eqv? msg 'empty?) (null? ls))
          ((eqv? msg 'push!)
           (set! ls (cons (car args) ls)))
          ((eqv? msg 'top) (car ls))
          ((eqv? msg 'pop!)
           (set! ls (cdr ls)))
          (else "oops"))))))
```

Each stack is stored as a list bound to the variable `ls`; `set!` is used to change this binding by `push!` and `pop!`. Notice that the argument list of the inner `lambda` expression uses the improper list syntax to bind `args` to a list of all arguments but the first. This is useful here because in the case of `empty?`, `top`, and `pop!` there is only one argument (the message), but in the case of `push!` there are two (the message and the object to push onto the stack).

```
(define stack1 (make-stack))
(define stack2 (make-stack))

(stack1 'empty?)  ⇒  #t
(stack2 'empty?)  ⇒  #t

(stack1 'push! 'a)
(stack1 'empty?)  ⇒  #f
(stack2 'empty?)  ⇒  #t

(stack1 'push! 'b)
(stack2 'push! 'c)
(stack1 'top)  ⇒  b
(stack2 'top)  ⇒  c

(stack1 'pop!)
(stack2 'empty?)  ⇒  #f
(stack1 'top)  ⇒  a

(stack2 'pop!)
(stack2 'empty?)  ⇒  #t
```

As with the counters created by `make-counter`, the state maintained by each stack object is directly accessible only within the object. Each reference or change to this state is made explicitly by the object itself. One important benefit is that we can change the internal structure of the stack, perhaps to use a vector (see Section 6.6) instead of a list to hold the elements, without changing its external behavior. Because the behavior of the object is known abstractly (not operationally), it is known as an *abstract object*. See Section 9.8 for more about creating abstract objects.

Exercise 2.9.1. Modify `make-counter` to take two arguments: an initial value for the counter to use in place of 0 and an amount to increment the counter by each time.

Exercise 2.9.2. Look up the description of `case` in Section 5.4. Replace the `cond` expression in `make-stack` with an equivalent `case` expression.

Exercise 2.9.3. Modify the `stack` object to allow the two messages `ref` and `set!`. (*stack* `'ref` *i*) should return the *i*th element from the top of the stack; (*stack* `'ref` 0) should be equivalent to (*stack* `'top`). Similarly, (*stack* `'set!` *i* *v*) should change the *i*th element from the top of the stack to *v*. [*Hint*: Use `list-ref` to implement `ref` and `list-tail` with `set-car!` to implement `set!`.]

Exercise 2.9.4. Modify the stack object to use vectors interally without changing the external (abstract) interface. Either enforce a limit on the overall stack size or make the vector small initially and allocate a new, larger vector as necessary.

Exercise 2.9.5. Using `set-cdr!`, it is possible to create *cyclic lists*. For example, the following expression evaluates to a list whose car is the symbol a and whose cdr is the list itself:

```
(let ((ls (cons 'a '())))
  (set-cdr! ls ls)
  ls)
```

What happens when you enter the above expression during an interactive Scheme session? What will the implementation of `length` given earlier in this chapter do when given a cyclic list? What does the built-in `length` primitive do?

Exercise 2.9.6. Define the predicate `list?`, which returns `#t` if its argument is a proper list and `#f` otherwise (see Section 6.2). It should return `#f` for cyclic lists as well as for lists terminated by objects other than ().

```
(list? '())   ⇒   #t
(list? '(1 2 3))   ⇒   #t
(list? '(a . b))   ⇒   #f
(list? (let ((ls (cons 'a '())))
         (set-cdr! ls ls)
         ls))   ⇒   #f
```

First write a simplified version of `list?` that does not handle cyclic lists, then extend this to handle cyclic lists correctly. Revise your definition until you are satisfied that it is as clear and concise as possible. [*Hint*: Use the following "hare and tortoise" algorithm to detect cycles. Define a recursive help procedure of two arguments, the hare and the tortoise. Start both the hare and the tortoise at the beginning of the list. Have the hare advance by two cdrs each time the tortoise advances by one cdr. If the hare catches the tortoise, there must be a cycle.]

CHAPTER 3

Going Further

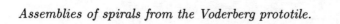
Assemblies of spirals from the Voderberg prototile.

The preceding chapter prepared you to write Scheme programs using a small set of the most useful primitive syntactic forms and procedures. This chapter introduces a number of additional features and programming techniques that will allow you to write more sophisticated and efficient programs.

3.1. Syntactic Extension

As we saw in Section 2.5, the `let` syntactic form is merely a *syntactic extension* defined in terms of a `lambda` expression and a procedure application, both core syntactic forms. At this point, you might be wondering which syntactic forms are core forms and which are syntactic extensions, and how new syntactic extensions may be defined. This section provides some answers to both questions.

In truth, it is not necessary for us to draw a distinction between core forms and syntactic extensions, since once defined, a syntactic extension has exactly the same status as a core form. Drawing a distinction, however, makes understanding the language easier, since it allows us to focus attention on the core forms and to understand all others in terms of them.

It *is* necessary for a Scheme implementation to distinguish between core forms and syntactic extensions. A Scheme implementation typically expands syntactic extensions into core forms prior to compilation or interpretation, allowing the compiler or interpreter to focus only on the core forms. The set of core forms remaining after expansion to be handled directly by the compiler or interpreter is implementation-dependent, however, and may be different from the set of forms described as core here.

The exact set of syntactic forms making up the core of the language is thus subject to debate, although it must be possible to derive all other forms from any set of forms declared to be core forms. The set described here is among the simplest for which this constraint is satisfied. It also closely matches the set described as "primitive" in the ANSI/IEEE Scheme standard and Revised Reports.

The core syntactic forms include top-level `define` forms, constants, variables, procedure applications, `quote` expressions, `lambda` expressions, `if` expressions, and `set!` expressions. The grammar below describes the core syntax of Scheme in terms of these definitions and expressions. In the grammar, vertical bars (|) separate alternatives, and a form followed by an asterisk (*) represents zero or more occurrences of the form, ⟨variable⟩ is any Scheme identifier. ⟨datum⟩ is any Scheme object, such as a number, list, symbol, or vector. ⟨boolean⟩ is either `#t` or `#f`, ⟨number⟩ is any number, ⟨character⟩ is any character, and ⟨string⟩ is any string. We have already seen examples of numbers, strings, lists, symbols, and booleans. See Chapter 6 or the more detailed grammar at the back of this book for more on the object-level syntax of these and other objects.

⟨program⟩ ⟶ ⟨form⟩*
⟨form⟩ ⟶ ⟨definition⟩ | ⟨expression⟩
⟨definition⟩ ⟶ ⟨variable definition⟩ | (**begin** ⟨definition⟩*)
⟨variable definition⟩ ⟶ (**define** ⟨variable⟩ ⟨expression⟩)
⟨expression⟩ ⟶ ⟨constant⟩
    | ⟨variable⟩
    | (**quote** ⟨datum⟩)
    | (**lambda** ⟨formals⟩ ⟨expression⟩ ⟨expression⟩*)
    | (**if** ⟨expression⟩ ⟨expression⟩ ⟨expression⟩)
    | (**set!** ⟨variable⟩ ⟨expression⟩)
    | ⟨application⟩
⟨constant⟩ ⟶ ⟨boolean⟩ | ⟨number⟩ | ⟨character⟩ | ⟨string⟩
⟨formals⟩ ⟶ ⟨variable⟩
    | (⟨variable⟩*)
    | (⟨variable⟩ ⟨variable⟩* . ⟨variable⟩)
⟨application⟩ ⟶ (⟨expression⟩ ⟨expression⟩*)

The grammar is ambiguous in that the syntax for procedure applications conflicts
with the syntaxes for `quote`, `lambda`, `if`, and `set!` expressions. In order to qualify
as a procedure application, the first ⟨expression⟩ must not be one of these keywords,
unless the keyword has been redefined or locally bound.

   The "defun" syntax for `define` given in Section 2.6 is not included in the core,
since definitions in that form are straightforwardly translated into the simpler
`define` syntax. Similarly, the core syntax for `if` does not permit the *alternative*
to be omitted, as did one example in Section 2.9. An `if` expression lacking an
alternative can be translated into the core syntax for `if` merely by replacing the
missing subexpression with an arbitrary constant, such as `#f`.

   A `begin` that contains only definitions is considered to be a definition in the
grammar; this is permitted in order to allow syntactic extensions to expand into
more than one definition. `begin` expressions, i.e., `begin` forms containing expressions, are not considered core forms. A `begin` expression of the form

(**begin** e_1 e_2 ...)

is equivalent to the `lambda` application

((**lambda** () e_1 e_2 ...))

and hence need not be considered core.

   Now that we have established a set of core syntactic forms, let's turn to a
discussion of syntactic extensions. Syntactic extensions are so called because they
extend the syntax of Scheme beyond the core syntax. All syntactic extensions in
a Scheme program must ultimately be derived from the core forms. One syntactic
extension, however, may be defined in terms of another syntactic extension, as long
as the latter is in some sense "closer" to the core syntax. Syntactic forms may
appear anywhere an expression or definition is expected, as long as the extended
form expands into a definition or expression as appropriate.

Syntactic extensions are defined with `define-syntax`. `define-syntax` is similar to `define`, except that `define-syntax` associates a syntactic transformation procedure, or *transformer*, with a keyword (such as `let`), rather than associating a value with a variable. Here is how we might define `let` with `define-syntax`:

```
(define-syntax let
  (syntax-rules ()
    ((_ ((x v) ...) e1 e2 ...)
     ((lambda (x ...) e1 e2 ...) v ...))))
```

The identifier appearing after `define-syntax` is the name, or keyword, of the syntactic extension being defined, in this case `let`. The `syntax-rules` form is an expression that evaluates to a transformer. The item following `syntax-rules` is a list of *auxiliary keywords* and is nearly always `()`. An example of an auxiliary keyword is the `else` of `cond`. Definitions requiring the use of auxiliary keywords are given in Chapter 8. Following the list of auxiliary keywords is a sequence of one or more *rules*, or *pattern/template* pairs. Only one rule appears in our definition of `let`. The pattern part of a rule specifies the form that the input must take, and the template specifies to what the input should be transformed.

The pattern should always be a structured expression whose first element is an underscore (_). (As we shall see in Chapter 8, the use of _ is only a convention, but it is a good one to follow.) If more than one rule is present, the appropriate one is chosen by matching the patterns, in order, against the input during expansion. An error is signaled if none of the patterns match the input.

Identifiers appearing within a pattern are *pattern variables*, unless they are listed as auxiliary keywords as described in Chapter 8. Pattern variables match any substructure and are bound to that substructure within the corresponding template. The notation *pat* ... in the pattern allows for zero or more expressions matching the ellipsis prototype *pat* in the input. Similarly, the notation *exp* ... in the template produces zero or more expressions from the ellipsis prototype *exp* in the output. The number of *pats* in the input determines the number of *exps* in the output; in order for this to work, any ellipsis prototype in the template must contain at least one pattern variable from an ellipsis prototype in the pattern.

The single rule in our definition of `let` should be fairly self-explanatory, but a few points are worth mentioning. First, the syntax of `let` requires that the body contain at least one expression; hence, we have specified `e1 e2 ...` instead of `e ...`, which might seem more natural. On the other hand, `let` does not require that there be at least one variable/value pair, so we were able to use, simply, `(x v) ...`. Second, the pattern variables `x` and `v`, though together within the same prototype in the pattern, are separated in the template; any sort of rearrangement or recombination is possible. Finally, the three pattern variables `x`, `v`, and `e2` that appear in ellipsis prototypes in the pattern also appear in ellipsis prototypes in the template. This is not a coincidence; it is a requirement. In general, if a pattern variable appears within an ellipsis prototype in the pattern, it cannot appear outside an ellipsis prototype in the template.

The definition of **and** below is somewhat more complex than the one for `let`.

```
(define-syntax and
  (syntax-rules ()
    ((_) #t)
    ((_ e) e)
    ((_ e1 e2 e3 ...)
     (if e1 (and e2 e3 ...) #f))))
```

This definition is recursive and involves more than one rule. Recall that (and) evaluates to #t; the first rule takes care of this case. The second and third rules specify the base case and recursion steps of the recursion and together translate and expressions with two or more subexpressions into nested if expressions. For example, (and a b c) expands first into

```
(if a (and b c) #f)
```

then

```
(if a (if b (and c) #f) #f)
```

and finally

```
(if a (if b c #f) #f)
```

With this expansion, if a and b evaluate to a true value, then the value is the value of c, otherwise #f, as desired.

The definition of or below is similar to the one for and except that a temporary variable must be introduced for each intermediate value so that we can both test the value and return it if it is a true value. (A similar temporary is not needed for and since there is only one false value, #f.)

```
(define-syntax or
  (syntax-rules ()
    ((_) #f)
    ((_ e) e)
    ((_ e1 e2 e3 ...)
     (let ((t e1))
       (if t t (or e2 e3 ...))))))
```

Like variables bound by lambda or let, identifiers introduced by a template are lexically scoped, i.e., visible only within expressions introduced by the template. Thus, even if one of the expressions e2 e3 ... contains a reference to t, the introduced binding for t does not "capture" those references. This is typically accomplished via automatic renaming of introduced identifiers.

Exercise 3.1.1. Write out the expansion steps necessary to expand

```
(let ((x (memv 'a ls)))
  (and x (memv 'b x)))
```

into core forms.

Exercise 3.1.2. Write out the expansion steps necessary to expand

```
(or (memv x '(a b c)) (list x))
```

into core forms.

Exercise 3.1.3. Look up the description of `let*` in Chapter 4 and define it using `define-syntax`.

Exercise 3.1.4. As we saw in Section 2.9, it is legal to omit the third, or *alternative*, subexpression of an `if` expression. Doing so, however, often leads to confusion. Some Scheme systems provide two syntactic forms, `when` and `unless`, that may be used in place of such "one-armed" `if` expressions.

```
(when test exp₁ exp₂ ...)
(unless test exp₁ exp₂ ...)
```

With both forms, `test` is evaluated first. For `when`, if `test` evaluates to true, the remaining forms are evaluated in sequence as if enclosed in an implicit `begin` expression. If `test` evaluates to false, the remaining forms are not evaluated, and the result is unspecified. `unless` is similar except that the remaining forms are evaluated only if `test` evaluates to false.

```
(let ((x 3))
  (unless (= x 0) (set! x (+ x 1)))
  (when (= x 4) (set! x (* x 2)))
  x)  ⇒  8
```

Define `when` as a syntactic extension in terms of `if` and `begin`, and define `unless` in terms of `when`.

3.2. More Recursion

In Section 2.8, we saw how to define recursive procedures using top-level definitions. Before that, we saw how to create local bindings for procedures using `let`. It is natural to wonder whether a `let`-bound procedure can be recursive. The answer is no, at least not in a straightforward way. If you try to evaluate the expression

```
(let ((sum (lambda (ls)
             (if (null? ls)
                 0
                 (+ (car ls) (sum (cdr ls)))))))
  (sum '(1 2 3 4 5)))
```

you will probably receive an error message to the effect that `sum` is undefined. This is because the variable `sum` is visible only within the body of the `let` expression and not within the `lambda` expression whose value is bound to `sum`. We can get around this problem by passing the procedure `sum` to itself as follows:

```
(let ((sum (lambda (sum ls)
             (if (null? ls)
                 0
                 (+ (car ls) (sum sum (cdr ls)))))))
  (sum sum '(1 2 3 4 5)))  ⇒  15
```

This works and is a clever solution, but there is an easier way, using `letrec`. Like `let`, the `letrec` syntactic form includes a set of variable-value pairs, along with a sequence of expressions referred to as the *body* of the `letrec`.

```
(letrec ((var val) ...) exp₁ exp₂ ...)
```

Unlike `let`, the variables *var* ... are visible not only within the body of the `letrec` but also within *val* .... Thus, we can rewrite the expression above as follows.

```
(letrec ((sum (lambda (ls)
                (if (null? ls)
                    0
                    (+ (car ls) (sum (cdr ls)))))))
  (sum '(1 2 3 4 5)))   ⇒   15
```

Using `letrec`, we can also define mutually recursive procedures, such as the procedures `even?` and `odd?` that were the subject of Exercise 2.8.6.

```
(letrec ((even?
           (lambda (x)
             (or (= x 0)
                 (odd? (- x 1)))))
         (odd?
           (lambda (x)
             (and (not (= x 0))
                  (even? (- x 1))))))
  (list (even? 20) (odd? 20)))   ⇒   (#t #f)
```

In a `letrec` expression, *val* ... are most commonly `lambda` expressions, though this need not be the case. One restriction on the expressions must be obeyed, however. It must be possible to evaluate each *val* without evaluating any of the variables *var* .... This restriction is always satisfied if the expressions are all `lambda` expressions, since even though the variables may appear within the `lambda` expressions, they cannot be evaluated until the resulting procedures are invoked in the body of the `letrec`. The following `letrec` expression obeys this restriction:

```
(letrec ((f (lambda () (+ x 2)))
         (x 1))
  (f))   ⇒   3
```

while the following does not.

```
(letrec ((y (+ x 2))
         (x 1))
  y)
```

The behavior in this case depends upon the implementation. The expression may return 3, it may return any other value, or it may result in an error being signaled.

We can use `letrec` to hide the definitions of "help" procedures so that they do not clutter the top-level name space. This is demonstrated by the definition of `list?` below, which follows the "hare and tortoise" algorithm outlined in Exercise 2.9.6.

```
(define list?
  (lambda (x)
    (letrec ((race
               (lambda (h t)
                 (if (pair? h)
                     (let ((h (cdr h)))
                       (if (pair? h)
                           (and (not (eq? h t))
                                (race (cdr h) (cdr t)))
                           (null? h)))
                     (null? h)))))
      (race x x))))
```

When a recursive procedure is called in only one place outside the procedure, as in the example above, it is often clearer to use a *named* let expression. Named let expressions take the following form.

```
(let name ((var val) ...)
  exp₁ exp₂ ...)
```

Named let is similar to unnamed let in that it binds the variables *var* ... to the values of *val* ... within the body *exp₁ exp₂* .... As with unnamed let, the variables are visible only within the body and not within *val* .... In addition, the variable *name* is bound within the body to a procedure that may be called to recur; the arguments to the procedure become the new values for the variables *var* ....

The definition of list? has been rewritten below to use named let.

```
(define list?
  (lambda (x)
    (let race ((h x) (t x))
      (if (pair? h)
          (let ((h (cdr h)))
            (if (pair? h)
                (and (not (eq? h t))
                     (race (cdr h) (cdr t)))
                (null? h)))
          (null? h)))))
```

Just as let can be expressed as a simple direct application of a lambda expression to arguments, named let can be expressed as the application of a recursive procedure to arguments. A named let of the form

```
(let name ((var val) ...)
  exp₁ exp₂ ...)
```

can be rewritten in terms of letrec as follows.

```
((letrec ((name (lambda (var ...) exp₁ exp₂ ...)))
   name)
 val ...)
```

Alternatively, it can be rewritten as

```
(letrec ((name (lambda (var ...) exp₁ exp₂ ...))))
  (name val ...))
```

provided that the variable *name* does not appear free within *val* ....

As we discussed in Section 2.8, some recursion is essentially iteration and executes as such. When a procedure call is in tail position (see below) with respect to a `lambda` expression, it is considered to be a *tail call*, and Scheme systems must treat it *properly*, as a "goto" or jump. When a procedure tail calls itself or calls itself indirectly through a series of tail calls, the result is *tail recursion*. Because tail calls are treated as jumps, tail recursion can be used for indefinite iteration in place of the more restrictive iteration constructs provided by other programming languages, without fear of overflowing any sort of recursion stack.

A call is in tail position with respect to a `lambda` expression if its value is returned directly from the `lambda` expression, i.e., if nothing is left to do after the call but to return from the `lambda` expression. For example, a call is in tail position if it is the last expression in the body of a `lambda` expression, the *consequent* or *alternative* part of an `if` expression in tail position, the last subexpression of an `and` or `or` expression in tail position, the last expression of a `let` or `letrec` in tail position, etc. Each of the calls to `f` in the expressions below are tail calls, but the calls to `g` are not.

```
(lambda () (f (g)))
(lambda () (if (g) (f) (f)))
(lambda () (let ((x 4)) (f)))
(lambda () (or (g) (f)))
```

In each case, the values of the calls to `f` are returned directly, whereas the calls to `g` are not.

Recursion in general and named `let` in particular provide a natural way to implement many algorithms, whether iterative, recursive, or partly iterative and partly recursive; the programmer is not burdened with two distinct mechanisms.

The following two definitions of `factorial` use named `let` expressions to compute the factorial, $n!$, of a nonnegative integer n. The first employs the recursive definition $n! = n \times (n-1)!$, where $0!$ is defined to be 1.

```
(define factorial
  (lambda (n)
    (let fact ((i n))
      (if (= i 0)
          1
          (* i (fact (- i 1)))))))

(factorial 0)   ⇒   1
(factorial 1)   ⇒   1
(factorial 2)   ⇒   2
(factorial 3)   ⇒   6
(factorial 10)  ⇒   3628800
```

The second is an iterative version that employs the iterative definition $n! = n \times (n - 1) \times (n-2) \times \ldots \times 1$, using an accumulator, a, to hold the intermediate products.

```
(define factorial
  (lambda (n)
    (let fact ((i n) (a 1))
      (if (= i 0)
          a
          (fact (- i 1) (* a i))))))
```

A similar problem is to compute the nth Fibonacci number for a given n. The *Fibonacci numbers* are an infinite sequence of integers, 0, 1, 1, 2, 3, 5, 8, etc., in which each number is the sum of the two preceding numbers in the sequence. A procedure to compute the nth Fibonacci number is most naturally defined recursively as follows:

```
(define fibonacci
  (lambda (n)
    (let fib ((i n))
      (cond
        ((= i 0) 0)
        ((= i 1) 1)
        (else (+ (fib (- i 1)) (fib (- i 2))))))))
```

```
(fibonacci 0)   ⇒   0
(fibonacci 1)   ⇒   1
(fibonacci 2)   ⇒   1
(fibonacci 3)   ⇒   2
(fibonacci 4)   ⇒   3
(fibonacci 5)   ⇒   5
(fibonacci 6)   ⇒   8
(fibonacci 20)  ⇒   6765
(fibonacci 30)  ⇒   832040
```

This solution requires the computation of the two preceding Fibonacci numbers at each step and hence is *doubly recursive*. For example, to compute (fibonacci 4) requires the computation of both (fib 3) and (fib 2), to compute (fib 3) requires computing both (fib 2) and (fib 1), and to compute (fib 2) requires computing both (fib 1) and (fib 0). This is very inefficient, and it becomes more inefficient as n grows. A more efficient solution is to adapt the accumulator solution of the factorial example above to use two accumulators, a1 for the current Fibonacci number and a2 for the preceding one.

```
(define fibonacci
  (lambda (n)
    (if (= n 0)
        0
        (let fib ((i n) (a1 1) (a2 0))
          (if (= i 1)
              a1
              (fib (- i 1) (+ a1 a2) a1))))))
```

Here, zero is treated as a special case, since there is no preceding value. This allows us to use the single base case (= i 1). The time it takes to compute the *n*th Fibonacci number using this iterative solution grows linearly with *n*, which makes a significant difference when compared to the doubly recursive version. To get a feel for the difference, try computing (fibonacci 30) and (fibonacci 35) using both definitions to see how long each takes.

We can also get a feel for the difference by looking at a trace for each on small inputs. The first trace below shows the calls to fib in the non-tail-recursive version of fibonacci, with input 5.

```
|(fib 5)
| (fib 4)
| |(fib 3)
| | (fib 2)
| | |(fib 1)
| | |1
| | |(fib 0)
| | |0
| | 1
| | (fib 1)
| | 1
| |2
| |(fib 2)
| | (fib 1)
| | 1
| | (fib 0)
| | 0
| |1
| 3
| (fib 3)
| |(fib 2)
| | (fib 1)
| | 1
| | (fib 0)
| | 0
| |1
| |(fib 1)
| |1
| 2
|5
```

Notice how there are several calls to fib with arguments 2, 1, and 0. The second trace shows the calls to fib in the tail-recursive version, again with input 5.

```
|(fib 5 1 0)
|(fib 4 1 1)
|(fib 3 2 1)
|(fib 2 3 2)
|(fib 1 5 3)
|5
```

Clearly, there is quite a difference.

The named `let` examples shown so far are either tail-recursive or not tail-recursive. It often happens that one recursive call within the same expression is tail-recursive while another is not. The definition of `factor` below computes the prime factors of its nonnegative integer argument; the first call to `f` is not tail-recursive, but the second one is.

```
(define factor
  (lambda (n)
    (let f ((n n) (i 2))
      (cond
        ((> i n) '())
        ((integer? (/ n i))
         (cons i (f (/ n i) i)))
        (else (f n (+ i 1))))))))
```

```
(factor 12)   ⇒  (2 2 3)
(factor 3628800)  ⇒  (2 2 2 2 2 2 2 2 3 3 3 3 5 5 7)
(factor 9239)  ⇒  (9239)
```

The trace of the calls to `f` in the evaluation of `(factor 120)` below highlights the difference between the nontail calls and the tail calls.

```
|(f 120 2)
| (f 60 2)
| |(f 30 2)
| | (f 15 2)
| | (f 15 3)
| | |(f 5 3)
| | |(f 5 4)
| | |(f 5 5)
| | | (f 1 5)
| | | ()
| | |(5)
| | (3 5)
| |(2 3 5)
| (2 2 3 5)
|(2 2 2 3 5)
```

A nontail call to `f` is shown indented relative to its caller, since the caller is still active, whereas tail calls appear at the same level of indentation.

Exercise 3.2.1. Which of the procedures defined in Section 3.2 are tail-recursive, and which are not?

Exercise 3.2.2. Rewrite `factor` using `letrec` to bind `f` in place of named `let`.

Exercise 3.2.3. Can the `letrec` expression defining **even?** and **odd?** on page 54 be rewritten using named `let`? If not, why not? If so, do it.

Exercise 3.2.4. Rewrite both definitions of `fibonacci` given in this section to count the number of recursive calls to `fib`, using a counter similar to the one used in the `cons-count` example of Section 2.9. Count the number of recursive calls made in each case for several input values. What do you notice?

Exercise 3.2.5. Augment the definition of `let` given in Section 3.1 to handle named `let` as well as unnamed `let`, using two rules.

Exercise 3.2.6. The following definition of `or` is simpler than the one given in Section 3.1.

```
(define-syntax or
  (syntax-rules ()
    ((_) #f)
    ((_ e1 e2 ...)
     (let ((t e1))
       (if t t (or e2 ...))))))
```

Say why it is not correct. [*Hint*: Think about what would happen if this version of `or` were used in the `even?` and `odd?` example given in this section, for very large inputs.]

Exercise 3.2.7. The definition of `factor` is not the most efficient possible. First, no factors of n besides n itself can possibly be found beyond $\sqrt{n}$. Second, the division `(/ n i)` is performed twice when a factor is found. Third, after 2, no even factors can possibly be found. Recode `factor` to correct all three problems. Which is the most important problem to solve? Are there any additional improvements you can make?

3.3. Continuations

During the evaluation of a Scheme expression, the implementation must keep track of two things: (1) what to evaluate and (2) what to do with the value. Consider the evaluation of `(null? x)` within the expression below.

```
(if (null? x) (quote ()) (cdr x))
```

The implementation must first evaluate `(null? x)` and, based on its value, evaluate either `(quote ())` or `(cdr x)`. "What to evaluate" is `(null? x)`, and "what to do with the value" is to make the decision which of `(quote ())` and `(cdr x)` to evaluate and do so. We call "what to do with the value" the *continuation* of a computation.

Thus, at any point during the evaluation of any expression, there is a continuation ready to complete, or at least *continue*, the computation from that point. Let's assume that `x` has the value `(a b c)`. Then we can isolate six continuations during the evaluation of `(if (null? x) (quote ()) (cdr x))`, the continuations waiting for:

1. the value of `(if (null? x) (quote ()) (cdr x))`,
2. the value of `(null? x)`,

3. the value of `null?`,

4. the value of `x`,

5. the value of `cdr`, and

6. the value of `x` (again).

The continuation of `(cdr x)` is not listed because it is the same as the one waiting for `(if (null? x) (quote ()) (cdr x))`.

Scheme allows the continuation of any expression to be obtained with the procedure `call-with-current-continuation`, which may be abbreviated `call/cc` in most implementations. (We use the shorter name here. If the implementation you are using does not recognize `call/cc`, simply define it to be `call-with-current-continuation` or use the longer name in your code.)

`call/cc` must be passed a procedure *p* of one argument. `call/cc` obtains the current continuation and passes it to *p*. The continuation itself is represented by a procedure *k*. Each time *k* is applied to a value, it returns the value to the continuation of the `call/cc` application. This value becomes, in essence, the value of the application of `call/cc`.

If *p* returns without invoking *k*, the value returned by the procedure becomes the value of the application of `call/cc`.

Consider the simple examples below.

```
(call/cc
  (lambda (k)
    (* 5 4)))   ⇒   20
(call/cc
  (lambda (k)
    (* 5 (k 4))))   ⇒   4
(+ 2
  (call/cc
    (lambda (k)
      (* 5 (k 4)))))   ⇒   6
```

In the first example, the continuation is obtained and bound to `k`, but `k` is never used, so the value is simply the product of 5 and 4. In the second, the continuation is invoked before the multiplication, so the value is the value passed to the continuation, 4. In the third, the continuation includes the addition by 2; thus, the value is the value passed to the continuation, 4, plus 2.

Here is a less trivial example, showing the use of `call/cc` to provide a nonlocal exit from a recursion.

```
(define product
  (lambda (ls)
    (call/cc
      (lambda (break)
        (let f ((ls ls))
          (cond
            ((null? ls) 1)
            ((= (car ls) 0) (break 0))
            (else (* (car ls) (f (cdr ls)))))))))))
```

```
(product '(1 2 3 4 5))  ⇒  120
(product '(7 3 8 0 1 9 5))  ⇒  0
```

The nonlocal exit allows **product** to return immediately, without performing the pending multiplications, when a zero value is detected.

Each of the continuation invocations above returns to the continuation while control remains within the procedure passed to **call/cc**. The following example uses the continuation after this procedure has already returned.

```
(let ((x (call/cc (lambda (k) k))))
  (x (lambda (ignore) "hi")))  ⇒  "hi"
```

The continuation obtained by this invocation of **call/cc** may be described as "Take the value, bind it to x, and apply the value of x to the value of **(lambda (ignore) "hi")**." Since **(lambda (k) k)** returns its argument, x is bound to the continuation itself; this continuation is applied to the procedure resulting from the evaluation of **(lambda (ignore) "hi")**. This has the effect of binding x (again!) to this procedure and applying the procedure to itself. The procedure ignores its argument and returns "hi".

The following variation of the example above is probably the most confusing Scheme program of its size; it may be easy to guess what it returns, but it takes some work to verify that guess.

```
(((call/cc (lambda (k) k)) (lambda (x) x)) "HEY!")  ⇒  "HEY!"
```

The value of the **call/cc** is its own continuation, as in the preceding example. This is applied to the identity procedure **(lambda (x) x)**, so the **call/cc** returns a second time with this value. Then, the identity procedure is applied to itself, yielding the identity procedure. This is finally applied to "HEY!", yielding "HEY!".

Continuations used in this manner are not always so puzzling. Consider the following definition of **factorial** that saves the continuation at the base of the recursion before returning 1, by assigning the top-level variable **retry**.

```
(define retry #f)
```

```
(define factorial
  (lambda (x)
    (if (= x 0)
        (call/cc (lambda (k) (set! retry k) 1))
        (* x (factorial (- x 1))))))
```

With this definition, `factorial` works as we expect `factorial` to work, except it has the side effect of assigning `retry`.

```
(factorial 4)  ⇒  24
(retry 1)  ⇒  24
```

The continuation bound to `retry` might be described as "Multiply the value by 1, then multiply this result by 2, then multiply this result by 3, then multiply this result by 4." If we pass the continuation a different value, i.e., not 1, we will cause the base value to be something other than 1 and hence change the end result.

```
(retry 2)  ⇒  48
(retry 5)  ⇒  120
```

This mechanism could be the basis for a breakpoint package implemented with `call/cc`; each time a breakpoint is encountered, the continuation of the breakpoint is saved so that the computation may be restarted from the breakpoint (more than once, if desired).

Continuations may be used to implement various forms of multitasking. The simple "light-weight process" mechanism defined below allows multiple computations to be interleaved. Since it is *nonpreemptive*, it requires that each process voluntarily "pause" from time to time in order to allow the others to run.

```
(define lwp-list '())
(define lwp
  (lambda (thunk)
    (set! lwp-list (append lwp-list (list thunk)))))
(define start
  (lambda ()
    (let ((next (car lwp-list)))
      (set! lwp-list (cdr lwp-list))
      (next))))
(define pause
  (lambda ()
    (call/cc
      (lambda (k)
        (lwp (lambda () (k #f)))
        (start)))))
```

The following light-weight processes cooperate to print an indefinite sequence of the string `"hey!"`.

```
(lwp (lambda () (let f () (pause) (display "h") (f))))
(lwp (lambda () (let f () (pause) (display "e") (f))))
(lwp (lambda () (let f () (pause) (display "y") (f))))
(lwp (lambda () (let f () (pause) (display "!") (f))))
(lwp (lambda () (let f () (pause) (newline) (f))))
(start)
```

See Section 9.11 for an implementation of *engines*, which support preemptive multitasking, with `call/cc`.

Exercise 3.3.1. Use `call/cc` to write a program that loops indefinitely, printing a sequence of numbers beginning at zero.

Exercise 3.3.2. Rewrite `product` without `call/cc`, retaining the feature that no multiplications are performed if any of the list elements are zero.

Exercise 3.3.3. What would happen if a process created by `lwp` as defined above were to terminate, i.e., simply return without calling `pause`? Define a `quit` procedure that allows a process to terminate properly. Be sure to handle the case in which the only remaining process terminates.

Exercise 3.3.4. Each time `lwp` is called, the list of processes is copied because `lwp` uses `append` to add its argument to the end of the process list. Design and implement a queue abstraction that does not suffer from this problem and use it in the implementation of light-weight processes.

Exercise 3.3.5. The light-weight process mechanism allows new processes to be created dynamically, although the example given in this section does not do so. Design an application that requires new processes to be created dynamically and implement it using the light-weight process mechanism.

3.4. Continuation Passing Style

As we discussed in the preceding section, a continuation waits for the value of each expression. In particular, a continuation is associated with each procedure call. When one procedure invokes another via a nontail call, the called procedure receives an implicit continuation that is responsible for completing what is left of the calling procedure's body plus returning to the calling procedure's continuation. If the call is a tail call, the called procedure simply receives the continuation of the calling procedure.

We can make the continuations explicit by encapsulating "what to do" in an explicit procedural argument passed along on each call. For example, the continuation of the call to `f` in

```
(letrec ((f (lambda (x) (cons 'a x)))
         (g (lambda (x) (cons 'b (f x))))
         (h (lambda (x) (g (cons 'c x)))))
  (cons 'd (h '()))))   ⇒   (d b a c)
```

conses the symbol b onto the value returned to it, then returns the result of this cons to the continuation of the call to `g`. This continuation is the same as the continuation of the call to `h`, which conses the symbol d onto the value returned to it. We can rewrite this in *continuation-passing style*, or CPS, by replacing these implicit continuations with explicit procedures.

```
(letrec ((f (lambda (x k) (k (cons 'a x))))
         (g (lambda (x k)
              (f x (lambda (v) (k (cons 'b v))))))
         (h (lambda (x k) (g (cons 'c x) k))))
  (h '() (lambda (v) (cons 'd v))))
```

Like the implicit continuation of h and g in the preceding example, the explicit continuation passed to h and on to g,

```
(lambda (v) (cons 'd v))
```

conses the symbol d onto the value passed to it. Similarly, the continuation passed to f,

```
(lambda (v) (k (cons 'b v)))
```

conses b onto the value passed to it, then passes this on to the continuation of g.

Expressions written in CPS are more complicated, of course, but this style of programming has some useful applications. CPS allows a procedure to pass more than one result to its continuation, because the procedure that implements the continuation can take any number of arguments.

```
(define car&cdr
  (lambda (p k)
    (k (car p) (cdr p))))
(car&cdr '(a b c)
  (lambda (x y)
    (list y x)))    ⇒   ((b c) a)
(car&cdr '(a b c) cons)   ⇒   (a b c)
(car&cdr '(a b c a d) memv)   ⇒   (a d)
```

(This can be done with multiple values as well; see Section 5.8.) CPS also allows a procedure to take separate "success" and "failure" continuations, which may accept different numbers of arguments. An example is integer-divide below, which passes the quotient and remainder of its first two arguments to its third, unless the second argument (the divisor) is zero, in which case it passes an error message to its fourth argument.

```
(define integer-divide
  (lambda (x y success failure)
    (if (= y 0)
        (failure "divide by zero")
        (let ((q (quotient x y)))
          (success q (- x (* q y)))))))
(integer-divide 10 3 list (lambda (x) x))   ⇒   (3 1)
(integer-divide 10 0 list (lambda (x) x))   ⇒   "divide by zero"
```

The procedure quotient, employed by integer-divide, returns the quotient of its two arguments, truncated towards zero.

Explicit success and failure continuations can sometimes help to avoid the extra communication necessary to separate successful execution of a procedure from unsuccessful execution. Furthermore, it is possible to have multiple success or failure continuations for different flavors of success or failure, each possibly taking different numbers and types of arguments. See Sections 9.10 and 9.11 for extended examples that employ continuation-passing style.

At this point you may be wondering about the relationship between CPS and the continuations obtained via `call/cc`. It turns out that any program that uses `call/cc` can be rewritten in CPS without `call/cc`, but a total rewrite of the program (sometimes including even system-defined primitives) may be necessary. Try to convert the **product** example on page 61 into CPS before looking at the version below.

```
(define product
  (lambda (ls k)
    (let ((break k))
      (let f ((ls ls) (k k))
        (cond
          ((null? ls) (k 1))
          ((= (car ls) 0) (break 0))
          (else (f (cdr ls)
                   (lambda (x)
                     (k (* (car ls) x)))))))))))

(product '(1 2 3 4 5) (lambda (x) x))     ⇒   120
(product '(7 3 8 0 1 9 5) (lambda (x) x))  ⇒   0
```

Exercise 3.4.1. Rewrite the `reciprocal` example first given in Section 2.1 to accept both success and failure continuations, like `integer-divide` above.

Exercise 3.4.2. Rewrite the `retry` example from the preceding section in CPS.

Exercise 3.4.3. Rewrite the following expression in CPS to avoid using `call/cc`.

```
(define reciprocals
  (lambda (ls)
    (call/cc
      (lambda (k)
        (map (lambda (x)
               (if (= x 0)
                   (k "zero found")
                   (/ 1 x)))
             ls)))))

(reciprocals '(2 1/3 5 1/4))    ⇒   (1/2 3 1/5 4)
(reciprocals '(2 1/3 0 5 1/4))  ⇒   "zero found"
```

[*Hint*: A single-list version of **map** is defined on page 39.]

3.5. Internal Definitions

In Section 2.6, we discussed top-level definitions. Definitions may also appear at
the front of a `lambda`, `let`, or `letrec` body, in which case the bindings they create
are local to the body.

```
(define f (lambda (x) (* x x)))
(let ((x 3))
  (define f (lambda (y) (+ y x)))
  (f 4))  ⇒  7
(f 4)  ⇒  16
```

Procedures bound by internal definitions can be mutually recursive, as with `letrec`.
For example, we can rewrite the `even?` and `odd?` example from Section 3.2 using
internal definitions as follows.

```
(let ()
  (define even?
    (lambda (x)
      (or (= x 0)
          (odd? (- x 1)))))
  (define odd?
    (lambda (x)
      (and (not (= x 0))
           (even? (- x 1)))))
  (even? 20))  ⇒  #t
```

Similarly, we can replace the use of `letrec` to bind `race` with an internal definition
of `race` in our first definition of `list?`.

```
(define list?
  (lambda (x)
    (define race
      (lambda (h t)
        (if (pair? h)
            (let ((h (cdr h)))
              (if (pair? h)
                  (and (not (eq? h t))
                       (race (cdr h) (cdr t)))
                  (null? h)))
            (null? h))))
    (race x x)))
```

In fact, internal definitions and `letrec` are practically interchangeable. It should
not be surprising, therefore, that a `lambda`, `let`, or `letrec` body containing internal
definitions can be replaced with an equivalent `letrec` expression. A body of the
form

```
(define var val)
   ⋮
exp₁
exp₂
   ⋮
```

is equivalent to a `letrec` expression binding the defined variables to the associated values in a body comprising the expressions.

```
(letrec ((var val) ...) exp₁ exp₂ ...)
```

Conversely, a `letrec` of the form

```
(letrec ((var val) ...) exp₁ exp₂ ...)
```

can be replaced with a `let` expression containing internal definitions and the expressions from the body as follows.

```
(let ()
  (define var val)
     ⋮
  exp₁
  exp₂
     ⋮
)
```

The seeming lack of symmetry between these transformations is due to the fact that `letrec` expressions can appear anywhere an expression is valid, whereas internal definitions can appear only at the front of a body. Thus, in replacing a `letrec` with internal definitions, we must generally introduce a `let` expression to hold the definitions.

Syntax definitions may also appear at the front of a `lambda`, `let`, or `letrec` body.

```
(let ((x 3))
  (define-syntax set-x!
    (syntax-rules ()
      ((_ e) (set! x e))))
  (set-x! (+ x x))
  x)  ⇒  6
```

The scope of a syntactic extension established by an internal syntax definition, as with an internal variable definition, is limited to the body in which the syntax definition appears.

Internal definitions may be used in conjunction with top-level definitions and assignments to help modularize programs. Each module of a program should make visible only those bindings that are needed by other modules, while hiding other bindings that would otherwise clutter the top-level namespace and possibly result in unintended use or redefinition of those bindings. A common way of structuring a module is shown below.

```
(define export-var #f)
    ⋮
(let ()
  (define var val)
     ⋮
  init-exp
     ⋮
  (set! export-var export-val)
     ⋮
)
```

The first set of definitions establish top-level bindings for the variables we desire to export (make visible globally). The second set of definitions establish local bindings visible only within the module. The expressions *init-exp* ... perform any initialization that must occur after the local bindings have been established. Finally, the `set!` expressions assign the exported variables to the appropriate values. Some of the extended examples in Chapter 9 use this modularization technique.

One advantage of this form of modularization is that the bracketing `let` expression may be removed or "commented out" during program development, making the internal definitions top-level to facilitate interactive testing.

The following module exports a single variable, `calc`, which is bound to a procedure that implements a simple four-function calculator.

```
(define calc #f)
(let ()
  (define apply-op
    (lambda (ek op args)
      (op (do-calc ek (car args)) (do-calc ek (cadr args)))))
  (define complain
    (lambda (ek msg exp)
      (ek (list msg exp))))
  (define do-calc
    (lambda (ek exp)
      (cond
        ((number? exp) exp)
        ((and (list? exp) (= (length exp) 3))
         (let ((op (car exp)) (args (cdr exp)))
           (case op
             ((add) (apply-op ek + args))
             ((sub) (apply-op ek - args))
             ((mul) (apply-op ek * args))
             ((div) (apply-op ek / args))
             (else (complain ek "invalid operator" op)))))
        (else (complain ek "invalid expression" exp)))))
  (set! calc
    (lambda (exp)
      ; grab an error continuation ek
```

```
      (call/cc
        (lambda (ek)
          (do-calc ek exp))))))
```

```
(calc '(add (mul 3 2) -4))  ⇒  2
(calc '(div 1/2 1/6))  ⇒  3
(calc '(add (mul 3 2) (div 4)))  ⇒  ("invalid expression" (div 4))
(calc '(mul (add 1 -2) (pow 2 7)))  ⇒  ("invalid operator" pow)
```

This example uses a **case** expression to determine which operator to apply. **case** is similar to **cond** except that the test is always the same: (**memv** *val* (*key* ...)), where *val* is the value of the first **case** subform and (*key* ...) is the list of items at the front of each **case** clause. The **case** expression in the example above could be rewritten using **cond** as follows.

```
(let ((temp op))
  (cond
    ((memv temp '(add)) (apply-op ek + args))
    ((memv temp '(sub)) (apply-op ek - args))
    ((memv temp '(mul)) (apply-op ek * args))
    ((memv temp '(div)) (apply-op ek / args))
    (else (complain ek "invalid operator" op))))
```

Exercise 3.5.1. Replace **complain** in the **calc** example with an equivalent syntactic extension.

Exercise 3.5.2. In the **calc** example, the error continuation **ek** is passed along on each call to **apply-op**, **complain**, and **do-calc**. Move the definitions of **apply-op**, **complain**, and **do-calc** to within the scope of the binding for **ek** established within **calc**. Then eliminate the **ek** argument from the definitions and applications of **apply-op**, **complain**, and **do-calc**.

Exercise 3.5.3. Determine the error-signaling facilities provided by the Scheme implementation you are using. Eliminate the **call/cc** from **calc** and rewrite **complain** to signal an error.

Exercise 3.5.4. Extend **calc** to handle unary minus expressions, e.g.,

```
(minus (add 2 3))  ⇒  -5
```

and other operators of your choice.

CHAPTER 4

Variable Binding

A three-armed spiral.

This chapter describes the small set of syntactic forms whose primary purpose is to bind or to assign variables. Other forms that bind or assign variables for which the binding or assignment is not the primary purpose (such as do) are found in later chapters, especially in Chapter 5. This chapter begins with variable references and the lambda syntactic form. All variable binding operations in Scheme are derived from lambda, except top-level occurrences of define, which establishes top-level bindings.

4.1. Variable References

variable   **syntax**
returns: the value of *variable*

Any unquoted identifier appearing in an expression is a keyword or variable reference. It is a keyword reference if a lexical or top-level keyword binding for the identifier is visible; otherwise, it is a variable reference. It is an error to evaluate a top-level variable reference before the variable is defined at top-level, but it is not an error for a variable reference to appear within an expression that has not yet been evaluated.

```
list  ⇒  #<procedure>
(define x 'a)
(list x x)  ⇒  (a a)
(let ((x 'b))
  (list x x))  ⇒  (b b)
(let ((let 'let)) let)  ⇒  let

(define f
  (lambda (x)
    (g x)))
(define g
  (lambda (x)
    (+ x x)))
(f 3)  ⇒  6
```

4.2. Lambda

(lambda *formals* *exp*$_1$ *exp*$_2$ ...)   **syntax**
returns: a procedure

The lambda syntactic form is used to create procedures. Any operation that creates a procedure or establishes local variable bindings is ultimately defined in terms of lambda.

The variables in *formals* are the formal parameters of the procedure, and the sequence of expressions *exp*$_1$ *exp*$_2$ ... is its body.

The body may begin with a sequence of definitions, in which case the established bindings are local to the procedure. If definitions are present, the body is replaced by a letrec expression formed from the definitions and the remaining expressions.

Consult Section 3.5 or Section 4.4 for more details. The remainder of this discussion on `lambda` assumes that this transformation has taken place, if necessary, so that the body is a sequence of expressions without definitions.

When the procedure is created, the bindings of all variables occurring free within the body, excluding the formal parameters, are retained with the procedure. Subsequently, whenever the procedure is applied to a sequence of actual parameters, the formal parameters are bound to the actual parameters, the retained bindings are restored, and the body is evaluated.

Upon application, the formal parameters defined by *formals* are bound to the actual parameters as follows.

- If *formals* is a proper list of variables, e.g., (x y z), each variable is bound to the corresponding actual parameter. It is an error if too few or too many actual parameters are supplied.

- If *formals* is a single variable (not in a list), e.g., z, it is bound to a list of the actual parameters.

- If *formals* is an improper list of variables terminated by a variable, e.g., (x y . z), each variable but the last is bound to the corresponding actual parameter. The last variable is bound to a list of the remaining actual parameters. It is an error if too few actual parameters are supplied.

When the body is evaluated, the expressions exp_1 exp_2 ... are evaluated in sequence. The value of the last expression is the value of the procedure.

Procedures do not have a printed representation in the usual sense. Scheme systems print procedures in different ways; this book uses the notation `#<procedure>`.

```
(lambda (x) (+ x 3))  ⇒  #<procedure>
((lambda (x) (+ x 3)) 7)  ⇒  10
((lambda (x y) (* x (+ x y))) 7 13)  ⇒  140
((lambda (f x) (f x x)) + 11)  ⇒  22
((lambda () (+ 3 4)))  ⇒  7

((lambda (x . y) (list x y))
 28 37)  ⇒  (28 (37))
((lambda (x . y) (list x y))
 28 37 47 28)  ⇒  (28 (37 47 28))
((lambda (x y . z) (list x y z))
 1 2 3 4)  ⇒  (1 2 (3 4))
((lambda x x) 7 13)  ⇒  (7 13)
```

4.3. Local Binding

(let (((*var* *val*) ...) exp_1 exp_2 ...)   **syntax**
returns: the value of the final expression

`let` establishes local variable bindings. Each variable *var* is bound to the value of the corresponding expression *val*. The body of the `let`, in which the variables are bound, is the sequence of expressions exp_1 exp_2 ....

The forms let, let*, and letrec (let* and letrec are described after let) are similar but serve slightly different purposes. With let, in contrast with let* and letrec, the expressions *val* ... are all outside the scope of the variables *var* .... Also, in contrast with let*, no ordering is implied for the evaluation of the expressions *val* .... They may be evaluated from left to right, from right to left, or in any other order at the discretion of the implementation. Use let whenever the values are independent of the variables and the order of evaluation is unimportant.

The body of a let expression may begin with a sequence of definitions, which establish bindings local to the body of the let. See Section 3.5 or Section 4.4.

The following definition of let shows the typical derivation of let from lambda.

```
(define-syntax let
  (syntax-rules ()
    ((_ ((x v) ...) e1 e2 ...)
     ((lambda (x ...) e1 e2 ...) v ...))))

(let ((x (* 3.0 3.0)) (y (* 4.0 4.0)))
  (sqrt (+ x y)))  ⇒   5.0

(let ((x 'a) (y '(b c)))
  (cons x y))  ⇒   (a b c)

(let ((x 0) (y 1))
  (let ((x y) (y x))
    (list x y)))  ⇒   (1 0)
```

Another form of let, *named* let, is described in Section 5.5.

(let* ((*var val*) ...) *exp*₁ *exp*₂ ...)   **syntax**
returns: the value of the final expression

let* is similar to let except that the expressions *val* ... are evaluated in sequence from left to right, and each of these expressions is within the scope of the variables to the left. Use let* when there is a linear dependency among the values or when the order of evaluation is important.

Any let* expression may be converted to a set of nested let expressions. The following definition of let* demonstrates the typical transformation.

```
(define-syntax let*
  (syntax-rules ()
    ((_ () e1 e2 ...)
     (let () e1 e2 ...))
    ((_ ((x1 v1) (x2 v2) ...) e1 e2 ...)
     (let ((x1 v1))
       (let* ((x2 v2) ...) e1 e2 ...)))))

(let* ((x (* 5.0 5.0))
       (y (- x (* 4.0 4.0))))
  (sqrt y))  ⇒   3.0

(let ((x 0) (y 1))
  (let* ((x y) (y x))
    (list x y)))  ⇒   (1 1)
```

(letrec ((*var val*) ...) *exp₁ exp₂* ...)   **syntax**
returns: the value of the final expression

letrec is similar to **let** and **let***, except that all of the expressions *val* ... are within the scope of all of the variables *var* .... **letrec** allows the definition of mutually recursive procedures.

The order of evaluation of the expressions *val* ... is unspecified, so it is an error to reference any of the variables bound by the **letrec** expression before all of the values have been computed. (Occurrence of a variable within a **lambda** expression does not count as a reference, unless the resulting procedure is applied before all of the values have been computed.)

Choose **letrec** over **let** or **let*** when there is a circular dependency among the variables and their values and when the order of evaluation is unimportant.

A **letrec** expression of the form

(letrec ((*var val*) ...) *body*)

may be expressed in terms of **let** and **set!** as

```
(let ((var #f) ...)
  (let ((temp val) ...)
    (set! var temp) ...
    (let () body)))
```

where *temp* ... are unique variables, one for each (*var val*) pair. The outer **let** expression establishes the variable bindings. The initial value given each variable is unimportant, so any value suffices in place of **#f**. The bindings are established first so that the values may contain occurrences of the variables, i.e., so that the values are computed within the scope of the variables. The middle **let** evaluates the values and binds them to the temporary variables, and the **set!** expressions assign each variable to the corresponding value. The inner **let** is present in case *body* contains internal definitions.

This transformation does not enforce the restriction that the values must not directly reference one of the variables.

A definition of **letrec** performing this transformation is shown on page 176.

```
(letrec ((sum (lambda (x)
                (if (zero? x)
                    0
                    (+ x (sum (- x 1)))))))
  (sum 5))  ⇒  15
```

4.4. Variable Definitions

(define *var exp*)   **syntax**
(define (*var₀ var₁* ...) *exp₁ exp₂* ...)   **syntax**
(define (*var₀* . *varᵣ*) *exp₁ exp₂* ...)   **syntax**
(define (*var₀ var₁ var₂* ... . *varᵣ*) *exp₁ exp₂* ...)   **syntax**
returns: unspecified

In the first form, **define** creates a new binding of *var* to the value of *exp*. The remaining are shorthand forms for binding variables to procedures; they are identical to the following definition in terms of `lambda`:

```
(define var
  (lambda formals
    exp₁ exp₂ ...))
```

where *formals* is $(var_1 \ldots)$, var_r, or $(var_1\ var_2\ \ldots\ .\ var_r)$ for the second, third, and fourth `define` formats.

Definitions often appear at "top level," i.e., outside the scope of any `lambda` or any form derived from `lambda`, such as `let`, `let*`, or `letrec`. A variable bound at top level is visible within any expression typed at the keyboard or loaded from a file, except where shadowed by a local binding.

Definitions may also appear at the front of a `lambda` body or body of any form derived from `lambda`. These *internal definitions* must precede the expressions in the body. Any `lambda` expression whose body begins with definitions may be transformed into an equivalent `lambda` expression without such definitions, by rewriting the body as a `letrec` expression. That is, a `lambda` expression of the form

```
(lambda formals
  (define var val) ...
  exp₁ exp₂ ...)
```

may be expressed in the equivalent form below.

```
(lambda formals
  (letrec ((var val) ...)
    exp₁ exp₂ ...))
```

Although this shows the transformation for the first and simpler form of definition, either form may appear within a `lambda` body.

Syntax definitions may appear along with variable definitions wherever variable definitions may appear; see Chapter 8.

```
(define x 3)
x  ⇒  3
(define f
  (lambda (x y)
    (* (+ x y) 2)))
(f 5 4)  ⇒  18
(define (sum-of-squares x y)
  (+ (* x x) (* y y)))
(sum-of-squares 3 4)  ⇒  25
```

```
(define f
  (lambda (x)
    (+ x 1)))
(let ((x 2))
  (define f
    (lambda (y)
      (+ y x)))
  (f 3))  ⇒  5
(f 3)  ⇒  4
```

A set of definitions may be grouped by enclosing them in a **begin** form. Definitions grouped in this manner may appear wherever ordinary variable and syntax definitions may appear. They are treated as if written separately, i.e., without the enclosing **begin** form. This feature allows syntactic extensions to expand into groups of definitions.

```
(define-syntax multi-define-syntax
  (syntax-rules ()
    ((_ (var exp) ...)
     (begin
       (define-syntax var exp)
       ...))))
(let ()
  (define plus
    (lambda (x y)
       (if (zero? x)
           y
           (plus (sub1 x) (add1 y)))))
  (multi-define-syntax
    (add1 (syntax-rules () ((_ e) (+ e 1))))
    (sub1 (syntax-rules () ((_ e) (- e 1)))))
  (plus 7 8))  ⇒  15
```

4.5. Assignment

(set! *var exp*)   **syntax**
returns: unspecified

set! assigns a new value to an existing variable. The value of the variable *var* is changed to the value of *exp*. Any subsequent reference to *var* evaluates to the new value.

This form is different from the forms described earlier in this chapter because it does not establish a new binding for *var* but rather changes the value of an existing binding. It is an error to assign a top-level variable that has not yet been defined, although many implementations do not enforce this restriction.

Assignments are not employed as frequently in Scheme as in most traditional languages, but they are useful for updating the state of a system and in creating recursive structures (as with **letrec**).

```
(let ((x 3) (y 4))
  (set! x 5)
  (+ x y))  ⇒  9
(define f
  (lambda (x y)
    (cons x y)))
(f 'a 'b)  ⇒  (a . b)
(set! f
  (lambda (x y)
    (cons y x)))
(f 'a 'b)  ⇒  (b . a)
```

CHAPTER 5

Control Operations

Three warped, two-armed spirals.

This chapter introduces the syntactic forms and procedures that serve as control structures for Scheme programs.

5.1. Constants and Quotation

constant   **syntax**
returns: *constant*

constant is any self-evaluating constant, i.e., a number, boolean, character, or string. Constants are immutable; see the note in the description of **quote** below.

```
3.2  ⇒  3.2
#f  ⇒  #f
#\c  ⇒  #\c
"hi"  ⇒  "hi"
```

(**quote** *obj*)   **syntax**
'obj   **syntax**
returns: *obj*

'obj is equivalent to (**quote** *obj*). The abbreviated form is converted into the longer form by the Scheme reader (see **read**).

  quote inhibits the normal evaluation rule for *obj*, allowing *obj* to be employed as data. Although any Scheme object may be quoted, quotation is not necessary for self-evaluating constants, i.e., numbers, booleans, characters, and strings.

  Quoted and self-evaluating constants are immutable. That is, it is an error to alter a constant via **set-car!**, **string-set!**, etc. An implementation may choose to share storage among different constants to save space.

```
(+ 2 3)  ⇒  5
'(+ 2 3)  ⇒  (+ 2 3)
(quote (+ 2 3))  ⇒  (+ 2 3)
'a  ⇒  a
'cons  ⇒  cons
'()  ⇒  ()
'7  ⇒  7
```

(**quasiquote** *obj*)   **syntax**
`obj   **syntax**
(**unquote** *obj*)   **syntax**
,obj   **syntax**
(**unquote-splicing** *obj*)   **syntax**
,@obj   **syntax**
returns: see explanation

`obj is equivalent to (**quasiquote** *obj*), *,obj* is equivalent to (**unquote** *obj*), and *,@obj* is equivalent to (**unquote-splicing** *obj*). The abbreviated forms are converted into the longer forms by the Scheme reader (see **read**).

quasiquote is similar to quote, but it allows parts of the quoted text to
be "unquoted." Within a quasiquote expression, subforms of unquote and
unquote-splicing forms are evaluated, and everything else is quoted, i.e., left unevaluated. The value of each unquote subform is inserted into the output in place
of the unquote form, while the value of each unquote-splicing subform is spliced
into the surrounding list or vector structure. unquote and unquote-splicing are
valid only within quasiquote expressions.

quasiquote expressions may be nested, with each quasiquote introducing a new
level of quotation and each unquote or unquote-splicing taking away a level of
quotation. An expression nested within n quasiquote expressions must be within
n unquote or unquote-splicing expressions to be evaluated.

```
'(+ 2 3)  ⇒  (+ 2 3)

'(+ 2 ,(* 3 4))  ⇒  (+ 2 12)
'(a b (,(+ 2 3) c) d)  ⇒  (a b (5 c) d)
'(a b ,(reverse '(c d e)) f g)  ⇒  (a b (e d c) f g)
(let ((a 1) (b 2))
  '(,a . ,b))  ⇒  (1 . 2)

'(+ ,@(cdr '(* 2 3)))  ⇒  (+ 2 3)
'(a b ,@(reverse '(c d e)) f g)  ⇒  (a b e d c f g)
(let ((a 1) (b 2))
  '(,a ,@b))  ⇒  (1 . 2)
'#(,@(list 1 2 3))  ⇒  #(1 2 3)

'',(cons 'a 'b)  ⇒  ',(cons 'a 'b)
'',(cons 'a 'b)  ⇒  '(a . b)
```

5.2. Procedure Application

(*procedure exp* ...)   **syntax**
returns: result of applying the value of *procedure* to the values of *exp* ...

Procedure application is the most basic Scheme control structure. Any structured
form without a syntax keyword in the first position is a procedure application.
The expressions *procedure* and *exp* ... are evaluated and the value of *procedure* is
applied to the values of *exp* ....

The order in which the procedure and argument expressions are evaluated is
unspecified. It may be left to right, right to left, or some arbitrary order. The
evaluation is guaranteed to be sequential, however; whatever order is chosen, each
expression will be fully evaluated before evaluation of the next is started.

```
(+ 3 4)  ⇒  7
((if (odd? 3) + -) 6 2)  ⇒  8
((lambda (x) x) 5)  ⇒  5
(let ((f (lambda (x) (+ x x))))
  (f 8))  ⇒  16
```

(apply *procedure obj* ... *list*)   **procedure**
returns: the result of applying *procedure* to *obj* ... and the elements of *list*

apply invokes *procedure*, passing the first *obj* as the first argument, the second *obj* as the second argument, and so on for each object in *obj* ..., and passing the elements of *list* in order as the remaining arguments. Thus, *procedure* is called with as many arguments as there are *objs* plus elements of *list*.

apply is useful when some or all of the arguments to be passed to a procedure are in a list, since it frees the programmer from explicitly destructuring the list.

```
(apply + '(4 5))   ⇒   9

(apply min '(6 8 3 2 5))   ⇒   2

(apply min  5 1 3 '(6 8 3 2 5))   ⇒   1

(apply vector 'a 'b '(c d e))   ⇒   #5(a b c d e)

(define first
  (lambda (l)
    (apply (lambda (x . y) x)
           l)))
(define rest
  (lambda (l)
    (apply (lambda (x . y) y) l)))
(first '(a b c d))   ⇒   a
(rest '(a b c d))   ⇒   (b c d)
```

5.3. Sequencing

(begin *exp$_1$ exp$_2$* ...)   **syntax**
returns: the result of the last expression

The expressions *exp$_1$ exp$_2$* ... are evaluated in sequence from left to right. begin is used to sequence assignments, input/output, or other operations that cause side effects.

The bodies of many syntactic forms, including lambda, let, let*, and letrec, as well as the result clauses of cond, case, and do, are treated as if they were inside an implicit begin; that is, the expressions making up the body or result clause are executed in sequence.

A begin form may contain zero or more definitions in place of the expressions *exp$_1$ exp$_2$* ..., in which case it is considered to be a definition and may appear only where definitions are valid.

```
(define x 3)
(begin
  (set! x (+ x 1))
  (+ x x))   ⇒   8
```

```
(define swap-pair!
  (lambda (x)
    (let ((temp (car x)))
      (set-car! x (cdr x))
      (set-cdr! x temp)
      x)))
(swap-pair! (cons 'a 'b))  ⇒  (b . a)
```

5.4. Conditionals

(if *test consequent alternative*)   **syntax**
(if *test consequent*)   **syntax**
returns: the value of *consequent* or *alternative* depending on the value of *test*

test, *consequent*, and *alternative* are expressions. If no *alternative* is supplied and
test evaluates to false, the result is unspecified.

```
(let ((l '(a b c)))
  (if (null? l)
      '()
      (cdr l)))  ⇒  (b c)
(let ((l '()))
  (if (null? l)
      '()
      (cdr l)))  ⇒  ()
(let ((abs
        (lambda (x)
          (if (< x 0)
              (- 0 x)
              x))))
  (abs -4))  ⇒  4
(let ((x -4))
  (if (< x 0)
      (list 'minus (- 0 x))
      (list 'plus 4)))  ⇒  (minus 4)
```

(not *obj*)   **procedure**
returns: #t if *obj* is false, #f otherwise

not is equivalent to (lambda (x) (if x #f #t)).

The Revised[4] Report (but not the ANSI/IEEE Standard) permits the empty
list and #f to be identical. If they are identical, not returns #t for (); otherwise, it
returns #f for ().

```
(not #f)   ⇒   #t
(not #t)   ⇒   #f
(not '(a b))   ⇒   #f
(if (eq? #f '())
    (not '())
    (not (not '()))))   ⇒   #t
```

(and *exp* ...)   syntax
returns: see explanation

and evaluates its subexpressions in sequence from left to right and stops immediately
(without evaluating the remaining expressions) if any expression evaluates to false.
The value of the last expression evaluated is returned. **and** may be defined as
follows.

```
(define-syntax and
  (syntax-rules ()
    ((_) #t)
    ((_ e) e)
    ((_ e1 e2 e3 ...)
     (if e1 (and e2 e3 ...) #f))))
(let ((x 3))
  (and (> x 2) (< x 4)))   ⇒   #t

(let ((x 5))
  (and (> x 2) (< x 4)))   ⇒   #f

(and #f '(a b) '(c d))   ⇒   #f
(and '(a b) '(c d) '(e f))   ⇒   (e f)
```

(or *exp* ...)   syntax
returns: see explanation

or evaluates its subexpressions in sequence from left to right and stops immediately
(without evaluating the remaining expressions) if any expression evaluates to a true
value. The value of the last expression evaluated is returned. **or** may be defined as
follows.

```
(define-syntax or
  (syntax-rules ()
    ((_) #f)
    ((_ e) e)
    ((_ e1 e2 e3 ...)
     (let ((t e1)) (if t t (or e2 e3 ...))))))
(let ((x 3))
  (or (< x 2) (> x 4)))   ⇒   #f

(let ((x 5))
  (or (< x 2) (> x 4)))   ⇒   #t

(or #f '(a b) '(c d))   ⇒   (a b)
```

(cond *clause*₁ *clause*₂ ...)   **syntax**
returns: see explanation

Each *clause* but the last must take one of the forms below.

(*test*)
(*test* *exp*₁ *exp*₂ ...)
(*test* => *exp*)

The last clause may be in either of the above forms or it may be an "**else** clause"
of the form

(**else** *exp*₁ *exp*₂ ...)

Each *test* is evaluated in order until one evaluates to a true value or until all of the
tests have been evaluated. If the first clause whose *test* evaluates to a true value is
in the first form given above, the value of *test* is returned.

If the first clause whose *test* evaluates to a true value is in the second form given
above, the expressions *exp*₁ *exp*₂... are evaluated in sequence and the value of the
last expression is returned.

If the first clause whose *test* evaluates to a true value is in the third form given
above, the expression *exp* is evaluated. The value should be a procedure of one
argument, which is applied to the value of *test*. The result of this application is
returned.

If none of the tests evaluates to a true value and an **else** clause is present, the
expressions *exp*₁ *exp*₂ ... of the **else** clause are evaluated in sequence and the
value of the last expression is returned.

If none of the tests evaluates to a true value and no **else** clause is present, the
value is unspecified.

See page 173 for a definition of **cond** as a syntactic extension.

```
(let ((x 0))
  (cond
    ((< x 0) (list 'minus (abs x)))
    ((> x 0) (list 'plus x))
    (else (list 'zero x))))   ⇒   (zero 0)
(define select
  (lambda (x)
    (cond
      ((not (symbol? x)))
      ((assq x '((a . 1) (b . 2) (c . 3)))
       => cdr)
      (else 0))))
(select 3)  ⇒  #t
(select 'b)  ⇒  2
(select 'e)  ⇒  0
```

(**case** *exp*$_0$ *clause*$_1$ *clause*$_2$ ...)   **syntax**
returns: see explanation

Each clause but the last must take the form

((*key* ...) *exp*$_1$ *exp*$_2$ ...)

where each *key* is a datum distinct from the other keys. The last clause may be in the above form or it may be an **else** clause of the form

(**else** *exp*$_1$ *exp*$_2$ ...)

exp$_0$ is evaluated and the result is compared (using **eqv?**) against the keys of each clause in order. If a clause containing a matching key is found, the expressions *exp*$_1$ *exp*$_2$ ... are evaluated in sequence and the value of the last expression is returned.

If none of the clauses contains a matching key and an **else** clause is present, the expressions *exp*$_1$ *exp*$_2$ ... of the **else** clause are evaluated in sequence and the value of the last expression is returned.

If none of the clauses contains a matching key and no **else** clause is present, the value is unspecified.

See page 173 for a definition of **case** as a syntactic extension.

```
(let ((x 4) (y 5))
  (case (+ x y)
    ((1 3 5 7 9) 'odd)
    ((0 2 4 6 8) 'even)
    (else 'out-of-range)))   ⇒   odd
```

5.5. Recursion, Iteration, and Mapping

(**let** *name* ((*var val*) ...) *exp*$_1$ *exp*$_2$ ...)   **syntax**
returns: value of the last expression

This form of **let**, called *named* **let**, is a general-purpose iteration and recursion construct. It is similar to the more common form of **let** (see Section 4.3) in the binding of the variables *var* ... to the values *val* ... within the body *exp*$_1$ *exp*$_2$ .... In addition, the variable *name* is bound within the body to a procedure that may be called to recur or iterate; the arguments to the procedure become the new values for the variables *var* ....

A named **let** expression of the form

```
(let name ((var val) ...)
  exp₁ exp₂ ...)
```

can be rewritten with **letrec** as follows:

```
((letrec ((name (lambda (var ...) exp₁ exp₂ ...)))
   name)
 val ...)
```

The procedure `divisors` defined below uses named `let` to compute the nontrivial divisors of a nonnegative integer.

```
(define divisors
  (lambda (n)
    (let f ((i 2))
      (cond
        ((>= i n) '())
        ((integer? (/ n i))
         (cons i (f (+ i 1))))
        (else (f (+ i 1)))))))
```

```
(divisors 5)   ⇒  ()
(divisors 32)  ⇒  (2 4 8 16)
```

The above version is non-tail-recursive when a divisor is found and tail-recursive when a divisor is not found. The version below is fully tail-recursive. It builds up the list in reverse order, but this is easy to remedy, either by reversing the list on exit or by starting at $n - 1$ and counting down to 1.

```
(define divisors
  (lambda (n)
    (let f ((i 2) (ls '()))
      (cond
        ((>= i n) ls)
        ((integer? (/ n i))
         (f (+ i 1) (cons i ls)))
        (else (f (+ i 1) ls))))))
```

(do ((*var val update*) ...) (*test res* ...) *exp* ...)   **syntax**
returns: the value of the last *res*

`do` allows a common restricted form of iteration to be expressed succinctly. The variables *var* ... are bound initially to the values of *val* ... and are rebound on each subsequent iteration to the values of *update* .... The expressions **test**, *update* ..., *exp* ..., and *res* ... are all within the scope of the bindings established for *var* ....

On each step, the test expression *test* is evaluated. If the value of *test* is true, iteration ceases, the result expressions *res* ... are evaluated in sequence, and the value of the last expression is returned. If no result expressions are present, the value of the `do` expression is unspecified.

If the value of *test* is false, the expressions *exp* ... are evaluated in sequence, the expressions *update* ... are evaluated, new bindings for *var* ... to the values of *update* ... are created, and iteration continues.

The expressions *exp* ... are evaluated only for effect and are often omitted entirely. Any *update* expression may be omitted, in which case the effect is the same as if the *update* were simply the corresponding *var*.

Although looping constructs in most languages require that the loop iterands be updated via assignment, do requires the loop iterands *val* ... to be updated via rebinding. In fact, no side effects are involved in the evaluation of a do expression unless they are performed explicitly by its subexpressions.

See page 177 for a definition of do as a syntactic extension.

The definitions for `factorial` and `fibonacci` below are straightforward translations of the tail-recursive named-`let` versions given in Section 3.2.

```
(define factorial
  (lambda (n)
    (do ((i n (- i 1)) (a 1 (* a i)))
        ((zero? i) a))))
```

```
(factorial 10)   ⇒   3628800
```

```
(define fibonacci
  (lambda (n)
    (if (= n 0)
        0
        (do ((i n (- i 1)) (a1 1 (+ a1 a2)) (a2 0 a1))
            ((= i 1) a1)))))
```

```
(fibonacci 6)   ⇒   8
```

The definition of `divisors` below is similar to the tail-recursive definition of divisors given with the description of named `let` above.

```
(define divisors
  (lambda (n)
    (do ((i 2 (+ i 1))
         (ls '()
             (if (integer? (/ n i))
                 (cons i ls)
                 ls)))
        ((>= i n) ls))))
```

The variant of `divisors` below, which prints the divisors one per line, demonstrates a nonempty do body.

```
(define divisors
  (lambda (n)
    (do ((i 2 (+ i 1)))
        ((>= i n))
      (if (integer? (/ n i))
          (begin
            (write i)
            (newline))))))
```

(map *procedure* *list*$_1$ *list*$_2$ ...)   **procedure**
returns: list of results

map applies *procedure* to corresponding elements of the lists *list*$_1$ *list*$_2$ ... and returns a list of the resulting values. The lists *list*$_1$ *list*$_2$ ... must be of the same
length, and *procedure* must accept as many arguments as there are lists.

While the order in which the applications themselves occur is not specified, the
order of the values in the output list is the same as that of the corresponding values
in the input lists.

```
(map abs '(1 -2 3 -4 5 -6))  ⇒  (1 2 3 4 5 6)
(map (lambda (x y) (* x y))
     '(1 2 3 4)
     '(8 7 6 5))  ⇒  (8 14 18 20)
```

map might be defined as follows.

```
(define map
  (lambda (f ls . more)
    (if (null? more)
        (let map1 ((ls ls))
          (if (null? ls)
              '()
              (cons (f (car ls))
                    (map1 (cdr ls)))))
        (let map-more ((ls ls) (more more))
          (if (null? ls)
              '()
              (cons (apply f (car ls) (map car more))
                    (map-more (cdr ls)
                              (map cdr more)))))))))
```

No error checking is done by this version of map; f is assumed to be a procedure
and the other arguments are assumed to be proper lists of the same length. An
interesting feature of this definition is that map uses itself to pull out the cars and
cdrs of the list of input lists; this works because of the special treatment of the
single-list case.

(for-each *procedure* *list*$_1$ *list*$_2$ ...)   **procedure**
returns: unspecified

for-each is similar to map except that for-each does not create and return a list
of the resulting values, and for-each guarantees to perform the applications in
sequence over the lists from left to right. for-each may be defined as follows.

```
(define for-each
  (lambda (f ls . more)
    (do ((ls ls (cdr ls)) (more more (map cdr more)))
        ((null? ls))
      (apply f (car ls) (map car more)))))
```

```
(let ((same-count 0))
  (for-each
    (lambda (x y)
      (if (= x y)
          (set! same-count (+ same-count 1)))))
    '(1 2 3 4 5 6)
    '(2 3 3 4 7 6))
  same-count)  ⇒  3
```

5.6. Continuations

Continuations in Scheme are procedures that represent the remainder of a computation from a given point in the continuation. They may be obtained with `call-with-current-continuation`, which can be abbreviated `call/cc` in most Scheme implementations.

(call-with-current-continuation *procedure*)	**procedure**
(call/cc *procedure*)	**procedure**

returns: the result of applying *procedure* to the current continuation

`call-with-current-continuation` and `call/cc` are two names for the same procedure; the abbreviation `call/cc` is often used for the obvious reason that it requires fewer keystrokes to type.

`call/cc` obtains its continuation and passes it to *procedure*, which must accept one argument. The continuation itself is represented by a procedure of one argument. (In the context of multiple values, a continuation may actually accept zero or more than one argument; see Section 5.8.) Each time this procedure is applied to a value, it returns the value to the continuation of the `call/cc` application. That is, when the continuation procedure is given a value, it returns the value as the result of the application of `call/cc`.

If *procedure* returns normally when passed the continuation procedure, the value returned by `call/cc` is the value returned by *procedure*.

Continuations allow the implementation of nonlocal exits, backtracking [11, 24], coroutines [13], and multitasking [8, 25].

The example below illustrates the use of a continuation to perform a nonlocal exit from a loop.

```
(define member
  (lambda (x ls)
    (call/cc
      (lambda (break)
        (do ((ls ls (cdr ls)))
            ((null? ls) #f)
          (if (equal? x (car ls))
              (break ls)))))))
(member 'd '(a b c))  ⇒  #f
(member 'b '(a b c))  ⇒  (b c)
```

Additional examples are given in Section 3.3.

The current continuation is typically represented internally as a stack of procedure activation records, and obtaining the continuation involves encapsulating the stack within a procedural object. Since an encapsulated stack has indefinite extent, some mechanism must be used to preserve the stack contents indefinitely. This can be done with surprising ease and efficiency and with no impact on programs that do not use continuations [14].

(dynamic-wind *in body out*)   **procedure**
returns: result of applying *body*

dynamic-wind offers "protection" from continuation invocation. It is useful for performing tasks that must be performed whenever control enters or leaves *body*, either normally or by continuation application.

The three arguments *in*, *body*, and *out* must be procedures of no arguments, i.e., *thunks*. Before applying *body*, and each time *body* is entered subsequently by the application of a continuation created within *body*, the *in* thunk is applied. Upon normal exit from *body* and each time *body* is exited by the application of a continuation created outside *body*, the *out* thunk is applied.

Thus, it is guaranteed that *in* is invoked at least once. In addition, if *body* ever returns, *out* is invoked at least once.

dynamic-wind has been approved for inclusion in the Revised[5] Report but is not in the ANSI/IEEE standard or the Revised[4] Report.

The following example demonstrates the use of dynamic-wind to be sure that an input port is closed after processing, regardless of whether the processing completes normally.

```
(let ((p (open-input-file "input-file")))
  (dynamic-wind
    (lambda () #f)
    (lambda () (process p))
    (lambda () (close-input-port p))))
```

Common Lisp provides a similar facility (unwind-protect) for protection from nonlocal exits. This is often sufficient. unwind-protect provides only the equivalent to *out*, however, since Common Lisp does not support fully general continuations. Here is how unwind-protect might be specified with dynamic-wind:

```
(define-syntax unwind-protect
  (syntax-rules ()
    ((_ body cleanup ...)
     (dynamic-wind
       (lambda () #f)
       (lambda () body)
       (lambda () cleanup ...)))))
```

```
((call/cc
    (let ((x 'a))
      (lambda (k)
        (unwind-protect
          (k (lambda () x))
          (set! x 'b))))))) ⇒  b
```

Some Scheme implementations support a controlled form of assignment known as *fluid binding*, in which a variable takes on a temporary value during a given computation and reverts to the old value after the computation has completed. The syntactic form `fluid-let` defined below in terms of `dynamic-wind` permits the fluid binding of a single variable x to a value v within a sequence of expressions e1 e2 ....

```
(define-syntax fluid-let
  (syntax-rules ()
    ((_ ((x v)) e1 e2 ...)
     (let ((y v))
       (let ((swap (lambda ()
                     (let ((t x))
                       (set! x y)
                       (set! y t)))))
         (dynamic-wind
           swap
           (lambda () e1 e2 ...)
           swap)))))))
```

(Implementations that support `fluid-let` generally extend it to allow an indefinite number of (x v) pairs, as with `let`.)

If no continuations are invoked within the body of a `fluid-let`, the behavior is the same as if the variable were simply assigned the new value on entry and assigned the old value on return.

```
(let ((x 3))
  (+ (fluid-let ((x 5))
       x)
     x)) ⇒  8
```

A fluid-bound variable also reverts to the old value if a continuation created outside of the `fluid-let` is invoked.

```
(let ((x 'a))
  (let ((f (lambda () x)))
    (cons (call/cc
            (lambda (k)
              (fluid-let ((x 'b))
                (f))))
          (f)))) ⇒  (b . a)
```

If control has left a `fluid-let` body, either normally or by the invocation of a continuation, and control reenters the body by the invocation of a continuation, the temporary value of the fluid-bound variable is reinstated. Furthermore, any changes to the temporary value are maintained and reflected upon reentry.

```
(define reenter #f)
(define x 0)
(fluid-let ((x 1))
  (call/cc (lambda (k) (set! reenter k)))
  (set! x (+ x 1))
  x)  ⇒  2
x  ⇒  0
(reenter '*)  ⇒  3
(reenter '*)  ⇒  4
x  ⇒  0
```

An implementation of `dynamic-wind` is given below. In addition to defining `dynamic-wind`, the code redefines `call/cc` (`call-with-current-continuation`). Together, `dynamic-wind` and `call/cc` manage a list of *winders*. A winder is a pair of *in* and *out* thunks established by a call to `dynamic-wind`. Whenever `dynamic-wind` is invoked, the *in* thunk is invoked, a new winder containing the *in* and *out* thunks is placed on the winders list, the *body* thunk is invoked, the winder is removed from the winders list, and the *out* thunk is invoked. This ordering ensures that the winder is on the winders list only when control has passed through *in* and not yet entered *out*. Whenever a continuation is obtained, the winders list is saved, and whenever the continuation is invoked, the saved winders list is reinstated. During reinstatement, the *out* thunk of each winder on the current winders list that is not also on the saved winders list is invoked, followed by the *in* thunk of each winder on the saved winders list that is not also on the current winders list. The winders list is updated incrementally, again to ensure that a winder is on the current winders list only if control has passed through its *in* thunk and not entered its *out* thunk.

```
(define dynamic-wind #f)
(let ((winders '()))
  (define common-tail
    (lambda (x y)
      (let ((lx (length x)) (ly (length y)))
        (do ((x (if (> lx ly) (list-tail x (- lx ly)) x) (cdr x))
             (y (if (> ly lx) (list-tail y (- ly lx)) y) (cdr y)))
            ((eq? x y) x)))))
  (define do-wind
    (lambda (new)
      (let ((tail (common-tail new winders)))
        (let f ((l winders))
          (if (not (eq? l tail))
              (begin
                (set! winders (cdr l))
                ((cdar l))
                (f (cdr l)))))
        (let f ((l new))
```

```
            (if (not (eq? l tail))
                (begin
                  (f (cdr l))
                  ((caar l))
                  (set! winders l)))))))
  (set! call/cc
    (let ((c call/cc))
      (lambda (f)
        (c (lambda (k)
             (f (let ((save winders))
                  (lambda (x)
                    (if (not (eq? save winders)) (do-wind save))
                    (k x))))))))
  (set! call-with-current-continuation call/cc)
  (set! dynamic-wind
    (lambda (in body out)
      (in)
      (set! winders (cons (cons in out) winders))
      (let ((ans (body)))
        (set! winders (cdr winders))
        (out)
        ans))))
```

The test (not (eq? save winders)) performed in call/cc is not strictly necessary but makes invoking a continuation less costly whenever the saved winders list is the same as the current winders list.

5.7. Delayed Evaluation

The syntactic form delay and the procedure force may be used in combination to implement *lazy evaluation*. An expression subject to lazy evaluation is not evaluated until its value is required and once evaluated is never reevaluated. delay and force are in the Revised[4] Report but not the ANSI/IEEE standard.

(delay *exp*)   **syntax**
returns: a promise

The first time the promise is *forced* (with force), it evaluates *exp*, "remembering" the resulting value. Thereafter, each time the promise is forced, it returns the remembered value instead of reevaluating *exp*. See the examples given for force below.

(force *promise*)   **procedure**
returns: result of forcing *promise*

delay may be defined as

```
(define-syntax delay
  (syntax-rules ()
    ((_ exp) (make-promise (lambda () exp)))))
```

where `make-promise` is defined as

```
(define make-promise
  (lambda (p)
    (let ((val #f) (set? #f))
      (lambda ()
        (if (not set?)
            (let ((x (p)))
              (if (not set?)
                  (begin (set! val x)
                         (set! set? #t)))))
        val)))))
```

With this definition of `delay`, `force` simply invokes the promise to force evaluation or to retrieve the saved value.

```
(define force
  (lambda (promise)
    (promise)))
```

The second test of the variable `set?` in `make-promise` is necessary in the unlikely event that, as a result of applying p, the promise is recursively forced. Since a promise must always return the same value, the result of the first application of p to complete is returned.

   `delay` and `force` are typically used only in the absence of side effects, e.g., assignments, so that the order of evaluation is unimportant.

   The benefit of using `delay` and `force` is that some amount of computation might be avoided altogether if it is delayed until absolutely required. Delayed evaluation may be used to construct conceptually infinite lists, or *streams*. The example below shows how a stream abstraction may be built with `delay` and `force`. A stream is a promise that, when forced, returns a pair whose cdr is a stream.

```
(define stream-car
  (lambda (s)
    (car (force s))))
(define stream-cdr
  (lambda (s)
    (cdr (force s))))
(define counters
  (let next ((n 1))
    (delay (cons n (next (+ n 1))))))
(stream-car counters)  ⇒  1

(stream-car (stream-cdr counters))  ⇒  2
```

```
(define stream-add
  (lambda (s1 s2)
    (delay (cons
             (+ (stream-car s1) (stream-car s2))
             (stream-add (stream-cdr s1) (stream-cdr s2))))))))
(define even-counters
  (stream-add counters counters))

(stream-car even-counters)  ⇒  2

(stream-car (stream-cdr even-counters))  ⇒  4
```

5.8. Multiple Values

This section describes support for multiple values. Two procedures, values and
call-with-values, comprise the multiple values interface. The multiple values
interface has been approved for inclusion in the Revised[5] Report but is not in the
ANSI/IEEE standard or the Revised[4] Report.

(call-with-values *producer consumer*)   **procedure**
returns: see discussion following

producer may be any procedure accepting zero arguments, and *consumer* may be
any procedure. call-with-values applies *consumer* to the values returned by
invoking *producer* without arguments. See the examples under values below.

(values *obj* ...)   **procedure**
returns: see discussion following

The procedure *values* accepts any number of arguments and simply passes (returns)
the arguments to its continuation.

The following simple examples demonstrate how call-with-values and values
interact:

```
(call-with-values (lambda () (values 1 2)) +)  ⇒  3

(call-with-values values (lambda args args))  ⇒  ()
```

In the second example, values itself serves as the producer. It receives no arguments
and thus returns no values.

The more realistic example below employs multiple values to divide a list non-
destructively into two sublists of alternating elements.

```
(define split
  (lambda (ls)
    (if (or (null? ls) (null? (cdr ls)))
        (values ls '())
        (call-with-values
          (lambda () (split (cddr ls)))
          (lambda (odds evens)
            (values (cons (car ls) odds)
                    (cons (cadr ls) evens)))))))
(split '(a b c d e f))   ⇒   (a c e)
                             (b d f)
```

At each level of recursion, the procedure `split` returns two values: a list of the odd-numbered elements from the argument list and a list of the even-numbered elements.

The continuation of a call to `values` need not be one established by a call to `call-with-values`, nor must only `values` be used to return to a continuation established by `call-with-values`. In particular, (`values` *v*) and *v* are equivalent in all situations. For example:

```
(+ (values 2) 4)   ⇒   6

(if (values #t) 1 2)   ⇒   1

(call-with-values
  (lambda () 4)
  (lambda (x) x))   ⇒   4
```

Similarly, `values` may be used to pass any number of values to a continuation that ignores the values, as in:

```
(begin (values 1 2 3) 4)   ⇒   4
```

Because a continuation may accept zero or more than one value, continuation objects obtained via `call-with-current-continuation` (`call/cc`) may accept zero or more than one argument:

```
(call-with-values
  (lambda ()
    (call/cc (lambda (k) (k 2 3))))
  (lambda (x y) (list x y)))   ⇒   (2 3)
```

Many Scheme operators pass along multiple values. Most of these are "automatic," in the sense that nothing special must be done by the implementation to make this happen. The usual expansion of `let` into a direct `lambda` call automatically propagates multiple values produced by the body of the `let`. Other operators must be coded specially to pass along multiple values. For example, if the computation delayed by `delay` produces multiple values, all of the values must be retained so that `force` can return them. This is easily accomplished via `call-with-values`, `apply`, and `values`, as the following alternative definition of `make-promise` (see Section 5.7) demonstrates.

```
(define make-promise
  (lambda (p)
    (let ((vals #f) (set? #f))
      (lambda ()
        (if (not set?)
            (call-with-values p
              (lambda x
                (if (not set?)
                    (begin (set! vals x)
                           (set! set? #t)))))))
        (apply values vals)))))
(define p (delay (values 1 2 3)))
(force p)  ⇒  1
                2
                3
(call-with-values (lambda () (force p)) +)  ⇒  6
```

Other operators that must be coded similarly to pass along multiple return values
include `call-with-input-file`, `call-with-output-file`, `with-input-from-file`,
`with-output-to-file`, and `dynamic-wind`.

The behavior is unspecified when a continuation expecting exactly one value
receives zero values or more than one value. For example, the behavior of each of
the following expressions is unspecified.

```
(if (values 1 2) 'x 'y)
```

```
(+ (values) 5)
```

Similarly, since there is no requirement to signal an error when the wrong number
of arguments is passed to a procedure (although most implementations do so), the
behavior of each of the following expressions is also unspecified.

```
(call-with-values
  (lambda () (values 2 3 4))
  (lambda (x y) x))
```

```
(call-with-values
  (lambda () (call/cc (lambda (k) (k 0))))
  (lambda (x y) x))
```

In the interests of catching possible coding errors and for consistency with the
signaling of errors when procedures receive incorrect numbers of arguments, some
implementations, including *Chez Scheme*, signal an error whenever an unexpected
number of values is received. This includes the case where too few or too many are
passed to the consumer of a `call-with-values` call and the case where zero or more
than one value is passed to a single-value continuation, such as in the test part of
an `if` expression. An implementation may, however, silently suppress additional
values or supply defaults for missing values.

Programs that wish to force extra values to be ignored in particular contexts
can do so easily by calling `call-with-values` explicitly. A syntactic form, which

we might call `first`, can be defined to abstract the discarding of more than one value when only one is desired:

```
(define-syntax first
  (syntax-rules ()
    ((_ expr)
     (call-with-values
       (lambda () expr)
       (lambda (x . y) x)))))
```

```
(if (first (values #t #f)) 'a 'b)  ⇒  a
```

Since *producer* is most often a `lambda` expression, it is often convenient to use a syntactic extension that suppresses the lambda expression in the interest of readability.

```
(define-syntax with-values
  (syntax-rules ()
    ((_ expr consumer)
     (call-with-values (lambda () expr) consumer))))
```

```
(with-values (values 1 2) list)  ⇒  (1 2)
(with-values (split '(1 2 3 4))
  (lambda (odds evens)
    evens))  ⇒  (2 4)
```

If the *consumer* is also a `lambda` expression, the multiple-value variant of `let` defined below might be even more convenient.

```
(define-syntax mvlet
  (syntax-rules ()
    ((_ ((x ...) e0) e1 e2 ...)
     (with-values e0
       (lambda (x ...) e1 e2 ...)))))
```

```
(mvlet ((odds evens) (split '(1 2 3 4)))
  evens)  ⇒  (2 4)
```

The definitions of `values` and `call-with-values` (and concomitant redefinition of `call/cc`) below demonstrate that the multiple return values interface can be implemented entirely in Scheme. No error checking can be done, however, for the case in which more than one value is returned to a single-value context such as the test part of an `if` expression.

```
(define call/cc call/cc)
(define values #f)
(define call-with-values #f)
(let ((magic (cons 'multiple 'values)))
  (define magic?
    (lambda (x)
      (and (pair? x) (eq? (car x) magic)))))
```

```
(set! call/cc
  (let ((primitive-call/cc call/cc))
    (lambda (p)
      (primitive-call/cc
        (lambda (k)
          (p (lambda args
               (k (apply values args)))))))))
(set! values
  (lambda args
    (if (and (not (null? args)) (null? (cdr args)))
        (car args)
        (cons magic args))))
(set! call-with-values
  (lambda (producer consumer)
    (let ((x (producer)))
      (if (magic? x)
          (apply consumer (cdr x))
          (consumer x)))))))
```

Multiple values can be implemented much more efficiently [2], but this code serves to illustrate the meanings of the operators and can be used to provide multiple values in implementations that do not support them.

5.9. Eval

(eval *obj*)   **procedure**
returns: the result of evaluating *obj* as a Scheme program

obj may be any Scheme object that corresponds to a valid Scheme program. The current lexical environment is not visible within *obj*; instead, *obj* behaves as if it appeared at top level or in some other implementation-dependent environment containing the top-level bindings for (at least) the standard syntactic forms and procedures.

At the time of this writing, eval has been accepted for inclusion in the Revised[5] Report on Scheme, but its interface has not been fully specified. The form described here is recognized by most Scheme systems, however. eval is not in the ANSI/IEEE standard or the Revised[4] Report.

```
(eval 3)  ⇒  3
(eval '(+ 3 4))  ⇒  7
(eval ''(+ 3 4))  ⇒  (+ 3 4)
(eval (list '+ 3 4))  ⇒  7
(let ((k 4))
  ((eval '(lambda (x) (+ x ,k))) 3))  ⇒  7
```

CHAPTER 6

Operations on Objects

A large warped spiral and small satellite.

This chapter describes the operations on objects, including lists, numbers, characters, strings, vectors, and symbols. The first section describes generic equivalence predicates for comparing two objects and predicates for determining the *type* of an object. Later sections describe procedures that deal primarily with one of the object types mentioned above. There is no section treating operations on procedures, since the only operation defined specifically for procedures is application, and this is described in Chapter 5. Operations on ports are covered in the more general discussion of input and output in Chapter 7.

6.1. Generic Equivalence and Type Predicates

This section describes the basic Scheme predicates (procedures returning one of the boolean values #t or #f) for determining the type of an object or the equivalence of two objects. The equivalence predicates eq?, eqv?, and equal? are discussed first, followed by the type predicates.

(eq? obj_1 obj_2)   **procedure**
returns: #t if obj_1 and obj_2 are identical, #f otherwise

In most Scheme systems, two objects are considered identical if they are represented internally by the same pointer value and distinct (not identical) if they are represented internally by different pointer values, although other criteria, such as time-stamping, are possible.

Although the particular rules for object identity vary somewhat from system to system, the following rules always hold:

- Two objects of different types (booleans, the empty list, pairs, numbers, characters, strings, vectors, symbols, and procedures) are distinct. The Revised[4] Report (but not the ANSI/IEEE standard) permits one exception to this rule: the empty list and the boolean #f may be identical.

- Two objects of the same type with different contents or values are distinct.

- The boolean object #t is identical to itself wherever it appears, and #f is identical to itself wherever it appears, but #t and #f are distinct.

- The empty list () is identical to itself wherever it appears.

- Two symbols (created by read or by string->symbol) are identical if and only if they have the same name (by string=?).

- A quoted pair, vector, or string is identical to itself, as is a pair, vector, or string created by an application of cons, vector, string, etc. Two pairs, vectors, or strings created by different applications of cons, vector, string, etc., are distinct. One consequence is that cons, for example, may be used to create a unique object distinct from all other objects.

- Two procedures that may behave differently are distinct. A procedure created by an evaluation of a `lambda` expression is identical to itself. Two procedures created by the same `lambda` expression at different times, or by similar `lambda` expressions, may or may not be identical.

`eq?` cannot be used to compare numbers and characters reliably. Although every inexact number is distinct from every exact number, two exact numbers, two inexact numbers, or two characters with the same value may or may not be identical.

Since constant objects are immutable, i.e., it is an error to modify one, all or portions of different quoted constants or self-evaluating literals may be represented internally by the same object. Thus, `eq?` may return `#t` when applied to equal parts of different immutable constants.

```
(eq? 'a 3)   ⇒  #f
(eq? #t 't)  ⇒  #f
(eq? "abc" 'abc)  ⇒  #f
(eq? "hi" '(hi))  ⇒  #f
(eq? "()" '())  ⇒  #f

(eq? 9/2 7/2)  ⇒  #f
(eq? 3.4 53344)  ⇒  #f
(eq? 3 3.0)  ⇒  #f
(eq? 1/3 #i1/3)  ⇒  #f

(eq? 9/2 9/2)  ⇒  unspecified
(eq? 3.4 (+ 3.0 .4))  ⇒  unspecified
(let ((x (* 12345678987654321 2)))
  (eq? x x))  ⇒  unspecified

(eq? #\a #\b)  ⇒  #f
(eq? #\a #\a)  ⇒  unspecified
(let ((x (string-ref "hi" 0)))
  (eq? x x))  ⇒  unspecified

(eq? #t #t)  ⇒  #t
(eq? #f #f)  ⇒  #t
(eq? #t #f)  ⇒  #f
(eq? (null? '()) #t)  ⇒  #t
(eq? (null? '(a)) #f)  ⇒  #t

(eq? (cdr '(a)) '())  ⇒  #t

(eq? 'a 'a)  ⇒  #t
(eq? 'a 'b)  ⇒  #f
(eq? 'a (string->symbol "a"))  ⇒  #t

(eq? '(a) '(b))  ⇒  #f
(eq? '(a) '(a))  ⇒  unspecified
(let ((x '(a . b))) (eq? x x))  ⇒  #t
(let ((x (cons 'a 'b)))
  (eq? x x))  ⇒  #t
(eq? (cons 'a 'b) (cons 'a 'b))  ⇒  #f
```

```
(eq? "abc" "cba")   ⇒   #f
(eq? "abc" "abc")   ⇒   unspecified
(let ((x "hi")) (eq? x x))   ⇒   #t
(let ((x (string #\h #\i))) (eq? x x))   ⇒   #t
(eq? (string #\h #\i)
     (string #\h #\i))   ⇒   #f

(eq? '#(a) '#(b))   ⇒   #f
(eq? '#(a) '#(a))   ⇒   unspecified
(let ((x '#(a))) (eq? x x))   ⇒   #t
(let ((x (vector 'a)))
  (eq? x x))   ⇒   #t
(eq? (vector 'a) (vector 'a))   ⇒   #f

(eq? car car)   ⇒   #t
(eq? car cdr)   ⇒   #f
(let ((f (lambda (x) x)))
  (eq? f f))   ⇒   #t
(let ((f (lambda () (lambda (x) x))))
  (eq? (f) (f)))   ⇒   unspecified
(eq? (lambda (x) x) (lambda (y) y))   ⇒   unspecified

(let ((f (lambda (x)
           (lambda ()
             (set! x (+ x 1))
             x))))
  (eq? (f 0) (f 0)))   ⇒   #f
```

(eqv? *obj₁* *obj₂*)   **procedure**

returns: #t if *obj₁* and *obj₂* are equivalent, #f otherwise

eqv? is similar to eq? except that eqv? is guaranteed to return #t for two exact
numbers, two inexact numbers, or two characters with the same value (by = or
char=?). eqv? is less implementation-dependent but generally more expensive than
eq?. eqv? might be defined as follows:

```
(define eqv?
  (lambda (x y)
    (cond
      ((eq? x y))
      ((number? x)
       (and (number? y)
            (if (exact? x)
                (and (exact? y) (= x y))
                (and (inexact? y) (= x y)))))
      ((char? x) (and (char? y) (char=? x y)))
      (else #f))))
```

```
(eqv? 'a 3)  ⇒  #f
(eqv? #t 't)  ⇒  #f
(eqv? "abc" 'abc)  ⇒  #f
(eqv? "hi" '(hi))  ⇒  #f
(eqv? "()" '())  ⇒  #f

(eqv? 9/2 7/2)  ⇒  #f
(eqv? 3.4 53344)  ⇒  #f
(eqv? 3 3.0)  ⇒  #f
(eqv? 1/3 #i1/3)  ⇒  #f

(eqv? 9/2 9/2)  ⇒  #t
(eqv? 3.4 (+ 3.0 .4))  ⇒  #t
(let ((x (* 12345678987654321 2)))
  (eqv? x x))  ⇒  #t

(eqv? #\a #\b)  ⇒  #f
(eqv? #\a #\a)  ⇒  #t
(let ((x (string-ref "hi" 0)))
  (eqv? x x))  ⇒  #t

(eqv? #t #t)  ⇒  #t
(eqv? #f #f)  ⇒  #t
(eqv? #t #f)  ⇒  #f
(eqv? (null? '()) #t)  ⇒  #t
(eqv? (null? '(a)) #f)  ⇒  #t

(eqv? (cdr '(a)) '())  ⇒  #t

(eqv? 'a 'a)  ⇒  #t
(eqv? 'a 'b)  ⇒  #f
(eqv? 'a (string->symbol "a"))  ⇒  #t

(eqv? '(a) '(b))  ⇒  #f
(eqv? '(a) '(a))  ⇒  unspecified
(let ((x '(a . b))) (eqv? x x))  ⇒  #t
(let ((x (cons 'a 'b)))
  (eqv? x x))  ⇒  #t
(eqv? (cons 'a 'b) (cons 'a 'b))  ⇒  #f

(eqv? "abc" "cba")  ⇒  #f
(eqv? "abc" "abc")  ⇒  unspecified
(let ((x "hi")) (eqv? x x))  ⇒  #t
(let ((x (string #\h #\i))) (eqv? x x))  ⇒  #t
(eqv? (string #\h #\i)
      (string #\h #\i))  ⇒  #f

(eqv? '#(a) '#(b))  ⇒  #f
(eqv? '#(a) '#(a))  ⇒  unspecified
(let ((x '#(a))) (eqv? x x))  ⇒  #t
(let ((x (vector 'a)))
  (eqv? x x))  ⇒  #t
(eqv? (vector 'a) (vector 'a))  ⇒  #f
```

```
(eqv? car car)  ⇒  #t
(eqv? car cdr)  ⇒  #f
(let ((f (lambda (x) x)))
  (eqv? f f))  ⇒  #t
(let ((f (lambda () (lambda (x) x))))
  (eqv? (f) (f)))  ⇒  unspecified
(eqv? (lambda (x) x) (lambda (y) y))  ⇒  unspecified

(let ((f (lambda (x)
           (lambda ()
             (set! x (+ x 1))
             x))))
  (eqv? (f 0) (f 0)))  ⇒  #f
```

(equal? *obj₁* *obj₂*)   **procedure**

returns: #t if *obj₁* and *obj₂* have the same structure and contents, #f otherwise

Two objects are equal if they are equivalent according to eqv? or if they are strings
that are string=?, pairs whose cars and cdrs are equal, or vectors of the same
length whose corresponding elements are equal.

   equal? is recursively defined and must compare not only numbers and characters
for equivalence but also pairs, strings, and vectors. The result is that equal? is less
discriminating than either eq? or eqv?. It is also likely to be more expensive.

   equal? might be defined as follows:

```
(define equal?
  (lambda (x y)
    (cond
      ((eqv? x y))
      ((pair? x)
       (and (pair? y)
            (equal? (car x) (car y))
            (equal? (cdr x) (cdr y))))
      ((string? x) (and (string? y) (string=? x y)))
      ((vector? x)
       (and (vector? y)
            (let ((n (vector-length x)))
              (and (= (vector-length y) n)
                   (let loop ((i 0))
                     (or (= i n)
                         (and (equal? (vector-ref x i) (vector-ref y i))
                              (loop (+ i 1)))))))))
      (else #f))))

(equal? 'a 3)  ⇒  #f
(equal? #t 't)  ⇒  #f
(equal? "abc" 'abc)  ⇒  #f
(equal? "hi" '(hi))  ⇒  #f
(equal? "()" '())  ⇒  #f
```

```
(equal? 9/2 7/2)  ⇒  #f
(equal? 3.4 53344)  ⇒  #f
(equal? 3 3.0)  ⇒  #f
(equal? 1/3 #i1/3)  ⇒  #f

(equal? 9/2 9/2)  ⇒  #t
(equal? 3.4 (+ 3.0 .4))  ⇒  #t
(let ((x (* 12345678987654321 2)))
  (equal? x x))  ⇒  #t

(equal? #\a #\b)  ⇒  #f
(equal? #\a #\a)  ⇒  #t
(let ((x (string-ref "hi" 0)))
  (equal? x x))  ⇒  #t

(equal? #t #t)  ⇒  #t
(equal? #f #f)  ⇒  #t
(equal? #t #f)  ⇒  #f
(equal? (null? '()) #t)  ⇒  #t
(equal? (null? '(a)) #f)  ⇒  #t

(equal? (cdr '(a)) '())  ⇒  #t

(equal? 'a 'a)  ⇒  #t
(equal? 'a 'b)  ⇒  #f
(equal? 'a (string->symbol "a"))  ⇒  #t

(equal? '(a) '(b))  ⇒  #f
(equal? '(a) '(a))  ⇒  #t
(let ((x '(a . b))) (equal? x x))  ⇒  #t
(let ((x (cons 'a 'b)))
  (equal? x x))  ⇒  #t
(equal? (cons 'a 'b) (cons 'a 'b))  ⇒  #t

(equal? "abc" "cba")  ⇒  #f
(equal? "abc" "abc")  ⇒  #t
(let ((x "hi")) (equal? x x))  ⇒  #t
(let ((x (string #\h #\i))) (equal? x x))  ⇒  #t
(equal? (string #\h #\i)
        (string #\h #\i))  ⇒  #t

(equal? '#(a) '#(b))  ⇒  #f
(equal? '#(a) '#(a))  ⇒  #t
(let ((x '#(a))) (equal? x x))  ⇒  #t
(let ((x (vector 'a)))
  (equal? x x))  ⇒  #t
(equal? (vector 'a) (vector 'a))  ⇒  #t

(equal? car car)  ⇒  #t
(equal? car cdr)  ⇒  #f
(let ((f (lambda (x) x)))
  (equal? f f))  ⇒  #t
(let ((f (lambda () (lambda (x) x))))
  (equal? (f) (f)))  ⇒  unspecified
(equal? (lambda (x) x) (lambda (y) y))  ⇒  unspecified
```

```
(let ((f (lambda (x)
           (lambda ()
             (set! x (+ x 1))
             x))))
  (equal? (f 0) (f 0)))  ⇒  #f
```

(boolean? *obj*)   **procedure**
returns: #t if *obj* is either #t or #f, #f otherwise

boolean? is equivalent to (lambda (x) (or (eq? x #t) (eq? x #f))).

The Revised[4] Report (but not the ANSI/IEEE Standard) permits the empty list and #f to be identical. If they are identical, boolean? returns #t for (); otherwise, it returns #f for ().

```
(boolean? #t)  ⇒  #t
(boolean? #f)  ⇒  #t
(boolean? 't)  ⇒  #f
(if (eq? #f '())
    (boolean? '())
    (not (boolean? '()))))  ⇒  #t
```

(null? *obj*)   **procedure**
returns: #t if *obj* is the empty list, #f otherwise

null? is equivalent to (lambda (x) (eq? x '())).

The Revised[4] Report (but not the ANSI/IEEE Standard) permits the empty list and #f to be identical. If they are identical, null? returns #t for #f; otherwise, it returns #f for #f.

```
(null? '())  ⇒  #t
(null? '(a))  ⇒  #f
(null? (cdr '(a)))  ⇒  #t
(null? 3)  ⇒  #f
(if (eq? #f '())
    (null? #f)
    (not (null? #f)))  ⇒  #t
```

(pair? *obj*)   **procedure**
returns: #t if *obj* is a pair, #f otherwise

```
(pair? '(a b c))  ⇒  #t
(pair? '(3 . 4))  ⇒  #t
(pair? '())  ⇒  #f
(pair? '#(a b))  ⇒  #f
(pair? 3)  ⇒  #f
```

(number? *obj*)   **procedure**
returns: #t if *obj* is a number, #f otherwise
(complex? *obj*)   **procedure**
returns: #t if *obj* is a complex number, #f otherwise
(real? *obj*)   **procedure**
returns: #t if *obj* is a real number, #f otherwise
(rational? *obj*)   **procedure**
returns: #t if *obj* is a rational number, #f otherwise
(integer? *obj*)   **procedure**
returns: #t if *obj* is an integer, #f otherwise

These predicates form a hierarchy: any integer is rational, any rational is real, any
real is complex, and any complex is numeric. Most implementations do not provide
internal representations for irrational numbers, so all real numbers are typically
rational as well.

```
(integer? 1901)   ⇒   #t
(rational? 1901)   ⇒   #t
(real? 1901)   ⇒   #t
(complex? 1901)   ⇒   #t
(number? 1901)   ⇒   #t

(integer? -3.0)   ⇒   #t
(rational? -3.0)   ⇒   #t
(real? -3.0)   ⇒   #t
(complex? -3.0)   ⇒   #t
(number? -3.0)   ⇒   #t

(integer? 7.0+0.0i)   ⇒   #t
(rational? 7.0+0.0i)   ⇒   #t
(real? 7.0+0.0i)   ⇒   #t
(complex? 7.0+0.0i)   ⇒   #t
(number? 7.0+0.0i)   ⇒   #t

(integer? -2/3)   ⇒   #f
(rational? -2/3)   ⇒   #t
(real? -2/3)   ⇒   #t
(complex? -2/3)   ⇒   #t
(number? -2/3)   ⇒   #t

(integer? -2.345)   ⇒   #f
(rational? -2.345)   ⇒   #t
(real? -2.345)   ⇒   #t
(complex? -2.345)   ⇒   #t
(number? -2.345)   ⇒   #t

(integer? 3.2-2.01i)   ⇒   #f
(rational? 3.2-2.01i)   ⇒   #f
(real? 3.2-2.01i)   ⇒   #f
(complex? 3.2-2.01i)   ⇒   #t
(number? 3.2-2.01i)   ⇒   #t
```

```
(integer? 'a)  ⇒  #f
(rational? '(a b c))  ⇒  #f
(real? "3")  ⇒  #f
(complex? #(1 2))  ⇒  #f
(number? #\a)  ⇒  #f
```

(char? *obj*)   **procedure**
returns: #t if *obj* is a character, #f otherwise

```
(char? 'a)  ⇒  #f
(char? 97)  ⇒  #f
(char? #\a)  ⇒  #t
(char? "a")  ⇒  #f
(char? (string-ref (make-string 1) 0))  ⇒  #t
```

(string? *obj*)   **procedure**
returns: #t if *obj* is a string, #f otherwise

```
(string? "hi")  ⇒  #t
(string? 'hi)  ⇒  #f
(string? #\h)  ⇒  #f
```

(vector? *obj*)   **procedure**
returns: #t if *obj* is a vector, #f otherwise

```
(vector? '#())  ⇒  #t
(vector? '#(a b c))  ⇒  #t
(vector? (vector 'a 'b 'c))  ⇒  #t
(vector? '())  ⇒  #f
(vector? '(a b c))  ⇒  #f
(vector? "abc")  ⇒  #f
```

(symbol? *obj*)   **procedure**
returns: #t if *obj* is a symbol, #f otherwise

```
(symbol? 't)  ⇒  #t
(symbol? "t")  ⇒  #f
(symbol? '(t))  ⇒  #f
(symbol? #\t)  ⇒  #f
(symbol? 3)  ⇒  #f
(symbol? #t)  ⇒  #f
```

(procedure? *obj*)   **procedure**
returns: #t if *obj* is a procedure, #f otherwise

Continuations obtained via `call-with-current-continuation` are procedures, so
`procedure?` can be used to distinguish them from nonprocedures but not from
other procedures.

```
(procedure? car)   ⇒   #t
(procedure? 'car)  ⇒   #f
(procedure? (lambda (x) x))   ⇒   #t
(procedure? '(lambda (x) x))  ⇒   #f
(call/cc procedure?)   ⇒   #t
```

6.2. Lists and Pairs

The pair, or *cons cell*, is the most fundamental of Scheme's structured object types. The most common use for pairs is to build lists, which are ordered sequences of pairs linked one to the next by the *cdr* field. The elements of the list occupy the *car* field of each pair. The cdr of the last pair in a *proper list* is the empty list, ( ); the cdr of the last pair in an *improper list* can be anything other than ( ).

Pairs may be used to construct binary trees. Each pair in the tree structure is an internal node of the binary tree; its car and cdr are the children of the node.

Proper lists are printed as sequences of objects separated by whitespace (that is, blanks, tabs, and newlines) and enclosed in parentheses. Brackets ([ ]) may also be used in some Scheme systems. For example, (1 2 3) and (a (nested list)) are proper lists. The empty list is written as ().

Improper lists and trees require a slightly more complex syntax. A single pair is written as two objects separated by whitespace and a dot, e.g., (a . b). This is referred to as *dotted-pair notation*. Improper lists and trees are also written in dotted-pair notation; the dot appears wherever necessary, e.g., (1 2 3 . 4) or ((1 . 2) . 3). Proper lists may be written in dotted-pair notation as well. For example, (1 2 3) may be written as (1 . (2 . (3 . ()))).

Unless otherwise stated, it is an error to pass an improper list to a procedure requiring a list argument.

It is possible to create a circular list or a cyclic graph by destructively altering the car or cdr field of a pair, using `set-car!` or `set-cdr!`. Some of the procedures listed in this section may loop indefinitely when handed a cyclic structure.

(cons *obj₁ obj₂*)   **procedure**
returns: a new pair whose car and cdr are *obj₁* and *obj₂*

cons is the pair constructor procedure. *obj₁* becomes the car and *obj₂* becomes the cdr of the new pair.

```
(cons 'a '())    ⇒   (a)
(cons 'a '(b c)) ⇒   (a b c)
(cons 3 4)   ⇒   (3 . 4)
```

(car *pair*)   **procedure**
returns: the car of *pair*

It is an error to ask for the car of the empty list.

```
(car '(a))  ⇒  a
(car '(a b c))  ⇒  a
(car (cons 3 4))  ⇒  3
```

(cdr *pair*)   procedure

returns: the cdr of *pair*

It is an error to ask for the cdr of the empty list.

```
(cdr '(a))  ⇒  ()
(cdr '(a b c))  ⇒  (b c)
(cdr (cons 3 4))  ⇒  4
```

(set-car! *pair obj*)   procedure

returns: unspecified

set-car! changes the car of *pair* to *obj*.

```
(let ((x '(a b c)))
  (set-car! x 1)
  x)  ⇒  (1 b c)
```

(set-cdr! *pair obj*)   procedure

returns: unspecified

set-cdr! changes the cdr of *pair* to *obj*.

```
(let ((x '(a b c)))
  (set-cdr! x 1)
  x)  ⇒  (a . 1)
```

(caar *pair*)   procedure
(cadr *pair*)   procedure
⋮
(cddddr *pair*)   procedure

returns: the caar, cadr, ..., or cddddr of *pair*

These procedures are defined as the composition of up to four cars and cdrs. The a's and d's between the c and d represent the application of car or cdr in order from right to left. For example, the procedure cadr applied to a pair yields the car of the cdr of the pair and is equivalent to (lambda (x) (car (cdr x))).

```
(caar '((a)))  ⇒  a
(cadr '(a b c))  ⇒  b
(cdddr '(a b c d))  ⇒  (d)
(cadadr '(a (b c)))  ⇒  c
```

(list *obj* ...)   **procedure**
returns: a list of *obj* ...

list is equivalent to (lambda x x).

```
(list)  ⇒  ()
(list 1 2 3)  ⇒  (1 2 3)
(list 3 2 1)  ⇒  (3 2 1)
```

(list? *obj*)   **procedure**
returns: #t if *obj* is a proper list, #f otherwise

list? must return #f for all improper lists, including cyclic lists. A definition of
list? is shown on page 55.

```
(list? '())  ⇒  #t
(list? '(a b c))  ⇒  #t
(list? 'a)  ⇒  #f
(list? '(3 . 4))  ⇒  #f
(list? 3)  ⇒  #f
(let ((x (list 'a 'b 'c)))
  (set-cdr! (cddr x) x)
  (list? x))  ⇒  #f
```

(length *list*)   **procedure**
returns: the number of elements in *list*

length may be defined as follows.

```
(define length
  (lambda (ls)
    (let loop ((ls ls) (n 0))
      (if (null? ls)
          n
          (loop (cdr ls) (+ n 1))))))
(length '())  ⇒  0
(length '(a b c))  ⇒  3
```

(list-ref *list* *n*)   **procedure**
returns: the *n*th element (zero-based) of *list*

n must be an exact nonnegative integer strictly less than the length of *list*. list-ref
may be defined as follows.

```
(define list-ref
  (lambda (ls n)
    (if (= n 0)
        (car ls)
        (list-ref (cdr ls) (- n 1)))))
```

```
(list-ref '(a b c) 0)  ⇒  a
(list-ref '(a b c) 1)  ⇒  b
(list-ref '(a b c) 2)  ⇒  c
```

(list-tail *list* *n*)   **procedure**
returns: the *n*th tail (zero-based) of *list*

n must be an exact nonnegative integer less than or equal to the length of *list*. The
result is not a copy; the tail is **eq?** to the *n*th cdr of *list* (or to *list* itself, if *n* is
zero).

list-tail is in the Revised[4] Report but not the ANSI/IEEE standard. It may
be defined as follows.

```
(define list-tail
  (lambda (ls n)
    (if (= n 0)
        ls
        (list-tail (cdr ls) (- n 1)))))
```
```
(list-tail '(a b c) 0)  ⇒  (a b c)
(list-tail '(a b c) 2)  ⇒  (c)
(list-tail '(a b c) 3)  ⇒  ()
(list-tail '(a b c . d) 2)  ⇒  (c . d)
(list-tail '(a b c . d) 3)  ⇒  d
(let ((x (list 1 2 3)))
  (eq? (list-tail x 2)
       (cddr x)))  ⇒  #t
```

(append *list* ...)   **procedure**
returns: the concatenation of the input lists

append returns a new list consisting of the elements of the first list followed by the
elements of the second list, the elements of the third list, and so on. The new list
is made from new pairs for all arguments but the last; the last (which need not
actually be a list) is merely placed at the end of the new structure. **append** may be
defined as follows.

```
(define append
  (lambda args
    (let f ((ls '()) (args args))
      (if (null? args)
          ls
          (let g ((ls ls))
            (if (null? ls)
                (f (car args) (cdr args))
                (cons (car ls) (g (cdr ls)))))))))
```

```
(append '(a b c) '())   ⇒   (a b c)
(append '() '(a b c))   ⇒   (a b c)
(append '(a b) '(c d))  ⇒   (a b c d)
(append '(a b) 'c)  ⇒   (a b . c)
(let ((x (list 'b)))
  (eq? x (cdr (append '(a) x))))  ⇒   #t
```

(reverse *list*)   procedure
returns: a new list containing the elements of *list* in reverse order

reverse may be defined as follows.

```
(define reverse
  (lambda (ls)
    (let rev ((ls ls) (new '()))
      (if (null? ls)
          new
          (rev (cdr ls) (cons (car ls) new))))))
(reverse '())  ⇒   ()
(reverse '(a b c))  ⇒   (c b a)
```

(memq *obj* *list*)   procedure
(memv *obj* *list*)   procedure
(member *obj* *list*)   procedure
returns: the first tail of *list* whose car is equivalent to *obj*, or #f

These procedures traverse the argument *list* in order, comparing the elements of
list against *obj*. If an object equivalent to *obj* is found, the tail of the list whose
first element is that object is returned. If the list contains more than one object
equivalent to *obj*, the first tail whose first element is equivalent to *obj* is returned.
If no object equivalent to *obj* is found, #f is returned. The equivalence test for memq
is eq?, for memv is eqv?, and for member is equal?.

These procedures are most often used as predicates, but their names do not end
with a question mark because they return a useful true value in place of #t. memq
may be defined as follows.

```
(define memq
  (lambda (x ls)
    (cond
      ((null? ls) #f)
      ((eq? (car ls) x) ls)
      (else (memq x (cdr ls))))))
```

memv and member may be defined similarly, with eqv? and equal? in place of eq?.

```
(memq 'a '(b c a d e))  ⇒   (a d e)
(memq 'a '(b c d e g))  ⇒   #f
(memq 'a '(b a c a d a))  ⇒   (a c a d a)
```

```
(memv 3.4 '(1.2 2.3 3.4 4.5))  ⇒  (3.4 4.5)
(memv 3.4 '(1.3 2.5 3.7 4.9))  ⇒  #f
(let ((ls (list 'a 'b 'c)))
  (set-car! (memv 'b ls) 'z)
  ls)  ⇒  (a z c)

(member '(b) '((a) (b) (c)))  ⇒  ((b) (c))
(member '(d) '((a) (b) (c)))  ⇒  #f
(member "b" '("a" "b" "c"))  ⇒  ("b" "c")
```

(assq *obj alist*)	procedure
(assv *obj alist*)	procedure
(assoc *obj alist*)	procedure

returns: first element of *alist* whose car is equivalent to *obj*, or #f

The argument *alist* must be an *association list*. An association list is a proper list whose elements are key-value pairs of the form (**key . value**). Associations are useful for storing information (values) associated with certain objects (keys).

These procedures traverse the association list, testing each key for equivalence with *obj*. If an equivalent key is found, the key-value pair is returned. Otherwise, #f is returned.

The equivalence test for **assq** is **eq?**, for **assv** is **eqv?**, and for **assoc** is **equal?**. **assq** may be defined as follows.

```
(define assq
  (lambda (x ls)
    (cond
      ((null? ls) #f)
      ((eq? (caar ls) x) (car ls))
      (else (assq x (cdr ls))))))
```

assv and **assoc** may be defined similarly, with **eqv?** and **equal?** in place of **eq?**.

```
(assq 'b '((a . 1) (b . 2)))  ⇒  (b . 2)
(cdr (assq 'b '((a . 1) (b . 2))))  ⇒  2
(assq 'c '((a . 1) (b . 2)))  ⇒  #f

(assv 2/3 '((1/3 . 1) (2/3 . 2)))  ⇒  (2/3 . 2)
(assv 2/3 '((1/3 . a) (3/4 . b)))  ⇒  #f

(assoc '(a) '(((a) . a) (-1 . b)))  ⇒  ((a) . a)
(assoc '(a) '(((b) . b) (a . c)))  ⇒  #f

(let ((alist '((2 . a) (3 . b))))
  (set-cdr! (assv 3 alist) 'c)
  alist)  ⇒  ((2 . a) (3 . c))
```

6.3. Numbers

Scheme numbers may be classified as integers, rational numbers, real numbers, or complex numbers, although an implementation may support only a subset of these numeric classes. This classification is hierarchical, in that all integers are rational, all rational numbers are real, and all real numbers are complex. The predicates `integer?`, `rational?`, `real?`, and `complex?` described in Section 6.1 are used to determine into which of these classes a number falls.

A Scheme number may also be classified as *exact* or *inexact*, depending upon the quality of operations used to derive the number and the inputs to these operations. The predicates `exact?` and `inexact?` may be used to determine the exactness of a number. Most operations on numbers in Scheme are *exactness preserving*: if given exact operands they return exact values, and if given inexact operands or a combination of exact and inexact operands they return inexact values.

Exact integer and rational arithmetic is typically supported to arbitrary precision; the size of an integer or of the denominator or numerator of a ratio is limited only by system storage constraints. Although other representations are possible, inexact numbers are typically represented by *floating-point* numbers supported by the host computer's hardware or by system software. Complex numbers are typically represented as ordered pairs (*real-part*, *imag-part*), where *real-part* and *imag-part* are exact integers, exact rationals, or floating-point numbers.

Scheme numbers are written in a straightforward manner not much different from ordinary conventions for writing numbers. An exact integer is normally written as a sequence of numerals preceded by an optional sign. For example, 3, +19, -100000, and 208423089237489374 all represent exact integers.

An exact rational number is normally written as two sequences of numerals separated by a slash (/) and preceded by an optional sign. For example, 3/4, -6/5, and 1/1208203823 are all exact rational numbers. A ratio is reduced immediately when it is read and may in fact reduce to an exact integer.

Inexact integers and rational numbers are normally written in either floating-point or scientific notation. Floating-point notation consists of a sequence of numerals followed by a decimal point and another sequence of numerals, all preceded by an optional sign. Scientific notation consists of an optional sign, a sequence of numerals, an optional decimal point followed by a second string of numerals, and an exponent; an exponent is written as the letter e followed by an optional sign and a sequence of numerals. For example, 1.0 and -200.0 are valid inexact integers, and 1.5, 0.034, -10e-10 and 1.5e-5 are valid inexact rational numbers. The exponent is the power of ten by which the number preceding the exponent should be scaled, so that 2e3 is equivalent to 2000.0.

The special digit # (hash) may be used in place of a normal digit in certain contexts to signify that the value of the digit is unknown. Numbers that include hash digits are naturally inexact, even if they are written in the style of exact integers or rational numbers. Hash digits may appear after one or more nonhash digits to signify an inexact integer; after one or more nonhash digits in the first or second part of a ratio to specify an inexact rational number; or after one or more nonhash digits before or after the decimal point of an inexact number written in floating-point or scientific notation. No significant (known) digit may follow a hash digit. For example, 1####, -1#/2#, .123### and 1#.### all specify inexact quantities.

Exact and inexact real numbers are written as exact or inexact integers or rational numbers; no provision is made in the syntax of Scheme numbers for nonrational real numbers, i.e., irrational numbers.

Complex numbers may be written in either rectangular or polar form. In rectangular form, a complex number is written as $x+y$i or $x-y$i, where x is an integer, rational, or real number and y is an unsigned integer, rational, or real number. The real part, x, may be omitted, in which case it is assumed to be zero. For example, 3+4i, 3.2-3/4i, +i, and -3e-5i are complex numbers written in rectangular form. In polar form, a complex number is written as x@yi, where x and y are integer, rational, or real numbers. For example, 1.1@1.764 and -1@-1/2 are complex numbers written in polar form.

The exactness of a numeric representation may be overridden by preceding the representation by either #e or #i. #e forces the number to be exact, and #i forces it to be inexact. For example, 1, #e1, 1/1, #e1/1, #e1.0, #e1e0, and #e1.## all represent the exact integer 1, and #i3/10, 3#/100, 0.3, #i0.3, and 3e-1 all represent the inexact rational 0.3.

Numbers are written by default in base 10, although the special prefixes #b (binary), #o (octal), #d (decimal), and #x (hexadecimal) can be used to specify base 2, base 8, base 10, or base 16. For radix 16, the letters a through f or A through F serve as the additional numerals required to express digit values 10 through 15. For example, #b10101 is the binary equivalent of 21_{10}, #o72 is the octal equivalent of 58_{10}, and #xC7 is the hexadecimal equivalent of 199_{10}. Numbers written in floating-point and scientific notations are always written in base 10.

If both are present, radix and exactness prefixes may appear in either order.

A Scheme implementation may support more than one size of internal representation for inexact quantities. The exponent markers s (*short*), f (*single*), d (*double*), and l (*long*) may appear in place of the default exponent marker e to override the default size for numbers written in scientific notation. In implementations that support multiple representations, the default size has at least as much precision as *double*.

A precise grammar for Scheme numbers is included in the description of the formal syntax of Scheme at the back of this book.

Any number can be written in a variety of different ways, but the system printer (see **write** and **display**) and **number->string** express numbers in a compact form, using the fewest number of digits possible while retaining the property that, when read, the printed number is identical to the original number.

Scheme implementations are permitted to support only a subset of the numeric datatypes, in which case certain of the procedures described in this section need not be implemented. Implementors should consult the ANSI/IEEE standard or Revised[4] Report for a detailed description of what constitutes a valid subset.

The remainder of this section describes procedures that operate on numbers. The type of numeric arguments accepted by these procedures is implied by the name given to the arguments: *num* for complex numbers (that is, all numbers), *real* for real numbers, *rat* for rational numbers, and *int* for integers.

(exact? *num*)   **procedure**
returns: #t if *num* is exact, #f otherwise

```
(exact? 1)   ⇒  #t
(exact? -15/16)  ⇒  #t
(exact? 2.01)  ⇒  #f
(exact? #i77)  ⇒  #f
(exact? #i2/3)  ⇒  #f
(exact? 1.0-2i)  ⇒  #f
(exact? -1#i)  ⇒  #f
```

(inexact? *num*)   **procedure**
returns: #t if *num* is inexact, #f otherwise

```
(inexact? -123)  ⇒  #f
(inexact? #i123)  ⇒  #t
(inexact? 1e23)  ⇒  #t
(inexact? 1###)  ⇒  #t
(inexact? 1#/2#)  ⇒  #t
(inexact? #e1#/2#)  ⇒  #f
(inexact? +i)  ⇒  #f
```

(= *num$_1$ num$_2$ num$_3$* ...)   **procedure**
(< *real$_1$ real$_2$ real$_3$* ...)   **procedure**
(> *real$_1$ real$_2$ real$_3$* ...)   **procedure**
(<= *real$_1$ real$_2$ real$_3$* ...)   **procedure**
(>= *real$_1$ real$_2$ real$_3$* ...)   **procedure**
returns: #t if the relation holds, #f otherwise

The predicate = returns #t if its arguments are equal. The predicate < returns #t
if its arguments are monotonically increasing, i.e., each argument is greater than
the preceding ones, while > returns #t if its arguments are monotonically decreasing. The predicate <= returns #t if its arguments are monotonically nondecreasing,
i.e., each argument is not less than the preceding ones, while >= returns #t if its
arguments are monotonically nonincreasing.

As implied by the names of the arguments, = is defined for complex arguments
while the other relational predicates are defined only for real arguments. Two
complex numbers are considered equal if their real and imaginary parts are equal.

```
(= 7 7)   ⇒  #t
(= 7 9)   ⇒  #f

(< 2e3 3e2)  ⇒  #f
(<= 1 2 3 3 4 5)  ⇒  #t
(<= 1 2 3 4 5)  ⇒  #t

(> 1 2 2 3 3 4)  ⇒  #f
(>= 1 2 2 3 3 4)  ⇒  #f
```

```
(= -1/2 -0.5)  ⇒  #t
(= 2/3 .667)  ⇒  #f
(= 7.2+0i 7.2)  ⇒  #t
(= 7.2-3i 7)  ⇒  #f

(< 1/2 2/3 3/4)  ⇒  #t
(> 8 4.102 2/3 -5)  ⇒  #t

(let ((x 0.218723452))
  (< 0.210 x 0.220))  ⇒  #t

(let ((i 1) (v (vector 'a 'b 'c)))
  (< -1 i (vector-length v)))  ⇒  #t

(apply < '(1 2 3 4))  ⇒  #t
(apply > '(4 3 3 2))  ⇒  #f
```

(+ *num* ...)   **procedure**
returns: the sum of the arguments *num* ...

When called with no arguments, + returns 0.

```
(+)  ⇒  0
(+ 1 2)  ⇒  3
(+ 1/2 2/3)  ⇒  7/6
(+ 3 4 5)  ⇒  12
(+ 3.0 4)  ⇒  7.0
(+ 3+4i 4+3i)  ⇒  7+7i
(apply + '(1 2 3 4 5))  ⇒  15
```

(- *num₁*)   **procedure**
(- *num₁* *num₂* *num₃* ...)   **procedure**
returns: see explanation

When called with one argument, - returns the negative of num_1. Thus, (- num_1) is an idiom for (- 0 num_1).

When called with two or more arguments, - returns the result of subtracting the sum of the numbers num_2 ... from num_1.

The ANSI/IEEE standard includes only one- and two-argument variants. The more general form is included in the Revised[4] Report.

```
(- 3)  ⇒  -3
(- -2/3)  ⇒  2/3
(- 4 3.0)  ⇒  1.0
(- 3.25+4.25i 1/4+1/4i)  ⇒  3.0+4.0i
(- 4 3 2 1)  ⇒  -2
```

(* *num* ...)   **procedure**
returns: the product of the arguments *num* ...

When called with no arguments, * returns 1.

```
(*)  ⇒  1
(* 3.4)  ⇒  3.4
(* 1 1/2)  ⇒  1/2
(* 3 4 5.5)  ⇒  66.0
(* 1+2i 3+4i)  ⇒  -5+10i
(apply * '(1 2 3 4 5))  ⇒  120
```

(/ num_1)   **procedure**
(/ num_1 num_2 num_3 ...)   **procedure**
returns: see explanation

When called with one argument, / returns the reciprocal of num_1. That is,
(/ num_1) is an idiom for (/ 1 num_1).

When called with two or more arguments, / returns the result of dividing num_1
by the product of the remaining arguments num_2 ....

The ANSI/IEEE standard includes only one- and two-argument variants. The
more general form is included in the Revised[4] Report.

```
(/ -17)  ⇒  -1/17
(/ 1/2)  ⇒  2
(/ .5)  ⇒  2.0
(/ 3 4)  ⇒  3/4
(/ 3.0 4)  ⇒  .75
(/ -5+10i 3+4i)  ⇒  1+2i
(/ 60 5 4 3 2)  ⇒  1/2
```

(zero? *num*)   **procedure**
returns: #t if *num* is zero, #f otherwise

zero? is equivalent to (lambda (x) (= x 0)).

```
(zero? 0)  ⇒  #t
(zero? 1)  ⇒  #f
(zero? (- 3.0 3.0))  ⇒  #t
(zero? (+ 1/2 1/2))  ⇒  #f
(zero? 0+0i)  ⇒  #t
(zero? 0.0-0.0i)  ⇒  #t
```

(positive? *real*)   **procedure**
returns: #t if *real* is greater than zero, #f otherwise

positive? is equivalent to (lambda (x) (> x 0)).

```
(positive? 128)  ⇒  #t
(positive? 0.0)  ⇒  #f
(positive? 1.8e-15)  ⇒  #t
(positive? -2/3)  ⇒  #f
(positive? .001-0.0i)  ⇒  #t
```

(negative? *real*)   **procedure**
returns: #t if *real* is less than zero, #f otherwise

negative? is equivalent to (lambda (x) (< x 0)).

(negative? -65) ⇒ #t
(negative? 0) ⇒ #f
(negative? -0.0121) ⇒ #t
(negative? 15/16) ⇒ #f
(negative? -7.0+0.0i) ⇒ #t

(even? *int*)   **procedure**
returns: #t if *int* is even, #f otherwise

(even? 0) ⇒ #t
(even? 1) ⇒ #f
(even? 2.0) ⇒ #t
(even? -120762398465) ⇒ #f
(even? 2.0+0.0i) ⇒ #t

(odd? *int*)   **procedure**
returns: #t if *int* is odd, #f otherwise

(odd? 0) ⇒ #f
(odd? 1) ⇒ #t
(odd? 2.0) ⇒ #f
(odd? -120762398465) ⇒ #t
(odd? 2.0+0.0i) ⇒ #f

(quotient *int₁* *int₂*)   **procedure**
returns: the integer quotient of *int₁* and *int₂*

(quotient 45 6) ⇒ 7
(quotient 6.0 2.0) ⇒ 3.0
(quotient 3.0 -2) ⇒ -1.0

(remainder *int₁* *int₂*)   **procedure**
returns: the integer remainder of *int₁* and *int₂*

The result of **remainder** has the same sign as *int₁*.

(remainder 16 4) ⇒ 0
(remainder 5 2) ⇒ 1
(remainder -45.0 7) ⇒ -3.0
(remainder 10.0 -3.0) ⇒ 1.0
(remainder -17 -9) ⇒ -8

(modulo int_1 int_2)   **procedure**
returns: the integer modulus of int_1 and int_2

The result of modulo has the same sign as int_2.

```
(modulo 16 4)   ⇒   0
(modulo 5 2)   ⇒   1
(modulo -45.0 7)   ⇒   4.0
(modulo 10.0 -3.0)   ⇒   -2.0
(modulo -17 -9)   ⇒   -8
```

(truncate *real*)   **procedure**
returns: the integer closest to *real* toward zero

```
(truncate 19)   ⇒   19
(truncate 2/3)   ⇒   0
(truncate -2/3)   ⇒   0
(truncate 17.3)   ⇒   17.0
(truncate -17/2)   ⇒   -8
```

(floor *real*)   **procedure**
returns: the integer closest to *real* toward $-\infty$

```
(floor 19)   ⇒   19
(floor 2/3)   ⇒   0
(floor -2/3)   ⇒   -1
(floor 17.3)   ⇒   17.0
(floor -17/2)   ⇒   -9
```

(ceiling *real*)   **procedure**
returns: the integer closest to *real* toward $+\infty$

```
(ceiling 19)   ⇒   19
(ceiling 2/3)   ⇒   1
(ceiling -2/3)   ⇒   0
(ceiling 17.3)   ⇒   18.0
(ceiling -17/2)   ⇒   -8
```

(round *real*)   **procedure**
returns: the integer closest to *real*

If *real* is exactly between two integers, the closest even integer is returned.

```
(round 19)   ⇒   19
(round 2/3)   ⇒   1
(round -2/3)   ⇒   -1
(round 17.3)   ⇒   17.0
(round -17/2)   ⇒   -8
(round 2.5)   ⇒   2.0
(round 3.5)   ⇒   4.0
```

(abs *real*)   **procedure**
returns: the absolute value of *real*

abs is equivalent to (lambda (x) (if (< x 0) (- x) x)). abs and magnitude (see page 132) are identical for real inputs.

```
(abs 1)  ⇒  1
(abs -3/4)  ⇒  3/4
(abs 1.83)  ⇒  1.83
(abs -0.093)  ⇒  0.093
```

(max *real*$_1$ *real*$_2$ ...)   **procedure**
returns: the maximum of *real*$_1$ *real*$_2$ ...

```
(max 4 -7 2 0 -6)  ⇒  4
(max 1/2 3/4 4/5 5/6 6/7)  ⇒  6/7
(max 1.5 1.3 -0.3 0.4 2.0 1.8)  ⇒  2.0
(max 5 2.0)  ⇒  5.0
(max -5 -2.0)  ⇒  -2.0
(let ((ls '(7 3 5 2 9 8)))
  (apply max ls))  ⇒  9
```

(min *real*$_1$ *real*$_2$ ...)   **procedure**
returns: the minimum of *real*$_1$ *real*$_2$ ...

```
(min 4 -7 2 0 -6)  ⇒  -7
(min 1/2 3/4 4/5 5/6 6/7)  ⇒  1/2
(min 1.5 1.3 -0.3 0.4 2.0 1.8)  ⇒  -0.3
(min 5 2.0)  ⇒  2.0
(min -5 -2.0)  ⇒  -5.0
(let ((ls '(7 3 5 2 9 8)))
  (apply min ls))  ⇒  2
```

(gcd *int* ...)   **procedure**
returns: the greatest common divisor of its arguments *int* ...

The result is always nonnegative, i.e., factors of −1 are ignored. When called with no arguments, gcd returns 0.

```
(gcd)  ⇒  0
(gcd 34)  ⇒  34
(gcd 33.0 15.0)  ⇒  3.0
(gcd 70 -42 28)  ⇒  14
```

(lcm *int* ...)   **procedure**
returns: the least common multiple of its arguments *int* ...

The result is always nonnegative, i.e., common multiples of −1 are ignored. Although lcm should probably return ∞ when called with no arguments, it is defined to return 1. If one or more of the arguments is 0, lcm returns 0.

```
(lcm)  ⇒  1
(lcm 34)  ⇒  34
(lcm 33.0 15.0)  ⇒  165.0
(lcm 70 -42 28)  ⇒  420
(lcm 17.0 0)  ⇒  0
```

(expt *num$_1$ num$_2$*)   **procedure**
returns: *num$_1$* raised to the *num$_2$* power

If both arguments are 0, **expt** returns 1.

```
(expt 2 10)  ⇒  1024
(expt 2 -10)  ⇒  1/1024
(expt 2 -10.0)  ⇒  9.765625e-4
(expt -1/2 5)  ⇒  -1/32
(expt 3.0 3)  ⇒  27.0
(expt +i 2)  ⇒  -1
```

(exact->inexact *num*)   **procedure**
returns: an inexact representation for *num*

If *num* is already inexact, it is returned unchanged.

If no inexact representation for *num* is supported by the implementation, an
error may be signaled.

```
(exact->inexact 3)  ⇒  3.0
(exact->inexact 3.0)  ⇒  3.0
(exact->inexact -1/4)  ⇒  -.25
(exact->inexact 3+4i)  ⇒  3.0+4.0i
(exact->inexact (expt 10 20))  ⇒  1e20
```

(inexact->exact *num*)   **procedure**
returns: an exact representation for *num*

If *num* is already exact, it is returned unchanged.

If no exact representation for *num* is supported by the implementation, an error
may be signaled.

```
(inexact->exact 3.0)  ⇒  3
(inexact->exact 3)  ⇒  3
(inexact->exact -.25)  ⇒  -1/4
(inexact->exact 3.0+4.0i)  ⇒  3+4i
(inexact->exact 1e20)  ⇒  100000000000000000000
```

(rationalize $real_1$ $real_2$)   **procedure**
returns: see below

rationalize returns the simplest rational number that differs from $real_1$ by no more than $real_2$. A rational number $q_1 = n_1/m_1$ is simpler than another rational number $q_2 = n_2/m_2$ if $|n_1| \leq |n_2|$ and $|m_1| \leq |m_2|$ and either $|n_1| < |n_2|$ or $|m_1| < |m_2|$.

```
(rationalize 3/10 1/10)  ⇒  1/3
(rationalize .3 1/10)  ⇒   0.3333333333333333
(eqv? (rationalize .3 1/10) #i1/3)  ⇒   #t
```

(numerator rat)   **procedure**
returns: the numerator of rat

If rat is an integer, the numerator is rat.

```
(numerator 9)  ⇒  9
(numerator 9.0)  ⇒  9.0
(numerator 2/3)  ⇒  2
(numerator -9/4)  ⇒  -9
(numerator -2.25)  ⇒  -9.0
```

(denominator rat)   **procedure**
returns: the denominator of rat

If rat is an integer, the denominator is 1.

```
(denominator 9)  ⇒  1
(denominator 9.0)  ⇒  1.0
(denominator 2/3)  ⇒  3
(denominator -9/4)  ⇒  4
(denominator -2.25)  ⇒  4.0
```

(real-part num)   **procedure**
returns: the real component of num

If num is real, real-part returns num.

```
(real-part 3+4i)  ⇒  3
(real-part -2.3+0.7i)  ⇒  -2.3
(real-part -i)  ⇒  0
(real-part 17.2)  ⇒  17.2
(real-part -17/100)  ⇒  -17/100
```

(imag-part num)   **procedure**
returns: the imaginary component of num

If num is real, imag-part returns zero.

```
(imag-part 3+4i)  ⇒  4
(imag-part -2.3+0.7i)  ⇒  0.7
(imag-part -i)  ⇒  -1
(imag-part 17.2)  ⇒  0.0
(imag-part -17/100)  ⇒  0
```

(make-rectangular *real₁ real₂*)   **procedure**
returns: a complex number with real component *real₁* and imaginary component *real₂*

```
(make-rectangular -2 7)  ⇒  -2+7i
(make-rectangular 2/3 -1/2)  ⇒  2/3-1/2i
(make-rectangular 3.2 5.3)  ⇒  3.2+5.3i
```

(make-polar *real₁ real₂*)   **procedure**
returns: a complex number with magnitude *real₁* and angle *real₂*

```
(make-polar 2 0)  ⇒  2
(make-polar 2.0 0.0)  ⇒  2.0+0.0i
(make-polar 1.0 (asin -1.0))  ⇒  0.0-1.0i
(eqv? (make-polar 7.2 -0.588) 7.2@-0.588)  ⇒  #t
```

(angle *num*)   **procedure**
returns: the angle part of the polar representation of *num*

The range of the result is $-\pi$ (exclusive) to $+\pi$ (inclusive).

```
(angle 7.3@1.5708)  ⇒  1.5708
(angle 5.2)  ⇒  0.0
```

(magnitude *num*)   **procedure**
returns: the magnitude of *num*

magnitude and **abs** (see page 129) are identical for real arguments. The magnitude of a complex number $x + yi$ is $\sqrt{x^2 + y^2}$.

```
(magnitude 1)  ⇒  1
(magnitude -3/4)  ⇒  3/4
(magnitude 1.83)  ⇒  1.83
(magnitude -0.093)  ⇒  0.093
(magnitude 3+4i)  ⇒  5
(magnitude 7.25@1.5708)  ⇒  7.25
```

(sqrt *num*)   **procedure**
returns: the principal square root of *num*

Implementations are encouraged, but not required, to return exact results for exact inputs to **sqrt** whenever feasible.

```
(sqrt 16)  ⇒  4
(sqrt 1/4)  ⇒  1/2
(sqrt 4.84)  ⇒  2.2
(sqrt -4.84)  ⇒  0.0+2.2i
(sqrt 3+4i)  ⇒  2+1i
(sqrt -3.0-4.0i)  ⇒  1.0-2.0i
```

(exp *num*)   **procedure**

returns: e to the *num* power

```
(exp 0.0)  ⇒  1.0
(exp 1.0)  ⇒  2.7182818284590455
(exp -.5)  ⇒  0.6065306597126334
```

(log *num*)   **procedure**

returns: the natural log of *num*

The log of a complex number z is defined as follows:

$$\log(z) = \log(\text{magnitude}(z)) + i\,\text{angle}(z).$$

```
(log 1.0)  ⇒  0.0
(log (exp 1.0))  ⇒  1.0
(/ (log 100) (log 10))  ⇒  2.0
(log (make-polar (exp 2.0) 1.0))  ⇒  2.0+1.0i
```

(sin *num*)   **procedure**
(cos *num*)   **procedure**
(tan *num*)   **procedure**

returns: the sine, cosine, or tangent of *num*

The argument is specified in radians.

(asin *num*)   **procedure**
(acos *num*)   **procedure**

returns: the arc sine or the arc cosine of *num*

The result is in radians. The arc sine and arc cosine of a complex number z are defined as follows:

$$\sin^{-1}(z) = -i\log(iz + \sqrt{1 - z^2})$$
$$\cos^{-1}(z) = \pi/2 - \sin^{-1}(z)$$

(atan *num*)   procedure
(atan *real₁ real₂*)   procedure
returns: see explanation

When passed a single complex argument *num* (the first form), atan returns the arc tangent of *num*. The arc tangent of a complex number z is defined as follows:

$$\tan^{-1}(z) = (\log(1 + iz) - \log(1 - iz))/(2i)$$

When passed two real arguments (the second form), atan is equivalent to (lambda (x y) (angle (make-rectangular x y))).

(string->number *string*)   procedure
(string->number *string radix*)   procedure
returns: the number represented by *string*, or #f

If *string* is a valid representation of a number, that number is returned, otherwise #f is returned. The number is interpreted in radix *radix*, which must be an exact integer in the set $\{2, 8, 10, 16\}$. If not specified, *radix* defaults to 10. Any radix specifier within *string*, e.g., #x, overrides the *radix* argument.

```
(string->number "0")  ⇒  0
(string->number "3.4e3")  ⇒  3400.0
(string->number "#x#e-2e2")  ⇒  -738
(string->number "#e-2e2" 16)  ⇒  -738
(string->number "#i15/16")  ⇒  0.9375
(string->number "10" 16)  ⇒  16
```

(number->string *num*)   procedure
(number->string *num radix*)   procedure
returns: an external representation of *num* as a string

The num is expressed in radix *radix*, which must be an exact integer in the set $\{2, 8, 10, 16\}$. If not specified, *radix* defaults to 10. In any case, no radix specifier appears in the resulting string.

The external representation is such that, when converted back into a number using string->number, the resulting numeric value is equivalent to *num*. That is, for all inputs:

```
(eqv? (number->string
        (string->number num radix)
        radix)
      num)
```

returns #t. Inexact results are expressed using the fewest number of significant digits possible without violating the above restriction.

```
(number->string 3.4)    ⇒   "3.4"
(number->string 1e2)    ⇒   "100.0"
(number->string 1e23)   ⇒   "1e23"
(number->string -7/2)   ⇒   "-7/2"
(number->string 220/9 16)  ⇒   "DC/9"
```

6.4. Characters

Characters are atomic objects representing letters, digits, special symbols such as $ or -, and certain nongraphic control characters such as space and newline. Characters are written with a #\ prefix. For most characters, the prefix is followed by the character itself. The written character representation of the letter A, for example, is #\A. The characters newline and space may be written in this manner as well, but they can also be written as #\newline or #\space.

This section describes the operations that deal primarily with characters. See also the following section on strings and Chapter 7 on input and output for other operations relating to character objects.

(char=? *char₁ char₂ char₃* ...)	**procedure**
(char<? *char₁ char₂ char₃* ...)	**procedure**
(char>? *char₁ char₂ char₃* ...)	**procedure**
(char<=? *char₁ char₂ char₃* ...)	**procedure**
(char>=? *char₁ char₂ char₃* ...)	**procedure**

returns: #t if the relation holds, #f otherwise

These predicates behave in a similar manner to the numeric predicates =, <, >, <=, and >=. For example, char=? returns #t when its arguments are equivalent characters, and char<? returns #t when its arguments are monotonically increasing character values.

Independent of the particular representation employed, the following relationships are guaranteed to hold:

- The lowercase letters #\a through #\z are in order from low to high; e.g., #\d is less than #\e.

- The uppercase letters #\A through #\Z are in order from low to high; e.g., #\Q is less than #\R.

- The digits #\0 through #\9 are in order from low to high; e.g., #\3 is less than #\4.

- All digits precede all lowercase letters, or all lowercase letters precede all digits.

- All digits precede all uppercase letters, or all uppercase letters precede all digits.

The tests performed by char=?, char<?, char>?, char<=?, and char>=? are case-sensitive. That is, the character #\A is not equivalent to the character #\a according to these predicates.

The ANSI/IEEE standard includes only two-argument versions of these procedures. The more general versions are included in the Revised[4] Report.

```
(char>? #\a #\b)  ⇒  #f
(char<? #\a #\b)  ⇒  #t
(char<? #\a #\b #\c)  ⇒  #t
(let ((c #\r))
  (char<=? #\a c #\z))  ⇒  #t
(char<=? #\Z #\W)  ⇒  #f
(char=? #\+ #\+)  ⇒  #t
(or (char<? #\a #\0)
    (char<? #\0 #\a))  ⇒  #t
```

(char-ci=? $char_1$ $char_2$ $char_3$ ...)   **procedure**
(char-ci<? $char_1$ $char_2$ $char_3$ ...)   **procedure**
(char-ci>? $char_1$ $char_2$ $char_3$ ...)   **procedure**
(char-ci<=? $char_1$ $char_2$ $char_3$ ...)   **procedure**
(char-ci>=? $char_1$ $char_2$ $char_3$ ...)   **procedure**
returns: #t if the relation holds, #f otherwise

These predicates are identical to the predicates char=?, char<?, char>?, char<=?,
and char>=? except that they are case-insensitive. This means that when two letters
are compared, case is unimportant. For example, char=? considers #\a and #\A to
be distinct values; char-ci=? does not.

The ANSI/IEEE standard includes only two-argument versions of these procedures. The more general versions are included in the Revised[4] Report.

```
(char-ci<? #\a #\B)  ⇒  #t
(char-ci=? #\W #\w)  ⇒  #t
(char-ci=? #\= #\+)  ⇒  #f
(let ((c #\R))
  (list (char<=? #\a c #\z)
        (char-ci<=? #\a c #\z)))  ⇒  (#f #t)
```

(char-alphabetic? *char*)   **procedure**
returns: #t if *char* is a letter, #f otherwise

```
(char-alphabetic? #\a)  ⇒  #t
(char-alphabetic? #\T)  ⇒  #t
(char-alphabetic? #\8)  ⇒  #f
(char-alphabetic? #\$)  ⇒  #f
```

(char-numeric? *char*)   **procedure**
returns: #t if *char* is a digit, #f otherwise

```
(char-numeric? #\7)  ⇒  #t
(char-numeric? #\2)  ⇒  #t
(char-numeric? #\X)  ⇒  #f
(char-numeric? #\space)  ⇒  #f
```

(char-lower-case? *letter*)   **procedure**
returns: #t if *letter* is lowercase, #f otherwise

If *letter* is not alphabetic, the result is unspecified.

(char-lower-case? #\r) ⇒ #t
(char-lower-case? #\R) ⇒ #f
(char-lower-case? #\8) ⇒ *unspecified*

(char-upper-case? *letter*)   **procedure**
returns: #t if *letter* is uppercase, #f otherwise

If *letter* is not alphabetic, the result is unspecified.

(char-upper-case? #\r) ⇒ #f
(char-upper-case? #\R) ⇒ #t
(char-upper-case? #\8) ⇒ *unspecified*

(char-whitespace? *char*)   **procedure**
returns: #t if *char* is whitespace, #f otherwise

Whitespace consists of spaces and newlines and possibly other nongraphic characters, depending upon the Scheme implementation and the underlying operating system.

(char-whitespace? #\space) ⇒ #t
(char-whitespace? #\newline) ⇒ #t
(char-whitespace? #\Z) ⇒ #f

(char-upcase *char*)   **procedure**
returns: the uppercase character equivalent to *char*

If *char* is a lowercase character, **char-upcase** returns the uppercase equivalent. If *char* is not a lowercase character, **char-upcase** returns **char**.

(char-upcase #\g) ⇒ #\G
(char-upcase #\Y) ⇒ #\Y
(char-upcase #\7) ⇒ #\7

(char-downcase *char*)   **procedure**
returns: the lowercase character equivalent to *char*

If *char* is an uppercase character, **char-downcase** returns the lowercase equivalent. If *char* is not an uppercase character, **char-downcase** returns **char**.

(char-downcase #\g) ⇒ #\g
(char-downcase #\Y) ⇒ #\y
(char-downcase #\7) ⇒ #\7

`(char->integer` *char*`)`   **procedure**
returns: an integer representation for *char*

`char->integer` is useful for performing table lookups, with the integer representation of *char* employed as an index into a table. The integer representation of
a character is typically the integer code supported by the operating system for
character input and output.

Although the particular representation employed depends on the Scheme implementation and the underlying operating system, the same rules regarding the
relationship between character objects stated above under the description of `char=?`
and its relatives is guaranteed to hold for the integer representations of characters
as well.

The following examples assume that the integer representation is the ASCII
code for the character.

`(char->integer #\h)` ⇒ `104`
`(char->integer #\newline)` ⇒ `10`

The definition of `make-dispatch-table` below shows how the integer codes returned by `char->integer` may be used portably to associate values with characters
in vector-based dispatch tables, even though the exact correspondence between
characters and their integer codes is unspecified.

`make-dispatch-table` accepts two arguments: an association list (see `assv` in
Section 6.2) associating characters with values and a default value for characters
without associations. It returns a lookup procedure that accepts a character and
returns the associated (or default) value. `make-dispatch-table` builds a vector
that is used by the lookup procedure. This vector is indexed by the integer codes
for the characters and contains the associated values. Slots in the vector between
indices for characters with defined values are filled with the default value. The
code works even if `char->integer` returns negative values or both negative and
nonnegative values, although the table can get large if the character codes are not
tightly packed.

```
(define make-dispatch-table
  (lambda (alist default)
    (let ((codes (map char->integer (map car alist))))
      (let ((first-index (apply min codes))
            (last-index (apply max codes)))
        (let ((n (+ (- last-index first-index) 1)))
          (let ((v (make-vector n default)))
            (for-each
              (lambda (i x) (vector-set! v (- i first-index) x))
              codes
              (map cdr alist))
            ;; table is built; return the table lookup procedure
            (lambda (c)
              (let ((i (char->integer c)))
                (if (<= first-index i last-index)
                    (vector-ref v (- i first-index))
                    default)))))))))
```

```
(define-syntax define-dispatch-table
  ;; define-dispatch-table is a handy syntactic extension for
  ;; associating sets of characters in strings with values in a
  ;; call to make-dispatch-table.  It is used below.
  (syntax-rules ()
    ((_ default (str val) ...)
     (make-dispatch-table
       (append (map (lambda (c) (cons c 'val))
                    (string->list str))
               ...)
       'default)))))

(define t
  (define-dispatch-table
    unknown
    ("abcdefghijklmnopqrstuvwxyz" letter)
    ("ABCDEFGHIJKLMNOPQRSTUVWXYZ" letter)
    ("0123456789" digit)))

(t #\m)  ⇒  letter
(t #\0)  ⇒  digit
(t #\*)  ⇒  unknown
```

(integer->char *int*)   **procedure**
returns: the character object corresponding to the integer *int*

This procedure is the functional inverse of char->integer. It is an error for *int* to be outside the range of valid integer character codes.

The following examples assume that the integer representation is the ASCII code for the character.

```
(integer->char 48)   ⇒  #\0
(integer->char 101)  ⇒  #\e
```

6.5. Strings

Strings are sequences of characters and are typically used as messages or character buffers. Scheme provides operations for creating strings, extracting characters from strings, obtaining substrings, concatenating strings, and altering the contents of strings.

A string is written as a sequence of characters enclosed in double quotes, e.g., "hi there". A double quote may be introduced into a string by preceding it by a backward slash, e.g., "two \"quotes\" within". A backward slash may also be included by preceding it with a backward slash, e.g., "a \\slash".

Strings are indexed by exact nonnegative integers, and the index of the first element of any string is 0. The highest valid index for a given string is one less than its length.

(string=? *string₁ string₂ string₃* ...)	**procedure**
(string<? *string₁ string₂ string₃* ...)	**procedure**
(string>? *string₁ string₂ string₃* ...)	**procedure**
(string<=? *string₁ string₂ string₃* ...)	**procedure**
(string>=? *string₁ string₂ string₃* ...)	**procedure**

returns: #t if the relation holds, #f otherwise

As with =, <, >, <=, and >=, these predicates express relationships among all of the arguments. For example, `string>?` determines if the lexicographic ordering of its arguments is monotonically decreasing.

The comparisons are based on the character predicates `char=?`, `char<?`, `char>?`, `char<=?`, and `char>=?`. Two strings are lexicographically equivalent if they are the same length and consist of the same sequence of characters according to `char=?`. If two strings differ only in length, the shorter string is considered to be lexicographically less than the longer string. Otherwise, the first character position at which the strings differ determines which string is lexicographically less than the other, according to `char<?`.

The ANSI/IEEE standard includes only two-argument versions of these procedures. The more general versions are included in the Revised[4] Report.

Two-argument `string=?` may be defined as follows.

```
(define string=?
  (lambda (s1 s2)
    (let ((n (string-length s1)))
      (and (= (string-length s2) n)
           (let loop ((i 0))
             (or (= i n)
                 (and (char=? (string-ref s1 i) (string-ref s2 i))
                      (loop (+ i 1)))))))))
```

Two-argument `string<?` may be defined as follows.

```
(define string<?
  (lambda (s1 s2)
    (let ((n1 (string-length s1)) (n2 (string-length s2)))
      (let loop ((i 0))
        (and (not (= i n2))
             (or (= i n1)
                 (let ((c1 (string-ref s1 i)) (c2 (string-ref s2 i)))
                   (or (char<? c1 c2)
                       (and (char=? c1 c2)
                            (loop (+ i 1)))))))))))
```

These definitions may be extended straightforwardly to support three or more arguments. `string<=?`, `string>?`, and `string>=?` may be defined similarly.

```
(string=? "mom" "mom")  ⇒  #t
(string<? "mom" "mommy")  ⇒  #t
(string>? "Dad" "Dad")  ⇒  #f
(string=? "Mom and Dad" "mom and dad")  ⇒  #f
(string<? "a" "b" "c")  ⇒  #t
```

(string-ci=? *string*$_1$ *string*$_2$ *string*$_3$ ...)	**procedure**
(string-ci<? *string*$_1$ *string*$_2$ *string*$_3$ ...)	**procedure**
(string-ci>? *string*$_1$ *string*$_2$ *string*$_3$ ...)	**procedure**
(string-ci<=? *string*$_1$ *string*$_2$ *string*$_3$ ...)	**procedure**
(string-ci>=? *string*$_1$ *string*$_2$ *string*$_3$ ...)	**procedure**

returns: #t if the relation holds, #f otherwise

These predicates are case-insensitive versions of string=?, string<?, string>?, string<=?, and string>=?. That is, the comparisons are based on the character predicates char-ci=?, char-ci<?, char-ci>?, char-ci<=?, and char-ci>=?.

The ANSI/IEEE standard includes only two-argument versions of these procedures. The more general versions are included in the Revised[4] Report.

Two-argument versions of these procedures may be defined in a manner similar to string=? and string<? above.

```
(string-ci=? "Mom and Dad" "mom and dad")  ⇒  #t
(string-ci<=? "say what" "Say What!?")  ⇒  #t
(string-ci>? "N" "m" "L" "k")  ⇒  #t
```

(string *char* ...)	**procedure**

returns: a string containing the characters *char* ...

```
(string)  ⇒  ""
(string #\a #\b #\c)  ⇒  "abc"
(string #\H #\E #\Y #\!)  ⇒  "HEY!"
```

(make-string *n*)	**procedure**
(make-string *n* *char*)	**procedure**

returns: a string of length *n*

n must be an exact nonnegative integer. If *char* is supplied, the string is filled with *char*, otherwise the characters contained in the string are unspecified.

```
(make-string 0)  ⇒  ""
(make-string 0 #\x)  ⇒  ""
(make-string 5 #\x)  ⇒  "xxxxx"
```

(string-length *string*)	**procedure**

returns: the number of characters in *string*

The length of a string is always an exact nonnegative integer.

```
(string-length "abc")  ⇒  3
(string-length "")  ⇒  0
(string-length "hi there")  ⇒  8
(string-length (make-string 1000000))  ⇒  1000000
```

`(string-ref string n)`   **procedure**
returns: the *n*th character (zero-based) of *string*

n must be an exact nonnegative integer strictly less than the length of *string*.

```
(string-ref "hi there" 0)  ⇒  #\h
(string-ref "hi there" 5)  ⇒  #\e
```

`(string-set! string n char)`   **procedure**
returns: unspecified

n must be an exact nonnegative integer strictly less than the length of *string*.
string-set! changes the *n*th element of *string* to *char*.

```
(let ((str "hi three"))
  (string-set! str 5 #\e)
  (string-set! str 6 #\r)
  str)  ⇒  "hi there"
```

`(string-copy string)`   **procedure**
returns: a new copy of *string*

string-copy is equivalent to `(lambda (s) (string-append s))`. string-copy is in
the Revised[4] Report but not the ANSI/IEEE standard.

```
(string-copy "abc")  ⇒  "abc"
(let ((str "abc"))
  (eq? str (string-copy str)))  ⇒  #f
```

`(string-append string ...)`   **procedure**
returns: a new string formed by concatenating the strings *string* ...

The following implementation of **string-append** recurs down the list of strings to
compute the total length, then allocates the new string and fills it up as it unwinds
the recursion.

```
(define string-append
  (lambda args
    (let f ((ls args) (n 0))
      (if (null? ls)
          (make-string n)
          (let* ((s1 (car ls))
                 (m (string-length s1))
                 (s2 (f (cdr ls) (+ n m))))
            (do ((i 0 (+ i 1)) (j n (+ j 1)))
                ((= i m) s2)
              (string-set! s2 j (string-ref s1 i))))))))
(string-append)  ⇒  ""
(string-append "abc" "def")  ⇒  "abcdef"
(string-append "Hey " "you " "there!")  ⇒  "Hey you there!"
```

(substring *string start end***)**   **procedure**
returns: a copy of *string* from *start* (inclusive) to *end* (exclusive)

start and *end* must be exact nonnegative integers; *start* must be strictly less than
the length of *string*, while *end* may be less than or equal to the length of *string*.
If *end* $\leq$ *start*, a string of length zero is returned. **substring** may be defined as
follows.

```
(define substring
  (lambda (s1 m n)
    (let ((s2 (make-string (- n m))))
      (do ((j 0 (+ j 1)) (i m (+ i 1)))
          ((= i n) s2)
          (string-set! s2 j (string-ref s1 i))))))
```

```
(substring "hi there" 0 1)  ⇒  "h"
(substring "hi there" 3 6)  ⇒  "the"
(substring "hi there" 5 5)  ⇒  ""
```

```
(let ((str "hi there"))
  (let ((end (string-length str)))
    (substring str 0 end)))  ⇒  "hi there"
```

(string-fill! *string char***)**   **procedure**
returns: unspecified

string-fill! sets every character in *string* to *char*. **string-fill!** is in the
Revised[4] Report but not the ANSI/IEEE standard. It may be defined as follows:

```
(define string-fill!
  (lambda (s c)
    (let ((n (string-length s)))
      (do ((i 0 (+ i 1)))
          ((= i n))
          (string-set! s i c)))))
```

```
(let ((str (string-copy "sleepy")))
  (string-fill! str #\Z)
  str)  ⇒  "ZZZZZZ"
```

(string->list *string***)**   **procedure**
returns: a list of the characters in *string*

string->list allows a string to be converted into a list, so that Scheme's list-
processing operations may be applied to the processing of strings. **string->list**
is in the Revised[4] Report but not the ANSI/IEEE standard. It may be defined as
follows.

```
(define string->list
  (lambda (s)
    (do ((i (- (string-length s) 1) (- i 1))
         (ls '() (cons (string-ref s i) ls)))
        ((< i 0) ls))))
```

```
(string->list "")   ⇒   ()
(string->list "abc")   ⇒   (#\a #\b #\c)
(apply char<? (string->list "abc"))   ⇒   #t
(map char-upcase (string->list "abc"))   ⇒   (#\A #\B #\C)
```

(list->string *list*)   **procedure**
returns: a string of the characters in *list*

list must consist entirely of characters.

list->string is the functional inverse of string->list. A program might use both procedures together, first converting a string into a list, then operating on this list to produce a new list, and finally converting the new list back into a string.

list->string is in the Revised[4] Report but not the ANSI/IEEE standard. It may be defined as follows.

```
(define list->string
  (lambda (ls)
    (let ((s (make-string (length ls))))
      (do ((ls ls (cdr ls)) (i 0 (+ i 1)))
          ((null? ls) s)
          (string-set! s i (car ls))))))
```

```
(list->string '())   ⇒   ""
(list->string '(#\a #\b #\c))   ⇒   "abc"
(list->string
  (map char-upcase
       (string->list "abc")))   ⇒   "ABC"
```

6.6. Vectors

Vectors are more convenient and efficient than lists for some applications. Whereas accessing an arbitrary element in a list requires a linear traversal of the list up to the selected element, arbitrary vector elements are accessed in constant time. The *length* of a vector in Scheme is the number of elements it contains. Vectors are indexed by exact nonnegative integers, and the index of the first element of any vector is 0. The highest valid index for a given vector is one less than its length.

As with lists, the elements of a vector may be of any type; a single vector may even hold more than one type of object.

A vector is written as a sequence of objects separated by whitespace, preceded by the prefix #(and followed by). For example, a vector consisting of the elements a, b, and c would be written #(a b c).

```
(vector obj ...)                                            procedure
```
returns: a vector of the objects *obj* ...

```
(vector)  ⇒  #()
(vector 'a 'b 'c)  ⇒  #(a b c)
```


```
(make-vector n)                                             procedure
(make-vector n obj)                                         procedure
```
returns: a vector of length *n*

n must be an exact nonnegative integer. If *obj* is supplied, each element of the vector is filled with *obj*; otherwise, the elements are unspecified.

```
(make-vector 0)  ⇒  #()
(make-vector 0 'a)  ⇒  #()
(make-vector 5 'a)  ⇒  #(a a a a a)
```


```
(vector-length vector)                                      procedure
```
returns: the number of elements in *vector*

The length of a vector is always an exact nonnegative integer.

```
(vector-length '#())  ⇒  0
(vector-length '#(a b c))  ⇒  3
(vector-length (vector 1 2 3 4))  ⇒  4
(vector-length (make-vector 300))  ⇒  300
```


```
(vector-ref vector n)                                       procedure
```
returns: the *n*th element (zero-based) of *vector*

n must be an exact nonnegative integer strictly less than the length of *vector*.

```
(vector-ref '#(a b c) 0)  ⇒  a
(vector-ref '#(a b c) 1)  ⇒  b
(vector-ref '#(x y z w) 3)  ⇒  w
```


```
(vector-set! vector n obj)                                  procedure
```
returns: unspecified

n must be an exact nonnegative integer strictly less than the length of *vector*.
vector-set! changes the *n*th element of *vector* to *obj*.

```
(let ((v (vector 'a 'b 'c 'd 'e)))
  (vector-set! v 2 'x)
  v)  ⇒  #(a b x d e)
```

(vector-fill! *vector obj*)   **procedure**
returns: unspecified

vector-fill! replaces each element of *vector* with *obj*. vector-fill! is in the
Revised[4] Report but not the ANSI/IEEE standard. It may be defined as follows:

```
(define vector-fill!
  (lambda (v x)
    (let ((n (vector-length v)))
      (do ((i 0 (+ i 1)))
          ((= i n))
          (vector-set! v i x)))))
(let ((v (vector 1 2 3)))
  (vector-fill! v 0)
  v)   ⇒   #(0 0 0)
```

(vector->list *vector*)   **procedure**
returns: a list of the elements of *vector*

vector->list provides a convenient method for applying list-processing operations
to vectors. vector->list is in the Revised[4] Report but not the ANSI/IEEE standard. It may be defined as follows.

```
(define vector->list
  (lambda (s)
    (do ((i (- (vector-length s) 1) (- i 1))
         (ls '() (cons (vector-ref s i) ls)))
        ((< i 0) ls))))
(vector->list (vector))   ⇒   ()
(vector->list '#(a b c))   ⇒   (a b c)
(let ((v '#(1 2 3 4 5)))
  (apply * (vector->list v)))   ⇒   120
```

(list->vector *list*)   **procedure**
returns: a vector of the elements of *list*

list->vector is the functional inverse of vector->list. The two procedures are
often used in combination to take advantage of a list-processing operation. A vector
may be converted to a list with vector->list, this list processed in some manner to
produce a new list, and the new list converted back into a vector with list->vector.

   list->vector is in the Revised[4] Report but not the ANSI/IEEE standard. It
may be defined as follows.

```
(define list->vector
  (lambda (ls)
    (let ((s (make-vector (length ls))))
      (do ((ls ls (cdr ls)) (i 0 (+ i 1)))
          ((null? ls) s)
          (vector-set! s i (car ls))))))
```

```
(list->vector '())  ⇒  #()
(list->vector '(a b c))  ⇒  #(a b c)

(let ((v '#(1 2 3 4 5)))
  (let ((ls (vector->list v)))
    (list->vector (map * ls ls))))  ⇒  #(1 4 9 16 25)
```

6.7. Symbols

Symbols are used for a variety of purposes as symbolic names in Scheme programs. Strings could be used for most of the same purposes, but an important characteristic of symbols makes comparisons between symbols much more efficient. This characteristic is that two symbols with the same name are identical in the sense of eq?. The reason is that the Scheme reader (see **read** in Section 7.1) and the procedure **string->symbol** catalog symbols in an internal symbol table and always return the same symbol whenever the same name is encountered. Thus, no character-by-character comparison is needed, as would be needed to compare two strings.

The property that two symbols may be compared quickly for equivalence makes them ideally suited for use as identifiers in the representation of programs, allowing fast comparison of identifiers. This property also makes symbols useful for a variety of other purposes. For example, symbols might be used as messages passed between procedures, labels for list-structured records, or names for objects stored in an association list (see **assq** in Section 6.2).

Symbols are written without double quotes or other bracketing characters. Parentheses, double quotes, spaces, and most other characters with a special meaning to the Scheme reader are not allowed within the printed representation of a symbol. Some implementations, however, support the use of backward slashes to escape special characters occurring in symbols, in a manner similar to the use of backward slashes in strings.

Refer to Section 1.1 or the formal syntax of Scheme at the back of this book for a precise description of the syntax of symbols.

(**string->symbol** *string*)   **procedure**
returns: a symbol whose name is *string*

string->symbol records all symbols it creates in an internal table that it shares with the system reader, **read**. If a symbol whose name is equivalent to string (according to the predicate **string=?**) already exists in the table, this symbol is returned. Otherwise, a new symbol is created with *string* as its name; this symbol is entered into the table and returned.

The system reader arranges to convert all symbols to a single case (lowercase is assumed in this book), before entering them into the internal table. **string->symbol** does not. Thus, it is possible to produce symbols in lowercase, uppercase, or even mixed-case, using **string->symbol**. It is also possible to create symbols with names that contain special characters, such as spaces or parentheses.

```
(string->symbol "x")  ⇒  x
(eq? (string->symbol "x") 'x)  ⇒  #t
(eq? (string->symbol "X") 'x)  ⇒  #f
(eq? (string->symbol "x")
     (string->symbol "x"))  ⇒  #t
```

(symbol->string *symbol*)   **procedure**
returns: a string, the name of *symbol*

The string returned by `symbol->string` for a symbol created by an earlier call to `string->symbol` may or may not be the same string (by `eq?`) as the string passed to `string->symbol`. That is, an implementation is free to copy or not to copy a string it uses as the name of a symbol. Unpredictable behavior can result if a string passed to `string->symbol` is altered with `string-set!` or by any other means.

```
(symbol->string 'xyz)  ⇒  "xyz"
(symbol->string (string->symbol "Hi"))  ⇒  "Hi"
(symbol->string (string->symbol "()"))  ⇒  "()"
```

CHAPTER 7

Input and Output

A six-armed spiral.

This chapter describes input and output operations. All input and output operations are performed through *ports*. A port is a pointer into a (possibly infinite) stream of characters (typically a file), an opening through which programs may draw characters or objects from the stream or place characters or objects into the stream.

Ports are first-class objects, like any other object in Scheme. Like procedures, ports do not have a printed representation the way strings and numbers do, so they are shown here with the notation #<port>. There are initially two ports in the system, the current input port and the current output port. In an interactive session, these ports usually point to the terminal input and output streams. Several ways to open new ports are provided.

An input port often points to a finite stream, e.g., an input file stored on disk. If one of the input operations (read, read-char, or peek-char) is asked to read from a port that has reached the end of a finite stream, it returns a special *eof* (end of file) *object*. The predicate eof-object? may be used to determine if an object returned from read, read-char, or peek-char is an eof object.

7.1. Input Operations

This section describes operations for manipulating input ports.

(input-port? *obj*)   **procedure**
returns: #t if *obj* is an input port, #f otherwise

Ports need not be distinct from other object types.

```
(input-port? '(a b c)))   ⇒   unspecified
(input-port? (current-input-port))   ⇒   #t
(input-port? (open-input-file "infile.ss"))   ⇒   #t
```

The last example assumes that "infile.ss" may be opened for input.

(current-input-port)   **procedure**
returns: the current input port

Most procedures involving input ports may be called with or without an explicit port argument. If called without an explicit port argument, the current input port is used. For example, (read-char) and (read-char (current-input-port)) both return the next character from the current input port.

(open-input-file *filename*)   **procedure**
returns: a new input port

filename must be a string. open-input-file creates a new input port for the file named by *filename*. An error is signaled if the file does not exist or cannot be opened for input. See the example given for close-input-port.

(`close-input-port` *input-port*)   **procedure**
returns: unspecified

`close-input-port` closes an input port. Once an input port has been closed, no
more input operations may be performed on that port. Because the operating
system may place limits on the number of ports open at one time or restrict access
to an open port, it is a good practice to close any port that will no longer be used
for input or output. Some Scheme implementations close ports automatically after
they become inaccessible to the program or when the Scheme program exits, but
it is best to close ports explicitly whenever possible.

It is not an error to close a port that has already been closed; doing so has no
effect.

The following shows the use of `open-input-file` and `close-input-port` in an
expression that gathers a list of objects from the file `"myfile.ss"`. It is functionally
equivalent to the example given for `call-with-input-file` below.

```
(let ((p (open-input-file "myfile.ss")))
  (let f ((x (read p)))
    (if (eof-object? x)
        (begin
          (close-input-port p)
          '())
        (cons x (f (read p))))))
```

(`call-with-input-file` *filename proc*)   **procedure**
returns: the result of invoking *proc*

filename must be a string. *proc* must be a procedure of one argument.

`call-with-input-file` creates a new input port for the file named by *filename*
and passes this port to *proc*. An error is signaled if the file does not exist or cannot
be opened for input. If *proc* returns, `call-with-input-file` closes the input port
and returns the value returned by *proc*.

`call-with-input-file` does not automatically close the input port if a continuation created outside of *proc* is invoked, since it is possible that another continuation
created inside of *proc* will be invoked at a later time, returning control to *proc*. If
proc does not return, an implementation is free to close the input port only if
it can prove that the input port is no longer accessible. As shown in Section 5.6,
`dynamic-wind` may be used to ensure that the port is closed if a continuation created
outside of *proc* is invoked.

`call-with-input-file` might be defined as follows.

```
(define call-with-input-file
  (lambda (filename proc)
    (let ((p (open-input-file filename)))
      (let ((v (proc p)))
        (close-input-port p)
        v))))
```

The following example shows the use of `call-with-input-file` in an expression that gathers a list of objects from the file `"myfile.ss"`. It is functionally equivalent to the example given for `close-input-port` above.

```
(call-with-input-file "myfile.ss"
  (lambda (p)
    (let f ((x (read p)))
      (if (eof-object? x)
          '()
          (cons x (f (read p)))))))
```

(with-input-from-file *filename* *thunk*)   **procedure**
returns: the value returned by *thunk*

filename must be a string.

with-input-from-file temporarily changes the current input port to be the result of opening the file named by *filename* for input during the application of *thunk*. If *thunk* returns, the port is closed and the current input port is restored to its old value.

The behavior of `with-input-from-file` is unspecified if a continuation created outside of *thunk* is invoked before *thunk* returns. An implementation may close the port and restore the current input port to its old value—but it may not.

with-input-from-file is in the Revised[4] Report but not the ANSI/IEEE standard.

(read)   **procedure**
(read *input-port*)   **procedure**
returns: the next object from *input-port*

If *input-port* is not supplied, it defaults to the current input port. If *input-port* is at end of file, an eof object is returned. See the examples given for `close-input-port` and `call-with-input-file`.

(read-char)   **procedure**
(read-char *input-port*)   **procedure**
returns: the next character from *input-port*

If *input-port* is not supplied, it defaults to the current input port. If *input-port* is at end of file, an eof object is returned. See the examples given for `peek-char` and `write-char`.

(peek-char)   **procedure**
(peek-char *input-port*)   **procedure**
returns: the next character from *input-port*

If *input-port* is not supplied, it defaults to the current input port. If *input-port* is at end of file, an eof object is returned.

In contrast to `read-char`, `peek-char` does not consume the character it reads from *input-port*; a subsequent call to `peek-char` or `read-char` returns the same character.

`peek-char` is provided for applications requiring one character of lookahead. The procedure `read-word` defined below returns the next word from an input port as a string, where a word is defined to be a sequence of alphabetic characters. Since `read-word` does not know until it sees one character beyond the word that it has read the entire word, it uses `peek-char` to determine the next character and `read-char` to consume the character.

```
(define read-word
  (lambda (p)
    (list->string
      (let f ()
        (let ((c (peek-char p)))
          (cond
            ((eof-object? c) '())
            ((char-alphabetic? c)
             (read-char p)
             (cons c (f)))
            (else '())))))))
```

`(eof-object? ` *obj*`)`	**procedure**

returns: `#t` if *obj* is an eof object, `#f` otherwise

An end-of-file object is returned by `read`, `read-char`, or `peek-char` when an input port has reached the end of input. Although end-of-file objects need not be distinct from other object types, they are unique in the sense that they cannot be confused with objects that may be returned by `read`, `read-char`, or `peek-char` when the input port has not reached the end of input. For example, if `(eof-object? x)` is `#t`, `(eq? x #\a)` must be false but `(char? x)` may be true or false.

`(char-ready?)`	**procedure**
`(char-ready? ` *input-port*`)`	**procedure**

returns: `#t` if a character is available on *input-port*, `#f` otherwise

If *input-port* is not supplied, it defaults to the current input port.

`char-ready?` allows a program to look for character input on an interactive port without hanging. If `char-ready?` returns `#t`, the next `peek-char` or `read-char` operation on *input-port* will not be delayed. If *input-port* is at end of file, `char-ready?` returns `#t`. `char-ready?` is in the Revised[4] Report but not the ANSI/IEEE standard.

7.2. Output Operations

This section describes operations for manipulating output ports.

(output-port? *obj*)   **procedure**
returns: #t if *obj* is an output port, #f otherwise

Ports need not be distinct from other object types.

(output-port? '(a b c)))   ⇒   *unspecified*
(output-port? (current-output-port))   ⇒   #t
(output-port? (open-output-file "outfile.ss"))   ⇒   #t

The last example assumes that "outfile.ss" may be opened for output.

(current-output-port)   **procedure**
returns: the current output port

Most procedures involving output ports may be called with or without an explicit
port argument. If called without an explicit port argument, the current output
port is used. For example, (write *obj*) and (write *obj* (current-output-port))
both write to the current output port.

(open-output-file *filename*)   **procedure**
returns: a new output port

filename must be a string. open-output-file creates a new output port for the file
named by *filename*. An error is signaled if the file cannot be opened for output.
See the example given for close-output-port.

(close-output-port *output-port*)   **procedure**
returns: unspecified

close-output-port closes an output port. Once an output port has been closed,
no more output operations may be performed on that port. Because the operating
system may place limits on the number of ports open at one time or restrict access
to an open port, it is a good practice to close any port that will no longer be used
for input or output. Also, because the system may buffer output for efficiency,
some of the output may not appear on the file until the file has been closed. Some
Scheme implementations close ports automatically after they become inaccessible
to the program or when the Scheme program exits, but it is best to close ports
explicitly whenever possible.

It is not an error to close a port that has already been closed; doing so has no
effect.

The following shows the use of open-output-file and close-output-port to
write a list of objects (the value of list-to-be-printed), separated by newlines,
to the file "myfile.ss". It is functionally equivalent to the example given for
call-with-output-file below.

```
(let ((p (open-output-file "myfile.ss")))
  (let f ((ls list-to-be-printed))
    (if (not (null? ls))
        (begin
          (write (car ls) p)
          (newline p)
          (f (cdr ls)))))
  (close-output-port p))
```

(call-with-output-file *filename proc*)   **procedure**
returns: the result of invoking *proc*

filename must be a string. *proc* must be a procedure of one argument.

   `call-with-output-file` creates a new output port for the file named by *filename*
and passes this port to *proc*. An error is signaled if the file cannot be opened for
output. If *proc* returns, `call-with-output-file` closes the output port and returns
the value returned by *proc*.

   `call-with-output-file` does not automatically close the output port if a continuation created outside of *proc* is invoked, since it is possible that another continuation created inside of *proc* will be invoked at a later time, returning control
to *proc*. If *proc* does not return, an implementation is free to close the output
port only if it can prove that the output port is no longer accessible. As shown
in Section 5.6, `dynamic-wind` may be used to ensure that the port is closed if a
continuation created outside of *proc* is invoked.

   `call-with-output-file` might be defined as follows.

```
(define call-with-output-file
  (lambda (filename proc)
    (let ((p (open-output-file filename)))
      (let ((v (proc p)))
        (close-output-port p)
        v))))
```

The following shows the use of `call-with-output-file` to write a list of objects
(the value of `list-to-be-printed`), separated by newlines, to the file `"myfile.ss"`.
It is functionally equivalent to the example given for `close-output-port` above.

```
(call-with-output-file "myfile.ss"
  (lambda (p)
    (let f ((ls list-to-be-printed))
      (if (not (null? ls))
          (begin
            (write (car ls) p)
            (newline p)
            (f (cdr ls)))))))
```

(`with-output-to-file` *filename thunk*) **procedure**
returns: the value returned by *thunk*

filename must be a string.

    `with-output-to-file` temporarily rebinds the current output port to be the result of opening the file named by *filename* for output during the application of *thunk*. If *thunk* returns, the port is closed and the current output port is restored to its old value.

    The behavior of `with-output-to-file` is unspecified if a continuation created outside of *thunk* is invoked before *thunk* returns. An implementation may close the port and restore the current output port to its old value—but it may not.

    `with-output-to-file` is in the Revised[4] Report but not the ANSI/IEEE standard.

(`write` *obj*) **procedure**
(`write` *obj output-port*) **procedure**
returns: unspecified

If *output-port* is not supplied, it defaults to the current output port.

    `write` prints *obj* to *output-port* in such a way that it can later be read by the procedure `read`, unless it contains unprintable objects such as procedures, ports, or symbols containing nonstandard characters. Strings are printed within quote marks, using slashes where necessary, and characters are printed with the #\ notation. See Section 9.5 for an implementation of `write` and `display`.

(`display` *obj*) **procedure**
(`display` *obj output-port*) **procedure**
returns: unspecified

If *output-port* is not supplied, it defaults to the current output port.

    `display` is similar to `write` but prints strings and characters found within *obj* directly. Strings are printed without quotation marks or slashes, and characters are printed without the #\ notation. For example, both (`display` "(a b c)") and (`display` '("a b" c)) would print (a b c). Because of this, `display` should not be used to print objects that are intended to be read with `read`. `display` is useful primarily for printing messages, with *obj* most often being a string. See Section 9.5 for an implementation of `write` and `display`.

(`write-char` *char*) **procedure**
(`write-char` *char output-port*) **procedure**
returns: unspecified

If *output-port* is not supplied, it defaults to the current output port. `write-char` writes the single character *char* to *output-port*, without the #\ notation. The following example copies the contents of one file to another, one character at a time.

```
(call-with-input-file "infile"
  (lambda (ip)
    (call-with-output-file "outfile"
      (lambda (op)
        (do ((c (read-char ip) (read-char ip)))
            ((eof-object? c))
          (write-char c op))))))
```

(newline)   **procedure**
(newline *output-port*)   **procedure**
returns: unspecified

If *output-port* is not supplied, it defaults to the current output port. `newline` sends
a newline character to *output-port*. It may be defined as follows:

```
(define newline
  (lambda args
    (apply write-char #\newline args)))
```

7.3. Loading Programs

(load *filename*)   **procedure**
returns: unspecified

filename must be a string. `load` reads and evaluates in sequence each expression in the file specified by *filename*. `load` is in the Revised[4] Report but not the
ANSI/IEEE standard.

7.4. Transcript Files

A transcript file is a record of an interactive session. It is also useful as a "quick-and-
dirty" alternative to opening an output file and using explicit output operations.

`transcript-on` and `transcript-off` are in the Revised[4] Report but not the
ANSI/IEEE standard.

(transcript-on *filename*)   **procedure**
returns: unspecified

filename must be a string.

`transcript-on` opens the file named by *filename* for output, and it copies to
this file all input from the current input port and all output to the current output
port. An error is signaled if the file cannot be opened for output.

(transcript-off)   **procedure**
returns: unspecified

`transcript-off` ends transcription and closes the transcript file.

CHAPTER 8

Syntactic Extension

A warped, two-armed spiral.

Syntactic extensions are used to simplify and regularize repeated patterns in a program, to introduce syntactic forms with new evaluation rules, and to perform transformations that help make programs more efficient. Nearly all Scheme implementations provide some sort of syntactic extension, or *macro*, system. The most up-to-date implement the high-level pattern-based mechanism described in Section 8.2. This mechanism has been adopted for inclusion in the Revised[5] Report on Scheme but is not in the ANSI/IEEE standard. Preliminary versions were described in an appendix to the Revised[4] Report. Some implementations also support the compatible and more general mechanism described in Section 8.3. Examples demonstrating both mechanisms appear throughout this chapter, with several more detailed examples appearing in Section 8.4.

A portable implementation of the complete syntactic extension system is available via ftp from `ftp.cs.indiana.edu` in `pub/scheme/syntax-case`. A description of the motivations behind and implementation of the system can be found in the article "Syntactic Abstraction in Scheme" [9].

A syntactic extension typically takes the form (*keyword subform* ...), where *keyword* is the identifier that names the syntactic extension. The syntax of each *subform* varies from one syntactic extension to another. Syntactic extensions can also take the form of improper lists (or even singleton identifiers; see Section 8.3), although this is less common.

New syntactic extensions are defined by associating keywords with transformation procedures, or *transformers*. Syntactic extensions are defined globally using top-level **define-syntax** forms or within the scope of particular expressions using **let-syntax**, **letrec-syntax**, internal **define-syntax**, or **fluid-let-syntax**. Transformers are created with **syntax-rules**, **syntax-case**, or some implementation-dependent mechanism.

Syntactic extensions are expanded into core forms at the start of evaluation (before compilation or interpretation) by a syntax *expander*. The expander is invoked once for each top-level form in a program. If the expander encounters a syntactic extension, it invokes the associated transformer to expand the syntactic extension, then repeats the expansion process for the form returned by the transformer. If the expander encounters a core syntactic form, it recursively processes the subforms, if any, and reconstructs the form from the expanded subforms. Information about identifier bindings is maintained during expansion to enforce lexical scoping for variables and keywords.

8.1. Keyword Bindings

This section describes forms that establish bindings between keywords and transformers. Keyword bindings may be established at top level, using **define-syntax**, or locally, using **let-syntax**, **letrec-syntax**, or internal **define-syntax**. Existing bindings may be rebound temporarily with **fluid-let-syntax**. **define-syntax**, **let-syntax**, and **letrec-syntax** have been adopted for inclusion in the Revised[5]

Report on Scheme. `fluid-let-syntax` is an extension supported by the portable `syntax-case` system.

(define-syntax *keyword exp*)   syntax
returns: unspecified

exp must evaluate to a transformer.

The following example defines `let*` as a syntactic extension, specifying the transformer with `syntax-rules` (see Section 8.2).

```
(define-syntax let*
  (syntax-rules ()
    ((_ () e1 e2 ...) (let () e1 e2 ...))
    ((_ ((i1 v1) (i2 v2) ...) e1 e2 ...)
     (let ((i1 v1))
       (let* ((i2 v2) ...) e1 e2 ...)))))
```

`define-syntax` forms appearing at top level behave similarly to top-level variable definitions, and `define-syntax` forms appearing at the front of a `lambda` or other body behave similarly to internal variable definitions. That is, a binding established by a top-level `define-syntax` form is visible globally, whereas one established by an internal `define-syntax` form is visible only within the body in which the `define-syntax` form appears.

All bindings established by a set of internal definitions, whether keyword or variable definitions, are visible within the definitions themselves. For example, the expression

```
(let ()
  (define even?
    (lambda (x)
      (or (= x 0) (odd? (- x 1)))))
  (define-syntax odd?
    (syntax-rules ()
      ((_ x) (not (even? x)))))
  (even? 10))
```

is valid and should return #t. It must be possible for the expander to determine the set of syntax and variable definitions that appears at the front of a body without referring to any of the locally defined identifiers. It is not legal, therefore, for an internal definition to affect the status of a (potential) internal definition in the same sequence of forms. For example,

```
(let ()
  (define-syntax bind-to-zero
    (syntax-rules ()
      ((_ id) (define id 0))))
  (bind-to-zero x)
  x)
```

is not valid, since it would require the expander to expand (bind-to-zero x) in order to recognize it as a syntax definition. Rewritten as follows it returns 0:

```
(let ()
  (define-syntax bind-to-zero
    (syntax-rules ()
      ((_ id) (define id 0))))
  (let ()
    (bind-to-zero x)
    x))
```

A top-level syntactic definition must be established before its first use in order for that use to be recognized.

(let-syntax (((*keyword exp*) ...) *form₁ form₂* ...)	**syntax**
(letrec-syntax (((*keyword exp*) ...) *form₁ form₂* ...)	**syntax**

returns: see explanation

Each *exp* must evaluate to a transformer. For both let-syntax and letrec-syntax, each *keyword* is bound within the forms *form₁ form₂* .... For letrec-syntax the binding scope also includes each *exp*.

A let-syntax or letrec-syntax form may expand into one or more expressions anywhere expressions are permitted, in which case the resulting expressions are treated as if enclosed in a begin expression.

A let-syntax or letrec-syntax form may expand into a definition or sequence of definitions anywhere are permitted, in which case the definitions are treated as if they appeared in place of the let-syntax or letrec-syntax form.

The following example highlights how let-syntax and letrec-syntax differ.

```
(let ((f (lambda (x) (+ x 1))))
  (let-syntax ((f (syntax-rules ()
                    ((_ x) x)))
               (g (syntax-rules ()
                    ((_ x) (f x)))))
    (list (f 1) (g 1))))  ⇒  (1 2)

(let ((f (lambda (x) (+ x 1))))
  (letrec-syntax ((f (syntax-rules ()
                       ((_ x) x)))
                  (g (syntax-rules ()
                       ((_ x) (f x)))))
    (list (f 1) (g 1))))  ⇒  (1 1)
```

The two expressions are identical except that the let-syntax form in the first expression is a letrec-syntax form in the second. In the first expression, the f occurring in g refers to the let-bound variable f, whereas in the second it refers to the keyword f whose binding is established by the letrec-syntax form.

```
(fluid-let-syntax ((keyword exp) ...) form₁ form₂ ...)                          syntax
```
returns: see explanation

Each *exp* must evaluate to a transformer. `fluid-let-syntax` is similar to `let-syntax`, except that instead of introducing new bindings for the keywords *keyword* ..., `fluid-let-syntax` temporarily alters the existing bindings for the keywords during the expansion of its body. That is, during the expansion of *form₁ form₂* ..., the visible lexical (or top-level) binding for each `keyword` is temporarily replaced by a new association between the keyword and the corresponding transformer. This affects any references to the keyword that resolve to the same lexical (or top-level) binding whether the references occur in the text of the body or are introduced during its expansion. In contrast, `let-syntax` captures only those references that occur within the text of its body.

The following example shows how `fluid-let-syntax` differs from `let-syntax`.

```
(let ((f (lambda (x) (+ x 1))))
  (let-syntax ((g (syntax-rules ()
                    ((_ x) (f x)))))
    (let-syntax ((f (syntax-rules ()
                      ((_ x) x))))
      (g 1))))   ⇒   2
(let ((f (lambda (x) (+ x 1))))
  (let-syntax ((g (syntax-rules ()
                    ((_ x) (f x)))))
    (fluid-let-syntax ((f (syntax-rules ()
                           ((_ x) x))))
      (g 1))))   ⇒   1
```

The two expressions are identical except that the inner `let-syntax` form in the first expression is a `fluid-let-syntax` form in the second. In the first expression, the `f` occurring in the expansion of `(g 1)` refers to the `let`-bound variable `f`, whereas in the second it refers to the keyword `f` by virtue of the fluid syntax binding for `f`.

8.2. Syntax-Rules Transformers

The `syntax-rules` form described in this section permits simple transformers to be specified in a convenient manner. These transformers may be bound to keywords using the mechanisms described in Section 8.1. While it is much less expressive than the mechanism described in Section 8.3, it is sufficient for defining many common syntactic extensions. `syntax-rules` has been adopted for inclusion in the Revised[5] Report on Scheme.

```
(syntax-rules (literal ...) clause ...)                                          syntax
```
returns: a transformer

Each *literal* must be an identifier. Each clause takes the form:

(pattern template)

Each *pattern* specifies one possible syntax that the input form might take, and the corresponding *template* specifies how the output should appear in each case.

Patterns consist of list structure, vector structure, identifiers, and constants. Each identifier within a pattern is either a *literal*, a *pattern variable*, or an *ellipsis*. The identifier ... is an ellipsis. Any identifier other than ... is a literal if it appears in the list of literals (*literal* ...); otherwise, it is a pattern variable. Literals serve as auxiliary keywords, such as `else` in `case` and `cond` expressions. List and vector structure within a pattern specifies the basic structure required of the input, pattern variables specify arbitrary substructure, and literals and constants specify atomic pieces that must match exactly. Ellipses specify repeated occurrences of the subpatterns they follow.

An input form F matches a pattern P if and only if

- P is a pattern variable,

- P is a literal identifier and F is an identifier with the same binding (see `free-identifier=?` in Section 8.3),

- P is of the form $(P_1 \ldots P_n)$ and F is a list of n elements that match P_1 through P_n,

- P is of the form $(P_1 \ P_2 \ldots P_n \ . \ P_x)$ and F is a list or improper list of n or more elements whose first n elements match P_1 through P_n and whose nth cdr matches P_x,

- P is of the form $(P_1 \ldots P_n \ P_x \ldots)$ and F is a proper list of n or more elements whose first n elements match P_1 through P_n and whose remaining elements each match P_x,

- P is of the form $\#(P_1 \ldots P_n)$ and F is a vector of n elements that match P_1 through P_n,

- P is of the form $\#(P_1 \ldots P_n \ P_x \ldots)$ and F is a vector of n or more elements whose first n elements match P_1 through P_n and whose remaining elements each match P_x, or

- P is a pattern datum (any nonlist, nonvector, nonsymbol object) and F is equal to P in the sense of the `equal?` procedure.

The outermost structure of a `syntax-rules` *pattern* must actually be in one of the list-structured forms above, although subpatterns of the pattern may be in any of the above forms. Furthermore, the first element of the outermost pattern is ignored, since it is always assumed to be the keyword naming the syntactic form. (These statements do not apply to `syntax-case`; see Section 8.3.)

If an input form passed to a `syntax-rules` transformer matches the pattern for a given clause, the clause is accepted and the form is transformed as specified by the associated template. As this transformation takes place, pattern variables appearing in the pattern are bound to the corresponding input subforms. Pattern variables appearing within a subpattern followed by one or more ellipses may be bound to a set or sets of zero or more input subforms.

A template is a pattern variable, an identifier that is not a pattern variable, a pattern datum, a list of subtemplates $(S_1 \ldots S_n)$, an improper list of subtemplates $(S_1\ S_2\ \ldots\ S_n\ .\ T)$, or a vector of subtemplates $\#(S_1\ \ldots\ S_n)$. Each subtemplate S_i is either a template or a template followed by one or more ellipses. The final element T of an improper subtemplate list is a template.

Pattern variables appearing within a template are replaced in the output by the input subforms to which they are bound. Pattern data and identifiers that are not pattern variables are inserted directly into the output. List and vector structure within the template remains list and vector structure in the output. A subtemplate followed by an ellipsis expands into zero or more occurrences of the subtemplate. The subtemplate must contain at least one pattern variable from a subpattern followed by an ellipsis. (Otherwise, the expander could not determine how many times the subform should be repeated in the output.) Pattern variables that occur in subpatterns followed by one or more ellipses may occur only in subtemplates that are followed by (at least) as many ellipses. These pattern variables are replaced in the output by the input subforms to which they are bound, distributed as specified. If a pattern variable is followed by more ellipses in the template than in the associated pattern, the input form is replicated as necessary.

A template of the form (**...** *template*) is identical to *template*, except that ellipses within the template have no special meaning. That is, any ellipses contained within *template* are treated as ordinary identifiers. In particular, the template (**...** **...**) produces a single ellipsis, **...**. This allows syntactic extensions to expand into forms containing ellipses.

The definition of **or** below demonstrates the use of **syntax-rules**.

```
(define-syntax or
  (syntax-rules ()
    ((_) #f)
    ((_ e) e)
    ((_ e1 e2 e3 ...)
     (let ((t e1)) (if t t (or e2 e3 ...)))))))
```

The input patterns specify that the input must consist of the keyword and zero or more subexpressions. An underscore (_), which is an ordinary pattern variable, is used by convention for the keyword position to remind the programmer and anyone reading the definition that the keyword position never fails to contain the expected keyword and need not be matched. (In fact, as mentioned above, **syntax-rules** ignores what appears in the keyword position.) If more than one subexpression is present (third clause), the expanded code must both test the value of the first subexpression and return the value if it is not false. In order to avoid evaluating the expression twice, the transformer introduces a binding for the temporary variable **t**.

The expansion algorithm maintains lexical scoping automatically by renaming local identifiers as necessary. Thus, the binding for **t** introduced by the transformer is visible only within code introduced by the transformer and not within subforms of the input. Similarly, the references to the identifiers **let** and **if** are unaffected by any bindings present in the context of the input.

```
(let ((if #f))
  (let ((t 'okay))
    (or if t)))  ⇒  okay
```

This expression is transformed during expansion to the equivalent of the expression below.

```
((lambda (if1)
   ((lambda (t1)
      ((lambda (t2)
         (if t2 t2 t1))
       if1))
    'okay))
 #f)  ⇒  okay
```

In this sample expansion, if1, t1, and t2 represent identifiers to which if and t in the original expression and t in the expansion of or have been renamed.

The definition of a simplified version of cond below (simplified because it requires at least one output expression per clause and does not support the auxiliary keyword =>) demonstrates how auxiliary keywords such as else are recognized in the input to a transformer, via inclusion in the list of literals.

```
(define-syntax cond
  (syntax-rules (else)
    ((_ (else e1 e2 ...)) (begin e1 e2 ...))
    ((_ (e0 e1 e2 ...)) (if e0 (begin e1 e2 ...)))
    ((_ (e0 e1 e2 ...) c1 c2 ...)
     (if e0 (begin e1 e2 ...) (cond c1 c2 ...)))))
```

8.3. Syntax-Case Transformers

This section describes a more expressive mechanism for creating transformers, based on syntax-case, a generalized version of syntax-rules. This mechanism permits more complex transformations to be specified, including transformations that "bend" lexical scoping in a controlled manner, allowing a much broader class of syntactic extensions to be defined. Any transformer that may be defined using syntax-rules may be rewritten easily to use syntax-case instead; in fact, syntax-rules itself may be defined as a syntactic extension in terms of syntax-case, as demonstrated within the description of syntax below.

With this mechanism, transformers are procedures of one argument. The argument is a *syntax object* representing the form to be processed. The return value is a syntax object representing the output form. A syntax object contains contextual information about a form in addition to its structure. This contextual information is used by the expander to maintain lexical scoping.

A syntax object representing an identifier is itself referred to as an identifier; thus, the term *identifier* may refer either to the syntactic entity (symbol, variable, or keyword) or to the concrete representation of the syntactic entity as a syntax object. It is rarely necessary to distinguish the two uses.

Transformers destructure their input with `syntax-case` and rebuild their output with `syntax`. These two forms alone are sufficient for defining many syntactic extensions, including any that can be defined using `syntax-rules`. They are described below along with a set of additional forms and procedures that provide added functionality.

The forms and procedures described in this section are extensions supported by the portable `syntax-case` system.

(syntax-case *exp* (*literal* ...) *clause* ...**)**   syntax
returns: see below

Each *literal* must be an identifier. Each *clause* must take one of the following two forms:

(*pattern* *output-expression*)
(*pattern* *fender* *output-expression*)

`syntax-case` patterns may be in any of the forms described in Section 8.2.

`syntax-case` first evaluates *exp*, then attempts to match the resulting value against the pattern from the first *clause*. This value is usually a syntax object, but it may be any Scheme object. If the value matches the pattern and no *fender* is present, *output-expression* is evaluated and its value returned as the value of the `syntax-case` expression. If the value does not match the pattern, the value is compared against the next clause, and so on. An error is signaled if the value does not match any of the patterns.

If the optional *fender* is present, it serves as an additional constraint on acceptance of a clause. If the value of the `syntax-case` *exp* matches the pattern for a given clause, the corresponding *fender* is evaluated. If *fender* evaluates to a true value, the clause is accepted; otherwise, the clause is rejected as if the input had failed to match the pattern. Fenders are logically a part of the matching process, i.e., they specify additional matching constraints beyond the basic structure of an expression.

Pattern variables contained within a clause's `pattern` are bound to the corresponding pieces of the input value within the clause's `fender` (if present) and `output-expression`. Pattern variables occupy the same name space as program variables and keywords; pattern variable bindings created by `syntax-case` can shadow (and be shadowed by) program variable and keyword bindings as well as other pattern variable bindings. Pattern variables, however, can be referenced only within **syntax** expressions.

See the examples following the description of **syntax**.

(**syntax** *template*)   **syntax**
returns: see below

A **syntax** expression is like a **quote** expression except that the values of pattern variables appearing within *template* are inserted into *template*, and contextual information associated with any nonlist, nonvector items from the template is retained in the output. A **syntax** *template* is identical to a **syntax-rules** *template* and is treated similarly.

The definition of **or** below is equivalent to the one given in Section 8.2 except that it employs **syntax-case** and **syntax** in place of **syntax-rules**.

```
(define-syntax or
  (lambda (x)
    (syntax-case x ()
      ((_) (syntax #f))
      ((_ e) (syntax e))
      ((_ e1 e2 e3 ...)
       (syntax (let ((t e1)) (if t t (or e2 e3 ...)))))))))
```

In this version, the **lambda** expression that produces the transformer is explicit, as are the **syntax** forms in the output part of each clause. Any **syntax-rules** form can be expressed with **syntax-case** by making the **lambda** expression and **syntax** expressions explicit. This observation leads to the following definition of **syntax-rules** in terms of **syntax-case**.

```
(define-syntax syntax-rules
  (lambda (x)
    (syntax-case x ()
      ((_ (i ...) ((keyword . pattern) template) ...)
       (syntax (lambda (x)
                 (syntax-case x (i ...)
                   ((dummy . pattern) (syntax template))
                   ...)))))))
```

The unreferenced pattern variable **dummy** is used in place of each **keyword** since the first position of each **syntax-rules** pattern is always ignored.

Since the **lambda** and **syntax** expressions are implicit in a **syntax-rules** form, definitions expressed with **syntax-rules** are often shorter than the equivalent definitions expressed with **syntax-case**. The choice of which to use when either suffices is a matter of taste, but many transformers that can be written easily with **syntax-case** cannot be written easily or at all with **syntax-rules** (see Section 8.4).

(identifier? *obj*)   **procedure**
returns: #t if *obj* is an identifier, #f otherwise

identifier? is often used within fenders to verify that certain subforms of an input
form are identifiers, as in the definition of unnamed let below.

```
(define-syntax let
  (lambda (x)
    (define ids?
      (lambda (ls)
        (or (null? ls)
            (and (identifier? (car ls))
                 (ids? (cdr ls))))))
    (syntax-case x ()
      ((_ ((i v) ...) e1 e2 ...)
       (ids? (syntax (i ...)))
       (syntax ((lambda (i ...) e1 e2 ...) v ...))))))
```

Syntactic extensions ordinarily take the form (*keyword subform* ...), but the
syntax-case system permits them to take the form of singleton identifiers as well.
For example, the keyword pcar in the expression below may be used both as an
identifier (in which case it expands into a call to car) or as a structured form (in
which case it expands into a call to set-car!).

```
(let ((p (cons 0 #f)))
  (define-syntax pcar
    (lambda (x)
      (syntax-case x ()
        (_ (identifier? x) (syntax (car p)))
        ((_ v) (syntax (set-car! p v))))))
  (let ((a pcar))
    (pcar 1)
    (list a pcar)))   ⇒   (0 1)
```

The fender (identifier? x) is used to recognize the singleton identifier case.

(free-identifier=? *identifier₁ identifier₂*)   **procedure**
(bound-identifier=? *identifier₁ identifier₂*)   **procedure**
returns: see below

Symbolic names alone do not distinguish identifiers unless the identifiers are
to be used only as symbolic data.   The predicates free-identifier=? and
bound-identifier=? are used to compare identifiers according to their *intended
use* as free references or bound identifiers in a given context.

`free-identifier=?` is used to determine whether two identifiers would be equivalent if they were to appear as free identifiers in the output of a transformer. Because identifier references are lexically scoped, this means that (`free-identifier=?` id_1 id_2) is true if and only if the identifiers id_1 and id_2 refer to the same lexical or top-level binding. (For this comparison, all variables are assumed to have top-level bindings, whether defined yet or not.) Literal identifiers (auxiliary keywords) appearing in `syntax-case` patterns (such as `else` in `case` and `cond`) are matched with `free-identifier=?`.

Similarly, `bound-identifier=?` is used to determine if two identifiers would be equivalent if they were to appear as bound identifiers in the output of a transformer. In other words, if `bound-identifier=?` returns true for two identifiers, a binding for one will capture references to the other within its scope. In general, two identifiers are `bound-identifier=?` only if both are present in the original program or both are introduced by the same transformer application (perhaps implicitly—see `datum->syntax-object`). `bound-identifier=?` can be used for detecting duplicate identifiers in a binding construct or for other preprocessing of a binding construct that requires detecting instances of the bound identifiers.

Two identifiers that are `bound-identifier=?` are also `free-identifier=?`, but two identifiers that are `free-identifier=?` are not necessarily `bound-identifier=?`. An identifier introduced by a transformer may refer to the same enclosing binding as an identifier not introduced by the transformer, but an introduced binding for one will not capture references to the other.

The definition below is equivalent to the earlier definition of a simplified version of `cond` with `syntax-rules`, except that `else` is recognized via an explicit call to `free-identifier?` within a fender rather than via inclusion in the literals list.

```
(define-syntax cond
  (lambda (x)
    (syntax-case x ()
      ((_ (e0 e1 e2 ...))
       (and (identifier? (syntax e0))
            (free-identifier=? (syntax e0) (syntax else)))
       (syntax (begin e1 e2 ...)))
      ((_ (e0 e1 e2 ...)) (syntax (if e0 (begin e1 e2 ...))))
      ((_ (e0 e1 e2 ...) c1 c2 ...)
       (syntax (if e0 (begin e1 e2 ...) (cond c1 c2 ...)))))))
```

With either definition of `cond`, `else` is not recognized as an auxiliary keyword if an enclosing lexical binding for `else` exists. For example,

```
(let ((else #f))
  (cond (else (write "oops"))))
```

does *not* write "oops", since `else` is bound lexically and is therefore not the same `else` that appears in the definition of `cond`.

The following definition of unnamed `let` uses `bound-identifier=?` to detect duplicate identifiers.

```
(define-syntax let
  (lambda (x)
    (define ids?
      (lambda (ls)
        (or (null? ls)
            (and (identifier? (car ls))
                 (ids? (cdr ls))))))
    (define unique-ids?
      (lambda (ls)
        (or (null? ls)
            (and (let notmem? ((x (car ls)) (ls (cdr ls)))
                   (or (null? ls)
                       (and (not (bound-identifier=? x (car ls)))
                            (notmem? x (cdr ls)))))
                 (unique-ids? (cdr ls))))))
    (syntax-case x ()
      ((_ ((i v) ...) e1 e2 ...)
       (and (ids? (syntax (i ...)))
            (unique-ids? (syntax (i ...))))
       (syntax ((lambda (i ...) e1 e2 ...) v ...))))))
```

With the definition of `let` above, the expression

```
(let ((a 3) (a 4)) (+ a a))
```

results in a syntax error, whereas

```
(let-syntax ((dolet (lambda (x)
                      (syntax-case x ()
                        ((_ b)
                         (syntax (let ((a 3) (b 4))
                                   (+ a b)))))))) 
  (dolet a))
```

evaluates to 7 since the identifier `a` introduced by `dolet` and the identifier `a` extracted from the input form are not `bound-identifier=?`. Since both occurrences of `a`, however, if left as free references, would refer to the same (top-level) binding for `a`, `free-identifier=?` would not distinguish them.

(with-syntax ((*pattern val*) ...) *exp₁ exp₂* ...)   **syntax**
returns: the value of the last *expᵢ*

It is sometimes useful to construct a transformer's output in separate pieces, then put the pieces together. `with-syntax` facilitates this by allowing the creation of local pattern bindings.

pattern is identical in form to a `syntax-case` pattern. The value of each *val* is computed and destructured according to the corresponding *pattern*, and pattern variables within the *pattern* are bound as with `syntax-case` to appropriate portions of the value within *exp₁ exp₂* ....

`with-syntax` may be defined as a syntactic extension in terms of `syntax-case`.

```
(define-syntax with-syntax
  (lambda (x)
    (syntax-case x ()
      ((_ ((p e0) ...) e1 e2 ...)
       (syntax (syntax-case (list e0 ...) ()
                 ((p ...) (begin e1 e2 ...)))))))))
```

The following definitions of full cond and case demonstrate the use of
with-syntax to support transformers that employ recursion internally to construct
their output.

```
(define-syntax cond
  (lambda (x)
    (syntax-case x ()
      ((_ c1 c2 ...)
       (let f ((c1 (syntax c1)) (cmore (syntax (c2 ...))))
         (if (null? cmore)
             (syntax-case c1 (else =>)
               ((else e1 e2 ...) (syntax (begin e1 e2 ...)))
               ((e0) (syntax (let ((t e0)) (if t t))))
               ((e0 => e1) (syntax (let ((t e0)) (if t (e1 t)))))
               ((e0 e1 e2 ...) (syntax (if e0 (begin e1 e2 ...)))))
             (with-syntax ((rest (f (car cmore) (cdr cmore))))
               (syntax-case c1 (=>)
                 ((e0) (syntax (let ((t e0)) (if t t rest))))
                 ((e0 => e1) (syntax (let ((t e0)) (if t (e1 t) rest))))
                 ((e0 e1 e2 ...)
                  (syntax (if e0 (begin e1 e2 ...) rest)))))))))))
(define-syntax case
  (lambda (x)
    (syntax-case x ()
      ((_ e c1 c2 ...)
       (with-syntax ((body
           (let f ((c1 (syntax c1)) (cmore (syntax (c2 ...))))
             (if (null? cmore)
                 (syntax-case c1 (else)
                   ((else e1 e2 ...) (syntax (begin e1 e2 ...)))
                   (((k ...) e1 e2 ...)
                    (syntax (if (memv t '(k ...)) (begin e1 e2 ...))))
                   (with-syntax ((rest (f (car cmore) (cdr cmore))))
                     (syntax-case c1 ()
                       (((k ...) e1 e2 ...)
                        (syntax (if (memv t '(k ...))
                                    (begin e1 e2 ...)
                                    rest)))))))))
         (syntax (let ((t e)) body)))))))
```

(syntax-object->datum *obj*)   **procedure**
returns: *obj* stripped of syntactic information

The procedure `syntax-object->datum` strips all syntactic information from a syntax object and returns the corresponding Scheme "datum." Identifiers stripped in this manner are converted to their symbolic names, which can then be compared with eq?. Thus, a predicate `symbolic-identifier=?` might be defined as follows:

```
(define symbolic-identifier=?
  (lambda (x y)
    (eq? (syntax-object->datum x)
         (syntax-object->datum y))))
```

Two identifiers that are `free-identifier=?` are `symbolic-identifier=?`; in order to refer to the same binding, two identifiers must have the same name. The converse is not always true, since two identifiers may have the same name but different bindings.

(datum->syntax-object *template-identifier obj*)   **procedure**
returns: a syntax object

`datum->syntax-object` constructs a syntax object from *obj* that contains the same contextual information as *template-identifier*, with the effect that the syntax object behaves as if it were introduced into the code when *template-identifier* was introduced. The template identifier is often the keyword of an input form, extracted from the form, and the object is often a symbol naming an identifier to be constructed.

`datum->syntax-object` allows a transformer to "bend" lexical scoping rules by creating *implicit identifiers* that behave as if they were present in the input form, thus permitting the definition of syntactic extensions that introduce visible bindings for or references to identifiers that do not appear explicitly in the input form. For example, we can define a `loop` expression that binds the variable `break` to an escape procedure within the loop body.

```
(define-syntax loop
  (lambda (x)
    (syntax-case x ()
      ((k e ...)
       (with-syntax ((break (datum->syntax-object (syntax k) 'break)))
         (syntax (call-with-current-continuation
                   (lambda (break)
                     (let f () e ... (f)))))))))))

(let ((n 3) (ls '()))
  (loop
    (if (= n 0) (break ls))
    (set! ls (cons 'a ls))
    (set! n (- n 1))))  ⇒  (a a a)
```

Were we to define `loop` as

```
(define-syntax loop
  (lambda (x)
    (syntax-case x ()
      ((_ e ...)
       (syntax (call-with-current-continuation
                 (lambda (break)
                   (let f () e ... (f)))))))))
```

the variable `break` would not be visible in `e` ....

It is also useful for *obj* to represent an arbitrary Scheme form, as demonstrated by the following definition of `include`, an expand-time version of `load`.

```
(define-syntax include
  (lambda (x)
    (define read-file
      (lambda (fn k)
        (let ((p (open-input-file fn)))
          (let f ((x (read p)))
            (if (eof-object? x)
                (begin (close-input-port p) '())
                (cons (datum->syntax-object k x)
                      (f (read p))))))))
    (syntax-case x ()
      ((k filename)
       (let ((fn (syntax-object->datum (syntax filename))))
         (with-syntax (((exp ...) (read-file fn (syntax k))))
           (syntax (begin exp ...))))))))
```

`(include "filename")` expands into a `begin` expression containing the forms found in the file named by `"filename"`. For example, if the file `f-def.ss` contains the expression `(define f (lambda () x))`, the expression

```
(let ((x "okay"))
  (include "f-def.ss")
  (f))
```

evaluates to `"okay"`.

The definition of `include` uses `datum->syntax-object` to convert the objects read from the file into syntax objects in the proper lexical context, so that identifier references and definitions within those expressions are scoped where the `include` form appears.

(generate-temporaries *list***)**   **procedure**
returns: a list of distinct generated identifiers

Transformers can introduce a fixed number of identifiers into their output by naming each identifier. In some cases, however, the number of identifiers to be introduced depends upon some characteristic of the input expression. A straightforward definition of `letrec`, for example, requires as many temporary identifiers as there are binding pairs in the input expression. The procedure `generate-temporaries` is used to construct lists of temporary identifiers.

list may be any list; its contents are not important. The number of temporaries generated is the number of elements in *list*. Each temporary is guaranteed to be different from all other identifiers.

A definition of `letrec` that uses `generate-temporaries` is shown below.

```
(define-syntax letrec
  (lambda (x)
    (syntax-case x ()
      ((_ ((i v) ...) e1 e2 ...)
       (with-syntax (((t ...) (generate-temporaries (syntax (i ...)))))
         (syntax (let ((i #f) ...)
                   (let ((t v) ...)
                     (set! i t) ...
                     (let () e1 e2 ...)))))))))
```

Any transformer that uses `generate-temporaries` in this fashion can be rewritten to avoid using it, albeit with a loss of clarity. The trick is to use a recursively defined intermediate form that generates one temporary per expansion step and completes the expansion after enough temporaries have been generated. A definition of `letrec` that does not use `generate-temporaries` is left as an exercise for the reader.

8.4. Examples

This section presents a series of illustrative syntactic extensions defined with either `syntax-rules` or `syntax-case`, starting with a few simple but useful syntactic extensions and ending with a fairly complex mechanism for defining structures with automatically generated constructors, predicates, field accessors, and field setters.

The simplest example in this section is the following definition of `rec`. `rec` is a syntactic extension that permits internally recursive anonymous (not externally named) procedures to be created with minimal effort.

```
(define-syntax rec
  (syntax-rules ()
    ((_ x e) (letrec ((x e)) x))))
(map (rec sum
       (lambda (x)
         (if (= x 0)
             0
             (+ x (sum (- x 1))))))
     '(0 1 2 3 4 5))  ⇒  (0 1 3 6 10 15)
```

Using `rec`, we can define the full `let` (both unnamed and named) as follows.

```
(define-syntax let
  (syntax-rules ()
    ((_ ((x v) ...) e1 e2 ...)
     ((lambda (x ...) e1 e2 ...) v ...))
    ((_ f ((x v) ...) e1 e2 ...)
     ((rec f (lambda (x ...) e1 e2 ...)) v ...))))
```

This definition relies upon the fact that the first pattern cannot match a named let, since the first subform of a named let must be an identifier, not a list of bindings. The following definition uses a fender to make this check more robust:

```
(define-syntax let
  (lambda (x)
    (syntax-case x ()
      ((_ ((x v) ...) e1 e2 ...)
       (syntax ((lambda (x ...) e1 e2 ...) v ...)))
      ((_ f ((x v) ...) e1 e2 ...)
       (identifier? (syntax f))
       (syntax ((rec f (lambda (x ...) e1 e2 ...)) v ...))))))
```

Of course, to be completely robust, the ids? and all-ids? checks employed in the definition of unnamed let in Section 8.3 should be employed here as well.

The precise syntax of do cannot be expressed directly with a single pattern because some of the bindings in a do expression's binding list may take the form (var val) while others take the form (var val update). The following definition of do uses syntax-case internally to parse the bindings separately from the overall form.

```
(define-syntax do
  (lambda (x)
    (syntax-case x ()
      ((_ (binding ...) (test res ...) exp ...)
       (with-syntax ((((var val update) ...)
                      (map (lambda (b)
                             (syntax-case b ()
                               ((var val)
                                (syntax (var val var)))
                               ((var val update)
                                (syntax (var val update)))))
                           (syntax (binding ...)))))
         (syntax (let doloop ((var val) ...)
                   (if test
                       (begin (if #f #f) res ...)
                       (begin exp ... (doloop update ...))))))))))
```

The odd looking expression (if #f #f) is inserted before the result expressions res ... in case no result expressions are provided, since begin requires at least one subexpression. The value of (if #f #f) is unspecified, which is what we want since the value of do is unspecified if no result expressions are provided. At the expense of a bit more code, we could use syntax-case to determine whether any result expressions are provided and to produce a loop with either a one- or two-armed if as appropriate. The resulting expansion would be cleaner but semantically equivalent.

As mentioned in Section 8.2, ellipses lose their special meaning within templates of the form (... *template*), This fact allows syntactic extensions to expand into syntax definitions containing ellipses. This usage is illustrated by the definition below of `be-like-begin`:

```
(define-syntax be-like-begin
  (syntax-rules ()
    ((_ name)
     (define-syntax name
       (syntax-rules ()
         ((_ e0 e1 (... ...))
          (begin e0 e1 (... ...))))))))
```

With `be-like-begin` defined in this manner, `(be-like-begin sequence)` has the same effect as the following definition of `sequence`.

```
(define-syntax sequence
  (syntax-rules ()
    ((_ e0 e1 ...)
     (begin e0 e1 ...))))
```

That is, a `sequence` form becomes equivalent to a `begin` form.

The following example shows how one might restrict `if` expressions within a given expression to require the "else" (alternative) subexpression by defining the local `if` in terms of the top-level `if`:

```
(let-syntax ((if (lambda (x)
                   (syntax-case x ()
                     ((_ e1 e2 e3)
                      (syntax (if e1 e2 e3)))))))
  (if 1 2 3))   ⇒  2
(let-syntax ((if (lambda (x)
                   (syntax-case x ()
                     ((_ e1 e2 e3)
                      (syntax (if e1 e2 e3)))))))
  (if 1 2))   ⇒  *error*
```

Although this local definition of `if` looks simple enough, there are a few subtle ways in which an attempt to write it might go wrong. If `letrec-syntax` were used in place of `let-syntax`, the identifier `if` inserted into the output would refer to the local `if` rather than the top-level `if`, and expansion would loop indefinitely.

Similarly, if the underscore were replaced with the identifier `if`, expansion would again loop indefinitely. The `if` appearing in the template `(if e1 e2 e3)` would be treated as a pattern variable bound to the corresponding identifier `if` from the input form, which denotes the local version of `if`.

Placing if in the list of literals in an attempt to patch up the latter version would not work either. This would cause syntax-case to compare the literal if in the pattern, which would be scoped outside the let-syntax expression, with the if in the input expression, which would be scoped inside the let-syntax. Since they would not refer to the same binding, they would not be free-identifier=?, and a syntax error would result.

The conventional use of underscore (_) helps the programmer avoid situations like these in which the wrong identifier is matched against or inserted by accident.

It is an error to generate a reference to an identifier that is not present within the context of an input form, which can happen if the "closest enclosing lexical binding" for an identifier inserted into the output of a transformer does not also enclose the input form. For example,

```
(let-syntax ((divide (lambda (x)
                       (let ((/ +))
                         (syntax-case x ()
                           ((_ e1 e2)
                            (syntax (/ e1 e2)))))))))
  (let ((/ *)) (divide 2 1)))
```

results in an error to the effect that / is referenced in an invalid context, since the occurrence of / in the output of divide is a reference to the variable / bound by the let expression within the transformer.

As noted in the description of identifier? in Section 8.3, singleton identifiers can be treated as syntactic extensions and expanded into arbitrary forms. Often, it is necessary to treat the case where an identifier appears in the first position of a structured expression differently from the case where it appears elsewhere, as in the pcar example given in the description for identifier?. In other situations, both cases must or may be treated the same. The form identifier-syntax defined below can make doing so more convenient.

```
(define-syntax identifier-syntax
  (lambda (x)
    (syntax-case x ()
      ((_ e)
       (syntax
         (lambda (x)
           (syntax-case x ()
             (id
              (identifier? (syntax id))
              (syntax e))
             ((id x (... ...))
              (identifier? (syntax id))
              (syntax (e x (... ...)))))))))))
```

```
(let ((x 0))
  (define-syntax x++
    (identifier-syntax
      (let ((t x)) (set! x (+ t 1)) t)))
  (let ((a x++))
    (list a x)))   ⇒   (0 1)
```

The following example uses `identifier-syntax`, `datum->syntax-object`, and
local syntax definitions to define a form of *method*, one of the basic building blocks
of object-oriented programming (OOP) systems. A `method` expression is similar to
a `lambda` expression, except that in addition to the formal parameters and body,
a `method` expression also contains a list of instance variables (`ivar ...`). When
a method is invoked, it is always passed an *object* (*instance*), represented as a
vector of *fields* corresponding to the instance variables, and zero or more additional
arguments. Within the method body, the object is bound implicitly to the identifier
`self` and the additional arguments are bound to the formal parameters. The fields
of the object may be accessed or altered within the method body via instance
variable references or assignments.

```
(define-syntax method
  (lambda (x)
    (syntax-case x ()
      ((k (ivar ...) formals e1 e2 ...)
       (with-syntax (((index ...)
                      (let f ((i 0) (ls (syntax (ivar ...))))
                        (if (null? ls)
                            '()
                            (cons i (f (+ i 1) (cdr ls))))))
                     (self (datum->syntax-object (syntax k) 'self))
                     (set! (datum->syntax-object (syntax k) 'set!)))
         (syntax
           (lambda (self . formals)
             (let-syntax ((ivar (identifier-syntax
                                  (vector-ref self index)))
                          ...)
               (let-syntax ((set! (syntax-rules (ivar ...)
                                    ((_ ivar e)
                                     (vector-set! self index e))
                                    ...
                                    ((_ x e) (set! x e)))))
                 e1 e2 ...)))))))))
```

Local bindings for `ivar ...` and for `set!` make the fields of the object appear
to be ordinary variables, with references and assignments translated into calls to
`vector-ref` and `vector-set!`. `datum->syntax-object` is used to make the introduced bindings of `self` and `set!` visible in the method body. Nested `let-syntax`
expressions are needed so that the identifiers `ivar ...` serving as auxiliary keywords
for the local version of `set!` are scoped properly. The examples below demonstrate
simple uses of `method`.

```
(let ((m (method (a) (x) (list a x self))))
  (m #(1) 2))  ⇒  (1 2 #(1)))
(let ((m (method (a) (x)
          (set! a x)
          (set! x (+ a x))
          (list a x self))))
  (m #(1) 2))  ⇒  (2 4 #(2)))
```

In a complete OOP system based on `method`, the instance variables `ivar` ... would likely be drawn from class declarations, not listed explicitly in the `method` forms, although the same techniques would be used to make instance variables appear as ordinary variables within method bodies.

The next example defines a `define-integrable` form that is similar to `define` for procedure definitions except that it causes the code for the procedure to be *integrated*, or inserted, wherever a direct call to the procedure is found. No semantic difference is visible between procedures defined with `define-integrable` and those defined with `define`, except that a top-level `define-integrable` form must appear before the first reference to the defined identifier, and syntactic extensions within the body of the defined procedure are expanded at the point of call. Lexical scoping is preserved, the actual parameters in an integrated call are evaluated once and at the proper time, integrable procedures may be used as first-class values, and recursive procedures do not cause indefinite recursive expansion.

A `define-integrable` has the following form.

(`define-integrable` *name lambda-expression*)

A `define-integrable` form expands into a pair of definitions: a syntax definition of *name* and a variable definition of a generated name, `residual-`*name*. The transformer for *name* converts apparent calls to *name* into direct calls to *lambda-expression*. Since the resulting forms are merely direct `lambda` applications (the equivalent of `let` expressions), the actual parameters are evaluated exactly once and before evaluation of the procedure's body, as required. All other references to *name* are replaced with references to `residual-`*name*. The definition of `residual-`*name* binds it to *lambda-expression*. This allows the procedure to be used as a first-class value. Within *lambda-expression*, wherever it appears, *name* is rebound to a transformer that expands all references into references to `residual-`*name*. The use of `fluid-let-syntax` for this purpose prevents indefinite expansion from indirect recursion among integrable procedures. This allows the procedure to be recursive without causing indefinite expansion. Nothing special is done by `define-integrable` to maintain lexical scoping, since lexical scoping is maintained automatically by the expander.

```
(define-syntax define-integrable
  (lambda (x)
    (define make-residual-name
      (lambda (name)
        (datum->syntax-object name
          (string->symbol
            (string-append "residual-"
              (symbol->string (syntax-object->datum name)))))))
    (syntax-case x (lambda)
      ((_ name (lambda formals form1 form2 ...))
       (identifier? (syntax name))
       (with-syntax ((xname (make-residual-name (syntax name))))
         (syntax
           (begin
             (define-syntax name
               (lambda (x)
                 (syntax-case x ()
                   (_ (identifier? x) (syntax xname))
                   ((_ arg (... ...))
                    (syntax
                      ((fluid-let-syntax
                         ((name (identifier-syntax xname)))
                         (lambda formals form1 form2 ...))
                       arg (... ...)))))))
             (define xname
               (fluid-let-syntax ((name (identifier-syntax xname)))
                 (lambda formals form1 form2 ...)))))))))
```

The final example of this section defines a simple structure definition facility that represents structures as vectors with named fields. Structures are defined with **define-structure**, which takes the form:

(define-structure *name field* ...)

where *name* names the structure and *field* ... names its fields. **define-structure** expands into a series of generated definitions: a constructor **make-*name***, a type predicate *name*?, and one accessor *name-field* and setter **set-*name-field*!** per field name. The constructor accepts as many arguments as there are fields in the structure and creates a vector whose first element is the symbol *name* and whose remaining elements are the argument values. The type predicate returns true if its argument is a vector of the expected length whose first element is *name*.

Since a **define-structure** form expands into a **begin** containing definitions, it is itself a definition and can be used wherever definitions are valid.

The generated identifiers are created with **datum->syntax-object** to allow the identifiers to be visible where the **define-structure** form appears.

```
(define-syntax define-structure
  (lambda (x)
    (define gen-id
      (lambda (template-id . args)
        (datum->syntax-object template-id
          (string->symbol
            (apply string-append
                   (map (lambda (x)
                          (if (string? x)
                              x
                              (symbol->string
                                (syntax-object->datum x))))
                        args))))))
    (syntax-case x ()
      ((_ name field ...)
       (with-syntax
         ((constructor (gen-id (syntax name) "make-" (syntax name)))
          (predicate (gen-id (syntax name) (syntax name) "?"))
          ((access ...)
           (map (lambda (x) (gen-id x (syntax name) "-" x))
                (syntax (field ...))))
          ((assign ...)
           (map (lambda (x) (gen-id x "set-" (syntax name) "-" x "!"))
                (syntax (field ...))))
          (structure-length (+ (length (syntax (field ...))) 1))
          ((index ...) (let f ((i 1) (ids (syntax (field ...))))
                         (if (null? ids)
                             '()
                             (cons i (f (+ i 1) (cdr ids)))))))
         (syntax (begin
                   (define constructor
                     (lambda (field ...)
                       (vector 'name field ...)))
                   (define predicate
                     (lambda (x)
                       (and (vector? x)
                            (= (vector-length x) structure-length)
                            (eq? (vector-ref x 0) 'name))))
                   (define access
                     (lambda (x)
                       (vector-ref x index)))
                   ...
                   (define assign
                     (lambda (x update)
                       (vector-set! x index update)))
                   ...)))))))
```

The examples below demonstrate the use of `define-structure`.

```
(define-structure tree left right)
(define t
  (make-tree
    (make-tree 0 1)
    (make-tree 2 3)))
```

```
t  ⇒  #(tree #(tree 0 1) #(tree 2 3))
(tree? t)  ⇒  #t
(tree-left t)  ⇒  #(tree 0 1)
(tree-right t)  ⇒  #(tree 2 3)
(set-tree-left! t 0)
t  ⇒  #(tree 0 #(tree 2 3))
```

Since the bodies of the generated procedures are short and simple, it may be desirable to use `define-integrable` as defined above in place of `define` for some or all of the generated procedure definitions.

CHAPTER 9

Extended Examples

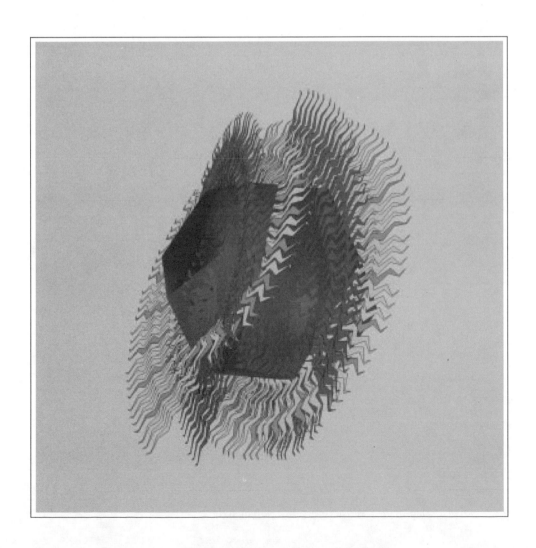

Two warped, two-armed spirals and one polyhedron.

This chapter presents a series of programs that perform more complicated tasks than most of the simpler examples found throughout the earlier chapters of the book. They illustrate a variety of programming techniques and demonstrate a particular programming style.

Each section of this chapter describes one program in detail. The program to be displayed is first described along with examples of its use. This is followed by a listing of the code. At the end of each section are exercises intended to stimulate thought about the program and to suggest possible extensions. These exercises are generally more difficult than those found in Chapters 2 and 3, and a few are major projects.

Section 9.1 presents a simple matrix multiplication package. It demonstrates a set of procedures that could be written in almost any language. Its most interesting features are that all multiplication operations are performed by calling a single *generic* procedure, `mul`, which calls the appropriate help procedure depending upon the dimensions of its arguments, and that it dynamically allocates results of the proper size. Section 9.2 presents a useful merge sorting algorithm for ordering lists according to arbitrary predicates. Section 9.3 describes a syntactic form that is used to construct sets. It demonstrates a simple but efficient syntactic transformation from set notation to Scheme code. Section 9.4 presents a word counting program borrowed from *The C Programming Language* [16], translated from C into Scheme. It shows character and string manipulation, data structure creation and manipulation, and basic file input and output. Section 9.5 presents a basic Scheme printer that supports both `write` and `display` for all standard object types. Section 9.6 presents a simple formatted output facility similar to those found in many Scheme systems and in other languages. Section 9.7 presents a simple interpreter for Scheme that illustrates Scheme as a language implementation vehicle while giving an informal operational semantics for Scheme as well as a useful basis for investigating extensions to Scheme. Section 9.8 presents a small, extensible abstract object facility that could serve as the basis for an entire object-oriented subsystem. Section 9.9 presents a recursive algorithm for computing the Fourier transform of a sequence of input values. It highlights the use of Scheme's complex arithmetic. Section 9.10 presents a concise unification algorithm that shows how procedures can be used as continuations and as substitutions (unifiers) in Scheme. Section 9.11 describes a multitasking facility and its implementation in terms of continuations.

9.1. Matrix and Vector Multiplication

This example program involves mostly basic programming techniques. It demonstrates simple arithmetic and vector operations, looping with the `do` syntactic form, dispatching based on object type, and generating error messages.

Multiplication of scalar to scalar, scalar to matrix, or matrix to matrix is performed by a single *generic* procedure, called `mul`. Because scalar multiplication uses Scheme's multiplication procedure, `*`, `mul` scalars can be any built-in numeric type (exact or inexact complex, real, rational, or integer).

The product of an $m \times n$ matrix A and an $n \times p$ matrix B is the $m \times p$ matrix C whose entries are defined by

$$C_{ij} = \sum_{k=0}^{n-1} A_{ik} B_{kj}.$$

The product of a scalar x and an $m \times n$ matrix A is the $m \times n$ matrix C whose entries are defined by the equation:

$$C_{ij} = x A_{ij}.$$

That is, each element of C is the product of x and the corresponding element of A. Vector-vector, vector-matrix, and matrix-vector multiplication may be considered special cases of matrix-matrix multiplication, where a vector is represented as a $1 \times n$ or $n \times 1$ matrix.

The structure of the code is worth explaining briefly. The first few definitions establish a set of procedures that support the matrix datatype. A matrix is a vector of vectors. Included are a procedure to create matrices, procedures to access and assign matrix elements, and a matrix predicate. Following these definitions is the definition of `mul` itself. Inside the `lambda` expression for `mul` are a set of definitions for help procedures that support `mul`.

The generic procedure `mul` checks the type of its arguments and chooses the appropriate help procedure to do the work. Each help procedure operates on arguments of specific types. For example, `mat-sca-mul` multiplies a matrix by a scalar. If the type of either argument is invalid or the arguments are incompatible, e.g., rows or columns do not match up, `mul` or one of the help procedures signals an error. Since standard Scheme does not include any mechanism for signaling errors, we use the *Chez Scheme* `error` procedure briefly described in Section 2.7.

The `mul` procedure is called with two arguments. Here are a few examples, each preceded by the equivalent operation in standard mathematical notation.

- Scalar times scalar:

$$3 \times 4 = 12$$

```
(mul 3 4)   ⟹   12
```

- Scalar times vector (1×3 matrix):

$$1/2 \times (1 \quad 2 \quad 3) = (1/2 \quad 1 \quad 3/2)$$

```
(mul 1/2 #(#(1 2 3)))   ⟹   #(#(1/2 1 3/2))
```

- Scalar times matrix:

$$-2 \times \begin{pmatrix} 3 & -2 & -1 \\ -3 & 0 & -5 \\ 7 & -1 & -1 \end{pmatrix} = \begin{pmatrix} -6 & 4 & 2 \\ 6 & 0 & 10 \\ -14 & 2 & 2 \end{pmatrix}$$

```
(mul -2
     #(#(3 -2 -1)
       #(-3 0 -5)
       #(7 -1 -1)))   ⇒   #(#(-6 4 2)
                             #(6 0 10)
                             #(-14 2 2))
```

- Vector times matrix:

$$(1 \quad 2 \quad 3) \times \begin{pmatrix} 2 & 3 \\ 3 & 4 \\ 4 & 5 \end{pmatrix} = (20 \quad 26)$$

```
(mul #(#(1 2 3))
     #(#(2 3)
       #(3 4)
       #(4 5)))   ⇒   #(#(20 26))
```

- Matrix times vector:

$$\begin{pmatrix} 2 & 3 & 4 \\ 3 & 4 & 5 \end{pmatrix} \times \begin{pmatrix} 1 \\ 2 \\ 3 \end{pmatrix} = \begin{pmatrix} 20 \\ 26 \end{pmatrix}$$

```
(mul #(#(2 3 4)
       #(3 4 5))
     #(#(1) #(2) #(3)))   ⇒   #(#(20) #(26))
```

- Matrix times matrix:

$$\begin{pmatrix} 1 & 2 & 3 \\ 4 & 5 & 6 \end{pmatrix} \times \begin{pmatrix} 1 & 2 & 3 & 4 \\ 2 & 3 & 4 & 5 \\ 3 & 4 & 5 & 6 \end{pmatrix} = \begin{pmatrix} 14 & 20 & 26 & 32 \\ 32 & 47 & 62 & 77 \end{pmatrix}$$

```
(mul #(#(1 2 3)
       #(4 5 6))
     #(#(1 2 3 4)
       #(2 3 4 5)
       #(3 4 5 6)))   ⇒   #(#(14 20 26 32)
                             #(32 47 62 77))
```

Exercises appear after the code at the end of the section.

```
;;; make-matrix creates a matrix (a vector of vectors).
(define make-matrix
  (lambda (rows columns)
    (do ((m (make-vector rows))
         (i 0 (+ i 1)))
        ((= i rows) m)
      (vector-set! m i (make-vector columns)))))
```

```
;;; matrix? checks to see if its argument is a matrix.
;;; It isn't foolproof, but it's generally good enough.
(define matrix?
  (lambda (x)
    (and (vector? x)
         (> (vector-length x) 0)
         (vector? (vector-ref x 0)))))

;;; matrix-ref returns the jth element of the ith row.
(define matrix-ref
  (lambda (m i j)
    (vector-ref (vector-ref m i) j)))

;;; matrix-set! changes the jth element of the ith row.
(define matrix-set!
  (lambda (m i j x)
    (vector-set! (vector-ref m i) j x)))

;;; mul is the generic matrix/scalar multiplication procedure
(define mul
  (lambda (x y)
    ;; type-error is called to complain when mul receives an invalid
    ;; type of argument.
    (define type-error
      (lambda (what)
        (error 'mul
          "~s is not a number or matrix"
          what)))

    ;; match-error is called to complain when mul receives a pair of
    ;; incompatible arguments.
    (define match-error
      (lambda (what1 what2)
        (error 'mul
          "~s and ~s are incompatible operands"
          what1
          what2)))

    ;; matrix-rows returns the number of rows in a matrix.
    (define matrix-rows
      (lambda (x)
        (vector-length x)))

    ;; matrix-columns returns the number of columns in a matrix.
    (define matrix-columns
      (lambda (x)
        (vector-length (vector-ref x 0))))
```

```scheme
;; mat-sca-mul multiplies a matrix by a scalar.
(define mat-sca-mul
   (lambda (m x)
      (let* ((nr (matrix-rows m))
             (nc (matrix-columns m))
             (r  (make-matrix nr nc)))
         (do ((i 0 (+ i 1)))
             ((= i nr) r)
             (do ((j 0 (+ j 1)))
                 ((= j nc))
                 (matrix-set! r i j
                    (* x (matrix-ref m i j))))))))

;; mat-mat-mul multiplies one matrix by another, after verifying
;; that the first matrix has as many columns as the second
;; matrix has rows.
(define mat-mat-mul
   (lambda (m1 m2)
      (let* ((nr1 (matrix-rows m1))
             (nr2 (matrix-rows m2))
             (nc2 (matrix-columns m2))
             (r   (make-matrix nr1 nc2)))
         (if (not (= (matrix-columns m1) nr2))
             (match-error m1 m2))
         (do ((i 0 (+ i 1)))
             ((= i nr1) r)
             (do ((j 0 (+ j 1)))
                 ((= j nc2))
                 (do ((k 0 (+ k 1))
                      (a 0
                         (+ a
                            (* (matrix-ref m1 i k)
                               (matrix-ref m2 k j)))))
                     ((= k nr2)
                      (matrix-set! r i j a))))))))

;; body of mul; dispatch based on input types
(cond
  ((number? x)
   (cond
     ((number? y) (* x y))
     ((matrix? y) (mat-sca-mul y x))
     (else (type-error y))))
  ((matrix? x)
   (cond
     ((number? y) (mat-sca-mul x y))
     ((matrix? y) (mat-mat-mul x y))
     (else (type-error y))))
  (else (type-error x))))
```

Exercise 9.1.1. Make the necessary changes to rename `mul` to `*`.

Exercise 9.1.2. The predicate `matrix?` is usually sufficient but not completely reliable, since it may return `#t` for objects that are not matrices. In particular, it does not verify that all of the matrix rows are vectors, that each row has the same number of elements, or that the elements themselves are numbers. Modify `matrix?` to perform each of these additional checks.

Exercise 9.1.3. Write similar generic procedures for addition and subtraction. Devise a generic `dispatch` procedure or syntactic form so that the type dispatching code need not be rewritten for each new operation.

Exercise 9.1.4. This version of `mul` uses vectors of vectors to represent matrices. Rewrite the system, using nested lists to represent matrices. What efficiency is gained or lost by this change?

9.2. List Sorting

This section illustrates a list sorting algorithm based on a simple technique known as merge sorting. The procedure `sort` defined here accepts two arguments: a predicate and a list. It returns a list containing the elements of the old list sorted according to the predicate. The predicate should be a procedure that expects two arguments and returns `#t` if and only if its first argument must precede its second in the sorted list. That is, if the predicate is applied to two elements x and y, where x appears after y in the input list, it should return true only if x should appear before y in the output list. If this constraint is met, `sort` will perform a *stable sort*; with a stable sort, two elements that are already sorted with respect to each other will appear in the output in the same order in which they appeared in the input. Thus, sorting a list that is already sorted will result in no reordering, even if there are equivalent elements.

```
(sort < '(3 4 2 1 2 5))   ⇒   (1 2 2 3 4 5)
(sort > '(0.5 1/2))   ⇒   (0.5 1/2)
(sort > '(1/2 0.5))   ⇒   (1/2 0.5))
(list->string
  (sort char>?
        (string->list "coins")))   ⇒   "sonic"
```

A companion procedure, `merge`, is also defined by the code. `merge` accepts a predicate and two sorted lists and returns a merged list in sorted order of the elements of the two lists. With a properly defined predicate, `merge` is also stable in the sense that an item from the first list will appear before an item from the second list unless it is necessary that the item from the second list appear first.

```
(merge char<?
       '(#\a #\c)
       '(#\b #\c #\d))  ⇒  (#\a #\b #\c #\c #\d)
(merge <
       '(1/2 2/3 3/4)
       '(0.5 0.6 0.7))  ⇒  (1/2 0.5 0.6 2/3 0.7 3/4)
```

The merge sorting algorithm works quite simply. The input list is split into two approximately equal sublists. These sublists are sorted recursively, yielding two sorted lists. The sorted lists are then merged to form a single sorted list. The base cases for the recursion are lists of one and two elements, which can be sorted trivially.

```
(define sort #f)
(define merge #f)
(let ()
  (define dosort
    (lambda (pred? ls n)
      (cond
        ((= n 1) (list (car ls)))
        ((= n 2) (let ((x (car ls)) (y (cadr ls)))
                   (if (pred? y x) (list y x) (list x y))))
        (else
          (let ((i (quotient n 2)))
            (domerge pred?
                     (dosort pred? ls i)
                     (dosort pred? (list-tail ls i) (- n i)))))))))
  (define domerge
    (lambda (pred? l1 l2)
      (cond
        ((null? l1) l2)
        ((null? l2) l1)
        ((pred? (car l2) (car l1))
         (cons (car l2) (domerge pred? l1 (cdr l2))))
        (else (cons (car l1) (domerge pred? (cdr l1) l2))))))
  (set! sort
    (lambda (pred? l)
      (if (null? l) l (dosort pred? l (length l)))))
  (set! merge
    (lambda (pred? l1 l2)
      (domerge pred? l1 l2))))
```

Exercise 9.2.1. In dosort, when n is 1, why is (list (car ls)) returned instead of ls? Similarly, when n is 2 and (pred? y x) is false, why is (list x y) returned instead of ls?

Exercise 9.2.2. Taking into account the answer to the previous exercise, how much work is actually saved by not copying the first part of the input list when splitting it in dosort?

Exercise 9.2.3. All or nearly all allocation could be saved if the algorithm were to work destructively, using set-cdr! to separate and join lists. Write destructive versions sort! and merge! of the sort and merge. Determine the difference between the two sets of procedures in terms of allocation and run time for various inputs.

9.3. A Set Constructor

This example describes a syntactic extension, set-of, that allows the construction of sets represented as lists with no repeated elements [19]. It uses define-syntax and syntax-rules to compile set expressions into recursion expressions. The expanded code is often as efficient as that which can be produced by hand.

A set-of expression takes the following form.

(set-of *value exp* ...)

value describes the elements of the set in terms of the bindings established by the expressions *exp* .... Each of the expressions *exp* ... can take one of three forms:

1. An expression of the form (x in s) establishes a binding for x to each element of the set s in turn. This binding is visible within the remaining expressions *exp* ... and the expression *value*.

2. An expression of the form (x is e) establishes a binding for x to e. This binding is visible within the remaining expressions *exp* ... and the expression *value*. This form is essentially an abbreviation for (x in (list e)).

3. An expression taking any other form is treated as a predicate; this is used to force refusal of certain elements as in the second of the examples below.

```
(set-of x
  (x in '(a b c)))  ⇒  (a b c)
(set-of x
  (x in '(1 2 3 4))
  (even? x))  ⇒  (2 4)
(set-of (cons x y)
  (x in '(1 2 3))
  (y is (* x x)))  ⇒  ((1 . 1) (2 . 4) (3 . 9))
```

```
(set-of (cons x y)
  (x in '(a b))
  (y in '(1 2)))   ⇒   ((a . 1) (a . 2) (b . 1) (b . 2))
```

A set-of expression is transformed into nested let, named let, and if expressions, corresponding to each is, in, or predicate subexpression. For example, the simple expression

```
(set-of x (x in '(a b c)))
```

is transformed into

```
(let loop ((set '(a b c)))
  (if (null? set)
      '()
      (let ((x (car set)))
        (set-cons x (loop (cdr set))))))
```

The expression

```
(set-of x (x in '(1 2 3 4)) (even? x))
```

is transformed into

```
(let loop ((set '(1 2 3 4)))
  (if (null? set)
      '()
      (let ((x (car set)))
        (if (even? x)
            (set-cons x (loop (cdr set)))
            (loop (cdr set))))))
```

The more complicated expression

```
(set-of (cons x y) (x in '(1 2 3)) (y is (* x x)))
```

is transformed into

```
(let loop ((set '(1 2 3)))
  (if (null? set)
      '()
      (let ((x (car set)))
        (let ((y (* x x)))
          (set-cons (cons x y)
                    (loop (cdr set)))))))
```

Finally, the expression

```
(set-of (cons x y) (x in '(a b)) (y in '(1 2)))
```

is transformed into nested named let expressions:

```
(let loop1 ((set1 '(a b)))
  (if (null? set1)
      '()
      (let ((x (car set1)))
        (let loop2 ((set2 '(1 2)))
          (if (null? set2)
              (loop1 (cdr set1))
              (let ((y (car set2)))
                (set-cons (cons x y)
                          (loop2 (cdr set2)))))))))
```

These are fairly straightforward transformations, except that the base case for the recursion on nested named `let` expressions varies depending upon the level. The base case for the outermost named `let` is always the empty list (), while the base case for an internal named `let` is the recursion step for the next outer named `let`. In order to handle this, the definition of `set-of` employs a help syntactic extension `set-of-help`. `set-of-help` takes an additional expression, `base`, which is the base case for recursion at the current level.

```
;;; set-of uses helper syntactic extension set-of-help, passing it
;;; an initial base expression of '()
(define-syntax set-of
  (syntax-rules ()
    ((_ e m ...)
     (set-of-help e '() m ...))))

;;; set-of-help recognizes in, is, and predicate expressions and
;;; changes them into nested named let, let, and if expressions.
(define-syntax set-of-help
  (syntax-rules (in is)
    ((_ e base)
     (set-cons e base))
    ((_ e base (x in s) m ...)
     (let loop ((set s))
       (if (null? set)
           base
           (let ((x (car set)))
             (set-of-help e (loop (cdr set)) m ...)))))
    ((_ e base (x is y) m ...)
     (let ((x y)) (set-of-help e base m ...)))
    ((_ e base p m ...)
     (if p (set-of-help e base m ...) base))))

;;; set-cons returns the original set y if x is already in y.
(define set-cons
  (lambda (x y)
    (if (memv x y)
        y
        (cons x y))))
```

Exercise 9.3.1. Write a procedure, **union**, that takes an arbitrary number of sets (lists) as arguments and returns the union of the sets, using only the **set-of** syntactic form. For example:

```
(union)  ⇒  ()
(union '(a b c))  ⇒  (a b c)
(union '(2 5 4) '(9 4 3))  ⇒  (2 5 9 4 3)
(union '(1 2) '(2 4) '(4 8))  ⇒  (1 2 4 8)
```

Exercise 9.3.2. A single-list version of **map** can (almost) be defined as follows:

```
(define map1
  (lambda (f ls)
    (set-of (f x) (x in ls))))
(map1 - '(1 2 3 2))  ⇒  (-1 -3 -2)
```

Why does this not work? What could be changed to make it work?

Exercise 9.3.3. Devise a different definition for **set-cons** that maintains sets in some sorted order, making the test for set membership, and hence **set-cons** itself, potentially more efficient.

9.4. Word Frequency Counting

This program demonstrates several basic programming techniques, including string and character manipulation, file input/output, data structure manipulation, and recursion. As was mentioned in the introduction to this chapter, the program is adapted from Chapter 6 of *The C Programming Language* [16]. One reason for using this particular example is to show how a C program might look when converted almost literally into Scheme.

A few differences between the Scheme program and the original C program are worth noting. First, the Scheme version employs a different protocol for file input and output. Rather than implicitly use the standard input and output ports, it requires that filenames be passed in, thus demonstrating the opening and closing of files. Second, the procedure **get-word** returns one of three values: a string (the word), a nonalphabetic character, or an eof value. The original C version returned a flag for letter (to say that a word was read) or a nonalphabetic character. Furthermore, the C version passed in a string to fill and a limit on the number of characters in the string; the Scheme version builds a new string of whatever length is required (the characters in the word are held in a list until the end of the word has been found, then converted into a string with **list->string**). Finally, **char-type** uses the primitive Scheme character predicates **char-alphabetic?** and **char-numeric?** to determine whether a character is a letter or digit.

The main program, **frequency**, takes an input filename and an output filename as arguments, e.g., **(frequency "pickle" "freq.out")** prints the frequency count for each word in the file **"pickle"** to the file **"freq.out"**. As **frequency** reads words from the input file, it inserts them into a binary tree structure (using a binary sorting algorithm). Duplicate entries are recorded by incrementing the count associated with each word. Once end of file is reached, the program traverses the tree, printing each word with its count.

Assume that the file `"pickle"` contains the following text.

```
Peter Piper picked a peck of pickled peppers;
A peck of pickled peppers Peter Piper picked.
If Peter Piper picked a peck of pickled peppers,
Where's the peck of pickled peppers Peter Piper picked?
```

Then, after typing `(frequency "pickle" "freq.out")`, the file `"freq.out"` should contain the following.

```
1 A
1 If
4 Peter
4 Piper
1 Where
2 a
4 of
4 peck
4 peppers
4 picked
4 pickled
1 s
1 the
```

(On some systems, the capitalized words may appear after the others.)

```
;;; If the next character on p is a letter, get-word reads a word
;;; from p and returns it in a string.  If the character is not a
;;; letter, get-word returns the character (on eof, the eof-object).
(define get-word
  (lambda (p)
    (let ((c (read-char p)))
      (if (eq? (char-type c) 'letter)
          (list->string
            (let loop ((c c))
              (cons c
                (if (memq (char-type (peek-char p)) '(letter digit))
                    (loop (read-char p))
                    '()))))
          c))))
```

```
;;; char-type tests for the eof-object first, since the eof-object
;;; may not be a valid argument to char-alphabetic? or char-numeric?
;;; It returns the eof-object, the symbol letter, the symbol digit,
;;; or the argument itself if it is not a letter or digit.
(define char-type
  (lambda (c)
    (cond
      ((eof-object? c) c)
      ((char-alphabetic? c) 'letter)
      ((char-numeric? c) 'digit)
      (else c))))

;;; Trees are represented as vectors with four fields: word, left,
;;; right, and count.  Only one field, word, is initialized by an
;;; argument to the constructor procedure make-tree.  The remaining
;;; fields are explicitly initialized and changed by subsequent
;;; operations.  Most Scheme systems provide structure definition
;;; facilities that automate creation of structure manipulation
;;; procedures, but we simply define the procedures by hand here.
(define make-tree
  (lambda (word)
    (vector word '() '() 1)))

(define tree-word (lambda (tree) (vector-ref tree 0)))

(define tree-left (lambda (tree) (vector-ref tree 1)))
(define set-tree-left!
  (lambda (tree new-left)
    (vector-set! tree 1 new-left)))

(define tree-right (lambda (tree) (vector-ref tree 2)))
(define set-tree-right!
  (lambda (tree new-right)
    (vector-set! tree 2 new-right)))

(define tree-count (lambda (tree) (vector-ref tree 3)))
(define set-tree-count!
  (lambda (tree new-count)
    (vector-set! tree 3 new-count)))

;;; If the word already exists in the tree, tree increments its
;;; count.  Otherwise, a new tree node is created and put into the
;;; tree.  In any case, the new or modified tree is returned.
(define tree
  (lambda (node word)
    (cond
      ((null? node) (make-tree word))
      ((string=? word (tree-word node))
       (set-tree-count! node (+ (tree-count node) 1))
       node)
      ((string<? word (tree-word node))
       (set-tree-left! node (tree (tree-left node) word))
       node)
```

```
        (else
         (set-tree-right! node (tree (tree-right node) word))
         node)))))
;;; tree-print prints the tree in "in-order," i.e., left subtree,
;;; then node, then right subtree.  For each word, the count and the
;;; word are printed on a single line.
(define tree-print
  (lambda (node p)
    (if (not (null? node))
        (begin
          (tree-print (tree-left node) p)
          (write (tree-count node) p)
          (write-char #\space p)
          (display (tree-word node) p)
          (newline p)
          (tree-print (tree-right node) p)))))
;;; frequency is the driver routine.  It opens the files, reads the
;;; words, and enters them into the tree.  When the input port
;;; reaches end-of-file, it prints the tree and closes the ports.
(define frequency
  (lambda (infn outfn)
    (let ((ip (open-input-file infn))
          (op (open-output-file outfn)))
      (let loop ((root '()))
        (let ((w (get-word ip)))
          (cond
            ((eof-object? w) (tree-print root op))
            ((string? w) (loop (tree root w)))
            (else (loop root)))))
      (close-input-port ip)
      (close-output-port op))))
```

Exercise 9.4.1. Replace the procedures used to implement the tree datatype with a structure definition, using the facilities provided by the Scheme system you are using or define-structure from Section 8.4.

Exercise 9.4.2. In the output file shown earlier, the capitalized words appeared before the others in the output file, and the capital A was not recognized as the same word as the lowercase a. Modify tree to use the case-insensitive versions of the string comparisons so that this does not happen.

Exercise 9.4.3. The "word" s appears in the file "freq.out", although it is really just a part of the contraction Where's. Adjust get-word to allow embedded single quote marks.

Exercise 9.4.4. Modify this program to "weed out" certain common words such as a, an, the, is, of, etc., in order to reduce the amount of output for long input files. Try to devise other ways to cut down on useless output.

Exercise 9.4.5. get-word buffers characters in a list, allocating a new pair (with cons) for each character. Make it more efficient by using a string to buffer the characters. Devise a way to allow the string to grow if necessary. [*Hint*: Use string-append.]

Exercise 9.4.6. This tree algorithm works by creating trees and later filling in its left and right fields. This requires many unnecessary assignments. Rewrite the tree procedure to avoid set-tree-left! and set-tree-right! entirely.

9.5. Scheme Printer

Printing Scheme objects may seem like a complicated process, but in fact a rudimentary printer is quite straightforward, as this example demonstrates. Both write and display are supported by the same code. Sophisticated Scheme implementations often support various printer controls and handle printing of cyclic objects, but the one given here is completely basic.

The main driver for the program is a procedure wr, which takes an object to print x, a flag d?, and a port p. The flag d? is #t if the code is to *display* the object, #f if it is to *write* the object. The d? flag is important only for characters and strings. Recall from Section 7.2 that display prints strings without the enclosing quote marks and characters without the #\ syntax.

The entry points write and display handle the optionality of the second (port) argument, passing the value of current-output-port when no port argument is provided.

Procedures, ports, and end-of-file objects are printed as #<procedure>, #<port>, and #<eof>. The tests for the end-of-file objects and ports are made early, since implementations are permitted to implement these object types as special cases of other object types. Objects of types not recognized by the printer are printed as #<unknown>; this can occur if the Scheme implementation provides extensions to the standard set of object types.

The code follows the module structure outlined in Section 3.5.

```
(define write #f)
(define display #f)
```

```scheme
(let ()
  ;; wr is the driver, dispatching on the type of x
  (define wr
    (lambda (x d? p)
      (cond
        ((eof-object? x) (write-string "#<eof>" p))
        ((port? x) (write-string "#<port>" p))
        ((symbol? x) (write-string (symbol->string x) p))
        ((pair? x) (wrpair x d? p))
        ((number? x) (write-string (number->string x) p))
        ((null? x) (write-string "()" p))
        ((boolean? x) (write-string (if x "#t" "#f") p))
        ((char? x) (if d? (write-char x p) (wrchar x p)))
        ((string? x) (if d? (write-string x p) (wrstring x p)))
        ((vector? x) (wrvector x d? p))
        ((procedure? x) (write-string "#<procedure>" p))
        (else (write-string "#<unknown>" p)))))

  ;; write-string writes each character of s to p
  (define write-string
    (lambda (s p)
      (let ((n (string-length s)))
        (do ((i 0 (+ i 1)))
            ((= i n))
          (write-char (string-ref s i) p)))))

  ;; wrpair handles pairs and nonempty lists
  (define wrpair
    (lambda (x d? p)
      (write-char #\( p)
      (let loop ((x x))
        (wr (car x) d? p)
        (cond
          ((pair? (cdr x))
           (write-char #\space p)
           (loop (cdr x)))
          ((null? (cdr x)))
          (else
           (write-string " . " p)
           (wr (cdr x) d? p))))
      (write-char #\) p)))

  ;; wrchar handles characters, recognizing and printing the
  ;; special syntaxes for #\space and #\newline.  Used only when
  ;; d? is #f.
  (define wrchar
    (lambda (x p)
      (case x
        ((#\newline) (write-string "#\\newline" p))
        ((#\space) (write-string "#\\space" p))
```

```
          (else (write-string "#\\" p)
                (write-char x p)))))

;; wrstring handles strings, inserting slashes where
;; necessary.  Used only when d? is #f.
(define wrstring
  (lambda (x p)
    (write-char #\" p)
    (let ((n (string-length x)))
      (do ((i 0 (+ i 1)))
          ((= i n))
          (let ((c (string-ref x i)))
            (if (or (char=? c #\") (char=? c #\\))
                (write-char #\\ p))
            (write-char c p))))
    (write-char #\" p)))

;; wrvector handles vectors
(define wrvector
  (lambda (x d? p)
    (write-string "#(" p)
    (let ((size (vector-length x)))
      (if (not (= size 0))
          (let ((last (- size 1)))
            (let loop ((i 0))
              (wr (vector-ref x i) d? p)
              (if (not (= i last))
                  (begin
                    (write-char #\space p)
                    (loop (+ i 1))))))))
    (write-char #\) p)))

;; write calls wr with d? set to #f
(set! write
  (lambda (x . rest)
    (if (null? rest)
        (wr x #f (current-output-port))
        (wr x #f (car rest)))))

;; display calls wr with d? set to #t
(set! display
  (lambda (x . rest)
    (if (null? rest)
        (wr x #t (current-output-port))
        (wr x #t (car rest))))))
```

Exercise 9.5.1. Numbers are printed with the help of number->string. Correct printing of all Scheme numeric types, especially inexact numbers, is a complicated task. Handling exact integers and rational numbers is fairly straightforward, however. Modify the code to print exact integers and rational numbers directly (without `number->string`), but continue to use `number->string` for inexact and complex numbers.

Exercise 9.5.2. Modify `wr` and its helpers to direct their output to an internal buffer rather than to a port. Use the modified versions to implement a procedure `object->string` that, like `number->string`, returns a string containing a printed representation of its input. For example:

```
(object->string '(a b c))  ⇒  "(a b c)"
(object->string "hello")  ⇒  "\"hello\""
```

You may be surprised just how easy this change is to make.

9.6. Formatted Output

It is often necessary to print strings containing the printed representations of Scheme objects, especially numbers. Doing so with Scheme's standard output routines can be tedious. For example, the `tree-print` procedure of Section 9.4 requires a sequence of four calls to output routines to print a simple one-line message:

```
(write (tree-count node) p)
(write-char #\space p)
(display (tree-word node) p)
(newline p)
```

The formatted output facility defined in this section allows these four calls to be replaced by the single call to `fprintf` below:

```
(fprintf p "~s ~a~%" (tree-count node) (tree-word node))
```

`fprintf` expects a port argument, a *control string*, and an indefinite number of additional arguments that are inserted into the output as specified by the control string. In the example, the value of `(tree-count node)` is written first, in place of `~s`. This is followed by a space and the displayed value of `(tree-word node)`, in place of `~a`. The `~%` is replaced in the output with a newline.

The procedure `printf`, also defined in this section, is like `fprintf` except that no port argument is expected and output is sent to the current output port.

`~s`, `~a`, and `~%` are *format directives*; `~s` causes the first unused argument after the control string to be printed to the output via `write`, `~a` causes the first unused argument to be printed via `display`, and `~%` simply causes a newline character to be printed. The simple implementation of `fprintf` below recognizes only one other format directive, `~~`, which inserts a tilde into the output. For example,

```
(printf "The string ~s displays as ~~.~%" "~")
```

prints

```
The string "~" displays as ~.
```

Uppercase `~A` and `~S` are equivalent to lowercase `~a` and `~s`.

```
(let ()
  ;; dofmt does all of the work.  It loops through the control
  ;; string, recognizing format directives and printing all other
  ;; characters without interpretation.  A tilde at the end of
  ;; a control string is treated as an ordinary character.  No
  ;; checks are made for proper inputs.
  (define dofmt
    (lambda (p cntl args)
      (let ((nmax (- (string-length cntl) 1)))
        (let loop ((n 0) (a args))
          (if (<= n nmax)
              (let ((c (string-ref cntl n)))
                (if (and (char=? c #\~) (< n nmax))
                    (case (string-ref cntl (+ n 1))
                      ((#\a #\A)
                       (display (car a) p)
                       (loop (+ n 2) (cdr a)))
                      ((#\s #\S)
                       (write (car a) p)
                       (loop (+ n 2) (cdr a)))
                      ((#\%)
                       (newline p)
                       (loop (+ n 2) a))
                      ((#\~)
                       (write-char #\~ p)
                       (loop (+ n 2) a))
                      (else
                       (write-char c p)
                       (loop (+ n 1) a)))
                    (begin
                      (write-char c p)
                      (loop (+ n 1) a)))))))))
  ;; printf and fprintf differ only in that fprintf passes its
  ;; port argument to dofmt while printf passes the current output
  ;; port.
  (set! printf
    (lambda (control . args)
      (dofmt (current-output-port) control args)))
  (set! fprintf
    (lambda (p control . args)
      (dofmt p control args))))
```

Exercise 9.6.1. Using the optional radix argument to number->string, augment printf and fprintf with support for the following new format directives:

    a. ~b or ~B: print the next unused argument, which must be a number, in binary;

    b. ~o or ~O: print the next unused argument, which must be a number, in octal; and

  c. ˜x or ˜X: print the next unused argument, which must be a number, in
   hexadecimal.

For example:

(printf "#x˜x #o˜o #b˜b˜%" 16 8 2)

would print

#x10 #o10 #b10

Exercise 9.6.2. Add an "indirect" format directive, ˜@, that treats the next
unused argument, which must be a string, as if it were spliced into the current
format string. For example:

(printf "--- ˜@ ---" "> ˜s <" '(a b c))

would print

---> (a b c) <---

Exercise 9.6.3. Implement format, a version of fprintf that places its output
into a string instead of writing to a port. Make use of object->string from Exercise 9.5.2 to support the ˜s and ˜a directives.

(let ((x 3) (y 4))
 (format "˜s + ˜s = ˜s" x y (+ x y))) ⇒ "3 + 4 = 7"

Exercise 9.6.4. Modify format, fprintf, and printf to allow a field size to
be specified after the tilde in the ˜a and ˜s format directives. For example, the
directive ˜10s would cause the next unused argument to be inserted into the output
left-justified in a field of size 10. If the object requires more spaces than the amount
specified, allow it to extend beyond the field.

(let ((x 'abc) (y '(def)))
 (format "(cons '˜5s '˜5s) = ˜5s"
  x y (cons x y))) ⇒ "(cons 'abc '(def)) = (abc def)"

[*Hint*: Use format recursively.]

9.7. A Meta-Circular Interpreter for Scheme

The program described in this section is a *meta-circular* interpreter for Scheme, i.e.,
it is an interpreter *for* Scheme written *in* Scheme. The interpreter shows how small
Scheme is when the core structure is considered independently from its syntactic
extensions and primitives. It also illustrates interpretation techniques that can be
applied equally well to languages other than Scheme.

  The relative simplicity of the interpreter is somewhat misleading. An interpreter
for Scheme written in Scheme can be quite a bit simpler than one written in most
other languages. Here are a few reasons why this one is simpler.

- Tail calls are handled properly only because tail calls in the interpreter are handled properly by the host implementation. All that is required is that the interpreter itself be tail-recursive.

- First-class procedures in interpreted code are implemented by first-class procedures in the interpreter, which in turn are supported by the host implementation.

- First-class continuations created with `call/cc` are provided by the host implementation's `call/cc`.

- Primitive procedures such as `cons` and `assq` and services such as storage management are provided by the host implementation.

Converting the interpreter to run in a language other than Scheme may require explicit support for some or all of these items.

The interpreter stores lexical bindings in an *environment*, which is simply an *association list* (see `assq`). Evaluation of a `lambda` expression results in the creation of a procedure within the scope of variables holding the environment and the `lambda` body. Subsequent application of the procedure combines the new bindings (the actual parameters) with the saved environment.

The interpreter handles only the core syntactic forms described in Section 3.1, and it recognizes bindings for only a handful of primitive procedures. It performs no error checking.

```
(interpret 3)  ⇒  3

(interpret '(cons 3 4))  ⇒  (3 . 4)

(interpret
  '((lambda (x . y)
      (list x y))
    'a 'b 'c 'd))  ⇒  (a (b c d))

(interpret
  '(((call/cc (lambda (k) k))
     (lambda (x) x))
    "HEY!"))  ⇒  "HEY!"

(interpret
  '((lambda (memq)
      (memq memq 'a '(b c a d e)))
    (lambda (memq x ls)
      (if (null? ls) #f
          (if (eq? (car ls) x)
              ls
              (memq memq x (cdr ls)))))))  ⇒  (a d e)
```

```
(interpret
  '((lambda (reverse)
      (set! reverse
        (lambda (ls new)
          (if (null? ls)
              new
              (reverse (cdr ls) (cons (car ls) new)))))
      (reverse '(a b c d e) '())))
  #f))  ⇒  (e d c b a)
```

```
(define interpret #f)
(let ()
  ;; primitive-environment is an environment containing a small
  ;; number of primitive procedures; it can be extended easily
  ;; to include additional primitives.
  (define primitive-environment
    (list (cons 'apply apply)
          (cons 'assq assq)
          (cons 'call/cc call/cc)
          (cons 'car car)
          (cons 'cadr cadr)
          (cons 'caddr caddr)
          (cons 'cadddr cadddr)
          (cons 'cddr cddr)
          (cons 'cdr cdr)
          (cons 'cons cons)
          (cons 'eq? eq?)
          (cons 'list list)
          (cons 'map map)
          (cons 'memv memv)
          (cons 'null? null?)
          (cons 'pair? pair?)
          (cons 'read read)
          (cons 'set-car! set-car!)
          (cons 'set-cdr! set-cdr!)
          (cons 'symbol? symbol?)))

  ;; new-env returns a new environment from a formal parameter
  ;; specification, a list of actual parameters, and an outer
  ;; environment.  The symbol? test identifies "improper"
  ;; argument lists.  Environments are association lists,
  ;; associating variables with values.
  (define new-env
    (lambda (formals actuals env)
      (cond
        ((null? formals) env)
        ((symbol? formals) (cons (cons formals actuals) env))
        (else
         (cons (cons (car formals) (car actuals))
               (new-env (cdr formals) (cdr actuals) env))))))
```

```
;; lookup finds the value of the variable var in the environment
;; env, using assq.  Assumes var is bound in env.
(define lookup
  (lambda (var env)
    (cdr (assq var env))))

;; assign is similar to lookup but alters the binding of the
;; variable var in the environment env by changing the cdr of
;; association pair
(define assign
  (lambda (var val env)
    (set-cdr! (assq var env) val)))

;; exec evaluates the expression, recognizing all core forms.
(define exec
  (lambda (exp env)
    (cond
      ((symbol? exp) (lookup exp env))
      ((pair? exp)
       (case (car exp)
         ((quote) (cadr exp))
         ((lambda)
          (lambda vals
            (let ((env (new-env (cadr exp) vals env)))
              (let loop ((exps (cddr exp)))
                (if (null? (cdr exps))
                    (exec (car exps) env)
                    (begin
                      (exec (car exps) env)
                      (loop (cdr exps))))))))
         ((if)
          (if (exec (cadr exp) env)
              (exec (caddr exp) env)
              (exec (cadddr exp) env)))
         ((set!)
          (assign (cadr exp)
                  (exec (caddr exp) env)
                  env))
         (else
          (apply (exec (car exp) env)
                 (map (lambda (x) (exec x env))
                      (cdr exp))))))
      (else exp))))

;; interpret starts execution with the primitive environment.
(set! interpret
  (lambda (exp)
    (exec exp  primitive-environment)))
```

Exercise 9.7.1. As written, the interpreter cannot interpret itself because it does not support several of the syntactic forms used in its implementation: `let` (named and unnamed), internal `define`, `case`, `cond`, and `begin`. Rewrite the code for the interpreter, using only core syntactic forms.

Exercise 9.7.2. After completing the preceding exercise, use the interpreter to run a copy of the interpreter, and use the copy to run another copy of the interpreter. Repeat this process to see how many levels deep it will go before the Scheme system grinds to a halt.

Exercise 9.7.3. At first glance, it might seem that the `lambda` case could be written more simply as follows:

```
((lambda)
 (lambda vals
   (let ((env (new-env (cadr exp) vals env)))
     (let loop ((exps (cddr exp)))
       (let ((val (exec (car exps) env)))
         (if (null? (cdr exps))
             val
             (loop (cdr exps))))))))
```

Why would this be incorrect? [*Hint*: What property of Scheme would be violated?]

Exercise 9.7.4. Try to make the interpreter more efficient by looking for ways to ask fewer questions or to allocate less storage space. [*Hint*: Before evaluation, convert lexical variable references into (`access` n), where n represents the number of values in the environment association list in front of the value in question.]

Exercise 9.7.5. Scheme evaluates arguments to a procedure before applying the procedure and applies the procedure to the values of these arguments (*call-by-value*). Modify the interpreter to pass arguments unevaluated and arrange to evaluate them upon reference (*call-by-name*). [*Hint*: Use `lambda` to delay evaluation.] You will need to create versions of the primitive procedures (`car`, `null?`, etc.) that take their arguments unevaluated.

9.8. Defining Abstract Objects

This example demonstrates a syntactic extension that facilitates the definition of simple abstract objects (see Section 2.9). This facility has unlimited potential as the basis for a complete object-oriented subsystem in Scheme.

Abstract objects are similar to basic data structures such as pairs and vectors. Rather than being manipulated via access and assignment operators, however, abstract objects respond to *messages*. The valid messages and the actions to be taken for each message are defined by code within the object itself rather than by code outside the object, resulting in more modular and potentially more secure programming systems. The data local to an abstract object is accessible only through the actions performed by the object in response to the messages.

A particular type of abstract object is defined with `define-object`, which has the general form

```
(define-object (name var₁ ...)
  ((var₂ val) ...)
  ((msg action) ...))
```

The first set of bindings $((var_2 \ val) \ ...)$ may be omitted. `define-object` defines a procedure that is called to create new abstract objects of the given type. This procedure is called *name*, and the arguments to this procedure become the values of the local variables var_1 .... After the procedure is invoked, the variables var_2 ... are bound to the values *val* ... in sequence (as with `let*`) and the messages *msg* ... are bound to the procedure values *action* ... in a mutually recursive fashion (as with `letrec`). Within these bindings, the new abstract object is created; this object is the value of the creation procedure.

The syntactic form `send-message` is used to send messages to abstract objects. (`send-message` *object msg arg* ...) sends *object* the message *msg* with arguments *arg* .... When an object receives a message, the *arg* ... become the parameters to the action procedure associated with the message, and the value returned by this procedure is returned by `send-message`.

The following examples should help to clarify how abstract objects are defined and used. The first example is a simple `kons` object that is similar to Scheme's built-in pair object type, except that to access or assign its fields requires sending it messages.

```
(define-object (kons kar kdr)
  ((get-car (lambda () kar))
   (get-cdr (lambda () kdr))
   (set-car! (lambda (x) (set! kar x)))
   (set-cdr! (lambda (x) (set! kdr x)))))

(define p (kons 'a 'b))
(send-message p get-car)   ⇒   a
(send-message p get-cdr)   ⇒   b
(send-message p set-cdr! 'c)
(send-message p get-cdr)   ⇒   c
```

The simple `kons` object does nothing but return or assign one of the fields as requested. What makes abstract objects interesting is that they can be used to restrict access or perform additional services. The following version of `kons` requires that a password be given with any request to assign one of the fields. This password is a parameter to the `kons` procedure.

```
(define-object (kons kar kdr pwd)
  ((get-car (lambda () kar))
   (get-cdr (lambda () kar))
   (set-car!
     (lambda (x p)
       (if (string=? p pwd)
           (set! kar x))))
   (set-cdr!
     (lambda (x p)
       (if (string=? p pwd)
           (set! kar x)))))
(define p1 (kons 'a 'b "magnificent"))
(send-message p1 set-car! 'c "magnificent")
(send-message p1 get-car)  ⇒  c
(send-message p1 set-car! 'd "please")
(send-message p1 get-car)  ⇒  c

(define p2 (kons 'x 'y "please"))
(send-message p2 set-car! 'z "please")
(send-message p2 get-car)  ⇒  z
```

One important ability of an abstract object is that it can keep statistics on messages sent to it. The following version of **kons** counts accesses to the two fields. This version also demonstrates the use of explicitly initialized local bindings.

```
(define-object (kons kar kdr)
  ((count 0))
  ((get-car
    (lambda ()
      (set! count (+ count 1))
      kar))
   (get-cdr
    (lambda ()
      (set! count (+ count 1))
      kdr))
   (accesses
    (lambda () count))))
(define p (kons 'a 'b))
(send-message p get-car)   ⇒  a
(send-message p get-cdr)   ⇒  b
(send-message p accesses)  ⇒  2
(send-message p get-cdr)   ⇒  b
(send-message p accesses)  ⇒  3
```

The implementation of **define-object** is straightforward. The object definition is transformed into a definition of the object creation procedure. This procedure is the value of a **lambda** expression whose arguments are those specified in the definition. The body of the **lambda** consists of a **let*** expression to bind the local variables and a **letrec** expression to bind the message names to the action procedures. The body of the **letrec** is another **lambda** expression whose value represents the new object. The body of this `lambda` expression compares the messages passed in with the expected messages using a `case` expression and applies the corresponding action procedure to the remaining arguments.

For example, the definition

```
(define-object (kons kar kdr)
  ((count 0))
  ((get-car
    (lambda ()
      (set! count (+ count 1))
      kar))
   (get-cdr
    (lambda ()
      (set! count (+ count 1))
      kdr))
   (accesses
    (lambda () count))))
```

is transformed into

```
(define kons
  (lambda (kar kdr)
    (let* ((count 0))
      (letrec ((get-car
                 (lambda ()
                   (set! count (+ count 1)) kar))
               (get-cdr
                 (lambda ()
                   (set! count (+ count 1)) kdr))
               (accesses (lambda () count)))
        (lambda (msg . args)
          (case msg
            ((get-car) (apply get-car args))
            ((get-cdr) (apply get-cdr args))
            ((accesses) (apply accesses args))
            (else
             (error 'kons "invalid message ~s"
               (cons msg args)))))))))
```

```
;;; define-object creates an object constructor that uses let* to bind
;;; local fields and letrec to define the exported procedures.  An
;;; object is itself a procedure that accepts messages corresponding
;;; to the names of the exported procedures.  The second pattern is
;;; used to allow the set of local fields to be omitted.
(define-syntax define-object
  (syntax-rules ()
    ((_ (name . varlist)
        ((var1 val1) ...)
        ((var2 val2) ...))
     (define name
```

```
      (lambda varlist
        (let* ((var1 val1) ...)
          (letrec ((var2 val2) ...)
            (lambda (msg . args)
              (case msg
                ((var2) (apply var2 args)) ...
                (else
                 (error 'name "invalid message ~s"
                     (cons msg args))))))))))))
  ((_ (name . varlist)
      ((var2 val2) ...))
   (define-object (name . varlist)
     ()
     ((var2 val2) ...)))))
```
```
;;; send-message abstracts the act of sending a message from the act
;;; of applying a procedure and allows the message to be unquoted.
(define-syntax send-message
  (syntax-rules ()
    ((_ obj msg arg ...)
     (obj 'msg arg ...))))
```

Exercise 9.8.1. Use `define-object` to define the `stack` object type from Section 2.9.

Exercise 9.8.2. Use `define-object` to define a `queue` object type. A `queue` object should accept the messages `empty?`, `get!` (removes and returns the first element), and `put!` (adds an element to the end of the queue). Elements should be removed in the same order as they are entered.

Exercise 9.8.3. It is often useful to describe one object in terms of another. For example, the second `kons` object type could be described as the same as the first but with a password argument and different actions associated with the `set-car!` and `set-cdr!` messages. This is called *inheritance*; the new type of object is said to *inherit* attributes from the first. Modify `define-object` to support inheritance by allowing the optional declaration (`inherit object-name`) to appear after the message/action pairs. This will require saving some information about each object definition for possible use in subsequent object definitions. Conflicting argument names should be disallowed, but other conflicts should be resolved by using the initialization or action specified in the new object definition.

Exercise 9.8.4. What if we want to describe an object type in terms not of just one but of two or more existing object types? Further modify `define-object` to support *multiple inheritance* by extending the `inherit` expression to allow multiple object names. What should happen if two or more inherited objects initialize a conflicting variable or message name differently?

9.9. Fast Fourier Transform

The program described in this section uses Scheme's complex arithmetic to compute the discrete *Fourier transform* (DFT) of a sequence of values [3]. Discrete Fourier transforms are used to analyze and process sampled signal sequences in a wide variety of digital electronics applications such as pattern recognition, bandwidth compression, radar target detection, and weather surveillance.

The DFT of a sequence of N input values,

$$\{x(n)\}_{n=0}^{N-1},$$

is the sequence of N output values,

$$\{X(m)\}_{m=0}^{N-1},$$

each defined by the equation

$$X(m) = \sum_{n=0}^{N-1} x(n)e^{-i\frac{2\pi mn}{N}}.$$

It is convenient to abstract away the constant amount (for given N)

$$W_N = e^{-i\frac{2\pi}{N}},$$

in order to obtain the more concise but equivalent equation

$$X(m) = \sum_{n=0}^{N-1} x(n)W_N^{mn}.$$

A straightforward computation of the N output values, each as a sum of N intermediate values, requires on the order of N^2 operations. A *fast* Fourier transform (FFT), applicable when N is a power of 2, requires only on the order of $N \log_2 N$ operations. Although usually presented as a rather complicated iterative algorithm, the fast Fourier transform is most concisely and elegantly expressed as a recursive algorithm [6]. The recursive algorithm can be derived by manipulating the preceding summation as follows. We first split the summation into two summations and recombine them into one summation from 0 to $N/2 - 1$.

$$
\begin{aligned}
X(m) &= \sum_{n=0}^{N/2-1} x(n)W_N^{mn} + \sum_{n=N/2}^{N-1} x(n)W_N^{mn} \\
&= \sum_{n=0}^{N/2-1} [x(n)W_N^{mn} + x(n+N/2)W_N^{m(n+N/2)}]
\end{aligned}
$$

We then pull out the common factor W_N^{mn}.

$$
X(m) = \sum_{n=0}^{N/2-1} [x(n) + x(n+N/2)W_N^{m(N/2)}]W_N^{mn}
$$

We can reduce $W_N^{m(N/2)}$ to 1 when m is even and -1 when m is odd, since

$$W_N^{m(N/2)} = W_2^m = e^{-i\pi m} = \begin{cases} 1, & m \text{ even} \\ -1, & m \text{ odd}. \end{cases}$$

This allows us to specialize the summation for the even and odd cases of $m = 2k$ and $m = 2k + 1$, $0 \le k \le N/2 - 1$.

$$X(2k) = \sum_{n=0}^{N/2-1} [x(n) + x(n + N/2)] W_N^{2kn}$$

$$= \sum_{n=0}^{N/2-1} [x(n) + x(n + N/2)] W_{N/2}^{kn}$$

$$X(2k+1) = \sum_{n=0}^{N/2-1} [x(n) - x(n + N/2)] W_N^{(2k+1)n}$$

$$= \sum_{n=0}^{N/2-1} [x(n) - x(n + N/2)] W_N^n W_{N/2}^{kn}$$

The resulting summations are DFTs of the $N/2$-element sequences

$$\{x(n) + x(n + N/2)\}_{n=0}^{N/2-1}$$

and

$$\{[x(n) - x(n + N/2)] W_N^n\}_{n=0}^{N/2-1}.$$

Thus, the DFT of an N-element sequence can be computed recursively by interlacing the DFTs of two $N/2$-element sequences. If we select a base case of two elements, we can describe a recursive fast Fourier transformation (RFFT) algorithm as follows. For $N = 2$,

$$RFFT\{x(n)\}_{n=0}^1 = \{X(m)\}_{m=0}^1$$

$$= \{x(0) + x(1), [x(0) - x(1)] W_2^0\}$$

$$= \{x(0) + x(1), x(0) - x(1)\},$$

since $W_2^0 = e^0 = 1$. For $N > 2$,

$$RFFT\{x(n)\}_{n=0}^{N-1} = \{X(m)\}_{n=0}^{N-1}$$

$$= \begin{cases} RFFT\{x(n) + x(n + N/2)\}_{n=0}^{N/2-1}, & m \text{ even} \\ RFFT\{(x(n) - x(n + N/2)) W_N^n\}_{n=0}^{N/2-1}, & m \text{ odd} \end{cases}$$

with the attendant interlacing of even and odd components.

The diagram below, adapted from [6], shows the computational structure of the RFFT algorithm. The first stage computes pairwise sums and differences of the first and second halves of the input; this stage is labeled the *butterfly* stage. The second stage recurs on the resulting subsequences. The third stage interlaces the output of the two recursive calls to RFFT, thus yielding the properly ordered seqence $\{X(m)\}_{m=0}^{N-1}$.

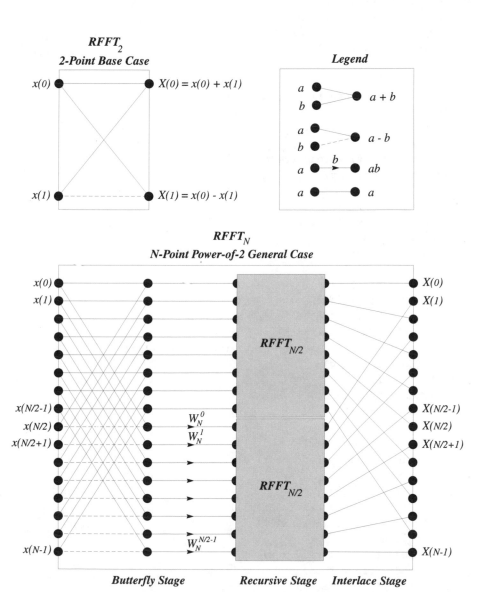

The procedure dft defined by the code below accepts a sequence (list) of values, x, the length of which is assumed to be a power of 2. dft precomputes a sequence of powers of W_N, $\{W_N^n\}_{n=0}^{N/2-1}$, and initiates the recursion. The code for rfft follows the algorithm outlined above.

```
(define (dft x)
  (define (w-powers n)
    (let ((pi (* (acos 0.0) 2)))
      (let ((delta (/ (* -2.0i pi) n)))
        (let f ((n n) (x 0.0))
          (if (= n 0)
              '()
              (cons (exp x) (f (- n 2) (+ x delta)))))))))
  (define (evens w)
    (if (null? w)
        '()
        (cons (car w) (evens (cddr w)))))
  (define (interlace x y)
    (if (null? x)
        '()
        (cons (car x) (cons (car y) (interlace (cdr x) (cdr y))))))
  (define (split ls)
    (let split ((fast ls) (slow ls))
      (if (null? fast)
          (values '() slow)
          (call-with-values
            (lambda () (split (cddr fast) (cdr slow)))
            (lambda (front back)
              (values (cons (car slow) front) back))))))
  (define (butterfly x w)
    (call-with-values
      (lambda () (split x))
      (lambda (front back)
        (values
          (map + front back)
          (map * (map - front back) w)))))
  (define (rfft x w)
    (if (null? (cddr x))
        (let ((x0 (car x)) (x1 (cadr x)))
          (list (+ x0 x1) (- x0 x1)))
        (call-with-values
          (lambda () (butterfly x w))
          (lambda (front back)
            (let ((w (evens w)))
              (interlace (rfft front w) (rfft back w)))))))
  (rfft x (w-powers (length x))))
```

Exercise 9.9.1. Alter the algorithm to employ a base case of four points. What simplifications can be made to avoid multiplying any of the base case outputs by elements of w?

Exercise 9.9.2. Recode `dft` to accept a vector rather than a list as input, and have it produce a vector as output. Use lists internally if necessary, but do not simply convert the input to a list on entry and the output to a vector on exit.

Exercise 9.9.3. Rather than recomputing the powers of `w` on each step for a new number of points, the code simply uses the even numbered elements of the preceding list of powers. Show that doing so yields the proper list of powers. That is, show that `(evens (w-powers n))` is equal to `(w-powers (/ n 2))`.

Exercise 9.9.4. The recursion step creates several intermediate lists that are immediately discarded. Recode the recursion step to avoid any unnecessary allocation.

Exercise 9.9.5. Each element of a sequence of input values may be regenerated from the discrete Fourier transform of the sequence via the equation

$$x(n) = \frac{1}{N} \sum_{m=0}^{N-1} X(m) e^{i\frac{2\pi mn}{N}}.$$

Noting the similarity between this equation and the original equation defining $X(m)$, create a modified version of `dft`, `inverse-dft`, that performs the inverse transformation. Verify that `(inverse-dft (dft seq))` returns *seq* for several input sequences *seq*.

9.10. A Unification Algorithm

Unification [20] is a pattern-matching technique used in automated theorem proving, type-inference systems, computer algebra, and logic programming, e.g., Prolog [5].

A unification algorithm attempts to make two symbolic expressions equal by computing a unifying substitution for the expressions. A *substitution* is a function that replaces variables with other expressions. A substitution must treat all occurrences of a variable the same way, e.g., if it replaces one occurrence of the variable x by a, it must replace all occurrences of x by a. A unifying substitution, or *unifier*, for two expressions e_1 and e_2 is a substitution, σ, such that $\sigma(e_1) = \sigma(e_2)$.

For example, the two expressions $f(x)$ and $f(y)$ can be unified by substituting x for y (or y for x). In this case, the unifier σ could be described as the function that replaces y with x and leaves other variables unchanged. On the other hand, the two expressions $x + 1$ and $y + 2$ cannot be unified. It might appear that substituting 3 for x and 2 for y would make both expressions equal to 4 and hence equal to each other. The symbolic expressions, $3 + 1$ and $2 + 2$, however, still differ.

Two expressions may have more than one unifier. For example, the expressions $f(x, y)$ and $f(1, y)$ can be unified to $f(1, y)$ with the substitution of 1 for x. They may also be unified to $f(1, 5)$ with the substitution of 1 for x and 5 for y. The first substitution is preferable, since it does not commit to the unnecessary replacement of y. Unification algorithms typically produce the *most general unifier*, or *mgu*, for two expressions. The mgu for two expressions makes no unnecessary substitutions;

all other unifiers for the expressions are special cases of the mgu. In the example above, the first substitution is the mgu and the second is a special case.

For the purposes of this program, a symbolic expression can be a variable, a constant, or a function application. Variables are represented by Scheme symbols, e.g., x; a function application is represented by a list with the function name in the first position and its arguments in the remaining positions, e.g., (f x); and constants are represented by zero-argument functions, e.g., (a).

The algorithm presented here finds the mgu for two terms, if it exists, using a continuation passing style, or CPS (see Section 3.4), approach to recursion on subterms. The procedure unify takes two terms and passes them to a help procedure, uni, along with an initial (identity) substitution, a success continuation, and a failure continuation. The success continuation returns the result of applying its argument, a substitution, to one of the terms, i.e., the unified result. The failure continuation simply returns its argument, a message. Because control passes by explicit continuation within unify (always with tail calls), a return from the success or failure continuation is a return from unify itself.

Substitutions are procedures. Whenever a variable is to be replaced by another term, a new substitution is formed from the variable, the term, and the existing substitution. Given a term as an argument, the new substitution replaces occurrences of its saved variable with its saved term in the result of invoking the saved substitution on the argument expression. Intuitively, a substitution is a chain of procedures, one for each variable in the substitution. The chain is terminated by the initial, identity substitution.

```
(unify 'x 'y)  ⇒  y
(unify '(f x y) '(g x y))  ⇒  "clash"
(unify '(f x (h)) '(f (h) y))  ⇒  (f (h) (h))
(unify '(f (g x) y) '(f y x))  ⇒  "cycle"
(unify '(f (g x) y) '(f y (g x)))  ⇒  (f (g x) (g x))
(unify '(f (g x) y) '(f y z))  ⇒  (f (g x) (g x))
```

```
(define unify #f)
(let ()
  ;; occurs? returns true if and only if u occurs in v
  (define occurs?
    (lambda (u v)
      (and (pair? v)
           (let f ((l (cdr v)))
             (and (pair? l)
                  (or (eq? u (car l))
                      (occurs? u (car l))
                      (f (cdr l)))))))))
```

```
;; sigma returns a new substitution procedure extending s by
;; the substitution of u with v
(define sigma
  (lambda (u v s)
    (lambda (x)
      (let f ((x (s x)))
        (if (symbol? x)
            (if (eq? x u) v x)
            (cons (car x) (map f (cdr x)))))))))

;; try-subst tries to substitute u for v but may require a
;; full unification if (s u) is not a variable, and it may
;; fail if it sees that u occurs in v.
(define try-subst
  (lambda (u v s ks kf)
    (let ((u (s u)))
      (if (not (symbol? u))
          (uni u v s ks kf)
          (let ((v (s v)))
            (cond
              ((eq? u v) (ks s))
              ((occurs? u v) (kf "cycle"))
              (else (ks (sigma u v s)))))))))

;; uni attempts to unify u and v with a continuation-passing
;; style that returns a substitution to the success argument
;; ks or an error message to the failure argument kf.  The
;; substitution itself is represented by a procedure from
;; variables to terms.
(define uni
  (lambda (u v s ks kf)
    (cond
      ((symbol? u) (try-subst u v s ks kf))
      ((symbol? v) (try-subst v u s ks kf))
      ((and (eq? (car u) (car v))
            (= (length u) (length v)))
       (let f ((u (cdr u)) (v (cdr v)) (s s))
         (if (null? u)
             (ks s)
             (uni (car u)
                  (car v)
                  s
                  (lambda (s) (f (cdr u) (cdr v) s))
                  kf))))
      (else (kf "clash")))))
```

```
;; unify shows one possible interface to uni, where the initial
;; substitution is the identity procedure, the initial success
;; continuation returns the unified term, and the initial failure
;; continuation returns the error message.
(set! unify
  (lambda (u v)
    (uni u
         v
         (lambda (x) x)
         (lambda (s) (s u))
         (lambda (msg) msg)))))
```

Exercise 9.10.1. Modify unify so that it returns its substitution rather than printing the unified term. Apply this substitution to both input terms to verify that it returns the same result for each.

Exercise 9.10.2. As mentioned above, substitutions on a term are performed sequentially, requiring one entire pass through the input expression for each substituted variable. Represent the substitution differently so that only one pass through the expression need be made. Make sure that substitutions are performed not only on the input expression but also on any expressions you insert during substitution.

Exercise 9.10.3. Extend the continuation-passing style unification algorithm into an entire continuation-passing style logic programming system.

9.11. Multitasking with Engines

Engines are a high-level process abstraction supporting *timed preemption* [8, 12]. Engines may be used to simulate multiprocessing, implement light-weight threads, implement operating system kernels, and perform nondeterministic computations. The engine implementation is one of the more interesting applications of continuations in Scheme.

An engine is created by passing a thunk (procedure of no arguments) to make-engine. The body of the thunk is the computation to be performed by the engine. An engine itself is a procedure of three arguments:

1. *ticks*, a positive integer that specifies the amount of *fuel* to be given to the engine. An engine executes until this fuel runs out or until its computation finishes.

2. *complete*, a procedure of two arguments that specifies what to do if the computation finishes. Its arguments will be the amount of fuel left over and the result of the computation.

3. *expire*, a procedure of one argument that specifies what to do if the fuel runs out before the computation finishes. Its argument will be a new engine capable of continuing the computation from the point of interruption.

When an engine is applied to its arguments, it sets up a timer to fire in *ticks* time units. If the engine computation completes before the timer goes off, the system invokes *complete*, passing it the number of *ticks* left over and the value of the computation. If, on the other hand, the timer goes off before the engine computation completes, the system creates a new engine from the continuation of the interrupted computation and passes this engine to *expire*. *complete* and *expire* are invoked in the continuation of the engine invocation.

The following example creates an engine from a trivial computation, 3, and gives the engine 10 ticks.

```
(define eng
  (make-engine
    (lambda () 3)))

(eng 10
  (lambda (ticks value) value)
  (lambda (x) x))   ⇒   3
```

It is often useful to pass `list` as the *complete* procedure to an engine, causing the engine to return a list of the ticks remaining and the value if the computation completes.

```
(eng 10
  list
  (lambda (x) x))   ⇒   (9 3)
```

In the example above, the value was 3 and there were 9 ticks left over, i.e., it took only one unit of fuel to evaluate 3. (The fuel amounts given here are for illustration only. The actual amount may differ.)

Typically, the engine computation does not finish in one try. The following example displays the use of an engine to compute the 10th Fibonacci number (see Section 3.2) in steps.

```
(define fibonacci
  (lambda (n)
    (if (< n 2)
        n
        (+ (fibonacci (- n 1))
           (fibonacci (- n 2))))))
(define eng
  (make-engine
    (lambda ()
      (fibonacci 10))))
```

```
(eng 50
  list
  (lambda (new-eng)
    (set! eng new-eng)
    "expired"))   ⇒   "expired"
(eng 50
  list
  (lambda (new-eng)
    (set! eng new-eng)
    "expired"))   ⇒   "expired"
(eng 50
  list
  (lambda (new-eng)
    (set! eng new-eng)
    "expired"))   ⇒   "expired"
(eng 50
  list
  (lambda (new-eng)
    (set! eng new-eng)
    "expired"))   ⇒   (23 55)
```

Each time the engine's fuel ran out, the *expire* procedure assigned **eng** to the new engine. The entire computation required four allotments of 50 ticks to complete; of the last 50 it used all but 23. Thus, the total amount of fuel used was 177 ticks. This leads us to the following procedure, **mileage**, which uses engines to "time" a computation.

```
(define mileage
  (lambda (thunk)
    (let loop ((eng (make-engine thunk)) (total-ticks 0))
      (eng 50
        (lambda (ticks value)
          (+ total-ticks (- 50 ticks)))
        (lambda (new-eng)
          (loop new-eng (+ total-ticks 50)))))))
(mileage (lambda () (fibonacci 10)))   ⇒   177
```

The choice of 50 for the number of ticks to use each time is arbitrary, of course. It might make more sense to pass a much larger number, say 10000, in order to reduce the number of times the computation is interrupted.

The next procedure, **round-robin**, could be the basis for a simple time-sharing operating system. **round-robin** maintains a queue of processes (a list of engines) and cycles through the queue in a *round-robin* fashion, allowing each process to run for a set amount of time. **round-robin** returns a list of the values returned by the engine computations in the order that the computations complete.

```
(define round-robin
  (lambda (engs)
    (if (null? engs)
        '()
        ((car engs) 1
          (lambda (ticks value)
            (cons value (round-robin (cdr engs))))
          (lambda (eng)
            (round-robin
              (append (cdr engs) (list eng)))))))))
```

Assuming the amount of computation corresponding to one tick is constant, the effect of round-robin is to return a list of the values sorted from the quickest to complete to the slowest to complete. Thus, when we call round-robin on a list of engines, each computing one of the Fibonacci numbers, the output list is sorted with the earlier Fibonacci numbers first, regardless of the order of the input list.

```
(round-robin
  (map (lambda (x)
         (make-engine
           (lambda ()
             (fibonacci x))))
       '(4 5 2 8 3 7 6 2)))  ⇒  (1 1 2 3 5 8 13 21)
```

More interesting things could happen if the amount of fuel varied each time through the loop. In this case, the computation would be nondeterministic, i.e., the results would vary from call to call.

The following syntactic form, por (parallel-or), returns the first of its expressions to complete with a true value. por is implemented with the procedure first-true, which is similar to round-robin but quits when any of the engines completes with a true value. If all of the engines complete, but none with a true value, first-true (and hence por) returns #f.

```
(define-syntax por
  (syntax-rules ()
    ((_ x ...)
     (first-true
       (list (make-engine (lambda () x)) ...)))))
(define first-true
  (lambda (engs)
    (if (null? engs)
        #f
        ((car engs) 1
          (lambda (ticks value)
            (or value (first-true (cdr engs))))
          (lambda (eng)
            (first-true
              (append (cdr engs) (list eng)))))))))
```

Even if one of the expressions is an infinite loop, por can still finish (as long as one of the other expressions completes and returns a true value).

```
(por 1 2)  ⇒  1
(por ((lambda (x) (x x)) (lambda (x) (x x)))
     (fibonacci 10))  ⇒  55
```

The first subexpression of the second por expression is nonterminating, so the answer is the value of the second subexpression.

Let's turn to the implementation of engines. Any preemptive multitasking primitive must have the ability to interrupt a running process after a given amount of computation. This ability is provided by a primitive timer interrupt mechanism in some Scheme implementations. We will construct a suitable one here.

Our timer system defines three procedures: start-timer, stop-timer, and decrement-timer, which can be described operationally as follows.

- (start-timer *ticks* *handler*) initializes the timer to *ticks* and installs *handler* as the procedure to be invoked (without arguments) when the timer expires.

- (stop-timer) resets the timer and returns the number of ticks remaining.

- (decrement-timer) decrements the timer by one tick if the timer is on, i.e., if it is not zero. When the timer reaches zero, decrement-timer invokes the saved handler. If the timer has already reached zero, decrement-timer returns without changing the timer.

Code to implement these procedures is given along with the engine implementation below.

Using the timer system requires inserting calls to decrement-timer in appropriate places. Consuming a timer tick on entry to a procedure usually provides a sufficient level of granularity. This can be accomplished by using timed-lambda as defined below in place of lambda. timed-lambda simply invokes decrement-timer before executing the expressions in its body.

```
(define-syntax timed-lambda
  (syntax-rules ()
    ((_ formals exp1 exp2 ...)
     (lambda formals (decrement-timer) exp1 exp2 ...))))
```

It may be useful to redefine named let and do to use timed-lambda as well, so that recursions expressed with these constructs are timed. If you use this mechanism, do not forget to use the timed versions of lambda and other forms in code run within an engine, or no ticks will be consumed.

Now that we have a suitable timer, we can implement engines in terms of the timer and continuations. We use call/cc in two places in the engine implementation: (1) to obtain the continuation of the computation that invokes the engine so that we can return to that continuation when the engine computation completes or the timer expires, and (2) to obtain the continuation of the engine computation when the timer expires so that we can return to this computation if the newly created engine is subsequently run.

The state of the engine system is contained in two variables local to the engine system: `do-complete` and `do-expire`. When an engine is started, the engine assigns to `do-complete` and `do-expire` procedures that, when invoked, return to the continuation of the engine's caller to invoke *complete* or *expire*. The engine starts (or restarts) the computation by invoking the procedure passed as an argument to `make-engine` with the specified number of ticks. The ticks and the local procedure `timer-handler` are then used to start the timer.

Suppose that the timer expires before the engine computation completes. The procedure `timer-handler` is then invoked. It initiates a call to `start-timer` but obtains the ticks by calling `call/cc` with `do-expire`. Consequently, `do-expire` is called with a continuation that, if invoked, will restart the timer and continue the interrupted computation. `do-expire` creates a new engine from this continuation and arranges for the engine's *expire* procedure to be invoked with the new engine in the correct continuation.

If, on the other hand, the engine computation completes before the timer expires, the timer is stopped and the number of ticks remaining is passed along with the value to `do-complete`; `do-complete` arranges for the engine's *complete* procedure to be invoked with the ticks and value in the correct continuation.

Let's discuss a couple of subtle aspects to this code. The first concerns the method used to start the timer when an engine is invoked. The code would apparently be simplified by letting `new-engine` start the timer before it initiates or resumes the engine computation, instead of passing the ticks to the computation and letting it start the timer. Starting the timer within the computation, however, prevents ticks from being consumed prematurely. If the engine system itself consumes fuel, then an engine provided with a small amount of fuel may not progress toward completion. (It may, in fact, make negative progress.) If the software timer described above is used, this problem is actually avoided by compiling the engine-making code with the untimed version of `lambda`.

The second subtlety concerns the procedures created by `do-complete` and `do-expire` and subsequently applied by the continuation of the `call/cc` application. It may appear that `do-complete` could first invoke the engine's *complete* procedure, then pass the result to the continuation (and similarly for `do-expire`) as follows:

```
(escape (complete value ticks))
```

This would result in improper treatment of tail recursion, however. The problem is that the current continuation would not be replaced with the continuation stored in `escape` until the call to the `complete` procedure returns. Consequently, both the continuation of the running engine and the continuation of the engine invocation could be retained for an indefinite period of time, when in fact the actual engine invocation may appear to be tail-recursive. This is especially inappropriate because the engine interface encourages use of continuation-passing style and hence tail recursion. The round-robin scheduler and `first-true` provide good examples of this, since the *expire* procedure in each invokes engines tail-recursively.

We maintain proper treatment of tail recursion by arranging for `do-complete` and `do-expire` to escape from the continuation of the running engine before invoking the `complete` or `expire` procedures. Since the continuation of the engine

invocation is a procedure application, passing it a procedure of no arguments results
in application of the procedure in the continuation of the engine invocation.

```
(define start-timer #f)
(define stop-timer #f)
(define decrement-timer #f)
(let ((clock 0) (handler #f))
  (set! start-timer
    (lambda (ticks new-handler)
      (set! handler new-handler)
      (set! clock ticks)))
  (set! stop-timer
    (lambda ()
      (let ((time-left clock))
        (set! clock 0)
        time-left)))
  (set! decrement-timer
    (lambda ()
      (if (> clock 0)
          (begin
            (set! clock (- clock 1))
            (if (= clock 0) (handler)))))))
(define make-engine
  (let ((do-complete #f) (do-expire #f))
    (define timer-handler
      (lambda ()
        (start-timer (call/cc do-expire) timer-handler)))
    (define new-engine
      (lambda (resume)
        (lambda (ticks complete expire)
          ((call/cc
             (lambda (escape)
               (set! do-complete
                 (lambda (ticks value)
                   (escape (lambda () (complete ticks value)))))
               (set! do-expire
                 (lambda (resume)
                   (escape (lambda ()
                             (expire (new-engine resume))))))
               (resume ticks)))))))
    (lambda (proc)
      (new-engine
        (lambda (ticks)
          (start-timer ticks timer-handler)
          (let ((value (proc)))
            (let ((ticks (stop-timer)))
              (do-complete ticks value))))))))
```

Exercise 9.11.1. It may appear that the nested `let` expressions in the body of `make-engine`:

```
(let ((value (proc)))
  (let ((ticks (stop-timer)))
    (do-complete ticks value)))
```

could be replaced with:

```
(let ((value (proc)) (ticks (stop-timer)))
  (do-complete value ticks))
```

Why is this not correct?

Exercise 9.11.2. It would also be incorrect to replace the nested `let` expressions discussed in the preceding exercise with:

```
(let ((value (proc)))
  (do-complete value (stop-timer)))
```

Why?

Exercise 9.11.3. Modify the engine implementation to provide a procedure, `engine-return`, that returns immediately from an engine.

Exercise 9.11.4. Implement the kernel of a small operating system using engines for processes. Processes should request services (such as reading input from the user) by evaluating an expression of the form `(trap 'request)`. Use `call/cc` and `engine-return` from the preceding exercise to implement `trap`.

Exercise 9.11.5. Write the same operating-system kernel without using engines, building instead from continuations and timer interrupts.

Exercise 9.11.6. This implementation of engines does not allow one engine to call another, i.e., nested engines [8]. Modify the implementation to allow nested engines.

Bibliography

[1] Harold Abelson and Gerald J. Sussman with Julie Sussman. *Structure and Interpretation of Computer Programs*, second edition. MIT Press and McGraw-Hill, 1996.

[2] J. Michael Ashley and R. Kent Dybvig. An efficient implementation of multiple return values in Scheme. In *Proceedings of the 1994 ACM Conference on Lisp and Functional Programming*, pages 140–149, June 1994.

[3] William Briggs and Van Emden Henson. *The DFT: An Owner's Manual for the Discrete Fourier Transform*. Society for Industrial and Applied Mathematics, Philadelphia, 1995.

[4] William Clinger, Jonathan Rees, et al. The revised[4] report on the algorithmic language Scheme. *LISP Pointers*, 4(3), 1991.

[5] William F. Clocksin and Christopher S. Mellish. *Programming in Prolog*, second edition. Springer-Verlag, 1984.

[6] Sam M. Daniel. Efficient recursive FFT implementation in Prolog. In *Proceedings of the Second International Conference on the Practical Application of Prolog*, pages 175–185, 1994.

[7] R. Kent Dybvig. *Chez Scheme System Manual, Rev. 3.0*. Cadence Research Systems, Bloomington, Indiana, December 1995.

[8] R. Kent Dybvig and Robert Hieb. Engines from continuations. *Computer Languages*, 14(2):109–123, 1989.

[9] R. Kent Dybvig, Robert Hieb, and Carl Bruggeman. Syntactic abstraction in Scheme. *Lisp and Symbolic Computation*, 5(4):295–326, 1993.

[10] Daniel P. Friedman and Matthias Felleisen. *The Little Schemer*, fourth edition. MIT Press, 1996.

[11] Daniel P. Friedman, Christopher T. Haynes, and Eugene E. Kohlbecker. Programming with continuations. In P. Pepper, editor, *Program Transformation and Programming Environments*, pages 263–274. Springer-Verlag, 1984.

[12] Christopher T. Haynes and Daniel P. Friedman. Abstracting timed preemption with engines. *Computer Languages*, 12(2):109–121, 1987.

[13] Christopher T. Haynes, Daniel P. Friedman, and Mitchell Wand. Obtaining coroutines with continuations. *Computer Languages*, 11(3/4):143–153, 1986.

[14] Robert Hieb, R. Kent Dybvig, and Carl Bruggeman. Representing control in the presence of first-class continuations. In *Proceedings of the SIGPLAN '90 Conference on Programming Language Design and Implementation*, pages 66–77, June 1990.

[15] IEEE Computer Society. *IEEE Standard for the Scheme Programming Language*, May 1991. IEEE Std 1178-1990.

[16] Brian W. Kernighan and Dennis M. Ritchie. *The C Programming Language*, second edition. Prentice Hall, 1988.

[17] Vincent S. Manis and James J. Little. *The Schematics of Computation*. Prentice Hall, 1995.

[18] Peter Naur et al. Revised report on the algorithmic language ALGOL 60. *Communications of the ACM*, 6(1):1–17, January 1963.

[19] David A. Plaisted. Constructs for sets, quantifiers, and rewrite rules in Lisp. Technical Report UIUCDCS-R-84-1176, University of Illinois at Urbana-Champaign Department of Computer Science, June 1984.

[20] J. A. Robinson. A machine-oriented logic based on the resolution principle. *Journal of the ACM*, 12(1):23–41, 1965.

[21] George Springer and Daniel P. Friedman. *Scheme and the Art of Programming*. MIT Press and McGraw-Hill, 1989.

[22] Guy L. Steele Jr. *Common Lisp, the Language*, second edition. Digital Press, 1990.

[23] Guy L. Steele Jr. and Gerald J. Sussman. The revised report on Scheme, a dialect of Lisp. MIT AI Memo 452, Massachusetts Institute of Technology, January 1978.

[24] Gerald J. Sussman and Guy L. Steele Jr. Scheme: An interpreter for extended lambda calculus. MIT AI Memo 349, Massachusetts Institute of Technology, May 1975.

[25] Mitchell Wand. Continuation-based multiprocessing. In *Conference Record of the 1980 Lisp Conference*, pages 19–28, August 1980.

Formal Syntax of Scheme

The formal grammars and accompanying text appearing here describe the syntax of Scheme programs and data. Consult the Summary of Forms and Procedures and the individual descriptions given in Chapters 4 through 8 for additional details on specific syntactic forms.

Programs and data are formed from tokens, whitespace, and comments. Tokens include identifiers, booleans, numbers, characters, strings, open and close parentheses, the open vector parenthesis #(, the dotted pair marker . (dot), the quotation marks ' and `, and the unquotation marks , and ,@. Whitespace consists of spaces and newline characters and in some implementations also consists of other characters, such as tabs or form feeds. A comment consists of a semicolon (;) followed by any number of characters up to the next line break. A token may be surrounded by any number of whitespace characters and comments. Identifiers, numbers, characters, and dot are delimited by whitespace, the start of a comment, an open or close parenthesis, or a string quote.

In the productions below, ⟨empty⟩ stands for the empty string. An item followed by an asterisk (*) represents zero or more occurrences of the item, and an item followed by a raised plus sign (+) represents one or more occurrences. Spacing between items within a production appears for readability only and should be treated as if it were not present.

Programs. A program consists of a sequence of definitions and expressions.

⟨program⟩ ⟶ ⟨form⟩*
⟨form⟩ ⟶ ⟨definition⟩ | ⟨expression⟩

Definitions. Definitions include variable and syntax definitions, `begin` forms containing zero or more definitions, `let-syntax` and `letrec-syntax` forms expanding into zero or more definitions, and derived definitions. Derived definitions are syntactic extensions that expand into some form of definition. A transformer expression is a `syntax-rules` form or some other expression that produces a transformer.

⟨definition⟩ ⟶ ⟨variable definition⟩
    | ⟨syntax definition⟩
    | (**begin** ⟨definition⟩*)
    | (**let-syntax** (⟨syntax binding⟩*) ⟨definition⟩*)
    | (**letrec-syntax** (⟨syntax binding⟩*) ⟨definition⟩*)
    | ⟨derived definition⟩
⟨variable definition⟩ ⟶ (**define** ⟨variable⟩ ⟨expression⟩)
    | (**define** (⟨variable⟩ ⟨variable⟩*) ⟨body⟩)
    | (**define** (⟨variable⟩ ⟨variable⟩* . ⟨variable⟩) ⟨body⟩)
⟨variable⟩ ⟶ ⟨identifier⟩
⟨body⟩ ⟶ ⟨definition⟩* ⟨expression⟩⁺
⟨syntax definition⟩ ⟶ (**define-syntax** ⟨keyword⟩ ⟨transformer expression⟩)
⟨keyword⟩ ⟶ ⟨identifier⟩
⟨syntax binding⟩ ⟶ (⟨keyword⟩ ⟨transformer expression⟩)

Expressions. Expressions include core expressions, **let-syntax** or **letrec-syntax** forms expanding into a sequence of one or more expressions, and derived expressions. The core expressions are self-evaluating constants, variable references, applications, and **quote**, **lambda**, **if**, and **set!** expressions. Derived expressions include **and**, **begin**, **case**, **cond**, **delay**, **do**, **let**, **let***, **letrec**, **or**, and **quasiquote** expressions plus syntactic extensions that expand into some form of expression.

⟨expression⟩ ⟶ ⟨constant⟩
    | ⟨variable⟩
    | (**quote** ⟨datum⟩) | ' ⟨datum⟩
    | (**lambda** ⟨formals⟩ ⟨body⟩)
    | (**if** ⟨expression⟩ ⟨expression⟩ ⟨expression⟩) | (**if** ⟨expression⟩ ⟨expression⟩)
    | (**set!** ⟨variable⟩ ⟨expression⟩)
    | ⟨application⟩
    | (**let-syntax** (⟨syntax binding⟩*) ⟨expression⟩⁺)
    | (**letrec-syntax** (⟨syntax binding⟩*) ⟨expression⟩⁺)
    | ⟨derived expression⟩
⟨constant⟩ ⟶ ⟨boolean⟩ | ⟨number⟩ | ⟨character⟩ | ⟨string⟩
⟨formals⟩ ⟶ ⟨variable⟩ | (⟨variable⟩*) | (⟨variable⟩⁺ . ⟨variable⟩)
⟨application⟩ ⟶ (⟨expression⟩ ⟨expression⟩*)

Identifiers. Identifiers may denote variables, keywords, or symbols, depending upon context. They are formed from sequences of letters, digits, and special characters. With three exceptions, identifiers cannot begin with a character that can also begin a number, i.e., they cannot begin with ., +, -, or a digit. The three exceptions are the identifiers ..., +, and -. Case is insignificant in symbols so that, for example, **newspaper**, **NewsPaper**, and **NEWSPAPER** all represent the same identifier.

⟨identifier⟩ ⟶ ⟨initial⟩ ⟨subsequent⟩* | + | - | ...
⟨initial⟩ ⟶ ⟨letter⟩ | ! | \$ | % | & | * | / | : | < | = | > | ? | ˜ | _ | ^
⟨subsequent⟩ ⟶ ⟨initial⟩ | ⟨digit⟩ | . | + | -
⟨letter⟩ ⟶ a | b | ... | z
⟨digit⟩ ⟶ 0 | 1 | ... | 9

Data. Data include booleans, numbers, characters, strings, symbols, lists, and vectors. Case is insignificant in the syntax for booleans, numbers, and character names, but it is significant in other character constants and in strings. For example, #T is equivalent to #t, #E1E3 is equivalent to #e1e3, #X2aBc is equivalent to #x2abc, and #\NewLine is equivalent to #\newline; but #\A is distinct from #\a and "String" is distinct from "string".

⟨datum⟩ ⟶ ⟨boolean⟩ | ⟨number⟩ | ⟨character⟩ | ⟨string⟩ | ⟨symbol⟩ | ⟨list⟩ | ⟨vector⟩
⟨boolean⟩ ⟶ #t | #f
⟨number⟩ ⟶ ⟨num 2⟩ | ⟨num 8⟩ | ⟨num 10⟩ | ⟨num 16⟩
⟨character⟩ ⟶ #\ ⟨any character⟩ | #\newline | #\space
⟨string⟩ ⟶ " ⟨string character⟩* "
⟨string character⟩ ⟶ \" | \\ | ⟨any character other than " or \⟩
⟨symbol⟩ ⟶ ⟨identifier⟩
⟨list⟩ ⟶ (⟨datum⟩*) | (⟨datum⟩$^+$. ⟨datum⟩) | ⟨abbreviation⟩
⟨abbreviation⟩ ⟶ ' ⟨datum⟩ | ` ⟨datum⟩ | , ⟨datum⟩ | ,@ ⟨datum⟩
⟨vector⟩ ⟶ #(⟨datum⟩*)

Numbers. Numbers can appear in one of four radixes: 2, 8, 10, and 16, with 10 the default. The first several of productions below are parameterized by the radix, r, and each represents four productions, one for each of the four possible radixes. Numbers that contain radix points or exponents are constrained to appear in radix 10, so ⟨decimal r⟩ is valid only when r is 10.

⟨num r⟩ ⟶ ⟨prefix r⟩ ⟨complex r⟩
⟨complex r⟩ ⟶ ⟨real r⟩ | ⟨real r⟩ @ ⟨real r⟩
   | ⟨real r⟩ + ⟨imag r⟩ | ⟨real r⟩ - ⟨imag r⟩
   | + ⟨imag r⟩ | - ⟨imag r⟩
⟨imag r⟩ ⟶ i | ⟨ureal r⟩ i
⟨real r⟩ ⟶ ⟨sign⟩ ⟨ureal r⟩
⟨ureal r⟩ ⟶ ⟨uinteger r⟩ | ⟨uinteger r⟩ / ⟨uinteger r⟩ | ⟨decimal r⟩
⟨uinteger r⟩ ⟶ ⟨digit r⟩$^+$ #*
⟨prefix r⟩ ⟶ ⟨radix r⟩ ⟨exactness⟩ | ⟨exactness⟩ ⟨radix r⟩
⟨decimal 10⟩ ⟶ ⟨uinteger 10⟩ ⟨exponent⟩
   | . ⟨digit 10⟩$^+$ #* ⟨suffix⟩
   | ⟨digit 10⟩$^+$. ⟨digit 10⟩* #* ⟨suffix⟩
   | ⟨digit 10⟩$^+$ #$^+$. #* ⟨suffix⟩
⟨suffix⟩ ⟶ ⟨empty⟩ | ⟨exponent⟩
⟨exponent⟩ ⟶ ⟨exponent marker⟩ ⟨sign⟩ ⟨digit 10⟩$^+$
⟨exponent marker⟩ ⟶ e | s | f | d | l
⟨sign⟩ ⟶ ⟨empty⟩ | + | -

⟨exactness⟩ ⟶ ⟨empty⟩ | #i | #e
⟨radix 2⟩ ⟶ #b
⟨radix 8⟩ ⟶ #o
⟨radix 10⟩ ⟶ ⟨empty⟩ | #d
⟨radix 16⟩ ⟶ #x
⟨digit 2⟩ ⟶ 0 | 1
⟨digit 8⟩ ⟶ 0 | 1 | ... | 7
⟨digit 10⟩ ⟶ ⟨digit⟩
⟨digit 16⟩ ⟶ ⟨digit⟩ | a | b | c | d | e | f

Summary of Forms

The table that follows summarizes the Scheme syntactic forms and procedures described in Chapters 4 through 8. It shows the category of the form and the page number where it is defined. The category states whether the form describes a syntactic form or a procedure.

Form	Category	Page
'obj	syntax	83
(* num ...)	procedure	125
(+ num ...)	procedure	125
,obj	syntax	83
,@obj	syntax	83
(- num_1)	procedure	125
(- num_1 num_2 num_3 ...)	procedure	125
(/ num_1)	procedure	126
(/ num_1 num_2 num_3 ...)	procedure	126
(< $real_1$ $real_2$ $real_3$ ...)	procedure	124
(<= $real_1$ $real_2$ $real_3$ ...)	procedure	124
(= num_1 num_2 num_3 ...)	procedure	124
(> $real_1$ $real_2$ $real_3$ ...)	procedure	124
(>= $real_1$ $real_2$ $real_3$ ...)	procedure	124
`obj	syntax	83
(abs $real$)	procedure	129
(acos num)	procedure	133
(and exp ...)	syntax	87
(angle num)	procedure	132
(append $list$ ...)	procedure	119
(apply $procedure$ obj ... $list$)	procedure	85
(asin num)	procedure	133
(assoc obj $alist$)	procedure	121
(assq obj $alist$)	procedure	121
(assv obj $alist$)	procedure	121
(atan num)	procedure	134
(atan $real_1$ $real_2$)	procedure	134
(begin exp_1 exp_2 ...)	syntax	85

`(boolean? obj)`	procedure	113
`(bound-identifier=? identifier₁ identifier₂)`	procedure	170
`(caaaar pair)`	procedure	117
`(caaadr pair)`	procedure	117
`(caaar pair)`	procedure	117
`(caadar pair)`	procedure	117
`(caaddr pair)`	procedure	117
`(caadr pair)`	procedure	117
`(caar pair)`	procedure	117
`(cadaar pair)`	procedure	117
`(cadadr pair)`	procedure	117
`(cadar pair)`	procedure	117
`(caddar pair)`	procedure	117
`(cadddr pair)`	procedure	117
`(caddr pair)`	procedure	117
`(cadr pair)`	procedure	117
`(call-with-current-continuation procedure)`	procedure	93
`(call-with-input-file filename proc)`	procedure	152
`(call-with-output-file filename proc)`	procedure	156
`(call-with-values producer consumer)`	procedure	99
`(call/cc procedure)`	procedure	93
`(car pair)`	procedure	116
`(case exp₀ clause₁ clause₂ ...)`	syntax	89
`(cdaaar pair)`	procedure	117
`(cdaadr pair)`	procedure	117
`(cdaar pair)`	procedure	117
`(cdadar pair)`	procedure	117
`(cdaddr pair)`	procedure	117
`(cdadr pair)`	procedure	117
`(cdar pair)`	procedure	117
`(cddaar pair)`	procedure	117
`(cddadr pair)`	procedure	117
`(cddar pair)`	procedure	117
`(cdddar pair)`	procedure	117
`(cddddr pair)`	procedure	117
`(cdddr pair)`	procedure	117
`(cddr pair)`	procedure	117
`(cdr pair)`	procedure	117
`(ceiling real)`	procedure	128
`(char->integer char)`	procedure	138
`(char-alphabetic? char)`	procedure	136
`(char-ci<=? char₁ char₂ char₃ ...)`	procedure	136
`(char-ci<? char₁ char₂ char₃ ...)`	procedure	136
`(char-ci=? char₁ char₂ char₃ ...)`	procedure	136
`(char-ci>=? char₁ char₂ char₃ ...)`	procedure	136
`(char-ci>? char₁ char₂ char₃ ...)`	procedure	136

Index

Leads against a Trump Contract

- ❏ Top of a three-card sequence
- ❏ Top of two touching honors
- ❏ Singleton or doubleton
- ❏ Partner's suit
- ❏ The unbid suit
- ❏ The stronger of two unbid suits
- ❏ Your longest suit with four trump cards

Long Suit Leads against a Notrump Contract

- ❏ The A from suits headed by the AKQ or the AKJ
- ❏ The K from suits headed by the KQJ or the KQ10
- ❏ The Q from suits headed by the QJ10, QJ9, or AQJ
- ❏ The J from suits headed by the J109, J108, AJ109, AJ108, KJ109, or KJ108
- ❏ The 10 from suits headed by the 1098, 1097, A1098, A1097, K1098, K1097, Q1098, Q1097, AK109, or AQ109
- ❏ The highest card from four small cards

Short Suit Leads against a Notrump Contract

(Look to these leads if your partner bids a suit or if your opponents bid your longest suit.)

- ❏ The top of a doubleton
- ❏ The top of three small cards
- ❏ Low from three cards headed by one honor
- ❏ Low from three cards headed by two nontouching honors, such as the A104, KJ2, K105, or Q104
- ❏ Top of two touching honors with exactly three cards, such as the KQ3, QJ5, J104, or 1093

Bridge For Dummies®

Cheat Sheet

Points Scored by Contract

Tricks Taken	7	8	9	10	11	12	13
Notrump	40	70	100	130	160	190	220
Spades	30	60	90	120	150	180	210
Hearts	30	60	90	120	150	180	210
Diamonds	20	40	60	80	100	120	140
Clubs	20	40	60	80	100	120	140

(Game = 100 points)

Trick Points by Suit

Hearts or spades: 30 points per trick

Clubs or diamonds: 20 points per trick

Notrump: First trick 40 points,
each subsequent trick 30 points

Undertrick Penalty Points

Not Vulnerable: 50 points per trick

Vulnerable: 100 points per trick

For Dummies: Bestselling Book Series for Beginners

Praise for Bridge For Dummies

"Among the talented and authoritative bridge writers, Eddie Kantar is the most informal. His friendly personality and deep appreciation of the beauties and fascinations of the game shine through in his work, beacons along the path to entertainment."

— Jeff Rubens, *The Bridge World*

"World Champion Eddie Kantar has taught thousands to play the world's most popular card game. His easy-going style makes him the perfect pick to write *Bridge For Dummies*. Kantar entertains you while cutting through the complexities. I'm happy to recommend this fine book."

— Frank R. Stewart, Bridge Columnist, "Sheinwold's Bridge"

"Eddie Kantar's writing and teaching are unusual, to the point, and simply the best. He has now fit his talent to the perfect format, which features laid-back bridge advice presented with his keen sense of humor."

— Bobby Wolff, President of the World Bridge Federation and Bridge Columnist

"Eddie Kantar's *Bridge For Dummies* is one of the very best of the thousands of books that introduce the beginner to the game. It takes the beginner from the structure of the deck to bridge in clubs, in tournaments, and on the Internet."

— Alan Truscott, Bridge Columnist, *The New York Times*

TM

...FOR DUMMIES

References for the Rest of Us!®

BESTSELLING BOOK SERIES

Do you find that traditional reference books are overloaded with technical details and advice you'll never use? Do you postpone important life decisions because you just don't want to deal with them? Then our *For Dummies*® business and general reference book series is for you.

For Dummies business and general reference books are written for those frustrated and hard-working souls who know they aren't dumb, but find that the myriad of personal and business issues and the accompanying horror stories make them feel helpless. *For Dummies* books use a lighthearted approach, a down-to-earth style, and even cartoons and humorous icons to dispel fears and build confidence. Lighthearted but not lightweight, these books are perfect survival guides to solve your everyday personal and business problems.

"More than a publishing phenomenon, 'Dummies' is a sign of the times."

— The New York Times

"...you won't go wrong buying them."

— Walter Mossberg, Wall Street Journal, on For Dummies books

"A world of detailed and authoritative information is packed into them..."

— U.S. News and World Report

Already, millions of satisfied readers agree. They have made For Dummies the #1 introductory level computer book series and a best-selling business book series. They have written asking for more. So, if you're looking for the best and easiest way to learn about business and other general reference topics, look to For Dummies to give you a helping hand.

Wiley Publishing, Inc.

5/09

Bridge FOR DUMMIES®

by Eddie Kantar

Wiley Publishing, Inc.

Bridge For Dummies®
Published by
Wiley Publishing, Inc.
909 Third Avenue
New York, NY 10022
www.wiley.com

Copyright, 1997 by Wiley Publishing, Inc., Indianapolis, Indiana

For general information on our other products and services or to obtain technical support, please contact our Customer Care Department within the U.S. at 800-762-2974, outside the U.S. at 317-572-3993, or fax 317-572-4002.

Wiley also publishes its books in a variety of electronic formats. Some content that appears in print may not be available in electronic books.

Library of Congress Cataloging-in-Publication Data:

Library of Congress Control Number: 97-72424

ISBN: 0-7645-5015-2

Manufactured in the United States of America

20 19 18 17 16 15 14

About the Author

Eddie Kantar, a transplanted Californian, is one of the best known bridge writers in the world. He has more than 20 bridge books in print and is a regular contributor to the *Bulletin, The Bridge World, Bridge Today,* and many other bridge publications.

Eddie, a two-time World Champion, is highly regarded as a player, and he still plays regularly at major tournaments. He is known as one of bridge's great ambassadors.

Eddie learned to play bridge at age 11. By the time he was 17, he was teaching the game to his friends. Eddie was so enthusiastic about bridge that he often took his bridge books to school, hiding them behind his textbooks so that the teachers couldn't see him reading about bridge during class. At the University of Minnesota, where Eddie studied foreign languages, he taught bridge to pay his tuition.

Eddie gained stature as a player by winning two World Championship titles and 13 North American Championships. His North American titles include wins in the Spingold Knockout Teams, the Reisinger Board-a-Match Teams, the Vanderbilt Knockout Teams, and the Grand National Teams. Eddie is a Grand Master in World Bridge Federation rankings and an ACBL Grand Life Master.

Today, Eddie is best known as a writer, and many of his books are considered classics. When not playing bridge or writing about the subject, he can be found playing paddle tennis (an offshoot of tennis) at Venice Beach (come and join the game). By the way, Eddie is the only person ever to have played in both a World Bridge Championship and a World Table Tennis Championship (he did better at bridge).

Eddie was inducted into the Bridge Hall of Fame in 1996, the same year he was inducted into the Minnesota State Table Tennis Hall of Fame.

Acknowledgments

I would first like to thank Carolyn Krupp for suggesting to the powers that be that I write this book.

And not to forget my friend Gary Miller who struggled valiantly trying to teach me how to use my computer: a hopeless undertaking.

I would also like to thank my Project Editor, Mary Goodwin, who warmed my heart by telling me that she wants to start playing bridge after working on the book. We came a long way, Mary. I forgive you for shortening my book — I know you had to! Special thanks also go to Diane Giangrossi and Joe Jansen for their excellent copy editing.

I would also like to thank Ron Garber for helping me through the early stages of the book by making helpful suggestions as only he can. Norman Cressy also looked at several chapters of the book and made pertinent suggestions and corrections.

And a special thanks to Richard Aronson, my computer expert, who clued me in on the latest developments in computer bridge.

But it wasn't until Barry Rigal, a British export (and expert), came on the scene that we really got the ball rolling. Thank you, Barry — I would still be slaving away if it weren't for you.

And finally, I save the biggest thanks of all for Yvonne Snyder. Her encouragement was above and beyond the call of duty; there would have been no book without Yvonne.

Publisher's Acknowledgments

We're proud of this book; please register your comments through our online registration form located at www.dummies.com/register.

Some of the people who helped bring this book to market include the following:

Acquisitions, Development, and Editorial

Project Editor: Mary Goodwin

Acquisitions Editor: Mark Butler

Copy Editors: Diane L. Giangrossi, Joe Jansen

Technical Editors: Barry Rigal, Ron Garber

Editorial Manager: Mary C. Corder

Editorial Assistants: Donna Love, Darren Meiss

Special Help
   Joyce Pepple

Production

Project Coordinator: Valery Bourke

Layout and Graphics: Lou Boudreau, Maridee V. Ennis, Kelly Hardesty, Angela F. Hunckler, Todd Klemme, Brian Massey, Tom Missler, Brent Savage, M. Anne Sipahimalani, Rashell Smith, Michael A. Sullivan

Special Art: Shelley Lea

Proofreaders: Christine Berman, Melissa D. Buddendeck, Renee Kelty, Christine Sabooni, Joel K. Draper, Nancy Price, Robert Springer, Karen York

Indexer: Sharon Hilgenberg

Publishing and Editorial for Consumer Dummies
   Diane Graves Steele, Vice President and Publisher, Consumer Dummies
   Joyce Pepple, Acquisitions Director, Consumer Dummies
   Kristin A. Cocks, Product Development Director, Consumer Dummies
   Michael Spring, Vice President and Publisher, Travel
   Brice Gosnell, Publishing Director, Travel
   Suzanne Jannetta, Editorial Director, Travel

Publishing for Technology Dummies
   Andy Cummings, Acquisitions Director

Composition Services
   Gerry Fahey, Executive Director of Production Services
   Debbie Stailey, Director of Composition Services

Contents at a Glance

Cartoons at a Glance

By Rich Tennant

"I THOUGHT SHE WAS COUNTING TRICKS TOO, UNTIL SHE STARTED SNORING."

page 57

"OK, I'LL LET HIM PLAY AS LONG AS YOU STOP SAYING, 'YOU CAN'T TAKE AN OLD DOGS NEW TRICKS'."

page 283

"...AND DO YOU PROMISE TO LOVE, HONOR, AND ALWAYS LEAD THE HIGHEST CARD FROM THE SHORT SIDE?"

page 331

"BETTY—DON'T YOU DARE USE THIS AS AN EXCUSE NOT TO CONCENTRATE!"

page 5

"I DON'T CARE WHAT KIND OF CLOWNS YOU TWO ARE, I KNOW A SIGNAL WHEN I HEAR ONE! YOU HONK THAT THING ONE MORE TIME AND I'M LEAVING THE TABLE!"

page 109

"MY CURRENT DISTRIBUTION IS 4, 3, 3, AND 1. 4 KIDS, 3 TUITIONS, 3 MORTGAGES AND 1 JOB."

page 349

Fax: 978-546-7747
E-mail: richtennant@the5thwave.com
World Wide Web: www.the5thwave.com

Table of Contents

• •

Introduction

● ●

*B*ridge, quite simply, is the best card game ever. No other game even comes close. Of course, I may be a little biased on this point. I've been playing since I was 11 years old, when my best friend's father asked our gambling group, "Why don't you guys find a good game to play?" What I found was a great game, and I've never played another game since then.

What exactly is it about bridge that fascinates countless millions, has fascinated countless millions, and will continue to fascinate countless millions? Let me count the ways:

✔ **Bridge is a social game:** You play with a partner and two opponents. Right off the bat you have four people together. Inevitably, you meet a host of new friends with a strong common bond, the game of bridge. Bridge is not an "I" game — bridge is a "we" game.

✔ **Bridge is a challenging game:** Each hand is an adventure; each hand presents a unique set of conditions that you react to and solve. You have to do a little thinking.

✔ **Bridge is a game of psychology:** If you fancy yourself a keen observer of human behavior, look no further. You have found your niche. Players aren't supposed to show any emotion during the play, but there are always a few leaks in the dam.

✔ **Bridge is fun:** Hours become minutes! Playing bridge can mean endless hours of pleasure, a host of new friends, and many laughs.

Do You Really Need a Book about Bridge?

Yes! If you're an absolute beginner, you need the hand-held tour of the game that this book can give you. I take the time to explain the fundamentals in terms you can understand. I walk you through the different aspects of the game, showing you real-life examples, so that you can feel comfortable with the basics before you start to play.

If you have played (or tried to play) bridge before, this book still has much to offer you. I condense my years of experience with the game into tips and hints that can make you a better player.

If you're a bridge novice, eventually you'll have to play a few hands in order to feel like a real bridge player. This book offers an easy-to-follow path to your first (of if you've played before, your best) hand.

How to Use This Book

I describe many plays and sample hands throughout this book. To get a real feel for the game, you should read the book with a deck of cards nearby. In fact, you can save yourself weeks or months of time if you lay out the cards that you see in the sample hands and play those cards as I tell you to in the text.

Better yet, try to find three other players who want to play this exciting game. You can read the book together and actually play the hands as you read. Experience is the best teacher, and if you're not ready for a real hand, you can use the material in this book as a kind of dry run.

If, during the course of reading this book, you feel like you just have to get in on the action, feel free to jump into any game you can find. Play as often as you can.

How This Book Is Organized

You find the book divided into six parts, each focusing on a different aspect of the game.

Part I: The Play of the Hand at Notrump

Chapter 1 starts at ground zero and describes the mechanics of the game, giving you a birds-eye view of bridge. The rest of the part discusses various techniques for taking tricks in a notrump contract.

Part II: The Play of the Hand at Trump

In this part, you discover the special know-how you need to bring home the tricks when you end up in a trump contract.

Part III: Bidding to Win

This part also teaches you the fundamentals of bidding — when to bid and how high to go when you do. You can also find out all about the scoring in bridge.

Part IV: Playing Defense

You can't just let your opponents walk all over you! In this part, I tell you how to stick out your foot and really trip up your opponents.

Part V: Getting Hooked on Bridge

You will come to love this game. In this part, you can read up on playing in clubs and tournaments and on the Internet.

Part VI: The Part of Tens

In this part, you can read about the most important factor in any hand — your partner. You can also pick a little bridge background by reading about some of the greatest bridge players of all time. Finally, this part also offers a list of some really great bridge resources that you can use after you put this book back on the shelf.

Icons Used in This Book

The icons used in this book highlight important topics and help you pick out what you want to know.

Bridge has a language all its own, and I point you to a few key terms in this new language.

If you can't remember everything you read in this book, please try to keep these items in mind.

I pack this book full of helpful hints that make you a smarter player, faster.

Watch out! You could lose many tricks or something equally disastrous if you ignore items marked with this icon.

Before You Get Started

In this book, I use a few symbols when referring to cards and bids.

In a deck of cards, you have four suits: spades (♠), hearts (♥), diamonds (♦), and clubs (♣). When I refer to a particular card, I use abbreviations. For example, the six of spades becomes ♠6 and the jack of hearts transforms into ♥J.

I talk a lot about cards in this book. Sometimes I want to show you all the cards in your hand, and sometimes I want to show you the cards in every player's hand (that's 52 cards!). Instead of listing those cards in the text, I set them aside in figures so that you can more easily see who has which cards. The cards in a hand are separated by suit, making it even easier to see each player's holdings.

In these figures, you may notice that I've assigned a "direction" to each of the four players: You see a North, South, East, and West. Again, I use directions to make it easier for you to follow the play as it goes around the table. For most of the book, you are South. If I want you to see things from a different perspective, I tell you where you are seated.

When I talk about bidding (especially in Part III), I use a table like the following to show you how a bidding sequence progresses:

South	West	North	East
1♣	1NT	Pass	Pass
Pass			

Don't worry about what this bidding means. For now, I just want you to understand that you read these tables starting at the upper left-hand corner, continuing to the right until the fourth player, and then back to the second line and the first player. For example, for the preceding sequence, the bidding starts with the first player, South (who bids 1♣), and continues to the right until the fourth player, East (who passes). Then the sequence goes back to South, the first player, who passes.

At times, it may seem that I overrun you with rules. I'm just giving you guidelines, something to get you started with the game. After you begin to play, you will see many exceptions to the guidelines you read in this book. Just remember that bridge is based most of all on common sense. After reading this book, you'll have a good idea of what to do when you encounter new situations.

Part I
The Play of the Hand at Notrump

The 5th Wave   By Rich Tennant

"BETTY—DON'T YOU DARE USE THIS AS AN EXCUSE NOT TO CONCENTRATE!"

In this part . . .

Don't get scared off by the title of the first chapter — Bridge Boot Camp. I promise I won't ask you to drop and give me 20 sit-ups. But you can consider this chapter a kind of induction into the world of bridge; I cover all the fundamentals you need to get a quick start with the game.

In the rest of the part, I go over the various elements of playing a hand at a notrump contract where the highest card in the suit wins the shootin' match (the trick).

Chapter 1

Bridge Boot Camp

*W*elcome to bridge boot camp! In this chapter, I talk about some basic concepts that you need under your belt to get started playing bridge. Consider this chapter your first step into the game of bridge.

By the way, I want you to know that you made a good choice, a very good choice, about playing bridge. Perhaps I'm biased, but bridge is the best card game ever. You can play bridge all over the world, and wherever you go, you can make new friends automatically by starting up a game of bridge. Bridge can be more than a game — it can be a common bond.

Getting a Game Started: What You Need

Before you can begin to play bridge, you need to outfit yourself with some basic supplies. Actually, you may already have some of these items around the house, just begging for you to use them in your bridge game. What do you need? Here's your bottom-line list:

▶ Four warm bodies, including yours.

▶ A table — a square one is best. In a pinch, you can play on a blanket, on a bed, indoors, outdoors, or even on a computer if you can't find a game.

▶ One deck of playing cards, preferably two decks (remove the jokers).

▶ A pencil and a piece of paper to keep score on. You can use any old piece of paper— a legal pad, the back of a grocery list, or even an ancient piece of papyrus will do.

Eddie's quick-start tips

I've been playing bridge for a long time now, so let me offer you a few hints on how you can make getting started with the game a little easier:

- ✔ Watch a real bridge game to observe the mechanics of the game.

- ✔ Round up three friends who are interested in playing. Not to worry if you all don't know what you're doing. We all begin knowing nothing; some of us even end up that way.

- ✔ Follow the sample hands in this book by laying out the cards to correspond to the cards in the figures. Doing so gives you a feel for the cards and makes the explanations easier to follow.

Ranking the Cards

A deck has 52 cards divided up into four suits: spades (♠), hearts (♥), diamonds (♦), and clubs (♣).

Each suit has 13 cards: the AKQJ10 (which are called the *honor cards*) and 98765432 (the *spot cards*).

The 13 cards in a suit all have a rank — that is, they have a pecking order. The ace is the highest-ranking card, followed by the king, the queen, the jack, and the 10, on down to the lowly 2 (which is also called the *deuce*).

Because each card has a ranking, the more high-ranking cards you have in your hand, the better. The more honor cards you have, the stronger your hand. You can never have too many honor cards.

Knowing Your Directions

In bridge, the players are nameless souls — they're known by directions. When you sit down at a table with your three pals to play bridge, imagine that the table is a compass. You're sitting at due South, your partner sits across from you in the North seat, and your opponents sit East and West.

In Chapters 1 through 7 of this book, you're South for every hand, and your partner is North. Just as in the opera where the tenor always gets the girl, in a bridge diagram, you're represented as South — you are called the *declarer*, and you always get to play the hand. Your partner, North, is always the *dummy*. Don't worry about what these terms mean just yet — the idea is that you play every hand from the South position.

Figure 1-1 diagrams the playing table. You should get acquainted with this little diagram: You see some form of it many, many times in this book, not to mention in newspaper columns and magazines. For me, this diagram was a blessing in disguise — I never could get my directions straight until I started playing bridge.

Figure 1-1:
You're
South, your
partner is
North, and
your
opponents
are East
and West.

North (Your Partner)

West   East

South (You)

Playing the Game

Obviously, there's more to playing a game of bridge than I can tell you in this section. If playing bridge were that simple, it wouldn't be half as challenging, rewarding, and fun (and you certainly would not need this book). In this section, I'd like to give you a fast-forwarded view of one bridge hand so that you can get acquainted with how it all works.

First and foremost, bridge is a partnership game — you swim together and you sink together. Your opponents are in the same boat. In bridge, you don't score points individually — you score points as a team.

To get the drift of the first chapters of this book, don't worry about keeping score. See Chapter 16 to find out more about scoring if you can't wait.

Each hand of bridge is divided into four phases, which always occur in the same order:

1. The deal
2. The bidding
3. The play
4. The scoring

Phase 1: the deal

The game starts with each player seated facing her partner. The cards are shuffled and placed on the table face down. Each player selects a card, and the one who picks the highest card deals the first hand. (After each hand, the deal rotates to the left so that one person doesn't get stuck doing all the dealing.)

The cards are dealt one at a time starting with the player to the dealer's left and moving in a clockwise rotation until each player has 13 cards (you deal out the entire deck of cards).

You should wait until the dealer distributes all the cards before you pick up your hand. That's bridge etiquette Lesson #1. I give you some other etiquette tips throughout the book to help you polish your form.

When each player has 13 cards, pick up and sort your hand. You can sort the cards in any number of ways, but I recommend sorting your cards into the four suits. You should also alternate your black suits (clubs and spades) with your red suits (diamonds and hearts) so that you don't confuse a black suit for another black suit or a red suit for another red suit. It's a bit disconcerting to think you're playing a heart only to see a diamond come floating out of your hand. In addition, hold your cards back so that only you can see them. It's difficult to be a winning bridge player when your opponents can see your hand.

Phase 2: the bidding for tricks

Bidding in bridge can be compared to an auction. The auctioneer tells you what the minimum bid is, and the first bid starts from that point or higher. Each successive bid must be higher than the last until someone bids so high that everyone else wants out. When you want out of the bidding, you say "pass." After three consecutive players say "pass," the bidding is over. However, if you pass and someone else makes a bid, just as at an auction, you can reenter the bidding.

In real-life auctions, people often bid for silly things, such as John F. Kennedy's golf clubs or Andy Warhol's cookie jars. In bridge, you don't bid for cars, art treasures, or precious gems; you bid for something really valuable — tricks. Because the whole game revolves around tricks, you really need to understand the term.

Some of you may remember the game of War from when you were a kid. If you don't remember, just pretend that you do and follow along. In War, two players divide the deck between them. Each player takes a turn placing a card face up on the table. The player with the higher card *takes the trick*.

In bridge, four people each place a card face up on the table, and the highest card in the suit that has been led takes the trick. Because each player has 13 cards, 13 tricks must be fought over and won in each hand.

Think of bidding as an estimation of how many of those 13 tricks your side (or their side) thinks it can take. The bidding starts with the dealer and moves to his left in a clockwise rotation. Each player gets a chance to bid. The least you can bid is for seven tricks, and the maximum you can bid is for all 13. A player can either bid or pass at his turn.

The bidding goes around and around the table, each player either bidding or passing, until three players in a row say "pass."

The last bid (the one followed by three passes) is called the *final contract.* No, that's not something the Mafia puts out on you. It's simply the number of tricks that the bidding team must take in order to score points (see Part III for more about bidding and Chapter 16 for more about scoring).

Phase 3: the play of the hand

After the bidding for tricks, the play begins. Either your team or the other team makes the final bid. Because you are the star of this book, pretend that you make the final bid — for nine tricks. Therefore, your goal is to win at least nine tricks in the hand.

If you take nine (or more) tricks, your team scores points. If you take fewer than nine tricks, you are penalized, and your opponents score points. See Chapter 16 for the details on scoring.

The opening lead and the dummy

The person who makes the last bid (you, in this case) usually becomes the *declarer,* and that person's partner becomes the *dummy* (no offense intended). The person to declarer's left (West, assuming that you're South) *leads,* or puts down, the first card, called the *opening lead,* faceup in the middle of the table.

After the opening lead lands on the table, things really begin to roll. The next person to "play" is the dummy — but instead of playing a card, the dummy puts her hand faceup on the table in four neat vertical rows, one row for each suit, and then bows out of the action entirely. After she puts down her cards, she says and does nothing, leaving the other three people to play the rest of the hand. Ever heard of the Sphinx?

The 13 cards that the dummy puts down are also called *the dummy.* Yes, the dummy puts down the dummy. I know it doesn't make much sense — I didn't make these terms up.

Because the dummy is no longer involved in the action, each time it is the dummy's turn to play, you, the declarer, must physically take a card from the dummy and put it in the middle of the table. In addition, you must play a card from your own hand when it's your turn.

The fact that the declarer gets stuck with playing all the team's cards while the dummy is off munching on snacks may seem a bit unfair. But you do have an advantage over the defenders: You get to see your partner's cards before you play, which allows you to plan a strategy of how to win those nine tricks (or however many tricks you need in order to make the final contract).

Now hear this: following suit

The opening lead determines which suit the other three players must play. Each of the players must *follow suit,* meaning that they must play a card in the suit that's led if they have one. For example, pretend that the opening lead is a heart. Down comes the dummy, and you (and everyone else at the table) can see the dummy's hearts as well as your own hearts. Because you must play the same suit that is led if you have one, you have to play some heart, any heart you wish, from the dummy. You place the heart of your choice face up on the table and wait for your right-hand opponent (East, assuming that the dummy is North) to play a heart. After she plays a heart, you play a heart from your hand. Voilà: Four hearts now sit on the table. A trick! Whoever has played the highest heart takes the trick. One trick down and only 12 to go — you're on a roll!

What if a player doesn't have a card in the suit that has been led? Then, and only then, can a player choose a card, any card, from another suit and play it, which is called a *discard.* When you discard, you're literally throwing your card away, knowing that it's worthless because it's not in the proper suit. A discard can never win a trick.

In general, you discard worthless cards that can't take tricks, saving good-looking cards that may take tricks later.

If you can follow suit, you must. If you have a card in the suit that's been led but you play a card in another suit by mistake, you *revoke.* Not good; if you are detected, penalties may be involved. Don't worry, though — everybody revokes once in a while. I once lost a National Championship by revoking on the last hand of the tournament.

Winning and stacking tricks

The player who plays the highest card in the suit that has been led wins the trick. That player sweeps up the four cards and puts them in a neat stack, facedown a little off to the side. The declarer "keeps house" for his team by stacking tricks into piles so that anyone can see how many tricks that team has won. The defender (your opponent) who wins the first trick does the same for his or her side.

The player who takes the first trick *leads first*, or plays the first card, to the second trick. That person can lead any card in any suit she wishes, and the other three players must follow suit if they can.

The play continues until all 13 tricks have been played. After you play to the last trick, each team counts up the number of tricks it has won.

Phase 4: the scoring

After the smoke clears and the tricks are counted, you know soon enough whether the declarer's team made its contract. You then register the score — see Chapter 16 for more about scoring.

After the hand has been scored up, the deal moves one player to the left. So if South dealt the first hand, West is now the dealer. Then North deals the next hand, then East, and then the deal reverts back to South.

Play continues until one team bids and makes two game contracts, which is called winning a *rubber*. Once the rubber is over, everyone can go home or start playing another rubber. If you play tennis, think of winning a rubber as *winning a set*.

Understanding Notrump and Trump

The names of the first two parts of this book have some funny words in them: *trump* and *notrump*. You can't get very far playing bridge if you don't decode these funny phrases. Take a few minutes to read this section and be in the know.

Have you ever played a card game that has wild cards? When you play with wild cards, playing a wild card automatically wins the trick for you. Sometimes wild cards can be jokers, deuces, or aces. It doesn't matter what the card is; if you have one, you know you have a sure winner. In bridge, you have wild cards, too, called *trump cards*. Only in bridge, the trump cards are really wild because they change from hand to hand, depending on the bidding.

The bidding determines whether a hand will be played with trump cards or in a notrump contract (a hand with no trump cards). If the final bid names a trump suit, that suit is the "wild" suit for the hand. For example, suppose that the final bid is 4♠ — this bid determines that spades are *trump* (or wild) for the entire hand. For more about playing a hand at a trump contract, see Part II.

When the final bid ends in notrump, the highest card played in the suit that has been led wins the trick. All the hands that you play in Part I are played at notrump.

More contracts are played at notrump than in any of the four suits.

Graduating from Bridge Boot Camp

Congratulations! If you read this whole chapter, you just graduated from Bridge Boot Camp. Sorry — you don't get a diploma. But you do get the thrill of knowing what you need to know to start playing bridge.

If you haven't read the chapter, I strongly recommend that you do, because it explains a few key concepts that will help you understand the rest of this book.

So what's the fascination?

You may have met a few unfortunates who are totally hooked on playing bridge. They just can't get enough of it. Being a charter member of that breed, I can offer a few words on why people can get so wrapped up in the game.

One fascination is the bidding. Bidding involves a lot of partner-to-partner communication skills, and cleverly exchanging information between you and your partner in the special language of the game is a great challenge. Your opponents also pass information back and forth during the bidding, so figuring out what they're telling each other is another challenge. Bidding is such an art that some bridge books deal entirely with bidding.

Another hook for the game is taking tricks. You get to root out all kinds of devious ways to take tricks, both as a declarer and as a defender.

And don't forget the human element. Bridge is much more than a game of putting down and picking up cards. Emotions enter into the picture — sooner or later, every emotion or personality trait that you see in life emerges at the bridge table.

Chapter 2

Counting and Taking Sure Tricks

●●

In This Chapter

▶ Recognizing the sure tricks in each suit

▶ Adding sure tricks to your trick pile

●●

*I*f you are sitting at a blackjack table in Las Vegas, you're a goner if you get caught counting cards. However, if you are at a bridge table and you don't count cards, you are one dead duck.

When you play a bridge hand, you need to count several things — most important, you need to count your tricks. The game of bridge revolves around tricks; you bid for tricks; you take as many tricks as you can in the play of the hand, and the opponents try to take as many tricks as they can on defense. Tricks, tricks, tricks.

In this chapter, I show you how to spot a sure trick in its natural habitat — in your hand or in the dummy.

Before the play of the hand begins, the bidding determines the final contract. In Parts I and II of this book, I purposely omit the bidding process from the scenarios that I discuss; for the hands in these chapters, the bidding has already taken place and the dummy has already come down. In Parts I and II, I want you to concentrate on both how to count and take your tricks to your best advantage. After you discover the trick-taking capabilities of honor cards and long suits, the bidding will make much more sense. You can turn to Part III of the book to discover the wonders of bidding for tricks.

Counting Sure Tricks after the Dummy Comes Down

The old phrase "You need to know where you are to know where you're going" comes to mind when playing bridge. After you know your *final contract* (how many tricks you need to take), you then need to figure out how to win all the tricks you need to make your contract.

Depending on which cards you and your partner hold, you may hold some sure winners, called *sure tricks,* from the beginning of the hand. Of course, you want as many of these sure tricks as possible, and you should be very happy to see them in your hand. You can never have too many sure tricks.

Sure tricks (tricks that you can take at any time) depend on whether you have the ace in a particular suit (either in your hand or the dummy's hand). Because you get to see the dummy after the opening lead, you can see quite clearly if any aces are lurking over there in the dummy. If you notice an ace, you can get greedy and look for a king in that same suit (either in your hand or the dummy). Basically, counting sure tricks boils down to this:

- ✔ If you have the ace in a suit (but no king), count one sure trick.

- ✔ If you have both the ace and the king in the same suit (between the two hands), count two sure tricks.

- ✔ If you have the ace, king, and queen in the same suit (between the two hands), count three sure tricks.

In the following sections, I use a sample hand to demonstrate how to count sure tricks by looking at your honor cards and their distribution.

In Figure 2-1 your final contract is for nine tricks. After you settle on the final contract, the play begins. West makes the opening lead. She decides to lead the ♠Q. Down comes the dummy, and you swing into action, but first a little planning. You need to count your sure tricks.

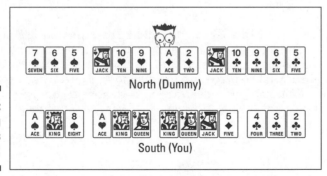

Figure 2-1:
Counting
sure tricks
sure is fun!

Eyeballing your sure tricks in each suit

You count your sure tricks one suit at a time. After you know how many tricks you have, you can make further plans about how to win additional tricks. I walk you through each suit in the following sections, showing you how to count sure tricks.

Be a world-class dummy

The dummy doesn't do much to help you count and take sure tricks except lay down her cards. After her cards are on the table, the dummy shouldn't contribute anything else to the hand — except good dummy etiquette.

As the play progresses, the dummy is not supposed to make faces, utter strange noises, or make disjointed body movements such as

jerks or twitches. Sometimes this takes super-human willpower, particularly when her partner, the declarer, screws up big time. A good dummy learns to control his baser instincts.

If you end up as the dummy and get fidgety, you can always leave the table. The kitchen and TV room offer ideal visitation possibilities.

Walking you through the spades

When the dummy comes down, you can see that your partner has three small spades and you have the ♠A and ♠K, as you see in Figure 2-2.

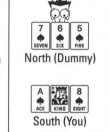

Figure 2-2: Digging up sure spade tricks.

North (Dummy): 7♠ 6♠ 5♠

South (You): A♠ K♠ 8♠

Because the ♠A and the ♠K are the two highest spades in the suit, you can count two sure spade tricks. If you also held the ♠Q, you could count three sure spade tricks.

When you have sure tricks in a suit, you don't have to play them right away. You can take sure tricks at any point during the play of the hand.

Counting some equally divided hearts

Figure 2-3 shows the hearts that you hold in this hand. Notice that hearts is literally loaded with honor cards: You have the ♥AKQJ10.

This wonderful array of hearts is only worth three sure tricks because both hands have the same number of cards. When you play a heart from one hand, you must play a heart from the other hand. As a result, after you play the ♥AKQ, the dummy won't have any more hearts left (and neither will you). You wind up with only three heart tricks because the suit is *equally divided* (you have the same number of cards in both hands).

Figure 2-3: Your hearts are heavy with honor cards.

North (Dummy)

South (You)

When you have an equal number of cards on each side, you can never take more tricks than the number of cards in each hand. For example, if you both hold four hearts, it doesn't matter how many high hearts you have between your hand and the dummy, you can never take more than four heart tricks. Take a look at Figure 2-4 to see how the tragic story of an equally divided suit unfolds.

Figure 2-4: An honor collision causes some honor cards to become worthless.

North (Dummy)

South (You)

In Figure 2-4, you have one heart on each side, the ♥A and the ♥K. All you can take is one lousy heart trick. If you lead the ♥A, you have to play the ♥K from the dummy. If the dummy leads the ♥K first, you have to "overtake" it with your ♥A. It's too sad for words.

Checking out some unequally-divided diamonds

In Figure 2-5, you can see that South holds four diamonds, while North only holds two. When one partner holds more cards in a suit, the suit is said to be *unequally divided.*

Figure 2-5:
Some diamonds in the rough; an unequally divided suit can be a gem.

North (Dummy)

South (You)

Strong unequally divided suits offer oodles of tricks, providing that you play the suit correctly. For example, take a look at how things play out with the cards in Figure 2-5. You begin by leading the ♦5 from your hand, and then you play the ♦A from the dummy — that's one trick. Now the lead is in the dummy because the dummy has taken the trick. Continue by playing ♦2 and then play the ♦K from your hand. Now that the lead is back in your hand, play the ♦Q and then the ♦J. Don't look now, but you just won tricks with all your honor cards — four in all.

Lean a little closer to hear a 5-star tip: If you want to live a long and happy life with unequally divided suits that contain a number of *equal* honors (touching honors such as a king and a queen), play the high honor cards from the short side first. What does *short side* mean? In an unequally divided suit, the player with fewer cards is the short side. In Figure 2-5, the dummy has two diamonds to your four diamonds, making the dummy the short side. When you play the high honors from the short side first, you end up playing the high honors from the hand that started with more cards in the suit (the *long side*). When the lead ends up in the long hand, you get the maximum number of tricks possible.

Counting tricks in a suit with no aces: the clubs

When the dummy comes down, you may see that neither you nor the dummy has the ace in a particular suit, such as the club suit shown in Figure 2-6.

Not all that pretty are they? The opponents have the ♣AKQ. You have no sure tricks in clubs because you don't have the ♣A. If neither your hand nor the dummy has the ace in a particular suit, you can't count any sure tricks in that suit.

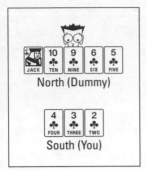

Figure 2-6:
Counting
sure tricks
in a suit
with no
aces.
Forget it.

North (Dummy)

South (You)

Adding up your sure tricks

After you assess how many sure tricks you have in each suit, it's reckoning time. You need to add up all your sure tricks and see if you have enough to make your final contract.

Just to get some practice at adding up tricks, go ahead and add up your sure tricks from the hand shown in Figure 2-1. The total number of tricks is what's important, and you have the following:

- **Spades:** Two sure tricks, the ♠A and the ♠K.
- **Hearts:** Three sure tricks, the ♥AKQ.
- **Diamonds:** Four sure tricks, the ♦AKQJ.
- **Clubs:** No sure tricks because you have no ace. Bad break, buddy.

You are in luck — you have the nine tricks that you need to make your final contract. Now all you have to do is take those nine tricks. You can do it.

Taking Sure Tricks

Having sure tricks is only half the battle; *converting,* or taking, those sure tricks is the other half. In this section, I show you how to do it.

Starting with the strongest suit

When you have enough sure tricks between the two hands to make your contract, you *don't* have to take those tricks in any particular order. However, a reliable guideline to get you off on the right foot is to start by first playing the cards in your strongest suit (the suit that offers you the most tricks). In the case of the hand shown in Figure 2-1, you start by playing your diamonds.

For a moment, backtrack to West's opening lead of the ♠Q. Say that you take this trick with the ♠A, and now the lead is in your hand. You then take your four diamond tricks, and then you can take three more heart tricks by playing the ♥AKQ. Finally, you take your ninth trick with the ♠K. Your opponents take the last four tricks. No big deal — you've taken nine tricks and made your contract.

Taking sure tricks with unequally divided suits

Strong suits are a good source of tricks — the stronger, the better. If those strong suits are unequally divided with equal (or touching) honor cards in both hands, you should play the high honors from the short side first. The cards in Figure 2-7 show you the advantage of starting with the short-side honor cards.

Figure 2-7:
Serving up
sure tricks,
starting
with the
short-side
honor
cards.

North (Dummy)

South (You)

In the example shown in Figure 2-7, you decide to play spades, an unequally divided suit. You have also (smartly) decided to play the high honors from the short side (your hand is the short side because you have three cards to dummy's four cards). Play the ♠A and then the ♠K. You remain with the ♠2, and the dummy has two winning tricks, the ♠QJ. Lead your ♠2 and take the trick with the dummy's ♠J. The lead is now in the dummy, and you can take a fourth spade trick with the ♠Q. You have just added four tricks to your trick pile. There is no stopping you now!

Chapter 3

Playing at Notrump

● ●

In This Chapter

▶ Getting the most out of your lower honor cards

▶ Squeezing tricks from your small cards

▶ Getting around your opponents' honor cards

▶ Interfering with your opponents' tricks

● ●

*W*inning at bridge would be a breeze if you always had enough sure tricks to make your contract. The sad news is that you *seldom* have enough sure tricks to make your contract. You must come up with other ways of taking tricks, ways that may mean temporarily surrendering the lead to your opponents. In this chapter, I show you clever techniques to win those extra tricks that you need to make your contract.

Throughout this chapter, you may notice that many figures show cards in only one suit. Sometimes, I want you to focus on one suit at a time: In the following figures, you see suits that are ideal for creating the extra tricks you need. Don't forget: I always put you in the hot seat by making you South — that's where the action is!

Establishing Tricks with Lower Honor Cards

When you don't have the ace in a suit, you're in bad shape as far as sure tricks. Not to worry. Your new friend, *establishing tricks,* will see you through the tough times and help you win the tricks you need in order to make your contract.

Establishing tricks is all about sacrificing one of your honor cards to drive out one of your opponents' higher honor cards. You can then swoop in later with *your* remaining honor cards and take a bundle of tricks.

Driving the ace out of its hole

The all-powerful ace wins a trick for you every time. But no matter how hard you pray for aces, sometimes you just don't get any, and you can't count any sure tricks in a suit with no aces (see Chapter 2 for the skinny on sure tricks). Sometimes you get tons of honor cards, but no ace, and you still can't count even one sure trick in that suit. Ah, the inhumanity!

Cheer up — you can still create winning tricks in such a suit. When you have all the honors in a suit except the ace, you can *attack* that suit early and *drive out the ace* from your opponent's hand. Here's what you do:

1. **Lead an honor card in the suit in which you are missing the ace.**

   In order to get rid of the ace, you have to play one of your equal honor cards. If you lead a low card, your opponents won't play their ace to take the trick. They would instead take the trick with a lower card.

2. **Continue playing the suit until your opponents play the ace and take the trick.**

3. **After that ace is out of the way, you can count all your remaining equal (touching) honor cards as sure tricks.**

Driving out the ace is a great way of setting up extra tricks. The cards in Figure 3-1 provide an example of a suit that you can attack in order to drive out the ace.

Figure 3-1:
Get the shovel — you're digging for aces.

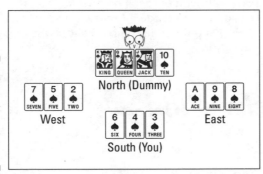

In Figure 3-1, you can't count a single sure spade trick because your opponent (East) has the ♠A. Yet, the spades in the dummy are extremely powerful. (Any suit that contains four honor cards is considered powerful.)

Say that the lead is in your hand from the preceding trick and you lead a low spade (the lowest spade you have). West plays a low spade, you play the ♠10 from the dummy, and East decides to win the trick with the ♠A. You may have lost the lead, but you have also driven out the ♠A. The dummy remains with the ♠KQJ, all winning tricks. You have *established* three sure spade tricks where before there were none — that is, you're set up to win three tricks with the dummy's ♠KQJ because nobody else at the table now has any spades that can beat these honor cards.

Suits with three or more equal honor cards between the two hands are ideal for suit establishment. When you see the KQJ or the QJ10 between your hand and the dummy, don't think twice about attacking that suit.

Doubling your (dis)pleasure

When you're missing just the ace, you can establish the suit easily by just leading one honor after another until your opponent gives up the ace. However, if you're missing both the ace and the king, you have to give up the lead twice in order to take later tricks.

Bridge is a game of giving up the lead to get tricks back. Don't fear giving up the lead. Your high honor cards in the other suits protect you by allowing you to eventually regain the lead and pursue your goal of establishing tricks.

Figure 3-2 shows just such a suit, where you have to swallow your pride twice before you can establish your lower honor cards.

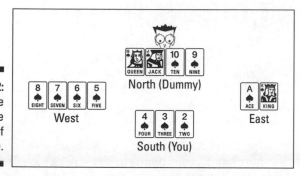

Figure 3-2: Chasing the ace and the king out of their castle.

Notice that the dummy in Figure 3-2 has a sequence of cards headed by three *equal* honors — the ♠QJ10 (and the ♠9). When you have a sequence of cards in one equal suit, all the cards have equal power to take tricks — or to drive out opposing honor cards. For example, you can use the ♠9 or the ♠Q to drive out your opponent's ♠K or ♠A.

In Figure 3-2, your opponents hold the ♠AK. To compensate, you have the ♠QJ109, four equals headed by three honors — a very good sign. You lead a low spade; West plays a low spade; you play the ♠9 from the dummy, and East takes the trick with the ♠K. You have driven out one spade honor. One more to go. Your spades are still not established, but you're halfway home! The next time you have the lead, lead a low spade and then play the ♠10 from the dummy, driving out the ♠A. Guess what? You started with zero sure spade tricks, but now you have two.

Remembering the short-side honors

Never forget this simple and powerful rule: When attacking an unequally divided suit, play the high equal honors from the short side first (the side with the fewest cards). Doing so enables you to end up in the long side where the remainder of the honors, and therefore the remainder of the tricks, are located. If you remember to play your equal honors from the short side first, your partner will kneel down and declare you Ruler of the Universe.

Even if you don't want to be the Ruler of the Universe, you still need to remember that playing the honors from the short side first enables you to end up in the hand holding the remainder of the honors — and therefore the remainder of the tricks. If you remember "short-side honors first," you'll know what to do when faced with cards like those shown in Figure 3-3.

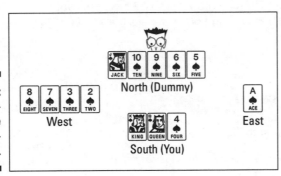

Figure 3-3: Don't short-change your short-side honors.

Liberation time! The short hand (your hand) has two honor cards, the ♠KQ. Start by playing the ♠K, the highest honor on the short side, and a low spade from the dummy. As it happens, East must take the trick with the ♠A because she doesn't have any other spades.

No mutual admiration society

In case you're wondering, your opponents don't just sit around and admire your dazzling technique of establishing tricks. Oh, no — they're busy trying to establish tricks of their own.

In bridge, turnabout is fair play. Whatever you can do, your opponents can also do. Many a

hand turns into a race for tricks. In order to win the race, you must establish your tricks earlier rather than later. Remembering this rule will keep you focused and help you edge out your opponents.

You have established your spades because the ♠A is gone, but you still need to remember the five-star tip of playing the high equal honor from the short side. Play the ♠Q, which takes the trick, and then the ♠4. The dummy can then play the ♠9 to win the trick. With the lead now in the dummy, you can play the ♠J10 to win the rest of the spade tricks on the table. You establish four spade tricks by playing the high card from the short side twice.

Looking for length with no high honor in sight

In this section, you hit the jackpot — I show you how to establish tricks in a suit where you have the J1098, but you're missing the ace, king, and queen! If you don't have any of the three top dogs, but you have four or more cards in the suit, you can still scrape a trick or two out of the suit. When you have length, you know that even after your opponents win all their tricks with the ace, king, and queen, you still hold cards in that suit, which become — voilà! — instant winners.

Perhaps you're wondering why you would ever want to squeeze some juice out of a suit in which you lack the ace, king, and queen? The answer: You may need tricks from an anemic suit like this in order to make your contract. It happens. Sometimes you just get the raw side of the deal, and you need to pick up tricks wherever you can eke them out.

When you look at the dummy and see a suit such as the one in Figure 3-4, try not to shriek with horror.

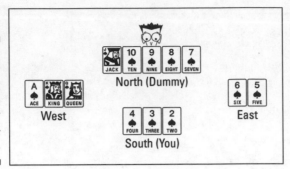

Figure 3-4: Taking the ace, king, and queen out for dinner — your treat.

North (Dummy)

West

East

South (You)

Do those spades in Figure 3-4 make you a little queasy? True, it's not the most appetizing suit you'll ever have to deal with, but don't judge a book by its cover. You can get some tricks out of this suit because you have the advantage of length: You have a total of eight spades between the two hands. The strength you get from numbers helps you outlast the ace, king, and queen.

Say you need to develop two tricks from this hopeless-looking, forsaken suit. You start with a low spade, which is taken by West's ♠Q (the dummy and East contribute the ♠7 and ♠5, respectively). After you regain the lead in some other suit, lead another spade, which is taken by West's ♠K (the dummy plays the ♠8 and East plays her last spade, the ♠6). After you gain the lead again in another suit, lead a third spade, which loses to West's ♠A. You have lost the lead again, but you have accomplished your ultimate goal. Don't look now, but the dummy holds two winning spades — the ♠J10. Nobody at the table holds any more spades; when the dummy wins a trick in another suit, you can go right ahead and claim those two spade tricks.

Practicing establishment

Practice makes perfect, they say, so I want you to practice making your contract by establishing tricks. In this section, you hold the hand shown in Figure 3-5. Your final contract is for 12 tricks. West leads the ♠J. Now you need to do your thing and establish some tricks.

Before you even think of playing a card from the dummy, count your sure tricks. Give it a whirl (see Chapter 2 if you need some help counting sure tricks):

- **Spades:** You have three sure tricks — the AKQ.
- **Hearts:** You have another three sure tricks — the AKQ. (Don't count the ♥J; you have three hearts in each hand, so you can't take more than three tricks.)
- **Diamonds:** Sad. No sure tricks — no ace, no sure tricks.
- **Clubs:** You have three sure tricks — the AKQ.

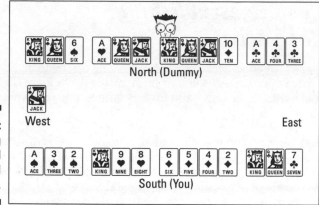

Figure 3-5:
Establishing
a powerful
diamond
suit.

You have 9 sure tricks, but you need 12 tricks to make your contract. You must establish 3 more tricks. Look no further than the dummy's magnificent diamond suit. If you can drive out the ♦A, you can establish three diamond tricks just like that.

When you need to establish extra tricks, pick the suit you plan to work with and start establishing immediately. Do not take your sure tricks until you establish your extra needed tricks. Then take all your tricks in one giant cascade.

First you need to deal with West's opening lead, the ♠J. You have a choice. You can win the trick in either your hand with the ♠A or in the dummy with the ♠Q. Your objective is to establish tricks in your target suit: the diamonds. Say that you decide to save your ♠A for later, and you take the ♠J with the ♠Q in the dummy.

Following your game plan, you lead the ♦K from the dummy. Pretend that West takes the trick with the ♦A and then leads the ♠10. Presto — your three remaining diamonds in the dummy, the ♦QJ10, have just become three sure tricks. Your sure trick count has just ballooned from 9 to 12. Don't look now, but you've just made your contract.

After you have enough sure tricks to make your contract, do not pass Go, do not collect $200, just take your tricks.

Next comes the best part: the mop-up and taking your winning tricks. Say that you take West's return of ♠10 with the ♠K. Then you take your three established diamonds, your three winning hearts, your three winning clubs and, finally, your ♠A. It all comes to 12 tricks, 3 in each suit. Ah, the thrill of victory.

Taking before establishing: you will be sorry

Establishing extra, needed tricks is all about giving up the lead. Sometimes you need to drive out an ace, a king, or both an ace *and* a king. Giving up the lead to establish tricks can be painful for a beginner, but you must steel yourself to do it.

You may hate to give up the lead for fear that something terrible may happen. And you're right. Something terrible is going to happen — if you're afraid to give up the lead to establish a suit. Most of the time, beginners fail to make their contracts because they don't establish extra tricks soon enough. Very often, beginners fall into the trap of taking tricks before establishing tricks.

I know that you would never commit such a grievous error, but just for the fun of it, take a look at Figure 3-6 to see what happens when you take tricks before establishing tricks. This isn't going to be pretty, so clear out the children.

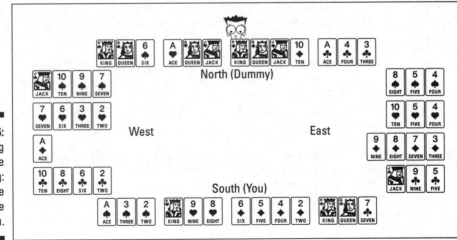

Figure 3-6:
Taking before establishing: The apocalypse is upon you.

In this hand (showing all the cards from the hand shown in Figure 3-5), the opening lead is the ♠J, and you need to take 12 tricks. Say you take the first three spade tricks with the ♠AKQ, then the next three heart tricks with the ♥AKQ, and finally the next three club tricks with the ♣AKQ. Figure 3-7 shows what's left after you take the first nine tricks (Remember: You need to take 12 tricks.)

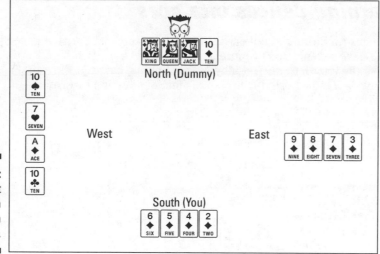

Figure 3-7: It doesn't get much uglier than this.

Now, finally you lead a low diamond. But guess what — West takes the trick with the ♦A. The hairs standing up on the back of your neck may tell you what I'm going to say next: West has all the rest of the tricks! West remains with a winning spade, a winning heart, and a winning club. Nobody else at the table has any of those suits, so all the other players are forced to discard. West's three cards are all winning tricks, and those great diamonds in the dummy are nothing but deadweight.

A word to the wise: Nothing good can happen to you if you take your sure tricks before establishing extra needed tricks.

Taking Tricks with Small Cards

Grab a man off the street, and he'll be able to take tricks with aces and kings. But can that same man take tricks with small cards, such as 2s and 3s?

Only very rarely do you get a hand dripping with all the honor cards you need to make your contract. Therefore, you must know how to take tricks with the smaller cards. You seldom have enough firepower (aces and kings) to make your contract without these little fellows.

Small, or *low*, cards take tricks when attached to long suits. Small cards start out looking pretty innocuous, but they sort of hang out with the higher honors hoping to get into the action. Eventually, after all the high honors in a suit have been played, the little guys start making appearances. They may be bit actors when the play begins, but before the final curtain is drawn, they're out there taking the final bows — and taking tricks.

Turning deuces into aces

Deuces (and other small cards, for that matter) can take tricks for you when you have seven cards or more in a suit between the two hands. You may then have the length to outlast all your opponents' cards in the suit. Figure 3-8 shows a hand where this incredible feat of staying power takes place.

Figure 3-8:
The ugly duckling becomes a swan.

	North (Dummy)	
	♠A ♠K ♠Q ♠2	
West		East
♠J ♠9 ♠8		♠10 ♠7 ♠4
	South (You)	
	♠6 ♠5 ♠3	

You have chosen to attack spades in this hand. Because the ♠AKQ in the dummy are all equals (see "Doubling your (dis)pleasure" in this chapter for more on equals), the suit can be started from either your hand or the dummy. Pretend that the lead is in your hand, and you begin by leading a low spade to the ♠Q in the dummy, and both opponents follow suit. With the lead in the dummy, continue by leading the ♠A and then the ♠K from the dummy. As it happens, the opponents both started with three spades, meaning that they now have no more spades. That ♠2 in the dummy is a winning trick. The frog has turned into a prince.

Whenever you have four cards in a suit in one hand and three in the other, and the opponents have six cards in the suit divided three in each hand, you are destined to take a trick with any small card attached to your four-card suit.

Don't expect that fourth card to turn into a trick every time. Your opponents' six cards may not be divided 3-3 after all. They may be divided 4-2, as you see in Figure 3-9.

When you play the ♠AKQ as you do in Figure 3-9, East turns up with four spades, so your ♠2 won't be a trick. After you play the ♠AKQ, East remains with the ♠J, a higher spade than your ♠2. Learn to live with it.

Bridge is a game of strategy and luck. When it comes to taking tricks with small cards, you just have to hope that chance is on your side.

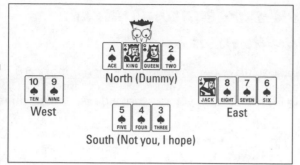

Figure 3-9:
Dealing
with an
unfriendly
split.

TIP

Subtracting your way to stardom

Happiness is having small cards that turn into winning tricks; misery is having small cards that are winning tricks and not knowing it; total misery is thinking your small cards are winning tricks only to find out they aren't.

In order to know when your small cards are winners, you must become familiar with the dreaded "c" word, *counting.* If you count the cards in the suit you're playing, you can tell whether your little guys have a chance. You have to do a little simple subtraction as well, but I can assure you it's well worth the effort.

A neat way of counting the suit you're attacking is with the *subtraction-by-two method.* Follow these steps for successful counting every time:

1. **Count how many cards you and the dummy have in the suit.**

2. **Subtract the number of cards you have from 13 (the total number of cards in a suit) to get the total number of cards your opponents have in the suit.**

3. **Each time you lead the suit and both opponents follow suit, subtract two from the number of cards your opponents have left.**

4. **When the number of cards your opponents hold gets to 0, all your remaining small cards are winning tricks.**

With this method, the numbers get smaller and become easier to work with. Some people think doing stuff like this is fun — with any luck, you're one of these people.

You may discover an easier way of counting, but for most people the subtraction-by-two method works just fine. If you just have to be different, here are a few other methods:

✔ **The digital (fingers and toes) method:** This method requires playing with open-air sandals so that you can see your digits clearly.

✔ **The faking-a-count method:** You look intently at the cards that have been played as if you're counting them. Then you look up at the ceiling as if the count is written up there, and finally, you nod sagely even though you don't have the vaguest idea of how many cards your opponents have left.

Turning low cards into winners by driving out high honors

Sometimes you have to drive out an opponent's high honor card before you can turn your frogs into princes (or turn your deuces into tricks). Figure 3-10 shows you how (with a little luck) you can turn a deuce into a winner.

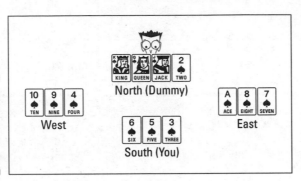

Figure 3-10: Another frog, another prince.

With the cards shown in Figure 3-10, your plan is to develop (or *establish*) as many spade tricks as possible, keeping a wary eye on turning that ♠2 in the dummy into a winner. Say that you begin by leading a low spade, and West follows with a low spade. You play the ♠J from the dummy, which loses to East's ♠A. At this point, you note the following:

- The ♠KQ in the dummy are now both winning tricks because your opponents' ♠A is gone.

- Your opponents started with six spades. By using Kantar's subtraction method (see the nearby "Subtracting your way to stardom" sidebar), you know that your opponents now have only four spades left. Four is the new key number.

After regaining the lead by winning a trick in another suit, you can lead one of your low spades to the ♠Q in the dummy (with both opponents following suit). Your opponents now have two spades left between them. When you continue with the ♠K, both opponents follow suit again. They now have zero spades left — triumph! The ♠2 in the dummy is now a sure trick. Deuces love to take tricks — it makes them feel wanted.

Make sure that you count the cards in the suit you are attacking. It's pretty sad if you don't know (or aren't sure) whether a low card in your hand or in the dummy could be a winner and leave it untouched because it is such a small card.

Losing a trick early: the ducking play

Suits that have seven or eight cards between your hand and the dummy, including the ace and the king, lend themselves to taking extra tricks with lower cards, even though you have to lose a trick in the suit.

Why do you have to lose a trick in the suit? Because the opponents have the queen, the jack, and the ten. After you play the ace and the king, the opponent with the queen is looking at a winning trick.

When you know you have to lose at least one trick in a suit that includes the ace and king, you should face the inevitable. You should intentionally lose that trick early by playing low cards from both your hand and the dummy. Taking this dive early on is called *ducking a trick*.

Ducking a trick is a necessary evil when playing bridge. Paradoxically, it affords you control over the play later in the game. Ducking a trick in a suit that has an inevitable loser allows you to keep your controlling cards (the ace and the king) in the suit so that you can use them in a late rush of tricks.

When you duck a trick and then play the ace and king of your long suit, you wind up in the hand where the small cards are — just where you want to be.

The cards in Figure 3-11 show how successful ducking a trick can be.

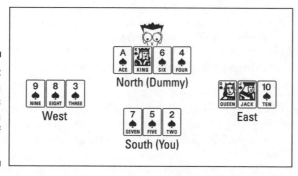

Figure 3-11: Ducking a trick leaves you in control of the suit.

In Figure 3-11, you have seven cards between the two hands with the ♠AK in the dummy — a perfect setup for ducking a trick. You can only hope that your opponents' six cards are divided 3-3. In order to find out, you have to play the suit three times.

You know you have to lose at least one spade trick because your opponents hold the ♠QJ10. Because you have to lose at least one spade trick, you should lose the trick right away.

Try this: Play a low spade from both hands! No, you aren't giving out presents; actually you're making a very clever ducking play by letting your opponents have a trick they're entitled to early on.

After you concede the trick, you can come roaring back with your big guns, the ♠A and the ♠K, the next time you regain the lead. Notice that because their spades are divided 3-3, that little ♠6 in the dummy takes a third trick in the suit — neither opponent has any more spades.

If the dummy has a five-card suit headed by the ace and the king, you can take two extra tricks with a ducking play. See Figure 3-12, where you can use a ducking play to make the tricks come flowing in.

Figure 3-12:
Setting
up an
avalanche
of tricks via
a ducking
play.

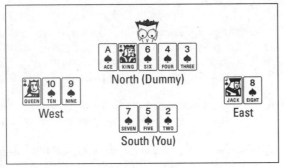

In Figure 3-12, the opponents have five spades between the two hands, including the ♠QJ. You have to lose a spade trick no matter what, so lose it right away by making one of your patented ducking plays. Lead the ♠2; West plays the ♠9, you play the ♠3 from the dummy, and East plays the ♠8. West wins the trick. Not to worry — you will soon show them who's boss!

The next time either you or the dummy regains the lead, play the ♠A and ♠K, thus removing all their remaining spades. You have the lead in the dummy, and the dummy remains with the ♠64, both winning tricks.

When you have five cards in one hand and three in the other, including the ace and the king, you have a chance to take four tricks by playing a low card from both hands at your first opportunity. This ducking play allows you to retain control (control = the highest cards in the suit); it allows you to come swooping in later to take the remaining tricks.

Finding heaven with seven

Having any seven cards may mean an extra trick for you — if your opponents' cards are divided 3-3. The hand in Figure 3-13 shows you how any small card can become a winner when your opponents' cards are split evenly.

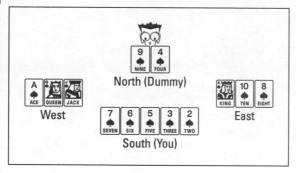

Figure 3-13:
Winning
against all
odds: You
hold no
honor
cards, but
you have
length in
one hand.

You have seven cards between your hand and dummy, the signal that something good may happen for your small cards. Of course, you would be a little happier if you had some higher cards in the suit (such as an honor or two), but beggars can't be choosers.

Remember Cinderella and how her sisters dressed her up to look ugly even though she was beautiful? Well, those five cards in South are like Cinderella — you just have to cast off the rags to see the beauty underneath.

Say you lead a low spade, and West takes the trick with the ♠J. Later, you lead a second spade, and West takes that trick with the ♠Q. You have played spades twice, and because you have been counting those spades, you know that your opponents have two spades left.

After you regain the lead, you again lead a *rag* (low card). Crash, bang! West plays the ♠A, and East plays the ♠K. Now they have no more spades, and the two remaining spades in your hand are winning tricks. You concede three tricks in the suit (tricks they always had coming) but get back two tricks in return by persistence.

Blocking a suit

Even when length is on your side, you need to play the high equal honor cards from the short side first. Doing so ensures that the lead ends up in the hand with the length — and therefore the winning tricks. If you don't play the high honors from the short side first, you run the risk of *blocking a suit*. A suit is blocked when you have winning cards stranded in one hand and no way to get over to that hand in order to play those winning cards. Figure 3-14 shows you a suit that's blocked from the very start.

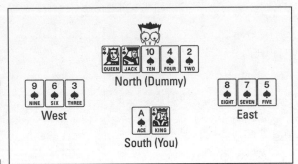

Figure 3-14:
Some suits are born blocked.

Figure 3-14 features a bridge tragedy: seeing the dummy come down with a strong suit only to realize that it's blocked and can't be used. You have five spade tricks, but you may be able to take only two of those five. After you play the ♠AK, you are fresh out of spades, and the dummy remains with the ♠QJ10.

If you don't have an *entry* (a winning card) in another suit to get over to the dummy, the dummy's three winning spades will die on the vine.

The more poignant tragedy is when you block your own suits by forgetting to play the high card(s) from the short side. When you forget to play the high honors from the short side first, you wind up with the lead in the short hand, thus nullifying any winning tricks you have left in the long hand. Read the following sidebar, "The tragic, true story of blocking your own suit" for more on the horrible consequences of blocking your own suit.

Figure 3-15:
Going, going, gone! Blocking suits blows away your tricks.

The tragic, true story of blocking your own suit

Blocking your own suit brings to mind a true story that took place in a swanky London Bridge Club some 60-odd years ago. I call this story my own personal "Gone with the Wind." I want to tell you this story to show you how treacherous it can be to block your own suits by forgetting to play the high honors from the short side first.

It was a high-stakes game, and North was the pro playing with the worst player in the club, a rich young man. The idea when playing with this man wasn't to win — that was impossible — but to hold your losses to as little as possible. It was a scorchingly hot day, and all the windows in the club were wide open. The pro happened to be sitting with his back to one of the windows.

The pro tried never to let his partner play a hand if he could help it. It was just too painful to watch. Then came the ill-fated Hand to End All Hands, shown in Figure 3-15. Going against his better judgment, the pro allowed this gentleman to play the hand, in which the final contract was for nine tricks (a staggering total for the young gentleman).

The opening lead was the ♦K. After the pro put down the dummy, he went to get a drink but couldn't resist walking behind his partner to peek at what he had. When he saw what the young man had, the pro was ecstatic. His partner was actually going to take 10 tricks: 7 clubs (by playing the ♣A and then a low club to the dummy's ♣10, followed by five more winning clubs) plus 3 other aces. The pro was going to win a bundle. Unheard of! He returned to his seat to enjoy the hand and also to figure out how many pounds (the game was in England, remember) he was about to win.

The young gentleman took the first trick with the ♦A and immediately led the ♣2. Instead of playing the high card from the short side (the ♣A), he played the low card from the short side. By this one stroke, the young man had *blocked* the club suit.

Here's what happened: After playing the ♣2 and winning the trick in the dummy with the ♣10, the young man then led a low club from the dummy back to the ♣A in his hand. Unfortunately, the dummy now held five — count 'em, five — winning clubs. Poor South had no more clubs in his hand and no way to get to the dummy in another suit (rendering all the remaining clubs in North's hand worthless). The club suit in the dummy was dead, totally dead. The inexperienced young man had blocked the club suit and converted seven club tricks into only two club tricks, which is something you would never do, right? Nod your head, for goodness sake.

When the pro saw the mistake the young man had made, he took his remaining 10 cards and tossed them out the window. "Why are you doing that?" the young man asked. "You won't need them anymore," the pro replied.

Slipping Lower Honors Past Higher Honors: The Finesse

In this section, I discuss another technique for establishing tricks; this technique requires you to start by leading the suit from a particular hand.

When you have the ace in a suit, you can just take the trick any time you want. But what if you have a king in a suit, but no ace? If you lead the king, the opponent with the ace will zap it. In cases such as these, you need to *lead toward* the king, meaning that you need to lead the suit from the side opposite the king.

Welcome to the world of the *finesse,* a technique for taking tricks with lower honor cards when the opponents have higher honor cards. Think of their higher honors as big bullies that you have to sidestep.

The gentle art of the finesse is based on which opponent holds the missing honor cards. Finesses succeed only when the opponent who plays second to the trick has the missing honor card; finesses fail when the opponent who plays fourth (or last to the trick) holds the missing honor card. For example, if you (South) lead a low card toward a king in the dummy (hoping to take a trick with the king), the finesse works only if West (second to play) holds the ace. If East (last to play) holds the ace, your king is history.

Finesses are a 50-50 proposition. Because you can't see your opponents' cards, you can never be sure that your finesse will work. Each time that you attempt a finesse, you think to yourself, "Will my finesse work, or will it be a bad day at the office?" Sometimes your only chance for extra tricks is to attempt a finesse and hope that it works. After all, a 50-50 chance is better than no chance.

When you want to take tricks with lower honor cards, such as the king, queen, or jack, you need to lead from the side opposite the honor card you want to take a trick with. Think of leading from weakness toward strength. The following sections show you a few examples of finesses so that you can get acquainted with this new kid on the block.

Slipping a king by an ace

Figure 3-16 shows a classic finesse position. You have the ♠K in the dummy; your opponents have the ♠A. You want to take a trick with the ♠K. Lead a low spade from your hand — from weakness toward strength.

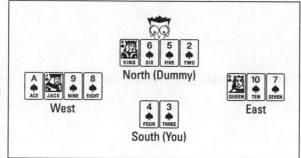

Figure 3-16:
Giving the ace the slip.

West happens to have the ♠A. If West plays the ♠A, your ♠K becomes a sure trick. If West plays a low spade, you take a trick immediately with the ♠K. Your finesse works; you have taken a trick with the ♠K.

Now check out Figure 3-17, which presents a scenario just as likely as the one shown in Figure 3-16.

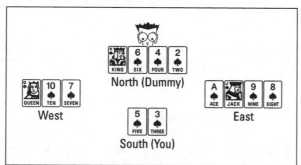

Figure 3-17:
Finesses fail when the fourth hand holds the important missing honor.

When you lead a low spade and then play the ♠K in the dummy, East (the last to play to the trick) takes your ♠K with the ♠A. Your ♠K does not take a trick. Your finesse has lost. Don't grieve — it happens about half the time.

Slipping a queen past the king

Queens are akin to kings. If you want to take a trick with a queen, do her a favor and lead toward her; she may be able to escape the clutches of the king. Figure 3-18 shows you how the queen can elude the king.

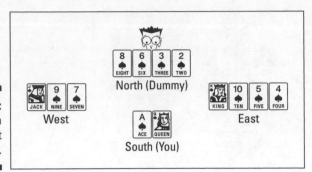

Figure 3-18:
The queen getting past the king.

You want to take a trick with your ♠Q, but you don't know who has the ♠K. Yes, you can see the ♠K in East's hand in the figure, but if you were playing for real, you couldn't see that ♠K unless you were Superman.

Say you lead a low spade from the dummy — again, weakness toward strength. East, the second to play after the lead, usually plays low so as not to give away any information about her hand. You, South, play the ♠Q, which wins the trick. Your finesse works. If West (the fourth to play to the trick) has the ♠K, your finesse loses.

Figure 3-19 shows another very common finesse involving the queen. This time, the ♠Q is in the dummy separated from her guardian, the ♠A. Begin by leading a low spade from your hand, the hand opposite the ♠Q, the card you want to take the trick with. You're hoping that West, second hand, has the missing honor, the ♠K. In this case, West does have the ♠K. Am I good to you, or what?

If West plays a low spade, you take the trick with the ♠Q; if West takes the trick with the ♠K, your ♠Q becomes a later trick. Of course, if East, fourth hand, has the ♠K, it gobbles up your ♠Q, and your finesse loses. *C'est la vie.*

Figure 3-19:
Looking at a very common finesse involving the queen and the ace.

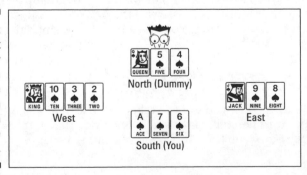

Combining length with a finesse

When you take finesses in suits that have seven or more cards between your hand and the dummy, you always have the chance of developing an extra trick(s) with small cards, as shown in Figure 3-20.

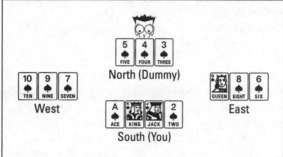

Figure 3-20:
The best of two worlds: finessing in a long suit.

You have the ♠A and ♠K between the two hands, but you want more than two tricks. You also want to take a trick with your ♠J. You even want to take a trick with your ♠2. May as well think big when you have seven or more cards in the same suit.

You lead a low spade from the dummy (from weakness toward strength), East plays the ♠6, and then you play the ♠J. The ♠J wins! You can then play the ♠A and ♠K, which both win tricks. You're the only person left at the table with any spades, so even that lowly ♠2 takes a trick for you. You've managed to take four spade tricks because you combined the finesse with length.

Of course, if West has the ♠Q, your finesse doesn't work. I hope you can handle losing finesses because it's going to happen about 50 percent of the time. When your finesse fails, you need to keep your cool. Try hard to avoid showing emotion during the play — it gives your opponents too big a high.

Don't let the risk involved with finesses scare you away from trying them, especially if you're finessing in a long suit. Finesses in longer suits have the advantage of setting up small cards in the suit, even if the finesse doesn't work.

The story of Too Tall Tex

Once upon a time, there lived a bridge player called Too Tall Tex. Tex was so tall that he could easily look down into his opponents' hands and see all their cards. It didn't take Tex long to figure out that he played much better when he knew where all the missing honor cards were before he started to play. Too Tall Tex never lost a finesse!

When the hand in Figure 3-21 was played, Too Tall Tex was sitting South. In this particular hand, Too Tall Tex knew from his partner's bidding that his team should try for either 12 or 13 tricks. Tex was afraid that North didn't have the ♠K they would need to make 13 tricks, and he didn't want to bid for 13 tricks until he took a "surveillance." So Too Tall Tex went out on a scouting mission.

West knew all about Too Tall. When Tex went out on his scouting mission, West tucked the ♠9 in with his clubs, making Too Tall Tex believe that the ♠K was a *singleton*, or a single card in the suit.

When Tex saw that the ♠K was a singleton, he quickly bid for 13 tricks, thinking he had all the tricks in the bag. The opening lead was the ♣Q, which Tex won in the dummy with the ♣K. For the next trick, Tex led a spade to the ♠A, expecting to snag West's ♠K (if West had only the ♠K, he would have had to play it in order to follow suit). When West produced the ♠9 instead, Too Tall Tex stormed away from the table, shouting, "I can't play in a game with cheaters!"

Figure 3-21: Even Too Tall Tex loses a finesse when his opponents are on the lookout.

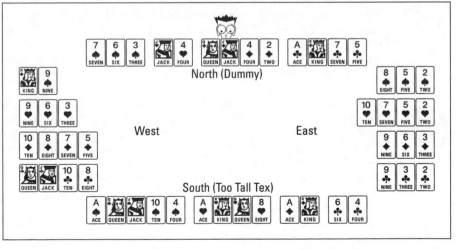

Some finesses bear repeating

Sometimes, the honor cards that you hold dictate that you lead from weakness toward strength *twice*. I want to show you one particular situation, one with a romantic pairing: the king and the queen.

The only thing better than taking one finesse in a suit is taking two finesses in the same suit. It sounds tricky, but I assure you it can be done: Just remember to lead from weakness toward strength, and watch yourself slide right by their honor cards. The cards in Figure 3-22 show you a hand where you can pull off this stunt.

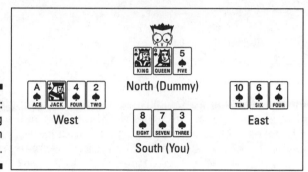

Figure 3-22:
Keeping love alive in the dummy.

North (Dummy)

West

East

South (You)

In Figure 3-22, you have an item going on in the dummy between the ♠K and the ♠Q. Bridge nuts try to clean everything up, so some call this coupling a *marriage,* which is actually a pinochle term.

Forgetting the social aspects of the suit, you need to take as many spade tricks as you can. Start by leading a low spade from your hand, from weakness to strength. West can simplify your life by playing the ♠A right away, a friendly play that immediately makes both the ♠K and the ♠Q in the dummy winning tricks. West thinks better of such a gift and plays the ♠2, allowing you to take the trick with the ♠Q.

You took a trick with the ♠Q by leading toward it, and you must repeat the process if you want to take a trick with the ♠K. Return to your hand (South) in another suit and lead another low spade. If West takes the trick with his ♠A, your ♠K becomes a later trick; if West plays a low spade again, you take the trick with the ♠K. You prevail because the second hand to play (West) has the missing honor; keep in mind that you would not be so lucky if East had the ♠A.

Figure 3-23 shows you another suit where you can repeat your finesse to great success. This particular finesse has "holy overtones."

You have three honor cards in your hand, but they are not equal (touching) honors. Do you see that hole (missing honor) between the ♠A and the ♠Q? A "holy" suit is a finessable suit.

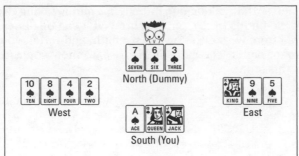

Figure 3-23:
The ♠K is trapped.

Lead a low spade from the dummy (from weakness toward strength), and when East plays a low spade, play the ♠Q to win the trick. You remain with the ♠AJ in your hand, and if you want to take a trick with the ♠J, you need to return to the dummy in another suit and lead another low spade. When East plays low again, you play the ♠J and take three tricks in the suit. Nor does it do East any good to play the ♠K — you just zap it with your ♠A.

When you have equal honor cards in your hand, such as the ♠QJ, play the higher equal first. Doing so is more deceptive — just trust me on this. However, when you have equal honors in the dummy, the hand that both your opponents can see, it doesn't matter which honor you play first.

Finessing against split honors

Sometimes your opponents have two important honors in the suit that you want to attack. You should assume that those honors are split and that each opponent has one honor. When you make this assumption and plan your play accordingly, you're *playing for split honors.*

You have a chance to play for split honors with the cards shown in Figure 3-24, a hand where you can take two finesses.

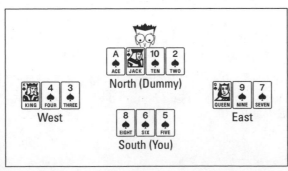

Figure 3-24:
Doubling your tricks by playing for split honors.

In Figure 3-24, you have a powerful three-card honor combination in the dummy, the ♠AJ10. Suits with powerful honor combinations should be attacked early. Because you are missing both the ♠K and the ♠Q, two important honors, assume that the honors are split between the two opposing hands.

Start by leading a low spade from your hand, weakness to strength. West, second to play, sees that the dummy has a higher spade (the ♠A) than West has (the ♠K), so West properly plays low. You insert the ♠10 from the dummy, and East wins the trick with the ♠Q, as expected (split honors, remember?). Hang on though; it ain't over 'til it's over.

After you regain the lead in another suit, you persist by leading another low spade from your hand. Once again, West properly plays low and this time you insert the ♠J from the dummy. Success! Your second finesse has worked. The missing spade honors were split after all (the ♠K in one hand and the ♠Q in the other). Of course they were split; I set them up that way!

You have a little bonus in store for you, to boot. After your ♠J wins the trick, you take the next trick by playing the ♠A. After both opponents follow, that little ♠2 in the dummy also becomes a trick (because nobody has any more spades). Of course, you were counting cards, so you already knew that.

Showing out: the big tip-off

Finessing is a risky business. On a good day, they all work, but on a bad day, don't ask. However, you can take some of the risk out of finessing by watching which cards your opponents play.

Finesses work best when you know who has the missing honors (like Too Tall Tex in the preceding sidebar). However, at times you can be as smart as Too Tall Tex, without peeking over your opponents' shoulders. Say that you lead a suit and one of your opponents *shows out* (your opponent discards from another suit because he or she has no cards left in the suit that you're playing). Now, you can be sure that your other opponent has all the missing cards in that suit, including any vital honor cards that you may be missing.

Figure 3-25 shows a suit where you can take a sure-fire finesse after your opponent shows out.

In this hand, you begin by playing the ♠AK, the high honors from the short side. On the second lead of spades, East, who has no more spades, makes a discard (shows out).

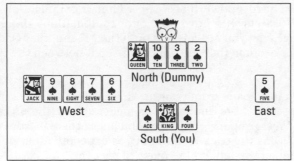

Figure 3-25:
Showing out gives you the green light on a finesse.

Aha! you say to yourself. If East has no more spades, West must then have all the missing spades, including the ♠J. When you lead the ♠4 and West plays a low spade, you can rest 100 percent assured that you can play the ♠10 from the dummy and take the trick. After the ♠10 wins, you can take a fourth trick with the dummy's ♠Q.

Corralling a missing honor

Sometimes you attempt a finesse when you have one, two, or three of the five honor cards between the two hands. Sometimes you strike gold and have a suit with four of the top honors, including the ace, but missing the king or queen.

In order to corral the missing honor card, start the suit by leading an honor card from the side opposite the ace. Then hopefully watch your left-hand opponent squirm. Figure 3-26 gives you a chance to make West very uneasy. In this suit, you're missing the ♠K.

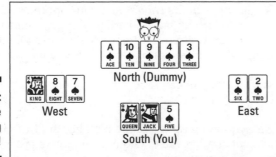

Figure 3-26:
Let the squirming begin!

The dreaded finesseaholic

Some players become addicted to the finesse. If you fear your partner may be obsessed with the finesse, look for these give-away signs:

✔ A finesseaholic prowls around looking for every opportunity to finesse, needed or not.

✔ A finesseaholic even takes practice finesses — finesses she doesn't need just to see whether they work.

✔ A finesseaholic takes finesses for the sheer joy of it all.

If your partner exhibits one or more of these signs, he may need help. In extreme cases, finesseaholics may need to be enrolled in F.A. (Finesseaholics Anonymous). People enrolled in F.A. are not allowed to take any finesses until they graduate.

Begin by leading the ♠Q from your hand. Have you ever been caught in a vise? Ask West. He knows how it feels right about now. If West plays ♠K, the dummy wins the trick with the ♠A. Then you can lead a low spade back to the ♠J in your hand. Finally, you lead your remaining spade over to the dummy's three winning spades (the ♠9, the ♠10, and the ♠4). What fun. You take five tricks.

If West doesn't play the ♠K when you lead the ♠Q, you play a low card from the dummy and take the trick. Next, you play the ♠J (the high card from the short side). West is caught in a real pickle. If West plays the ♠K, you can zap it with dummy's ♠A. If West plays a low spade, the ♠J takes the trick. West can kiss that ♠K so long, auf Wiedersehen, and good-bye.

Of course, you can corral any missing king or queen just as long as you hold the rest of the honor cards. You start the suit by leading an honor from the side opposite the ace — and hope that the second hand has the missing honor.

Cutting Communications with the Hold-Up Play

When you play a notrump contract, the highest card in the suit that has been led takes the trick. In a notrump contract, you typically establish tricks by driving out an opponent's ace when you have the lower honor cards between your hand and the dummy.

Driving out the ace is great strategy, but don't forget your opponents. They have the opening lead and are also trying to set up tricks — perhaps by driving out one of your aces. The *nerve!* After they get rid of the ace in the suit they're attacking, they remain with winning tricks in that suit. Not good. Is there anything you can do about it? Yes, you do have countermeasures. Enter the *hold-up play,* a technique that may stop your opponents dead in their tracks.

No, the hold-up play doesn't involve robbing a bank. The successful hold-up play allows you to cut the lifeline between the opponents' hands.

The typical hold-up play involves taking an ace in the suit that your opponents have led, but waiting until the third round of the suit (rather than taking the ace in the first round). The idea behind the hold-up play is to try to void one opponent in this suit. Later, if that opponent gets the lead, he won't have any cards left in the suit to lead over to his partner, who is sitting there with winning tricks.

A hold-up play usually follows this sequence:

1. **Your opponents attack your weakest suit, in which you have the ace, but no other significant honor cards.**

2. **You see that you have to drive out an opposing honor card to make your contract. In other words, you are going to have to surrender the lead.**

   In order to neutralize the suit that your opponents lead, it is to your advantage to take the third round of the suit, allowing your opponents to win the first two tricks. This is your hold-up play in action.

3. **Drive out the opposing honor in order to establish your extra needed tricks.**

4. **Pray that the opponent who wins the trick doesn't have any more cards in the suit that was led originally.**

Figure 3-27 shows a hand where you can commit the perfect crime — a successful hold-up play.

In the hand shown in Figure 3-27, you need to take nine tricks. West leads the ♠K with the intention of driving out your ♠A and making the rest of his spades into winning tricks. After the lead, the dummy comes down, and it's your turn to enter center stage by counting your sure tricks suit by suit:

- ✔ **Spades:** One sure trick — the ace
- ✔ **Hearts:** Three sure tricks — the AKQ
- ✔ **Diamonds:** No sure tricks — no ace
- ✔ **Clubs:** One sure trick — the ace

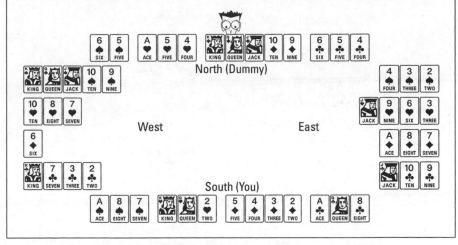

Figure 3-27:
Putting their
spades to
sleep with a
hold-up
play.

You have five sure tricks; you need nine, and those diamonds in the dummy offer your only chance of making your contract. If you can drive out the ♦A, you get four diamond tricks just like that. But life is not quite that easy. There is that little matter of that ♠K lead.

Paying attention to their opening lead

When you play a hand, the opening lead is a very important card because it tells you a lot about what your opponents are up to. Make sure to take a good look at the opening lead. Speaking from experience, the opening lead can come back to haunt you if you don't pay attention to it.

In the case of the cards in Figure 3-27, the lead of an honor card, such as the ♠K, sends a special message around the table. It says "Partner, I almost surely have three or four equal honor cards, and I'm leading my highest honor card." In other words, West is saying loud and clear that she has the ♠KQJ or the ♠KQJ10. (For more information on the opening lead, see Chapter 17.)

Even though West holds some pretty ominous spades, you don't have to just sit there and take it. You should at least try to plot a countermeasure. Take a look at those spades again, which you can see in Figure 3-28.

The two key suits in this hand are spades and diamonds. Spades is the suit they're establishing, and diamonds is the suit you want to establish. Because they have the opening lead, they're ahead in the race.

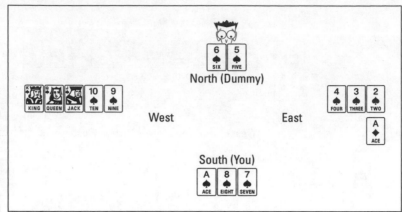

Figure 3-28:
Taking a closer look at West's spades.

More contracts are lost at trick one than at all the other tricks combined! Keeping that terrifying statistic in mind, take yet another look at those spades. Notice that East has the ♦A, the card you must drive out in order to develop those four extra tricks you need.

The good news is that your spade stopper is the ♠A (a *stopper card* is a card that keeps your opponents from taking their winning tricks). The bad news is that your opponents have attacked a suit in which you have only one stopper: the ♠A. If you win the first trick with your ♠A, West remains with four winning spades and East remains with two spades. If you win the second spade, West remains with three winning spades and East has one spade. And if you win the third spade, West remains with two winning spades and East has no more spades.

West has been able to set up (establish) his spades before you can even begin to set up your diamonds. There's trouble right here in River City.

At least your spade stopper is the ♠A. The ♠A is a *flexible stopper*, the best kind. A flexible stopper is one you can take whenever you want to. You can take that ♠A at trick one, trick two, or trick three. Does it matter? It matters.

Say you win the ♠A at the first trick, and you then lead a low diamond from your hand and play the ♦9 from the dummy. East takes the trick with the ♦A and leads a spade over to those lovely spades in West. West has the ♠QJ109, all winning tricks, which she takes one by one as you watch in silent agony. You wind up losing four spade tricks, plus the ♦A. After you lose these five tricks, you can't take the nine tricks you need to make your contract. Your partner is not happy. What went wrong? Plenty.

Return to the scene of the crime (the first trick) and gaze once again at those spades. This time, you're going to let the bad guys have the first two spade tricks, and you're going to win the third round of the suit with the ♠A.

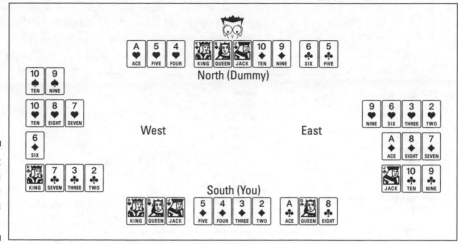

North (Dummy)

West　　　　　　　　East

Figure 3-29:
Holding up
your ace
averts
disaster.

South (You)

By winning the third round of the suit, you have just made a hold-up play and depleted East of spades. Now you can lead a diamond and drive out the ♦A, leaving the cards you see in Figure 3-29.

The moment East wins the trick with her ♦A, your sure trick count has just increased from five to nine because you established four winning diamond tricks in the dummy. Wait, there's even more good news: East doesn't have a spade, and West is sitting over there chomping at the bit with two winning spades. By winning the third round of spades, you cut the spade lifeline between East and West, forcing East to lead another suit. East shifts to the ♣J.

After you've driven out the ♦A and survived the spade onslaught, you have enough tricks to make your contract, so take them! Win the ♣A and take your four diamond tricks, your three heart tricks, and your two black aces for nine big ones.

Don't even think of risking your contract by trying to finesse clubs by playing the ♣Q. Only a finesseaholic makes such a play.

Coming to terms with the danger hand

In Bridgese, when a particular opponent has winning tricks and can hurt you by gaining the lead, that hand is called the *danger hand*. In Figure 3-29, after you win the third lead of spades, West is the danger hand because West has two winning spades. Stay clear of West.

East has no more spades, so East is called the *non-danger hand*. You can hang out with East because East can't hurt you even if East gets the lead in another suit.

When you make a hold-up play, your intent is to void one opponent in the suit that was led. Usually you're trying to void the partner of the opening leader — usually, but not always, as you can see in Figure 3-30.

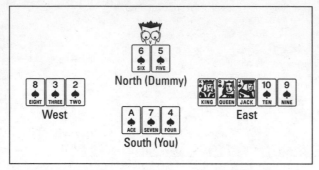

Figure 3-30:
A new danger hand.

In this hand, East bids spades and West leads a low spade. You win the third round of spades with your ♠A, a flexible stopper. In this case, East is the danger hand. If you have to lose a trick, you hope that West wins that trick because West has no more spades.

A *flexible stopper* is the highest remaining card in a suit. Aces are always flexible stoppers, but a king can be a flexible stopper if the ace has already been played. Figure 3-31 shows a hand where the king gets "upgraded" to flexible stopper status.

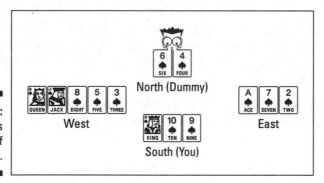

Figure 3-31:
Your king is now king of the hill.

In this hand, West leads the ♠5, and East plays the ♠A. After taking the trick, East then returns the ♠7. Your ♠K is the highest outstanding spade and is a flexible stopper. You don't have to take the trick just yet. You can play the ♠10 and allow West to take the trick with the ♠J. Say that West plays a third spade, which you must take with your ♠K. Fine. Because of your hold-up play, you have cut their spade lifeline. If East gets the lead later in the hand, East can't hurt you by playing a spade because she doesn't have a spade.

When your stopper isn't flexible, grab the trick while you can. Figure 3-32 shows you when not to hold up.

Figure 3-32: Sometimes you gotta grab for the gusto and not hold up.

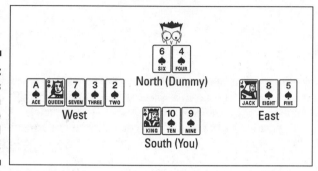

West leads the ♠3 and East plays the ♠J. Grab the ♠K! Your ♠K isn't the highest outstanding spade. The ♠A is still out there roaming around. If you don't take your ♠K, East's ♠J will take the trick. Now East returns a spade and your ♠K is mincemeat. You remain with the ♠K10. If you play the ♠10, West wastes no time or effort snatching it up with the ♠Q. If you play the ♠K, West will then trample all over it with the ♠A. East-West will take five spade tricks, and you won't take any!

You can only make a hold-up play when you have the highest card or the highest remaining card in the suit. If you don't have the highest card in the suit, just take the trick.

If you have enough tricks to make your contract, don't take any finesses into the player who has the setting trick(s), the danger hand.

Overtaking

When you're taking tricks, there will be times that you cannot afford to be miserly with your honor cards. With equal honors between the two hands, you may have to play two honors on the same trick (overtaking one with another) in order to wind up in the hand with the greater length in that suit. Figure 3-33 shows you what has to be done.

Figure 3-33:
Showing
largesse.

North (Dummy)

South (You)

At notrump, your goal is to take three spade tricks. Lead the ♠K, overtake with the ♠A, and then play the ♠Q and ♠J. Voila — three tricks. If you don't overtake the ♠K, you may not be able to reach dummy in another suit to take the other two spade tricks. Greed and miserliness will have beaten you.

Figure 3-34 is another example of where stinginess strikes out.

Figure 3-34:
Not being
a skinflint.

North (Dummy)

South (You)

At notrump, you wish to take four spade tricks. Begin with the ♠A (high card from the short side) and continue with the ♠J. Your hand remains with the ♠KQ10, all equal to the jack. Overtake the ♠J with the ♠Q (or ♠K) and take two more winning spades. If you play the ♠10 under your jack (ugly!), you are stuck in dummy and may not be able to reenter your hand in another suit to take your remaining spade winners.

When all of your honor cards (or even spot cards) are equals, you may have to overtake one with another in order to continue playing the suit. Just do it!

Part II
The Play of the
Hand at Trump

The 5th Wave — By Rich Tennant

"I THOUGHT SHE WAS COUNTING TRICKS TOO, UNTIL SHE STARTED SNORING."

In this part . . .

Υou've come to the right part of the book if you want to discover the beauty and glory of playing in a trump contract. The addition of wild (trump) cards can wreak havoc on your opponents. Unfortunately, it can backfire and wreak havoc upon you if you are not careful in the play of the hand. In this part, I show you how to get the most out of a hand when there is a trump suit involved.

Chapter 4

Working with Trump Suits

In this chapter you discover how to use your trump cards to your best advantage. I show you how to knock the wind out of your opponents' sails by preventing them from taking scads of tricks in their strong suits. I also show you the proper sequence of plays that allows you to take your winning tricks safely. In short, this chapter gives you your first taste of the wonderful powers of the trump suit.

Understanding Trump Suits

In bridge, the bidding often designates a suit as the *trump suit*. If the final contract has a suit associated with it, 4♠, 3♥, 2♦, or 1♣ for example, that suit is then declared the trump suit for the hand.

When a suit is selected as the trump suit, any card in that trump suit potentially has special powers; any card in the trump suit can win a trick over any card of another suit. For example, suppose that spades is the trump suit and West leads with the ♥A, you can still take the trick with the ♠2 (assuming that you have no hearts in your hand and therefore can't follow suit).

Because trump suits have so much power, naturally everyone at the table wants to have a say in determining which suit is declared the trump suit. Because bridge is a partnership game, the partnership determines which suit will be the best trump suit for their side.

Trumping saves the day

You can easily see the advantage of playing with a trump suit. For example, if you play a hand at a *notrump contract,* the highest card in the suit led always takes the trick (see Chapter 3 for more information on playing at notrump). If your opponent has a suit headed by all the high cards, it can wind up killing you. If your opponent has the lead, she can just keep playing all her winning cards — be it four, five, six, or seven of them — taking one trick after another as you watch helplessly. Such is the beauty and the horror of playing a hand at notrump. You see the beauty when your side is peeling off the tricks; you experience the horror when your opponents take trick after trick.

However, when the bidding designates a trump suit, you may well be in a position to neutralize your opponents' position of strength quite easily. After either you or your partner is *void* (has no cards left) in the suit that your opponents lead, you can just play any of your cards in the trump suit and take the trick. This little maneuver is called *trumping* your opponents' trick, (which your opponents really hate).

The hand in Figure 4-1 shows you the power of playing in a trump suit.

On this hand, suppose that you need nine tricks to make your contract of 3NT. Between your hand and the dummy, you can count 11 sure tricks: 5 spades, 3 diamonds, and 3 clubs.

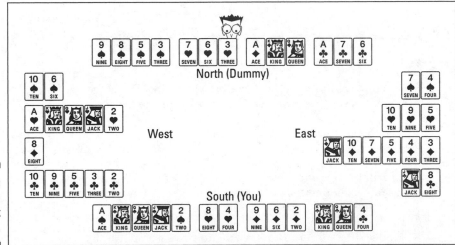

Figure 4-1: Avoiding a heart attack.

Bridge terms steeped in history

Trumping is also called *ruffing*. The words *trump* and *ruff* have a very interesting history. Trump derives from *Triomphe,* a French game, which may have something in common with *Trionfi,* an Italian word used to describe tarot cards in the 15th Century. *Ruff* derives from a variation of Whist (the predecessor of bridge), which was known as *Ruff and Honors,* for reasons lost in the mists of time.

If you play the hand shown in Figure 4-1 in notrump, it doesn't matter how many sure tricks you have: If you have a suit with no high cards in either hand, such as the hearts in this example, you are one dead duck. Playing in notrump, West can use the opening lead to win the first five heart tricks by leading the ♥AKQJ2, in that order. To put it mildly, this is not a good way for your side to start out the hand — you need to win nine tricks (you can only afford to lose four tricks), but you have already lost the first five tricks.

On this hand, you and your partner need to communicate effectively in the bidding to discover which suit (hearts, in this case) is woefully weak in both your hands (see Part III for more information on effective bidding). When you hold such a weak suit, you need to end the bidding in a trump suit so that you have some ammunition to fire against your opponents' long, strong suits.

In Figure 4-1, assume that the bidding ends in a contract of 4♠, meaning you must take ten tricks and spades is your trump suit. When West begins with the ♥AKQ, you can trump (or *ruff*) the third heart with your ♠2 and take the trick. Instead of losing five heart tricks, you only lose two heart tricks. *Remember:* You must follow suit if you can, so you can't trump either of your opponents' first two hearts.

Trumping your tricks: Your opponents have trump cards, too

Bear in mind that your opponents can also use their trump cards effectively; if they hold no cards in the suit that you or your partner lead, they can trump one of your tricks.

After you have the lead, you want to prevent them from trumping your winning tricks. You don't want your opponents to exercise the same strategy on you! You need to get rid of their trump cards before they can hurt you. I show you how to do that in the following section.

Getting Rid of Your Opponents' Trump Cards

BRIDGE TALK

If you can trump your opponents' winning tricks when you are void in the suit they are leading, it follows that your opponents can turn the tables and do the same thing to you. Instead of allowing your opponents to trump your sure tricks, you should play your high trump cards early on in the hand. Because the opponents must follow suit, you can remove their trump cards *before* you take your sure tricks. If you can extract their trump cards, you effectively remove their fangs. *Pulling* or *drawing* trump allows you to then take your winning tricks in peace, without fear of them being trumped.

Send the children out of the room and see what happens if you try to take your sure tricks *before* you draw trump. For example, in Figure 4-1 (where spades are trump), if you lead the ♦2, West would have to follow suit by playing the only diamond in his hand (the ♦8). You then play the ♦Q from the dummy, East plays one of her low diamonds, and you take the trick. However, if you follow up by playing the ♦A, West (having already played his only diamond) can trump your winning trick with the ♠6 (because spades is the trump suit in this hand).

The same misfortune befalls you if, instead of playing diamonds, you try to take three club tricks. East can trump the third round of clubs with the lowly ♠4. Imagine your discomfort when you see your opponents trump your sure tricks (although they don't think it's so unpleasant — they're thrilled about it!).

TIP

Try to draw trump as soon as possible. Get their pesky trump cards out of your hair. Then you can sit back and watch as your winning tricks come home safely to your trick pile.

To show you how drawing trump can work to your advantage, take a look at Figure 4-2, which shows only the spades (the trump suit) in the hand shown in Figure 4-1.

Figure 4-2:
Drawing trump removes their fangs.

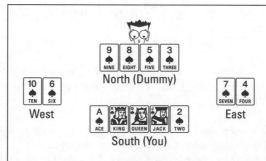

North (Dummy) — 9 8 5 3

West — 10 6

East — 7 4

South (You) — A K Q J 2

Drawing trump is just like playing any suit — you have to count the cards in the suit to know if you have successfully drawn all your opponents' trump cards. Sorry about that.

In the hand shown in Figure 4-2, you and your partner start life with nine spades between you, leaving only four spades that your opponents could possibly hold in their hands. Suppose that you play the ♠A — both opponents must then follow suit and play one of their spades. You win the trick, and you know that your opponents have only two spades left. Suppose that you then continue with the ♠K and both opponents follow. Now they have no more spades left (no more trump cards). You have *drawn trump*. See? That wasn't so bad.

Refer to Figure 4-1 (where West begins with the ♥AKQ, and you trump the third heart with your ♠2). After you trump the third heart trick, you draw trump by playing the ♠AK. You can then safely take your ♣AKQ and your ♦AKQ — you wind up losing only two heart tricks. You needed to make ten tricks to fulfill your contract, and in fact finished up with 11 tricks. Pretty good! Drawing trump helps you make your contract, doesn't it?

Looking at Distributions in the Trump Suit

In Part III, you discover when to play a hand with a trump suit and when to play a hand without a trump suit (notrump). In this section, keep in mind that if you have eight or more cards in a suit between your hand and the dummy, particularly in a *major suit* (either hearts or spades), you should make that suit your trump suit.

An *eight-card fit* (eight cards in a single suit between your hand and the dummy) gives you a safety net because you have many more trump cards than your opponents: Your trump cards outnumber theirs by eight to five. It is always to your advantage to have more trump cards than they do. You may be able to survive with a seven-card trump fit, but having an eight- or nine-card trump fit relieves tension. The more trump cards you have, the more tricks you can generate; the less chance your opponents have of taking any tricks with their trump cards.

The fewer trump cards your opponents have, the easier it is for you to get rid of their trump cards (or to *draw trump*).

The 4-4 trump fit

During the bidding, you may discover that you have an eight-card fit divided 4-4 between the two hands. Try to make such a fit your trump suit. A 4-4 trump fit almost always produces at least one extra trick in the play of the hand, as opposed to notrump (in notrump, if you have four cards in each hand, at most, you can only take four tricks in the suit.

At a notrump contract, the 4-4 fit shown in Figure 4-3 takes four tricks. At notrump, when each partner has four cards in the same suit, four tricks is your max.

Figure 4-3:
In a 4-4 trump fit, 4 + 4 = 5 tricks.

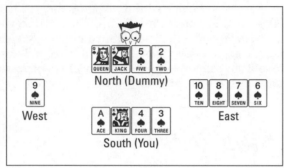

However, when spades is your trump suit, you can do better. In Figure 4-3 suppose that your opponents lead a suit that you don't have, which allows you to trump their lead with the ♠3. By drawing trump now (see "Getting Rid of Your Opponents' Trump Cards" for more on drawing trump), you can take four more spade tricks by playing the ♠A and the ♠K from your hand, and then playing the ♠J and ♠Q from the dummy. You wind up taking a total of five spade tricks — the card you trumped, plus four more high spades.

A 4-4 trump fit is primo. You can get more for your money from this trump fit. Make it a habit to keep your eyes open for 4-4 trump fits.

Other trump fits

Sometimes, eight-card trump fits come in different guises. Consider the eight-card trump fits shown in Figure 4-4.

Figure 4-4 shows examples of a 5-3 fit, a 6-2 fit, and a 7-1 fit. Good bidding uncovers eight-card (or longer) fits, which makes for safe trump suits. There is joy in numbers.

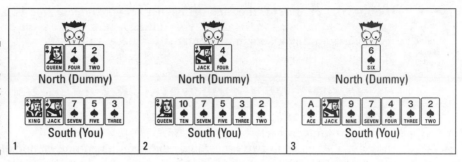

Figure 4-4:
The many
different
faces of the
eight-card
trump fit.

Using Extra Winners to Get Rid of Losers

When playing a hand at a trump contract, your strategy is to count how many losers you have. If you hold too many *losers* to make your contract, you then need to look in the dummy for *extra winners* that you can use to dispose of some of your losers.

You may find this approach a rather negative way of playing of a hand. But counting losers can have a very positive impact on your play at a trump contract. Your loser count tells you how many extra winners you need, if any. Extra winners are an indispensable security blanket to make your contract — extra winners help you get rid of losers.

Defining losers and extra winners

When playing a hand at a notrump contract, you count your sure tricks; however, when you play a hand at a trump contract, you count losers and extra winners. *Losers* are tricks you know you have to lose. For example, if neither you nor your partner holds the ace in a suit, you know you have to lose at least one trick in that suit.

Conversely, *extra winners* may allow you to get rid of some of your losers. What exactly is an extra winner? An *extra winner* is a winning trick in the dummy (North), upon which you can discard a loser from your own hand (South).

Get ready for some good news: When counting losers, you only have to count the losers in the long hand, which is the hand with more trump cards. The declarer's hand is almost always the long hand due to the bidding process (see Part III for the scoop on the bidding).

Do me a favor and, for the time being, just accept the fact that you don't have to count losers in the dummy. Counting losers in one hand is bad enough; counting losers in the dummy is unnecessary.

Recognizing immediate and eventual losers

Losers, ugh, come in two forms: immediate and eventual. *Immediate losers* are losers that your opponents can take when they have the lead. These losers have a special danger signal attached to them that reads "Danger — Unexploded Bomb!" Immediate losers spell bad news.

Of course, eventual losers are not exactly a welcome occurrence, either. Your opponents can't take your *eventual losers* right away because those losers are *protected* by an ace that you or your partner holds. In other words, with eventual losers, the opponents can't take their tricks right off the bat, which buys you a bit of breathing space (and some time to get rid of those eventual losers). One of the best homes for these eventual losers is to discard them on extra winners.

It helps to know which of your losers are eventual and which are immediate. Your game plan depends upon your immediate loser count. See "Drawing trump before taking extra winners" and "Taking extra winners before drawing trump" later in this chapter for more about how to proceed after counting your immediate losers.

Because identifying eventual and immediate losers is so important, take a look at the spades shown in Figures 4-5, 4-6, and 4-7 to spot some losers. Assume that in these figures, spades is a side suit and hearts is your trump suit.

Figure 4-5 shows a suit with two eventual losers.

Figure 4-5: Looking for eventual losers.

In the hand shown in Figure 4-5, as long as you have the ♠A protecting your two other spades, your spade losers are eventual. However, after your opponents lead a spade (which forces out your ace), your two remaining spades become immediate losers because they have no winning trick protecting them.

In Figure 4-6, you have one eventual spade loser.

Figure 4-6:
Even one eventual loser still hurts.

North (Dummy)

South (You)

With the spades shown in Figure 4-6, the dummy's ♠AK protects two of your three spades — but your third spade is on its own as a loser after the ♠A and ♠K have been removed from the dummy.

In Figure 4-7, you have two immediate spade losers.

Figure 4-7:
A pair of immediate losers — you don't want this couple at your dinner party.

North (Dummy)

South (You)

Notice that you count two, not three spade losers — you only count losers in the long trump hand (which is your hand).

Identifying extra winners

Enough with losers already — counting them can get depressing! You can get rid of some of these losers by using extra winners. Extra winners only work after you (South) are void in the suit being played — if you still have cards in the relevant suit, you have to follow suit and can't legally discard your dreaded losers. Therefore, extra winners can exist only in a suit that is unevenly divided between the two hands (and the greater length must be in the dummy). The stronger the extra winner suit (that is, the more high cards of that particular suit in the dummy's hand), the better.

Yes, it is possible to have extra winners in your own hand, on which you can discard a loser(s), but actually gaining an extra trick from this process is quite rare and won't be covered in this book.

Figure 4-8 shows you two extra winners in their natural habitat.

Figure 4-8: Looking for extra winners in all the right places.

North (Dummy)

South (You)

The cards shown in Figure 4-8 fit the bill for extra winners, because spades is an unevenly divided suit and the greater length is in the dummy. After you lead a spade and play the ♠Q from the dummy, you are now void in spades. You can then discard two losers from your own hand when you play the ♠A and the ♠K from the dummy. Therefore, you can count two extra winners in spades.

By contrast, the cards in Figure 4-9 look hopeful, but unfortunately, they can't offer you any extra winners.

Figure 4-9:
You won't find any extra winners in this suit, no matter how hard you squint.

North (Dummy)

South (You)

The cards shown in Figure 4-9 don't fit the mold for extra winners because you have the same number of spades in each hand. No matter how strong a suit is, if you have the same number of cards in each hand, you can't squeeze any extra winners out of the suit. You just have to follow suit all the time. True, the ♠AKQ aren't chopped liver; although this hand has no spade losers, it gives you no extra winners, either. Sorry!

The cards shown in Figure 4-10 contain no extra winners, either.

North (Dummy)

South (You)

Figure 4-10:
Striking out as far as extra winners.

The dummy's ♠AK take care of your two spades, but you have nothing "extra" over there — no ♠Q, for example — upon which you can discard one of your losers. This spade suit has no losers and no extra winners. You need to have "extra" winners to be able to throw a loser away. In Figure 4-10, your ♠A and ♠K do an excellent job of covering your two spade losers, but no more. You can't squeeze blood out of a turnip.

Drawing trump before taking extra winners

After counting your immediate losers (tricks you must lose), if you still have enough tricks to make your contract, go ahead and draw trump before taking extra winners. That way, you can make sure that your opponents don't swoop down on you with a trump card and ruin your plans.

Figure 4-11 illustrates this point by showing you a hand where spades is the trump suit.

In the hand shown in Figure 4-11, you need to take ten tricks to make your contract. West leads the ♥A.

Before playing a card from the dummy, count your losers one suit at a time, starting with the trump suit, the most important suit. You can't make a plan for the hand until your opponents make the opening lead, because you can't see the dummy until the opening lead is made. But as soon as the dummy comes down, try to curb your understandable eagerness to play a card from the dummy and do a little loser counting, instead.

In your trump suit (spades), you are well-heeled. You have ten spades between the two hands, including the ♠AKQ. Because your opponents have only three spades, you should have no trouble removing their spades. A suit with no losers is called a *solid suit*. You have a solid spade suit — you can never have too many solid suits.

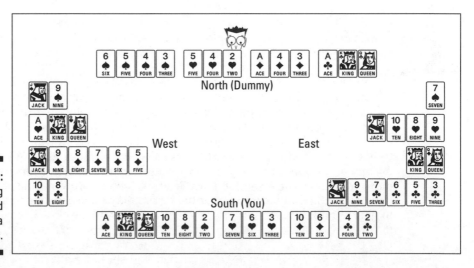

Figure 4-11: Counting losers and extra winners.

In hearts, however, you have trouble — big trouble. In this case, your own hand has three heart losers. But before you count three losers, check to see whether the dummy has any high cards in hearts to neutralize any of your losers. In this case, your partner doesn't come through for you at all, having only three baby hearts. You have three heart losers, and they are immediate ones.

In diamonds, you have two losers, but this time your partner does go to bat for you, with the ♦A as a winner. The ♦A negates one of your diamond losers, but you still have to count one diamond loser.

In clubs, you have two losers, but in this suit your partner really does come through. Not only does your partner take care of your two losers with the ♣AK, your partner also has an extra winner, the ♣Q. Count one extra winner in clubs.

Your mental box score for this hand reads as follows:

- ✔ **Spades:** You have a solid suit, no losers.
- ✔ **Hearts:** You must count three losers (the three cards in your hand).
- ✔ **Diamonds:** You have one loser because your partner covers one of your losers with the ace.
- ✔ **Clubs:** You count one extra winner.

Next, you determine how many losers you can lose and still make your contract. In this case, you need to take ten tricks, which means that you can afford to lose three tricks.

If you have more losers than you can afford, you then need to figure out how to get rid of those pesky deadbeats. One way to get rid of losers is by using extra winners — and you just happen to have an extra winner in clubs.

Follow the play: West starts out by leading the ♥AKQ, taking the first three tricks. You can do absolutely nothing about losing these heart tricks — that's why you call them *immediate* losers (tricks that your opponents can take whenever they want). Immediate losers are the pits.

After taking the first three heart tricks, West decides to shift to a low diamond, which establishes a potential winner for his side in diamonds. Assume that you take this trick with the ♦A; you are now staring at an immediate diamond loser in your hand. You may have a strong temptation to get rid of that loser immediately on the dummy's clubs — it may be making you nervous just to look at it. Don't do it. Draw trump first. If you play the ♣AKQ from the dummy before you draw trump, West will trump the third club and down you go in a contract you should make.

You should draw trump first and *then* play the ♣AKQ. West won't be able to trump any of your good tricks, nor will East — neither one of them will have any trump cards left. You wind up losing only three heart tricks — and making your contract!

The most favorable sequence of play, after losing the first three heart tricks and winning the ♦A, is as follows: Play the ♠A and ♠K, removing all their trump cards. Then you can play ♣AKQ and throw that diamond loser away. Now you have only trumps left, and you can sit back and take the rest of the tricks.

Any time you can draw trump before taking your extra winners, do it.

Taking extra winners before drawing trump

When you have more immediate losers than you can afford, and you have an extra winner, you must take your extra winner before you give up the lead. If your losers are immediate, you can't afford to let the opponents get the lead, or they will mow you down by taking their tricks all at once. Figure 4-12 shows you the importance of taking your extra winners before drawing trump. In this hand, your losers are immediate — if your opponents get the lead, you can pack up and go home.

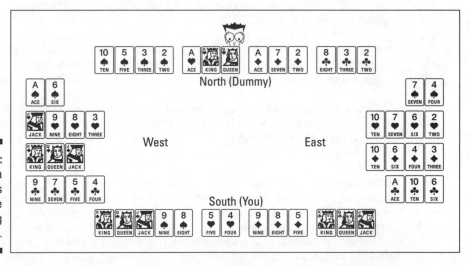

Figure 4-12: Taking extra winners before drawing trump.

In the hand shown in Figure 4-12, you need to make ten tricks with spades as the trump suit. West leads the ♦K, trying to establish diamond tricks (with the intention of driving out your ♦A). After the ♦A is gone, West's ♦Q and ♦J are then promoted to sure winners on subsequent tricks.

After you count your losers (see "Recognizing immediate and eventual losers" earlier in this chapter), you tally up the following losers and extra winners:

- ✔ **Spades:** You have one immediate loser — the ♠A.

- ✔ **Hearts:** You have one extra winner — the ♥Q.

- ✔ **Diamonds:** You count two losers, which are immediate after you play the ♦A.

- ✔ **Clubs:** You have one immediate loser — the ♣A.

You win the opening lead with the ♦A. Suppose that you then lead a low spade from the dummy and then play the ♠K from South, intending to draw trump, which is *usually* a good idea. (See "Getting Rid of Your Opponents' Trump Cards," earlier in this chapter, for more information on drawing trump.)

However, West wins the trick by playing the ♠A, takes the ♦QJ, and East still gets a trick with the ♣A. You lose four tricks. What happened? You went down in your contract while your extra winner, the ♥Q, was still sitting over there in the dummy, gathering dust.

You never got to use your extra winner in hearts because you drew trump too quickly. When you led a spade at the second trick, you had four losers, all immediate. *Immediate losers* are tricks that your opponents can take when they get the lead. And sure enough, they took them — all four of them.

If you want to make your contract on this hand, you need to play that extra winner *before* you draw trump. The winning play goes something like this: You win the ♦A at trick one, followed by the ♥AKQ at tricks two, three, and four. On the third heart (which comes from the dummy), you can discard one of your diamond losers. This play reduces your immediate loser count from an unwieldy four to a workable three. Now you can afford to lead a trump and give up the lead. After all, you do want to draw trump sooner or later.

If you play the hand properly, you wind up losing only one spade, one club, and one diamond — and you make your contract of ten tricks.

You may think that it's dangerous to play the ♥AKQ before you draw trump. But you have no choice. You have to get rid of one of your immediate losers before giving up the lead if you want to make your contract. Otherwise, it's like giving up the ship without a fight.

Chapter 5

Creating Extra Winners (Finding a Home for Your Losers)

Extra winners are a two-fold blessing: They allow you to take tricks while you discard losers. When you have an extra winner in the dummy, you can play that winner and at the same time discard a loser from your hand. (See "Using Extra Winners to Get Rid of Losers" in Chapter 4 for the details on discarding losers on extra winners.)

On a good day, you find extra winners perched in the dummy, just waiting to take tricks for you. Unfortunately, those good days are few and far between. On most days, you need to set up your own extra winners in order to make your contract. I show you just how to establish extra winners in this chapter.

Establishing Extra Winners in the Dummy

In order to create extra winners, the suit must look like this:

- ✔ The suit must be unequally divided (one hand holds more cards in that suit than the other hand does).
- ✔ The greater length must be in the dummy.

The more honor cards between your hand and the dummy, the better.

Figure 5-1 shows you a suit that's just prime for developing extra winners: The suit is unevenly divided, with the greater length in the dummy, plus the dummy holds three honors, a running head start.

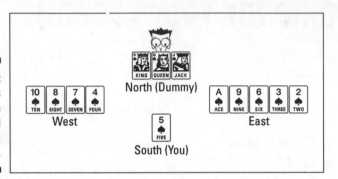

Figure 5-1:
This suit is laden with potential extra winners.

Start by leading the ♠5. West plays a low spade, and you play the dummy's ♠J. Assume that the ♠J drives out the ♠A in East's hand. (See Chapter 3 for more information on driving out the ace.) With the ♠A out of the way, you have created two extra winners: the ♠K and the ♠Q. The ♠K and the ♠Q are extra winners because they are the *boss* spades (the highest cards left in the suit), and you have no spades left. Later, when you play the ♠K and the ♠Q, you can discard two losers from your hand (see Chapter 4 to find out how to count the losers in your hand).

Determining when you can't create extra winners

Unfortunately, you can't create extra winners in every suit you play. Figure 5-2 shows you the sad case of a suit that can't yield any extra winners.

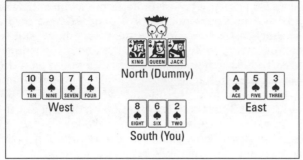

Figure 5-2:
This hand strikes out as far as extra winners.

The suit in Figure 5-2 can't produce any extra winners, no matter how hard you try — these cards are evenly divided (both you and the dummy hold three cards). You can't create any extra winners in evenly divided suits. Sorry about that.

In Figure 5-2, suppose that you lead the ♠2 to the ♠J in the dummy. Assuming that the ♠J drives out the ♠A in the East hand, you establish two tricks but no extra winners (see Chapter 3 for more information on establishing tricks). You can't use either of the dummy's spades to discard a loser from your hand because you have the same number of spades as the dummy. With both hands holding the same number of cards in the suit, neither hand runs out of cards in the suit before the other, which therefore gives you no chance to discard losers.

Driving out your opponents' honor cards first

On occasion, you have to do a little more work to make those extra winners appear. Sometimes you may need to drive out a few of your opponents' honor cards before you can count any extra winners. Take the cards in Figure 5-3 as an example.

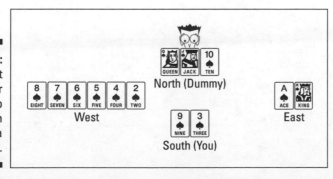

Figure 5-3:
Driving out some honor cards to create an extra winner.

The cards in Figure 5-3 offer the opportunity to create an extra winner, but first you need to drive out your opponents' ♠A and ♠K before you can claim the extra winner. Start by leading a low spade. West follows suit with another low spade. You then play the ♠10 from the dummy. Assume that the dummy's ♠10 loses to East, who plays the ♠K. After you regain the lead by winning a trick in another suit, lead your ♠9. West follows with another low spade. You then play the ♠J from the dummy, which drives out the ♠A from East's hand (see Chapter 3 for more information on driving out the ace). You're left with the ♠Q in the dummy — an extra winner because you have no more spades. After the dummy gains the lead by winning a trick in another suit, you can play the dummy's ♠Q and discard a loser.

Making sure you can reach those extra winners

When your suit fits the bill for creating extra winners but your equal (touching) honor cards are divided between the two hands, you need to play the high honor card from the short side first. Doing so makes it easier to reach the extra winner(s) you create.

Playing the honor cards from the short side is a bit like unblocking a logjam; if you leave the honor in the hand with shortness, you leave the log in place, and potentially create a fatal blockage. Be a beaver — unblock those honors!

In Figure 5-4, for example, you have three equal (touching) honor cards, but the honors are divided between the two hands. Start by playing the ♠K, the high honor card from the short side (South). Assume that your ♠K loses to West's ♠A. The dummy is left with the ♠QJ, and you're left with one small spade (♠5). When you regain the lead, you can lead your ♠5 to the dummy's ♠J. You can then discard one of your losers on the extra winner in spades (♠Q). Nice unblock.

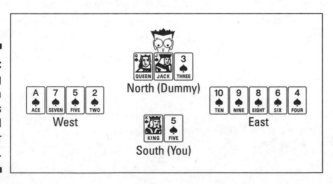

Figure 5-4: Creating extra winners with divided honor cards.

North (Dummy)

West

East

South (You)

Finessing for Extra Winners

When playing at a trump contract, you can take a *finesse* to create extra winners, just as you do at a notrump contract (see Chapter 3 for more information on finessing). This is what you need:

✔ An unevenly divided suit (the dummy holds more cards in the suit than you do).

✔ The majority of the honor cards are usually in the dummy.

✔ You are missing one or more of the top four honor cards.

When you behold such a treasure, you can create extra winners in that suit by taking a finesse, leading from weakness to strength. Luck plays a role when taking a finesse. Because you don't know who has the missing honor, finesses work about half the time. Shed no tears if your finesse doesn't pan out. If the suit you are finessing has enough honor cards between the two hands, even if the finesse loses, you can still create an extra winner.

Figure 5-5 shows you how this works.

Figure 5-5:
Finessing
for an extra
winner.

In Figure 5-5, you have the makings of an extra winner in spades because the dummy holds the majority of the cards, including three honor cards.

You begin by leading the ♠3: from weakness to strength. West also plays a low spade, and you then play the ♠J from the dummy.

If East plays the ♠K and your ♠J loses the trick, the ♠AQ in the dummy are the two highest remaining spades in the game — so you know you can win two tricks with those cards. When you or the dummy regain the lead by winning a trick in another suit, you can play the ♠A and then play the ♠Q. By the time the ♠Q is played from the dummy, you won't have any more spades in your hand, so you can discard a loser. Voilà — an extra winner!

If the ♠J wins the trick, indicating that West has the ♠K, repeat the finesse (see "Some finesses bear repeating" in Chapter 3 if you need help seeing the advantages of repeating a finesse). You must return to your hand with a winning trick in another suit and lead your remaining spade. Assuming West plays low again, play the ♠Q which wins the trick. Now, finally, you can discard a loser on the ♠A. In this scenario, you not only create an extra winner, your finesse also worked. Luck was on your side, and you didn't lose a trick.

On the other hand, in the cards shown in Figure 5-6, your honor strength is not strong enough to create any extra winners, so it's not such a hot suit to attack early on. If the finesse wins, you have no loser, but no extra winner, either.

And if the finesse loses (if East has the ♠K), you have lost one trick, and again you have not managed to create an extra winner.

In general, try to attack suits that at least have the potential for extra winners.

Figure 5-6:
Not enough
honor cards
to create
an extra
winner.

North (Dummy)

South (You)

In Figure 5-7, you have a suit with *one* extra winner, simply by first playing the ♠A and ♠K. Not only that, you can get that extra winner without losing a trick — an attractive prospect. But if the circumstances of the hand demand that you *need* two extra winners, one extra winner just won't cut it. If you need *two* extra winners, you have to take a chance on a finesse and lead a small card from your hand. With your heart in your mouth, try playing the dummy's ♠J! Again, you follow the general maxim of leading from weakness to strength. If the ♠J wins the trick, you create two extra winners; if the ♠J loses, at least you gave it your all. Bridge is not for the faint of heart.

Figure 5-7: Try to create two extra winners — no guts, no glory.

North (Dummy)

South (You)

In Figure 5-8, you have only one honor card in the dummy, but beggars can't be choosers. Lead low toward the ♠K. If West has the ♠A and plays it, your ♠K becomes an extra winner. If West doesn't play the ♠A, you take the trick with your ♠K, and your loser in that suit has suddenly become a winner. If East has the ♠A, and takes your ♠K with it, don't send me a tear-stained postcard bemoaning your fate; you took a risk that had a 50 percent chance of success. Sometimes it is just not your day!

Figure 5-8: This hand gives you a 50-50 shot at creating an extra winner.

North (Dummy)

South (You)

Knowing What You Have to Do and Doing It

In this section, I want you to look at a hand and determine if you need to create any extra winners. In Figure 5-9, you can see both your hand and the dummy's. Count your losers, suit by suit, and determine whether a straight-forward plan of attack will do or whether you need to create extra winners in order to make your contract.

For the hand in Figure 5-9, your contract is for ten tricks, spades are trump, and West leads the ♥K. You count up the following losers:

- ✔ **Spades:** One loser, the ♠A.
- ✔ **Hearts:** Two immediate losers (after you play the ♥A): The dummy can't cover your ♥7 and ♥4.
- ✔ **Diamonds:** No losers! In fact, you have one sure extra winner (the ♦A and ♦K cover your ♦2 and give you an extra winner). However, you may have two extra winners if you want to risk a finesse by leading a low diamond to the ♦J.
- ✔ **Clubs:** Two immediate losers: The dummy doesn't have any winners that can cover the ♣9 and ♣J.

The situation looks a little bleak, does it not? You have to take ten tricks, so you can only afford three losers. But you have five — count 'em, *five* — losers. To make matters worse, all your losers are *immediate* after your opponents lead the ♥K. The only resource that you have is that one extra winner in diamonds. Time to call out the militia.

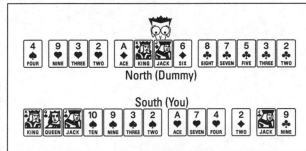

Figure 5-9:
Going for broke.

Although you can get rid of one of your heart or club losers by playing the ♦AK (while discarding a loser), it's still not enough. You need to get rid of *two* losers if you want to make your contract.

Go for a finesse! Win the first trick with the ♥A and then lead a low diamond to the ♦J in the dummy. If your finesse works, you can then play the ♦AK, and because you have no more diamonds in your hand, you can discard two of your losers in hearts or clubs. If the finesse loses (because East takes your ♦J with the ♦Q), you will lose your contract big-time. However, you can console yourself knowing that you made the right play, the gutsy play, the bridge play, by attempting the finesse.

Before leaving this hand, pretend for a moment that you need to take only nine tricks with the same opening lead. In this contract, you can afford to lose four tricks, so you only have to get rid of *one* of your five losers to make the hand. Now life is a lot less challenging; win the first trick with the ♥A and play the ♦AK, discarding one loser from your hand on the second winning diamond; then play a spade. No risky finesse is necessary in this contract — your loser count tells you how to play your diamond suit.

With all this finessing and creating extra winners going on, you may lose sight of your goal, which is making your final contract. Don't take any unnecessary risks, such as a finesse, when you don't need to do so in order to make your contract.

Letting Your Opponents Establish Extra Winners for You

When your opponents have the lead and take their tricks, they may unknowingly create extra winners for you. You may lose some tricks, but in the end, you will have the last laugh.

Don't look a gift horse in the mouth. Figure 5-10 shows you the rewards of having benevolent opponents who create extra winners for you — without your even asking them to do it!

In Figure 5-10, after West leads the ♠2, you play the ♠4 from the dummy, East plays the ♠A and wins the trick as you play the ♠J. Say East plays the ♠3. You follow suit by playing the ♠Q, West plays the ♠K, and you play the ♠5 from the dummy; West takes the trick.

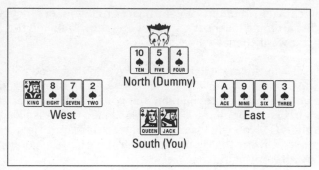

Figure 5-10: Thank your lucky stars for opponents who create extra winners for you.

Your opponents may be happy that they have taken the first two tricks, but you also have a reason to be happy. Look what happened: The ♠AKQJ have all been played, leaving the dummy's ♠10 as top banana in the suit. The ♠10 has become an extra winner, which you can use to discard a loser.

Your opponents played their two top spade tricks — not a bad idea in theory, but it came at a price this time. In the process, they did a lot of hard work for you by establishing your ♠10 as the highest remaining spade, thereby giving you a chance to cash an extra winner and throw away a loser from your own hand.

If your opponents had known what would happen, they may have led a different suit, leaving you to do your own hard work. How could your opponents have known that pesky ♠10 would turn into a valuable extra winner? These little surprises that pop up during the play make bridge the challenging game it is; you frequently find out your error after it's too late.

Getting Something for Nothing: A Free Finesse

A free finesse crops up when you are void (have no cards) in the suit that your opponent leads, but the dummy has several honor cards in that suit. You can play one of the dummy's lower honor cards (take a finesse), knowing that even if your right-hand opponent plays a higher honor card, you can trump it and still take the trick. A free finesse!

To see a free finesse unfold, check out the spades in Figure 5-11. Suppose that West leads a low spade. You're void in spades, so your first reaction may be to play the ♠A (an extra winner), on which you can discard a loser. But if one extra winner is good, aren't two extra winners better? Why not play the ♠Q at your first turn? If the ♠Q wins the trick, you can get rid of *two* losers, one on the ♠Q and one on the ♠A.

Figure 5-11:
A free
finesse
from your
opponents
— and it's
not even
your
birthday!

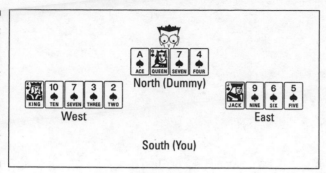

North (Dummy)

West   East

South (You)

This play is really a something-for-nothing play; if East has the ♠K instead of West, she will play it on your ♠Q — but you still have the last laugh. You can trump East's ♠K and later cross over to the dummy in another suit to use that ♠A to discard a loser.

Chapter 6

Establishing the Dummy's Long Suit

In this Chapter

▶ Establishing small cards in the dummy's long suit

▶ Keeping a path to the dummy

▶ Drawing trump

▶ Taking tricks with your established small cards

Most beginning bridge players rush to take their aces and kings with the speed of summer lightning. Once the high of taking those few tricks is over, reality sets in. What now? The truth is that you seldom have enough aces and kings to make any contract. If you think about it, all the aces (4) and all the kings (4) only add up to eight tricks, and most contracts require you to take more than that. And how often do you think you are going to have all the aces and all the kings between the two hands?

The answer to too many losers is taking tricks with the smaller cards that are attached to five (or six) card suits in the dummy. When your partner presents you with a five-card side suit (any suit that isn't the trump suit is called a side suit) he doesn't expect you to just sit there and admire it; he expects you to work with it so you can take extra tricks with the smaller cards in the suit.

Laying out the cards as you read can help you see the plays more clearly. Have your deck of cards at the ready as you read.

Knowing when to call on your small cards for winners

Whenever dummy presents you with a five- or six-card side suit (any suit that isn't the trump suit), there may be a chance to turn one or more of the small cards in that side suit into winning tricks. What you have to do is play the suit and keep playing the suit, trumping one or two of those small cards in your hand, until both opponents are void in the suit. That's what this chapter is all about.

Turning small cards into winners

In order to turn small cards in long suits into winning tricks, you need a three-point plan:

- ✔ A five- or six-card side suit in the dummy with fewer than three cards in that suit in your hand.

- ✔ A strong five- or six-card trump suit in your hand.

- ✔ Entries to the dummy, which are high cards in the dummy either in the trump suit or a side suit. You need the entries to get over to the dummy when necessary.

Squeezing tricks out of small cards in dummy's long suit requires a bit of effort, and you may ask yourself if it is really worth all the trouble. To spare yourself any unnecessary work, do not even think about messing with dummy's long suit unless you have too many losers to make your contract.

Figure 6-1 shows a hand where your three-point game plan is in place and you are trying to establish the dummy's side suit.

You and your partner have determined during the bidding that hearts should be your trump suit and you have contracted for ten tricks. West leads the ♠A.

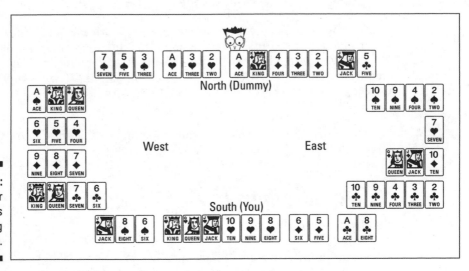

Figure 6-1: Mining your diamonds for winning small cards.

Remember the first rule of playing a hand; think before you do something silly. You'll thank yourself later for thinking about your plan of action before making a play.

If you need to take ten tricks, you can therefore afford to lose three tricks. First, see whether you have more than three losers, and if you do, whether you can get rid of some of those losers.

Take a look at your loser count for this hand (see Chapter 4 for more information on counting losers in your hand):

- ✔ **Hearts:** No losers — hearts is a *solid suit*. You can never have too many solid suits.

- ✔ **Diamonds:** No losers and some potential to establish small cards in the suit.

- ✔ **Clubs:** One loser, which is an eventual one rather than an immediate one. The loser is eventual because the ♣A allows you to control the suit, but your ♣8 is still a loser.

- ✔ **Spades:** The three small spades in your hand add up to three immediate losers because your partner also has three small spades — the kiss of death.

You need to win ten tricks, but you have four losers in your hand — one too many losers to make your contract. The potential answer to your club loser is that five-card diamond suit staring you in the face — your salvation. You need to turn at least one of those little diamonds into a winning trick and then use it to discard your losing ♣8. It sounds simple when I say it like that, doesn't it? Well, read on; the answer may not be as simple as ABC, but I think you will agree it's not rocket science either. You just keep playing diamonds, trumping losers in your hand if necessary, until the diamonds in the dummy are winners. Read the rest of this section to see how it works in practice.

Playing the long suit to the bitter end

West begins by taking the first three spade tricks with the ♠AKQ and then switches (smartly) to the ♣K, driving out your ♣A and turning your ♣8 into an immediate loser. Fortunately, you have the lead, and you also have a five-card diamond suit to work with. You want to establish the dummy's long suit (make at least one of the small cards over there into a winner), so you have to play the suit and keep playing it until both of your opponents run out of cards in the suit.

Start by leading a low diamond to the ♦K, and both of your opponents play low. Next you play the ♦A, and again both of your opponents play low. You remain with three little diamonds in the dummy and the opponents each have one diamond. Say that you trump a diamond in your hand. Do you see what happens? Each opponent has played his last diamond and suddenly both diamonds in the dummy are winning tricks! You have just set up a suit. But wait — you still have one more hurdle to clear.

If this were a notrump contract, all you would need to do is lead a heart to the ♥A in the dummy and take your two winning diamonds. Unfortunately, in this hand, hearts are trump and it isn't quite that easy.

Do you see those little hearts (four to be exact) in West and East? Until you remove all those hearts, your winning diamonds in the dummy are worthless. If you try to play one, one opponent or the other will trump your winning trick.

Getting rid of your opponents' trump cards

After you establish your small cards you can't use them until you *draw trump*. If you leave your opponents with trump cards, they will trump the dummy's established small-card tricks. Figure 6-2 shows only the trump suit (the hearts) from Figure 6-1 after you have trumped a diamond. You desperately need to draw trump in order to protect the small diamonds you have established as winners.

The opponents have four hearts between their two hands. Those four hearts are tiny, but until you get rid of them, they can pester you to death — or at least to the death of your contract. Your plan of attack is to lead hearts three times. After playing trump cards three times, your opponents won't have any hearts left with which to rain on your parade.

Figure 6-2:
Drawing
trump to
protect your
established
small cards.

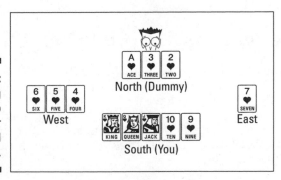

Ending up in the right place — the dummy

When drawing trump to protect established small cards, some players draw trump helter-skelter, ending up in one hand or the other without focusing on a game plan of where they need to be. These players run the risk of ending up in the wrong hand. The dummy's established small-card tricks are of absolutely no use until you draw trump, ending up in the dummy, if possible.

When drawing trump, keep the location of your established small-card winners in mind. Make sure that you end up in the hand that holds the established small card(s) so that you can play it immediately after you finish drawing trump. Keep a high card in the dummy until you need it. So if, as here, you only have the ♥A as a way to reach those beautiful diamonds, for heaven's sake, don't play the ♥A until the last possible moment.

In the case of the cards in Figure 6-1, you have two winning diamonds in the dummy, and you want to use at least one of them to get rid of your losing club. The only way to use those diamonds is by crossing over there *entering* with the ♥A. In bridge terms, that makes the ♥A your only *entry* (path) to the dummy. When your only entry to established tricks is in the trump suit, you have to draw trump carefully, ensuring that you end up by drawing the last of the opponent's trump as you finish up in the dummy — in this case, that means keeping the ♥A tucked away.

In Figure 6-2, you want to draw trump ending in the dummy. You play the ♥K, West plays the ♥4, the dummy contributes the ♥2, and East plays her only remaining trump card, the ♥7. You take the trick and then continue by playing the ♥Q. West follows with the ♥5, you play dummy's ♥3, and East discards a club. You take this trick, as well. West still has one heart left. No problem; you lead the ♥9, West plays the ♥6, the dummy plays the ♥A, and East discards another club.

Congratulations. You have drawn trump ending in the dummy, where your two established diamond tricks are waiting to take tricks for you.

Taking your established tricks

After you establish the dummy's long suit, and after you draw trump so that you end up in the hand with the established small-card winners, you can relax and enjoy taking your established tricks.

Establishing by Finessing

When you're missing a critical high card in the long suit you have chosen to attack, you may have to fall back on the finesse. A finesse involves leading from weakness up to strength, trying to win a trick relatively cheaply by hoping the missing honor card is held by the player who plays second to the trick.

Some five-card suits require a finesse before you can set them up. No problem, take the finesse! You want to dispose of losers by a one-two punch; the finesse allows you to exploit the position of your opponents' high cards. Then, later when you trump the suit, you create extra winners that provide a home for even more of your losers.

You need to take a finesse when you don't have a key top card, normally the ace or the king, in the suit you want to establish.

Also, you can't forget about entries when it comes to setting up suits. After you set up a suit by trumping the small cards, you need to reach the hand with the small cards again, in order to enjoy the fruits of your labor.

If you don't have at least two entries to the dummy, it may not be worthwhile trying to establish tricks in this suit.

Finessing in a side-suit requires the following basic steps:

1. **Determine which suit you want to work with and notice which of the high honor cards you are missing.**

2. **Determine how many cards your opponents have in that suit.**

3. **Lead from weakness to strength hoping that the opponent who plays second to the trick has the missing honor.**

4. **Eventually establish the suit by trumping dummy's small cards until the opponents are out of the suit.**

5. **Draw trump, ending up in the dummy. If you can't end up in the dummy, draw trump ending up in your hand and then enter the dummy in another suit. If you can't enter the dummy in another suit, you shouldn't have bothered setting up the suit in the first place.**

You must draw trump, before you take all your hard-earned winners in the side-suit you have set up. If your opponents have trump cards, you can kiss all those extra tricks good-bye.

6. Sit back and collect the tricks you have established by finessing.

Figure 6-3 shows a suit where finessing can establish an extra trick for you.

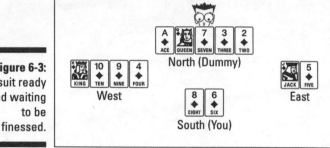

Figure 6-3:
A suit ready and waiting to be finessed.

North (Dummy)

West

East

South (You)

In Figure 6-3, you need to take three tricks from these diamonds; say that spades are trump, and you have high spades coming out of your ears. You want to take the finesse in diamonds, and you are missing the critical ♦K. You hope West, who plays second to the trick, has it.

Before you set up tricks by finessing in the diamond suit, ask yourself how many cards your opponents have in that suit. Otherwise, how will you know when your opponents are void in that suit? Because you have seven diamonds, you can be sure that they have six diamonds.

Start by leading a low diamond toward the ♦Q in the dummy (weakness to strength). This is the finesse, and like all finesses, it is not a sure thing. In fact, you have a 50/50 shot of making your finesse work, but today you are lucky because West, not East, has the ♦K. You therefore take the first diamond trick with the ♦Q, and because your opponents have each played a diamond, they now have four diamonds left. When you continue by playing the ♦A from the dummy, both opponents follow suit, and now they have two diamonds left. You then lead a low diamond from the dummy. Alas, East discards, meaning that West has both remaining diamonds. The nerve of West! Never mind. You trump this diamond in your hand with one of your spades, leaving the cards that you see in Figure 6-4.

Taking matters into your own hands

I once played with a woman who had established a long suit in the dummy, but she didn't have an entry to the dummy to play her established cards. She was very frustrated — she had worked so hard to set up the suit, but she had no entry, or path, to the cards in the dummy. The next time it was her turn to play, she solved the problem by leaving her seat, walking over to the dummy, and taking the established tricks. She fixed the problem of how to get to the cards in the dummy by taking matters into her own hands; she became the entry to the dummy! Please don't try this yourself.

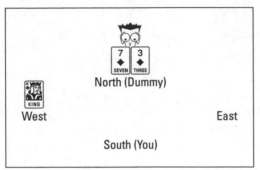

Figure 6-4: The case of the shrinking diamonds.

North (Dummy)

West

East

South (You)

You can still succeed, but you need a way to get back to the dummy two more times (two dummy *entries*). Cross over to the dummy in another suit, lead the ♦3, and trump it in your hand, removing West's last diamond. There, you've done it! You have set up the dummy's ♦7 by trumping twice in your hand. Nice going — almost. All you have to do to finish up the good work is to draw trump either ending in the dummy or being able to reach the dummy in another suit after trumps are drawn. Phew.

Trumping to Establish Small Cards

Trump cards can prove invaluable when establishing small cards in a *side-suit*, that is, any suit that is not the trump suit. Tiny trump cards can beat even the ace and the king in the suit which you want to establish.

You may not believe it, but you can win tricks in long suits, even if you don't hold a single honor card (the ace, king, queen, jack or ten) in that suit. All you need is enough length in the dummy, entries to the dummy, and patience.

When attempting to coax a trick or two out of such a scrawny suit, your strategy should be to play the suit and keep playing the suit until your opponents finally run out of cards in the suit. Eventually, they will.

In Figure 6-5, I spring a really anemic five-card suit on you — this is five-card suit appreciation time.

Figure 6-5:
Anything is possible — even getting some tricks out of this suit.

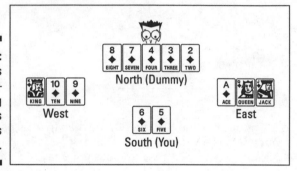

This is a side suit? Even a puny five-card suit such as the one in Figure 6-5 can be set up! No kidding. All you need is patience and dummy entries. You also have to play the suit and keep playing the suit.

Start by leading a diamond (one of your two kamikaze pilots that are about to sacrifice themselves for the greater good). East takes the trick with the ♦J. Say East leads some other suit, but you recapture the lead, and obstinately play your second diamond, which East takes with the ♦Q.

The opposition have only two diamonds left, and because East has the lead, he can plug on with another suit. But you will not be denied. Cross over to the dummy using a high card in another suit, and trump a diamond. Presto, they have no more diamonds and you have two extra diamond winners in the dummy. Of course, you still have to draw trump, and you still need a second entry to the dummy to enjoy those diamond winners. But it can be done!

After the trauma of setting up that last suit, you need a little breather; take a look at a five-card suit with a little more beef, such as the suit in Figure 6-6.

Start by leading a low diamond to the ♦Q (weakness toward strength). East wins the ♦A. Are you counting the diamonds? Big Brother is watching. They started with six diamonds and now they have four left.

Later, when you lead a diamond to the ♦K, both your opponents follow; now they have two diamonds left. When you trump a diamond, your opponents both follow — they now have no more diamonds. Both of the dummy's diamonds become winners. You are setting up suits like a veteran. People are noticing.

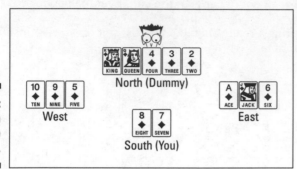

Figure 6-6:
A suit with a little more meat in it.

In the suits shown in Figures 6-5 and 6-6, the dummy has five cards, while you have two. Although this is a very common scenario, it is by no means the only one. The dummy may have a six-card suit; you may have a singleton (just one card in the suit) and so on. No matter, the technique is the same. Set up the suit, draw trump, and then mop up by taking your tricks.

Working with a six-card suit is easier and quicker than setting up a five-card suit; after you master setting up the five-card suit, six-card suits should be as easy as falling off a log.

On a good day, your partner will hand you a six-card side suit; on a beautiful day, you have enough dummy entries to allow you to set up and enjoy the suit as you can in Figure 6-7.

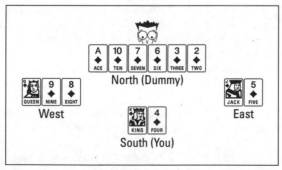

Figure 6-7:
On a sunny day, your opponents' cards divide as evenly as possible in the dummy's long suit.

Say you want to set up the dummy's six-card diamond suit. You notice that they have five diamonds. Start by playing the ♦K, the high equal honor from the short side. Both opponents play low diamonds so they have three diamonds left. You continue with the ♦4. West plays low and you play the ♦A. Again both opponents follow. They have one diamond left. You lead a low diamond from the dummy. If East trumps, you overtrump; if East discards, you trump and West's last diamond, the ♦Q, appears. Guess what? You have three, count 'em, three winning diamonds in the dummy. All you have to do is draw trump and get over to the dummy to use them. What a player you are turning into.

Setting up a side suit (any suit that is not the trump suit in a hand) entails certain risks. When you set up the small cards in a long suit, you often can't draw trump first because you need those entries to the dummy to reach your winners after you establish the suit. If the entries to the dummy are in the trump suit, you can't put the cart before the horse; you have to use the trump entries after setting up the suit. Hence drawing trump has to wait.

The dangers of trumping a side suit increase if the opponents still have trump cards. When you trump a card, the player who plays after you may also be void in the suit and may be able to play a higher trump card and take the trick, which is called *overtrumping*. Overtrumping can be a major pain — and you know where.

In addition, you may have the entry problems associated with long suit establishment; frequently you may be short of sufficient high cards in the dummy to both set up the dummy's winners and to be able to get back and enjoy the suit.

You also need enough trump cards in your hand to trump a card or two in the suit you are establishing *and* still have enough trump cards to remove all of your opponents' trump cards. Sometimes you are not dealt such an embarrassment of riches in the trump suit.

After all that, don't despair. I mention the downside to establishing a suit just to let you know that it doesn't always work out. Nevertheless, you should consider establishing a suit as a way to turn rags into riches.

Keeping Your Eyes on the Prize

Does establishing a suit seems like a whole lot of work? Sometimes it can be. But the rewards can be great.

You can achieve greatness by setting up a long suit. In Figure 6-8, you accomplish a grand slam by establishing a side suit. A grand slam (taking all 13 tricks) is the most exciting and one of the most difficult contracts to bring home (see Chapter 15 for the glorious details on slams). The risks when attempting a grand slam may be high, but it can sure pay off if you make your contract.

Before you get to slamming, listen in for a second. When you establish a suit and the dummy has entries in both the trump suit *and* a side suit, use the trump entry (entries) first; that way, you can use the side-suit entry at the very end, after you get all the trump cards out of the way.

Fasten your seat belt and take a look at the cards in Figure 6-8. There's nothing quite like bidding a *grand slam* (contracting for all 13 tricks) and then taking all 13 tricks. Your contract for this hand is 7♥ (hearts is the trump suit). West leads the ♠Q.

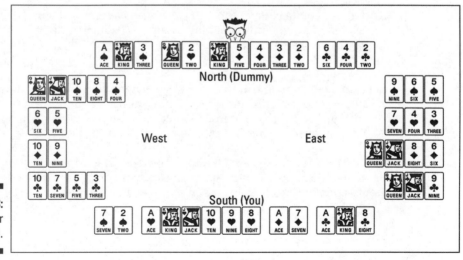

Figure 6-8: Going for the gold.

Whether you have to take 7 or 13 tricks, you still go through the same steps, counting your losers and looking for extra winners:

- ✔ **Hearts:** No losers, a solid suit
- ✔ **Spades:** No losers (the ♠AK take care of your two baby spades)
- ✔ **Diamonds:** No losers and a five-card suit (hint, hint, hint)
- ✔ **Clubs:** One loser, eventual

You have one loser in clubs, the fly in the ointment. You could get rid of losing club on one of the dummy's diamonds, but first you have to set up those diamonds.

Win the opening lead with the dummy's ♠K, and then lead a diamond to the ♦A (following the general principle of unblocking the log-jam by playing the high card from the short side). Then lead a diamond to the ♦K.

The opponents start with six diamonds; they have each played two diamonds, so they have a total of two diamonds left. When you play a third diamond, East follows, and you play a trump card. Fortunately, all of your trump are so high that West, who has no more diamonds, can't overtrump (trump higher). Assume that West discards a worthless spade.

Those two diamonds in the dummy still aren't winners because West has the ♦Q. Have some fortitude. Cross over to the dummy by using the ♥Q as an entry (using your trump entry first), and then trump the ♦4 in your hand, taking away the last obstacle to your happiness, East's ♦Q.

Now that the ♦5 in the dummy is an established trick, play the ♥AK, drawing the opponents' remaining trump cards, and then cross over to the dummy with the ♠A (dummy entry number two). You can then triumphantly play your ♦5, discarding your losing club.

You have just bid and made a grand slam by winning all 13 tricks, but you needed the dummy's ♦5 to do it. How does it feel?

Chapter 7

Using the Dummy's Trump Cards to Get Rid of Your Losers

*Y*ou find a bad apple in every barrel. You know the one I mean — that one rotten apple that ruins the entire barrel of apples. In bridge, you also come across some rotten apples — your losers, those losing cards that keep you from making your contract.

Just as you can throw out a rotten apple, you can also get rid of your losers. This chapter discusses a fun and easy technique for ridding your hand of unwanted losers.

Understanding the Concept

Playing a hand at a trump contract is all about getting rid of your side-suit losers (a side suit is any suit that is not the trump suit). One of the easiest ways to get rid of your losers is to put the dummy's trump cards to work. And exactly how do you do that?

You look for a side suit in the dummy that has a zero, one, or two cards (a void, singleton, or a doubleton), and then you check to make sure you have more cards in that suit than the dummy. After you find such an unequally divided suit, you are in business. The spades in Figure 7-1 show you why you can open up shop.

Assume that hearts is your trump suit and that the spade suit in Figure 7-1 is a side suit. Pretend that the dummy has three hearts.

Figure 7-1: Looking for a short suit in the dummy.

The spades in Figure 7-1 meet the criteria; you see two spades in the dummy and longer spades in your hand, an unequally divided suit. As it stands, you have three losing spades in your hand. However, if you lead spades twice and concede your opponents two spade tricks, the dummy won't have any more spades. After the dummy is void in a side suit, you can trump any remaining loser you have in that suit in the dummy. Hey, losing two spade tricks is better than losing three spade tricks.

Knowing When to Use the Short Hand

When you trump your loser(s) in the dummy, you are usually trumping in the hand that has fewer trump cards than you do. For that reason the dummy is called the short hand. Now I will let you in on a little secret: Each time you trump a loser in the short hand you gain a trick.

As you see in "Trumping Losers in the Long Hand" in this chapter, you don't gain a trick when you trump one of the dummy's losers in the long trump hand; it's an illusion. Clearly, your goal is to trump losers in the short hand. Figure 7-2 presents an absolute best case scenario of trumping losers in the short hand.

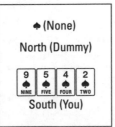

Figure 7-2: It doesn't get any better than this.

In this figure you hit the jackpot. The dummy starts out void in spades so you can just start trumping your spade losers as fast as you can.

The basic technique for trumping losers in the short hand, the dummy, is this:

1. **Identify a side suit in which you have more cards than the dummy, and the dummy has zero, one, or two cards in the suit.**

2. **Lead the suit until the dummy is void.**

3. **Once the dummy is void, trump your remaining losers in that suit.**

The cards in Figure 7-3 show you how the miracle of trumping losers in the short hand plays out in a sample hand.

In Figure 7-3, you have the following losers (see Chapter 4 for help on how to count losers):

✔ **Hearts:** You have one immediate loser because you don't have the ace.

✔ **Spades:** You have one eventual loser, the ♠2, unless you can find some way to cover it.

✔ **Diamonds:** You have no losers.

✔ **Clubs:** You have two losers, the ♣94.

On this hand, you need to win ten tricks, and hearts is the trump suit. West starts out the hand by playing the ♣AKQ. When West plays the ♣Q, you have run out of clubs, so you trump the ♣Q with a low heart and gain the lead.

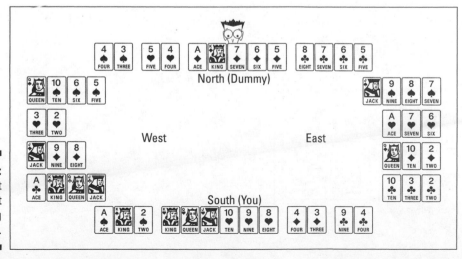

Figure 7-3:
Don't get caught consorting with losers.

You have lost two tricks, you have a certain loser in hearts, and you also have the little matter of the ♠2 to deal with. You have to find a way to get rid of that spade loser or you are doomed.

Sometimes losers can be discarded on the dummy's long suit (diamonds, in this case), using the technique discussed in Chapter 6, but not this time. Even if you could set up the diamonds by playing the ♦AK and then trumping one, you would have no entry to get back to the dummy to be able to take the winning diamonds. Scratch diamonds; this suit can't help you get rid of any losers. Try plan B. Your next plan is to search through your hand for a suit in which you have more cards than the dummy.

Take a closer look at that spade suit in Figure 7-3. You have three spades and the dummy has two spades, the signal that you may be able to trump your losing ♠2.

Play the ♠AK, which takes care of all of the dummy's spades, and now lead the ♠2, trumping it with the lowly ♥4 in the dummy. You just got rid of that losing spade. Your only remaining loser is the ♥A.

You obviously need to have trump cards in the dummy in order to trump losers. If you plan to trump one or more losers from your hand in the dummy, well then, you do have to keep some trump cards in the dummy. You may have to defer drawing trump until after you trump those losers.

In Figure 7-3, you need to trump one spade before you draw the opponents' hearts. If you play a trump card early in the hand and remove the dummy's trump cards, you would not be able to trump your spade loser in the dummy, and you would go down.

Frequently you have a side suit that looks like the spades shown in Figure 7-4.

Figure 7-4:
Keeping
your trump
cards
available
for use.

North (Dummy)

South (You)

You have two spade losers, but if you play the ♠A and void the dummy in spades, you can eventually trump your two remaining spades. Instead of two spade losers, you have no spade losers. Of course, you need two trump cards in the dummy to pull off this little caper.

Facing a Counterattack from Your Opponents

The opponents are also at the table. Your opponents watch you try to trump your losers in the dummy, and they don't like it. You are trumping tricks that they want to take. For every attempt you make to get rid of your losers your opponents may be planning a counterattack with their trump cards. For every strategy in bridge, there is a counter strategy.

Each time you give up the lead in the dummy's short suit, you can expect clever opponents to lead a trump card. After all, if you need to keep trump cards in the dummy, then you can expect your opponents to try to get rid of those trump cards. Each time they lead a trump card, that's one less trump card in the dummy you have to trump a loser. Of course, you can always hope that they haven't read this book . . . maybe they will lead something else, but I wouldn't count on it.

You can take the sting out of your opponents' trump leads by simply making sure that you have enough trump cards in the dummy to outlast their attack. Figure 7-5 shows you a hand where you can ward off any trump leads from the opponents.

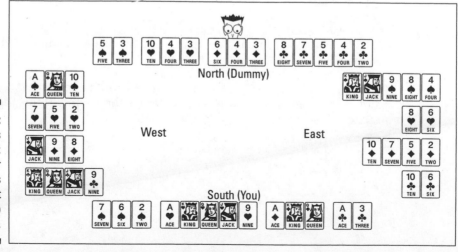

Figure 7-5: Barbarians at the gate: Your opponents plot against your trump cards.

In Figure 7-5, you need to take ten tricks, and hearts is the trump suit. West opens with the ♣K. First, you take stock of your losers (you can only afford to lose three tricks):

- ✔ **Hearts:** No losers
- ✔ **Spades:** Three losers, the ♠762
- ✔ **Diamonds:** No losers
- ✔ **Clubs:** One eventual loser

The nerve of your partner to present you with such a dummy! However, you do have a ray of hope. Did you notice that the dummy has two spades, one fewer spade than you have? If you play spades twice before you draw trump, you can void the dummy in spades. You could then trump your third spade with one of the dummy's hearts, reducing your loser count to three.

You have to give up the lead twice in spades, but even if your opponents lead a trump card each time they have the lead, you still have one trump card in the dummy you can use to trump your third spade. Strike one for the forces of light.

What about drawing trump first? Later, man, later. If you draw trump, you won't have a trump card in the dummy to care for your third spade.

Trumping Losers in the Long Hand

If you can get extra tricks by trumping losers in the dummy, perhaps you can generate extra tricks by trumping the dummy's losers in your hand. Sorry, it doesn't work that way.

In Figure 7-5, trumping a spade in the dummy gives your side six trump tricks (one spade trump in the dummy and five winning trump cards in your own hand).

For a moment, turn things around and think about trumping a loser in your hand — the long hand. Figure 7-6 gives you a chance to put this theory into practice. Assume hearts is your trump suit.

Figure 7-6:
Attempting
to trump a
loser in the
wrong
hand.

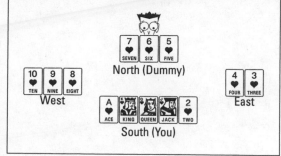

North (Dummy)

West

East

South (You)

You wish to draw trump, and you play the ♥AKQ, removing all of their trump cards. You remain with the ♥J2, both winners. You score five heart tricks. Agreed?

Now see what happens if they lead a suit you don't have and you trump the lead with your ♥2. You remain with the ♥AKQJ, four tricks, plus the deuce you have already used. Same five trump tricks. Trumping with the ♥2 doesn't give you an extra trick.

Trumping in the long hand is a break-even plan at best; you don't get any extra tricks. However, each time you trump in the short hand, you gain a trick.

Part III
Bidding to Win

The 5th Wave   By Rich Tennant

"I DON'T CARE WHAT KIND OF CLOWNS YOU TWO ARE,
I KNOW A SIGNAL WHEN I HEAR ONE! YOU HONK THAT
THING ONE MORE TIME AND I'M LEAVING THE TABLE!"

In this part . . .

The number one cause of bridge disasters is improper bidding. Think of the countless tricks that could be saved (from your opponents' trick pile) if you had a strong foundation in bidding.

In this part you discover when to bid and when to apply the brakes. In short, you see how to arrive at the best contract.

After you read this part, you'll find fewer of your tricks falling into the perilous hands of the opponents.

Chapter 8

Bidding Basics

● ●

In This Chapter

▶ Understanding bidding protocol

▶ Discovering the pecking order of suits

▶ Deciding how high to bid

▶ Finding out who plays and who watches

▶ Tallying up the strength of your hand

● ●

*B*idding for tricks is a very important part of the game of bridge. Successful bidding can either make or break your chances of fulfilling your contract.

In this chapter, you discover some of the fundamentals of bidding. You find out how the bidding progresses around the table, the proper way to call your bid, and how to assess the strength of your hand (so you can make good decisions about how many tricks you and your partner may be able to take). You certainly shouldn't pass on this chapter.

Grasping the Importance of Bidding

Bidding determines the *final contract* for a hand. The pressure is on the partnership who decides (or *buys*) the final contract — whoever buys the final contract has to win the number of tricks that they bid for. If the partnership fails to win the number of tricks they say they can make, penalty points are scored against them. If the partners do win the tricks they say they can take, they then score points. (You can read more about scoring in Chapter 16.)

In addition to determining how many tricks a partnership needs to win, the bidding also determines the following:

✔ **The declarer and the dummy for the hand:** For the partnership that buys the final contract, the bidding determines who will play the hand for the partnership (the *declarer*) and who gets to sit and watch (the *dummy*).

✔ **How many tricks a partnership needs to win:** Each bid corresponds to a number of tricks that a partnership thinks they can take. The partnership that buys the final contract is saying that they can win the number of tricks corresponding to their final bid. That partnership's only goal after buying the final contract is to win at least the number of tricks their final bid says that they can take.

✔ **The trump suit (if there is to be one) for the hand:** Depending on the cards held by the partnership that buys the final contract, there could be a trump suit (or the bidding could end in a notrump contract). See Chapter 3 to find out more about playing at notrump. Part III discusses playing at trump.

Bidding also allows the partners to exchange information about the strength (honor cards) and the distribution of their cards. Through bidding, you and your partner can tell each other which long suits you have and even perhaps in which suits you have honor cards.

Based on the information they exchange during the bidding, each partnership has to decide how many tricks they think they can take. The partnership with the greater combined strength usually *buys the contract* or makes the final bid. The declarer (the one who plays the hand) tries to take the number of tricks (or more tricks) that his side has contracted for. The opponents, on the other hand, do their darndest to prevent the declarer from winning those tricks.

Partnerships exchange vital information about the makeup of their hands through a *bidding system.* Because you can't tell your partner what you have by using plain English, you have to use a bidding system. You can think of a bidding system as a foreign language in which every bid you make carries some message. Although you can't say to your partner, "Hey partner, I have seven strong hearts, but only one ace and one king," the bidding system usually provides a bid that describes just such a hand.

The bidding (or *auction*) consists only of the permitted bids; you do not get the chance to describe your hand, either by facial expressions, kicking your partner under the table, or punching him in the nose. Your partner must also understand the conventional significance of your bids in order to make sense of what you are trying to communicate about your hand and to know how to respond properly.

Of course, everyone at the table hears your bid, as well as every other bid at the table. No secrets are allowed. Whatever your bid tells your partner, your opponents are also privy to the same information. Similarly, by listening to your opponents' bidding, you get a feel for the cards that your opponents have. You can then turn around and use this information when the play of the hand begins.

Bridge authorities universally agree that bidding is the most important aspect of the game. Using a simple system and making clear bids is the key to getting to the proper contract and racking up the points. Bidding incorrectly (giving your partner faulty information) leads to lousy contracts, which in turn let your opponents rack up the points after you fail to make your contract.

Understanding How Bidding Works

The bidding begins after the cards have been shuffled and dealt. Each player picks up his or her hand and assesses the strength of the hand (see "Valuing the Strength of Your Hand," later in this chapter, for more about evaluating the strength of your hand).

Opening the bidding

The player who deals the cards has the first opportunity to make a bid. The dealer looks at her hand, and if she sees that she has sufficient strength in her hand to make a bid, she makes a bid that begins to tell her partner (and everyone else at the table) how strong her hand is. The bid may also give some approximate idea of whether the player has a long suit, and if so, which suit that is. If she doesn't have enough strength to make the first bid, called the *opening bid,* she can *pass,* or not make a bid.

Being second in line

After the dealer either bids or passes, the bidding continues in a clockwise rotation. The next player can do one of two things: He can either make a bid higher than the dealer's bid (assuming that the dealer makes an opening bid) or he can pass. He can't make a bid unless he bids higher than the dealer's bid. See "Ranking the bids (ranking the suits)," later in this chapter, for more information on determining whether one bid is higher than another bid. If you've ever attended an auction, you can see why bidding is sometimes referred to as an auction — each bid must outrank the previous one, just like at an auction.

Responding to the opening bid

After the second player either makes a bid or passes, the bid follows a clockwise rotation to the next player at the table, who is the dealer's partner.

If the dealer opens the bidding, the third player (called the *responder*) can then make a bid called a *response*. This bid communicates whether the cards in her hand can work together with her partner's suit, or whether she has length and strength in a different suit. The responder also has the option to pass, which also communicates information (albeit of a rather depressing nature) about the strength of her hand.

Buying the contract

The bidding continues clockwise around the table, each player either making a bid higher than the last bid or passing. When a bid is followed by three passes, the bidding ends. After the bidding ends, the partnership that makes the last bid has *bought the contract* for the hand, meaning that they will play the hand, trying to take at least the number of tricks that corresponds to their bid.

During the bidding, think of yourself as being in an "up-only" elevator that doesn't stop until three of its passengers say "Stop!" (or in this case, "Pass") consecutively. Furthermore, this elevator has no down button. The only way you can refrain from driving the elevator up is by saying "Pass" when it is your turn to bid.

Passing the buck

I want you to note one special case that does come up occasionally during the bidding. Sometimes, no one wants to make a bid, as you can see in the following bidding sequence:

West	North (Your Partner)	East	South (You)
Pass	Pass	Pass	Pass

The hand has been *passed out*. Nobody wants to get on the elevator, not even on the lowly first floor! Four wimps; or more charitably perhaps, none of the players have a strong enough hand to open the bidding. When a hand is passed out (which is relatively unusual), the cards are reshuffled and the same person deals again.

Looking at the Structure and the Rank of a Bid

During the bidding, players call out their bids in order to communicate information about their hands to their partners.

Bids have a structure and special notation rules all their own. Bids also have a ranking, which tells you when your bid is high enough to enter the bidding. Remember that each new bid must outrank the previous ones.

Each bid corresponds to a predetermined "message" about your cards, a message that you're trying to send to your partner about the strength of your hand. Each bid also corresponds to a number of tricks that you're saying you can win.

In Chapters 9 through 15, you discover which bid to use in order to tell your partner what you want them to know about your hand. In this section, I just want you to get acquainted with the look and feel of these bids.

Building a bid

A bid consists of two elements:

- **The suit:** For bidding purposes, the cards actually have five "suits," which are spades, hearts, diamonds, clubs, and notrump. (Note this expanded meaning of a *suit*.)

- **The number of tricks you are bidding for in that suit:** You start with six tricks and build from there.

When people call out a bid, they don't say "I want to bid three in the spade suit." Instead, players use a special language when making a bid. You announce bids as "four notrump," "three clubs," or "two diamonds." When you see bids referred to in books (including in this one), the bids are abbreviated to their card number and suit symbol. For example, the written equivalent of the preceding bids would look like this: 4NT (four notrump), 3♣ (three clubs), and 2♦ (two diamonds).

Each bridge hand consists of exactly 13 tricks; the minimum opening bid must be for at least 7 of those 13 tricks. Therefore, each bid has an automatic six tricks built into it; thus a 1♥ bid actually says that you think you can take seven tricks, not one trick. In other words, your bridge elevator starts on the seventh floor.

The numbers associated with a bid correspond to bidding levels. For example, bids of 1♠, 1♥, 1♦, and 1♣ are called *one level bids*. If you see (or make) a bid that starts with a 3, that is a *three level bid*. The highest bidding level is the seven level; doing a little math tells you 7♠, 7♥, 7♦, and 7♣ must be the highest possible bids because 7 + 6 = 13.

Ranking the bids (ranking the suits)

During the bidding, players can't make a bid unless their bid is higher than the previous bid. In bridge, two factors determine whether your bid is legal, in the bridge sense:

- ✔ Which suit you are bidding
- ✔ How many tricks you are bidding for in that suit

During the actual play of a hand, the rank of the suits has no significance. The rank of the suits only matters during the bidding. To understand the progression of the bidding, you should become familiar with the rank of the suits, yet another pecking order (first the ranking order of the cards, and now the order of the suits).

The suits are ranked in the following order:

- ✔ **Notrump (NT):** Wait! You thought you were reading about the rank of suits. I bet you don't remember seeing a *notrump* suit in your deck of cards. Well, okay — so notrump isn't really a suit in the strictest sense of the word. But notrump *is* a type of bid; you have to use an expanded definition of the word *suits* when it comes to the bidding. In fact, notrump is the highest "suit" you can bid. Notrump is the king of the hill when it comes to bidding — you can score the most points with notrump bids.

- ✔ **Spades (♠):** Spades is the highest ranking suit (after notrump).

- ✔ **Hearts (♥):** Hearts ranks behind spades; hearts and spades are referred to as the *major suits,* not only because they carry more weight in the auction but because they are also worth more in the scoring (discussed in Chapter 16).

- ✔ **Diamonds (♦):** Diamonds don't carry so much weight; they outrank only the clubs.

- ✔ **Clubs (♣):** Clubs are the lowest suit on the totem pole. Diamonds and clubs are called *minor suits* for two reasons. First, you can't score as many points when you bid these two minor suits. Second, bridge players love to sit around and make up terms like major and minor suits.

To remember the rank of the suits (excluding notrump), look at the first letter of each suit. The *S* in *spades* is higher in the alphabet than the *H* in *hearts,* which is higher than the *D* in *diamonds,* which is higher than the *C* in *clubs.*

To see how the rank of the suits comes into play during the bidding, consider the following example. Assume that you are seated in the South position:

South (You)	West	North (Your Partner)	East
1♥	?		

Suppose that you open the bidding with 1♥ (check out opening bids in Chapter 9). Because the bidding goes in clockwise fashion, West has the next chance to bid. West doesn't have to bid if he doesn't want to; however, the most likely reason for not bidding would be that West simply does not have a strong enough hand. West can say "Pass" (which is not considered a bid).

However, if West does want to join in the fun, he must make some bid that is *higher* than 1♥. For example, West can bid 1♠, but not 1♣ or 1♦ — because spades is a higher ranking suit than hearts, a 1♠ bid is higher than a 1♥ bid.

On the other hand, if West wants to bid diamonds (a lower ranking suit than hearts), West must bid at least 2♦ for his bid to be legal. That is, only by upping the *level* of the bid (from 1 to 2) can West make a legal bid in diamonds (a lower ranking suit than hearts).

Figuring out the final bid (the final contract)

After a bid is followed by three consecutive passes, the last bid becomes the final bid, or the *final contract.* The final bid determines the following issues about how the cards will be played in the hand:

- ✔ **Notrump:** If the final bid is in notrump, no cards are designated as wild cards, or *trump cards,* during the hand (see Part I for more information on playing at notrump).

- ✔ **Trump:** If a suit is named in the final bid, that particular suit is then designated as the trump suit for the hand. For example, if the final bid is 4♥, the trump suit is hearts for that hand.

> ✔ **How many tricks need to be won:** By automatically adding six to the number of the bid, you know how many tricks you need to take. For example, if the final contract is the popular 3NT, the partnership needs to win 9 tricks to make their contract (6 + 3 = 9).

Putting it all together in a sample bidding sequence

In the following example, you can see the bids made by each player during a sample bidding sequence. You don't see the cards upon which each player bases his or her bid, which isn't important for now. I just want you to follow the bidding around the table, noting how each bid is higher than the one before it. Assume that you're in the South position:

South (You)	West	North (Your Partner)	East
1♥	Pass	2♣	2♦
3♣	3♦	4♥	Pass
Pass	Pass		

After your opening 1♥ bid, West passes, and your partner (North) bids 2♣. East joins right in with a bid of 2♦, a bid that is higher than 2♣. When it's your turn to bid again, you decide to show support for your partner's clubs by bidding 3♣. Then West comes to life and supports East's diamonds by bidding 3♦. Your partner (don't forget your partner) chimes in with 4♥, a bid which silences everybody. Both East and West pass, just as they would at an auction where the bidding had gotten too rich for their blood.

As you can see in this auction, both North and South introduced a suit, implying length in those suits. East bid her diamonds, you supported your partner's club suit, and West then raised his partner in diamonds. Notice that because diamonds outrank clubs, West had to bid at least 3♦. Finally, North (your partner) ended the auction by bidding 4♥.

It has been a somewhat lively auction and your side has *bought the contract* with your partner's 4♥ bid, which means that you need to take ten tricks to make your contract. If you don't make your contract, the opponents score penalty points and you get zilch. The final contract of 4♥ also designates hearts as the trump suit for the hand.

Notice the following points about the bidding sequence:

> ✔ Each bid made was higher than the previous bid. Either the bid was at a higher level or at the same level in a higher ranking suit.

> ✔ A player can pass on the first round and then bid later (as West did); or a player can bid on the first round and then pass later (as East did).

> ✔ After three players in a row pass, the bidding is over.

Settling Who Plays the Hand

If your partnership buys the final contract, the bidding also determines who gets to play the hand (the *declarer*) for the partnership and who get to kick back and watch the action (the *dummy*). Basically, whoever bid the suit of the final bid first gets to be the declarer. For example, take a look at this sample bidding sequence:

South (You)	West	North (Your Partner)	East
1♥	Pass	2♣	2♦
3♣	3♦	4♥	Pass
Pass	Pass		

The contract ends in 4♥, which is the final bid, because it is followed by three passes. Both you and your partner bid hearts at some point in the bidding. However, you bid hearts first, which makes *you* the declarer.

Had the final contract ended in clubs, your partner would play (declare) the hand because she bid clubs first. Likewise, if the auction had ended at 3♦, East would have been the declarer and West the dummy.

The player seated to the left of the declarer (in this case, West) makes the opening lead and the partner of the declarer (North) is the dummy. After the opening lead, the dummy puts down her cards and bows out of the action.

Valuing the Strength of Your Hand

During the bidding, you need to figure out the collective strength of your partnership's hands in order to accurately assess how many tricks you can take. Of course, you have to determine how strong your own hand is *before* you can tell that to your partner. You must consider two elements when valuing the strength of your hand:

- ✔ Your high card points (see the following section for a definition)
- ✔ The distribution of your cards (how your cards are divided into the various suits)

How do you know how high to bid — or if you should bid at all? The strength and distribution of your hand, combined with the strength and distribution of your partner's hand, tell you how many tricks you should shoot for in your bid, or whether you should enter the bidding at all.

Adding up your high card points

Your honor cards (the honor cards are the ace, king, queen, and jack in each suit) contribute to the strength of your hand. When you pick up your hand, assign the following points to each of your honor cards:

- ✔ **Aces:** For every ace, count 4 points (A = 4 points).
- ✔ **Kings:** For every king, count 3 points (K = 3 points).
- ✔ **Queens:** For every queen, count 2 points (Q = 2 points).
- ✔ **Jacks:** For every jack, count 1 point (J = 1 point).

These points are called *high card points* (HCPs). This point system is called the *4-3-2-1 point count* — everyone who plays bridge uses the same system to value the strength of his hand. The 10 is also an honor card; but alas, it counts for nothing when tallying up your HCPs.

Each suit contains 10 HCPs, adding up to 40 HCPs in the deck. After you know the total HCPs between the two hands in your partnership (which you find out through the bidding), it makes deciding how many tricks to bid for much easier.

Looking for an eight-card fit

Why should you care about the *distribution* of the cards (that is, how many cards you or your partner has in any one suit)? Because in order for you and your partner to land in a safe trump-suit contract, you need to have at least eight cards in the same suit between the two hands, which is called an *eight-card fit*. Most of your bids are geared toward locating such a fit.

Chapter 9
Opening Bids

● ●

In This Chapter

▶ Having the first say in the bidding

▶ Knowing your hand types

▶ Opening with the correct bid for your hand

● ●

Starting off on the right foot is essential to anything you do, but it's twice as important when bidding for tricks. In this chapter, I tell you everything you need to know about the opening bid — the bid that starts off the bidding process. I show you how to figure out if you can make the first bid and what to bid if you can.

If you aren't familiar with the basics of bidding, check out Chapter 8 to pick up some fundamentals.

Opening the Bidding

After the dealer deals the cards, you pick them up, sort them, and evaluate the strength of your hand. Depending on how strong your hand is, you may get a chance to make the first bid, called the *opening bid.* But how do you know whether your hand is good enough to make an opening bid? Just read on.

Knowing when to get in on the game

Two factors contribute to whether you have an opening bid:

✔ **Your high card points (HCPs):** You should have at least 12 high card points in your hand in order to make an opening bid. (See "Valuing the Strength of Your Hand" in Chapter 8 for more information on calculating your HCPs.)

✔ **The length of your suits:** You should have at least four cards in the suit you bid. Fortunately, all hands contain at least one four-card suit.

If your cards fulfill both of these criteria, you can make an opening bid in the suit in which you have four cards or more. For example, suppose that you deal yourself either of the hands you see in Figure 9-1.

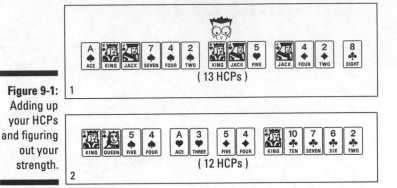

(13 HCPs)

1

Figure 9-1:
Adding up your HCPs and figuring out your strength.

2

(12 HCPs)

You can make an opening bid with either of these hands; both hands contain 12 HCPs or more, and both have a suit with four cards or more in it. So life is easy; you can open the bidding in your long suit, which is spades and clubs respectively.

REMEMBER

The player who makes the opening bid tries to show both her strength and her distribution to her partner. For example, if a player makes an opening bid of 1♣, you can bet that she has at least 12 high card points in her hand, and length (at least four cards) in clubs.

Playing with the rules

In "Knowing when to get in on the game," I tell you that you need at least 12 HCPs in order to make an opening bid. I try to give you definitive rules, but not all bridge concepts are cut-and-dry. Case in point, the strength require-ments for an opening bid can sometimes be shaded a little. For example, if you have a six-card suit or two five-card suits, you can open the bidding with as few as 11 HCPs. If you have a seven-card suit, you can dip as low as 10 HCPs to open the bidding. If your partner complains about you opening with fewer than 12 HCPs, just tell your partner that you don't need as many points because you play so well.

Getting in on the ground floor

The dealer gets the first chance to make a bid. If she has sufficient strength, she makes a bid. She can also choose to pass (passing is not considered a bid).

When it becomes your turn to bid (you may be first if you're the dealer or you may get a chance to make the opening bid if the other players before you pass) and your hand doesn't have enough strength to open, just say one word, "Pass," and don't look glum. You can frequently bid later.

Decoding the opening bid

The opening bid gets the bidding rolling and communicates the following messages about the opener's hand:

- ✓ **High card strength:** You usually have 12 HCPs to open the bidding, so if you open the bidding, you've got some high card strength.

- ✓ **The opener's longest suit:** With rare exception, when you open the bidding, you have four or more cards in the suit that you are bidding.

Remembering your goal: finding the eight-card fit

The first few bids in most bidding sequences are exploratory bids, like two fighters feeling each other out in the early rounds. Usually on the second bid, one of the players shows his strength within a few points. Good news. Then his partner can add the total HCPs between two hands to see how high to bid.

While all this telling and adding is going on, the partnership is trying to locate a suit they both like (one in which they have at least eight cards between the two hands); if they find one, they try to make that suit the trump suit. Because hearts and spades are the most rewarding suits to play in (turn to Chapter 16 for more information on scoring), the partnership initially tries to find an eight-card (or longer) suit in either hearts or spades. Much depends upon whether the eight-card fit exists or not; if a partnership doesn't have such a fit, they play the hand at notrump or in an eight-card or longer minor suit fit (diamonds or clubs).

When you open the bidding in a suit, your partner can't possibly know exactly how many cards you have in the suit. The opening bid is just the beginning of your picture. As you make a second bid (called the *rebid,* which you hear more about in Chapter 11) and, perhaps, on a third bid, the picture of your hand starts to come into focus. Be patient with yourself and your partner through the bidding process: Even the greatest of paintings begin with a single stroke of the brush.

Spies lurk everywhere — the place is bugged

Bidding is an exchange of information. During the bidding, you're trying to telegraph details about your cards to your partner.

But what about your opponents? What are they doing while you pass this coded information back and forth? They're not reading a book, you know — they listen to the bidding, too! This coded information you pass to your partner may be in a foreign language (the language of bidding), but your opponents also speak this language. Whatever you tell your partner, your opponents hear, and your opponents know. Your opponents have a decoder.

Your first impulse may be to develop some special bidding conventions that only you and your partner know. However, according to the rules of the game, you can't have any bidding secrets with your partner; the same goes for your opponents.

Your opponents can bid, as well. In fact, your opponents bid their heads off most of the time. They know how much it bugs you, so they do it constantly. You, too, can be a major league "buttinski," as you see in Chapter 14.

Bidding with 12 to 20 HCPs in Your Hand

In theory, opening bids can be made at any level you like (see "Building a bid" in Chapter 8 for more information on bidding levels). In practice, if you have enough points to open the bidding, you almost always start the bidding at the one level.

If your hand has 12 to 20 HCPs, start the bidding with a one level bid. If you have more than 20 HCPs, turn to "Opening with 20 HCPs or More in Your Hand" in this chapter to see how to handle such hands. If you keep picking up hands of more than 20 HCPs, give me a call — I need to know partners like you.

If both your HCPs and your distribution help you decide whether to make an opening bid, which factor is more important? One simple fact answers this question: The longer the suit you have, the more tricks you are likely to take. Based on this fact, you bid your longer, not necessarily your stronger, suit first. It's also why your partnership's ultimate goal during the bidding is to locate that all-important eight-card fit. Remember to put length before strength.

After you ascertain that you have 12 or more HCPs, you try to tell your partner how your cards are divided (how many cards you have in each suit), which is called your *distribution*.

The distribution of your cards (the length of your suits) plays a major part in how high you bid. You use an established bidding method, called a *system* to communicate your distribution. I discuss the various distributions, or *hand patterns;* and how to handle them in this section.

Eyeballing your distribution

The distribution of your cards determines which suit you bid first. Every hand you pick up will have one of the following characteristics:

- **One-suited:** A hand with one five-, six-, or seven-card suit.

- **Two-suited:** A hand with two five-card suits or a five- and a four-card suit.

- **Three-suited:** Three four-card suits.

- **Balanced:** A hand with no long suit and no really short suit. Balanced hands come in three types: a hand with only one four-card suit, a hand with two four-card suits, and a hand with a five-card suit. You can refer to balanced hand types numerically in terms of the suit-length, putting the long suit first; for example, a 4-3-3-3 shape, a 4-4-3-2 shape, and a 5-3-3-2 shape. These hands are balanced because you have length in every suit.

Astute readers may note that hands with a 5-3-3-2 distribution belong to two different families, because they could be put in the one-suiter hand-type, or the balanced hand category. Who'll get custody of the 5-3-3-2? See "Opening the bidding with balanced hands" in this chapter to find out the answer.

Opening with a one-suited hand

With one rare exception, in order to open the bidding in any suit, you need at least four cards in the suit. If your hand has only one suit with five cards or more, and your hand isn't balanced, then you have a one-suited hand. Take a look at the hands in Figure 9-2 to see some great-looking one-suited hands.

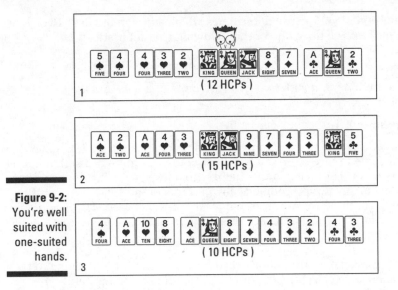

Figure 9-2: You're well suited with one-suited hands.

When you have a one-suited hand and 12 to 20 HCPs, you open with a one level bid in your longest suit. For example, in Figure 9-2, each hand is strong enough to open 1♦. (Notice that in the third hand, you can open the bidding with as few as 10 HCPs because you have a seven-card suit.) If you had a one-suited hand with clubs as the longest suit, then you would open with 1♣.

If you have a one-suited hand and between 12 and 20 points, you usually open at the one level and always bid your longest suit.

Opening with a two-suited hand

Hands with one five-card suit and one four-card suit (or two five-card suits) are the most common two-suited distributions (5-4 or 5-5 shape). However, hands with one six-card suit and one four- or five-card suit (6-4 or 6-5 shape) are also considered two-suited hands. Figure 9-3 shows you some real, live two-suited hands.

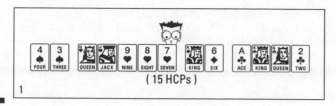

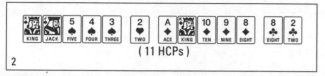

Figure 9-3: Two suits are better than one.

When you have a two-suited hand, you want to let your partner know that you have two long suits during the bidding. You open with the longer of the two suits, intending to tell your partner about the other long suit on your *rebid* (you can hear more about rebidding in Chapter 11).

If you have two suits with five cards apiece, you bid the higher-ranking suit first (the rank of the suits is spades, hearts, diamonds, clubs). See "Ranking a bid (ranking the suits)" in Chapter 8 for more information on ranking the suits.

Listen closely to the number one rule of bidding: You can never be too far off-base if you bid your longest suit first. Edgar Kaplan, one of the all-time bridge greats, says: "The answer to most bidding problems is to bid your longest suit." If you remember that you need 12 or more HCPs to open the bidding and you bid your longest suit first, you will be a survivor.

In the first hand in Figure 9-3 you open the bidding with 1♥ because your hearts are longer than your clubs. Yes, I can see that the clubs are stronger (clubs has more honor cards) than the hearts. Never mind — bid the longer suit first. You just read an important message; length comes before strength in the dictionary and it should come first in the bidding too.

In the second hand in Figure 9-3, you have two five-card suits. Which one should you bid first? You didn't think you were going to get out of this chapter without any rules, did you? Perish the thought. With two five-card suits, bid the higher-ranking suit first. In this case, you would open 1♠ with the intention of showing your diamonds at your next turn.

Opening with a three-suited hand

Talk about small families — this category of hands has 1¹/₂ members. The most common shape for a three-suited hand is one with three four-card suits in it. Less common is the hand with a five-card suit and two four-card suits, and absolutely zilch (a *void*) in the fourth suit.

If your hand contains one of these distributions, you have what's called a *three-suited hand*. Lucky you! These hands don't come along every day; in fact, they come along very rarely. But when they do, you'll be prepared.

The cards in Figure 9-4 show you some classic examples of three-suited hands.

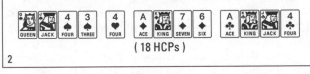
(12 HCPs)

1

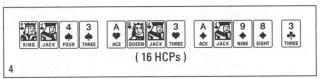
(18 HCPs)

2

Figure 9-4:
A full
house:
Three-
suited
hands
fill the
place up.

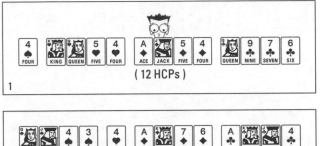
(14 HCPs)

3

(16 HCPs)

4

Three-suited hands present a unique challenge. Bridge should offer a special opening bid that tells your partner, "You won't believe this, but I have three four-card suits!" Unfortunately, no such bid exists. However, you can follow a very simple rule when opening with a three-suited hand.

When you have three four-card suits, open 1♦. However, if your *singleton* (the suit with one card) is a diamond, open 1♣. This doesn't mean that every time you open 1♦ your partner expects you to have three four-card suits. But he will be at least alive to that possibility.

TIP

Don't expect your partner to know with certainty that you have a three-suited hand after your opening bid unless your partner can read Tarot cards.

Opening the bidding with balanced hands

Balanced hands include hands with the following distributions in any suits:

- ✔ **4-4-3-2:** Two suits with four cards each, one suit with three cards, and one suit with two cards
- ✔ **4-3-3-3:** One suit with four cards and three suits with three cards
- ✔ **5-3-3-2:** One suit with five cards, two suits with three cards, and one suit with two cards

In this section, I discuss the opening bid with balanced hands that have 15 to 17 HCPs. I then focus on opening balanced hands with fewer HCPs (12 to 14 HCPs) or more HCPs (18 to 19 HCPs).

Opening balanced hands with 15 to 17 HCPs (1NT)

With 15 to 17 HCPs and no really long suit, life is so easy you would not believe it. Open 1NT. You then have almost all of your hand off your chest with one bid! You could open 1NT with any of the hands in Figure 9-5.

Each of the hands in Figure 9-5 is balanced, and each falls within the designated range of 15 to 17 HCPs. Open any balanced hand pattern with between 15 and 17 HCPs with 1NT.

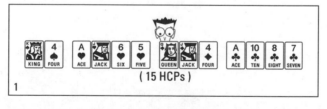

(15 HCPs)

1

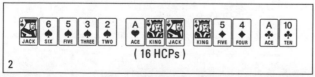

(16 HCPs)

2

Figure 9-5: 1NT pretty much says it all.

(17 HCPs)

3

In the interest of simplicity, for now, open 1NT even with a five-card major suit and 15 to 17 HCPs and a balanced hand. When you learn to hedge, you can pick and choose between opening INT or opening with your five-card major suit.

Opening with a 5-3-3-2 hand pattern outside the 1NT range

With a 5-3-3-2 pattern outside the range of a 1NT opening bid (15 to 17 HCPs), bid your five-card suit first. See, I am breaking you in gently.

Opening with a 4-4-3-2 hand pattern outside the 1NT range

The 4-4-3-2 hand pattern (any 4-4-3-2 distribution) is the most common of all hand patterns. You pick up this hand pattern in about one hand in five. Your main concern when you pick up a 4-4-3-2 hand pattern is bidding the right four-card suit first, assuming you are strong enough to open (that you have at least 12 HCPs).

If the hand contains a four-card major and a four-card minor, bid the minor suit first. So with clubs and hearts, or clubs and spades, bid the clubs first. With diamonds and hearts, or diamonds and spades, bid the diamonds first.

Figure 9-6 shows you two 4-4-3-2 hand patterns with both a minor and a major suit.

In both of the hands shown in Figure 9-6, you should bid the minor suit first. In the first example, you would open with 1♦, and in the second example, you would open with 1♣. Now you're on the right track.

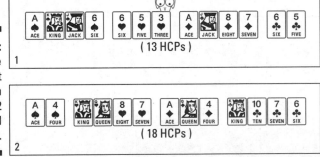

Figure 9-6: Bidding the minor suit first with 4-4-3-2 hand patterns.

When you have two four-card majors in a 4-4-3-2 hand pattern, open the bidding in your three-card minor. Take the hands in Figure 9-7 as an example.

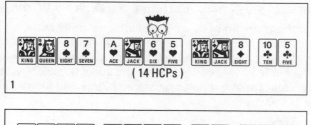

Figure 9-7:
What?
Opening
with a
three-card
minor when
you have
two four-
card
majors?

In these two 4-4-3-2 hand patterns, you would open with 1♦ and 1♣. Why? You normally open the bidding in your longest suit. Why would you bid a three-card suit when you have two four-card suits? When you open with a major suit, you guarantee at least five cards in the suit. So when you have a hand with four cards in each major suit, you don't have enough cards to bid either suit. Opening the three-card minor is considered the lesser evil.

Playing a five-card major system means making adjustments when you have an opening bid plus one or two four-card majors. The compromise solution holding four hearts and four spades is to open the bidding with your *three-card minor*. You tell a small lie, but you hope your deception is temporary, and that your partner responds in a major suit, allowing you to come out of the woodwork and show support for his suit. (See Chapter 10 for more information on responding.) Think of opening a three-card minor as the eggs you have to break to make an omelet.

Opening the bidding with a three-card minor is rare and is driven by the requirement that a major-suit opening shows five cards. A three-card minor opening is called *the short club* — or even rarer, *the short diamond.* People always ask if you play "a short club." Your answer should be: "Yes, but only when I have to."

When you have two four-card minors with a 4-4-3-2 hand pattern, open 1♦.

I have to level with you. Not even experts can agree on which suit to open with two four-card minors in a 4-4-3-2 hand pattern. Some experts insist on opening with 1♣, others say that you should go with 1♦. However, most bridge masters hedge (or use their own judgment), using their own brand of magic to determine which suit to open. When you first start out with bridge, make things easy on yourself and open with 1♦.

Opening with a 4-3-3-3 hand pattern outside the 1NT range

4-3-3-3 hand patterns are so blah: no long suits, no short suits, no nothing, which is why these hand patterns are called *flat hands* — kind of like a flat tire. When you look at these hands, don't think of them as one-suited hands (a one-suiter has at least five-cards in the long suit); these are closer to "no-suited" hands. Treat these hands as balanced hands and follow the guidelines outlined in this section.

Figure 9-8 shows you a few flat hands.

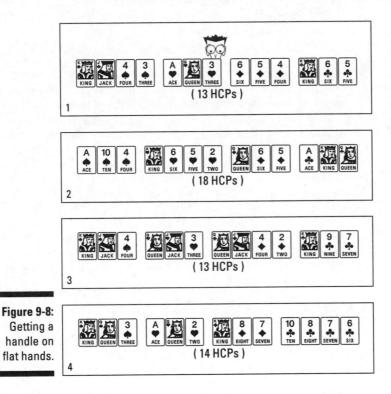

Figure 9-8: Getting a handle on flat hands.

In each case in Figure 9-8, you have enough HCPs to open the bidding. You have no long suit, but you do have too little (or too much) to open 1NT, which shows 15 to 17 HCPs. What do you do?

Because you can't bid a major (which would show five cards in the suit) with a 4-3-3-3 distribution and a four-card major, open 1♣; otherwise open the bidding in your four-card minor. With the first and second hands in Figure 9-8, open 1♣; with the third hand, open 1♦; with the fourth hand open 1♣.

Open 1♣ with any 4-3-3-3 outside the range of 15 to 17 HCPs unless the hand has four diamonds, in which case open 1♦.

Opening with balanced hands with 20 to 21 and 25 to 26 HCPs

If you have a (balanced) hand pattern of 4-4-3-2, 5-3-3-2, or 4-3-3-3 shape and 20 to 21 HCPs or 25 to 26 HCPs, you can open with the following sweet-sounding bids:

- ✔ **A balanced hand pattern and 20 to 21 HCPs:** Open 2NT
- ✔ **A balanced hand pattern and 25 to 26 HCPs:** Open 3NT

Figure 9-9 shows you three hands primed for 2NT and 3NT opening bids.

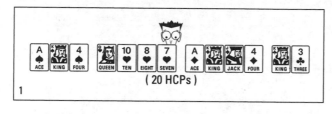

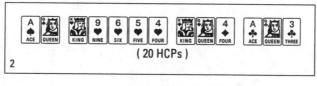

Figure 9-9: You have a bunch of notrump on your hands: bidding 2NT and 3NT.

In the first and second hands in Figure 9-9, open 2NT; in the third hand, open 3NT.

But what about hands in the 22 to 24 HCP range? Are they orphans? No, you can read about hands in the 22 to 24 range in "Opening 2♣ with a balanced hand" in this chapter. I know, you can hardly wait.

Opening with 20 or More HCPs in Your Hand

Sometimes you pick up a hand so wonderful that you think you must be dreaming; you can't believe that you have 20 HCPs or more in your hand. Your heart starts pounding a little faster and you mustn't do or say anything to let on what you have — it isn't ethical.

When you get a great hand like this, you almost always open with 2♣, the strongest opening bid in bridge. You can read about the exception to this rule in "Opening with balanced hands with 20 to 21 and 25 to 26 HCPs" in this chapter.

The 2♣ bid basically tells your partner that you can make game in your own hand. You may even have a slam — you may be able to take 12 or 13 tricks! (See Chapter 16 for the details on making game and slams.)

The 2♣ opening is completely artificial, which is to say the bid has nothing to do with the clubs in your hand; you may or may not have clubs. You use your second bid to tell your partner the reason for your strong opening bid: You have a very long suit.

Opening 2♣ with an unbalanced hand

You open most unbalanced hands with 20 or more HCPs with 2♣. (Unbalanced hands include all hands that don't fit into the balanced hand shapes as discussed in "Opening the bidding with balanced hands" in this chapter.) Very strong unbalanced hands could look like the examples shown in Figure 9-10.

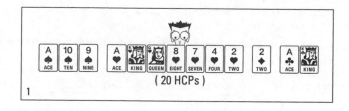

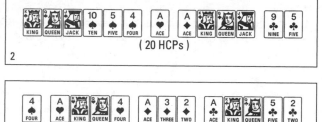

Figure 9-10: You can't get much more unbalanced than this and still be legal.

You could open each of the hands in Figure 9-10 with 2♣.

If you have a six- or seven-card suit with 20 or more HCPs, you have a 2♣ opening bid. If you have an unbalanced hand with a five-card suit with 21 or more HCPs, you also have a 2♣ opening bid. (If you have a five-card suit and a balanced hand, you open 2NT with 20 to 21 HCPs.)

Even a sleepy partner wakes up when the sound of a 2♣ opening bid comes from across the table. A 2♣ opening bid means that big happenings are in the air. All of the hands in Figure 9-10 are very powerful. These hands can do great things, no matter what garbage may be in their partner's hand.

For example, the first hand in Figure 9-10 shows a 20-point hand that can take 10 tricks: seven hearts, two clubs, and one spade. The second hand is another 20-point hand that can take 10 tricks: five spades, four diamonds, and one heart. In the third hand, you can see a 22-point hand that has a strong potential for 10 tricks.

If you open with 2♣, you have aces and kings coming out the kazoo. You want to make a forceful opening bid that tells your partner, "Partner, if you value your life, do not pass until we reach at least a game contract. I have enough tricks in my own hand to make game."

Opening 2♣ is easy on the central nervous system because you know that your partner can't pass until game is reached. You can relax and just bid your suits at the low levels until you find a fit.

I know that this chapter is about opening bids, but I want you to look a little further into the bidding process in order to see how this 2♣ bid really works.

The 2♣ opening bid is completely *artificial* — you may or may not have clubs. You just use the 2♣ opening bid to tell your partner that you have a really good hand.

You have to show your partner your "real" suit on your next bid. Unless your partner has a five- or six-card suit of her own with 7 or more HCPs, your partner's response is going to be 2♦, which is an artificial "waiting" response (you find out more about responses in Chapter 10). Your partner responds with this artificial bid because she is waiting to hear your real suit.

Nine times out of ten, your partner's response to your 2♣ opening will be 2♦. After those first two bids of 2♣ and 2♦, everything is on the up-and-up. You and your partner will then start bidding suits you really have. When it's your turn to bid again, you bid your longest suit.

For example, consider the following bidding sequence:

You	Your Partner
2♣	2♦
2♥	

In this sequence, your bids each communicate a specific message. Your 2♣ bid tells your partner, "Partner, I'm loaded, don't you dare pass!" Your partner's 2♦ bid says, "I wouldn't dream of it, tell me more." Then your 2♥ bid chimes in with, "Hearts is my real suit, I was kidding about clubs."

Why not just open 2♥ and be done with it? Remember that bidding takes place through conventions, and the meaning of an opening 2♥ bid is that you have a weak hand (see "Opening with 6 to 10 HCPs" in this chapter for more information on opening the bidding with a weak hand). You open with 2♣ because that's the convention that shows you have some real firepower in your hand. You also open 2♣ so that you can smoothly arrive at a game or a slam contract.

Opening 2♣ with a balanced hand

An opening bid of 2NT shows 20 to 21 HCPs, and an opening bid of 3NT shows 25 to 26 HCPs. What do you do with in-between hands (22 to 24 HCPs) or an even stronger hand with 27 to 28 HCPs? Answer: Start with 2♣ and follow up by bidding notrump.

About half the time that you open 2♣, you have a balanced hand in the 22 to 24 HCPs range. Don't expect to get many hands in the 27 to 28 point range. It's not going to happen. If you play day and night, you may get a hand like this by the turn of the century.

When the 2♣ bidder has a balanced hand in the normal 22 to 24 HCP range, the opener rebids 2NT to show her partner how strong her hand is. When you have such a hand, the bidding sequence looks like this:

You	Your Partner
2♣	2♦
2NT	

You use these bidding conventions to describe very specific aspects of your hands. For example, the opening 2♣ bid tells your partner, "I have a great hand." Upon hearing your 2♣ bid, your partner finally responds with 2♦, a "waiting" response which doesn't say anything about her hand (she just wants to get the bidding back to you to hear more about your hand). When it's your turn to bid again, you rebid 2NT, which tells your partner "My great hand is balanced and I have between 22 and 24 HCPs."

After your partner hears your 2NT bid, your partner now becomes the *captain* (the one who makes the final decision as to how high to bid), because you have *limited* your hand. *Limiting one's hand* means showing your partner both your point count and your distribution.

If your partner opens 2♣ and rebids 2NT you can pass that. It is the only rebid after a 2♣ opening that can be passed. However, do bear in mind that it is not how weak a hand you have, it's what you and your partner have together. Even a pitiful hand with only 3 HCPs is enough to bid game after your partner opens 2♣ and rebids 2NT.

If you have a hand like the one shown in Figure 9-11, you can open 2♣ and rebid 3NT to show your strength.

In Figure 9-11, the bidding would go like this:

You	Your Partner
2♣	2♦
3NT	

Figure 9-11:
Showing a
balanced
hand with
27 to 28
HCPs.

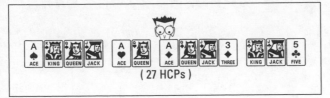

(27 HCPs)

These bids in combination show that you have a balanced hand with 27 or 28 HCPs. After you bid 3NT, your partner can pass or do whatever he pleases.

Because it takes about 33 HCPs to make a slam (slams involve bidding and making at least 12 of the 13 tricks), your partner looks for higher things with as little as 6 HCPs, facing your 27 points. It's what you have together that counts. Togetherness.

Opening with 6 to 10 HCPs

How does this sound? The less you have, the more you bid. Crazy, right? Not so crazy. If you don't have enough HCPs to open the bidding at the one level (you need at least 12 points to bid 1♣ or the like), you may still have enough in your hand to open the bidding. Alice in Wonderland in your own backyard.

With only 6 to 10 HCPs in your hand and a strong six- or seven-card suit, you should consider making a *weak* opening bid, which is also called a *preemptive opening bid*. A preemptive bid bypasses the one level and goes directly to the two, three, or four levels. When you make such a bid, you are said to *preempt* your opponents.

Preemptive opening bids are based primarily on tricks, not on HCPs. That is to say, your bid is based on a long suit (of at least six cards), which will be worth something if that suit is the trump suit, but otherwise may be worthless. The purpose of these preemptive bids is to obstruct the opposition from arriving at their proper contract by forcing them to enter the bidding for the first time at a very high level.

Understanding your goal

When you have a very weak hand (10 HCPs or less), it figures that your opponents have the majority of the strength in the hand. This strength means that your opponents can usually make some contract, perhaps a game contract, or perhaps even a slam contract (see Chapter 15 for more information on slam contracts). Of course, a preempt makes life tough for your partner as well; a preempt involves a risk for everyone at the table. Nevertheless, when looking at a long suit without many HCPs, you want to make that suit the trump suit, if possible.

Think of a preemptive opening bid (an opening bid that starts at the two, three, or four levels) as a sacrifice. When you make a preemptive opening bid, you are prepared to lose several hundred penalty points if you do not make your bid (see Chapter 16 for more on penalty points). But losing those several hundred penalty points is peanuts compared with what you can lose if the opponents bid and make game or a slam.

Face it, when you hold a weak hand, you are probably going to lose points. The best way to hold down your losses is to strike the first blow using a preemptive opening bid.

Your preemptive bid can also prevent your opponents from bidding a game or a slam. In order to arrive at a reasonable contract (that is, to know how many tricks to bid for), a partnership has to exchange information. Ideally, this exchange takes place at the one and two levels. However, if you start the bidding at the two, three, or four levels, you have stolen these levels from the opponents. Without these levels to exchange information, you steal from your opponents the opportunity to exchange information — your preemptive bid reduces your opponents to guesswork. Even the best players in the world have difficulty arriving at a reasonable contract when they have to guess.

Opponents hate preempts — and if they hate preempts, you know it must be right to make them. Personally, it seems that every time I have a strong hand, one opponent or another gums up the works for me by throwing in one of these darned preempts. However, being a nice fellow, I try to return the favor whenever I can, and so should you. Your partner will thank you for your efforts.

Counting your tricks

Tricks form the foundation of preemptive bidding. If you know approximately how many tricks you have, and you know about how many tricks your partner has, you get a good idea of how many tricks your side can take.

When making a preempt, try to make as accurate a preempt as possible in order to combine maximum safety with maximum messing-up-the-opponents. You want to show your partner approximately how many tricks you can take; your partner already knows you have a miserable hand when you preempt.

Suppose that you hold the hand shown in Figure 9-12.

Figure 9-12:
Looking at a
weak hand
with only
9 HCPs.

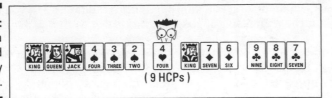

(9 HCPs)

The hand in Figure 9-12 is nothing to write home about. True, the hand has a six-card suit, but it has only 9 HCPs. With a six-card suit, you need at least 11 HCPs to open the bidding with a one level bid. If HCPs were the only criterion for opening, you would have to pass.

But take a closer look at that spade suit. Pretend that spades are trump and your partner has a couple of little spades — average expectancy when you have a six-card suit. How many spade tricks do you think you can take with this hand shown in Figure 9-13?

Figure 9-13:
Counting
tricks
in your
long suit.

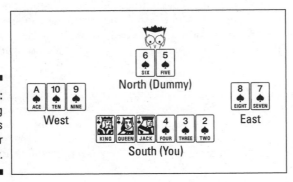

North (Dummy)

West   East

South (You)

When you have eight cards total, your opponents' five cards are usually divided 3-2. Suppose that you lead the ♠K and West takes the trick with the ♠A. Later, you play the ♠Q and ♠J. Now your opponents have no more spades. Your three remaining little spades are all tricks. You have taken five tricks from this spade suit. Any hand worth five tricks may be grounds for a preemptive bid.

Counting tricks in long suits is relatively easy. Assume that you have a six-card suit and you want to guesstimate the number of tricks that you can take from the suit (you can never be 100 percent sure because you can't see your partner's cards). Look at the honor cards at the head of your suit and estimate how many tricks you think you can take with those honors. Then add an automatic *three* to that number. The *three* represents the fourth, fifth, and sixth cards in the suit. After you play a long suit three times, the fourth, fifth, and sixth cards figure to be tricks because nobody else at the table has any more cards in that suit.

Suppose that you have a suit like this: AKQxxx (*x* means any small card). The AKQ are three sure tricks — add the three length-tricks to equal six tricks. Or try this suit, for example: QJ10xxx. The QJ10 is worth one trick so 1 + 3 = 4 — you can estimate four tricks. Estimating tricks is easiest when you have three equal honors at the head of your suit such as AKQ = 3, KQJ = 2, or QJ10 = 1.

Just to give you an idea of how many tricks you can expect to take with some other six-card suits, here is a little guide (which you don't need to memorize):

✔ AKJxxx or AQJxxx	5 to 6 tricks
✔ AKxxxx, AQ10xxx, AJ10xxx, KQ10xxxx	Close to 5 tricks
✔ AQxxxx, AJ9xxx, KQxxxx, KJ10xxx	4 to 5 tricks
✔ A109xxx, K109xxx, Q109xxx, KJxxxx, or QJ10xxx	4 tricks

Any 109 (the ten and the nine) combination in the middle of a suit enhances the suit. Suits headed by the A109, K109, Q109, or even the J109 can take more tricks than you would expect because of the 10 and the 9.

Knowing when to make a weak two bid

In the Standard American system that you are playing, an opening bid of 2♦, 2♥, or 2♠ is called a *weak two* bid. You use a weak two opening bid to tell your partner that your hand has the following characteristics:

✔ A six-card suit, headed by two of the top four honor cards, any three honors, or the A109, K109, Q109, or J109. In other words, a suit worth about four or five tricks.

✔ A hand with 6 to 10 HCPs (never more than 10 HCPs!)

✔ A hand with no five-card side suits, no voids, or no four card majors

An average opening weak two bid can take five or six tricks. If a hand can take more than six tricks, it is too strong for a weak two bid.

Notice that you don't see an opening bid of 2♣ on the weak two list. An opening bid of 2♣ is reserved for a truly powerful hand — hands in the 20 or more HCPs range (see "Opening with 20 or More HCPs in Your Hand" in this chapter for information on opening with strong hands). Don't open 2♣ with a weak hand unless you are in to catastrophes!

Suppose that you pick up the hand shown in Figure 9-14.

Figure 9-14: Your hand is ripe for a weak two bid.

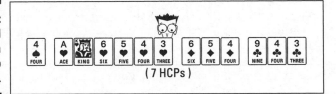

(7 HCPs)

You have fewer than 10 HCPs, a six-card suit, no void suit, and no five-card side suit — looking good. Count your tricks. At the head of the hearts (your longest suit), you have the ♥AK, which are worth two tricks. The fourth, fifth, and sixth hearts are all considered tricks (because of your length), so you have about five tricks. A perfect hand for a preemptive bid. Open 2♥.

You could also pick up a hand like the one shown in Figure 9-15.

Figure 9-15: Making a weak two bid with a weak hand.

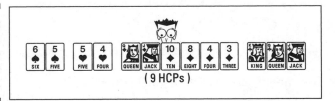

(9 HCPs)

In the hand shown in Figure 9-15, you have fewer than 10 HCPs, a six-card suit, no void, no side five-card suit, and no four-card major. Count your tricks — in diamonds, you have four tricks and in clubs you have two tricks. You have a six-trick hand, the maximum for making a weak two bid. Open 2♦.

Keeping within the parameters of the bid

If you have more than six tricks, your hand is too strong (trickwise) to open a weak two bid. If you have 11 or more HCPs, your hand is too strong (point-count-wise) to open a weak two bid. When making a weak two bid, you must stay within your trick and point count ranges. If you do, your partner can get an accurate picture of what you have; he can add his hand to what you have shown him, and start working out what is the best contract to play. When making a preempt, it's just as dangerous for you to be too strong as to be too weak.

A weak two bid should tell your partner that your hand is really of interest only in the suit you have just bid. If you have another five-card suit or four cards in a major, your preemptive bid may preempt your side out of uncovering your best fit!

Take a gander at the cards in Figure 9-16 to see some hands that may fool you into thinking you could open with a weak two bid.

Figure 9-16:
A side four-card major disqualifies your hand for a weak two bid.

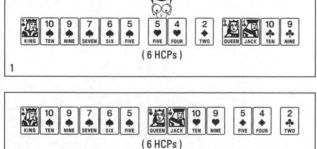

Both hands in Figure 9-16 may, at first, look ripe for a weak two bid, but only the first hand really qualifies for the bid. The second hand contains a side four-card major, and majors are so much more valuable than minors that you don't want to miss a fit there.

Don't open a weak two bid with a side four-card major. You may miss a 4-4 fit in that suit if your partner has length in that suit. Open 2♠ with the first hand in Figure 9-16; pass with the second.

Opening with a preemptive three bid

An opening three bid (3♠, 3♥, 3♦, or 3♣) is very similar to an opening weak two bid, except for the following three tiny differences:

- You have a seven-card suit.
- You have 6 to 9 HCPs.
- You can have a void (a suit in which you have no cards) in the hand.

If opening at the two level makes your opponents uncomfortable, imagine their aggravation level when you open at the three level. The higher you open, the more space you take away from them, and thus the more difficult you make it for them to communicate efficiently. They may not be able to bid at all.

You can make opening three bids in all four suits. The club suit finally gets to join the party, unlike in the weak two bid. Also, you can open with a three bid so long as you have a seven-card suit, pretty much no matter what your shape in the side-suits.

Figure 9-17 shows a hand in which you could open with a preemptive three bid.

Figure 9-17:
Stifling the opponents with your opening three bid.

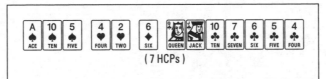

(7 HCPs)

In the hand shown in Figure 9-17, you have 7 HCPs; your club suit offers the chance to take five tricks (the ♣QJ10 are worth one trick, and you can count the four little clubs as tricks, as well). Throw in the ♠A, and you have a 6-trick hand; open 3♣.

As long as you are not strong enough to open the bidding (you have fewer than 10 HCPs) and you have a strong *seven-bagger* (a seven-card suit), preempt! Stick it to them every chance you get.

When you have a seven-card suit, count four tricks for the fourth, fifth, sixth, and seventh cards in the suit, no matter how small the cards are. The length of the suit turns those cards into tricks.

Opening with a preemptive four bid

An opening four bid is like an opening three bid, only the four bid features an eight-card suit (or a 7-4 hand pattern). If an opening weak two irritates your opponents, and an opening three bid drives them up the wall, an opening four bid sends a dagger straight into their hearts. Few partnerships can recover from one of these monster preempts because it's so difficult for your opponents to start a conversation when you start the bidding at such a dangerous level.

To open with a four bid (4♠, 4♥, 4♦, or 4♣), your hand must have the following:

- ✔ Between 6 and 10 HCPs (and no more than 10)
- ✔ 7 or 8 tricks (count an automatic five tricks for length)
- ✔ An eight-card suit or a seven-card suit with a four-card side suit

When you get a hand like this, make your opponents pay by opening with a four bid. The cards in Figure 9-18 give you a taste of the great feeling you get when you open a four bid.

Figure 9-18: Don't expect a birthday card: Your opponents won't like your opening four bid.

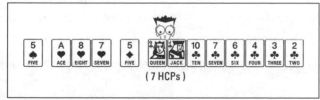

(7 HCPs)

The ♣QJ10 are worth one trick. Added to that, you get five length tricks — and don't forget to count the ♥A. You have a seven-trick hand — open 4♣ and watch the suffering begin.

Why will your opponents suffer? They either have to pass and possibly let you steal them blind, or one of them has to take a huge risk and come in at the four level before knowing what their partner has. Entering the bidding at the four level is like putting your head on the chopping block if your partner turns up with zilch. Your opponents will score a huge number of penalty points.

Opening with a four bid is such a delicious feeling, I want to show you the cards in Figure 9-19 as another tasty treat.

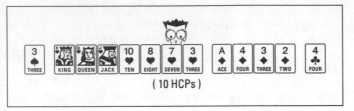

Figure 9-19:
Seven and
four, close
the door —
on your
opponents!

(10 HCPs)

You have a 7-4 hand pattern, acceptable for an opening four bid. You also have 10 HCPs, also acceptable. Count your tricks. In hearts, you have six tricks, missing only the ♥A. In diamonds, you have a trick and a half (that fourth card in the four-card side suit counts as half a trick). You have a seven-and-a-half-trick hand. Open 4♥.

If you make disciplined preempts (that is, your hand fulfills the criteria for making the bids you make), you will be a feared opponent. If you make undisciplined preempts (yielding to temptation), you will be a feared partner! Although you can have fun opening with a bombshell like a 4♥ bid in the hope of messing up the opponents, if you have the wrong sort of hand for the bid, you run the risk of losing your partner's trust — the one thing you can't afford to lose. On a bad day, your partner may also have a really weak hand, and you may lose big time when you preempt.

Responding to a weak two opening bid

Someone once said that bridge is a game of fits and misfits. How true.

When you are thinking about responding to a weak two bid, and you have a fit for your partner's suit (at least two cards), it is much easier to respond if you think of your partner's hand in terms of the number of tricks your partner has promised with his bid. In the case of a weak two bid, your partner has promised between 5 and 6 tricks. You need to determine how many tricks you have, add your tricks to your partner's tricks, and then decide if it's worthwhile to bid on.

First things first; you have to count your tricks:

✔ The ace, of course, counts as one trick.

✔ The ace and king of the same suit counts as two tricks.

✔ The king and queen or the king and jack of the same suit counts as one trick.

- The king or queen in your partner's suit counts as one trick.

- If you have three (or more) cards in your partner's suit, count one trick for a side-suit doubleton, and count two tricks for a side-suit singleton.

- If you have four cards in your partner's suit, give yourself a bonus trick no matter what else you have.

After you determine how many tricks you have, add them to the number of tricks your partner has and respond according to the following scale:

- **With 3 tricks or less:** Pass — you have no chance for game.

- **With 4 tricks:** Bid 2NT, an invitational bid that asks partner to bid game with a maximum (6 tricks) or to return to the original suit with a minimum (5 tricks).

- **With 5 or more tricks:** Bid game in your partner's suit.

When you have a singleton or void in your partner's suit, which are danger signs, you revert to counting HCPs. To even think about bidding, you need at least 15 HCPs plus a strong six-card suit of your own. With less, use the best bid in bridge — pass!

The hands in Figure 9-20 give you four chances to respond to a weak 2♥ opening bid by your partner.

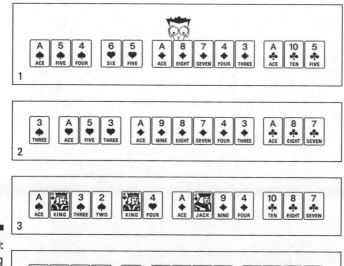

Figure 9-20:
Responding
to a weak
two bid.

For all of the hands in Figure 9-20, the bidding has gone like this:

North (Your Partner)	East	South (You)	West
2♥	Pass	?	

With the first hand, pass; three tricks is not enough to try for game facing a weak two bid.

With the second hand, leap all the way to 4♥; you have five tricks for your partner, including two for the singleton spade.

With the third hand, invite your partner to game by bidding 2NT; the rest is up to your partner. With six tricks, or close to it, your partner jumps to 4♥. With five tricks or a little less, your partner returns to 3♥.

With the fourth hand, get out while the getting is good! Pass! There is no fit, and 14 HCPs facing a likely 7 to 8 HCPs spells trouble if you get any higher.

The higher the level of your partner's preemptive bid, the more your partner promises not to mention his long, strong suit. Having support for your partner's suit is no longer your concern — side-suit tricks are. If your partner opens 3♥, showing 6 or 7 tricks, raise your partner to game with 3 or more tricks and hope for the best. After all, you don't have to play the hand — your partner does.

Chapter 10

Responding to an Opening Bid

In This Chapter

▶ Responding with a suit at the one level

▶ Responding at the two level

▶ Responding in notrump

▶ Raising your partner

Your partner has opened the bidding; congratulations! Your side has made the first step toward determining the best contract. Now it's your turn up to bat. Get ready to tell your partner, the opener, some details about the cards you have in your hand.

Your First Response

After your partner opens the bidding, the opponents get a chance to bid. Then you, the *responder*, begin to describe your hand with your response to the opening bid.

To make any response to an opening bid, you need at least 6 HCPs in your hand. If you have fewer than 6 HCPs, just pass. If you have 6 or more HCPs, your first obligation is to show your partner your longest suit. Not necessarily your strongest suit — your longest suit. Sometimes, however, you may wish to respond in notrump or support your partner's suit. I discuss all three of these response options in this chapter.

If you have 6 or more HCPs, you have to make some kind of response. You may have to get creative with your response, but with 6 HCPs, you owe it to your partner to show your strength.

Responding to a 1♣ Opening Bid

Your partner opens the bidding with a 1♣ bid — a very fine bid indeed. Read on to find out what you should do when it's your turn to bid after your partner has the guts and determination to open 1♣.

What you know about your partner's hand

When your partner opens the bidding with 1♣ (or any suit, for that matter), her opening bid tells you the following about her hand:

- Your partner usually has between 11 and 20 HCPs. (10 and 11 HCPs are an exception.)
- Your partner is, with rare exception, bidding her longest suit.

Your partner must have these requirements to open the bidding at 1♣. Unless your partner marches to the beat of a different drum, or she hasn't read this book, you can bet that the preceeding points accurately describe your partner's hand.

After the opening bid, you have some picture of what your partner's hand looks like, but the picture isn't very sharp. The preceeding points cover a wide range of possible hands. Typically, you can't find out too much about your partner's hand from an opening bid. As the responder, you need to start describing your own hand and wait for your partner to further describe her strength and distribution on subsequent bids.

With 6 or more HCPs and at least four cards in your suit

In order to respond to an opening bid of 1♣, you should have:

- 6 HCPs or more
- Four cards or more in the suit that you wish to bid

If you have fewer than 6 HCPs, you should pass. If you have 6 or more HCPs, your plan should be to show your partner your longest suit at the one level. The suit you bid must have at least four cards in it, hopefully five or six.

Suppose that you are gazing at the cards shown in Figure 10-1.

Figure 10-1:
Responding to an opening bid of 1♣.

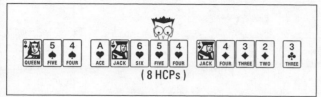

(8 HCPs)

In Figure 10-1, you would respond with 1♥. You have 6 or more HCPs and hearts is your longest suit.

When you respond to a one level bid with another one level bid, you are said to be bidding *one over one*. A one over one response shows that you have 6 or more HCPs, and length in the suit you bid. Because this bid doesn't show a maximum number of HCPs, it's called an *unlimited response*.

When you respond in any new suit, such as a 1♥ response to a 1♣ opening bid, your partner must bid again. Your partner can't pass; she must honor any unlimited response with another bid. You may turn out to hold a mountain (a great hand) and be on your way to the stratosphere. In that case, you wouldn't be too happy if your partner passes and grinds things to a halt at the one level. Sure, at the one level, you would make your contract, but you would also miss out on much tastier rewards, such as a game or a slam contract.

With suits of equal length

Responding at the one level in your longest suit first may become second nature. However, sometimes you may have two or even three suits of equal length, as the hands in Figure 10-2 show.

In the first hand in Figure 10-2, you have two five-card suits; in the second hand, you have two four-card suits; in the third hand, you have three four-card suits.

With two five-card suits, always bid the higher ranking suit first. A simple rule, no exceptions.

With two or three four-card suits, bid the suit closest in rank to your partner's suit, the most economical call. This is known as bidding your suits *up the line*. In other words, with four spades and four hearts, bid 1♥ in response to a 1♣ opening bid.

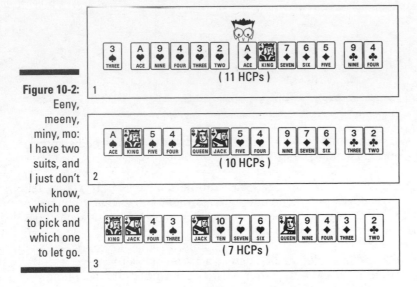

Figure 10-2:
Eeny,
meeny,
miny, mo:
I have two
suits, and
I just don't
know,
which one
to pick and
which one
to let go.

In the first hand in Figure 10-2, you would respond 1♥; in the second hand, you would also respond 1♥; and in the third hand, you would respond 1♦. That wasn't so bad, was it?

With 6 to 18 HCPs and a balanced hand

When you have a balanced hand with no four or five-card major suits (spades or hearts), respond in notrump according to the following scale:

- ✔ Respond 1NT if you have 6 to 10 HCPs
- ✔ Respond 2NT if you have 13 to 15 HCPs
- ✔ Respond 3NT if you have 16 to 18 HCPs

If you have four or five cards in a major suit, you should respond in that suit with the intention of bidding notrump later.

You can use this scale to respond to opening bids of 1♦, 1♥ ,and 1♠, as well as the 1♣ opening.

If you have precisely 11 or 12 HCPs with a balanced hand (as you do in Figure 10-3), your hand is too strong to respond 1NT and not strong enough to respond 2NT. What to do? You make a one level bid in your longest suit and then bid 2NT the next chance you get.

Figure 10-3:
Making the
best of an
awkward
situation.

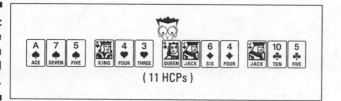

(11 HCPs)

In Figure 10-3, respond 1♦ and then bid 2NT the next time you get a chance to bid (see Chapter 12 for more information on bidding again when you are the responder).

If you have more than 18 HCPs, you can virtually guarantee a slam, which you can read more about in Chapter 15.

Take a look at the hands in Figure 10-4 to get some practice responding to a 1♣ opening bid if you pick up a balanced hand pattern.

In the first hand shown in Figure 10-4, respond 1♠; you should bid a major suit first, if you have one. In the second hand, you would respond 1NT because you have five cards in a minor suit and you have between 6 and 10 HCPs. In the third hand, you would respond 2NT; your four-card suit is a minor, and you have between 13 and 15 HCPs. In the fourth hand, you should respond with 1♦. You are too strong to respond 1NT and not strong enough to respond 2NT. You must bide your time by responding at the one level in your longest suit.

With 6 to 12 HCPs and real support for partner (adding support points)

Every so often, you have four or more clubs — the suit your partner bid. If your partner opens 1♣ and you don't have four or five cards in a major suit, you should normally show your club support at once.

When you have support for the suit your partner bids, you can add extra points, called *support points* (SPs), to your hand for your short suits. Short suits offer your partner a chance to trump his losing cards in your hand (see Chapter 5 for the details on trumping losers). How does this upgrade work? It all depends on how short you are in the side suits (the non-trump suits) and how many trump cards you have.

When supporting your partner's suit with four or more cards, use the 1-3-5 support point scale and add the following SPs to your HCPs:

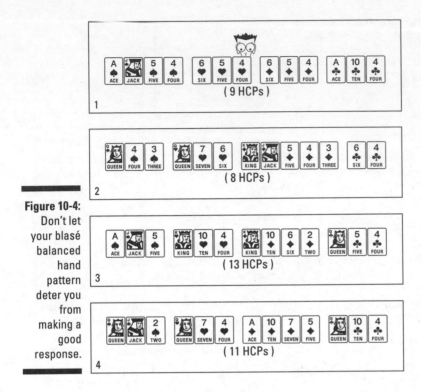

Figure 10-4:
Don't let your blasé balanced hand pattern deter you from making a good response.

> 〰 Add 1 point for each doubleton (a two-card holding in a side suit).
>
> 〰 Add 3 points for each singleton (a one-card holding in a side suit).
>
> 〰 Add 5 points for each void (a side suit in which you have zero, nada, zilch, zip cards).

After you add these SPs, you should think in terms of your "new" total. But remember, you can only add SPs to your HCPs when you are supporting a suit your partner has bid. Your shortness in side suits only becomes valuable when you have trump support; your shortness allows your partner to trump her losers in that suit with your trump cards (see Chapter 7).

After you count up your support points and add them to your HCPs, respond to a 1♣ opening bid according to the following scale:

> 〰 **6 to 9 combined SPs and HCPs:** Raise your partner from 1♣ to 2♣.
>
> 〰 **10 to 12 combined SPs and HCPs:** Raise your partner from 1♣ to 3♣.

Take a peek at the cards in Figure 10-5 to see how adding SPs figures into responding to a 1♣ opening bid.

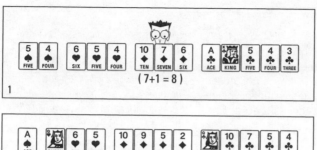

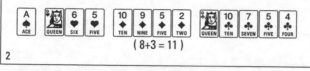

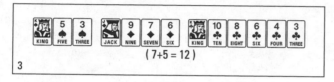

Figure 10-5:
Responding
with SPs.

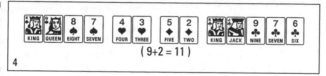

In the first hand in Figure 10-5, you pick up one point for having a doubleton, and your proper response is 2♣. In the second hand, you can add three support points for the singleton, which means that you should respond 3♣. In the third hand, you pick up five support points for the void you have in diamonds, and your response should be 3♣. In the fourth hand, you have four cards in a major suit (spades), so you should show your partner your major suit first (the major suits always get the red carpet treatment); respond 1♠ and then bid clubs the next time round.

Some bridge players fall in love with singletons and voids. They love them so much that they count extra points for them right off the bat. Do every-thing you can to avoid becoming one of these players. They are a tragedy waiting to happen, because they fail to appreciate that short suits are only good *when you have support for your partner's suit*.

Figure 10-6 illustrates the dangers of adding SPS to your HCPs prematurely.

In Figure 10-6, you have 8 HCPs plus four cards in each of three suits — potential excellent support for your partner if he bids any of those suits. Feel free to add SPs if your partner opens with spades, hearts, or diamonds.

No right answer

You can't always find one "right" bid for a hand. If only it were so. Many hands present close-call decisions. For many hands, you become like the baseball umpire who decides whether each pitch is a ball or a strike. Some calls are obvious, while others raise the dander of the pitcher or the batter.

One of the most popular bridge magazines in the world, Bridge World, features a great monthly column called the "Master Solver's Club." In this column, 25 top bridge experts answer questions about the bidding for eight sample hands. You'd think that most of the experts would come up with the same bid for the same hand, but it never happens. Each sample hand attracts three, four, and sometimes five different bids, plus lively (and funny) comments about the hand.

Sometimes the magazine tries to trick the experts by feeding them the same hands they gave them 20 or more years ago to see if they come up with the same bids. Most of the experts don't recognize the hands and come up with different bids and different comments, sometimes ridiculing bids they themselves suggested in the past for the same hand! (See Chapter 25 for more on bridge magazines from all around the world.)

Figure 10-6: Don't get smitten with your singletons, doubletons, and voids.

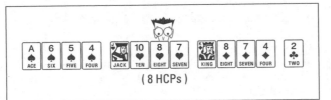

(8 HCPs)

But some partners (mine included) have the irritating habit of bidding your short suit. If this happens to you, keep cool and don't add any SPs to your hand. Later, if your partner mentions one of your four-card suits, then, and only then, can you count points for shortness.

Unless you are the seventh son of a seventh son, you can't tell whether or not your short suits will be worth anything until you hear the bidding. The bidding tells you whether your short suits will be valuable or worthless. Remember, support in your partner's suit makes your short suits more valuable; don't count for shortness until you find a fit.

Responding to a 1♦ Opening Bid

When your partner opens 1♦, you respond almost the same way you would respond if your partner opens 1♣ (as described in the preceding section). In fact, your response differs only in one case — when your long suit is clubs.

When clubs is your longest suit

Clubs is a lower-ranking suit than diamonds, so you can't respond 1♣ to show clubs as your long suit. Remember, during the bidding, each successive bid must be higher than the last bid. After your partner opens 1♦, you can't backtrack and respond 1♣.

If you want to respond with clubs, you have to bid 2♣. However, to make this response, which pushes up the level of the auction by a step, from one to two, you need to have 11 or more HCPs in your hand (or 10 HCPs if you have a six-card suit). A bid of 2♣ is an unlimited response (this bid doesn't show any upper limit to the HCPs in your hand), but it does show a respectable hand.

Naturally, problems arise when your long suit is clubs and you aren't strong enough to respond with 2♣. If you have less than 6 HCPs, you can always pass, but if you have more than 5 HCPs but less than 10 HCPs, then you have to come up with some response.

If you have at least four cards in a major suit, then you can respond with a one level bid in that suit. But if your only long suit is clubs, and you don't have enough strength to respond 2♣, and you don't have four cards in either major suit, respond 1NT.

The 1NT response to a 1♦ opening bid doesn't necessarily guarantee a balanced hand; only the 1NT response to a 1♣ opening bid promises a balanced hand (see "With 6 to 18 HCPs and a balanced hand," earlier in this chapter).

For example, the hand shown in Figure 10-7 is strong enough to respond (you have 6 HCPs), but it's not nearly strong enough to respond 2♣. Solution: Respond 1NT and hope that you can show your clubs later.

The cards in Figure 10-8 show several hands where clubs is your longest suit. Your partner has opened the bidding 1♦. What should you do?

Figure 10-7:
Responding
1NT to a 1♦
opening bid
when you
have a long
club suit.

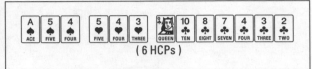

(6 HCPs)

In the first two hands in Figure 10-8, you meet the requirements to respond 2♣, although the first hand just barely makes the cut because of the six-card suit. On the third and fourth hands, you don't have enough HCPs to respond 2♣ (you need at least 11 HCPs). However, you need to make a bid because, in both cases, you have more than 6 HCPs. On the third hand, you can respond 1♠; although spades is not your longest suit, it is a major suit that you can bid. You would respond 1NT on the fourth hand because you don't have a four-card major suit to bid.

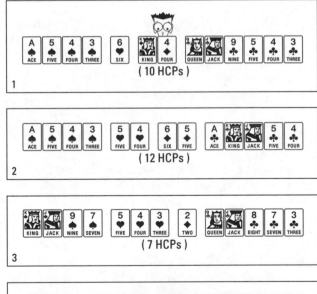

(10 HCPs)

1

(12 HCPs)

2

Figure 10-8:
Responding
to a 1♦
opening bid
when clubs
is your
longest suit.

3

(7 HCPs)

4

(9 HCPs)

When you want to make a game contract

Because you need at least 11 HCPs to make a 2♣ response to a 1♦ opening bid, much more often than not, you have opening bid strength when you respond at the two level (a *two over one* response).

Partners love to hear two over one responses, especially when you have what you're supposed to have for the bid — and we are solid citizens aren't we? When you respond two over one, your partner knows that you almost always have enough strength for an opening bid. Your partner's opening bid strength together with your opening bid strength is usually enough to arrive at a game contract.

Responding to a 1♥ Opening Bid

When your partner opens the bidding 1♣ or 1♦, she may have five, six, or even seven cards in the suit. She may also have a balanced hand with four (or in emergencies even three) cards in the suit. When your partner opens a major suit (1♥ or 1♠), just assume that your partner has at least five hearts or five spades.

Many times, you make the same response to a 1♥ opening bid as you would to a 1♠ opening bid. Turn to "Responding to a 1♠ Opening Bid" to see how responding to a 1♠ opening bid differs from responding to a 1♥ opening bid.

During the bidding, you and your partner would like to locate a suit in which you have eight or more cards between the two hands (an eight-card fit). You may not always have an eight-card fit, but if you do, things tend to work out well when you make that suit the trump suit.

If your partner opens 1♥ and you have three or more hearts, you have found your eight-card fit. It's blasphemous not to show your partner this fit at some point during the bidding.

Because locating an eight-card fit in a major suit is so important (you can score beaucoup points with such a fit), you should place your hand in one of the three following categories when you're formulating your response to a 1♥ opening bid:

- ✔ Hands with fewer than three hearts
- ✔ Hands with exactly three hearts
- ✔ Hands with four or more hearts

Things would be so much easier if you could just lean over and whisper the number of hearts and HCPs that you have, but the rules of the game forbid such direct communication. You have to use the special language of bidding — a bidding system — to tell your partner what you have.

With fewer than three hearts

Oh, great. Your partner has just opened with 1♥, and you have fewer than three hearts in your hand. What should you do?

When you have one or two hearts and at least 6 HCPs, you have to come up with some response. Your first instinct should be to look for your longest suit. If your longest suit is spades, you can respond with 1♠, because spades is a higher ranking suit than hearts. But what if your longest suit is clubs or diamonds?

If your longest suit is clubs or diamonds, you need 11 or more HCPs to respond 2♣ or 2♦. If you don't have the HCPs (if you have 6 to 10 HCPs), you then cough up a 1NT response, the catch-all response for all hands that can't respond to a one level opening bid with a two level response.

Each of the hands shown in Figure 10-9 shows a hand with fewer than three hearts.

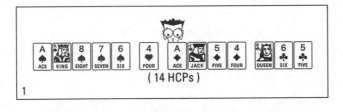

(14 HCPs)

1

Figure 10-9:
With fewer
than three
hearts,
you've got a
meeting of
the Lonely
Hearts Club.

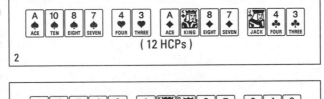

(12 HCPs)

2

(13 HCPs)

3

In the first hand in Figure 10-9, you would respond 1♠, your longest suit showing six or more HCPs. On the second hand, you would also respond 1♠; with two four-card suits, bid the suit that you can introduce more cheaply (see "With suits of equal length" in this chapter). On the third hand, you would respond 1♠; with two five-card suits, bid the higher-ranking suit first.

The cards in Figure 10-10 also feature some possible responding hands with fewer than three hearts.

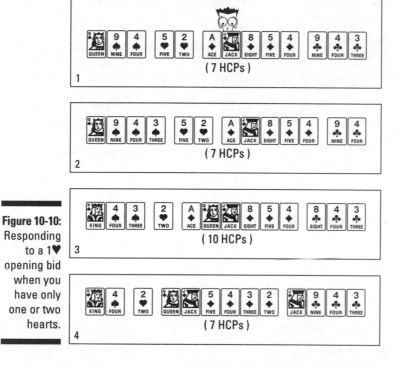

Figure 10-10: Responding to a 1♥ opening bid when you have only one or two hearts.

On the first hand in Figure 10-10, you would respond 1NT, showing 6 to 10 HCPs; you are not strong enough to bid 2♦, which shows 11 or more HCPs. On the second hand, you should respond 1♠; you aren't strong enough to respond with 2♦, but you are strong enough to respond 1♠, which shows 6 or more HCPs. On the third hand, you can respond 2♦ — although you only have 10 HCPs, you have a six-card suit. On the fourth hand, you respond 1NT because you don't have the 10 HCPs you need to introduce your longest suit at the two level.

If you have fewer than three hearts plus a balanced hand, you can use the 2NT and 3NT responses with the following HCPs ranges:

- ✔ Respond with 2NT if you have 13 to 15 HCPs
- ✔ Respond with 3NT if you have 16 to 18 HCPs

With exactly three hearts

If your partner opens the bidding with 1♥, and you have three hearts in your hand, you have just located that all-important eight-card fit. If you have an eight-card fit between the two hands, you can produce an extra trick or two during the play of the hand. When you find a fit, never let it go.

After you realize that you have an eight-card fit, this is what you do:

- ✔ Reevaluate your hand upwards. Even with three card support, you get to add points (support points, or SPs) for short suits. Give yourself one point for each doubleton, two points for each singleton, and three points for each void. Add these support points to your HCPs when you evaluate your strength. (See "With 6 to 12 HCPs and real support for partner (adding support points)" in this chapter for the details on support points.)
- ✔ Show your partner your support and your strength.

You can make one of three responses, depending on how many support points you have after you reevaluate your hand:

- ✔ **6 to 10 combined SPs and HCPs:** Respond 2♥.

- ✔ **11 to 12 combined SPs and HCPs:** Respond in your longest suit and then bid 3♥ at your next opportunity.

- ✔ **13 to 16 combined SPs and HCPs:** Respond in your longest suit and then bid 4♥ at your next opportunity.

The cards in Figure 10-11 show a few examples of responding hands with three hearts.

In the first hand, you would add one point for the doubleton diamond suit, bringing you up to 9 points and a response of 2♥. For the second hand, add two points for the singleton club, weighing in your hand at 11 points, enough to bid 2♦ with the intention of bidding hearts the next time you get a chance. You don't have any short suits in the third hand, but you still have enough HCPs to respond 2♥.

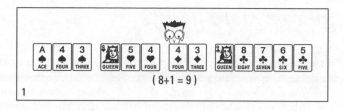

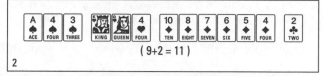

Figure 10-11:
Three
hearts
make an
eight-card
fit.

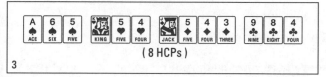

Signals create scandals

Most bridge players bend over backwards to be ethical, but every once in a while, you run across partners who can't resist the temptation to cheat by using illegal signals.

Many years ago, a famous cheating scandal arose at a World Championship. One partnership was accused of using illegal signals to tell each other how many hearts they had. It was alleged that they signaled each other by holding their cards so that a certain number of fingers showed when they had a certain number of hearts. The accused partnership denied the charges, even though the captain of the offending team forfeited all matches. The case eventually went to a court of law and the accused were found not guilty.

I was once witness to a famous cheating scandal during the 1975 World Championship in Bermuda. We were playing against two Italians who were accused of passing information by kicking each other under the table. In order to prevent this illegal spread of information, a huge board was secretly placed under the table. Not knowing about the board, I inadvertently crashed my leg into it the next day. Ouch.

Despite the use of the board to prevent cheating, the U.S. team considered withdrawing from the tournament. The offending pair was barred from play, so we stayed. The Italians did, however, go on to win the Championship in a very exciting finish. My friend, Walter Bingham, who covered the event for *Sports Illustrated,* wrote a great article about the scandal called "The Foot Soldiers."

Due to scandals such as these, some people watch every move they make at the bridge table to avoid any suspicion of signaling.

With four or more hearts

Having four or more hearts when your partner has opened with 1♥ should be near the top of your wish list. When you have such great support for your partner's major suit, you know you have a great fit, at least nine hearts between you. You get to add even more support points to your hand, because your short side suits will pay even higher dividends for your partner, who should be able to trump at least one or two of his losing cards in your hand (see Chapter 5 for the details on trumping losers).

If you have four or more hearts, add the following SPs to your HCPs:

- ✔ Add 1 point for each doubleton
- ✔ Add 3 points for each singleton
- ✔ Add 5 points for a void

After you reevaluate your hand, your response depends upon your new total. Your original HCP count is out of date; you add the old HCP to your support points and get a new improved product.

When you have four or more hearts, make one of the following responses based on your new point total:

- ✔ **With 6 to 8 combined SPs and HCPs:** Respond 2♥
- ✔ **With 9 to 12 combined SPs and HCPs:** Respond 3♥
- ✔ **With 12 to 16 combined SPs and HCPs:** Respond with another suit and then bid 4♥

The cards in Figure 10-12 show you several hands with four or more hearts.

In the first hand, after reevaluating your hand, you clock in with enough points (6) to squeak out a 2♥ response. In the second hand, your hand grows from 8 HCPs to 11. You can jump to 3♥. This jump support for a partner is called a *limit raise;* this bid shows a fair hand, but it doesn't force your partner to bid again. Your partner can pass if you make a limit raise, but only if he has a very minimum hand for his opening bid.

The opener only passes a limit raise with a minimum opening bid. Because the responder shows a pretty fair hand, the opener only wants to stay low at the three level rather than trying for game if he has nothing to spare for his opening bid.

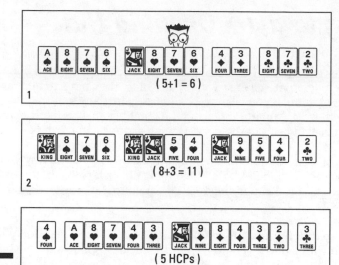

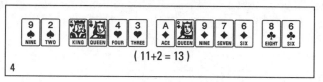

Figure 10-12:
Responding
when you
have four or
more
hearts.

The cards in the third hand in Figure 10-12 show a case where you can respond with a *weak freak,* which is a response that jumps to game. You have a hand with a lot of trump support and not much in the way of high cards, which means that you respond to a 1♥ opening bid with 4♥. In order to make a weak freak response, your hand must have the following characteristics:

- Four or more hearts
- 2 to 7 HCPs
- A total of 10 or 11 cards in two suits, including hearts

In the case of the third hand in Figure 10-12, your cards meet all three of these criteria — you can make a weak freak response of 4♥.

Weak freaks take a huge number of tricks. You don't have to worry about points when you have a freak hand. Get thee not to a nunnery, but to a game contract of four of your partner's major.

In the fourth hand in Figure 10-12, your hand blossoms from 11 HCPs to 13. In this case, you are too strong to make a limit raise. To get this message across to your partner, respond 2♦ (diamonds are your side suit), and then leap to 4♥ on your next bid. The rest is up to your partner; you have shown your strength and your support. Your partner can't sue you for non-support.

Responding to a 1♠ Opening Bid

Spades is the "boss" suit. Whichever partnership has the majority of the spades rules the world. If your partnership has the spades and your opponents wish to compete against your spade bids, they have to increase the level of the bidding. If you wish to compete against any suit they bid, you don't have to worry about increasing the level because you have spades — the highest ranking suit in the deck. Having spades can make your day.

Basically, you respond to a 1♠ opening bid exactly the same way you would respond to a 1♥ opening bid. Do I hear a big cheer forming in the background? Please see "Responding to a 1♥ Opening Bid" earlier in this chapter for the details.

When your partner opens the bidding with 1♠, you can't mention your longest suit with a one level bid — period. Lacking spade support but having 6 or more HCPs, you do have to bid something. If you aren't strong enough to respond in your longest suit with a two level response (you don't have 11 or more HCPs), you must respond 1NT. This means that responding 1NT to a 1♠ opening bid can show some really strange distributions, such as the cards shown in Figure 10-13.

Figure 10-13:
One weirdo distribution.

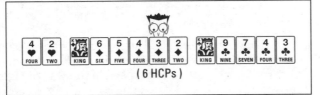

(6 HCPs)

Suppose that your partner opens 1♠ and you have the cards shown in Figure 10-13. You aren't strong enough to respond 2♦ by a long shot, but you have to bid something (you do have 6 or more HCPs). Welcome to the 1NT garbage-can response. You can make a 1NT response to a 1♠ opening bid with some really bizarre hands. When you respond with 1NT to a 1♠ opening bid, the opener expects anything!

If you have enough strength to bid at the two level (if you have 11 or more HCPs), your responses are identical to those to a 1♥ opening bid.

For example, if you have two five-card suits, you respond with the higher ranking of the two suits. The cards in Figure 10-14 provide a few examples of hands with two five-card suits.

In the first hand, you would respond 1NT because you don't have the 11 HCPs necessary to respond with 2♥. In the second hand, you would respond 2♥ because you have the HCPs to make a two level response.

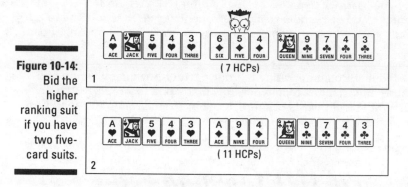

Figure 10-14:
Bid the higher ranking suit if you have two five-card suits.

If you have two or more four-card suits, you would bid the lower-ranking suit first. Check out Figure 10-15 for examples of hands with two or more four-card suits.

In the first hand, you respond 2♣ — the first four-card suit you come to — starting from spades and working your way up the ladder from the bottom rung. In the second hand, you would respond 2♦, the first four-card suit you come to starting from spades and going up the ladder from the bottom. You would respond 1NT with the third hand because you aren't strong enough to bid any of your four-card suits.

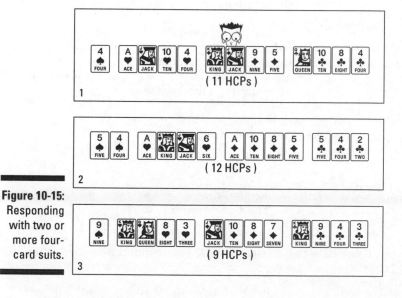

Figure 10-15:
Responding with two or more four-card suits.

Supporting your partner's spades or responding 1NT, 2NT, or 3NT is identical in meaning to those responses for a 1♥ opening. See "Responding to a 1♥ Opening Bid," earlier in this chapter, for more information on making those responses.

During the bidding, communicating to your partner how many trump you have is just as important as telling her how many points you have. If you have a trump fit of eight cards or more, let your partner in on the secret as soon as possible. Let joy be unconfined.

Responding to a 1NT Opening Bid

When your partner opens 1NT, you have a pretty clear picture of what cards your partner has. In order to make this 1NT opening bid, your partner must have a balanced hand and between 15 to 17 HCPs — no more, and no less.

When your partner opens 1NT, you should assume that your partner has 16 HCPs — that way, you can never be off of your partner's actual HCP total by more than a point.

When your partner opens 1NT, your own long suits take on a little extra luster because you know that your partner has at least two cards in your suit (your partner must have a balanced hand in order to open 1NT). If your partner has two cards in your suit, there is a good chance that at least one of them is an honor card.

After you estimate the strength of your partner's hand, you can start looking at your own hand. The fact that partner has a strong hand and at least something in every suit means your long suits are worth even more than usual. In fact, you can upgrade your hand by the following scale:

- A five-card suit headed by two honors is worth 1 extra point. For example, KJ976 = 5 points, not 4.
- A five-card suit headed by three honors is worth 2 extra points. For example, KQJ42 = 8 points, not 6.
- A six-card suit headed by the ace, king, or queen is worth 2 additional points. For example, Q97632 = 4 points, not 2.
- A six-card suit headed by two of the top three honors or any three honors is worth 3 extra points. KQ8432 = 8 points, not 5. AK10875 = 10 points, not 7.

Responding to 1NT is much easier than responding to any other bid, because your partner's high-card range is so narrowly defined. With all other bids the range of the opening is really wide; but 1NT has a very small range of only three points. Because a 1NT opening bid tells you so much about your partner's hand, you can formulate a pretty specific plan of attack for your response, which includes the following:

- ✔ If you have 10 points or more (using the preceding revaluation scale), you want to play in a game contract.

- ✔ If you have 9 points, you want to invite game by asking partner to bid game if he has 16 or 17 HCPs or stay out of game if he only has 15 HCPs.

- ✔ If you have 0 to 8 points, you want to stop as low as possible, either in 1NT or at the cheapest possible level in another suit.

Your distributional strategy:

- ✔ If you have a balanced hand, keep the bidding in notrump.

- ✔ If you have six cards in a major suit (spades or hearts), make that suit trump.

- ✔ If you have four or five cards in a major suit, try to determine whether you have an eight-card major suit fit before returning to notrump.

With a balanced hand or a six-card minor suit

In this section, I discuss how to respond to the 1NT opening if you have a balanced hand or a hand that includes a six-card minor suit (clubs or diamonds).

The cards in Figure 10-16 show some sample balanced hands.

When you have a balanced hand you can add extra points to your HCP tally according to the scale mentioned at the start of this section.

After you reevaluate your points, you can respond to a 1NT opening bid according to the following scale:

- ✔ **With 0 to 8 points:** Pass
- ✔ **With 9 points:** Bid 2NT
- ✔ **With 10 to 15 points:** Raise to 3NT

With a better hand you can start thinking about slams, which you hear more about in Chapter 15.

These counts assume that you have made any upward adjustments necessary for your long, strong suits.

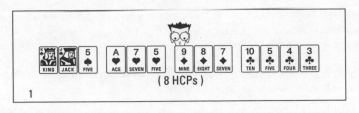

(8 HCPs)

1

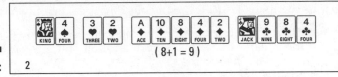

(8+1 = 9)

Figure 10-16:
Responding
to 1NT when
you have a
balanced
hand.

2

(8+3 = 11)

3

In the first hand in Figure 10-16, you would pass because you need 9 points to respond 2NT and look for a game; you have no reason to assume game will be sensible here, so stay low. On the second hand, you have 9 points, which you can show your partner by bidding 2NT. With the third hand in Figure 10-16, you would respond 3NT to show your partner that you have 10 to 15 points.

A 2NT response is called an *invitational bid.* When you respond 2NT, you show your partner 9 points and "invite" your partner to bid for game if she has enough points (she would need 16 to 17 points). If your partner only has 15 points, she should regretfully decline your invitation and pass.

With a five- or six-card major suit

With a five-card major suit, you normally consider making your suit the trump suit; and when you have a six-card major suit, your strategy is to definitely make the six-card suit the trump suit — no matter how weak your hand is. If you have a six-card major suit, you can respond with zero points! After all, the 1NT bid shows a balanced hand, so you know you have an eight-card fit.

The cards in Figure 10-17 show you a prime example of a six-card major suit.

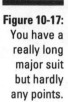

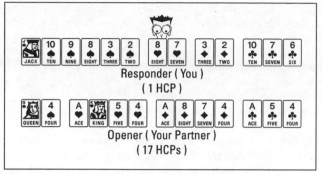

Responder (You)
(1 HCP)

Opener (Your Partner)
(17 HCPs)

Figure 10-17:
You have a
really long
major suit
but hardly
any points.

You may look at the cards in Figure 10-17 and think, "Why do I need to end up with spades as the trump suit? Couldn't I just pass and end up taking just as many tricks at notrump?" To answer this question, I want you to count the number of tricks you would take at notrump with this hand. Here's a list by suit:

- **Spades:** 0 tricks (no ♠A)
- **Hearts:** 2 tricks (you have the ♥AK)
- **Diamonds:** 1 trick (the ♦A)
- **Clubs:** 1 trick (the ♣A)

Even though your spades are long and reasonably strong, you can't take a single spade trick. After you drive out their ♠A and ♠K, even a blowtorch couldn't get the lead into the dummy; and the established spade tricks will wither on the vine. However, if you played this hand with spades as the trump suit, you could count the following number of tricks for each suit:

- **Spades:** 4 tricks
- **Hearts:** 2 tricks
- **Diamonds:** 1 trick
- **Clubs:** 1 trick

You would end up taking four more tricks if spades were the trump suit. Clearly, you need the bidding to end with spades as the trump suit without getting your partner too excited about your bid so that he heads for the stratosphere while you are trying to get out with your life at as low a level as possible.

When the responding hand has a six-card major suit facing an opening 1NT bid, that long suit of yours must be made the trump suit regardless. The 1NT bidder will always have at least two cards for you, sometimes even three or four cards to help you out. So play in your suit at all costs. But how do you do that? Ah, there's the rub.

I am about to tell you something rather shocking. For a moment, please put yourself in my hands entirely and trust me as you have never trusted me before.

When you have a six-card major suit, however many HCPs you have, you use a very strange convention to show your six-card major suit to your partner: You respond in the suit beneath your real suit! This means that you respond 2♥ if you have six spades and 2♦ when you have six hearts. Wild!

Responding in the suit beneath your real six-card suit may seem outlandishly strange to you. However, this is an established convention with a strong compelling reason behind it. Your partner knows what your response really means; your partner knows that you're really showing spade length when you respond with 2♥.

For the cards shown in Figure 10-17, the bidding would go like this:

Opener (Your Partner)	Responder (You)
1NT	2♥
2♠	Pass

During this bidding sequence, you and your partner communicate very important information. When your partner opens with 1NT, she's saying, "I have 15 to 17 HCPs and a balanced hand." Your 2♥ response says, "I can't believe that I'm doing this, but I have spades, not hearts! Can you hear me over there? Eddie Kantar told me to make this bid, and I hope that you understand it!" Your partner stays cool and bids 2♠, which says, "Will you please stop panicking? I know you have spades. That's the convention. I hear you loud and clear — here's a 2♠ bid to back up your spades." Responder passes, saying "Mission accomplished. We have reached the best spot; time to end the auction."

With a long suit (transferring)

You find out pretty quickly that the stronger of the two hands in a partnership should be the declarer (by bidding the trump suit first) whenever possible. When the declarer is the stronger hand, high cards are concealed from the opponents, making their defense that much harder.

When you respond to a 1NT opener by bidding the suit beneath your major suit, you end up *transferring* the play over to the strong hand. Instead of you playing the hand in your long suit, your partner does; you show the suit, and your partner bids it. Your partner becomes the declarer, and you get the coffee.

Your partner is programmed to bid 2♠ when you respond 2♥ and is similarly programmed to bid 2♥ when you bid 2♦. Your partner's programmed responses are called *completing the transfer*. By transferring, you achieve a number of aims, but the simplest of them is to make the strong hand the declarer.

Transfers are the brainchild of Oswald Jacoby and are often called Jacoby Transfers. Jacoby was one of the top players in the world in his day.

To see a Jacoby Transfer in action, take a peek at the cards in Figure 10-18.

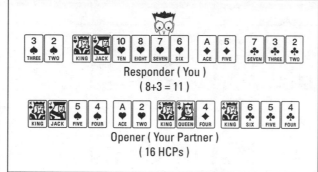

Figure 10-18:
Fixin' to
transfer.

For the cards in Figure 10-18, the bidding would look something like this:

Opener (Your Partner)	Responder (You)
1NT	2♦
2♥	4♥
Pass	

When the bidding opens with 1NT, you respond with 2♦, which tells your partner, "I want to play the hand in hearts. Eddie Kantar told me to bid 2♦, and he promised me that you would help me out by bidding 2♥." Your partner responds, "Yes, master," and bids 2♥. You have enough points and length in hearts to contract for game, so you respond with 4♥. Your partner then passes.

Notice how much easier it will be to play 4♥ from the strong hand (the hand with all the points). Whatever suit the opponents lead comes right up to your partner's strength. It's always an advantage for the strong hand to be the last person to play to the trick.

You can also use the Jacoby Transfer with a five-card major suit. If you have a five-card major suit, the bidding would go something like this:

Opener (Your Partner)	Responder (You)
1NT	2♦ (transfer to 2♥)
2♥	Pass (0 to 8 points)
	2NT (9 points)
	3NT (10 to 15 points)

Check out the cards in Figure 10-19 to see a hand where you can use the Jacoby Transfer with a five-card major suit.

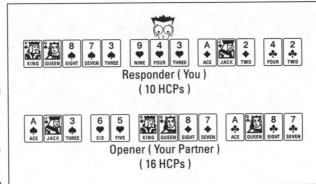

Figure 10-19: Transferring with a five-card major suit.

For the cards shown in Figure 10-19, the bidding would go like this:

Opener (Your Partner)	Responder (You)
1NT	2♥
2♠	3NT
4♠	Pass

Your 2♥ response tells your partner, "I only have five spades. Eddie Kantar says I could use the Jacoby Transfer with five or six spades. I hope you remember that this response means that I have spades." Your partner's 2♠ response confirms that she has, in fact, remembered. Your next bid of 3NT tells your partner, "I'm giving you a choice of contracts. I have a balanced hand with only five spades. You decide whether to play in 4♠ or 3NT."

Your partner has three spades, making her bid of 4♠ a very easy choice to make. If she had only two spades, she would pass after you bid 3NT.

If you've never played with someone before, it wouldn't hurt to ask them if they use Jacoby Transfers before you start playing. Bidding conventions only work when both players in a partnership know and use the same conventions! Amen.

You can also use Jacoby Transfers after your partner opens 2NT. Again, a bid of 3♦ shows at least five hearts, and a bid of 3♥ shows at least five spades. Again, the target is to get the strong hand to be the declarer as much as possible.

With one or two four-card majors (the Stayman Convention)

Your partner has just bid 1NT. If you have one four-card major with 9 or more HCPs, or two four-card majors with 8 or more HCPs, you are strong enough to respond; the question is with what bid?

Your goal is to find out if your partner also has four cards in the same major suit you do (you're looking for that eight-card fit). Thank goodness you can use a convention to find out just what you need to know.

Pull your chair up a little closer; you're about to join a group of millions of bridge players who use the *Stayman Convention,* an artificial response of 2♣ which has nothing to do with clubs, but which asks your partner if she has a four-card major. The object of the bid is to find out economically whether your partnership has a fit in either spades or hearts.

You may be familiar with some other artificial responses, such as the bids of 2♦ and 2♥, which transfer to your five- and six-card major suits when your partner opens with 1NT. An artificial response is just a bid that doesn't mean what it says. Instead, an artificial response conveys a preprogrammed message to your partner about your cards.

When you respond with 2♣ to a 1NT opening bid, you're asking your partner if she has a four-card major suit. If she does, she responds at the two level in the major suit in which she has four cards (the suit will be either spades or hearts). If she doesn't have a four-card major, she will respond with 2♦, which tells you, "Sorry. I don't have four cards in spades or hearts."

The cards in Figure 10-20 show you a hand where you can use the Stayman Convention quite effectively.

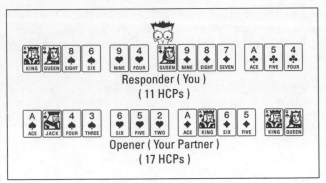

Figure 10-20:
Telling your partner about your four-card majors.

Responder (You)
(11 HCPs)

Opener (Your Partner)
(17 HCPs)

The bidding for the cards shown in Figure 10-20 would go something like this:

Opener (Your Partner)	*Responder (You)*
1NT	2♣
2♠	4♠
Pass	

In this hand, your 2♣ response is made with the following thoughts running through your head: "I have enough power in my hand to bid 3NT, but first I want to check to see if you have four spades. I hope you know I'm not trying to show you clubs." Your partner's response of 2♠ says, "Of course I know you're not showing clubs. Everybody in the world plays the Stayman Convention. I know you're asking whether I have a four-card major. I sure do, and it's spades. Is that the suit you're looking for?" Your 4♠ bid joyfully proclaims, "That's the suit I'm looking for!" And you're right to be happy; 4♠ is the best game contract for these two hands.

You can't expect to find the four-card suit you need each time you use the Stayman Convention. Sometimes your partner has the other four-card major; sometimes your partner doesn't have a four-card major at all. The cards in Figure 10-21 show you a case where using the Stayman doesn't make the desired connection.

For these two hands, the bidding should go like this:

Opener (Your Partner)	*Responder (You)*
1NT	2♣
2♥	3NT
Pass	

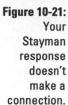

Figure 10-21:
Your
Stayman
response
doesn't
make a
connection.

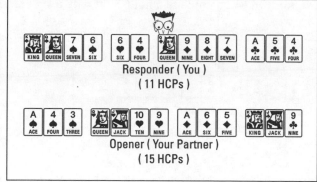

Responder (You)
(11 HCPs)

Opener (Your Partner)
(15 HCPs)

Your 2♣ response tells your partner, "I hope you remember that we use the Stayman Convention and I'm asking you if you have a four-card major." Your partner's 2♥ bid says loud and clear, "I have four hearts, how does that grab you?" That's not the response you were looking for, so you bid 3NT, which says, "Sorry man, that's not the major I was looking for. I'm heading back to notrump because we don't have an eight-card major suit fit." Your partner then passes, telling you, "You're the boss."

When your partner doesn't have the four-card major suit you're looking for, bid 2NT with 9 HCPs, or bid 3NT if you have 10 to 15 HCPs.

If you open the bidding 1NT, your partner's response of 2♣ asks if you have a four-card major. For example, if you bid 2♥ and your partner goes back to notrump, then you know that her four-card major is spades. If you bid 2♠ and she goes back to notrump, you know she has hearts. Good thinking.

The Jump Shift by Responder

When partner opens the bidding and catches you with 17+ HCPs, not only is game a certainty, but slam is a strong probability. In order to tell partner the good news, you usually *jump shift,* responding one level higher than necessary. Your jump shift is a game-force (neither player can pass until a game contract is reached). Indeed, you frequently wind up in a slam contract after a jump shift.

The two main reasons for jump shifting are

* to show a hand with a strong six-card (or seven-card) suit with 17+ HCPs

* to show a hand with four- or five-card support for opener's suit plus 17+ SPs

Figure 10-22 shows you an example of a jump shift with a six-card suit.

Figure 10-22: Partner, wake up — I'm jump shifting!

Responder (You)
(17 HCPs)

As you are busily adding up your points, you hear partner open 1♣. Respond 2♠ (not 1♠), a jump shift, alerting partner that game is a certainty and slam is on the horizon. At your next opportunity, repeat your spades (telling partner that your jump shift was based upon a long, strong suit).

Opener (Your Partner)	Responder (You)
1♣	2♠ (jump shift — one level higher than necessary)

A jump shift can also be based upon support (usually four or more cards) for partner's suit plus 17+ SPs. Jump shift in your longest *side* suit and then return to partner's suit.

Figure 10-23 gives you another chance to make partner happy.

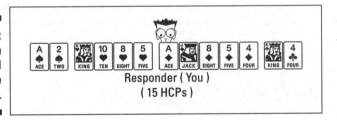

Figure 10-23: Partner, oh partner, have I got a surprise for you.

Responder (You)
(15 HCPs)

Your hand has just blossomed to 17 SPs (add one for each doubleton), enough to jump shift. Respond 3♦ and then return to hearts.

Opener (Your Partner)	Responder (You)
1♥	3♦ (jump shift — one level higher than necessary)

Most jump shifts show long, strong suits plus 17+ HCPs, or strong support for partner's suit with 17+ SPs. Responder's rebid clarifies.

A jump shift is forcing to game. Neither partner (if he values his life) can pass until a game contract is reached. Jump shifts frequently lead to slam contracts.

Chapter 11

Rebidding by the Opener

· ·

In This Chapter
- ▶ Figuring out when to rebid
- ▶ Deciding what to rebid

· ·

After you open the bidding and your partner makes a response, do you have to bid again, or can you just pass? I tell you everything you need to know about bidding after your partner's response (called *rebidding*), including when you can just pass and forget the whole thing.

What happened to your opponents? Have they taken a vow of silence not to come in and confuse your bidding? Of course not! However, I give your opponents the day off in this chapter. You may find it easier to work through the principles of bidding without any interference from your opponents. You can read about the nasty things your opponents can do to you (and what you can do to your opponents) during the bidding in Chapter 14.

Knowing When to Pass and When to Rebid

You made the opening bid and listened to your partner's response. After that, do you absolutely have to bid again? Your decision depends on what kind of response your partner makes.

Your partner's response can be *unlimited,* meaning that it shows any number of points with no upper limit. Or your partner's response can be *limited,* which shows a specific range of points.

You can't pass after an unlimited response. You *can* pass after a limited response, if you have a minimum hand, believe that you are in a safe contract, and you know that your side is unlikely to make game.

For example, if your partner responds in a new suit, you can't pass:

Opener (You)	Responder (Your Partner)
1♣ (12 to 20 HCPs)	1♥ (6 or more HCPs)

Because your partner has changed suits, your partner has made an unlimited response, so you dare not pass. Your partner may have a very strong hand and a game or a slam may be in your future. If you passed now, you'd miss the chance to find out about how strong a hand your partner has. If you drop your partner at the one level, be prepared to duck quickly.

Listen to your partner's response to your opening bid very carefully because you employ two completely different strategies on your second bid (*rebid*) depending on your partner's response.

As soon as your partner makes a limited bid, you can pass if you have nothing more to say — but not until then. You use your rebid to describe, and thereby limit, your own hand.

Rebidding After a One-Over-One Response

When your partner responds to an opening bid at the one level, she makes what is called a *one-over-one* response. Read on to figure out how to plan your next move after one of these one-over-one responses.

Before you rebid, you classify your hand by strength:

- ✔ **11 to 14 HCPs:** Minimum zone
- ✔ **15 to 18 HCPs:** Intermediate zone
- ✔ **19 to 20 HCPs:** Rock crushers, or hands with mondo points

Distributions or *hand patterns* (the way your cards are divided among suits) also influence your rebid:

- ✔ **A one-suiter:** A hand with a six- or seven-card suit
- ✔ **A two-suiter:** A hand with nine or more cards in two suits (the shorter suit must have at least four cards)
- ✔ **A three-suiter:** A hand with three four-card suits
- ✔ **Hands with support for a partner's suit**
- ✔ **Balanced hands**

When you open the bidding, you often have two or three chances to describe your hand. You can only have one of 635,013,559,600 possible hands, so how can you find it difficult to describe your hand to your partner? Yes, you face a daunting task, but after you get the hang of it, you can give your partner a pretty clear picture of your hand.

With a one-suited hand

You've got one long suit (with six or seven cards), and one long suit only. You open the bidding with a one level bid in your long suit, and your partner makes a one-over-one response. Now you want to show your partner that you have a *one-suited hand*.

However, you also must show your strength; if you have a minimum hand, you rebid your suit at the two level; if you have intermediate strength, you rebid your suit at the three level (called a *jump rebid*).

Figure 11-1 shows you a few hands that allow you to test these strategies.

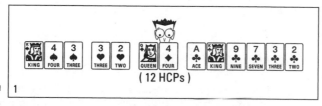

1

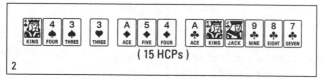

Figure 11-1:
Only one of your suits is long enough to rebid.

2

For each of the hands shown in Figure 11-1, suppose that the bidding begins as follows:

You	*Your Partner*
1♣	1♥
?	

In the first hand in Figure 11-1, you have a minimum-range opening bid, 12 to 14 HCPs, so you should make a minimum rebid. Rebid 2♣, the cheapest bid you can make to show that you have long (six or more) clubs.

In the second hand, you have an intermediate-range hand, 15 to 18 HCPs. When you have an intermediate one-suiter, jump to the three level in your suit. In this case, rebid 3♣ to tell your partner that your hand is in the 15 to 18 HCPs range.

After you rebid your suit, you have made a *limited rebid*. At that point, your partner knows your strength and distribution. Your partner becomes the *captain.* The captain knows his partner's strength and distribution and is frequently in a position to pass or to bid game. However, if the captain still doesn't know whether to bid game or not, he can make an invitational bid that asks his partner to make the final decision.

Notice that in the cards in Figure 11-1, you rebid a six-card club suit. You can also rebid a five-card suit, but you very rarely do because you almost always have something better to tell your partner. As a general rule, the responder assumes that the opener has a six-card suit when the opener rebids his original suit.

However, you can voluntarily rebid your suit if you have a five-card suit that's dripping with royalty — a suit with four honor cards and one small card, for example. When your five-card suit just reeks with honor cards, treat it as a six-card suit and rebid it.

With a two-suited hand

When you have two five-card suits or one five-card and one four-card suit, you have a classic case of the two-suited hand. When rebidding a two-suited hand, you tend to show your second suit (you already showed your first suit with your opening bid).

Bidding your second suit at the one level

Count your blessings if you have two suits to show during the bidding. Bidding two suits is great because it gives a partner a choice of trump suits. Bidding two suits can also be a challenge to your partner because it doesn't define your hand's strength all that narrowly — you are showing 12 to 18 HCPs, a very wide range.

Heaven is bidding both of your suits at the one level. However, you often find yourself in Hades, because the rank of your partner's response makes it impossible to get the second suit in at the one level.

The cards in Figure 11-2 allow you to spend some time in seventh heaven because you can show your second suit at the one level.

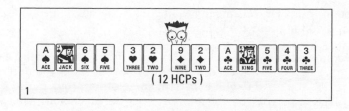

Figure 11-2:
Rebidding
your
second suit
at the one
level.

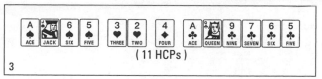

Opener (You)	Responder (Your Partner)
1♣	1♥
?	

In Figure 11-2, you would rebid 1♠ with all three hands; the rank of your second suit allows you to bid your second suit at the one level. You have just bid both of your suits at the one level. Very economical. Nice going. You've told most of your story and not climbed too high in the bidding; your partner can choose what to do and where to go starting from the first floor of the bidding elevator.

When the opener bids two suits, the opener's second suit is almost always a four-card suit. The responder shouldn't expect to have an eight-card fit in the opener's suit unless the responder also holds four cards in the suit.

Bidding your second suit at the two level

The rank of your two suits may not allow you to bid your second suit at the one level, and you may have to bid the second suit at the two level. Guess what? Bridge has a little rule for rebidding your second suit at the two level. How did I know you were longing for another rule?

If your second suit is lower ranking than your first suit, no problem. Just bid your second suit at the two level.

If your second suit is higher ranking than your first suit, you must have 17 HCPs or more to rebid your second suit at the two level. If you don't have those 17 HCPs, you need to come up with some other rebid. Perhaps you can rebid 1NT, or maybe you can support your partner's suit. What you can't do is show your second suit or worse, pass out of frustration.

The cards in Figure 11-3 ask you to decide whether or not to show your second suit.

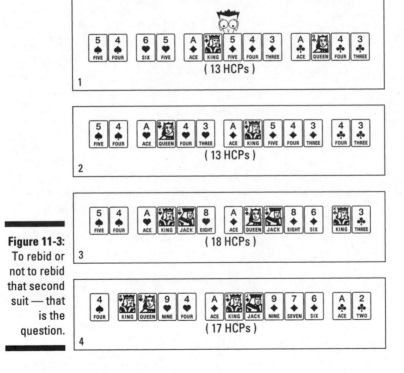

Figure 11-3: To rebid or not to rebid that second suit — that is the question.

Assume that the bidding begins like this:

Opener (You)	Responder (Your Partner)
1♦	1♠
?	

In the first hand in Figure 11-3, your second suit, clubs, is lower ranking than your first suit, diamonds. When your second suit is lower ranking than your first suit, you have no headache — just bid the suit at the two level — 2♣.

In the second, third, and fourth hands in Figure 11-3, your second suit, hearts, is higher ranking than your first suit. When your second suit is higher ranking than your first suit, you need 17 or more HCPs to bid the second suit. If you don't have those 17 HCPs, you can't show your second suit. You have to find some other rebid.

In the second hand, you don't have enough strength to show your second suit, hearts, because you only have 13 HCPs. You should rebid 2♦ as a last resort measure. In the third and fourth hands, you are strong enough to show your second suit, so you would rebid 2♥.

Bidding a higher ranking second suit at the two level is called *reversing*. After a one level response, reverses show a minimum of 17 HCPs. Your partner can't pass a reverse. In other words, a reverse is a *forcing* bid, and your partner must bid again. Your reverse shows a very strong hand and indicates that the bidding could go all the way to game and sometimes slam contracts.

When you have a 6-4 hand pattern, such as the one shown in the fourth hand in Figure 11-3, you can reverse with as few as 16 HCPs. You can also reverse with 16 HCPs if all your points are in your two long suits. When all of your strength lies in your two long suits, award yourself an extra point, which brings you to the 17 HCPs you need to rebid a second, higher-ranking suit.

With a three-suited hand

You've got a three-suited hand when you have three suits with four or more cards in them. Lucky you.

Are you the gambling type? If you are, you can bet that when you have a three-suited hand, your partner's response will be in your short suit. It never fails. However, if your partner responds in one of your four-card suits, your birthday has come early.

In Figure 11-4, you see two example hands in which you have a three-suited hand.

In the first hand in Figure 11-4, the bidding has gone as follows:

Opener (You)	Responder (Your Partner)
1♣	1♦ (Of course, your short suit)
?	

When your partner responds in your short suit, bid the next highest-ranking four-card suit (also called bidding *up the line*). In the case of the first hand in Figure 11-4, you would rebid 1♥.

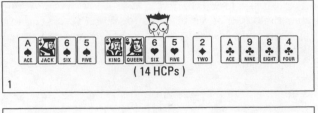

(14 HCPs)

1

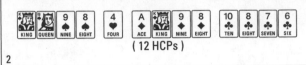

(12 HCPs)

2

Figure 11-4: Rebidding with three four-card suits and one short suit.

In the second hand in Figure 11-4, the bidding has gone as follows:

Opener (You)	Responder (Your Partner)
1♦	1♥ (What else?)
?	

In this case, you would rebid 1♠, your next higher-ranking four-card suit.

When you bid two suits without reversing, your range is wide — in the 12 to 18 HCP range.

Raising your partner's one level major-suit response

When your partner makes a major-suit response of 1♥ or 1♠, go out of your way to support your partner's suit by raising the suit if you can.

You can support a one level, major-suit response with either three or four cards in your partner's suit. However, if you only have three-card support, you must have a side-suit singleton or doubleton. If you don't have a side-suit singleton or doubleton, don't support your partner's suit just yet.

If you make a simple raise from the one level to the two level, you show a minimum hand with 13 to 15 SPs. (*Remember:* You get to add points to your hand for short suits whenever you support your partner's suit. See Chapter 10 for more information on support points.)

Take a look at the hands in Figure 11-5 to decide whether you can support your partner's one level, major-suit response.

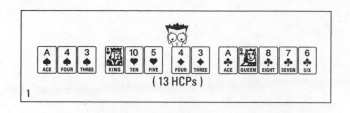

(13 HCPs)

1

Figure 11-5:
Looking for
the proper
rebid to a
one level,
major-suit
response.

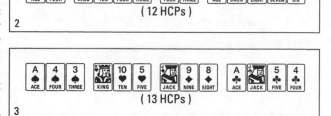

(12 HCPs)

2

(13 HCPs)

3

For each of the hands in Figure 11-5, the bidding has gone as follows:

Opener (You)	Responder (Your Partner)
1♣	1♥
?	

In the first two hands, you can comfortably raise your partner's response of
1♥ to 2♥. The raise from one to two shows a minimum hand (13 to 15 SPs)
with three- or four-card support.

Be sure to reevaluate when raising your partner. With the first hand in
Figure 11-5, add one extra point for your doubleton diamond, and with the
second hand, add two extra points, one for each doubleton. In the third
hand, you have no side-suit singleton or doubleton so you should not raise.
With a "flat" hand (a 4-3-3-3 distribution), a 1NT rebid showing 12 to 14 HCPs
more accurately describes your hand.

In Figure 11-6, you can *jump raise* your partner's suit to the three level to
show your extra strength.

Figure 11-6:
Jumping
over the
two level
straight to
the three
level.

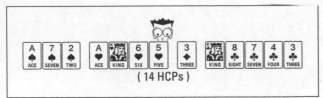

(14 HCPs)

The bidding for this hand has gone about its merry way like this:

Opener (You)	Responder (Your Partner)
1♣	1♥
?	

The hand in Figure 11-6 starts out as a minimum hand (you have 14 HCPs). If your partner had responded with the inevitable 1♦, your short suit, the hand would stay a minimum, and you would rebid 1♥.

Never add extra points to your hand when your partner bids your short suit.

However, if your partner responds 1♥, a suit for which you have four-card support, your stock goes way up. You can add three extra points for your singleton diamond, so your minimum hand has now blossomed into an intermediate hand.

The hand now evaluates to 17 SPs. With 16 to 18 SPs, you can jump raise to the three level; in this case, you would jump to 3♥.

Partners love to hear you raise their major suit responses; it means that your side has found a fit. In addition, your partner gets to play the hand, if the final contract ends in the "agreed" major suit.

Rebidding a balanced hand

Three classic shapes form a balanced hand: the 4-3-3-3 shape, the 4-4-3-2 shape, and the 5-3-3-2 shape. Balanced hands don't offer many options when it comes to rebidding. You can either support your partner's suit, rebid notrump at the minimum legal level, or introduce a second four-card suit at the one level.

With a 4-4-3-2 pattern

The most common balanced hand distribution is the 4-4-3-2 pattern. With 15 to 17 HCPs and this hand pattern, as the old joke goes, "you wouldn't have started from here" because you would have opened 1NT. If you open one of any suit with a balanced hand, your hand should be in the 12 to 14 or 18 to 19 HCP range.

The hands in Figure 11-7 show you a couple 4-4-3-2 hand patterns.

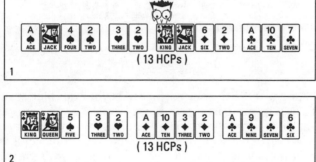

Figure 11-7:
Rebidding
with a
4-4-3-2
hand
pattern.

In both of the hands in Figure 11-7, the bidding sequence is:

Opener (You)	Responder (Your Partner)
1♦	1♥
?	

Anytime you can rebid your second suit at the one level with minimum or intermediate zone hands (with 12 to 18 HCPs), do it. On the first hand in Figure 11-7, rebid 1♠. If your partner responds in your doubleton suit, and you would have to introduce your other suit at the two level, rebid 1NT instead, as you would do in the second hand in Figure 11-7.

If you rebid a second suit at the two level, you should have at least nine cards between your two suits. If you only have eight cards, rebid 1NT instead.

With a 5-3-3-2 pattern

When you make a rebid with a 5-3-3-2 pattern, you should either rebid notrump or raise your partner's suit. Normally, to raise your partner directly with three-card support, your trump suit should be headed by at least one top honor (the ace, king, or queen). You can put your partner at ease if you present her with an honor card in the trump suit.

REMEMBER

In this section, I only discuss 5-3-3-2 patterns with 12 to 14 HCPs; with 15 to 17 HCPs, you would have opened 1NT in the first place.

The cards in Figure 11-8 give you a chance to make a rebid with a 5-3-3-2 hand pattern.

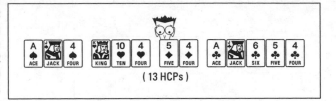

Figure 11-8:
Rebidding with a 5-3-3-2 hand pattern.

(13 HCPs)

Open the bidding with 1♣. If your partner bids your doubleton suit, diamonds, rebid 1NT. If your partner responds with 1♥ or 1♠, you can raise to 2♥ or 2♠. In each case, you have limited your hand and your partner has enough information about your hand to decide what contract is best. Notice that you do not rebid your five-card club suit. Raising your partner or rebidding notrump are higher priorities.

With a 4-3-3-3 pattern

Bid your four-card major suit (if you have one) at the one level if you possibly can. If your partner bids your four-card suit, raise it; otherwise, bid notrump at the lowest possible level.

The cards in Figure 11-9 give you a chance to make a rebid with a flat 4-3-3-3 hand pattern.

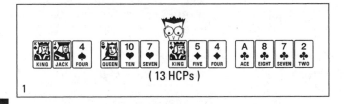

(13 HCPs)

1

Figure 11-9:
Making a rebid with a flat hand.

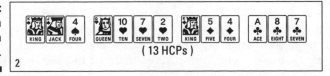

(13 HCPs)

2

You should open by bidding 1♣ with both hands in Figure 11-9. On the first hand, rebid 1NT over any one-level response because you don't have four-card support for whichever suit your partner bids. On the second hand in Figure 11-9, rebid 1♥ if your partner responds 1♦; raise a 1♥ response to 2♥; rebid 1NT if your partner responds 1♠.

If you have 18 or 19 HCPs with this distribution, jump to 2NT on your second bid. This bid will be music to your partner's ears!

Even with a flat hand, you can raise your partner's major suit response when you have four-card support in the suit. Why not cheer up your partner and tell him about the fit?

Handling rock crushers after your partner makes a one level response

If you have an unbalanced hand with two suits (typically with a 5-4, 6-4, or 5-5 distribution) and 19 to 20 HCPs, and your partner makes a one level response, you can show your strength by making a jump bid in a new suit. In bridge, you call such a jump bid a *jump shift*.

Do you want to see a typical jump shift rebid? I thought you'd never ask:

Opener (You)	Responder (Your Partner)
1♣	1♦
2♥	

In this sequence, you jumped (went up an extra level) in a new suit at your second turn. You could have bid 1♥, but you chose to jump. Why? Because you wanted to show your partner a rock crusher.

When your partner responds at the one level and you want to make sure that your partner bids again, jump shift. A jump shift forces your partner to game and shows a mountain of a hand!

You may, at one point, pick up a rock-crusher with four-card support for your partner. With that hand, you don't have to jump in a new suit because your partner has bid your second suit. Make him happy by jumping all the way to game. Jumping to game shows a great hand, naturally, because your partner could have as few as 6 HCPs. In fact, you need at least 19 SPs to pull off this jump all the way to game. The cards in Figure 11-10 show a hand where you can make this fantastic jump.

Figure 11-10:
Skip to
my Lou:
jumping to
game.

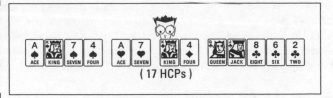

(17 HCPs)

For this hand, the bidding has gone as follows:

Opener (You)	Responder (Your Partner)
1♣	1♠
?	

Your partner's response allows you to reevaluate your hand upwards. You can count one additional point for each doubleton, so your point total zooms all the way to 19 SPs. You should rebid 4♠, a game bid.

TIP

When you have four-card support for your partner's one level major-suit response, jump to game in your partner's suit when you have 19 to 21 SPs.

Making a Rebid After a Two-over-One Response

You've hit the jackpot. Nothing bad can happen to you if your partner is strong enough to respond at the two level after you open at the one level. A two-over-one response has no upper limit of HCPs; it is an *unlimited* response. A two-over-one response can be your springboard to a game or a slam.

When your partner makes a two-over-one response, you know the following:

- ✔ She has a minimum of 11 HCPs.

- ✔ She promises to bid again. That promise, written in blood, allows you to relax knowing that your next bid can't be passed. So you can take your time describing your hand.

After a two-over-one response, you have options, all good ones, which I discuss in this section. Your basic goal after a two-over-one response is to limit your hand. You can do this by either rebidding some number of no-trump, supporting your partner's suit, or rebidding the suit in which you opened.

Rebidding 2NT after a two-over-one response

With 12 to 14 HCPs and a balanced hand, you plan to rebid 1NT over most one-over-one responses. But your partner may double-cross you and respond at the two level. No sweat — rebid 2NT, which still shows 12 to 14 HCPs.

Suppose that you deal yourself either of these hands shown in Figure 11-11.

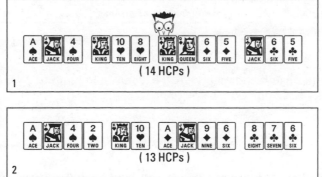

Figure 11-11: Rebidding 2NT after a two-over-one response.

On the first hand, you would open 1♦ intending to rebid 1NT over a 1♥ or 1♠ response. However, if your partner crosses you up and responds 2♣, rebid 2NT. On the second hand in Figure 11-11, you would also open with 1♦. If your partner responds 1♥, 1♠ is the proper rebid; if your partner responds 1♠, a raise to 2♠ is correct. However, if your partner responds 2♣, 2NT is the proper rebid. The hand is not strong enough to rebid 2♠; rebidding a higher-ranking suit at the two level after a two-over-one response shows 15 or more HCPs.

Jumping all the way to 3NT

With 18 to 19 HCPs, balanced, you're too strong to open 1NT (you should have 15 to 17 HCPs) and too weak to open 2NT (you need 20 to 21 HCPs). The solution: Open your longest suit and then jump in notrump on your rebid. After a two level response, you can jump directly to 3NT.

The cards in Figure 11-12 show you an example of jumping in notrump.

Figure 11-12:
It's a hop, skip, and a jump in notrump.

Opener (You)
(18 HCPs)

In Figure 11-12, the bidding has gone as follows:

Opener (You)	*Responder (Your Partner)*
1♦	2♣
?	

If your partner had responded 1♥ or 1♠, you would jump to 2NT. However, your partner responds 2♣, so you jump to 3NT.

Raising your partner's suit

If you have three- or four-card support for your partner's two level response, don't hold back; show this support by raising your partner's suit. Bear in mind that responder can make two level responses in clubs and diamonds with a four-card suit, so you normally need four cards to raise a two level minor suit response. However, a two level response of 2♥ guarantees at least a five-card suit, so you can raise your partner in hearts even if you only have three cards in the suit (three-card support).

The cards in Figure 11-13 show you a great example of when you have the support you need to raise your partner's two level response to the three level.

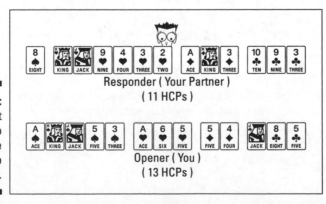

Responder (Your Partner)
(11 HCPs)

Figure 11-13:
You've got the gusto to go all the way to game.

Opener (You)
(13 HCPs)

I know this chapter is about rebidding, but I just have to show you how your giving your partner support simplifies the bidding:

Opener (You)	Responder (Your Partner)
1♠	2♥
3♥	4♥
Pass	

This bidding shows clear communication between the partners. Your partner's 2♥ response promises a minimum of a five-card heart suit with at least 11 HCPs. Your 3♥ rebid tells your partner, "I'm impressed. Well, I'm not about to rebid a five-card spade suit when I have three-card heart support for your five- or six-card heart suit." Your partner's 4♥ bid joyfully says, "I should hope not." When you pass, you're telling your partner, "What an easy game. You bid a suit, I support the suit, and we get to game. What could be better!"

If you want to win at bridge, raise your partner's major suit responses.

Rebidding a six-card suit

Whenever you have a hand with just one long suit, you normally rebid the suit. You want to show your partner a six-card suit and at the same time show your strength.

If you have a minimum zone hand of 12 to 14 HCPs, make a minimum rebid; if you have an intermediate zone hand of 15 to 17 HCPs, make a jump rebid.

For example, rebid your imaginary six-card heart suit as follows:

Opener (You)	Responder (Your Partner)
1♥	2♣
2♥ (11 to 14 HCPs)	

Opener (You)	Responder (Your Partner)
1♥	2♣
3♥ (15 to 17 HCPs)	

Rebidding a second, higher-ranking suit (reversing)

If you have a two-suited hand, you generally rebid the second suit and tell your partner the glad tidings as soon as you can.

If you have a second suit of four or more cards that is higher ranking than the suit you opened with, you need only 15 or more HCPs to rebid your second suit, not 17 or more HCPs as you do after a one-over-one response.

Rebidding a higher-ranking second suit is called *reversing*. If you don't have the necessary strength to reverse, don't bid your second suit. Find another rebid or perhaps raise your partner's suit. In that case, you could rebid your own suit or bid notrump; choose whichever option looks like the most accurate way to describe your hand.

Suppose that you pick up either of the two hands shown in Figure 11-14.

Figure 11-14:
Deciding whether or not to reverse.

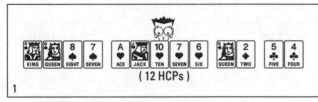

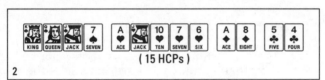

For both of these hands, the bidding has gone as follows:

Opener (You)	Responder (Your Partner)
1♥	2♣
?	

On the first hand, you aren't strong enough to rebid 2♠, a reverse, so you rebid 2♥. Your hearts are quite chunky, so you're only telling a little white lie to suggest that you may have six hearts. On the second hand, you are strong enough to reverse; rebid 2♠.

Rebidding a second suit at the three level (a three level reverse)

Sometimes, a partner's two level response forces you to the three level to show your second suit. Bidding a new suit at the three level is called *reversing at the three level*, and you need 15 or more HCPs to show your second suit at the three level. If you don't have 15 or more HCPs, find another rebid. Rebidding your first suit or rebidding 2NT, both minimum bids, present two live possibilities.

The hands in Figure 11-15 show you when you can reverse at the three level and when you need to take an alternative route.

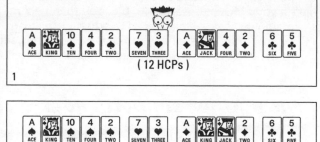

Figure 11-15:
Are you strong enough to rebid at the three level? If not, better get out your road map.

(12 HCPs)

1

(15 HCPs)

2

In both sample hands, the bidding has gone as follows:

Opener (You)	Responder (Your Partner)
1♠	2♣
?	

Perfect. In both cases in Figure 11-15, your second suit is lower ranking than your first, so you don't have to worry about any silly rules. Just rebid your second suit — rebid 2♦ with both hands.

Now, assume that you have the same two hands shown in Figure 11-15, but this time, the bidding goes like this:

Opener (You)	Responder (Your Partner)
1♠	2♥
?	

Your partner's 2♥ response forces you to the three level to show your second suit. You need 15 or more HCPs to show that second suit at the three level. On the first hand, you don't have the HCPs you need, so rebid 2♠. On the second hand, you have the necessary HCPs, so go ahead and show your second suit. Rebid 3♦.

You can't always show your second suit. If showing your second suit after a two-over-one response means going beyond the two level of your first suit, you need 15 or more HCPs. With fewer than 15 HCPs, find another rebid.

Rebidding After a Limited Response

When your partner makes a limited response, showing her strength within a few points, the fog clears. You can add the strength of the two hands together and have a good idea of how high to bid. You then become the captain. The captain makes the decisions as to whether to close up shop and pass, to bid game, or to issue an invitation to game. In this section, I discuss how you should rebid after the two most common limited responses.

When your partner supports your suit

When your partner supports your suit at the two level, you can assume that she has 6 to 10 support points. (Support points, or *SPs*, are HCPs plus a little something extra for voids, singletons, and doubletons.)

If you assume that your partner has 8 SPs when she raises you to the two level, you can never be off by more than two points.

Whenever your partner raises your suit, your hand improves because an eight-card (or longer) fit has been found. How do you know you have a fit? If your partner raises you voluntarily, that eight-card fit is like an elephant in your sock drawer — you just can't miss it.

Your partner has already added extra points for short suits to value her hand properly, and now you can add extra points for shortness. How many points should you add?

Reevaluating upwards

When you first pick up your hand, you just count your HCPs; you don't add for shortness because you haven't found a fit yet. However, if you find an eight-card fit, you can add extra points to your hand for shortness:

✔ Add one point for each doubleton

✔ Add two points for a singleton

✔ Add three points for a void

If you have a nine-card fit or longer (you have six trump cards and your partner shows three or more trump cards), take one more point as a sort of feel-good bonus, whatever you hold in the rest of your hand.

Figure 11-16 shows four hands where your partner has raised your 1♥ opening bid to 2♥, usually showing three-card support. You have to reevaluate your hand and decide what to do.

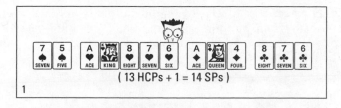
(14 HCPs + 2 = 16 SPs)

2

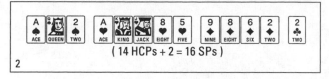
(13 HCPs + 1 = 14 SPs)

1

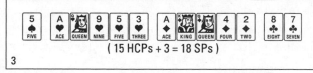
(15 HCPs + 3 = 18 SPs)

3

Figure 11-16:
Reevaluating
your hand
upward
after finding
a fit.

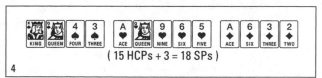
(15 HCPs + 3 = 18 SPs)

4

Making a winning decision

After you reevaluate your hand when you know you have an eight or nine-card fit, you can decide how high to bid according to the following scale:

- ✔ If there are 25 points between the two hands, even if your partner has a minimum (think of 7 SPs as being a minimum), bid game. (Your partner seldom has exactly 6 SPs.)

- ✔ If you can't possibly have 25 points between the two hands even if your partner has a maximum (think of 10 support points as being a maximum), pass.

- ✔ If you may have 25 points between the two hands if your partner has 8 to 10 support points, invite game by bidding 3♥.

On the first hand, with 14 reevaluated points, you would pass because you have no chance for game. On the second hand, with your reevaluated 16 count, you would invite game by bidding 3♥. On the third and fourth hands, you can leap all the way to 4♥, because your hand reevaluates to 18 or more points. The one who knows, goes.

If your partner makes a limit raise by jumping directly to 3♥, showing 9 to 11 SPs plus four-card trump support, give your hand an additional point, because you have a nine-card fit. In the case of Figure 11-16, you would bid 4♥ with all four hands.

When your partner responds 1NT

The 1NT response is a limited response, and as with all limited responses, the partner of the limited hand has a much better picture of the overall strength of the two hands and becomes the captain. When your partner responds with 1NT, you know the following:

- ✔ She has 6 to 10 HCPs.

- ✔ In response to a 1♣ opening bid, the 1NT response promises a balanced hand; in response to any other suit, the bid does not guarantee it.

- ✔ When the responder bids 1NT, she may have a long suit and may not be strong enough to bid it at the two level.

- ✔ The 1NT response to your major suit opening bid denies three-card support for your major suit.

The opener, the captain, must remember all these things when making a rebid after a 1NT response.

The cards in Figure 11-17 give you a chance to rebid after your partner has responded 1NT. When you have a balanced hand, add your points to your partner's total and see where you end up. Do two calculations, with the least (6 points) and the most (10 points) possible number of points; if you always have enough for game, bid 3NT. If you never have enough for game, pass. If you may want to play in 3NT opposite a maximum, bid 2NT as an invitation to the waltz.

Figure 11-17:
Rebidding after a 1NT response.

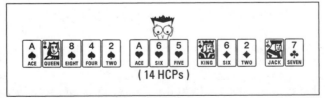

(14 HCPs)

So far, the bidding for this hand has gone as follows:

Opener (You)	Responder (Your Partner)
1♠	1NT
?	

Because you have a balanced hand and your partner has bid notrump, you should be content with a notrump contract.

The next question is how high should you bid? To figure out how high to go, add your HCPs to the most HCPs your partner can have; remember your partner has shown 6 to 10 points so she can't have more than that.

If the total doesn't come to 25 HCPs, stop adding, pass! In Figure 11-17, the total comes to 24 HCPs, so you should pass because your 14 points plus a maximum of 10 from your partner makes 24.

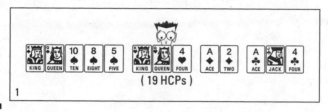

(19 HCPs)

1

Figure 11-18:
Deciding
how high
to bid.

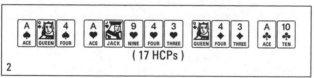

(17 HCPs)

2

The cards in Figure 11-18 give you another chance to rebid after a 1NT response.

In both hands, the bidding has gone as follows:

Opener (You)	Responder (Your Partner)
1♠	1NT (showing 6 to 10 HCPs)
?	

On the first hand in Figure 11-18, you have a balanced hand, making notrump your best contract. Add your HCPs to the most your partner can have, and you come up with 29 HCPs, more than enough for game (you need 25 points to try for 3NT). Now add your HCPs to the least your partner can have, and you still come up with 25 HCPs. You can bid 3NT.

On the second hand in Figure 11-18, you can also open 1NT (in Chapter 9, I advise you to open all 5-3-3-2 hands that have 15 to 17 HCPs with 1NT). Add your 17 HCPs to the most HCPs your partner can have and you come up with 27 total points, more than enough to bid 3NT. However, when you add your 17 HCPs to the least your partner can have, 6 HCPs, you only come up with 23 HCPs, not enough for game.

Because you have a game facing good news, but want to stay low facing a dog, you ask your partner to let you know which hand type she has by inviting with a bid of 2NT.

You must invite your partner to the ball — ask "Will you swing into the fox-trot and bid game with a maximum, or turn me down contemptuously with a minimum?" You ask this question by bidding 2NT. Your partner bids 3NT with a maximum (8 to 10 HCPs is considered a maximum) and passes with a minimum (6 to 7 HCPs).

What if your partner responds 1NT and you don't have a balanced hand? No problem. Bid your second suit. You know your partner doesn't have support for your first one.

Figure 11-19:
Making
a rebid
with an
unbalanced
hand when
your
partner has
responded
with 1NT.

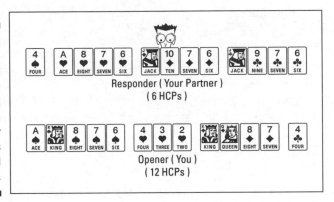

The cards in Figure 11-19 show an unbalanced hand.

Look how the bidding has gone so far with this hand:

Opener (You)	Responder (Your Partner)
1♠	1NT
?	

You have an unbalanced hand, and you know your partner doesn't have spade support (if she had support, she would have raised the bidding to 2♠). Look for a home in another suit. Rebid your other suit of four cards or more; bid 2♦. Bidding a new lower ranking suit does not necessarily show extra strength. The range of that 2♦ bid is 12 to 18 HCPs.

Guess what? You have found a home. Your partner can pass 2♦, and you end up in a very cozy contract, thank you very much.

Good bidders only rebid a six-card major suit after their partner responds 1NT. Rebidding a five-card major suit after a 1NT response has the earmarks of a death wish. Why head for a suit in which you can't possibly have an eight-card fit? It's suicidal.

Chapter 12
Rebidding by the Responder

In This Chapter
▶ Setting sail to a final contract
▶ Making the best rebid you can make

Your partner has opened the bidding, and you have responded. Your partner has bid again, and now it's your turn to bid again. You either need to pass or make another bid, called a *rebid*. In this chapter, I give you all kinds of tips and hints on what to bid at this stage of the game.

Becoming the Captain

During the bidding, each player tries to determine his partner's strength and distribution.

Your partner's hand (your partner opened the bidding) can fall into any of the following ranges:

- ✔ **12 to 14 HCPs:** Minimum range
- ✔ **15 to 17 HCPs:** Intermediate range
- ✔ **18 to 21 HCPs:** Rock-crusher range

Your hand, as the responder, can fall into any of the following four ranges:

- ✔ **6 to 10 HCPs:** Minimum range
- ✔ **11 to 12 HCPs:** Invitational range
- ✔ **13 to 17 HCPs:** Game or just possibly a slam range
- ✔ **18 or more HCPs:** Likely slam range

After either player reveals his range, which is called limiting one's hand, the partner of the player who has revealed his range becomes the *captain*. The captain knows how many total points are held by the partnership; the captain uses that number to determine how high to bid. And, of course, each player knows when he limits his own hand that his partner is the captain.

The captain can sometimes determine which trump suit is best for the hand after his partner has limited his hand. During the bidding, you're always trying to locate an eight-card (or longer) trump fit in a particular major suit (either hearts or spades). If you find one of these fits, make that suit your trump suit.

As the responder, you frequently have a pretty clear picture of your partner's hand after he bids a second time, particularly if his second bid is a limit bid. Before you make your rebid, the topic of this chapter, ask yourself the following two questions:

- What has my partner already told me about her hand with her first two bids?
- What have I already told my partner about my hand with my original response?

Your rebid depends on your answers to these two questions.

Limiting your hand

You may have already limited your hand with your first response. For example, you may have raised your partner's suit, or you may have responded some number of notrump, both limit bids. After you limit your hand, your partner becomes the captain. You are off the hook; no more decision making for you to add to the gray hairs — unless your partner turns the tables on you by making an invitational bid. If your partner makes an invitational bid, then you have to decide whether to bid game or hunker down in a part-score. Such an invitation transfers the responsibility (and also the blame) back to you; you are now about to become the hero . . . or the goat.

Pretend that you and your partner have exchanged the following bids:

Opener (Your Partner)	Responder (You)
1♥	2♥ (shows 6 to 10 SPs, a limit response)

Because you limit your hand by showing your HCPs and distribution, your partner becomes the captain. In this case, your partner usually makes one of the following three rebids:

- **Pass:** Telling you that the partnership doesn't have enough for game.
- **4♥:** Telling you that the partnership has 25 or more points between the two hands.

✔ **3♥:** An invitational bid that tells you that your partner isn't sure whether there are enough points to bid game.

The 3♥ asks for more information. It invites you to bid game (4♥) if you have a maximum (8 to 10 SPs) and asks you to pass if you have a minimum for your raise (6 to 7 SPs).

An invitational bid in this sequence reverses the captaincy. After an invitational bid, you must decide if your partnership has enough points for game.

When your partner limits her hand

Your partner can also limit her hand by supporting your suit, rebidding her suit, or even by bidding notrump. If your partner limits her hand, you become the captain.

In each of the hands in Figure 12-1, it's up to you to decide whether you have enough points to bid game.

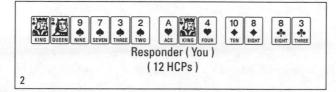

Opener (Your Partner)
(13 HCPs)

Responder (You)
(7 HCPs)

1

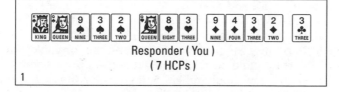

Responder (You)
(12 HCPs)

2

Figure 12-1:
Listening to
your
partner's
rebid.

Responder (You)
(10 HCPs)

3

For each of the hands in Figure 12-1, the bidding has gone as follows:

Opener (Your Partner)	Responder (You)
1♣ (12 or more HCPs)	1♠ (6 or more HCPs, an unlimited response)
2♠ (13 to 15 SPs)	?

In each case in Figure 12-1, you've made an unlimited response that shows 6 or more HCPs. Your partner still doesn't know which range your hand is in. However, when your partner raises your suit to 2♠, she makes a limit bid that shows a minimum range hand, and you become the captain.

If you feel that you have found a home for your partnership (an eight-card fit), add the two hands together and see whether you have a total of 25 or more points between the hands. If you do, you can bid game, which in the case of Figure 12-1 would be 4♠. If you don't have 25 or more points, then you should pass. If you can't be sure, you need to ask your partner for more information, perhaps by bidding 3♠. When you ask your partner for more information, she then becomes the captain.

In each of the hands in Figure 12-1, you have found a home. Even though your partner can have three spades to raise your one level major suit response, you know that you have at least eight spades between the two hands. Time to add the two hands together — almost.

Before you can add the two hands together, you must reevaluate your hand after your hand has been supported and you know that you have an eight-card fit (or longer). For more information on reevaluating your hand, see Chapter 10.

After reevaluating your hand, you can decide what to do with each of the hands in Figure 12-1. For the first hand, which reevaluates to 9 points, you don't have enough for game, so you pass. For the second hand, which reevaluates to 16 points, you have more than enough for game; you should rebid 4♠. For the third hand, which reevaluates to 11 points, you have invitational strength; you should rebid 3♠. If your partner has 14 to 15 SPs, she will accept your invitation. If she has 13 SPs, she passes. With the hand in Figure 12-1, which reevaluates to 14 SPs, your partner bids 4♠.

After any suit has been raised from the one level to the two level, a three level bid in that suit invites your partner to bid game. Your partner passes with a minimum hand (13 SPs) and bids game with a maximum (14 or 15 SPs).

When your partner raises your suit, he shows a minimum opening bid with at least three card support. This makes you the captain; you know his range — but he doesn't know yours. You can settle down at the two level if that seems high enough, or you can look for more if you aren't satisfied with a low level contract. In Figure 12-2, you see two hands where your partner raises your four-card major suit.

The bidding has gone as follows:

Opener (Your Partner)	Responder (You)
1♣ (12 or more HCPs)	1♥ (6 or more HCPs)
2♥ (13 to 15 SPs)	?

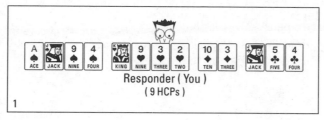

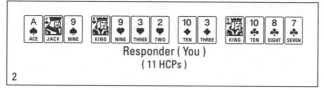

Responder (You)
(9 HCPs)

1

Figure 12-2:
Seven isn't heaven, but sometimes you have to make do.

Responder (You)
(11 HCPs)

2

After your partner raises your suit, you have found a seven-card heart fit (at least). At this point, you can either put up or shut up. In the first example in Figure 12-2, you have only 9 HCPs, and facing a maximum of 15 SPs, you have no ambition for game because you can't have more than 24 HCPs between you. Whether you have seven or eight hearts between you, you are in a comfortable spot, so why look for trouble?

When the opener shows a minimum opening bid, you need 11 or more points to continue the bidding.

With the second hand in Figure 12-2, you have enough to bid on, but not enough to drive to game. You can describe your hand accurately by bidding 2NT. What does this sound like to you? You have just found a fit in hearts, and here you are going to notrump. Did you mis-sort your hand and suddenly find that two of your red cards were diamonds, not hearts? No. Your 2NT rebid asks your partner, "Do you really want to play hearts? I only have four hearts and if you raised on three maybe we belong in notrump. I also have enough to try for game. Make the decision; game or part-score, hearts or notrump?" All those questions and inferences from just one bid!

After the opener raises your major suit, a 2NT rebid by you, the responder, shows 11 or 12 HCPs and four cards in your major suit.

Rebidding after Your Limited Response of 1NT

When you respond 1NT to your partner's opening bid, you limit your hand, showing 6 to 10 HCPs, and your partner is captain. Nevertheless, developments may force you to make yet another decision.

Take a look at the cards in Figure 12-3 to see some hands where your partner's rebid could force you to bid again.

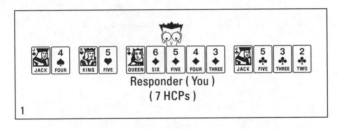

Responder (You)
(7 HCPs)

1

Responder (You)
(6 HCPs)

2

Figure 12-3:
You may still be up to bat after your 1NT response.

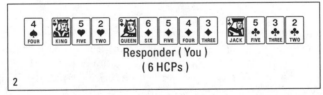

Responder (You)
(9 HCPs)

3

For each of the hands in Figure 12-3, the bidding has gone as follows:

Opener (Your Partner)	Responder (You)
1♠	1NT
?	

If your partner has a balanced hand and wants to keep the bidding in notrump, she will make one of the following bids:

- ✔ **Pass:** Your partner has no hope for game.

- ✔ **3NT:** She counts 25 points between the two hands.

- ✔ **2NT:** She invites you to game if you have between 8 and 10 HCPs.

If your partner invites you to game by bidding 2NT, refuse the invitation by passing with the first two hands. With the third hand, accept the invitation by bidding 3NT.

After your 1NT response, your partner may choose to bid a second suit. Unless you have a six-card suit of your own, your partner wants to know which of his suits you prefer.

If you have an equal number of cards in both suits, you absolutely, positively, must return to your partner's first suit, which is your partner's longer suit.

The cards in Figure 12-4 show you a hand where you must choose between two suits your partner bids.

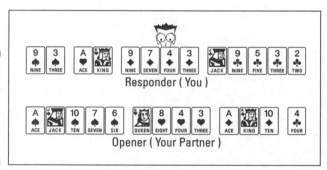

Figure 12-4:
Choosing
between
your
partner's
suits.

For this hand, the bidding has gone as follows:

Opener (Your Partner)	Responder (You)
1♠	1NT
2♥	2♠
Pass	

In this bidding sequence, your partner's opening bid of 1♠ says, "I like this chapter. I get an opening bid on every hand." Your 1NT response says, "Stop your crowing; I have nothing again." When your partner rebids 2♥, she asks you, "Which of my suits do you like better?" Your 2♠ response says, "I don't like either one, but I prefer spades to hearts because I have an equal number of cards in both suits. Besides, Kantar is watching my every move."

When your partner passes, the unspoken message is "Thanks for giving me a break and allowing me to play this hand in spades, where we have seven trump cards between our two hands, not in hearts where we only have six." Obviously, you need to outgun the opponents in the trump suit — not necessarily in terms of the high cards, more in the numerical department. You must have more trump cards than they do or bad things can happen. Very, very bad things. Don't ask.

Ideally, you would like to have eight or more trump cards between the two hands every time you play a trump contract. However, in the real world, you don't always get an eight-card fit. You may have to make do with a seven-card trump fit. If you wind up playing a contract with fewer than seven trump cards between the two hands, the wheels have come off. So when giving preferences to your partner, make sure that you concentrate on playing in the trump suit where you expect to have the most cards, not the one where you have the highest cards.

In Figure 12-5, you get a second chance to bid your own long suit.

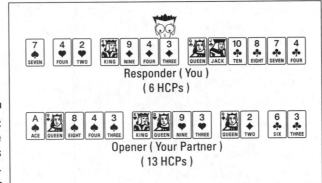

Figure 12-5: When the two hands don't mesh.

Responder (You)
(6 HCPs)

Opener (Your Partner)
(13 HCPs)

In this hand, the bidding has gone as follows:

Opener (Your Partner)	*Responder (You)*
1♠	1NT
2♥	3♣
Pass	

If your bids could talk, they'd be shouting the following messages to each other: 1♠: "I have five or more spades with 12 or more HCPs." 1NT: "Good for you. I have a weak hand with only 6 HCPs, but I have to respond, or you'll disown me; I am not nearly strong enough to bid 2♣ and show 10 or more points, so I will hedge with 1NT." 2♥: "Hey there. Hearts is my second suit. Which of my two suits do you like better?" 3♣: "I hate both of your suits, but I have a strong six-card suit of my own, which is clubs." Pass: "This is the end of the trail, amigo. You have shown six or more clubs, and we have an eight-card fit, but because you guarantee a weak hand and I have a minimum hand, I know enough to get out of this mess right now."

When your partner bids two suits, just remember the following points:

- With an equal number of cards in each suit your partner bids, take your partner back to her first suit. However, if you have a third, strong, six-card suit of your own that hasn't been heard from yet, then bid it!

- In order to raise your partner's second suit directly, you need four-card support because you assume that your partner has four cards in her second suit.

Rebidding after Your Partner Rebids 1NT

A 1NT rebid comes up frequently because balanced minimum hands are very common. Thus, you often hear this sort of bidding sequence:

Opener (Your Partner)	Responder (You)
1♣	1♥
1NT	?

Take a good look at this sequence. You hear this type of sequence so often that you may start to hum it in your sleep.

When your partner rebids 1NT, this is what you know:

- She has a minimum range hand (12 to 14 HCPs).
- She has a balanced hand. Her likely shapes are 4-3-3-3 or 4-4-3-2 or 5-3-3-2.

If you, too, have a balanced hand, add your points to your partner's (her rebid shows 12 to 14 HCPs, so assume 13 points as a ballpark figure). Your next move is to decide whether the two hands have a combined total of 25 HCPs, enough to try for game, 3NT.

The three examples in Figure 12-6 give you a chance to decide what to do after your partner's 1NT rebid.

You have a balanced hand in all the examples in Figure 12-6, so notrump is your home (you want the bidding to end in a notrump contract). Now you just need to decide how high to bid.

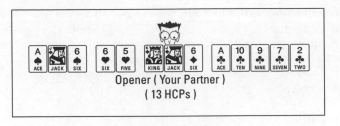

Opener (Your Partner)
(13 HCPs)

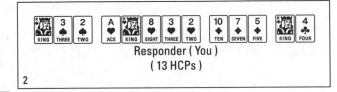

Responder (You)
(9 HCPs)

1

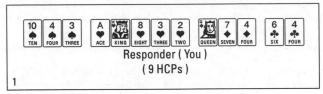

Responder (You)
(13 HCPs)

2

Figure 12-6:
Responding
to your
partner's
1NT rebid.

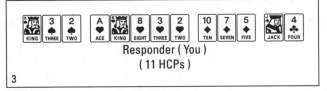

Responder (You)
(11 HCPs)

3

In the first hand in Figure 12-6, you would pass because you have no chance
for the 25 HCPs you need for game. In the second hand, you would bid 3NT
because you know of at least 25 HCPs between the two hands. In the third
hand, you would invite by bidding 2NT; you may or may not have 25 HCPs
between the two hands — you have to let your partner tell you whether you
do or not. If your partner has 13 HCPs and a good five-card suit or 14 HCPs,
she will accept your invitation and bid 3NT; with less, she will pass.

Rebidding Notrump after Your Partner Shows Two Suits

If your partner bids two suits and you're not thrilled with either of those
suits, you may wish to veer off into notrump. A notrump rebid gets you out
of the awkwardness of playing in a trump suit with only seven cards between the two hands. Just be sure to tell your partner your strength.

If you wish to make a notrump rebid, show your HCPs according to the following scale:

- **7 to 10 HCPs:** Rebid 1NT, a minimum range hand.

- **11 to 12 HCPs:** Rebid 2NT, an invitational range hand.

- **13 or more HCPs:** Rebid 3NT — go for game with this count.

The cards in Figure 12-7 show some hands where rebidding notrump is on target.

For each of the following hands, the bidding has gone as follows:

Opener (Your Partner)	*Responder (You)*
1♦	1♥
1♠	?

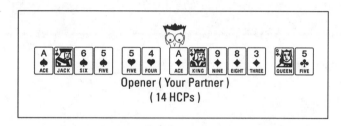

Opener (Your Partner)
(14 HCPs)

1

Responder (You)
(9 HCPs)

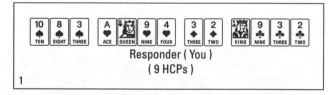

2

Responder (You)
(14 HCPs)

3

Responder (You)
(11 HCPs)

Figure 12-7:
Rebidding
notrump.

You have no support for either of your partner's suits, but you do have a balanced hand. A notrump rebid is called for in each of the hands shown in Figure 12-7. In the first hand, rebid 1NT, showing 7 to 10 HCPs. In the second hand, rebid 3NT, showing 13 or more HCPs. In the third hand, rebid 2NT, showing 11 to 12 HCPs. P.S.: The 2NT rebid showing 11 to 12 HCPs is one of your best friends. You use it in many sequences to invite game.

Rebidding after Your Partner Repeats Her Suit

If your partner has a six or seven-card suit, you can expect your partner to bid that suit at least two times, maybe three times. When your partner rebids a suit, she has limited her hand, meaning you are the captain. If you have support for the suit, you have found a home, but how high should you bid? It depends upon your partner's strength added to your strength.

Consider the following two bidding sequences:

Opener (Your Partner)	Responder (You)
1♥	1♠
2♥ (11 to 14 HCPs)	?

Opener (Your Partner)	Responder (You)
1♥	1♠
3♥ (15 to 17 HCPs)	?

In these two sequences, you know that your partner has at least six hearts, possibly seven. In the first sequence, your partner makes a simple rebid at the two level showing a minimum hand, while in the second sequence, she jumps to the three level, showing an intermediate hand.

Point count ranges aren't written in stone when it comes to long suits. Players often upgrade their hands a little when they hold a long, strong suit because such suits take so many tricks in the play of the hand.

The cards in Figure 12-8 illustrate an example of your partner making a jump rebid.

In Figure 12-8, the bidding has gone as follows:

Opener (Your Partner)	Responder (You)
1♠	1NT
3♠	4♠
Pass	

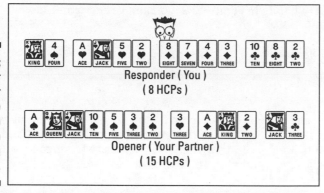

Figure 12-8:
Your
partner
sounds like
a broken
record with
her long
suit.

Responder (You)
(8 HCPs)

Opener (Your Partner)
(15 HCPs)

Your partner's opening bid of 1♠ shows that she has five or more spades with 12 or more HCPs. You respond 1NT because you aren't strong enough to bid at the two level, and you don't have three-card support for your partner.

When your partner bids a suit and then jumps the bidding in that suit, assume that your partner has an intermediate strength hand (15 to 17 HCPs) that can take about eight tricks on its own. Because you have two tricks in your hand, take a chance and bid game by bidding 4♠.

Rebidding Your Long Suit

Sometimes you (the responder) have a long, strong suit. Strong six-card suits, especially major suits, were put on this earth to be bid and bid again. But don't forget that you also have to tell your partner your strength. Also, your ranges change slightly when you have a six-card suit because your hand is automatically a little stronger.

If you have a minimum range hand (6 to 9 HCPs), rebid your suit at the cheapest level possible. With an intermediate range hand of 10 to 11 HCPs, jump to the three level in your suit, an invitational rebid. With a game-going range hand of 12 or more HCPs, get thee to game by jumping to game in your suit.

The cards in Figure 12-9 give you a chance to decide whether your long suit is long enough to rebid, and how high you should rebid if it is strong enough.

For each of the hands in Figure 12-9, you and your partner have the following dialog:

Opener (Your Partner)	*Responder (You)*
1♥	1♠
2♦	?

On the first hand in Figure 12-9, rebid 2♠ to show your minimum range hand. On the second hand, jump to 4♠ to show a game-going range hand. And on the third hand, jump to 3♠ to invite your partner to bid game. Your partner, with 14 HPs, accepts and bids 4♠, thank you very much.

Opener (Your Partner)
(14 HCPs)

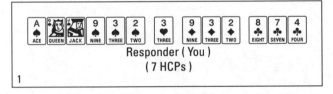

Responder (You)
(7 HCPs)

1

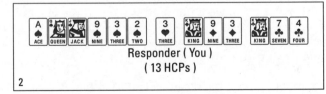

Responder (You)
(13 HCPs)

2

Figure 12-9:
Sticking
with your
long suit.

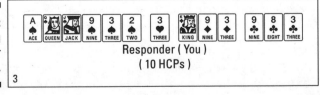

Responder (You)
(10 HCPs)

3

Playing the Waiting Game

After the opener bids twice, the responder may still not have enough information to place the final contract. In such cases, the responder bids a new suit, a waiting response, which forces her partner to bid again. The waiting response gives the opener another chance to tell the responder what she needs to know to seal the final contract.

The opener can't pass when the responder bids a new suit.

The cards in Figure 12-10 show an example of this waiting response in action.

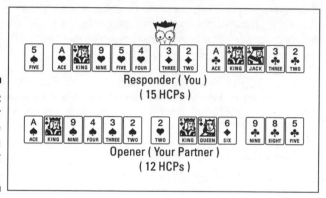

Figure 12-10: Waiting for more information from your partner.

Responder (You)
(15 HCPs)

Opener (Your Partner)
(12 HCPs)

Assume the bidding has gone as follows:

Opener (Your Partner)	Responder (You)
1♠	2♥
2♠	3♣
3NT	Pass

Your partner's opening bid of 1♠ tells you, "I have at least five spades. I happen to have six spades, but you don't know that yet." Your 2♥ response says, "Of course I don't know you have six spades. In the meantime, I want to tell you that I have a minimum of 11 HCPs, and so I'm expecting big action with this hand." Your partner then rebids 2♠, telling you, "I'm suggesting a six-card spade suit or five strong spades. I have a minimum range hand, so don't get too carried away. I have just limited my hand, making you the captain. Good luck!" Your 3♣ bid tells your partner, "I have some more to tell you about my hand. I'm bidding a new suit, which does not limit my hand, so you have to bid again." Your partner's 3NT response tells you, "I have strength in the unbid suit, diamonds, and I'm not in love with either of the suits you have shown me. After all, you have two suits under control, I have the other two suits, and 3NT is game." Your pass puts the cap on the sequence by saying, "So be it!"

In bridge, there's an old adage that says "3NT ends all auctions."

Rebidding after a Two-over-One Response

Most of the responder's rebidding headaches arise after a one-over-one response, followed by the opener mentioning a second suit. At that point, three bids have been made, and neither player has made a limit bid. Both hands have problems determining each other's strength.

However, if the initial response is two-over-one, the opener already knows that you have 11 or more HCPs. Suddenly the opener only has two ranges to deal with in the responder's hand, not three. The responder must have one of the following hand-types:

- ✔ **11 to 12 HCPs:** Invitational strength
- ✔ **13 or more HCPs:** Game-going strength, at least

The examples in Figure 12-11 show you how the responder defines his hand after a two-over-one response. Remember, the responder has shown at least 11 points already, so the opener can relax.

The bidding for this hand has gone as follows:

Opener (Your Partner)	Responder (You)
1♠	2♣
2♥	?

You must make a rebid because a two-over-one response promises a second bid. In addition, no one has limited her hand yet. No one has rebid a suit or raised a suit or bid notrump, so the traffic light is set firmly to green.

Ask yourself what you know about your partner's hand. So far, your partner has shown you the following:

- ✔ A range of 12 or more HCPs (an unlimited range)
- ✔ The likely possibility of five spades and four hearts

What does your partner know about your hand? So far you have shown your partner the following:

- 11 or more HCPs
- Four or more clubs

In the first hand in Figure 12-11, you should rebid 2NT, showing 11 to 12 HCPs. Notice that you can rebid 2NT with a singleton in your partner's first bid suit. When you don't like either of your partner's suits and you need to bid again, bidding notrump is an attractive option.

On the second hand, bid 2♠. You have 12 SPs for spades, and now is the time to let your partner in on that little secret. In the third hand, you have four-card support for your partner's second suit. You can reevaluate your hand, bringing it to 14 support points — go ahead and jump to 4♥.

After you make a two-over-one reponse, your partner already knows that you have at least 11 HCPs. With 11 or 12 HCPs, don't do any jumping — just make a minimum rebid.

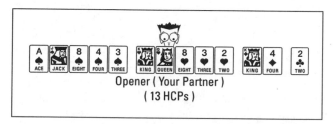

Opener (Your Partner)
(13 HCPs)

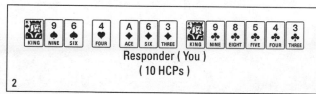

Responder (You)
(11 HCPs)

1

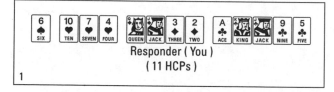

Responder (You)
(10 HCPs)

2

Figure 12-11:
The responder completes the picture after the two-over-one response.

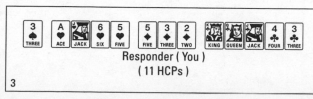

Responder (You)
(11 HCPs)

3

Chapter 13

Upping the Ante: Doubling and Redoubling

. . . .

In This Chapter

▶ Making them pay (doubling)

▶ Making them pay even more (redoubling)

. . . .

Some bidding conventions allow partners to exchange information with each other about their hands. Other bidding conventions, such as the double and redouble, allow you to tell your opponents what you think about their hands and the way they have bid their hands.

Doubling and redoubling may seem a little out of your league when you first start playing. You may have enough on your plate for a while, working with your bidding and making your contracts. You should still read this chapter, because doubling and redoubling, which "up the ante" in the bidding, add excitement and fun to the game.

Putting Your Money Where Your Mouth Is

Nobody bids perfectly. Accidents happen, and signals get crossed. Any of the following factors can cause the bidding to go awry between partners:

✔ **Hope springs eternal:** Some players see every hand through rose-colored glasses. Consequently, they bid too much most of the time. They wind up in stratospheric contracts that they can't possibly make.

✔ **Misunderstandings:** Each partner interprets a bid differently, sometimes very differently. Don't be surprised if at some point in an auction your partner thinks that you have a great hand when you've been trying to tell her all along that your hand couldn't take a trick even if your opponents got up and left the table. Trouble looms in the air.

✔ **Sacrifice bidding:** The opponents may decide that their hands just stink. They may prefer to lose points taking the contract away from you (even though they know that they can't make what they bid), rather than let you bid and make your contract. Because this can be a good defensive move, it happens all the time. See Chapter 14 for more on defensive bidding.

At some point it may become very obvious to you that your opponents have steered the bidding to a point of no return. When you suspect that your opponents are in way over their heads, you can trot out the dreaded penalty double.

A *penalty double* tells your partner (and your opponents) that you think your opponents have made a big mistake and that they can't make their bid. Penalty doubles usually take place toward the end of a bidding sequence.

The basic strategy of the penalty double is to let your opponents hang themselves. After you say "double" (just that one word), your partner usually passes. Of course, you can always double them again if they extract themselves from the frying-pan by escaping to another contract.

If you double the opponents and they do not make their contract, you get at least twice as many points as you would have received if you had not doubled.

Of course, if they make a doubled contract, they rack up twice the points they would normally get for winning the contract. (See Chapter 16 for more information about the points you win for making a contract.)

Knowing When to Double

The penalty double offers a formidable weapon that keeps your opponents from stepping all over you. If they know you won't double them, they take all kinds of liberties in the bidding.

However, you must use the penalty double wisely. You can't simply double "on spec." You need to know the proper times to unleash this lethal weapon.

Go ahead and double when you know the opponents have just gotten beyond their depth. For example, suppose that you pick up the hand shown in Figure 13-1.

This hand is not very promising. However, the opponents bid back and forth, and lo and behold they wind up in a contract of 6♠! The opponents have to take 12 tricks. You look at your hand and see that you have two sure spade tricks. Unless your opponents have a few cards up their sleeve, and then some, they can't possibly take 12 tricks because your ♠A and ♠K won't let them. Double! They can't make 6♠. You have just made a penalty double telling your partner to pass.

Figure 13-1:
Making a
silk purse
out of a
sow's ear:
Doubling
can turn a
sorry hand
into mucho
points.

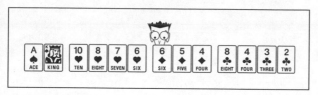

 Like everything else, you can get carried away with too much success. You double a few contracts, you defeat (or "set") the contracts, and suddenly you think that you created the game of bridge. Be careful. Don't double unless you have the proper hand. The worst possible moment to double a contract for penalties is when your partner expects a very different hand type than you have. Does that sound absurd? A prime example of the dangers appears in Figure 13-2.

Figure 13-2:
Doubling
can be
dangerous!
Proceed
with
caution.

You hear the following as the bidding progresses:

East	South (You)	West	North (Your Partner)
1♥	?		

The person to your right has actually opened 1♥, your longest and strongest suit. In addition, you have 15 HCPs. How can you show your partner all of these hearts? You can't just yet. Pass! If you double 1♥, it is not a penalty double, it is a *takeout double* showing short hearts with support for the other suits, plus at least 12 HCPs. (See Chapter 14 for more information on the takeout double.) Your partner, relying on you for spades, will bid spades for all eternity — until they double you!

 When the person to your right opens the bidding and you have five or more cards in the suit they open, you should pass. You may make a penalty double later; you can't double right now because a first-round double is a takeout double showing shortness in their suit plus support for the other suits.

For example, you have the cards shown in Figure 13-3.

Figure 13-3:
You can't
double
now — are
you angry?

The bidding for this hand is humming right along:

West	North (Your Partner)	East	South (You)
1♠	Pass	2♣	?

Are you going to teach them a lesson by doubling? You are? Better watch
out. When you double at your first opportunity (partner passing), you make
a *takeout double* showing the other suits. Your partner thinks that you have
diamonds and hearts, and you actually have clubs and spades. If you double
now, give me a break. I don't know you.

Talking Back: Redoubling

Some opponents don't like to be doubled. For some, doubling has the same
effect as waving a red flag at a bull. Your opponents may think that your
assessment is wrong. They may think that they can make their contract,
double or no double.

Your opponents have a very impressive way of telling you that they think
you have made a colossal mistake by doubling. One of your opponents can
say "redouble." If three passes follow the redouble, the deal is sealed — the
declarer is playing a redoubled contract.

If the redoubled contract is defeated, the doubling side scores four times
their normal score; if the contract is made, the redoubling side gets at least
four times their normal score. As a result, redoubled contracts tend to be
played very slowly.

The following bidding sequence shows a redouble in progress:

South (You)	West	North (Your Partner)	East
1♠	2♥	4♠	5♥
Double!	Redouble	Pass	Pass
Pass			

How do you tell a double from a double?

With two kinds of doubles, takeout and penalty, how can your partner know which double you mean (See "Taking a Chance on a Takeout Double" in Chapter 14 for the details on takeout doubles)? It would be nice if you could say, "This is a penalty double, partner! Don't bid!" In lieu of such illegal communication, use the following guidelines to help you tell a penalty double from a takeout double:

✔ If you double the opening bid, it's a takeout double.

✔ If you double at your first opportunity, partner passing, it's a takeout double.

✔ If you pass originally and then double at your first opportunity, partner passing, it's a takeout double.

✔ If you double a game or slam contract, it's a penalty double.

✔ If you double a 1NT opening bid, it's a penalty double.

✔ If you double after your partner has made a *positive bid* (anything but pass), it's a penalty double.

Remember not to say, "Double!" louder when you are making a penalty double, no matter how enthusiastic you are about the possibility of making your opponents pay. Changes in your voice are considered illegal signals; shouting "Double!" isn't the ethical way to tell your partner what your double means.

Oh boy! The final contract is 5♥, redoubled. To get to this point, each player's bid has broadcast some pretty clear messages to the table. When you doubled, your bid said, "I don't think you guys can make 5♥." West's redouble said, "Oh yeah, well I think that we can, and you are going to pay through the nose for your double!" Your partner then passed, which told West, "I trust my partner. Go ahead. We want to see you make your 5♥." East puts her two cents in by passing which says, "I trust my partner's assesment of the situation, too." Your final pass said, "We'll see who has made the mistake."

Temperatures can run high during the play of redoubled contracts because so many points are at stake. Keep your cool — you'll blow the respect of everyone at the table if you allow the excitement to get to you.

Of course, what is good for the goose is good for the gander; if the opponents double you in *your* contract, and you think that they are way off base, you can redouble them.

In addition to the redouble that follows a penalty double, bridge features a much more common use of the redouble. It occurs after your partner opens the bidding, the next hand makes a takout double, and you have 11 HCPs or more. This usually spells big trouble for your opponents. An example of this redouble appears in Figure 13-4.

Figure 13-4:
You have
the power
to redouble
their
double.

The bidding for this hand may go something like this:

North (Your Partner)	East	South (You)	West
1♥	Double	Redouble	

North's bid says, "I have 12 or more HCPs with at least five hearts." East chimes in with her takeout double, saying, "I have at least 12 or more HCPs plus support for the other suits." You counter with a redouble, saying, "Partner, I have 11 or more HCPs and we have the opponents outgunned point-wise big time. They could be in heaps of trouble if they don't have a fit. After all, they have to bid something, or let you play 1♥ redoubled, which you should make. You have hearts, and I have everything else. They may not have a home. Maybe we can lash them with a penalty double when they bid." Your partner will pass and await developments, and you hope in the end to take your opponents to the cleaners somewhere.

Chapter 14
Defensive Bidding

● ●

In This Chapter

▶ Butting in on the opponents' bidding

▶ Handling hands with tons of points but no long suit

● ●

*J*ust because an opponent opens the bidding doesn't mean that you and your partner lose the use of your vocal cords. You may be able to interfere with a bid (or bids) to make it that much harder for your opponents to reach a good contract.

Indeed, your side may have more strength than your opponents, and you or your partner may wind up playing the hand. However, even if your opponents do play the hand, your interference bid(s) may cause them to reach a lousy contract. They may not have located their best fit, and do they ever hate that! Equally important, your opponents may reach their best contract, but you may have tipped your partner off to the winning opening lead.

In this chapter, you discover how to use defensive bidding to your advantage. In short, you see how to become a difficult opponent. And you see what your opponents' bids mean if they try to do the same sort of thing to you; after all, turnabout is fair play.

Getting Nasty with the Bad Guys (Overcalling)

No matter how much you like your opponents, you should not resist the temptation to mess up their bidding. It's a jungle out there. Here's your short list of ways to really annoy your opponents after they open the bidding:

✔ Bidding a different suit, which is called an *overcall*. If you make a one level bid in another suit, you make a *one level overcall*.

✔ Bidding a suit at the two level, a *two level overcall*.

✔ Jumping the bidding in another suit, a *weak jump overcall*.

✔ Bidding 1NT, a *one notrump overcall*.

✔ Making a takeout double (see "Taking a Chance on a Takeout Double" in this chapter for more on the takeout double).

This chapter shows you how to get the most mileage out of your overcalls and takeout doubles. When bidding defensively after your opponents have opened, you want to achieve maximum irritation at minimum risk, while still hoping to bid constructively when you have a good hand. An ambitious target, but you can manage it.

You can start harassing the opposition as soon as they open the bidding. You should at least consider overcalling every time the opponents open the bidding. To overcall, you need a strong five- or six-card suit. If you have that strong suit, HCPs become less important.

Overcalls apply whether the player who opened the bidding is on your right (when you are second to bid) or on your left (when you become fourth to bid).

Bidding your long suit at the one level when the opponents open the bidding (a one level overcall)

When your opponents open the bidding, a one level overcall starts to get in their way. In order to bid a suit at the one level after an opponent has opened the bidding, you need

✔ 10 to 16 HCPs

✔ A five- or six-card suit headed by two of the top four honors, any three honors, or the A109, K109, Q109, or J109

In other words, a decent looking five-card suit, not one that looks like something the cat dragged home.

Pretend that your opponents open the bidding. You are seated South, and East opens the bidding with 1♦:

East	South (You)	West	North (Your Partner)
1♦	?		

You know that you want to interfere with East's bid if at all possible; after all, you want to help your partner find a good lead, bug your opponents, and maybe play the hand, don't you? In Figure 14-1, you see four different hands that you may hold when trying to decide whether to overcall East's opening bid of 1♦.

The first three hands in Figure 14-1 all fit the mold for an overcall: 1♥ in the first instance, 1♠ in the second and third examples.

The second hand in Figure 14-1 has two five-card suits. Whether you are the opener, responder, or overcaller, you always bid the higher ranking of two five-card suits first.

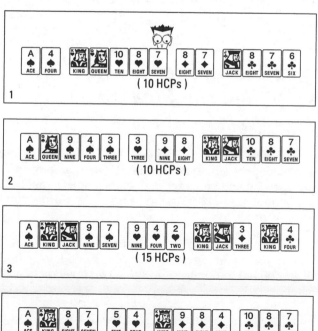

Figure 14-1:
What's that noise? Do you hear an overcall?

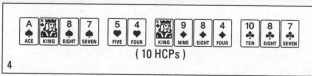

Notice that the third hand in Figure 14-1 has opening bid strength, which is very common. With a range of 10 to 16 HCPs, many overcalls show opening bid strength. Just because you have an opening bid doesn't mean that another player will not open before you get the chance to open.

The fourth hand in Figure 14-1 is the black sheep of the family. This hand doesn't have a five-card suit. No overcalls with four-card suits; you have to pass with this hand.

You make your one level overcalls in Figure 14-1 in the second seat. Your right hand opponent opened the bidding, and you were second to bid. You can also make overcalls in the fourth seat, when you are the last person at the table to bid.

For example, if you had either the second or third example hands shown in Figure 14-1, and the bidding had gone like this:

West	North (Your Partner)	East	South (You)
1♦	Pass	1♥	?

you would still overcall 1♠ in the fourth seat.

Bidding at the two level when the opponents open the bidding (a two level overcall)

Your opponents' bidding or the rank of your long suit may make it impossible for you to name that suit at the one level. For example, your right hand opponent may open 1♥ and you have diamonds, a lower ranking suit. To mention your diamonds, you have to bid 2♦. In other words, you have to make a *two level overcall*.

A two level overcall takes away some space from the opponents, but it ups your side's risk — you are at the two level not the one level, after all. You need a pretty good hand to up the ante with a two level overcall. Specifically, you need the following:

- ✔ A hand that would have opened the bidding if you had had the chance.
- ✔ More often than not, a six-card, not a five-card suit.
- ✔ If your overcall is based on a five-card suit, that suit must be headed by at least three honor cards.
- ✔ A six-card suit should be headed by two of the top four honors or the good old A109, K109, Q109, or J109.

You must have strong intermediate cards in your suit (eights, nines, and tens) when you make a two level overcall. You are sticking your neck out a bit when you make the bid — that is the time to have some stuffing in your suit that the intermediate cards provide.

A world of difference exists between these two suits: AQ743 and AQ1096. With the latter suit, you can make a two level overcall; the weak intermediate cards in the first suit increase the risk that you may get doubled (see Chapter 13 for more on doubling).

To get a better look at some two level overcalls, take a peek at the hands in Figure 14-2. For each of these hands, you are seated South and East, to your right, opens 1♥. It's your turn.

In the first hand in Figure 14-2, you can overcall 2♦; you have opening bid strength plus a strong six-card suit — just what the doctor ordered.

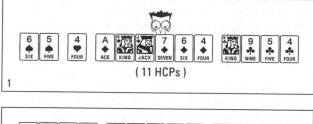

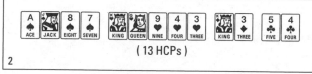

Figure 14-2: Attempting the feared two level overcall with no safety net.

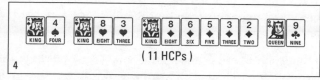

In the second hand in Figure 14-2, you can't overcall for the following reasons:

- ✔ No overcalls with four-card suits (you were looking at that spade suit, weren't you, and not the long hearts?). You can't — and should not want to — bid the opponent's suit. Why bid hearts knowing that the opponent to your right has five or more of them?
- ✔ The opponents open in your longest suit.

When the opponents bid your longest suit, the *trap pass* offers your best strategy. The trap pass allows you to hide in the bushes, waiting to pounce at a later date if your opponents have an accident and finish up in hearts. At that point, you can lower the boom on them with a penalty double; but wait until they have climbed a bit higher before you bring down the ax!

With the third hand in Figure 14-2, you also have to pass. Your hand is strong enough, your suit is long enough, but alas, your suit isn't strong enough because you don't have three honors. Most beginners fall into the trap of bidding 2♦ because they think they have the HCPs. But you can't overcall on a five-card suit unless you have some really good stuff. For example, the AQ843 doesn't qualify. When you overcall on a five-card suit, it sure helps to have nines and tens in your suit to back it up.

Sadly, on the fourth hand in Figure 14-2, you must also pass. Your hand is strong enough, your suit is long enough, but again your suit isn't strong enough. You also have an aceless wonder, which is a downer. Holding no aces in your own hand means that you have no sure tricks, not joyful news when risking an overcall.

Making a weak jump overcall

A weak jump overcall is not a simple overcall, such as a bid of 1♥ over your opponent's opening bid of 1♦. A weak jump overcall skips over one level of bidding and goes straight to 2♥, 2♠, or 3♣ over an opponent's 1♦ opening bid.

Despite its name, this bid actually has a lot of offensive power. A weak jump overcall forces your opponents to enter the bidding at a higher level than they may want to.

A weak jump's main aim is to screw up the opponents' bidding, and you can make one at your first opportunity, regardless of whether the opening bid comes on your right or on your left.

To see a weak jump overcall in the making, take a peek at Figure 14-3.

Figure 14-3:
A weak jump overcall is about to be in full effect.

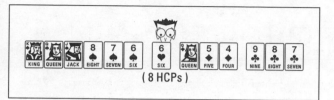

(8 HCPs)

With this hand, you would have opened 2♠, a weak two bid (see Chapter 9 for the details on weak two bids) if you had been allowed to get your blow in first.

However, an opponent may open the bidding before you can bid 2♠. No matter. Bid 2♠ anyway. Jump to 2♠. The jump means bidding at the two level, not bidding 1♠, which you would do with 10 or more HCPs. Notice that bidding 2♣ over the opponent's 1♦ is not a jump overcall because you bid clubs at the lowest legal level. A jump overcall would be to bid 3♣.

A jump overcall, or preemptive jump overcall, implies that you have a limited number of high cards. Jump overcalls make it that much harder for the opponents to find a fit, because you steal bidding space and foul up their constructive bidding. Weak jump overcalls are extremely effective defensive weapons; as usual, the combination of maximum irritation with minimum risk is your goal.

If your hands meet the following conditions, the time is ripe for making a weak jump overcall:

✔ 6 to 9 HCPs

✔ A six-card suit headed by two of the top four honors, three of the top five honors, or the A109, K109, Q109, or J109

If you have more than 9 HCPs, make a simple overcall by bidding the suit at the lowest possible level, without jumping.

You may be getting a sense of déjà vu. The requirements for making a weak jump overcall are exactly the same as they are for opening the bidding with a weak two bid. Think of a weak jump overcall at the two level as a weak two bid.

Check out the hands in Figure 14-4 to get a handle on making weak jump overcalls.

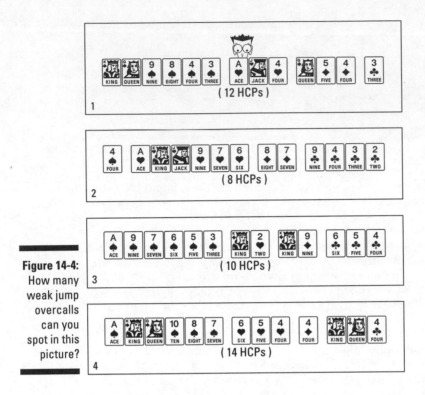

(12 HCPs)

1

(8 HCPs)

2

Figure 14-4:
How many
weak jump
overcalls
can you
spot in this
picture?

(10 HCPs)

3

(14 HCPs)

4

Assume that your right hand opponent (East) opens the bidding with 1♦;
you are South and thus next to speak.

In the first hand in Figure 14-4, you should overcall 1♠ — you're too strong
to make a weak jump overcall. In the second hand, everything is perfect for
a weak jump overcall, so you go for it and bid 2♥. Unfortunately, in the third
hand, you have too many points and your suit is too weak for a weak jump
overcall; in this case, you should overcall 1♠. In the fourth hand, you should
overcall 1♠ because you are way too strong for a weak jump overcall.

Making a three level weak jump overcall

A weak jump overcall at the three level is the equivalent of an opening bid of
three of a suit. Again, your defensive bid robs your opponents of a huge
amount of bidding space — generally good tactics.

In order to make a three level weak jump overcall, you need to have the following bullets in your gun:

- 6 to 9 HCPs
- A seven-card suit headed by the ace or any two honors

Show your opponents no mercy when you have a seven-card suit. Make them suffer. When you make a three level weak jump overcall, you can assume that your opponents will probably get derailed from here on in.

The cards in Figure 14-5 show you some hands where you need to decide whether you can make a weak jump overcall at the three level.

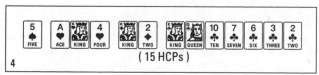
(7 HCPs)

1

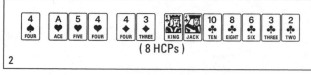
(8 HCPs)

2

Figure 14-5:
Make a
three level
weak jump
overcall
whenever
you can.

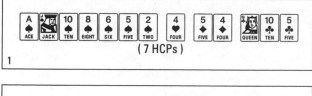
(12 HCPs)

3

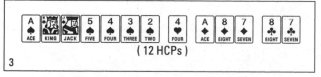
(15 HCPs)

4

For the hands in Figure 14-5, assume the bidding has proceeded as follows:

West	North (Your Partner)	East	South (You)
1♦	Pass	1♥	?

On the first hand in Figure 14-5, all the conditions are right to make a three level overcall — bid 3♠. On the second hand, you can make a three level overcall with 3♣ — stick it to them! In the third hand, you can overcall, but only with 1♠; you can't make a weak jump overcall with every seven-card suit. You may be too strong! You intend to bid again the next time it is your turn. In the fourth hand, overcall 2♣. You are too strong to make a weak jump overcall. You plan to bid again with this hand.

Making a four level overcall

If you hold an eight-card suit in the 6 to 12 HCPs range, make a jump overcall straight to the four level. For example, if you are fortunate enough to have the hand shown in Figure 14-6, bid 4♥ the first time you get a chance to bid.

Figure 14-6:
Thank your lucky stars and go for an overcall at the four level.

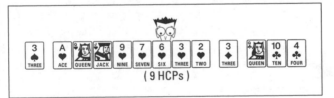

(9 HCPs)

What happens next? You have just jumped to game in the teeth of an opponent's opening bid, and you may find nothing from your partner. Will someone fall off their chair? Will you be doubled and find a heap of garbage coming down in the dummy? Or will the contract roll home with an overtrick or two? Who can say? That is the beauty of a preempt. No one knows how it will work out; but if you make the bid on the right sort of hands, you should come out on top. And if your four level overcall doesn't work, write to me, Alan P. Smith, in care of the publishers.

Respecting a two-over-one response

When the opponents respond two over one, be very careful about making a two level overcall.

When the responder bids two over one, the opponents usually have 24 or more HCPs between them. That leaves the good guys with 16 HCPs, maximum. Face it — you are outgunned. In order to enter the bidding after a two-over-one response, you need a powerful six-card suit, with most of your high-cards in that suit. Your overall strength is less important. You want to have at least two of the top three honors in your suit, if you can, to make the bid. Basically, you make the bid to indicate a good opening lead, as it is unlikely that your side will play the hand.

Say that you're faced with the following bidding sequence:

West	*North (Your Partner)*	*East*	*South (You)*
1♠	Pass	2♦	?

What would you do if you had the cards shown in Figure 14-7?

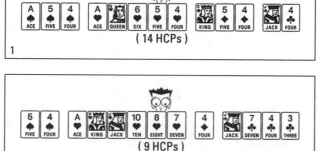

Figure 14-7: Jump back! You have to respect a two-over-one response — it's got power.

With the first hand in Figure 14-7, pass with the speed of summer lightning. Yes, I see your 14 HCPs, but I also see a mangy five-card suit instead of a powerful six-card suit. Also, with this hand, you would be lucky to find your partner with a stray jack or queen because the opponents apparently have at least 24 points between them. You can't take many tricks facing a whole heap of nothing.

Oftentimes your opponents' bidding tells you how strong your partner's hand is! When both opponents bid, add their supposed high card strength to yours and subtract the total from 40, which tells you how strong your partner is. Be prepared to be depressed.

In the second hand in Figure 14-7, bid 2♥. Look at that suit. That is what two level overcalls are all about — strong suits. Not a strong hand, only 9 HCPs, but a great suit; all those high hearts, it warms the heart.

If your two level overcalls are not all that strong in high cards, nobody will call the cops. However, if the suit that you bid isn't a six-card suit dripping with honors cards, even 911 won't be able to save you.

Making a 1NT overcall

When the opponents open the bidding, you may choose to bid a suit, of course. But you can also overcall 1NT. The overcall of 1NT is similar, almost identical, to the opening bid of 1NT. The 1NT overcall shows 15 to 18 HCPs, a balanced hand, plus strength in the suit that has been opened. So you need a pretty good hand to make the bid.

The hand in Figure 14-8 shows you a classic case of when you can overcall 1NT.

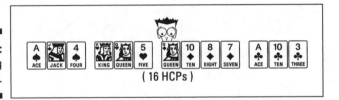

Figure 14-8:
Overcalling
1NT.

(16 HCPs)

No matter which suit your right-hand opponent opens, overcall 1NT. The same applies if the bidding gets around to you in the fourth seat.

Use the following rules to resist the urge to overcall 1NT at inopportune times:

- ✔ Do not overcall 1NT if you have more than 18 HCPs or less than 15 HCPs.
- ✔ Do not overcall 1NT unless you have a balanced hand.
- ✔ Do not overcall 1NT unless you have strength in any suit(s) bid by the opponents.

Responding to Your Partner's Overcall

After an opponent opens the bidding and your partner overcalls, you know that she has at least a five-card suit, whether she overcalls at the one level or two level. The strength of your hand plus the number of cards you hold in your partner's suit dictates your response.

Responding to a one level major suit overcall

If your partner overcalls 1♥ or 1♠, you know that she has at least five cards in her suit. If you have three or more cards in your partner's suit, you have found the Holy Grail.

With three or more cards in your partner's suit

If you have three or more cards in your partner's suit, you have located an eight-card fit. This is no time for secrets; raise your partner's suit!

This advice applies whatever the level of overcall you're responding to — in fact, the higher the level of the overcall, the faster you should raise!

You can respond to your partner's one level overcall according to the following scale:

- **7 to 10 combined SPs and HCPs:** Raise to the two level
- **11 to 14 combined SPs and HCPs:** Raise to the three level
- **15 or more combined SPs and HCPs:** Jump to game

After you locate an eight-card fit, you get to add points, called support points, for shortness in the side-suits (the non-trump suit). Add 1 point for every doubleton (two-card suit), 2 points for a singleton (one-card suit), and 3 points for a void (no cards in the suit).

Say that the bidding goes like this:

West	North (Your Partner)	East	South (You)
1♦	1♥	Pass	?

The cards in Figure 14-9 give you a chance to respond to this one level overcall with a variety of hands.

In the first hand, raise to 2♥. You have eight support points, giving yourself one extra for the doubleton club. Do not bid 1♠. You already have an eight-card major suit fit; be content.

When your partner overcalls in a major suit and you bid another suit, you deny three or more cards in your partner's major suit.

In the second hand in Figure 14-9, jump to 3♥. Your hand has sprouted to 13 points because you add three points for that singleton diamond because you have four-card support. (See "With 6 to 12 HCPs and real support for partner (adding support points)" in Chapter 10 for more information on adding support points.) The rest is up to your partner — he can pass or bid game depending on what he has.

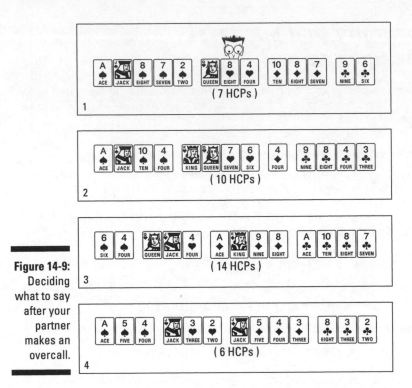

Figure 14-9:
Deciding what to say after your partner makes an overcall.

In the third hand, jump all the way to 4♥. You have 15 support points facing at least 10 HCPs in your partner's hand, putting you in the game zone (partner has a minimum of 10 HCPs for the overcall). The player who knows what to do should take the pressure off their partner.

On the fourth hand, you have to pass. You only have 6 support points, not to mention that your hand is also of the hated "flat as a pancake" variety, with the dreaded 4-3-3-3 shape. The disadvantage of this shape is that your partner can't trump anything in your hand because you have no short side suit. Don't punish your partner by raising to the two level with this piece of unmitigated junk.

With fewer than three cards in your partner's suit

When your partner overcalls and you have fewer than three cards in his suit, you know you can't support your partner. However if you have enough points to bid, you may feel like introducing a decent (headed by two or more honor cards) five- or six-card suit of your own. All you need is

✔ Eight or more points
✔ A decent five-card suit

If you have 8 to 12 HCPs, bid your suit at the lowest level possible; with 13 to 16 HCPs, jump the bidding in your own suit. A jump response (bidding your suit at one level higher than you need to) to a one level overcall is a highly invitational bid; your partner can pass only with a minimum hand.

Take a look at the following bidding sequence, where you find yourself responding to your partner's 1♥ overcall:

West	*North (Your Partner)*	*East*	*South (You)*
1♦	1♥	Pass	?

See what you would do to respond in each of the hands shown in Figure 14-10.

In the first hand, bid a peaceful 1♠. Your partner will know you have five decent spades, fewer than three hearts, plus 8 to 12 HCPs. Your partner can pass your 1♠ bid if she wishes.

On the second hand, jump to 2♠. A jump response to your partner's one level overcall typically shows a strong six-card suit with 13 to 16 HCPs. Just what you have! Your bid is highly invitational, meaning that your partner can pass with a really minimum hand and no support for your spades.

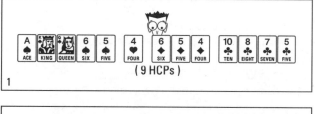

(9 HCPs)

1

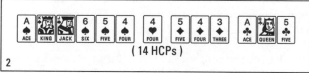

(14 HCPs)

2

Figure 14-10:
You have fewer than three cards in your partner's overcalled suit.

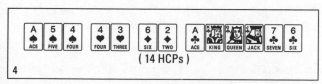

(9 HCPs)

3

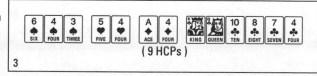

(14 HCPs)

4

On the third hand, bid 2♣. Bidding a new suit at the two level shows a six-card suit, again showing a moderate hand of 8 to 12 points. It is non-forcing (your partner can pass); your partner will bid with extra values for his overcall or for any other good reason.

On the fourth hand, jump to 3♣, an invitational bid. You want to show your partner you have the values for an opening bid plus a strong six-card suit. You just did.

Branching into notrump

When your partner overcalls at the one level, your hand may lack three-card support or a long suit, which suggests a balanced hand. If you have honor cards in the opponent's suit you can branch off into notrump according to the following scale:

- ✔ **9 to 12 HCPs:** Bid 1NT

- ✔ **13 to 15 HCPs:** Bid 2NT

- ✔ **16 or more HCPs:** Bid 3NT

When evaluating your hand, subtract one point if you have a singleton in your partner's overcalled suit. On the other hand, you can add a point to your hand if you have the queen or the king in your partner's suit.

Check your notrump responses to the one level overcall, shown in Figure 14-11. Assume that the bidding progresses as follows:

West	North (Your Partner)	East	South (You)
1♥	1♠	Pass	?

On the first hand in Figure 14-11, bid a quiet 1NT. You have the points and the strength in the opponent's suit, hearts.

Any notrump bid after the opponents have bid promises strength in their suit(s). You do not promise strength in the unbid suits (notice your clubs).

On the second hand, you can cough up a 2NT response, showing 13 to 15 HCPs. The bid is invitational. Your partner can pass if the hands don't add up to 25 HCPs.

On the third hand, don't fool around, bid a direct 3NT. Your partner should have at least 10 HCPs, bringing the total to 25 HCPs (the magic number for bidding game). Did you remember to give yourself an extra point for the ♠K?

With the fourth hand in Figure 14-11, get out while the getting is good. Pass. You do not have enough to bid. Did you remember to subtract one point for the small singleton in your partner's suit?

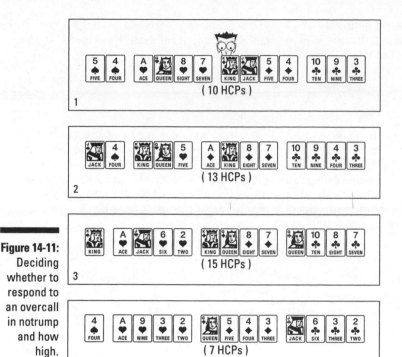

Figure 14-11:
Deciding
whether to
respond to
an overcall
in notrump
and how
high.

The best rule in all of bridge is this: When you don't have enough to bid, pass.

Responding to a two level overcall

Two level overcalls show the strength of an opening bid, typically with six-card suits. If your partner makes an overcall of 2♣ or 2♦, and you have strength in the opponent's suit, think about the possibility of playing in notrump. If you have a decent holding in the opponent's suit and a balanced hand, respond in notrump according to the following scale:

- ✔ **10 to 12 HCPs:** Bid 2NT
- ✔ **13 to 16 HCPs:** Bid 3NT

Of course, you have other options; you may have a strong five- or six-card heart or spade (major) suit you wish to show or, perhaps, raise your partner's suit to the three level, if you have 7 to 10 support points plus three-card support.

The cards in Figure 14-12 give you a chance to test your sea legs when responding to a two level overcall. For each of the hands in Figure 30-4, assume that the bidding has gone like this:

West	North (Your Partner)	East	South (You)
1♠	2♦	Pass	?

On the first hand, trot out 2NT; you have high cards in spades to control the opponent's suit, and you have enough points for this bid. On the second hand, try 2♥, a strong five-card suit. Maybe your partner has heart support. You'll never know unless you bid the suit. On the third hand, leap to 3NT. Clubs are for peasants. When you have a choice of bidding notrump or bidding a minor suit (clubs or diamonds), notrump prevails. On the fourth hand, raise to 3♦, a typical raise.

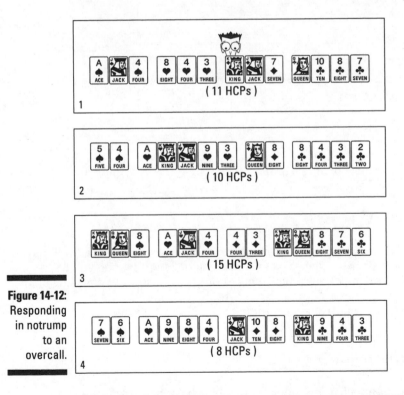

Figure 14-12: Responding in notrump to an overcall.

Responding to weak jump overcalls

Respond to weak jump overcalls exactly as you do to a weak two bid. See "Responding to a weak two opening bid" in Chapter 9 for more information.

Responding to a 1NT overcall

"The system is on," meaning that you respond to a 1NT overcall exactly as you do to a 1NT opening bid, which I discuss in "Responding to a 1NT Opening Bid" in Chapter 10. In other words, you can still use the Stayman and the Jacoby transfer responses.

Taking a Chance on a Takeout Double

What in the world do you do if you have tons of HCPs but no one long suit? You have an out with these hands — fasten your seat belt (it's going to be a bumpy ride!) and say "Double!"

You may think that you only double when you don't think that the opponents can make their contract (see Chapter 13 for more information on the penalty double). However, far more often you use that one word "double" to show your partner that you have an opening bid (12 or more HCPs), along with three- or four-card support for each of the unbid suits. This double, called a *takeout double,* is usually made directly after your right hand opponent opens the bidding. The takeout double is far and away the most powerful and flexible weapon in your entire armory of defensive bids because it gives you a way to describe strong hands with no long suit.

A takeout double forces your partner to bid — no excuses — if the next player passes. You use the takeout double to avoid guessing which of your two or three four-card suits to bid; the takeout double essentially allows you to bid all your suits at once.

Knowing when to make a takeout double

How do you know when to make a takeout double? Consider making a takeout double when your hand looks like this:

- 12 or more HCPs — no upper limit — you could have 20 HCPs

- Shortness (void, singleton, or doubleton) in the suit that your opponent has bid

- Three or four cards in each of the unbid suits

- Your distribution will usually be 4-4-3-2 or 4-4-4-1, but it can also be 5-4-3-1 or 5-4-4-0, the opponents having opened the bidding in your short suit

Making a takeout double after an opening bid

Figure 14-13 gives you a look at the most common takeout double sequence of all, the double of an opening bid.

Figure 14-13:
Making a
takeout
double after
an opening
bid.

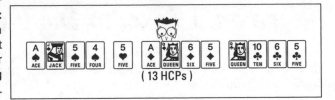

(13 HCPs)

The following bidding has taken place for this hand:

East	South (You)
1♥	Double

Figure 14-13 shows the ideal distribution for a takeout double; a singleton in the opponent's suit, an opening bid of your own, plus four-card support for each of the unbid suits. Now, assuming the next hand passes, your partner must bid, regardless of strength, and you find your fit; it works like a charm.

Making a takeout double after each opponent bids

Takeout doubles can also be made after each opponent bids a different suit. You would consider making a takeout double if you wish to show length in the two unbid suits. Figure 14-14 gives you a look at such a takeout double.

Figure 14-14:
Doubling to
show both
unbid suits.

The bidding for this hand progresses as follows:

West	North (Your Partner)	East	South (You)
1♦	Pass	1♠	Double

This time your double says that you have an opening bid with at least four-card support for each of the two unbid suits, clubs and hearts. Your double asks your partner for a choice of trump suits. It's as if you bid both suits at once!

Making a takeout double after you pass

If you pass originally, you can't have an opening bid, but you can still make a takeout double. If you make a takeout double after you pass, you show 10 to 11 HCPs with shortness in the opponent's suit. Figure 14-15 shows you a hand where you can make a takeout double after you pass.

Figure 14-15:
Passing and then coming to life.

The bidding for this hand takes this interesting turn:

South (You)	West	North (Your Partner)	East
Pass	Pass	Pass	1♣
Double			

Perfect! You have support for any suit that your partner cares to bid. Even though you passed originally, this hand has big trick-taking potential for any suit that your partner bids. Your hand will make a great dummy.

Notice you would not be able to make a takeout double in Figure 14-15 if your opponent had opened the bidding in another suit; takeout doubles work best when your opponent opens the bidding in your short suit.

Responding to a takeout double after the right hand opponent passes

When your partner makes a takeout double and the next player passes, your partner expects you to respond even though you may, and often will, have a very weak hand. Whatever you do, don't pass. You can't be too weak to respond to a takeout double.

Because you must answer a takeout double if the next hand passes, how will your partner know whether you are broke (and just coughed up a response because you were afraid your partner would ax you if you didn't), or if you really have a few goodies?

When your partner makes a takeout double and the next hand passes, use the following responses to tell your partner what you want her to know about your hand:

✔ **With 0 to 8 HCPs:** Bid your longest suit. Your partner assumes that you have about 4 or 5 HCPs when you make a minimum response, but you could have zero HCPs!

✔ **With 9 to 11 HCPs:** Jump the bidding one level in your longest suit. This lets your partner know that you aren't broke.

✔ **With 12 or more HCPs:** You may be so thrilled to have an opening bid of your own facing a takeout double that you almost have to control yourself from cheering out loud. Instead, you should leap to some game contract, usually with a five-card suit or longer.

With 12 or more HCPs, you have an additional option. Are you ready for this? You bid the opponent's suit! You read right. When you bid the opponent's suit, called a *cue bid,* you have a whale of a hand and you want to tell your partner there is game (or slam) in the hand. Your cue bid forces your partner to further describe her hand and buys time to arrive at the best contract. After you make your first cue bid, you know that you have arrived.

Figure 14-16 gives you a chance to practice your responses to a takeout double.

The bidding has gone as follows:

West	North (Your Partner)	East	South (You)
1♠	Double	Pass	?

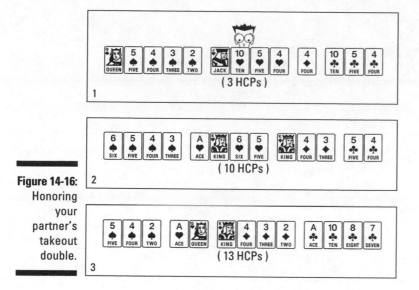

Figure 14-16:
Honoring
your
partner's
takeout
double.

On the first hand, respond ♥2. Just do it! On the second hand, jump to ♥3 to show 9 to 11 HCPs. On the third hand, respond ♠2, a cue bid, showing 12 or more HCPs, which tells your partner that the sky's the limit and to please bid!

Responding to a takeout double when you have strength in the opponent's suit

You may have strength in the opponent's suit. When you do, responding 1NT, 2NT, or 3NT can accurately describe your hand. You don't have to worry about having strength in the other suits; your partner has promised strength in those suits with her takeout double.

When you have strength in the opponent's suit, respond in notrump to your partner's takeout double according to this scale:

- **With 6 to 9 HCPs:** Respond 1NT
- **With 10 to 12 HCPs:** Respond 2NT
- **With 13 to 16 HCPs:** Respond 3NT

Figure 14-17 shows you how to handle responding hands to a takeout double when you have strength in the opponent's suit.

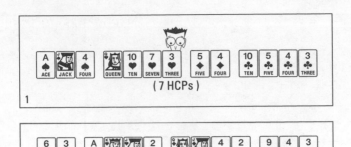

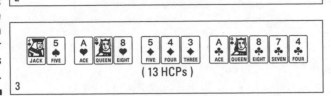

Figure 14-17:
You have
strength
in your
opponent's
suit.

Pretend that the bidding has gone as follows:

West	North (Your Partner)	East	South (You)
1♥	Double	Pass	?

With the first hand, respond 1NT, which is more descriptive than 2♣. With the second hand, respond 2NT, better than responding 3♦. (Remember, you have to jump the bidding in your suit when you have between 9 and 11 HCPs.) With the third hand, leap to 3NT in preference to showing your clubs. Besides, the minor suits are for peasants when you can safely bid notrump instead — just think about the scoring. It only takes 9 tricks to make game in notrump, but it takes 11 tricks to make game in either clubs or diamonds. Who doesn't like shortcuts?

Responding to a takeout double after your right hand opponent bids

When your partner makes a takeout and the next hand bids, you no longer have to bid; you know that your partner will get another chance to bid, and if she has a strong hand, she will bid again. (Remember that the bidding doesn't end until three players in a row pass.) You are off the hook!

Nevertheless, if you have 5 or more HCPs outside of the opponent's suit, plus a four- or five-card unbid suit, by all means let your voice be heard. In other words, bid your suit at the one or two level! Figure 14-18 shows you that courage is what the game is about.

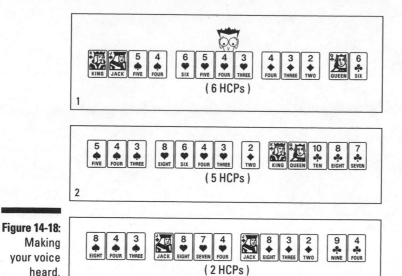

Figure 14-18: Making your voice heard.

The bidding has gone as follows:

West	North (Your Partner)	East	South (You)
1♦	Double	1♥	?

In the first hand, you have enough to bid 1♠. In the second hand, you have just barely enough to bid 2♣. In the third hand, pass and thank East for taking you off the hook.

Chapter 15

Slam Bidding

• •

In This Chapter

▶ Slam bidding at a notrump contract

▶ Slam bidding at a trump contract

▶ Asking for aces — the Blackwood Convention

• •

*O*nce in while, you and your partner have so much strength between your two hands that you can try for a small slam, which means bidding all the way to the six level. In this chapter, I show you what you need to know to climb to such heights.

Getting to Know Your Slams

"What is a slam?" you may justifiably ask. "First Kantar has me trying to get to game, and now he wants me to bid even higher?" Calm yourself; a *slam* comes in two varieties, small and grand. A small slam involves bidding and taking 12 of the 13 tricks, and therefore involves bidding to a six level contract. A grand slam requires you to successfully contract for all 13 tricks, a seven level contract. Grand slams are exciting . . . and scary.

Ninety-five percent of all the slam contracts you bid will be small slams (six level contracts). Bidding a grand slam means going for all 13 tricks, so you really have to have a lot of confidence that you and your partner have the World's Fair between you before you attempt one.

When you bid a small slam, you have a little breathing room. You can afford to lose a trick. Besides, it's such a downer to bid a grand slam and take 12 tricks — you score nothing and the opponents score points! Had you bid for 12 tricks, you would have scored in the neighborhood of 1,000 points. (See Chapter 16 for more information on scoring.)

Slam bidding falls into two groups: notrump slams and suit slams. I give you a look at both types in this chapter.

Bidding Notrump Slams

You need two main ingredients to bid all the way up to 6NT (to make a small slam).

✔ A balanced hand facing a balanced hand

✔ 33 HCPs between the two hands

Wouldn't you like to see a hand where you have the power to make a small slam at notrump? Look no further than Figure 15-1.

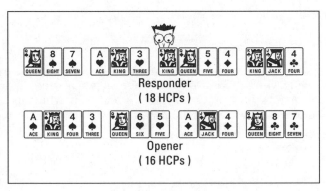

Figure 15-1:
You can take these cards all the way to a slam.

Responder
(18 HCPs)

Opener
(16 HCPs)

With your eyes on a small slam, the bidding would go as follows:

Opener	Responder
1NT	6NT

The responder can't always get such a quick, complete fix on her partner's values, but in this case, the responder sees enough points between the two hands to go for the gold at an early juncture. The responder has 18 HCPs. The responder knows that the opener has 15 to 17 HCPs plus a balanced hand because she opened with 1NT. Therefore, the two hands add up to at least 33 combined points without a shadow of a doubt.

Five- and six-card suits headed by honors increase in value facing a balanced hand. See Chapter 10 for more on responding to 1NT with long, strong suits.

An old bridge-playing sage once said, "The one who knows, goes." As soon as you have gathered enough information from the bidding to know that you have at least 33 HCPs between your hands, and both hands are reasonably balanced, don't waste any time in bidding 6NT. Do not beat around the bush when you know that you have 33 HCPs between the two hands. Just bid it. Practice saying "6NT" in front of a mirror if you think you will freak out by jumping all the way from the one level to the six level.

After you bid 6NT, you don't have to worry about further bidding; you are the captain because your partner made the first limit bid, 1NT. You make the decisions and your partner obeys.

Sometimes, the opener becomes the captain because the responder limits her hand first. Take the cards in Figure 15-2 as an example, where you are the opener, and your partner's response shows a limited number of HCPs.

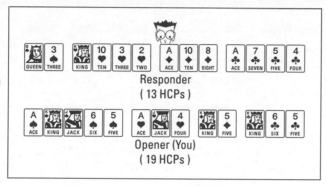

Figure 15-2: Opener knows and goes for the slam.

The bidding for this hand could go all the way to a slam, as in the following sequence:

Opener (You)	Responder
1♠	2NT (13 to 15 HCPs)
6NT	Pass

First things first. The opener is the captain because the responder has made a limit bid, 2NT, which signals 13 to 15 HCPs. Second, the opener adds two extra points for the strong five-card spade suit, because the opener knows that the responder has a balanced hand.

The opener's hand is now worth 21 points. With a count of 21 facing a minimum of 13 HCPs, the opener knows that the magic 33 HCP exists and bids 6NT.

Sometimes, the captain (who can be either the opener or the responder) can't be sure if there are 33 HCPS between the two hands. Rather than guess, the captain invites a slam by bidding 4NT, as she can with the hand shown in Figure 15-3.

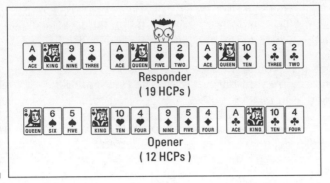

Figure 15-3:
Feeling
out the
possibility
of a slam.

The responder invites a slam in the following bidding sequence:

Opener	Responder
1♣	1♥
1NT	4NT
Pass	

The opener has a balanced hand with just 12 HCPs, but she scrapes the bottom of the barrel and comes up with a 1♣ opening bid. The responder, with 19 HCPs, has visions of a slam; but first she looks for an eight-card fit. An eight-card fit may make life easier.

If you have an eight-card fit (or longer), you don't need 33 HCPs between the two hands to make a slam. You can often make a slam with two or three points less.

Therefore, the responder responds 1♥ in Figure 15-3, the lower ranking of her two four-card suits, giving the opener a chance to raise hearts or rebid 1♠, bringing either fit to light.

The 1♥ response is unlimited; it shows 6 or more points with no upper limit, so the opener must bid again.

When the opener rebids 1NT (showing 12 to 14 HCPs), she shows a balanced hand and denies holding four spades or four hearts. Now the responder knows that no eight-card major suit fit is hiding in this hand. Nevertheless, with 19 HCPs, there could be a slam if the partner has a maximum of 14 points. The responder invites a slam by bidding 4NT. The responder declines the invitation.

When the previous bid is 1NT, 2NT, or 3NT, a bid of 4NT is an *invitational bid*. It asks the partner to bid 6NT with a maximum, but to please pass with a minimum. The meaning of 4NT is different in some other cases. I bet you're thrilled to hear that.

When your partner invites you to a slam by responding 4NT after you open with 1NT, make your rebid according to the following scale:

- **With 15 HCPs:** Pass.

- **With 17 HCPs:** Bid 6NT.

- **With 16 HCPs:** Make an educated guess; bid if you have anything positive. Otherwise pass.

Bidding Slams at a Trump Contract

When you bid a slam at notrump, you do it with power. You overwhelm your opponents with aces, kings, queens, and jacks. When you bid a slam at a suit contract, whether it be a small slam or a grand slam, you do it with a little finesse. You don't need quite so many HCPs. What you do need is a good trump fit plus a different short suit in each hand.

Here's a list of what you need to bid a slam at a trump contract:

- **A strong combined trump suit:** If you have any doubts about bidding a slam, particularly because of a mangy trump suit, sack the whole idea and play the hand in game.

- **31 or more reevaluated points between the two hands:** Both hands reevaluate after an eight-card fit or better has been found. Don't even think about bidding a slam unless you have a good trump fit and the two hands total at least 31 points after reevaluation.

- **At least three of the four aces between you:** Any ace can be missing.

- **No two immediate losers in any one suit:** I don't want your opponents rattling off the ace and king of any suit, defeating your contract!

Say that your partnership gets the hands shown in Figure 15-4. I know that you can't see your partner's hands while you're actually bidding — I just want you to see the building blocks that go into making a slam at a suit contract.

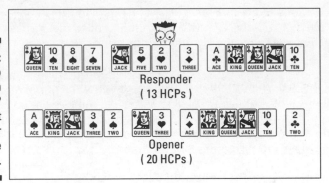

Figure 15-4:
Can you go
for a slam
or not?
Better put
on your
protective
helmet.

Go over the checklist and see if you have the power you need between the two hands to make 6♠:

✔ Strong combined trump suit? — Yes, in spades.

✔ 31 or more reevaluated points? — Yes, you have 33 points before reevaluation.

✔ At least three aces between the two hands? — Yes.

✔ Two immediate losers in any suit? Yes — and that's the wrong answer if you want to bid and make a slam. Look at the hearts in each hand. You don't have the ace or the king, which means that the bad guys have them.

You don't want to be in a slam contract with these two hands.

Reevaluating

When you find a good trump fit, both hands reevaluate their points, adding on support points for short suits, slam or no slam.

You may start with 25 to 26 HCPs between the two hands, but after reevaluation, you may cross into the 30 to 33 HCP zone. You may have a slam staring you in the face — if the hand passes the checklist test. So be awake; when you find your fit, start the reevaluation. A quiet game hand can tear off its shirt, and beneath its mild-mannered exterior be . . . a slam.

After you discover a fit, the wilder the distribution of the two hands, the better. If both hands are balanced, more losers have to be taken care of and you tack on fewer support points.

Solving the ace problem (the Blackwood Convention)

It's just too embarrassing to bid a slam only to find the opponents take the first two tricks with aces. That should not happen. There should be a way to find out if your partner has any missing aces that you need to complete your slam checklist. Of course, if they take two aces against a game contract, you do not mind too much, do you? You can afford to lose three tricks in a contract of 4♥ for example — but not in 6♥!

Consider the hands shown in Figure 15-5.

For each of the hands in Figure 15-5, the bidding has gone as follows:

Opener (You)	Responder (Your Partner)
1♠	3♠ (9 to 11 support points)

You are the opener, and your partner may have each of the three responding hands. On each hand your partner makes the same response of 3♠. Are you in the slam zone? You know that your partner has about 10 SPs, but what about you? You have 17 HCPs plus two singletons each worth two points. Your hand is worth about 21 points. More important, just look at your hand. What tricks can you possibly lose? Certainly you have no spade losers with 10 spades between the two hands, including the ♠A and ♠K. Certainly you have no diamond losers. The only possible losers you can have are one in hearts and one in clubs.

However, if your partner has the ace in either of those suits, you only have one loser. If your partner has the ace in both of those suits, you have no losers. If your partner has neither ace you have two losers. You must find out how many aces your partner has in order to know if you can make a slam or not! It would be nice to say: "Hey, partner, how many aces do you have — that's all I need to know." But unfortunately, the rules of the game forbid such direct questions. Would you believe it — bridge offers a very popular bidding convention that allows you to ask that burning question about missing aces, legally.

A bid of 4NT (as long as the previous bid is not 1NT, 2NT, or 3NT) asks your partner how many aces she has. This handy little convention is called the *Blackwood Convention,* after Easley Blackwood of Indianapolis, Indiana. Way back in 1933, Blackwood had a hand where he wanted to know how many aces his partner had. So he invented a bid of 4NT, called it the *Blackwood Convention,* and turned himself into a legend. With this simple bid, he invented the most beloved convention of all time.

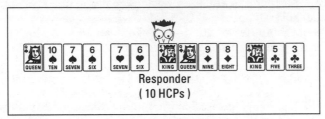

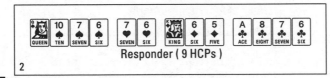

Figure 15-5:
Who's got
the missing
aces?

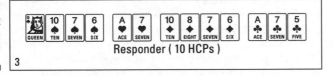

When you play the Blackwood Convention, you use the following responses
to 4NT to tell your partner how many aces you have:

- **5♣:** 0 or all 4 aces

- **5♦:** 1 ace

- **5♥:** 2 aces

- **5♠:** 3 aces

If your response to 4NT is 5♣ and your partner can't tell from your previous
bidding whether you have zero or all four aces, change partners — quickly!

The following bidding sequence shows you how the Blackwood Convention
would play out in the first hand in Figure 15-5:

Opener (You)	Responder (Your Partner)
1♠	3♠
4NT	5♣
5♠	Pass

Blackwood is a great convention for staying out of slams if you are missing two aces. On this hand, you have to give up on the slam because your partner's bid of 5♣ tells you that you're missing two aces.

In the second hand in Figure 15-5, the bidding would go like this:

Opener (You)	Responder (Your Partner)
1♠	3♠
4NT	5♦
6♠	Pass

In this hand, your partner's use of the Blackwood Convention shows one ace, so you can bid 6♠ and successfully contract for slam. Well done!

In the third hand in Figure 15-5, the bidding progresses as follows:

Opener (You)	Responder (Your Partner)
1♠	3♠
4NT	5♥
7♠	Pass

Your partner has two aces and responds 5♥. Bingo. You bid 7♠ because you don't have any losers. As easy as pie!

Just because you have all the aces doesn't mean that you can take all of the tricks. You have to be able to count 13 tricks before you bid a grand slam. Blackwood should carry a government health warning, really — aces on their own are not enough to ensure a slam.

Asking for kings

After you ask for aces and you find you have all four, you may suddenly be thinking about a grand slam! But first you may need to check on the number of kings your partner holds. Not to worry, Easley Blackwood has thought of everything. If the Blackwood bidder follows up a 4NT ace-ask with 5NT, he promises his partner all four aces and asks his partner for kings. If you have your eyes on a grand slam, you may also need to locate any missing kings.

You can bid 5NT after bidding 4NT to ask for kings. The responses are the same as for aces:

Use the following responses to tell your partner about your kings after she bids 5NT:

- **6♣:** 0 or all 4 kings
- **6♦:** 1 king
- **6♥:** 2 kings
- **6♠:** 3 kings

Take a look at the hands in Figure 15-6 to see the Blackwood Convention for kings in action.

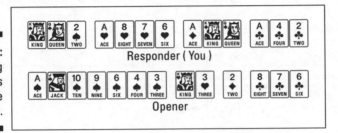

Figure 15-6: Casting your nets for some kings.

The bidding for this hand could proceed as follows:

Opener	Responder (You)
3♠	4NT
5♦	5NT
6♦	7NT
Pass	

The responder uses the Blackwood Convention and finds one ace and one king in the opener's hand. Armed with this information, the responder (you) can actually count 13 tricks:

- **Spades:** Seven tricks (your partner shows a seven-card suit for the 3♠ opening bid)
- **Hearts:** One trick — your ♥A
- **Diamonds:** Three tricks — your ♦AKQ
- **Clubs:** One trick — your ♣A
- **King:** One trick — your partner has either the ♥K or the ♣K

Add 'em up — your total number of tricks comes to 13!

Chapter 16

Keeping Score

Can you imagine playing a game without knowing how to keep score? You wouldn't know who was winning, how many points you needed to win, or when to stop playing.

Bridge is no different. You can't bid, play, or defend intelligently unless you know how to keep score. You need to know how high to bid and how many tricks you need to take to have a chance at winning. Read this chapter to discover everything you need to know about this important aspect of the game.

Achieving the Ultimate Goal

During the bidding, you hope to end up in a reasonable contract that you can make. If you make your contract, you score points towards *making game;* to make game, you need to score 100 points. The first team to score game twice wins the *rubber.* You get a big bonus for winning the rubber, so you may often take risks and shoot for game — even if there is only a 50 percent chance for success.

In bridge, whichever side wins the rubber does not necessarily win the match. If you play tennis, think of the relationship of sets and matches — whoever wins six games first wins the set, but not the match.

After a rubber is over and tallied, a new rubber begins; you can keep playing until someone falls asleep at the table, or to a specified time, or even to a specified number of rubbers. You don't have a limit — you play to whatever both parties agree. Assuming that you keep playing with the same partner, after the final rubber is scored, you know which team is the winner. If you change partners after each rubber, you should keep individual scores after each rubber.

I've seen people play all day and all night, but normally about three hours at a stretch is my limit; after that I lose a little focus.

Making Your Contract

Bridge scoring revolves around the final contract (as determined by the bidding) and the number of tricks actually taken by the side buying the contract.

If your final contract is 3♣, your goal is to win at least nine tricks and clubs are trump, the "wild" suit. If you take exactly nine tricks, you make your contract. If you take ten tricks, you have made your contract plus an extra trick, called an *overtrick*. In bridge, as the side buying the contract, you score points only if you make your contract or if you make your contract with overtrick(s). Overtricks score points for your side but don't contribute to winning the rubber.

To calculate the number of tricks you need to take to fulfill your final contract, add six to the number, or level, of the bid. For example, if your final contract is 5♠, you need to take 11 tricks to make your contract (5 + 6 = 11).

If you do not make your contract, the bad guys (the opponents) rack up penalty points and your side gets *nada* for your efforts. For example, if you take eight tricks in your contract of 3♣, you would be one trick short of making your contract (and concede one *undertrick*); your opponents would get to add points to their score.

Your goal on every hand is to make your contract; overtricks are icing on the cake, and undertricks are something you want to avoid.

Charting Your Points

Remember in grade school when your teacher gave you those awful multiplication problems? Did you find it easier to use a multiplication table rather then calculate things in your head? If so, the following table is for you. Just look up your score in Table 16-1 instead of fooling with a bunch of math every time you need to keep score.

Table 16-1 shows you how many points you score if you make your contract. If you don't make your contract, you don't have to worry about this table. If you don't make your contract, you don't score any points — your opponents do (see "Not Making Your Contract: Penalties" later in this chapter for more information about how to score when you don't make your contract)!

Your score for making your contract depends upon which suit your final contract is in and how many tricks you take.

Table 16-1			Charting Your Score				
Tricks Taken	*7*	*8*	*9*	*10*	*11*	*12*	*13*
Notrump	40	70	100	130	160	190	220
Spades	30	60	90	120	150	180	210
Hearts	30	60	90	120	150	180	210
Diamonds	20	40	60	80	100	120	140
Clubs	20	40	60	80	100	120	140

Eventually, you may want to keep score without having to carry this book around. In preparation for that wonderful day, you can use the following rules to calculate your score mentally. In addition, if you score any overtricks, you need to know how much each trick is worth in order to calculate how many points you earn in overtricks.

Keep in mind that the first six tricks (the six tricks you automatically add to your bid) don't count in the scoring:

✔ Each trick in hearts or spades is worth 30 points.

✔ Each trick in clubs or diamonds is worth 20 points.

✔ The first trick in notrump is worth 40 points, but each subsequent trick is worth 30 points.

Just use Table 16-1 for now to score the points you win for making your contract. When you first start to play bridge, you should concentrate on the game and how to play it, rather than fiddling with a bunch of math that's already been done for you!

Drawing Lines: Scoring a Rubber

Scoring in bridge is a cumulative process that takes in several factors. In this section, I discuss what contributes to your score and how to score these elements when you play an actual rubber. I walk you through the scoring of a rubber just to show you how the whole process comes together.

When scoring a rubber, think of you and your partner as "We" and the opponents as "They." Everyone uses this standard notation for scoring at bridge. Normally, everyone keeps a score of the rubber in front of them so that they can see how the rubber is progressing and how many points they need to make game. You can keep score on just about anything, but bridge score-pads are easily available if you can't be bothered to draw a few lines on a piece of paper for yourself.

The whole process starts by drawing a line, so that your score pad looks like the one shown in Figure 16-1.

We	They

Figure 16-1: Drawing a line on your score pad.

Do you see that horizontal line? The line isn't exactly sacred, but it is important. Beneath the line goes your score toward game (the 100 scoring points you are after); above the line go your overtricks, the penalty points you pick up when your opponents don't make their contract, and various bonuses you can pick up, such as for winning the rubber. Of course, your opponents get all those points above and below the line on their side if they defeat your contract, make their contract(s), and win the rubber. Fair is fair.

Compared to what goes on beneath the line, what goes on above the line is child's play. Looking beneath the line tells you where the real action is.

Starting the rubber

When either side makes a contract, the *trick score* for the bid goes under the line; the score for any overtricks goes above the line.

For example, on the first hand of this sample rubber, you and your partner arrive at a contract of 2♠ and take ten tricks. You have made your contract plus two extra tricks or overtricks. In order to make 2♠, you needed to take eight tricks, but by sheer brilliancy on your part, you took ten tricks. Drum roll, if you please. You enter your points so that your score pad looks like the one shown in Figure 16-2.

Of course, if your opponents had been the pair who had bid and made 2♠ with two overtricks, you would enter that pair of 60s on the They side of the score sheet instead.

Figure 16-2:
Entering
trick
scores and
overtricks
for the first
rubber.

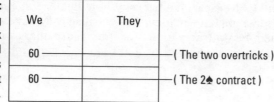

We	They
60 ——————	(The two overtricks)
60 ——————	(The 2♠ contract)

Assessing the situation

You need to score 100 points under the line to *make game*. When you begin the rubber, you have nothing under the line, so at the start, you need 100 points. But if you bid and make a contract for less than game, such as 2♠, you have a *partscore* or a *partial*. In this case, you have a partial of 60 points under the line, so you need 40 more points to reach your goal of 100 and make game.

The number of points that you score under the line dictates how high you need to bid (how many more points you need) in order to make a game. Conversely, you need to track your opponents' position as well to know what contract would be game for them, if they make it, of course.

For example, if you score 60 points below the line on the first hand, you need 40 more points for game. Referring to Table 16-1, you see that you can get 40 points by bidding 1NT, 2♣, 2♦, 2♥, or 2♠. In other words, you don't have to risk bidding higher because you only need 40 points to complete your partial and make game.

Your opponents, on the other hand, look at your partscore and try not to let you buy the contract too cheaply. In order to prevent you from making game, your opponents try to make you bid higher than you want to bid by making risky interference bids (see Chapter 14 for more on defensive bidding). They may try to force you up a level or two into a riskier contract.

Losing your beloved partscore

During the play of a rubber, partscores count toward making game. However, after a partnership makes game, the other partnership loses their partscore if they have one. If you lose your partscore, you have to start all over toward making game!

For example, in the sample rubber, pretend that on the second hand, your opponents bid 4♠ and take exactly ten tricks. When you look at Table 16-1, you see that your opponents have made game because they have scored 120 points for making their 4♠ contract. You enter their score under the They column and draw a line across the pad so that the score pad looks like the one shown in Figure 16-3.

Figure 16-3:
Making game, drawing a new line, and losing your partscore.

We	They
60	
60	120

On the first hand, you bid 2♠ and took ten tricks, giving you a 60 partscore toward game. On the second hand, they bid 4♠, took the same ten tricks, and made game. Remember, the points you win for making your bid go under the line, and extra tricks go above the line. They took the greater risk by contracting for game, ten tricks, so your opponents achieved a greater reward; they have bid and made a game contract. And what about your 60 partscore? Do you know what "history" means? Your 60 has just become history. You will get those 60 points later when the rubber is scored up, but for now, under the new bottom line, you have zilch. You have to start all over again for those 100 points you need to make game. Your opponents have killed your partial and are in the driver's seat. You need to bid and make two games to win the rubber; they only need to bid and make one more game to win the rubber.

Perhaps you are sorry now that you didn't bid 4♠ on the first hand, so that you could have made game. You will find it counterproductive to worry about what could have or should have been bid. Play to the future. The past is history. The top players have the exceptional quality of shrugging off both their own and their partners' mistakes and not worrying about them. (Yes, even the best players in the world make mistakes.) Mistakes can eat you up alive if you insist on dwelling upon them.

Drawing a new line

After either side scores 100 or more points beneath the first line, you draw a new line indicating that a game has been bid and made. Now both sides have to start all over again to score 100 points because neither side has any points under the new bottom line.

The goal is to bid and make two game contracts. So even though your opponents may be ahead in the race, it doesn't mean they have crossed the finish line. You must retain your fighting spirit.

Scoring bonus points for honors

If a hand is played at notrump and any one player (either the declarer, the dummy, or the defender) has all four aces, that team gets a bonus of 150 points above the line. If a hand is played at a suit contract and any one player has four of the top five trump honors (AKQJ, KQJ10, AQJ10, AKJ10), that team gets 100 points above the line. If any one player has all five trump honors (AKQJ10), that is worth a 150-point bonus above the line. I emphasize that these bonuses go above the line; they do not help you win the rubber. In a sense, these bonuses reward you solely for the luck of being dealt particular cards.

Declare the bonus points for honors only at the end of the hand, before the next hand begins. Don't declare them during the play of the hand because it gives the opponents (and your partner) too much information about your hand.

The team who scores two games first wins the rubber, and they get a big bonus for doing so. After a team wins the rubber, both sides add up the scores on their sheets, and whoever has the highest total wins. Sometimes you lose the battle (the rubber) but win the war (score more points than your opponents). If you defeat enough of their contracts, for example, before they bid and make two game contracts, you could have more points on your side of the verticle line than they do. It happens all the time.

Being vulnerable and not vulnerable

After a team bids and makes a game contract (100 points), that team is called *vulnerable*. Being vulnerable is like being halfway there. In the case of the sample rubber, after the second hand, your opponents are vulnerable and you are not. It seems strange to be vulnerable when you are ahead, but these are the terms.

If your side is vulnerable, you need to make only one more game contract to win the rubber and enjoy a large bonus. Is there a downside to being vulnerable? There's a downside to everything.

The penalties for not making a contract (going down) when you are vulnerable are twice as stiff as the penalties for going down not vulnerable (see "Not Making Your Contract: Penalties" in this chapter for more information on penalties). Now maybe you can see why it's called being vulnerable.

Getting closer to winning the rubber

After a game contract has been made, both partnerships begin anew trying to make another game contract. Of course, the partnership that made game first is closer to winning the rubber.

For example, on to the third hand of the sample rubber; the opponents bid 2♦ and take nine tricks, scoring 60 points (see Table 16-1 to see how many points you get for winning a contract). The score pad now looks like Figure 16-4.

Note that you always enter the score for overtricks above the first horizontal line. Your overtricks don't contribute to making game, so you can keep them out of the way.

Also note that things are getting a little hairy in the sample rubber. Not only are the opponents vulnerable (they made the first game contract), but now they have a partscore of 40, which means they only need 60 more points to make game and put you away by winning the rubber!

In order to complete their 40 partial, all they have to do is bid and make 2♥, 2♠, 2NT, 3♣, or 3♦, or more. Those first three contracts require taking eight tricks; the last two require nine tricks.

Why bid higher than necessary to make game? When you have a partscore, just bid enough to complete your partscore and make game. If you overbid, you risk going down and blowing it all.

One vulnerable kibitzer

When Harold Vanderbilt, an early bridge player, was on a cruise codifying the rules of the game, he was trying to find precisely the right term for the fact that the side who had scored up a game might lose larger penalties as a result. A young lady looking on (the Yiddish term for a looker-on is a *Kibitzer*) on the boat suggested "vulnerable" as the answer. Vanderbilt adopted her suggestion, and it is solemnly recorded that this is the first and last time that a kibitzer has ever made a useful suggestion.

Figure 16-4:
Making a
game
contract
takes a
partnership
halfway to
winning the
rubber.

We	They
60	20
60	
	120
	40

Lumping points after a game contract has been made

After a game contract has been made with or without overtricks, each partnership can enter the total score, including overtricks, beneath the line, just as long as the total score is 100 or greater. (Before a game contract has been made, each partnership can only enter their trick score under the line.) You can combine, or lump, all your points, rather than splitting them up above and below the line, if you wish.

When you eventually add up everyone's score at the end of the rubber, it doesn't matter whether the scores are above or beneath the line, the points all count the same. But during the rubber, the bottom line is the important line because it tells you if either side has a partial score toward game.

In the sample rubber, on the next hand (the fourth hand of the rubber) you and your partner finally arrive at the game contract of 3NT and take ten tricks. You have bid and made game! The score pad now looks like the one shown in Figure 16-5.

Figure 16-5:
Lumping
overtricks
and trick
points after
game has
been bid
and made.

We	They
60	20
60	120
130	40

You don't have to lump. Technically, you could still split your score up into overtricks and trick points. For example, in Figure 16-5, you could put 100 under the line and 30 above the line, but lumping is the way to go, because the score card looks less cluttered this way. It's not an issue of tactics or strategy, just saving space, and ink from your pen!

Aha! After this hand, you, too, are vulnerable (have bid and made game). In fact, both sides are now vulnerable.

As for your opponents' partial score of 40, it's history. Your opponents haven't lost their partscore completely; they just have to start all over in their quest for 100 game points. They can't use those 40 points as a stepping stone any longer. You have wiped out their partial — which is always gratifying when you do it, always irritating when they do it to you.

Finishing the rubber

Play continues until one partnership bids and makes two game contracts. The first partnership to make game twice wins the rubber and collects some mighty hefty bonus points.

In the sample rubber, both sides are vulnerable and neither side has a partscore. The suspense in this rubber is almost too much to bear, right? On the very next hand, your final contract is 4♥ and you take 11 tricks. Don't look now, but you have just bid and made your second game contract. Your side has won the rubber!

After a partnership wins the rubber, both sides add up the total number of points they scored during the rubber. You get to count all the points, regardless of whether they are above or below the line.

You won the sample rubber in the last hand. First things first. You bid 4♥ and took 11 tricks, so your trick score of 150, which includes your overtrick, can be lumped under the line. You have bid and made two games before the opponents so you have won the rubber.

Scoring bonus points

Now for the good news. You get 500 points for winning the rubber if your opponents are vulnerable. If your opponents are not vulnerable when you win the rubber, you score 700 bonus points. (For more details on vulnerability, see "Being vulnerable and not vulnerable," earlier in this chapter.)

Drawing a double line

After the rubber has been won, you draw a double line after the last game score and add up both partnerships' total points for the rubber. You add up all the points, both below and above the line.

The score sheet for the sample rubber now resembles Figure 16-6.

We	They
500	
60	20
60	120
130	40
150	
900	180

Figure 16-6: Adding up the total points after a rubber.

Splitting the difference or not: set and rotating games

If you decide beforehand that you will play more than one rubber with the same partner, you are playing what is called a *set game*. If you play a set game, the difference in the scores from the previous rubber(s) can be carried over and put above the line when the next rubber begins, which is called *carrying the score*.

In the sample rubber, it turns out your side has won 720 points (900 - 180 = 720). (You didn't think I was going to let you lose your first rubber, did you? This rubber was fixed!) If you went on to play another rubber with the same partner, you would start the second rubber with 720 points above the line. It's like having a head start, in that although these points do not count toward making game, they represent the running total in your favor. Opponents hate to see those "carry over" scores staring them in the face every time they glance at the score. If you carried over the points from the last rubber, the score pad would look like Figure 16-7 at the beginning of the next rubber.

If, however, you decide to switch partners after each rubber, you are playing in a *rotating game*. To decide who plays with whom in a rotating game, you can cut the cards for partners after every rubber, the two highest cards play against the two lowest. Rotating like this means that you could wind up playing with the same partner all night. If you want to make sure you have a variety of partners, play with each player in turn and do not cut for partners.

We	They
720	

Figure 16-7: Carrying over your score.

Not Making Your Contract: Penalties

BRIDGE TALK

In some rubbers, one or both partnerships can't make a contract, even if their lives depend upon it. When you don't make your contract, you are penalized when it comes to reckoning time at the end of the hand. Welcome to the sad world of *going set, going down,* or *failing.* All these terms mean the same thing — you didn't take enough tricks and didn't make your contract. When you come up short on your contract, the missing tricks are called *undertricks.*

When you don't make your contract, your opponents score points above the line according to the following scale:

✔ 50 points per trick if you're not vulnerable

✔ 100 points per trick if you're vulnerable

Note that the opponents' status is irrelevant — it is your status that determines the penalties you concede.

As an example, pretend that you have just started the second rubber of a set game (see "Splitting the difference or not: set and rotating games," earlier in this chapter for more on set games). You and your partner won big in the first rubber, and you get to carry over 720 points from the first rubber.

On the first hand of the second rubber, you go for broke and bid 3NT, trying for game. No luck. You only take eight tricks. You go down one trick not vulnerable. For each nonvulnerable undertrick, you lose 50 points. Those 50 points go above the line on your opponent's side. Had you gone down two tricks, they would have chalked up 100 points above the line. It doesn't hurt too much if they score points above the line, at 50 points a shot; it's the points below the line that kill you.

Your new score sheet looks like Figure 16-8.

Not so terrible. But in the next hand, you get more bad news to report. Your opponents bid 4♥ and take 11 tricks, scoring an overtrick. Now your opponents are vulnerable.

The new score looks like Figure 16-9.

Figure 16-8:
Adding
insult to
injury: Your
opponents
add points
above the
line when
you don't
make your
contract.

We	They
720	50

Figure 16-9:
Your
opponents
are
vulnerable:
time to get
serious.

We	They
720	50
	150

The next hand, they try to put you away by bidding 4♥, a game contract. This time your defense is razor-sharp and they take only 8 tricks. They have failed by two tricks, vulnerable. Vulnerable undertricks are worth 100 a pop, so you get to put 200 points above the line on your side. Now the score looks like Figure 16-10.

Figure 16-10:
Your
opponents
messed up,
and you add
points
above the
line.

We	They
200	
720	50
	150

In the following hand, your opponents bid 3♣ and take ten tricks. Your new score sheet looks like Figure 16-11.

Figure 16-11:
Your opponents make another partscore.

We	They
200	20
720	50
	150
	60

The noose is tightening. Your opponents are vulnerable with *60 on* (that is, they have a 60 partial). Record your opponents' overtrick above the line on the score pad. No lumping when no game contract has been bid and made.

Finally, you fight back and you put it all together on the next hand. You wind up in 4♥, taking 12 tricks. You record your score as shown in Figure 16-12.

Figure 16-12:
You are vulnerable at last.

We	They
200	20
720	50
	150
180	60

Finally, tragedy strikes as your opponents bid 3NT and take 11 tricks, which is the second game contract that they bid and make. Your opponents have won the rubber and get a 500-point bonus. Time to tally up, as shown in Figure 16-13.

Your carryover has shrunk from 720 points to 160 points (1100 – 940 = 160). At least you are still ahead.

We	They
	500
200	20
720	50
	150
	60
180	
	160
1100	940

Figure 16-13: You can't win 'em all!

Scoring Slams

Game contracts put you in line for eventual bonuses if you win the rubber. Slam contracts give you immediate bonuses. Bidding to the six level (a small slam) or bidding to the seven level (a grand slam) is exciting and also perilous. Bidding to the six level means you have to take 12 tricks, all the tricks in a hand but one; bidding to the seven level means you have to take all 13 tricks!

Clearly, if you are going to stick your neck out that far, you should be rewarded with a nice bonus if you make your contract. After all, you could have settled for a game contract with much less risk.

The number of bonus points that you receive for slams depend upon whether you are vulnerable at the time or not (see "Being vulnerable and not vulnerable" in this chapter for more information on vulnerability):

- Not vulnerable small slam = 500 points
- Vulnerable small slam = 750 points
- Not vulnerable grand slam = 1,000 points
- Vulnerable grand slam = 1,500 points

Slam bonuses are mouthwatering, but don't forget, you have to make your contract to get them. Not only do you get nothing if you fail, but worse, your opponents get penalty points if you don't make your contract (the usual 50/100 points a time for undertricks). The bottom line is you have to know what you are doing bidding at those rarefied levels.

Figure 16-14 shows you a small slam bonus in action. In Figure 16-14, you and a partner have just started a new rubber by bidding and making 6♠.

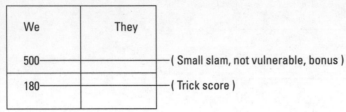

Figure 16-14:
Luck be your lady, tonight! Making a small slam right off the bat.

Suppose that good fortune visits you again, and you bid and make a second slam — back to back slams! On the very next hand, you bid and make 6♣, a vulnerable small slam. Take a look at your score now, as shown in Figure 16-14.

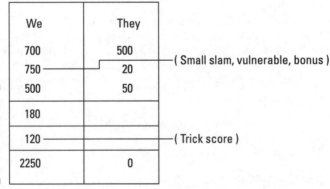

Figure 16-15:
You really sock it to them this time.

It doesn't get much better than this. The 750 above the line is your bonus for bidding and making a vulnerable small slam. The 700 above the line is your bonus for winning the rubber. Was that a big fat rubber, or what?

Playing for loot

You can play bridge for fun, which tends to result in rather undisciplined games, because nothing compels people to try and be sensible. Alternatively, you can play for a stake, at which point the game gets interesting and potentially expensive.

Most rubber bridge clubs offer only money tables (you play friendly bridge at home for the most part) and stakes vary enormously. In some clubs, you can play all day and finish up winning $20 or losing $10. At the other extreme, there are clubs in New York City where you can win or lose $3000 on a single hand!

A number of very successful tournament players also supplement their income from playing rubber bridge, but many successful rubber players would rather stick to winning money in the clubs instead of going to the tournaments.

Scoring Doubled and Redoubled Contracts

Your opponents may arrive at a final contract that either you or your partner think is just too high. For example, if the opponents bid 7NT, meaning that they must take all 13 tricks, and you have an ace, you know that they can't take all 13 tricks. You have a weapon (a bid) at your disposal to let the opponents know that they have made a big mistake. You can say "Double," (I dare you) when it is your turn to bid. (See Chapter 13 for the full scoop on doubling.) If you defeat the doubled contract, you get at least double your normal penalty score for the undertricks; if they make the doubled contract, they get double their trick score plus 50 for the insult.

Say the final contract is doubled (it often is). If the declarer fails to make the contract, losses are tabulated depending upon the vulnerability of the declaring side. The score for defeating the contract goes above the line of the doubling side.

Non-vulnerable undertricks in doubled contracts carry the following penalty points:

- Down 1 = 100 points
- Down 2 = 300 points
- Down 3 = 500 points
- Down 4 = 800 points

- Down 5 = 1100 points
- Down 6 = 1400 points
- Down 7 = 1700 points

Vulnerable undertricks in doubled contracts carry the following penalty points:

- Down 1 = 200 points
- Down 2 = 500 points
- Down 3 = 800 points
- Down 4 = 1100 points

Each subsequent undertrick is worth 300 more points to the doubling side. It gets pretty wild.

Scoring doubled overtricks

Sometimes the doubling side gets it all wrong and the declarer not only makes the contract but makes it with overtricks to boot. For these overtricks, the declarer gets the following bonus points:

- Each doubled overtrick, non-vulnerable = 100 points
- Each doubled overtrick, vulnerable = 200 points

Scoring redoubled contracts

Some players treat a penalty double as a personal insult. Those players are prone to say, "Redouble" (I double-dare you), quadrupling the stakes (see Chapter 13 for the details on redoubling)! When a contract is redoubled and not made, the penalties grow to behemoth proportions quickly. When the contract is made, the lucky declarer and his partner get four times the trick score and a bonus of 100 on top of that for the extra insult.

Score the following points for not vulnerable undertricks in redoubled contracts:

- Down 1 = 200 points
- Down 2 = 600 points
- Down 3 = 1000 points

The redoubled score is exactly double the score that it would be in a doubled contract.

Score the following points for vulnerable undertricks in redoubled contracts:

- ✔ Down 1 = 400 points
- ✔ Down 2 = 1000 points
- ✔ Down 3 = 1600 points

Double the score compared to going down in a doubled contract.

Scoring redoubled overtricks — bring a calculator

Sometimes the redoubling side makes overtricks. When this earth-shattering event happens, everything is quadrupled:

- ✔ Each non-vulnerable redoubled overtrick = 200 points.
- ✔ Each vulnerable redoubled overtrick = 400 points.

Should you be playing for money, bring quite a bit along if you or your partner make quite a few doubles and redoubles that don't work out. Of course, if they do, you will leave with pockets full.

Doubling Them into Game

When you double a partscore and the opponents make the contract, they get double their trick score below the line plus 50 points above the line for insult.

Say you double a contract of 2♣ and they make it. Instead of scoring 40 points beneath the line, they get 80 points beneath the line (plus 50 above the line for the insult), but they still need 20 more points to rack up a game.

But if you double a contract of 2♥ and they make it, instead of 60 points beneath the line, the opponents score 120 points beneath the line (plus 50 above the line). Disaster has struck. You have doubled the opponents into game! If they weren't vulnerable, they are now; if they were vulnerable, they have just won the rubber!

Be very careful about doubling a partscore contract that puts the opponents into game if they make it.

Part IV
Playing Defense

The 5th Wave   By Rich Tennant

©RICHTENNANT

"OK, I'LL LET HIM PLAY AS LONG AS YOU STOP SAYING, 'YOU CAN'T TAKE AN OLD DOG'S NEW TRICKS.'"

In this part . . .

After you play bridge for awhile, you discover that you are playing defense about half the time. Many of the contracts that the opponents reach can be defeated by accurate defense (providing that neither you nor your partner make a major goof). In this part I show you how to take all your defensive tricks so the declarer doesn't get away with murder during the play of the hand.

Chapter 17

Defending versus Notrump Contracts

In This Chapter

▶ Making the best opening lead

▶ Playing third hand like a pro

Defensive play is partnership play. Together with your partner, you can work to keep your opponents from making their contract.

As you read this chapter on defensive play, you may notice how similar defensive play is to declarer play. Both sides are trying to take tricks using the same techniques.

However, one significant compelling difference distinguishes declarer play from defensive play. When you play as the declarer, you have full access to your partnership's cards — you can see your own hand and your partner's hand, the dummy. As the declarer, you can easily plan your plays. When you play defense, planning your plays becomes much harder because you can't see your partner's hand. Obviously, more intuition and deduction has to go into defense.

Making the Opening Lead against a Notrump Contract

Even a strong defensive player can get lost without a little help from his partner. One way to pass information across the table legally is with the card(s) you lead. Your opening lead tells your partner quite a lot about what you have in the suit you are leading. That information, in turn, helps your partner plan the defense.

When you defend in a notrump contract, you and your opponent (the declarer) both try to accomplish the same things:

✔ You both want to establish tricks in strong suits. With the KQJ10, for example, you both want to drive out the ace and establish three tricks.

✔ You both want to take tricks with small cards in long suits by relentlessly playing the suit until your opponents run out of cards in the suit. After you get rid of their cards, all your remaining cards in that suit are winning tricks.

The defense has one big advantage: tempo. By virtue of the opening lead, the defense gets a vital opportunity to take the lead in the race to establish their suit. As the poet said, "Thrice blest is he who gets his blow in first." Starting with the opening lead, the defense hopes to strike at the declarer's weak point. Then the defense goes for the soft underbelly.

Appreciating the importance of the opening lead

The defenders make the first lead, called the *opening lead*. At times, an opening lead is pure guesswork. After all, you can't see your partner's hand, and you may not have a clear-cut lead.

On the other hand, you may be able to work out what to lead from your own hand; you may have a strong suit of your own to lead, for example. Your partner may have helped you out with the opening lead by making a bid, or you may have an inkling of the best lead by listening to your opponents' bidding; from their bidding you may have worked out in which suits they are well heeled and in which suits they have nothing.

For these reasons, the opening lead gives the defense an overwhelming advantage. Sometimes the declarer can't overcome the head start the defense gets with the opening lead. As a defender, if you find the declarer's Achilles' heel, you may find yourself working wonders and taking tricks from nowhere.

Statistically, the opening lead is far and away the most important single card the defense plays. You would be a World Champion if you made the best opening lead on every hand! You wouldn't even have any competition for the title.

Listening to the bidding

Before you make your opening lead, you have to listen to the bidding. Sometimes the bidding provides enough information about the hand to fill a library, and sometimes the bidding doesn't provide enough information to fill the side of a match box. However, most of the time the bidding furnishes you with some clues to the best opening lead.

During the bidding, the opponents frequently tell you how strong they are, and in which suits they do and don't have strength. The clearer the picture you get of both their hands, the more likely you can find the most lethal lead.

Just to show you how much you can find out from keeping a keen ear on the bidding, take a peek at the following bidding sequence. You are now West, and South is the declarer:

West (You)	North	East (Your Partner)	South
Pass	Pass	Pass	1NT
Pass	3NT	Pass	Pass
Pass			

These cats have told you nothing. No suits have been bid. All you know is that South has a balanced hand in the 15 to 17 HCPs range, and North, a *passed hand* (who couldn't open the bidding) has enough to raise to game, presumably 10 to 11 HCPs. However, you do know that North didn't bother to use the Stayman Convention (see Chapter 10 for information on using the Stayman Convention when responding to 1NT), so North probably doesn't have a four-card major.

Now check out this sequence:

South	West (You)	North	East (Your Partner)
1♣	Pass	1♦	Pass
3♣	Pass	3♦	Pass
3NT	Pass	Pass	Pass

Again, South is playing a contract of 3NT, but in the process of arriving at this contract, the opponents showed you two suits, clubs and diamonds. South has long and strong clubs and North has the same sort of holding in diamonds. The declarer will use these two suits to take tricks. You also know a little about your partner's hand, albeit through negative inferences; your partner didn't have enough points or a good enough suit to come into the bidding at his first turn. Don't expect the moon from him.

So which suit should you lead? Unless you are a close relative of the declarer, lead a heart or a spade. Which one? You can read all about making that decision in "Your MO," in this chapter.

In order to make a decent opening lead, listen to the bidding. If you watch TV or otherwise zone out during the bidding, don't expect to make a killer opening lead.

Your plan of attack

Before selecting your opening lead, first decide upon which suit to lead; then pick out the right card in that suit to lead. Nine times out of ten, you will either lead *fourth highest* or *top of a sequence* in your longest suit, providing that your opponents haven't bid the suit.

 Don't expect to make the winning lead on every hand. Nobody does. First of all, you can't trust the opponents, who may deliberately or accidentally misrepresent their hands. And even if you weigh up all the information perfectly, you can still be unlucky — at least that is my excuse whenever I find the worst possible opening lead after having done my calculations so carefully.

Leading from length

Because your goal is to establish tricks, and because tricks come from long suits, your best shot is usually to lead from your longest suit.

The hand in Figure 17-1 gives you a chance to kick off with your longest suit.

Figure 17-1:
Starting on your longest suit.

The bidding for this hand has gone as follows:

South	West (You)	North	East (Your Partner)
1NT	Pass	3NT	Pass
Pass	Pass		

Because neither opponent has bid a suit, you have no clues to help you sniff out their weakness. When the opponents haven't given you any tips on their favorite suits, try to take tricks by establishing winners in your long suit. You want to lead from your longest suit, spades. But which spade?

Leading low from a long suit

After you choose a suit to lead, you need to determine whether that suit is headed by three consecutive honor cards, such as the KQJ, QJ10, or J109. If your suit doesn't sport any consecutive honor cards, just lead the fourth highest card in your suit. Start from the highest card in the suit, count down four places, and throw that fourth highest card face up on the table.

In Figure 17-1, where your longest suit doesn't have any consecutive honor cards, you would lead the ♠4, the fourth highest card in your suit.

Say for a moment that you have the cards in Figure 17-1 again and the bidding has gone as follows:

South	West (You)	North	East (Your Partner)
1♠	Pass	2♣	Pass
2NT	Pass	3NT	Pass
Pass	Pass		

You must make the opening lead, and you have plenty of information from the bidding to help you decide which card to lead. The opponents have bid spades and clubs. Because you don't want to lead suits that the opponents have bid, lead a diamond or a heart, whichever suit is longer. In this case, you would lead ♥2, the fourth highest card in your suit.

If your opponents bid both of your long suits, so that you have only two or three cards in the unbid suits, you can lead from a short suit. If the opponents bid all four suits, you are on your own! You may treat the auction as if they had bid none of the suits, and fall back on your longest suit again.

Leading from the top when you have a string of honors

If your suit is headed by the AKQ, KQJ, QJ10, J109, or the 1098, you have been blessed with a three-card honor sequence. When you have such a sequence, lead the top honor. For example, if you have the ♥QJ1032, lead the ♥Q. You can never have too many sequences!

Before leading a suit, check to see whether you have an honor sequence at the head or in the middle of your suit. If you do, lead the top card in that sequence; if you don't, lead your fourth highest card in the suit.

Leading your partner's suit

If your partner bids a suit, try to lead the suit. However, if you have a suit of our own headed by a strong honor sequence, you can overrule your partner and lead your suit. Just how strong must your sequence be? It depends on how much you like your suit and how much you trust your partner! (And also whether you are bigger or can shout louder than your partner, if necessary!) Leading your partner's suit keeps her happy, but you have to go with what you think is best and let the chips fall where they may.

If the opponents bid your longest suit, you usually look elsewhere for another lead. However, if you have a strong honor sequence (AKJ, KQJ, QJ10) in that suit, go ahead and lead it anyway.

Leading your short suit

You may not always want to lead your longest suit. For example, you may not want to lead your longest suit if:

✔ An opponent bids your longest suit

✔ Your partner bids another suit

In the interest of partnership harmony (particularly marital partnership harmony), lead your partner's suit, especially if your partner has overcalled (see Chapter 14 for more on overcalls). Overcalls show strong five- or six-card suits. Your partner uses overcalls to tell you what to lead. Of course, if your partner bids two suits, you must choose between the suits. If you don't lead either of your partner's suits, the suit you lead had better be pretty strong, or you had better be a pretty fast runner. Say you have this hand shown in Figure 17-2.

Figure 17-2:
You may
have to lead
your short
suit.

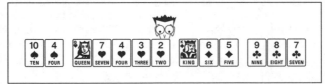

For Figure 17-2, the bidding has gone as follows:

North	East (Your Partner)	South	West (You)
1♣	1♠	2NT	Pass
3NT	Pass	Pass	Pass

Had your partner not bid, your lead would be ♥3, fourth highest from your longest suit. However, because your partner overcalled, by all means lead a spade, but which one?

Anytime you have two cards in the suit you want to lead, lead the higher card, period. In the case of Figure 17-2, lead the ♠10.

With three cards headed by one honor card, lead your lowest card. For example, from A83, lead the 3; from K72, lead the 2; and from Q65, lead the 5.

If you have three cards headed by two honors, lead a low card unless the honors are of equal value. If the honors are right next to each other in a sequence (touching), lead the higher honor. For example, from QJ4, lead the Q, because the two honors are touching. From the Q103, lead the 3 because the two honors aren't equals.

In bridge, the honor cards are the AKQJ10. The lower cards, meaning all the other cards in a suit, are called *spot cards*. If your suit has no honor card in it, but is topped by three or four spot cards, lead the top of the spot cards. This is called *leading top of nothing*. That is to say, from the 853 or the 8532, lead the 8. When you have four worthless cards, you don't lead the fourth best card. The lead of a low spot card promises at least one honor card in the suit.

Use top of nothing leads as a last resort. You may decide to lead top of nothing if it is the only unbid suit, for example.

Leading unbid major suits versus unbid minor suits

When you lead against a notrump contract and the choice of leads is between an unbid major suit (hearts or spades) and an unbid minor suit (clubs or diamonds), lead the unbid major. Opponents go out of their way to bid major suits. If they don't bid them, they don't have them. On the other hand, opponents routinely conceal minor suits.

For example, you have the cards shown in Figure 17-3.

Figure 17-3:
Choosing between an unbid major and unbid minor suit.

The bidding has gone as follows:

West (You)	North	East (Your Partner)	South
Pass	Pass	Pass	1NT
Pass	3NT	Pass	Pass
Pass			

Should you lead the ♠4 or the ♣4? Because your opponents haven't bid spades, a major suit, try the ♠4 — it's your best shot in the dark.

However, if your choice of leads is between an unbid major and an unbid minor, and you have a sequence of honor cards in the minor suit, lead the minor.

Playing Third Hand against a Notrump Contract

Your partner makes an opening lead. The dummy comes down, the declarer plays a card from the dummy, and suddenly it's your turn to play, making you *third hand*. By the time you have to play, you have heard the bidding, you have seen your partner's opening lead, and you have seen the dummy. Now you need to digest what all this information means.

Your play to the first trick, and possibly the next trick if you win the first one, are the two most important cards you play during the entire defense. They set the pattern for the whole hand; if you start off on the right foot, you may deal the declarer a blow from which he can't recover. If you mess up . . . but you won't, will you?

Your partner will either lead a low card, typically fourth highest from his longest suit, or an honor card, top of a sequence. Your play depends on whether your partner leads a low card or an honor card.

In this section, I use spades as the suit in most of the figures. You should dig up a deck of cards, remove the spade suit, and use those spades to follow the description of the play throughout the section. The play in this section relates absolutely equivalently to the play in any suit. Don't think you always have to lead spades, although I know some players who would be better off if they did just that!

When your partner leads a low card and the dummy has low cards

When your partner leads a low card and the dummy has only low cards, play your highest card. *Third hand high* is an easy term to remember, and playing third hand high is a great defensive rule.

To understand the idea behind playing third hand high, think about your partner's opening lead. You know your partner has an honor in her suit because she led a small card. Therefore, you should play the third hand high to prevent the declarer from winning a cheap trick.

Figure 17-4 shows you a hand where you should play third hand high.

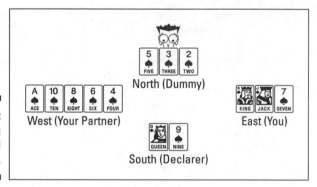

Figure 17-4: Playing third hand high.

Your partner leads the ♠6, his fourth highest spade; the dummy plays low and you hold the ♠KJ7. Which spade should you play? In Figure 17-4, you play the ♠K because the ♠K and ♠J are not equals. The ♠K takes the trick.

In Figure 17-4, if you had played the ♠J on the first trick, an ugly play, the declarer would have taken the trick with her ♠Q, a trick to which she is not entitled. You would only play the ♠J if you were playing against a very close relative. If you play the ♠K and then the ♠J, the higher of your two remaining spades, you take the first five spade tricks.

If your partner leads a low card and the dummy has small cards, play third hand high. If you remain with two cards in the suit, play the higher of the two cards.

When you have two or three equal honor cards

When you have touching honor cards (such as the KQ or J10) in the third seat, play the lower or the lowest equal. This play is essentially a conventional agreement, in just the same way as leading your fourth highest card is a convention. By playing the lowest equal, your partner can tell what cards you don't have. For example, if you play the king, then you can't have the queen.

The cards in Figure 17-5 give you a chance to choose between two equal honor cards in the suit your partner leads.

Figure 17-5:
Look low:
You want to
play your
lower
equal.

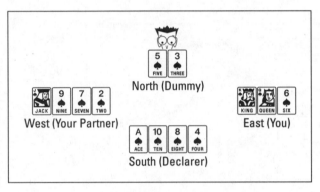

Your partner leads the ♠2, his fourth highest spade, the dummy plays low, and you expertly play the ♠Q, the lower of your equal honors (you intend to play the ♠K, the higher of your two remaining honor cards, the next time you get a chance).

Had you played the ♠K for the first trick, your partner would be fooled. Your partner would assume that the declarer has the ♠Q on the premise that you would have played the ♠Q if you had both the ♠KQ.

When everyone at the table plays by the rules, you can deduce who holds certain cards. For example, the third hand player should play the lower of two equal honors, if she has them. Knowing this, you can easily make out who has the missing ♠K in Figure 17-6.

You lead the ♠2, the dummy plays low, and your partner plays the ♠A. Who has the ♠K? Well, you don't have the ♠K and the dummy doesn't have it. The right answer must either be East, South, or the ♠K has fallen on the floor and no one has it.

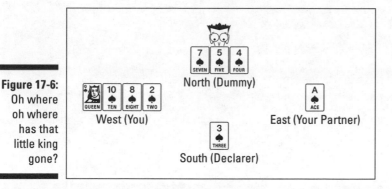

Figure 17-6:
Oh where
oh where
has that
little king
gone?

Remembering the rules of playing third hand, you know immediately that South has the ♠K. If your partner has the ♠AK, she plays the ♠K, not the ♠A, the lower of two equal honors. When she plays the ♠A, she's practically shouting that she doesn't have the ♠K. Elementary, my dear Watson.

As an aside, I once showed the cards in Figure 17-6 to a group of friends and asked who had the ♠K. Some said South and some said East. One of my friends decided she wasn't taking any chances, so she answered Southeast!

When you have a higher honor than the dummy's honor

The dummy doesn't always have just low cards. Sometimes the dummy comes down with an honor or two in the suit your partner leads, but you may nonetheless have a higher honor than the dummy's honor.

When the dummy has an honor and you have a higher honor, such as the ace or the king, but no other significant card in the suit, play your high card regardless. However, if you have a ten, a jack (or exceptionally a queen) with your high honor, keep your higher honor to zap the dummy's honor later on. Instead play your intermediate card and save your high honor. You don't want to waste your big guns for nothing; aces were meant to take kings and queens.

The cards in Figure 17-7 provide a prime example of when you should hold back your high honor when the dummy has a lower honor.

Your partner leads the ♠3, her lowest spade (you know the ♠3 is her lowest spade because you are looking smack at the ♠2) and the dummy plays low, saving her ♠K for a later trick. You have an honor that is higher than the dummy's honor and your next highest honor, the ♠Q, is also a winning trick with that ♠K in the dummy. No sense taking the trick with the ♠A when you can take the trick with the ♠Q. Play the ♠Q.

Figure 17-7:
Watch out
dummy!
I have a
higher
honor
waiting in
the wings.

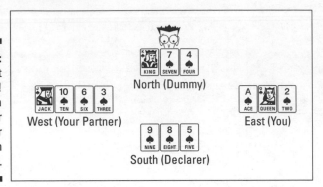

North (Dummy)

West (Your Partner)

East (You)

South (Declarer)

Holding back your higher honor doesn't always win the trick for you.
Sometimes the declarer has a higher honor than your honor. Take a peek at
Figure 17-8 to see what I mean.

Figure 17-8:
Sneak
attack:
South
steals your
thunder
with a
higher
honor.

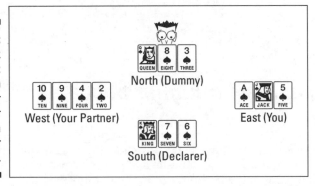

North (Dummy)

West (Your Partner)

East (You)

South (Declarer)

In Figure 17-8, your partner leads the ♠2, the dummy plays low, and you play
the ♠J. But this time the declarer (South) takes the trick with the ♠K. Don't
despair — despite this momentary setback, you've made a good play.

If you had erred by playing the ♠A, the declarer would have taken two tricks
with the ♠Q and the ♠K. This way, though, the declarer only takes one trick,
the ♠K. You are hovering over dummy's ♠Q with your ♠A, making it impossible for the declarer to take a second trick with the ♠Q. If you patiently wait
for your partner to lead the suit a second time, then your good play at trick
one will pay dividends. At that point, when the ♠Q is played from the
dummy, you will zero in on it with your ♠A, and the declarer takes only one
spade trick, not two.

When your partner leads an honor card

Your partner may lead an honor card, thus suggesting a sequence in the suit. The lead of an honor card shows a sequence of three equal (consecutive) honors, or the third card in the sequence can be missing by one link. For example, the KQJ or the KQ10 are considered sequences; the KQ9 is not a sequence.

Deducing what sequence your partner has

Your partner can lead five possible honor cards: the ace through the ten. Each honor card suggests a different sequence of cards that she may be holding.

After your partner leads an honor, assume that your partner has one of the following sequences:

- ✔ **The ace:** The lead of an ace, the strongest honor lead, shows a suit headed by the AKJ, or the AKQ.

- ✔ **The king:** The lead of a king shows a suit headed by the KQJ or the KQ10.

- ✔ **The queen:** The lead of a queen shows a suit headed by the QJ10 or the QJ9.

- ✔ **The jack:** This one is a little tricky. The lead of a jack can show a suit headed by the J109 or J108, or a suit headed by the AJ109, AJ108, KJ109, or KJ108.

- ✔ **The 10:** Are you ready for this? The lead of the ten shows suits headed by the 1098 and 1097 as well as suits headed by the A1098, A1097, K1098, K1097, Q1098, or Q1097.

Telling your partner what you have

When your partner leads an honor card, you may have any one of the following holdings in the suit your partner leads:

- ✔ An honor equal to the one your partner has led

- ✔ A higher unequal honor

- ✔ A doubleton honor (two cards headed by one honor card)

- ✔ No honors at all

Your job is to tell your partner which of these holdings you have.

Showing an equal honor

If your partner leads an honor card and you have an equal (touching) honor card, you want to let your partner in on the secret. In Figure 17-9, you want to tell your partner about your equal honor.

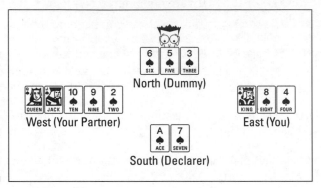

Figure 17-9: Go tell it on the mountain — you've got an equal honor.

Your partner leads the ♠Q, the dummy plays low, and you come out of your shell with the equal honor sign, playing the highest spot card you have. You play the ♠8. Now your partner assumes that you have a high honor. Had you played the ♠4, a low spot card, your partner would assume that you have no honors in spades.

Showing a doubleton honor

When you have a doubleton honor, play it. It only hurts for a little while. Although this may look like an unnecessary sacrifice of a high card just do it, and have courage.

Figure 17-10 shows you a case where you need to show your partner a doubleton honor.

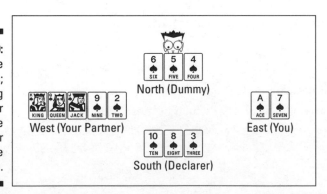

Figure 17-10: Clearing the debris; unblocking the honor for the greater good of the side.

Your partner leads the ♠K; you have just two spades, but you do have a high card, the ♠A. When you have a doubleton honor, play your honor, play that ♠A, even if you have to overtake your partner's trick. Just do it! After you win the trick and play a spade, your partner takes four more spade tricks, or five in all.

If you wimp out and play your seven on the first trick, you win the second round of spades with the ♠A. But then what? You have no more spades. Don't look at me. You blew it one trick earlier when you didn't overtake your partner's spade lead with your ♠A. It's almost too sad for words.

Overtaking a king with the ace is not as awful as it looks if you consider that your partner usually has the KQJ of the suit. You're actually doing your partner a favor by overtaking her king — you're clearing the way for her to take a bundle of tricks!

This same principle, of playing your high card when you hold any doubleton honor, applies whatever honor card your partner leads and whatever honor card you hold.

When your partner leads the 10 or jack

When your partner leads a 10 or jack, it may not be the top of a sequence — your partner may have higher honors in the suit. You must play third hand high if you have a higher unequal honor and the dummy has low cards, as in Figure 17-11.

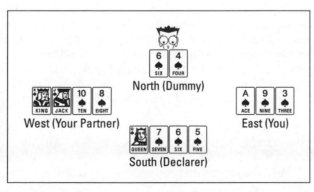

Figure 17-11: Don't let your partner down — go up!

North (Dummy)

West (Your Partner)

East (You)

South (Declarer)

Your partner leads the ♠J. You should play the ♠A and then the ♠9, the higher of your two remaining spades. South's ♠Q is caught and can't take a trick.

You play the same when your partner leads the 10 — play any higher unequal honor you may have to protect your partner's holding — if the dummy has small cards.

When your partner leads an honor, the dummy has an honor, but you have a higher honor

Frequently when your partner makes the opening lead of an honor card, the dummy also has an honor card, but you have a higher honor than the dummy's honor. Take the cards in Figure 17-12 as an example.

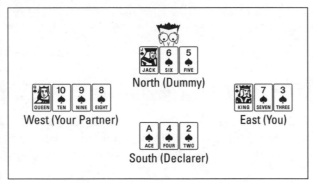

Figure 17-12: The dummy has an honor, but you have a higher honor.

In Figure 17-12, your partner leads the ♠10, the dummy plays low, and once again you have a higher honor than the dummy; but you need to save it. If the dummy has an honor that you can top, save your honor to zap the dummy's honor later. Your proper play is the ♠7, your highest spot card to say that you have an honor in your partner's suit. Let your partner's honor card do the dirty work of driving out the declarer's honor card.

If you play the ♠7, the declarer takes the trick with the ♠A, his only trick, and you and your partner remain with the ♠K and ♠Q. Had you played the ♠K at the first trick, the declarer would have won the ace and later been able to lead toward his ♠J for an undeserved second trick in the spade suit.

When your partner leads an honor card in your suit

During the bidding, you may have mentioned a suit, and your partner may lead in that suit. If your partner leads an honor card in your suit, give your partner either an encouraging signal (play a high spot card) if you want him to continue playing the suit or a discouraging signal (play a low spot card) if you don't want him to play the suit.

Figure 17-13 allows you to explore your options when your partner leads an honor in a suit you mentioned during the bidding.

The bidding for this hand has gone as follows:

East (You)	South	West (Your Partner)	North
1♠	1NT	Pass	3NT
Pass	Pass	Pass	

Your partner dutifully leads the ♠K, and now you can either make an encouraging or a discouraging signal. Do you want her to continue playing spades or do you want her to play something else?

See the ♥AKJ10 in your hand and the ♥Q in the dummy? If somehow your partner can be persuaded to lead a heart, your side can take four heart tricks, not to mention the two tricks from the ♠AK. Play the ♠2 to tell your partner to lead something else. How will your partner know "something else" means lead a heart?

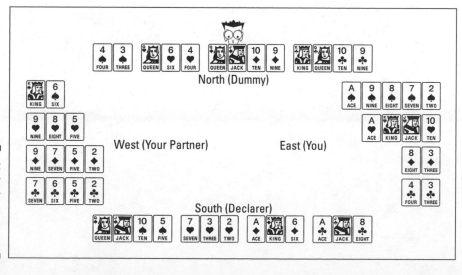

Figure 17-13: Your partner leads an honor in the suit you bid.

Your partner, being very observant, notices that your ♠2 is a discouraging signal and that you are asking for another suit. But which other suit? Your partner makes a quarter turn of his neck to the left and looks at the dummy, trying to figure out what you probably want.

Your partner sees strong clubs and strong diamonds in the dummy; if you don't want spades, and the clubs and diamonds in the dummy are strong, it must be logical that you want hearts. If your partner "reads" your signal and plays a heart, you can proceed to take enough heart and spade tricks to defeat your opponent's contract by two tricks. If your partner plays anything else, the declarer makes the 3NT contract by establishing a ninth trick in spades.

Pay attention to your partner's signal. Even though your partner has bid a suit, she may still want you to lead something else.

Chapter 18

Defending versus Suit Contracts

• •

In This Chapter

▶ Making the all-important good opening lead

▶ Playing third hand

• •

*A*fter your opponents arrive at a suit contract, you need to swing into defense. Depending on where you sit, you may need to make an opening lead against their trump contract, or you may need to play third hand. Both positions offer you the chance to stop your opponents' contract dead in its tracks.

Opening Leads versus a Suit Contract

When you defend a notrump contract, you tend to lead from your long suit, trying to establish your small cards in that suit. This strategy doesn't work against a suit contract because the declarer (or the dummy) can trump your established tricks. Bummer. To retaliate, you can trump the declarer's (or the dummy's) winning tricks if you are void in the suit that they lead. In practice, leading a short suit against a trump contract gives you a shot at trumping the declarer's winning tricks in that suit. However, the alternative of leading from a long suit still remains a sensible option, even against a trump contract.

Because you have the advantage of the opening lead, you can map out your defensive strategy depending upon the bidding and your own hand. In this section, I spell out your options for opening leads when defending against a suit contract. The opening lead is critical; you get the chance to play the hand on your terms by choosing the opening lead — don't waste the opportunity.

When you have a sequence of three honor cards

Sequences of honor cards (three adjacent honors) make such strong leads that you must have a good reason not to lead one if you have one. The stronger the sequence, the better. Suits headed by the AKQ, AKJ, KQJ, KQ10, QJ10, or QJ9 are particularly yummy.

When you are blessed with such a sequence, you lead the top (or highest) card from the sequence.

When you have two touching honors

Almost as good as three touching honors at the head of your suit are suits headed by two touching honors. Suits that have two touching honors, such as the AK632, KQ6, QJ82, or J1053, also warrant leading the top card.

Versus suit contracts, you lead the top of two touching honors, whereas at a notrump contract, you need three touching honors to lead the top card.

To see the power of leading the top card in a suit headed by two touching honors, look at Figure 18-1.

Figure 18-1:
Making the
opening
lead with
touching
honors.

The bidding for this hand has gone as follows:

South	West (You)	North	East (Your Partner)
1♥	Pass	3♥	Pass
Pass	Pass		

You must make the opening lead, and you know that the dummy has heart support for South and a moderate hand; South has a minimum opening bid because he passed an invitational bid from North. What should you lead?

Ah, look no farther than that ♠A. The lead of the ace from the AK is one of the strongest of all opening leads for three reasons:

- ✔ You take the trick (South and North are 99 percent sure to have at least one spade each).
- ✔ You can study the dummy while retaining the lead to plan what to do next.
- ✔ You see your partner's signal advising you what to do next.

It doesn't get much better than that.

I advise you to lead the ace from the AK at trick one only. For subsequent tricks, lead the king from the AK.

When you have a short suit

Leading a short suit (in which you only have one or two cards) against a trump contract is a very tempting lead — few can resist it. If your lead works out, you can trump one or two of the declarer's tricks before she can draw trump.

But don't rush to judgment every time you have a short suit lead available. At least glance at your trump suit first. You may not want to trump anything — your trump holding may be too strong. For example, if you have the QJ10 of their trump suit, trumping with one of these honor cards doesn't gain you a trick; you have a certain trump trick anyway.

Figure 18-2 shows you an example of when you do not want to lead a short suit.

Figure 18-2:
Phone the dog and wake up the neighbors: Leading a short suit seems crazy.

The bidding for this hand has gone as follows:

West (You)	North	East (Your Partner)	South
1♣	Double	Pass	2♠
Pass	4♠	Pass	Pass
Pass			

What is your opening lead? Listen to the opponents' bids. You expect South to have about 10 points and four or five spades, and North probably has a good hand with short clubs.

Because you have the ♠AK, the two highest cards in the trump suit, you have two sure trump tricks. It doesn't benefit you to trump a heart with either the ♠A or the ♠K. You will be trumping with a sure spade trick anyway. So a heart lead does not look like such a great idea. But if your spades had been something like ♠AK7, ♠A7, ♠A72, or ♠842, then, trumping a heart with a small spade would be a great idea.

When you have certain trump tricks (KQJ, QJ10, or J1092) don't bother leading a short suit; you don't want, or need, to trump anything. Lead something else. The proper opening lead for Figure 18-2 is the ♦K.

When your partner bids a suit

When your partner bids a suit, you should try to lead that suit. One of the reasons your partner bids a suit is to help you out on the opening lead. Unless you can find an overwhelmingly good alternative lead, look no farther than your partner's suit. Trust your partner — she'll appreciate it.

For example, take a look at the hand in Figure 18-3.

Figure 18-3:
Leading your partner's suit.

The bidding for this hand goes as follows:

South	West (You)	North	East (Your Partner)
1♥	Pass	2♦	3♣
3♥	Pass	4♥	Pass
Pass	Pass		

A good card to put on the table, assuming you value your life, is the ♣9, (you lead top of a doubleton) because your partner bid clubs.

When you lead your partner's suit and you have a doubleton, lead the higher card first. If you have three or four cards in your partner's suit, lead the lowest card unless those cards are headed by the ace (in which case you lead the ace). However, if you support your partner's suit and you have three or four small cards, lead your highest card.

After you play for a while, you may notice that at every table there is at least one self-designated teacher. Conservative estimates say that the advice given by these "teachers" is on target about 23 percent of the time. Be forewarned. You may hear one of these self-appointed teachers tell you to lead the highest card in your partner's suit no matter what you have. Don't believe it. You lead low when you have three or four cards headed by an honor in your partner's suit (or any suit for that matter).

The cards in Figure 18-4 show you why to disregard this advice.

Figure 18-4:
Walk the other way when someone tells you to always lead the highest card in your partner's suit.

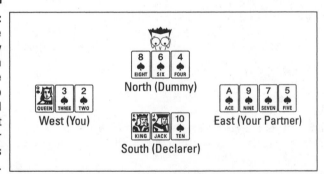

Say your partner has bid spades. If you lead the ♠Q (ugliness!), the declarer must wind up taking two tricks with the ♠KJ10. However, if you lead the ♠2, your partner wins with the ♠A (third hand high) and then plays a low spade. The declarer can only take one trick. If the declarer plays the ♠K, your ♠Q becomes the highest spade left out. If the declarer finesses the ♠J, you win with the ♠Q.

When one suit has not been bid

During the bidding, your opponents may mention three out of the four suits. When the opponents bid three suits, you should consider leading the unbid suit. That does not mean you should never lead a suit the opponents have bid; your own hand may tell you that it is right to lead one of their suits. If you have the AKQ in their suit, or a singleton, it may be clearly right to lead the suit. But as a general rule, you tend to look for the opening lead in places where the opponents have not advertised strength, and the unbid suit is a likely candidate.

The cards in Figure 18-5 give you a chance to make the opening lead in the only suit that your opponents haven't mentioned during the bidding.

Figure 18-5:
Go where no bidder has gone before: Leading an unbid suit.

The bidding for this hand is as follows:

South	West (You)	North	East (Your Partner)
1♣	Pass	1♠	Pass
3♣	Pass	3♦	Pass
5♣	Pass	Pass	Pass

Even on Mars, you lead a heart on this bidding. When the opponents bid three suits, the unbid suit is usually a good bet. Lead the ♥3, leading low from a suit headed by an honor.

When two suits haven't been bid

When two suits have gone unmentioned during the bidding, you usually lead one of those suits, but which one?

When you need to choose between two unbid suits, lead from your stronger suit, the suit in which you have the most honors; but don't lead from any suit headed by an ace, unless you have the AK.

The cards in Figure 18-6 give you a chance to choose between two unbid suits.

Figure 18-6:
Would the
best unbid
suit please
report for
the opening
lead?

Just look at the exciting bidding for this hand:

South	West (You)	North	East (Your Partner)
1♠	Pass	2♣	Pass
2♠	Pass	4♠	Pass
Pass	Pass		

Eliminate clubs and eliminate spades as possible lead choices because the opponents have bid these suits. You can choose between hearts and diamonds. Because your diamonds are headed by the ♦A, lead the ♥3, fourth highest from a long suit.

When you have four trump cards

Long suit leads are not quite as fashionable against suit contracts as they are against notrump contracts. However, long suit leads make good leads when you have four cards in their trump suit.

If you have four trump cards, try to make the declarer use his trump cards to trump your long suit once or twice. You may eventually wind up with more trump cards than the declarer. When that happens, the declarer is sunk. The declarer loses control of the hand when you have more trump cards than he does.

When you pick up the hand in Figure 18-7, you may be able to coax a few trump cards away from the declarer.

Figure 18-7:
Going for
the throat.

The bidding for this hand goes as follows:

South	West (You)	North	East (Your Partner)
1♠	Pass	2♠	Pass
3♠	Pass	Pass	Pass

Because you have four trump cards, you decide to lead from your longest suit rather than from one of your doubletons. The proper opening lead is the ♥4. You plan to make the declarer trump hearts until you wind up with more trump cards than the declarer — an intolerable situation for him.

When you have the ace of a suit

Yes, it's great fun to lead an ace and take a trick. But don't forget that aces were put on this planet to capture kings and queens, not deuces and threes. If you wait to play your ace, you usually get more for your money.

Nevertheless, you may come across any one of the following circumstances when you may need to bang down an ace on the opening lead:

- ✔ If your partner has bid the suit.

- ✔ If the opponents have arrived at a six or seven level (slam) contract.

- ✔ If you have a singleton ace (the ace is the only card you have in the suit).

- ✔ If you have a doubleton ace (the ace plus one low card), you may be lucky enough to find your partner with the king. Your partner wins the second lead of the suit and then plays the suit a third time, and you can trump this third round of the suit, generating an extra trick for your side. Whenever I try that lead, my partner never has the king; perhaps you will be luckier than I.

- ✔ If the opponents have bid every other suit.

If you need to lead a suit that is headed by the ace, lead the ace. If you "underlead" the ace, it may get away from you; one opponent may have a singleton, in which case, your ace is history.

When you want to remove the dummy's trump cards (leading a trump)

Trump opening leads should be saved for specific occasions; the old advice of "when in doubt lead a trump" really means that if you're too lazy to work out the right lead, lead a trump card!

All kidding aside, sometimes leading a trump card is a primo idea. For example, if the declarer bids two suits, and you are very strong in one of those suits, but the opponents wind up in the other suit, you should lead a trump card.

In Figure 18-8, you get a chance to lead a trump.

Figure 18-8:
Stealing their thunder — you open with a trump card.

The bidding has taken this interesting turn:

South	West (You)	North	East (Your Partner)
1♠	Pass	1NT	Pass
2♥	Pass	Pass	Pass

You can almost see the dummy's cards before they come down. The dummy has about seven points and is short in spades, perhaps a singleton spade, probably with three or maybe four hearts. The declarer, who bid spades first, has five spades and four or five hearts.

What is the declarer going to do with those five spades she has? She is going to try to trump as many of them as she can in the dummy (see Chapter 7 for more information on trumping losers in the dummy).

What can you do to stop the declarer from trumping those spades in the dummy? You can lead a trump card. Each time you lead a trump card, the dummy has fewer hearts for the declarer to use to trump a spade. After you get rid of the dummy's trump, your remaining spades are all winning tricks. In the case of Figure 18-8, lead a low heart. You are so tough on defense, your opponents may get scared.

When you have a suit with no honors

Welcome to the pits. It doesn't get much worse than having to lead from an empty suit with no honors in it. You have three or four cards, but for some reason or other every other suit is taboo. The right lead from this holding is the top card (called the top of nothing), but you do not have to like it.

When you lead the top of three or four small cards in an unbid suit, your partner may think you are leading from a doubleton and subsequently misdefend. If instead you lead your lowest card, your partner may think that you have an honor and may also misdefend. No matter what you lead, you get into trouble. For that reason, leading anything from a three- or four-card suit is near the bottom of the list. Leading the top of the three or four cards is the lesser of two evils, but I don't know you if it doesn't work out!

Selecting the proper card

After you select a suit to lead, then you need to select the right card in the suit. For the most part, you lead the same card against a suit contract as you do against a notrump contract. After you decide upon the suit, lead any of the following that apply to your suit:

- Top of any doubleton; for example, the 8 from the 83

- Low from three cards headed by one honor; for example, the 4 from the K64

- Top of three or four small cards; for example, the 7 from the 7643

- Top of a three-card sequence of honors; for example, the K from the KQJ4

- Top of two touching honors; for example, the Q from the QJ763

- Fourth highest from any four-card suit or longer that is not headed by a sequence or two touching honors; for example, the 3 from the Q10632

- The ace from any suit that includes the ace; for example, the A from the A8743

Third Hand Play versus Suit Contracts

Versus a notrump contract, more often than not your partner leads a low card, fourth highest. Versus a suit contract, more often than not your partner leads an honor card or from a short suit.

You see more honor card leads against suit contracts because the requirements for leading an honor are less severe than in a notrump contract. Versus a suit contract, you need two, not three, touching honors to lead an honor. As a result, the lead of the ace from the AK and the lead of the king from the KQ are regular customers versus a suit contract. Also, because you can trump the opponents' winning tricks when you are void in a suit, your partner may often lead a singleton or top of a doubleton against a suit contract.

Regardless of your partner's opening lead, you want to be prepared when it comes your turn to play *third hand*, which means you're the third person to play to the trick.

When your partner leads an honor card

When your partner leads an honor card (the ace, king, queen, or jack), she expects a little information from you in the form of an *attitude signal*. An attitude signal is a play that tells your partner whether you like the suit she has led or not.

You can make two types of attitude signals to convey your feelings about your partner's lead:

- ✓ **An encouraging signal:** By playing the highest spot card you can afford, you indicate that you want your partner to continue the suit.

- ✓ **A discouraging signal:** By playing the lowest spot card you have, you tell your partner that you have no interest in that suit.

What determines which signal you use? Broadly speaking, if you have an equal honor in the suit your partner has led, you give an encouraging signal. If you have three or more worthless cards in the suit, you give a discouraging signal. A lot of leeway exists between the two choices of course, so that the question of which signal to give may not be quite as obvious as all that. But those are the basic guidelines. Your partner will watch your attitude signal and proceed accordingly.

Sometimes the first card you play may not be all that easy for your partner to read; while he can tell that a nine is a big card, and a two a small one, what about a five or six? Your partner may be able to clarify the position by playing the suit a second time and observing whether your second card is higher or lower than the first. In the language of bridge, a *high-low signal* (playing a higher and then a lower spot card) is a come-on. It asks your partner to play the suit a third time. A *low-high signal* (first a low then a higher spot card) is a discouraging signal and says you are not interested in this suit.

The high-low signal

Versus a notrump contract, the high-low signal shows an honor, usually an equal honor. However, versus a suit contract, a high-low signal can also show a doubleton. The doubleton high-low signal is given primarily when your partner leads the ace from the AK.

A high-low signal in a suit contract tells your partner to play the suit a third time. When you make a high-low signal, you can either produce an equal honor or you can trump the third round, both winning scenarios.

The hand in Figure 18-9 gives you a chance to see an encouraging signal in action.

Your opponents have ended in a 4♥ contract, which means that hearts are the trump suit, and they need to win 10 tricks.

Your partner leads the ♠A, which allows you to assume that your partner has the ♠K as well. If your partner has the ♠AK and you have a doubleton spade, you can play a trump card when the third round of spades is played. Obviously, a good defensive move would be to trump your opponents' tricks as soon as possible — after all you only need to take four tricks to defeat their contract. Start by playing the ♠9 and then play the ♠3 when your partner continues with the ♠K, a high-low signal showing a doubleton. Nice signal.

When your partner sees that ♠9, she recognizes the start of a high-low signal showing either an equal honor or a doubleton. Because the only equal honor is the ♠Q, and because the dummy has the ♠Q, your partner brilliantly deduces that your high-low signal must be showing a doubleton.

Your partner continues with the ♠K and then a third spade, allowing you to trump the dummy's ♠Q. Now you have the lead. Make a quarter turn of your neck to the right and what do you see in the dummy? You see weak clubs and strong diamonds. I do not generally stoop to verse, but "When the dummy is to your right, lead the weakest suit in sight." Lead the ♣10, top of a sequence.

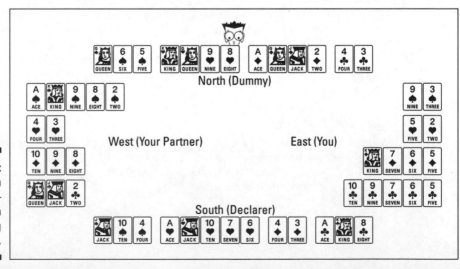

Figure 18-9:
Full steam ahead — giving an encouraging signal.

The declarer wins the trick, plays the ♥K and ♥A to take out all your trump cards, ending in his hand, and leads a low diamond to the ♦J, taking a finesse. He hopes to find your partner with the ♦K, in which case he will make his contract by avoiding a diamond loser altogether.

No luck, you have the ♦K, and you end up defeating the contract by one trick. You have actually taken two defensive tricks with that meatball hand of yours!

When you lead the ace from an AK combination, watch your partner's signal like a hawk to determine whether she's starting a high-low encouraging signal or a low-high discouraging signal.

The low-high signal

When your partner leads a high honor card, and you have worthless cards in that suit, waste no time in telling your partner to cease and desist with the suit. Play low.

Figure 18-10 shows a hand where you need to give the low-high signal to turn your partner off.

The opponents wind up in a contract of 4♥; hearts are trump and your opponents need to win 10 tricks to make their contract. Your mission: To defeat the contract by winning four tricks. Your partner leads the ♠A.

You have zilch in spades so you pass that message across the table to your partner by playing the lowest spade, the ♠4. After your partner determines that the ♠4 is your lowest spade (your partner has the ♠2 and can see the ♠3 in the dummy), your partner knows that you can't have a doubleton spade or even the ♠Q, or else you would have started a high-low encouraging signal.

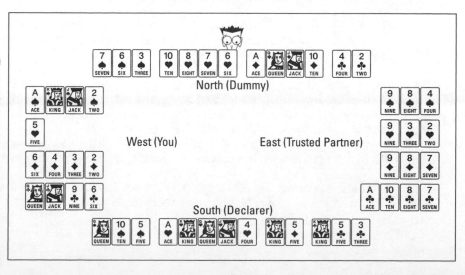

Figure 18-10:
You can't get there from here: telling your partner you have no support for her high honor card opening lead.

Rather than plunk down the ♠K and set up a trick for the ♠Q that the declarer surely has, your partner smartly shifts to the ♣Q, the top of the sequence. After you see the ♣Q, you know the declarer has the ♣K, so you take the trick with the ♣A (the declarer may have a singleton king). Now you play a spade, which is the suit your partner led. When the declarer plays the ♠10, your partner wins the trick by playing the ♠J, and then she continues with the ♠K, capturing South's ♠Q for the fourth and setting trick.

If your partner makes the Nervous Nellie play of the ♠K at the second trick, the declarer winds up losing two instead of three spade tricks and makes her 4♥ contract. Because of accurate defensive signaling, the declarer loses three spade tricks and one club trick, defeating the contract by a trick. Down one.

When your partner leads a short suit

The three most common leads versus suit contracts are the ace from AK, the king from KQ, and short suit leads. The first two are easy to spot because the size of the card hits you in the face. You have to be a bit more of a detective to spot a short suit lead. When your partner leads something like the five, you may have to wait until you see your partner's second card. If his second card is a three, a high-low, there is a good chance your partner has a doubleton. If your partner leads a five followed by a six, low-high, your partner cannot have a doubleton; your partner is leading low from an honor.

The trick is to watch the first card closely so you know whether the next one is higher or lower.

Avoiding common errors

I see two errors in third hand play against a trump contract that surface so frequently, I want to show them to you here so that you can avoid falling into either of these traps.

When your partner leads the queen, and you have the ace, and the king isn't in the dummy, the declarer must have the king. At times that king will be a singleton king, such as in Figure 18-11. In such cases, you should take the ♠Q with the ♠A. If you don't and the declarer has the singleton king, you will never hear the end of it — if the declarer wins with his king, he can proceed to trump spades until the cows come home, including trumping your ♠A.

When your partner leads the ♠Q, play the ♠A. If you don't, you may have to kiss your ♠A goodbye. Maybe you can use it on the next hand. Just kidding.

Figure 18-11:
If you don't play the ace, you will lose it.

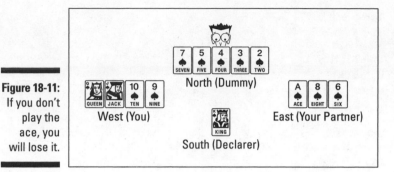

When your partner leads the king and you have an ace doubleton, overtake with the ace to unblock the suit just as you would at notrump. Just do it; the eyes of Texas (and your partner) are upon you. The cards in Figure 18-12 show you how vital this lead can be.

Figure 18-12:
Averting disaster by overtaking your partner's trick.

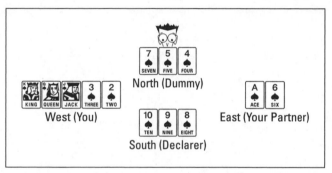

Your partner leads the ♠K, showing that he also has the ♠Q. When you have an ace doubleton, overtake the ♠K with the ♠A! It only hurts for a little while. By doing so, you give yourself a sure-fire way of taking three tricks in the suit. You have the ♠KQJ between the two hands, which takes two more tricks, or if the declarer has the ♠J, your partner takes the ♠Q and leads a low spade for you to trump. You can't lose if you overtake your partner's lead, and oh how impressed your partner will be.

Chapter 19

Playing Second Hand

● ●

In This Chapter

▶ Formulating your strategy

▶ Seeing the dummy's cards and acting accordingly

● ●

*W*hen you make an opening lead, you play first to the trick. When your partner makes an opening lead, you play third to the trick and are called *third hand*. When you are the last player to play to a trick, you are *fourth hand*.

This chapter discusses your strategy for defending when you play second to a trick, or *second hand*. The strategies outlined in this chapter apply for the most part both at trump and notrump. If your strategy should differ between defending a trump or a notrump contract, I let you know what to do.

Playing with Vision

Whenever you play second hand, either the declarer or the dummy has led the suit initially. Your plays are governed by which opponent leads the suit first.

When the dummy's on your right (blind man's bluff)

If, during the course of play, some suit is led from the dummy, the North hand, you are second to play, as shown in Figure 19-1. In this scenario, you can't see the hand that plays after you, the declarer's hand. Basically, you play second hand blind, meaning that you have to guess at what the declarer has in his hand.

Figure 19-1:
You have
the dummy
on your
right.

	North (Dummy)	
West (Your Partner)		East (You)
	South (Declarer)	

When the dummy's on your left (you can see)

When the declarer, South, leads the suit first, you are second hand, as shown in Figure 19-2. But this time you can see the dummy, the hand that plays after you, and that helps, because the declarer's options from the dummy are limited by the cards that you can see in the dummy. After all, if the dummy has no card higher than a 10 in the suit led, you can play the jack and take the trick.

Figure 19-2:
The dummy
ends up on
your left.

	North (Dummy)	
West (You)		East (Your Partner)
	South (Declarer)	

Because playing second-hand blind (the declarer plays after you do) differs from playing second-hand sighted (the dummy plays after you do), I divide the rest of this chapter into two sections that cover your course of action in each of these scenarios.

Haul out the spades from some handy deck. You can help yourself follow the explanations if you have the cards in front of you.

Defending with the Dummy on Your Right

When the dummy is on your right and leads a suit, you are second to play. In this section, you pick up some clever strategies for playing a smart second-hand defense.

Following a low lead with a low card

When the dummy leads a low card, you play the lowest card you have, which is called playing *second hand low*.

You can play second hand low most of the time. In fact, it is an exception not to play second hand low when the dummy leads a low card. You don't give away any secrets when you play second hand low.

Figure 19-3 shows you one good reason to play second hand low.

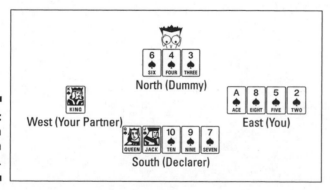

Figure 19-3:
Avoiding a
crash
landing.

In this hand, spades are trump and the dummy leads a low spade. You play a low spade, giving your partner a chance to take a trick, perhaps with a singleton honor. Had you played your ♠A, you would have brought your partner's ♠K down to earth with you.

Exceptions to playing low occur if you have a sequence of consecutive high honors. When the dummy leads a low card and you have a suit headed by the AK or the KQ, play the lower of those honors. Likewise, with a suit headed by three honors, you play your lowest card in that sequence. A different sort of exception occurs if the dummy leads a singleton (a one-card holding in a suit) in a side suit at a trump contract. In that case, play the ace if you have it.

TIP

If you decide not to play second hand low, and you turn out to have blown a trick, at least tell your partner that you meant to play low, but the wrong card fell out of your hand. It's your only way of saving face.

Covering with higher honors

When the dummy leads an honor card (ten or higher) and you have a higher honor card, play your higher honor and try to take the trick. In essence, you do not want to let the declarer make tricks separately with the high cards in his hand and in the dummy. By *covering* his high cards, you force him to combine the high cards on to a single trick. The cards in Figure 19-4 give you a chance to do just that.

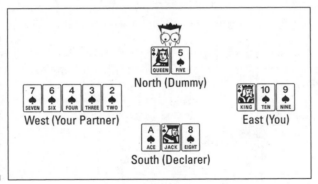

Figure 19-4: Take that — your honor is bigger than the dummy's honor.

North (Dummy)

West (Your Partner)

East (You)

South (Declarer)

If the dummy leads the ♠Q, play the ♠K, covering an honor with a higher honor. If you see the declarer take the trick with the ♠A, don't think that you have wasted your ♠K — think that you have promoted your ♠10. After the ♠QKA have been played, the ♠J becomes top dog in the suit. But after the ♠J is played, the ♠10 moves up a notch to top rank. You have the ♠10. Long live tens!

If you stubbornly refuse to play your ♠K, the ♠Q takes the trick, and the declarer remains with the ♠AJ. The declarer then takes the next two tricks by leading low to the ♠J. You wind up with nothing.

Covering an honor with a higher honor can work in strange and wonderful ways that save you from losing tricks. Take a look at Figure 19-5 to see what I mean.

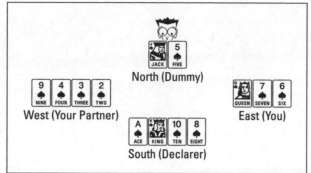

Figure 19-5:
Your
partner will
love you
for this.

North (Dummy)

West (Your Partner)

East (You)

South (Declarer)

If the dummy leads the ♠5, play the ♠6 (playing second hand low). However, if the dummy leads the ♠J, play the ♠Q. If you play the ♠Q, the declarer wins the ♠A. The ♠K and then the ♠10 are also high spades, but eventually your partner's ♠9 tops the declarer's ♠8. If you cover an honor with a higher honor, the declarer takes only three spade tricks.

If you don't cover, the ♠J wins the trick, and the declarer takes four spade tricks; his ♠10 becomes a winning trick after your ♠Q drops under the AK.

If you cover an honor with an honor and the declarer takes the trick with yet another honor, three of the top five honors vanish on one trick. Suddenly the lower honors and the eights and nines sit up and take notice because they soon become winning tricks. You cover an honor with an honor in order to promote lower honors (not to mention those eights and nines) for either you or your partner.

Covering the last of equal honors in the dummy

When the dummy leads one of several equal honors, do not cover the first honor; instead cover the last equal honor. For example, if the dummy has two equal honors, such as the QJ or the J10, cover the J and the 10, respectively. If the dummy has three equal honors, such as the QJ10 or the J109, cover the 10 or the 9, respectively.

In Figure 19-6, the dummy has two equal honors. Which one should you cover?

If either honor (♠Q or ♠J) is led from the dummy, play low. When the second honor is then led from the dummy, cover that one with your ♠K. Even though your ♠K loses to the ♠A, your partner's ♠10 becomes the highest remaining spade. If you cover the first honor, the declarer wins the ♠A and can lead a low spade, finessing the dummy's ♠9 and taking all three tricks. Trust me.

Figure 19-6:
Choosing
between
equal
honors.

North (Dummy)

West (Your Partner)

East (You)

South (Declarer)

Figure 19-7 gives you a look at a dummy that has three equal honors.

Figure 19-7:
Just like a
blanket, you
can cover
that honor
from the
dummy.

North (Dummy)

West (Your Partner)

East (You)

South (Declarer)

Whichever honor is played from the dummy, don't cover. When a second
honor is played, don't cover again. Now you can see how your patience pays
off. If you play low twice, the declarer takes the second trick with the ♠A and
winds up taking only two spade tricks. If you mistakenly cover the first or
the second honor, the declarer takes three tricks.

If the dummy leads a low card, play low; if the dummy has one honor card,
cover that honor with a higher honor if you have one. If the dummy has two
or more equal honors, cover the last equal honor.

Obviously, following these general guidelines doesn't guarantee that you'll
play the right card every time. But you will usually be right, and you won't
slow the game down to a crawl every time you play second hand.

Defending with the Dummy on Your Left

When the dummy is on your left, you can see what's in the hand that plays after you do. When the dummy is visible, you usually know what the declarer is planning to play from the dummy.

Using your bean

When the dummy is on your left, you can often just let common sense take over. The cards in Figure 19-8 show you a case where you can very easily think through your defense because you can see the dummy.

In Figure 19-8, no matter which spade South leads, play the ♠2 because you can see that the ♠A must be played on this trick.

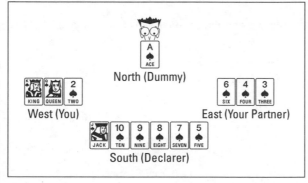

Figure 19-8: Sometimes you really can trust your instincts.

Letting the declarer take a losing finesse

When the dummy is on your left, give the declarer a chance to take a losing finesse when the dummy has a hole (broken honor strength) in it. Figure 19-9 shows a dummy that's missing the ♠Q.

Suppose that the declarer leads a low spade. When you can see broken honor strength, play low and give the declarer a chance to take a losing finesse. If the declarer finesses the ♠10, your partner wins with the ♠Q, and you can take another trick with your ♠A the next time you get a chance.

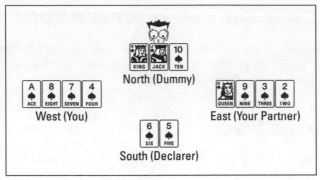

Figure 19-9:
Giving the declarer enough rope to hang himself.

Using your aces constructively

Use your ace to capture something worthwhile — don't use it to capture air (a low card) unless you just need one trick to beat the hand; then take it.

Figure 19-10 gives you a chance to make good use of your ace.

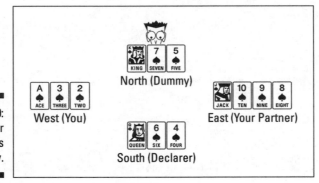

Figure 19-10:
Using your aces wisely.

Suppose that the declarer leads a low spade. If you play low, the dummy takes the trick with the ♠K — big deal. If you play your ♠A, the dummy not only takes a later trick with the ♠K but a trick with the ♠Q as well. By playing your ♠A, you capture air: You get the declarer's ♠4 and the dummy's ♠5. Aces were bred to do better than that.

Aces were meant to capture kings and queens, not fours and fives. If you play low, the declarer takes one spade trick, the ♠K, but you save your ♠A to capture the declarer's ♠Q.

Leaving the dummy's honors alone

When the declarer leads a low card toward the dummy, you generally don't have to waste your nines, tens, and jacks to force an honor out of the dummy; those honors will be played anyway. Does that sound unclear? The cards in Figure 19-11 show you what to do when the declarer leads up to an ace in the dummy.

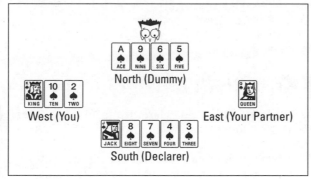

Figure 19-11: Waste not, want not.

If the declarer leads a low spade, don't (do not, not, not) play the ♠10 to force the ♠A out of the dummy. The declarer intends to play the ♠A anyway, and the card you play to force the ♠A out may be a card that can take a later trick if you keep it.

If you play low, the declarer plays the ♠A, dropping your partner's ♠Q, but you remain with the ♠K10 over the declarer's ♠J for two tricks. If you play the ♠10, the declarer plays the ♠A, which he was going to do anyway, and you only get one trick, the ♠K.

Knowing when you're beat

When the dummy's cards are higher than your cards, don't fight it — just play low. For example, you need to play low when you have the cards shown in Figure 19-12.

South leads a low spade. You see that whichever spade you play, the dummy has a higher one — play low. Don't waste an honor. For all you know, the declarer may intend to play the ♠A.

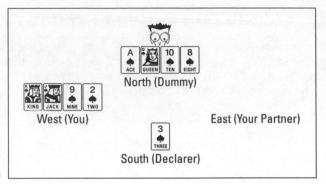

Figure 19-12:
You can't
fight city
hall.

Dealing with higher honors in the dummy

Your real problem arises when the declarer leads an honor, you have a higher honor, and the dummy has a higher honor yet.

If the declarer leads an honor in a side suit (any suit other than the trump suit), and you have one higher honor, follow these guidelines:

- If the dummy has one higher honor, don't play your honor.
- If the dummy has two higher honors, play your honor.

If the declarer leads an honor in the trump suit, don't cover, period.

When the dummy has one higher honor

In Figure 19-13, South leads the ♠J. Don't cover when the dummy has one higher honor.

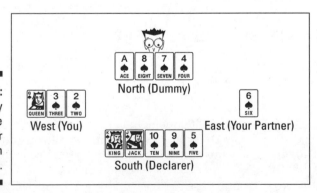

Figure 19-13:
The dummy
has one
higher
honor than
you have.

Sometimes the declarer leads an honor just to coax you into covering. In this case, for example, the declarer doesn't intend to take a finesse — the declarer intends to play the ♠AK. He's just offering you a little bait — don't bite!

When the dummy has two higher honors

In Figure 19-14, South leads the ♠J. If you cover, the declarer takes one trick, the ♠A. If you play low, your partner wins the ♠Q, but next time the declarer leads low to the ♠10 and takes two tricks.

Figure 19-14:
Watch out for the dummy's two higher honors.

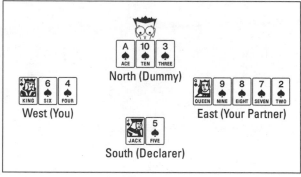

North (Dummy)

West (You)

East (Your Partner)

South (Declarer)

You cover an honor to promote nines and tens for either you or your partner. However, if you can see both of those cards in the dummy, no promotion is possible, so don't cover.

Overpowering them with honor cards

If the declarer leads an honor and you have higher honors, cover the declarer's honor with your lowest honor.

You need to play one of your honors in Figure 19-15.

If the declarer leads the ♠J or ♠10, cover with the ♠Q, your lower equal. If you do, you will take two more tricks with your ♠K and ♠9. In the world of promotion, nines are big cards

Whether you decide to cover or not to cover, do it nonchalantly as if you could care less about what is going on. If you start hemming and hawing and sweat starts appearing in various places and you finally play low, the declarer will pick up on your strange behavior and work out that you must have the missing honor. If you play low quickly, you can fool even the best declarers.

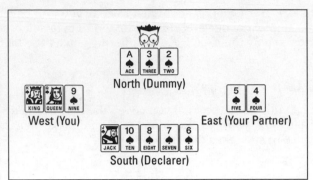

Part V
Getting Hooked on Bridge

The 5th Wave   By Rich Tennant

"...AND DO YOU PROMISE TO LOVE, HONOR, AND ALWAYS LEAD THE HIGHEST CARD FROM THE SHORT SIDE?"

In this part . . .

After you play a few hands, you may find that you can't stop playing bridge. If this happens, call a doctor — you may be a bridgeaholic. The only cure for your addiction is play, play, play.

In order to satisfy your craving for bridge, you can turn to this part to read about playing in bridge clubs (where other fanatics like you can be found), in tournaments (where the serious bridgeaholics hang out), on the computer, and on the Internet (where you can get support from fellow bridgeaholics as far away as China and, of course, play some bridge).

Chapter 20

Playing in Bridge Clubs and Entering the Tournament World

....

In This Chapter

▶ Finding a place close to home to play bridge

▶ Playing your way up in the tournament ranks

▶ Discovering the social side of bridge

....

*T*he title of this chapter may make you feel like you're being pushed out the door before you are ready, but that's not so. Although bridge clubs and tournaments often cater to more advanced players, both also offer services for novice players, both give you a chance to meet other newcomers to the game, and both give you the chance to play bridge against players of your own skill level.

Joining Your Local Bridge Club

Depending on where you live, you should be able to find a bridge club within striking distance. If you can't find the address and telephone number for a bridge club in your local telephone directory, call the American Contract Bridge League (901-332-5586) to obtain a club directory or a referral to the nearest club. (See "The American Contract Bridge League (ACBL)" in Chapter 24 for more information on the League.)

After you find your local bridge club, call them and see what they have to offer. Most clubs have beginner's lessons, as well as supervised play sessions — right up your alley. The club managers will treat you royally; beginners are the lifeblood of the game. The clubs need you!

Some services offered by local clubs may have fees attached to them, but the fees are most often minimal and well worth the expense.

Playing in Novice Tournaments

After you gain some confidence with your play, you may consider the next big step: playing in a novice tournament. You can find these novice tournaments staged at your local bridge club.

In most of these games, you can ask questions as you are playing. In short, you don't have to sweat bullets playing in novice tournaments — you can ask a more-advanced player if you aren't sure about your next move.

Heck, you may even enjoy the novice tournaments. Most people begin to enjoy these tournaments after they see they are going to survive.

Preparing to play with others

When you begin playing in novice tournaments, you'll find that 99 percent of the people that you meet and play against are pleasant and eager, and you are bound to make many friends who share bridge as a common interest. Of course, you can also expect to find the 1 percent who can't control themselves when something goes awry. These types like to lay the blame for their mistakes on their partner. Don't worry about these jokers. If they get out of line once too often, the club owner will bar them for a month or two — an eternity to a bridge player.

Accruing masterpoints

The American Contract Bridge League (ACBL) records the successes of its members in tournament play by awarding *masterpoints*. If you join the ACBL, the League tracks your masterpoints and sends you a record every few months so that you can see your progress.

You don't have to win (or even come in second) in tournaments in order to win points. You can garner fractional points by placing third, fourth, or even fifth, depending upon the number of players who are competing.

Masterpoints come in colors. You can win black, silver, red, or gold points, depending on the importance of the event. At first, you will probably be winning black points, the color you pick up in club games. When you start playing in larger tournaments, you can eventually win the prettier-colored points.

The ACBL gives you a title according to how many masterpoints you rack up. Table 20-1 shows how many masterpoints you need to achieve each title.

Table 20-1	Racking Up the Masterpoints
ACBL Title	*Masterpoint Requirement*
Rookie	0–4.99
Junior Master	5–19.99
Club Master	20–49.99
Sectional Master	50–99.99
Regional Master	100–199.99
NABC Master	199–299.99
Life Master	300 and higher

To reach the upper plateaus, some of your points must be in particular colors. In other words, you have to win some of your masterpoints in larger tournaments, which means leaving the safety net of your local bridge club to get them.

After you play through enough blood, sweat, and tears to amass 300 of these coveted masterpoints, the ACBL makes you a *Life Master* and rewards you by sending you a gold card with your name emblazoned upon it. What can you do with that gold card? You can board a bus, show the driver your card, and then pay your fare. After you pay, the driver will let you stay on the bus.

Seriously, you do get the following benefits from being a Life Master:

  ✔ Bragging rights for the rest of your life

  ✔ Eligibility to play in certain restricted events

  ✔ Reduced yearly membership dues in the ACBL

I got my gold card when I was 24 years old. Some players don't have to wait as long as I did — some child phenoms have become Life Masters at the age of 11! Of course, their parents taught them to play as soon as they uttered their first word. However, I have managed to accrue plenty of masterpoints; despite my "late" start, I have over 10,000.

After you start playing in novice tournaments, you will eventually start to win masterpoints. After you get your first masterpoint, you are hooked, baby.

Because everyone wants to get to that magic 300 points needed to become a Life Master, most everyone knows to the fraction of a point just how they stand. Of course they act as if it is not important to them. I once played with a lady who was approaching Life Masterdom (300 points) and I asked her: "Rea, how many masterpoints do you have?" She said, "Oh, I don't know, who cares? About 278.63."

Hooked at an early age

I started playing in local bridge tournaments when I was 14 years old. I was so hooked by the time I entered high school that I hid bridge books inside my regular school books so that I could study bridge during class. Once when the rest of the class was being raucous, my teacher pointed me out to the class as a shining example of good behavior, saying "Why can't you have study habits like Eddie? Look how quiet he is!" Thank goodness the teacher wasn't closer to my desk.

Advancing in the Tournament World

Tournaments come in many sizes, shapes, and locations, offering a variety of skill levels and prizes. One day, you may find yourself ascending in the tournament world. When you first begin to play bridge, you may want to attend the tournaments to meet other players and watch some of the best players in action. All the tournaments are ACBL-affiliated, and anyone can play in most of them (although some events may require a minimum number of masterpoints to enter).

Club tournaments

After you screw together your last ounce of courage and charge off to play in your first club tournament, there's no turning back. You'll soon be ringing the phone off the hook down at the club, asking for the latest tournament information.

Sectional tournaments

You may see many of the same people from your club tournaments when you enter a sectional tournament. However, your *card fees* (the fees for entering the tournament) are a little higher at sectional tournaments because you are playing in a larger venue and somebody has to pay the rent. The higher card fees may be worth your while if you're trying to accrue masterpoints: You receive more masterpoints for placing in sectional tournaments than in club tournaments.

Sectional tournaments usually last three days: Friday, Saturday, and Sunday. Most tournaments offer events for everyone, including novices, and you can play as much or as little as you like.

Regional tournaments

You are moving up in the world when you enter a regional event. Regional tournaments usually take place in a classy hotel or a convention center (the extra space is necessary because of the larger number of participants). Experts often come from out of state to play in regional tournaments. Masterpoints flow like champagne at these events.

Regional tournaments last one week, sometimes longer. Anyone can play, and often the tournaments offer events for players with any number of masterpoints — from zero to 50,000!

National Championship tournaments

The Nationals take place three times a year in the United States, and thousands of people descend from nowhere and everywhere to attend. If you get a chance to attend a National Championship, by all means do it. I went to 93 of them in a row before I finally missed one!

National tournaments are ten days of fun and/or hard work, depending upon which way you want to go. Although the Nationals do feature some big-time players doing what they do best, the tournaments also boast novice events every day and night.

If you don't feel quite up to playing at that level, you can *kibitz,* or watch some of the best players in the world. Non-American stars are now coming in droves to the National Championships and earning a living by playing on sponsored teams. Certain important National events help decide qualification for the U.S. Team in World Championship play.

There is no feeling like winning a National tournament. True, you don't play for money, but the glory and ego gratification can't be discounted! Paul Soloway and I once played on a team that won a National event. The event ended one day before the tournament was officially over, so I decided to head home. On the way out of the hotel, I saw Paul in the lobby and asked him why he wasn't going home. He said that he wanted to stay for the extra day of adulation.

International tournaments

International tournaments are glamorous affairs, usually held in phenomenal locales such as the French or Italian Riviera. The tournaments often take place in lush casinos, with large cash prizes going to the top finishers. The casino owners hope that after you win in the tournament, you may want to put some money into the casino slot machines or baccarat tables. Personally, the tournaments I like best were the ones in Monte Carlo, Paris, and Lido, a stone's throw from Venice.

International tournaments differ from the United States National Championships in a number of ways. In international tournaments:

- ✔ You compete for cash prizes, not masterpoints.
- ✔ You get to play in exotic locales.
- ✔ You play one long session per day, usually from 3 p.m. to 8 p.m., rather than two $3^1/_2$ hour sessions per day.
- ✔ You have a better chance of seeing Omar Sharif (an expert bridge player).

The ACBL is toying with the idea of initiating cash tournaments in the United States. Right now, you play only for glory and masterpoints when you play in U.S. tournaments.

Many celebrities (including Omar) attend International tournaments. Another heartthrob who is also making lots of waves on the international bridge circuit is Zia Mahmood. Zia is a world class player from Pakistan who currently lives in the U.S. and London. Inevitably, these two bridge masters attract the greatest number of kibitzers; incredibly, most of the kibitzers are women.

Keeping your cool

Winning a World Championship is the ultimate high for a bridge player — it's an experience that never fades from memory. The play is always exciting. For example, in Rio de Janeiro in 1979, the U.S. team played the mighty Italians in the finals of the World Championships. On the very last hand of the match, my partner, Billy Eisenberg, and I just managed to defeat the opponents' contract by one trick. Had the Italians made that contract, they would have walked away with the prize. To this day, that hand still sends shivers down my spine.

Of course, such high-stakes play can get to your nervous system. In another Championship, I made a costly bidding decision. Billy saw how upset I was and tried to calm me down by saying all the right things, such as "You couldn't be sure," "Don't let it get to you," and "It's only one hand." Then, to show me how calm he was about the situation, he picked up a gum wrapper on the table and lit it, thinking it was a cigarette. Sure, Billy, we were both cool.

Enjoying the Major Tournaments

Suppose that you aren't Omar or Zia or anyone even close to them. What are you going to do at these tournaments, where everyone looks like a bridge shark ready to eat you alive? Well, you do have several options, which I describe in the following sections.

Attending free lectures

All National Championship tournaments offer at least two free lectures a day, one before the afternoon session and one before the evening session. In addition, the Nationals offer two novice lectures each day. You don't even have to play in the tournament to attend the lectures. The lecturers are often world-renowned players who have quite humorous stories to tell.

Watching

Bridge is a strange game. The people who *kibitz* (or observe) don't pay a cent to attend the tournaments. Only the performers, the players themselves, pay the card fee to participate — sort of a role-reversal. If you get lucky, you can pull up a chair behind some of the best players in the world and watch them perform. But you have to be quiet — very, very quiet.

Pulling a late nighter

Once at a National Championship, I was on a late night panel flanked by three panelists and a moderator. We were being peppered with questions from people who never wanted to go to bed. Finally, mercifully, the moderator said there was time for just one more question. He recognized a player who asked, "Does anyone want to form a quorum for a membership meeting after the panel?" (A few people actually raised their hands.) The moderator said that wasn't the kind of question he was looking for, and he asked for one more question. A man in the back raised his hand and asked about a bid he had made (which some of his friends had criticized). The late Jim Jacoby, one of the panelists, offered to field the question. He said that anyone who would make such a bid would also vote to attend the meeting after the panel.

Playing

The major tournaments offer players a chance to play in four sessions a day. Of course, you need the endurance of a marathon runner to even think about playing this much. Major tournaments offer a morning, an afternoon, an evening, and a midnight session. Each session lasts about $3\frac{1}{2}$ hours. Would you believe that some people play three sessions a day and think nothing of it? A few nut cases (who are addicted beyond repair) play all four sessions.

I once played in a tournament that lasted 9 days (meaning that I could have conceivably played in 36 sessions if I had decided to forego sleeping entirely). At the end of the tournament, they awarded a prize to the only person who played in all 36 sessions. I expected to see a weight lifter come up and get the award — but no, it was a little old lady in her 70s!

Big tournaments have novice events for players with 0 to 5 masterpoints, as well as events for players who have many more masterpoints. The bottom line is that you wind up playing against people who play like you do.

You are charged by the session — *card fees* are currently eight to ten dollars a session, depending upon the importance of the event. (A *session* consists of 26 hands, played against 13 different pairs of opponents.) Novice events are a bit cheaper, and at the National Championships they even set aside one "free day" for novices.

After the session is over, you get a printout, called a *hand record,* of the hands you have just played. You get to review all your mistakes, if your partner hasn't already reminded you of them. Hand records are great for discussing hands with your partner or even with your opponents. If you have a guru, you can go over your bids and plays (if you can remember them) with him or her. Everyone likes hand records.

Going to the partnership desk

Suppose that you come to a tournament and you don't have a partner. Not to worry, most tournaments have professional matchmakers just waiting for you at the partnership desk.

Just tell the people at the partnership desk your vital statistics (how many masterpoints you have) and they will find someone with about the same number of masterpoints as you have. If they can, the matchmakers will even try to pair you up with someone of the same or opposite sex, depending upon your preference.

The greatest bridge stories of all come from pairings at the partnership desk. Don't be afraid to try it.

Eating, dancing, and partying

After every evening session at a National tournament, free food is offered — and it's good stuff. After the game, everybody is starving, but they seldom run out of food until you get to the front of the line. Just kidding.

Starting at about 11:30 p.m. at National events, the tournament organizers offer the players either dancing or professional entertainment. Sometimes, the local unit may put on a well-known musical with accompanying bridge lyrics. Again, it's all free. Of course, not everyone sticks around to enjoy it — some choose to go home, even though it means missing the midnight games. After all, some of these people have *only* played 10 or 11 hours by the time the midnight session rolls around.

Bridge players hate to go to sleep. When they finally do get a little sleep, they get up at noon. Each night at these tournaments, you can find parties all over the place. If you have social butterfly instincts, and you don't mind going to bed at about three or four in the morning, bridge tournaments are really for you.

Finding Out Where the Fun Is

How can you find out when and where these tournaments are, so that you can do a little planning? After you join the ACBL, you get the League's monthly magazine that gives you all the details on tournaments, plus much, much more.

Join the ACBL. Joining is your second good move — reading this book was your first, he said innocently. For more information on joining the ACBL, see Chapter 24.

The bottom line is that you have to get your feet wet by attending a tournament. Even if you only watch until you gather up your courage to play, so be it. You won't be sorry. After you give tournament play a whirl, you will be hooked like the rest of us. Furthermore, if I see you playing in the midnight game, I will understand.

Chapter 21

Playing Bridge on Your Computer and on the Internet

*Y*our computer isn't just for work, you know. Your computer also offers the opportunity to play a few hands, no matter who's around, no matter what time of day or night it is, and no matter where you are (if you have a laptop computer). In addition, if you have Internet access, you can tap into the online bridge world and play with bridge fanatics all over the planet (yes, they do play bridge in Iceland).

Playing Bridge with Computer Programs

Sorry to break the news to you, but so far, no one has come up with any software that can play bridge at an advanced level. Unlike your friends who play chess, you won't be reading about bridge Super Matches against the computer anytime in the near future.

However, bridge programs still give you a chance to practice your card counting, your bidding, and your play without risking the embarrassment of an angry partner. A computer program allows you an additional benefit: You'll always get the last word in a hand by simply quitting the program!

Computer bridge, like everything else to do with computers, changes fast enough to make your head spin. You can find dozens of new bridge programs at your local computer store. In this section, I tell you my current favorites.

Bridge Baron 7.0 (Windows or Macintosh)

The Bridge Baron plays the cards at a reasonably high level but with a fairly limited selection of conventions that make it a natural for less than expert players. Bridge Baron is programmed by Tom Throop and manufactured by Great Game Products Inc.

Bridge Buff 4.0 for Windows 95

Bridge Buff 4.0 offers practice routines for beginners and intermediate players. Bridge Buff provides an excellent way to pick up new conventions and improve your bidding and play. You can play Bridge Buff's random deals or enter a hand of your own. Bridge Buff is programmed by Doug Bennion and manufactured by BridgeWare.

Bridge Master and Bridge Master for Windows

Anything programmed by Fred Gitelman, a master programmer and a world class bridge player to boot, is top of the line. This software moves state of the art to a new level. The 180 deals range from elementary to expert, distributed among five levels. This means that you, regardless of player level, get roughly 120 deals at your level. You can also order 30-deal "refills" from the manufacturer, which is Bridge Base Inc.

Bridge Master for Novices for Windows 3.1 or Windows 95

You get 117 deals at beginner levels plus 30 more advanced deals prepared by Audrey Grant and programmed by Fred Gitelman. You can later add selected 36-deal refills. Bride Master for Novices is manufactured by Bridge Base Inc.

Bridge Mate 2 for Windows

Bridge Mate 2 doesn't play as well as some of the other programs listed in this section, but it does offer a superb assortment of systems and conventions to choose from. If you want to focus your attention on bidding, this program's the one for you. Bridge Mate 2 is programmed by Bob Richardson and manufactured by Bridge Mate.

Counting at Bridge for Windows 3.1 or Windows 95

Manufactured by Bridge Base Inc., this program is very user-friendly. The primary function of this software is teaching you how to count tricks. However, the wealth of information provided with each of the 100 deals may make you feel that you're getting private lessons from former World Champion Mike Lawrence.

Throughout the play, the program asks you questions, gives you hints, offers guidelines, and prods you into thinking and playing like a good player. Counting at Bridge is programmed by Fred Gitelman.

Playing Bridge Online

The Internet provides a vital forum for bridge players all over the world. Currently, you can find over 600 bridge-related Web sites that offer everything from bridge games to bridge instruction.

The Internet allows players all over the world to play against each other and talk about what matters in the bridge world: scoring options, system reliability, the quality of the players, and general kibitzing. All you need to tap into this amazing online bridge world is a computer, a modem, and Internet access.

The Bridge Companion Home Page

www.phoenix.net/~tbc/#Online

Come to this page to find the answer to your burning bridge questions: How would you expect the cards in two unseen hands to be divided? What are the odds of all four players being dealt all 13 cards in one suit? What is the frequency pattern of certain reoccurring hand patterns? You get the answer to these questions, plus much more, including a play of the hand summary, a bidding summary, bridge articles, and subscription information for the offline version of *The Bridge Companion*.

Bridge on the Web

www.cs.vu.nl/~sater/bridge/bridge-on-the-web.html

Don't expect any fancy graphics when you come to this site. The page doesn't offer much in the way of show, but it more than makes up for a lack of cosmetic appeal with an interesting array of information. For example, the site offers daily bulletins of tournaments past; the coverage provided by these bulletins goes beyond a trick-by-trick account of the play — one bulletin even lists the full text of a trial brought before the tournament director when one player accused his opponents of illegal signaling!

In addition, the site provides an impressive collection of links to home pages of bridge players, bridge clubs around the world, bridge magazines (including some Dutch and German publications), commercial bridge software companies, and National contract bridge organizations.

The Bridge World Home Page

www.bridgeworld.com

The popular offline publication puts a sampling of its content online at this site (see Chapter 24 for more information on the offline version of the magazine). Here you find a brief introduction to the game, bridge practice hands and puzzles for intermediate-level players (the site posts new puzzles at least twice a month), and the obligatory plea for subscriptions to the offline magazine.

You'll find the most helpful content at this site in its References and Miscellaneous section. You hit the jackpot in this section with a bridge glossary, which is hyperlinked for easy use. (And boy is this glossary detailed: If you ever wondered what an *Alcatraz coup* is, you can turn here to find out that it's an illegal, deliberate failure to follow suit in order to gain information from the opponents.) The section also offers the Bridge World Standard Summary, a standard system drawn from the help of over 100 top bridge experts, and links to many other bridge sites.

OKbridge

www.okbridge.com

OKbridge bills itself as the original and largest Internet bridge club. After spending a few minutes at this site, you see why the site easily lives up to this claim. The resources available here are easily among the finest offered on the Internet.

OKbridge centers around duplicate bridge. In duplicate bridge, any number of tables are given the same hand to play. Your success at taking tricks against the other tables playing the hand determines your point score. For a fee of around $80.00 a year, you can match wits at hand solving with some of the game's top players; if fact, the site boasts that over 25 percent of the top 500 ACBL masterpoint holders play on OKbridge. Some of the names associated with the site are truly stellar — the Sheinwold bridge column (now written by Frank Stewart) is published here, and Paul Soloway and Bobby Goldman have been known to show up for some hands.

In order to play, you need to download some software and sign up for an account. Windows and Unix users have it made; they can just click on a link and downloading begins immediately. Mac users not running Softwindows can only play OKbridge via Telnet; just click the Telnet link on the download page and follow the instructions onscreen.

In addition to the play, OKbridge also features a library with ethics and rules guidelines, convention cards, and back issues of bridge columns. If you intend to play OKbridge, don't forget to stop by the library to check out the glossary of abbreviations used during play — otherwise, how could you possibly know that "glp" stands for "Good luck partner!"

Finally, the site offers its own newsgroup (see "rec.games.bridge and rec.games.okbridge" in this section) and mailing list. The mailing list delivers updates of tournament play, solutions to bridge problems, and expert advice every day. To subscribe to the mailing list, send a message to `okbridge request@cs.ucsd.edu` and type **ADD; okbridge** in the message body.

The Internet Bridge Archive

`rgb.anu.edu.au/Bridge`

This site just may offer links to all 600 known bridge sites! Never fear the number of links — you won't have any trouble finding the site you need because everything is organized alphabetically by topic.

rec.games.bridge and rec.games.okbridge

One player in Dallas, Texas, asks for help solving a bridge problem that has left him stumped, and a string of responses come to his aid — each one offering a different solution! Another player announces an upcoming bridge tournament in New York City. Other players exchange stories on their latest and greatest hands.

You find a wide variety of bridge discussion taking place on these two newsgroups, but one factor remains consistent: the quality of the conversation. Chat is almost exclusively about the topic of the newsgroup (a rare occurrence in these public forums), and the discussions are not only educational — most are very witty and entertaining. New players may have to sit back and listen for a while; most of the discussions take place at a fairly high level. However, if you're looking for a place to meet and chat with other bridge players online, you'll find many willing participants in these newsgroups.

Other online services

In the early 1990s, the most popular online bridge service was the Imagination Network, which at its peak had more bridge players than even Okbridge. America Online, another popular online service, purchased the Imagination Network and incorporated it into America Online. America Online also offers backgammon, cribbage, hearts, and spades if you can't find four players for bridge. CompuServe and the Microsoft Network, two other online services, also enable you to play networked bridge.

If you subscribe to one of these services, just log on and browse your service's offerings.

Part VI
The Part of Tens

The 5th Wave   By Rich Tennant

"MY CURRENT DISTRIBUTION IS 4, 3, 3, AND 1. 4 KIDS, 3 TUITIONS, 3 MORTGAGES AND 1 JOB."

In this part . . .

It wouldn't be a ...*For Dummies* book without a Part of Tens. I found it very hard to keep the chapters in this part limited to only ten items apiece. After all, I can think of more than ten ways to be kind to your partner. And when it came to jotting down a list of the ten best bridge players of all time, I threw my hands up thinking it couldn't be done. I begged them to add another ten pages to the book so I could get all the players on this list who belong there, but they wouldn't let me do it! If you want to read about a player who isn't on the list, check with one of the bridge supply houses I list in Chapter 24.

Chapter 22

Ten Ways to Be Kind to Your Partner

Most bridge players value a reliable, happy partner above anything else. It's very important to the success of your play that you show your partner support and let her know that you are working together. You both want to win, so you can't gain anything from getting upset when things don't go exactly as planned.

In this chapter, I give you some tips on keeping the person sitting across from you one happy camper.

Treating Your Partner like Your Best Friend

Even if you don't know your partner that well, treating him or her like your best friend (getting her a soda, laughing at her jokes even if they aren't that funny, and so on) makes the whole table feel more relaxed. And you and your partner play better together, too. Treat your partner like your best friend, and you will be repaid in "spades." Always be a pleasant and courteous opponent and you will win everyone's "hearts."

Tolerating Your Partner's Errors

Don't keep harping on errors that your partner has made — just forgive and try to forget (at least until after the game). After all, do you want to be reminded of all the mistakes you've made? (*Everybody* makes mistakes, including you.)

If you really have constructive criticism, save it for after the session when you will both surely be calmer. Expect (demand) that your partner show you the same respect.

Offering Words of Encouragement

Give your partner a few words of support after the hand is over, particularly if you don't make your contract. "Tough luck" and "Nice try" go over bigger than "My great-grandmother could've made that hand in her sleep."

Keeping a Poker Face

Never show your partner any facial or body mannerisms that indicate whether you're pleased or displeased with a bid or play. You'll lose both your partner's and your opponents' respect. Remember, such facial and body mannerisms can be construed as illegal signals.

Treating Your Partner the Same Whether You Win or Lose

When the session is over, win or lose, keep your cool and tell your partner how much you enjoyed playing with him (no matter how you really feel). Your kind words can mean the world to a player who knows that he hasn't played that well. It also shows class.

Dealing Well with Disaster

A truly good partnership handles the inevitable disaster with a touch of humor. If your partner doesn't have to worry that you'll have an apoplectic fit whenever something goes wrong, she'll play better.

Playing the Conventions You Both Want to Play

Don't force your partner to play your favorite conventions if he's uncomfortable about playing them. A partner worried about remembering a convention inevitably makes more errors in the bidding, playing, and defending, not to mention messing up the convention itself if it comes up.

Picking up the Slack for the Weaker Player

In each partnership, inevitably one player is the better player. The better player should make the weaker player feel at ease. Follow these tips to help out a weaker partner:

- Make all your bids, leads, and defensive signals as simple and clear as possible.

- Don't give your partner tough contracts to play; bid for fewer tricks when playing with an inexperienced player.

Knowing When to Have Fun

When all is said and done, you play bridge to have fun, and so does your partner. You've done your job if your partner leaves the table happy. Angry partners are not fun to play with.

Chapter 23

The Ten Best Bridge Players of All Time

*W*hen asked to list the ten best bridge players and ten best partnerships of all time, I shuddered. After all, I know, or did know, all of the people on the list and many others who couldn't make it on the list because of space. To save my hide, I added five pairs to my list of ten best partnerships. I also want to make advanced apologies to at least a dozen players not mentioned on either list, especially Terence Reese of England, Christian Mari of France, and Tim Seres of Australia. Furthermore, the following ten players are listed alphabetically, for obvious reasons.

Giorgio Belladonna (1923–1996)

Giorgio Belladonna of Italy was a 16-time World Champion and a member of the legendary Italian "Blue Team," the strongest bridge team ever assembled. The Blue Team dominated world bridge from the late '50s to the early '70s. Giorgio was instrumental in the Blue Team's success. He was the primary inventor of the Roman System and also collaborated in the invention of Super Precision (both systems feature a forcing artificial opening bid that a partner can't pass regardless of strength). Giorgio also toured the United States in 1975 as a member of the Lancia team, which included Omar Sharif.

During his reign, Giorgio Belladonna was at once the most loved and most feared of players. Personally, my happiest moments playing against Giorgio were the moments before the last hand of the match. At least I knew it would be over soon.

Pietro Forquet (1925–)

The Italian Pietro Forquet is a 12-time World Champion and also a member of the fabled Blue Team. At one time, Pietro was considered by most bridge experts to be the best bridge player in the world. With movie-star looks and the calm demeanor of a riverboat gambler, nothing — but absolutely nothing — rattles this man. Take my word for it, it is murder playing against someone who doesn't make mistakes. He also authored one of my favorite books, *Bridge with the Blue Team* (published by A and B Publications, Sydney, Australia, 1983).

Benito Garozzo (1927–)

Considered to be the world's best player during his World Championship years, Benito Garozzo of Italy won three World Team Olympiad championships, plus ten World Championships as a member of the vaunted Blue Team. From 1972 to 1976, Benito paired with Giorgio Belladonna in what many bridge experts considered to be the strongest partnership in the world during those years.

Benito is an extremely deceptive declarer and defender. If you don't watch out, you will be playing without your underwear! He is also a master at solving *double-dummy* problems (you see all four hands and try to figure out how to take a certain number of tricks, but even that doesn't help!).

One time in Rome, I visited Belladonna's bridge club and happened to have a tough double-dummy problem, which I gave to the best players at the club. Finally, one of them said, *"Bisogna aspettare Garozzo,"* which means "We have to wait for Garozzo."

Robert D. Hamman (1938–)

Robert D. Hamman of the United States, a World Champion nine times over, has been the highest-ranking player in the world since 1985. As of this writing, Hamman is currently considered to be the best player in the world.

Bob was one of my first partners, and I was impressed when I first played with him over 40 years ago. Needless to say, I am still impressed. After yet another one of my overbidding ventures, Bob once said to me, "Edwin, I never have the hand you want me to have, so stop playing me for it!"

Jeffrey J. Meckstroth (1956–)

Jeffrey J. Meckstroth of the United States is the consummate bridge professional. Jeff rose from 1974's "King of Bridge" (a yearly honor awarded to the graduating high school senior in the American Contract Bridge League who has the best record in bridge) to the rank of World Champion in 1981. Since 1981, Jeff has won many other world titles.

Playing mainly with Eric Rodwell, the two have become the most feared partnership of the '80s and '90s. Happiness is leaving their table.

Eric V. Rodwell (1957–)

Eric V. Rodwell of the United States is a professional bridge player and writer, as well as an accomplished pianist and music composer. In major events, Eric plays almost exclusively with Jeff Meckstroth — the pair is even known as "Meckwell."

"Meckwell" are two of eight players who have ever won all three major World Championships. In addition, Eric has co-authored many books in collaboration with Audrey Grant, a well-known ambassador in the world of bridge.

Howard Schenken (1905–1979)

Howard Schenken of the United States was a real estate investor, bridge author, and bridge columnist. He is considered by many to be the best bridge player of all time. Howard was a three-time World Champion. He wrote several books on the game, including *Howard Schenken's Big Club* (published by Simon and Schuster, 1968) and *The Education of a Bridge Player* (published by Simon and Schuster, 1963).

Howard also developed the very popular *weak two bid,* an opening bid convention, which many players still use today. In his heyday, most experts named Schenken when asked, "Who would you play with if your life depended upon it?" The reason for their choice was clear: Howard was laid back at the table, but wily as a fox. Nothing — but nothing — escaped Howard Schenken.

Helen Sobel Smith (1910–1969)

Universally considered the greatest woman bridge player of all time, Helen Sobel Smith of the United States enjoyed a brief stage career as a chorus girl and appeared in *Animal Crackers* with the Marx brothers. Another chorus girl taught Helen how to play bridge and soon she rocketed to bridge stardom. The male bridge experts of her day considered Helen to be at least their equal.

Helen formed a lasting partnership with Charles Goren, a partnership considered the most successful in bridge history. After having won yet another tournament with Goren, Helen was asked, "What does it feel like to be playing with such a great expert?" She replied, "Ask Charlie." Helen also authored a successful book, *All the Tricks*. She was a pleasant opponent outwardly, but besting her at the table was close to impossible.

Paul Soloway (1941–)

Paul Soloway of the United States is considered the most successful tournament player ever. As of this writing, Paul has accrued some 45,000 masterpoints (see Chapter 20 for the details on master points). When you consider that it takes most people a lifetime to amass even 300 masterpoints, Paul's number stands out even more.

A three-time World Champion, Paul and his regular partner, Bobby Goldman (also a great player), are threats to win any team event that they enter. I was lucky enough to have played on teams with Soloway — when you play with Paul, all you have to do is follow suit.

Many years ago, Paul wanted to take off some extra pounds. Because I lived only a few blocks away, he frequently called me to go walking. He often called in the afternoon, and sometimes I wanted a snack while we were walking. It just so happened that we lived near some really fabulous bakeries. The first week we walked, I went in for a snack while Paul waited outside. The second week, Paul came into the bakery, but didn't buy anything. By the end of the third week, Paul bought more goodies than I did. The result of our power walks was that Paul gained only six pounds.

Robert S. Wolff (1932–)

Bobby Wolff of the United States is a syndicated bridge columnist, author, and former president of the ACBL (1987). Bobby is also a ten-time World Champion. He was one of the first three inductees into the Bridge Hall of

Fame in 1994, the first time such awards were bestowed in the modern era. In international competition, Bobby is the second most successful player in the world over the past 15 years, playing exclusively with Bob Hamman.

In addition, Bobby was one of the six original members of the "Dallas Aces," a professional bridge team financed by Dallas millionaire Ira Corn in 1965. Corn's dream was to dethrone the reigning Italian Blue Team. The Aces finally did beat the Blue Team in 1970 and again in 1971. The Aces even had an athletic trainer (championship bridge can be physically demanding).

"Wolffie" also has this irritating trait of always seeming to know what I have in my hand.

The Ten (Okay, Fifteen) Strongest Partnerships of All Time

Bridge is and always will be a partnership game. A strong partnership usually triumphs over two great individual players.

I cringe at the thought of the partnerships I couldn't get on the list. I list the partnerships alphabetically — not in any particular order of skill:

- ✔ Walter Avarelli — Giorgio Belladonna (Italy)
- ✔ Marcelo Branco — Gabriel Chagas (Brazil)
- ✔ Paul Chemla — Michel Perron (France)
- ✔ Billy Eisenberg — Eddie Kantar (U.S.A.)
- ✔ Pietro Forquet — Benito Garozzo (Italy)
- ✔ Bobby Goldman — Paul Soloway (U.S.A.)
- ✔ Charles Goren — Helen Sobel (U.S.A.)
- ✔ Bob Hamman — Bobby Wolff (U.S.A.)
- ✔ Sammy Kehela — Eric Murray (Canada)
- ✔ Alain Levy — Hèrve Mouiel (France)
- ✔ Zia Mahmood — Michael Rosenberg (U.S.A)
- ✔ Jeff Meckstroth — Eric Rodwell (U.S.A.)
- ✔ Charles (Chip) Martel — Lew Stansby (U.S.A.)
- ✔ George Rapee — Sidney Silodor (U.S.A)
- ✔ Alvin Roth — Tobias Stone (U.S.A.)

Chapter 24

The Ten Best Bridge Resources (Besides This Book)

• •

*T*his book tells you everything you need to know to sit down and start playing bridge. After you get hooked on the game, you may want to explore for bridge information that goes beyond the reach of this book. In this chapter, I point you toward some references and resources that you may find handy.

The American Contract Bridge League (ACBL)

Joining the ACBL is a must do. The ACBL is an excellent source of information about current events in the bridge community, bridge clubs all over America, and new plays and techniques.

The ACBL's monthly magazine (*The ACBL Bulletin*) that you get when you subscribe is worth many times more than the yearly dues. The magazine includes a special New Player Section as well as an Intermediate Section with monthly articles by various bridge writers, including yours truly.

Membership runs you about $14.00 for the first year; after that, membership runs about $28.00 a year. If you are 26 years old or younger, membership costs about only $10.00 per year. (The ACBL encourages younger players as much as it can.)

You can contact the ACBL at the following address:

The American Contract Bridge League
2990 Airways Boulevard
Memphis, Tennessee
38116-3847
Telephone: 800-264-2743

You can also find the ACBL on the Internet:

- ✔ e-mail: ACBL@CompuServe.com
- ✔ World Wide Web: www.acbl.org

The ACBL's Web site offers the following information, among other resources:

- ✔ **Membership Information:** Listings of the latest series and fees
- ✔ **Links to Bridge Sites:** Links to commercial Web sites, tournament schedules, and personal home pages related to bridge
- ✔ **Convention Charts:** All the help you need with bidding conventions
- ✔ **ACBL Club Listings:** Addressees, phone numbers, and schedules of events for clubs in all 50 states and Canada
- ✔ **Junior Page:** Junior membership information, tournament information for juniors, and links to international junior bridge organizations
- ✔ **The Bridge Teacher's Page:** Listings of ACBL Bridge Teachers in the United States and Canada, a column that answers questions posed by bridge teachers, links to teacher-related sites, and more

See Chapter 21 for more information about bridge resources on the Internet.

Your Local Library and Bookstore

Most libraries have a reasonable selection of bridge books, and borrowing a book is cheaper than buying one, especially if you're just starting out with the game. Of course, your local bookstore may also be stocked with the latest bridge books if you want one of your own.

Your Local Bridge Club

The local bridge club is a great place to go when you are starting out with bridge. Clubs offer all kinds of enticements, but best of all, you can get together and play with people that are at approximately your skill level. Nothing can supplant actual play for garnering experience with bridge: Suddenly the books you read, even this one, will make more sense because you will actually experience what you read about.

See "The American Contract Bridge League (ACBL)" in this chapter for more information about how to contact bridge clubs in your area.

Your Local YWCA and Adult Education Classes

Both of these venues offer bridge classes at modest prices and give you an opportunity to meet beginning bridge players like yourself.

The Daily Bridge Column in Your Newspaper

People who don't even play bridge read the bridge columns because they are amusing. A good column should be informative, instructive, and entertaining. The major bridge columnists usually come through on all three counts. Here are your five best bets, in no particular order (they are all good):

- ✔ "Sheinwold on Bridge" by Alfred Sheinwold and Frank Stewart
- ✔ "Goren Bridge" with Omar Sharif and Tannah Hirsch
- ✔ "The Aces on Bridge" by Bobby Wolff
- ✔ "Alder on Bridge" by Phillip Alder
- ✔ "Bridge" by Steve Becker

Shop around in other major newspapers if you can't find the column you want to read in your regular newspaper. (See "Your Local Library and Bookstore" for ideas on where to find additional newspapers.)

The Daily Bridge Calendar

The Daily Bridge Calendar is not only a regular calendar but also a valuable source of bridge tips. Each day features a bridge problem with a solution on the flip side of the page.

The Calendar has proved extremely popular since its inception in 1994. The problems are written by seven leading international experts (including moi). You can get The Daily Bridge Calendar at most bookstores, bridge clubs, bridge supply houses, or from the publisher at the following address:

Ashlar House
Copp Clark Longman LTD
2775 Matheson Boulevard East
Mississauga, Ontario, Canada
L4W 4P7
Phone: 800-749-3292

Bridge Supply Houses

Want a bridge book, bridge software, or a bridge-related gift? You can get all of these items, plus a friendly voice, if you call one of these 800 numbers. You can ask for a free catalog before you make any truly momentous decisions.

Baron Barclay Bridge Supplies
3600 Chamberlain Lane, Suite 230
Louisville, Kentucky
40241
Phone: 800-274-2221
Fax: 502-426-2044
e-mail: baronbarclay@baronbarclay.com

C and T Bridge Supplies
3838 Catalina Street
Los Alamitos, California
90720
Phone: 310-598-7010 or 800-525-4718
Fax: 310-430-8309
e-mail: tedinlosal@aol.com

Master Point Press Publishers
22 Lower Village Gate
Toronto, Ontario, Canada
M5P 3L7
Phone: 416-932-9766
Fax: 416-932-2816
e-mail: raylee@pathcom.com

Bridge Magazines

You can find scads of magazines at the newsstand. I tell you about my favorites in this section. Some of the information in these magazines may go a little over your head until you have played a little bridge, but all of them also offer articles for beginners.

The ACBL Bulletin

See "The American Contract Bridge League (ACBL)" in this chapter for more information on the ACBL and its offerings, which include this fabulous magazine.

Bridge Today

This wonderful bridge magazine caters mainly to intermediate and advanced players, but it also includes a few articles for beginners. The contributing bridge writers are top of the line.

Bridge Today can be ordered through any bridge supply house (see "Bridge Supply Houses" in this chapter for the details). The magazine costs approximately $27.00 for six issues a year.

The Bridge World

The Bridge World is the granddaddy of all bridge publications and the most respected bridge publication in the world. Unfortunately, the magazine is aimed primarily at advanced players. However, do not despair: *The Bridge World* offers information for players of all levels, including beginners, at its Web site (www.bridgeworld.com). See Chapter 21 for more information about bridge resources on the Internet.

You can contact *The Bridge World* at the following address for current subscription information:

The Bridge World
717 White Plains Road, Suite 106
Scarsdale, NY 10583-5009

Bridge On Board

Cruise ships offer an unequaled opportunity to immerse yourself in bridge. Each major cruise ship sets sail with a bridge teacher on board. When the ship is at sea, you get a lesson in the morning and the chance to enter a friendly tournament in the afternoon. However, you can just play bridge in the card room if you prefer. I currently do one cruise a year for the Cunard Line.

Bridge Tours

Bridge tours offer great opportunities to play bridge to your heart's content at some really great places. I can unhesitatingly recommend two such tours:

Finesse West Tours
P.O. 50166
Pasadena, California
91115
Telephone: 800-548-8062

Blue Water Bridge Festival
Bridge Pro Travel, Inc.
12223 Knobcrest Drive
Houston, Texas
77070
Telephone: 800-366-1689
(I do the instruction at this one.)

The Internet!

The Internet is such a great resource for bridge players, I devoted most of Chapter 21 to the subject. Please check there for more information on getting bridge information and playing bridge online.

Index

• *C* •

• *R* •

Notes

Notes

Notes